SCHOOLING IN AMERICA

SCHOOLING IN AMERICA
SOCIAL FOUNDATIONS OF EDUCATION

DANIEL SELAKOVICH
Oklahoma State University

Longman
New York & London

Schooling in America
Social Foundations of Education

Longman Inc., 1560 Broadway, New York, N.Y. 10036
Associated companies, branches, and representatives
throughout the world.

Developmental Editor: Lane Akers
Editorial and Design Supervisor: Joan Matthews
Production Supervisor: Ferne Y. Kawahara
Manufacturing Supervisor: Marion Hess

Library of Congress Cataloging in Publication Data

Selakovich, Daniel.
   Schooling in America.

   Includes index.
   1. Educational sociology—United States. 2. Educational
law and legislation—United States. I. Title.
LC191.4.S44   1984   370.19′0973   83–1149
ISBN 0-582-28439-2

MANUFACTURED IN THE UNITED STATES OF AMERICA
Printing: 9 8 7 6 5 4 3 2 1   Year: 92 91 90 89 88 87 86 85 84

Acknowledgments

Grateful acknowledgment is made to the following for their permission to reprint as noted from previously published material.

Excerpts from "Compulsory Education: An Idea Whose Time Has Passed," by Roger Sipher, are reprinted from USA TODAY, September 1978. Copyright 1978 by Society for the Advancement of Education.

Excerpts from "Compulsion and the Discourse on Compulsory School Attendance," by M. S. Katz, are reprinted from *Educational Theory*, Volume 27, No. 3, summer, 1977, pages 170–185. Copyright 1977 by The Board of Trustees of the University of Illinois. All Rights Reserved.

Figure 4.1, "Why Parents Choose Nonpublic Secondary Schools," is reprinted from American *Nonpublic Schools: Patterns of Diversity*, by Otto Krausaar, The Johns Hopkins Press, Baltimore, 1972.

Table 4.1, "Nonpublic School Enrollment Trends, 1970–1975," is reprinted from "Hard Times for Nonpublic Schools," by Richard I. Nault, Donald A. Erickson, and Bruce S. Cooper, *National Elementary Principal*, volume 56, number 6, July/August 1977, chart on p. 8. Copyright 1977, National Association of Elementary School Principals. All rights reserved.

Table 4.2, "Catholic School Enrollment—by Ethnic Background, 1970–71, 1978–79, 1979–80," is reprinted from *Catholic Schools in America*, National Catholic Educational Association, Fisher Publishing Co., Englewood, Colorado, 1980, p. xiv.

Figure 4.2, "The Seven Days of Creation Week," is reprinted from "Social Studies Unit: *God's Creation*," second edition, by Virginia Ford and Donald von Dohlen, Jr., Accelerated Christian Education, Garland, Texas, 1974, p. 3.

Table 5.1, "Policies of Highest State Control"; Table 5.2, "Policies in Which There

Is High State Control"; and Table 5.3, "Policies of Bimodal State Control Patterns"; are reprinted from "What State Laws Say about Local Control," by Frederick M. Wirt, *Phi Delta Kappan*, vol. 59, no. 8, April 1978, pp. 519–520.

Figure 7.1, "Continuous Systems of the Black and White Castes in the United States," is reprinted from *Minority Education and Caste*, by John Ogbu, Academic Press, New York, 1978, Figure 4.1, p. 104. Copyright 1978 by Carnegie Corporation of New York.

Portions of the discussion on pp. 283–284 are adapted from *Ethnicity and the Schools: Educating Minorities of Mainstream America*, by Daniel Selakovich, The Interstate Printers and Publishers, Inc., Danville, Illinois, 1978, pp. 50–52.

Excerpts from "Down the Bureaucracy," by Matthew P. Dumont, are published by permission of Transaction, Inc. from TRANSACTION, V.7 #12. Copyright © 1970 by Transaction, Inc.

Figure 9.2 is reprinted from THE STUDY OF TEACHING by Michael J. Dunkin and Bruce Biddle. Copyright © 1974 by Holt, Rinehart and Winston, CBS College Publishing.

Contents

Preface

This book is about schools in the United States. It is designed for those who are interested in becoming teachers or for those who have taught and want to reflect on the meaning of their experiences in the school system. The material presented here is what the author believes that prospective teachers and in-service teachers should know about the system generally.

As is the case with any such effort, the approach used here is subject to serious limitations. The general subject of schooling in America or, as it is sometimes called, "the foundations of education," is a developing discipline. Many scholars have addressed the subject but there is no general agreement on topics, concepts, or problems considered. That is, the subject matter of books on American schools vary widely. In a sense, the material here is an effort to more carefully define a developing discipline which might simply be called the nature and study of schooling in America.

Deciding what to include and what to leave out in a study of American schooling is difficult, and in the end, probably arbitrary. However, certain guidelines in making this decision were established at the outset of this project. The author reviewed surveys which are available on what is being taught in courses with titles such as: "Schooling in America," "Schools in American Society," and "Foundations of Education." The topics selected for consideration here were based on that review. Two other considerations were taken into account in the selection of topics for this book. First, the author was interested in presenting material which would help the classroom teacher understand why the classroom setting is what it is, and second, an attempt was made to avoid lengthy discussions of what might be called education "fads." Only those problems which have been around for some time and new problems which are unlikely to go away anytime soon were selected.

In this effort much attention has been given to the legal framework and court decisions on educational issues. This was done not only because the legal framework and court decisions reflect what constituted authority expects or permits from its schools and those who work in them but also because of the need for a sense of discipline in this subject. The legal framework and court decisions provide an excellent opportunity on many controversial areas to attain closure.

Rather than deal with endless arguments over what the schools ought to be, problems are described as accurately as possible and where these problems have been addressed by law or the courts these actions are noted. Every reader will not agree with the legal dispensation of school problems discussed here. However, whatever one thinks "ought" to be done, where the law or a court decision has at least temporarily dealt with the problem or issue in controversy, this provides a good starting point for analysis and discussion.

This book then is concerned with certain aspects of the following problems which promise to be around for some time and which should be of vital interest to those who would be teachers or who are presently teaching: the purposes of the schools, the relationship of the state to the schools, the school as a means of institutionalizing the values of society, the growing private school movement, the nature and problems of teaching, and the problem of inequality in American education.

Daniel Selakovich

SCHOOLING IN AMERICA

Part I
Problems and Approaches

The study of schooling has experienced some interesting developments in recent years. Early in the twentieth century, scholars concerned themselves with descriptions of the school and generally made efforts to explain by the use of history why the schools were the way they were. Thus, schools were reflections of the general development of society, which, as often as not, was viewed as a more or less orderly and progressively better society. Schools were functional in the sense that they were designed to prepare students for a growing and improving society.

More recently, critics of American schools have charged that while the schools may mirror the society, the society is seriously flawed. Thus, schools which mirror the society reflect not only the images of what is good and true and progressive, but also that which is petty and mean and destructive of human values.

The introductory chapter which follows presents an overview of what appear to be major schools of thought among contemporary scholars who attempt to explain why the schools are the way they are.

1

Studying Schools

Anyone who has kept abreast of current literature on American education must be impressed with the fact that there is not only great disagreement on what schooling should be as far as the public and school workers are concerned, but there is also a growing division among researchers who study schools.

Researchers study schools not only to understand the problems better, but more significantly, as far as the society is concerned, to provide some guidance in solving these problems. It would be easy to write a book on American education if everyone agreed on the nature and solution of school problems. Unfortunately, this is not the case. Researchers differ on the nature of the problems and of course, on policy decisions which should be made to solve them.

The purpose of this book is not to explain in any great detail the mysteries of scholarship on American schools. However the reader should have some general knowledge about recent scholarship in order to be able to understand that the way one looks at schools and the process of schooling determines, to a large extent, what things will be studied and which policies and practices will be implemented for the solution of the problems. The remainder of this chapter will outline the nature and direction of the study of American schools.

Perhaps greatly oversimplified, three major approaches have developed in the study of American schooling. These can be defined as functionalism, Marxist theory applied to schools, and the "new" sociology. None of these approaches is favored in this work but ideas from them are used in an effort to describe and analyze the problems selected.

THE STRUCTURAL FUNCTIONAL APPROACH

Structure is said to exist in all societies as an underlying and fundamental property. Everyone in society functions within some sort of structure. Interpersonal relationships are not accidental, but exist because of the nature of the basic structure of society. This does not mean that society is conceived as a huge monolithic structure. There are many structures. There is a political system which is structured in a certain way, an economic system with a definable structure, an educational system, a language system, and many others. Operating within these structures are human actors who must interact with each other in a variety of contexts and in a variety of ways.

According to Talcott Parsons, the actors in any social organization tend to become integrated into the organization which reflects the value system of the society. The value system of the society, as reflected in its goals, structures the way in which specific roles are defined. Individuals are socialized to the goals of society and rewarded and punished in terms of how well they accept the goals. Since all organizations, including the schools, are part of general society, their efficiency and stability are judged in terms of how well they adapt to the general goals of society and how well they contribute to the maintenance of the existing system.[1]

In its application to the study of schools, structural functionalism tends to emphasize the methodology of science. Actors such as students, teachers, and administrators are viewed as passive, their responses in given situations predictable, and their identities more or less fixed by environmental conditions and experiences.[2] Parsons viewed the school classroom as a basic agency of socialization,[3] although it was only one of many such agencies. He saw the school as the focal socializing agency from the first grade until entry into the labor force or marriage.

As a socializing agency the school teaches skills as well as roles. In this model the school is a true reflection of society. The structural functional model of Parsons views the school as accepting the existing arrangements in society—including the class system, values, differentiated roles which exist in the society, and the existing economic and political system. Following from this model, educational sociologists have tended to look for, and thus find, support for the idea that the schools are sifting and sorting agencies in the sense that they prepare students to enter the larger society without materially affecting or disturbing the arrangements which exist in that larger society. Teachers and administrators are conservative agents of the community.

The efforts of school people to conserve the values of society are not always successful. Some children simply do not fit the norms; they are alienated from the system in one way or another. For them, the schools are not functional. The assumptions of the functional model have become, in a very general way, the reflection of the goals and norms of the larger society, and these in turn seem to reflect the values of the mainstream—that is, white, middle-class society. Teachers and administrators are characterized as internalizing middle-class norms. The task of the school, that of teaching skills and morals, becomes the teaching of those mainstream skills which are needed to function in the society and those moral values which are embraced by the dominant class. Problems arise in this model since the schools must deal with so many pupils who are not socialized to these tasks. School populations in some places are anything but middle-class children. Instead there is a mixture of races, nationalities, cultures, and even languages in many elementary school classrooms. Functionalists recognize these discrepancies as problems. Merton and Nisbet suggest that a social problem exists whenever a serious discrepancy occurs between social standards and social reality. The standard may well be the existence of a school system whose major tasks are teaching skills and morals, while the reality of some classrooms might be the existence of large numbers of minority and poor children for whom the schools are not succeeding. Many students are unable, for a variety of reasons, to become socialized to the required skills and social norms.

Merton's model for functional analysis provides a framework for consideration of this problem.[4] He developed "middle range" theories which would enable researchers to be more effective in their analysis of failures in the system. His theoretical model expanded the definition of functionalism to include dysfunctions and nonfunctions. In Merton's words:

> Functions are those observed consequences which make for the adaptation or adjustment of a given system; and dysfunctions, those observed consequences which lessen the adaptation or adjustment of the system. There is also the empirical possibility of nonfunctional consequences, which are simply irrelevant to the system under consideration.[5]

This expanded model of functionalism permits one to explain almost any problem which exists in the school. The failure of the school to socialize students to the norms of the system can be explained by declaring the socialization process defective. The schools aren't working because the family has failed or because the teachers lack understanding or because the curriculum and materials are defective. The schools may fail to socialize because the pupils they get are not homogeneous enough.

SOME PROBLEMS WITH FUNCTIONALISM

Functionalism has many problems as an analytical tool for the study of schools. The critics of functionalism might agree that any society can be more or less accurately described. The critics may concur that subsystems and organizations within the society tend toward certain central goals. By definition, there must be some minimal level of harmony within the society, a certain level of consensus, or one does not have a society. The fact that there must be some harmony of goals and that divisions within the society get resolved through adaptation or through a change in the goals seems almost axiomatic.

However, critics of functionalism suggest that a central assumption of functionalists, that there is a consensus on values in any society, is open to serious question.[6] Even though a social system may operate as if there were, there may not be a consensus on central values at any given time. Even if one accepted the assumption that there is a consensus on central values, there still may be many groups and individuals within a pluralistic society who do not share these values.

On the practical level of a school setting, there are problems with the assumption that a central value consensus exists. Put perhaps too simply, functionalists see the need for general acceptance of goals by those in the organization if the organization is to operate efficiently. Since the goals of the organization must be in harmony with the general goals of the society, it must be assumed that someone within the organization understands what the goals of the society are and is able to interpret these for the organization. Thus school boards and/or administrators in schools understand what the consensus values of the society and the community are and, at least in a general way, understand how school goals fit into that picture. This assumes that however the goals are set by schools and whoever sets them, they are in harmony with the central value system of the society, and that individuals within the organization accept them almost without question. Functionalism would assume that if this harmony does not exist, adjustments and adaptations occur.

Within any school setting it is unlikely that the goals of society are ever really clearly perceived or that there is universal adherence to those which are. For example, teachers may have different goals than administrators. The major goal of teachers in a given school might be to impart the mysteries of their subject matter, whereas the major goal of the superintendent might be to maintain a good public image. In this example it is possible that neither party is much concerned about the goals of society.

A more serious problem in functional analysis occurs when teachers reject consensus values, or when students cannot be made to conform to them. Although consensus value assumptions may apply to teachers who hold Anglo middle-class values, all teachers are not easily classified. Some individual teachers within the organization might be antagonistic to this value system. Still, they can survive in the organization. Indeed, whole groups of teachers represented by a militant classroom teachers' association may be in basic conflict with so-called consensus values of the board and its administration, or for that matter with the public. Going one step further down the school hierarchy, individual students as well as groups of students may not accept the consensus values. Even assuming that the teacher accepts the consensus values and attempts to socialize students to the necessary skills and moral values, students may not be so pliable. This is a serious problem for minority group students in American schools. How does functionalism explain these anomalies?

One way the functional model deals with massive failures of minority group children in the system is to introduce the concept of alienation. Theoretically, when large numbers of individuals within the organization are not able to achieve the goals of the system, either the goals must be modified to accept the dissidents or the dissidents become alienated. Ogbu[7] explains this phenomenon by utilizing Cloward and Ohlin's[8] analysis, which suggests that frustrations generated within the social structure may lead to some form of adaptation as a solution. This "solution" may take the form of deviant behavior. Students can become labeled as deviant if the school seriously fails to socialize them to the mainstream of consensus goals. Unable to find a place within the framework of the system, those who cannot achieve any goals within the system abandon both the cultural goals and all efforts to achieve them, and create a "retreatist subculture" or a "retreatist adaptation." This does not result in a breakdown of the school system, or, for that matter, in any significant change in what the school does.

The fact that certain individuals and groups within the society fail to comply with the values of the dominant class or authority, as Alvin Gouldner[9] suggests, does not mean that functional analysis is fatally flawed. It simply means that there is something wrong with consensus values and the organizations within society which attempt to impose these values on individuals.

Where structural functional analysis may fail most seriously is in its attempts to treat the problems of conflict over goals and alienation of large numbers of people in the society as temporary. Structural functionalists see conflict as a temporary problem since organizations tend to seek equilibrium. A major criticism of this aspect of functionalism is that conflict, rather than consensus, may be a central feature of a stratified and racist society.[10] Because it is difficult to explain away these problems using the tools of functional analysis, some sociologists prefer to concentrate their efforts on the nature of conflict.

MARXISM: CLASS CONFLICT THEORY

In the following consideration of Marxist class conflict theory the reader should be aware that the division between functional and conflict theory is not a clean one. Functionalist theorists can be classified on the basis of their findings. The classification of conflict theorists is a bit arbitrary. As the term is used here, conflict theorists are those who argue that the schools correspond to the society and merely reflect its nature. This group includes various Marxist and neo-Marxist sociologists and economists who see contemporary schooling as a tool of the capitalist elite whose major function is to maintain existing social arrangements.

It should be said at the outset that Marxist conflict theorists and others who write about conflict do not necessarily reject the basic assumptions nor the model of structural functionalism. Conflict theorists tend to agree that the structural functional model is an accurate description of American society. Their argument is not with the model, per se; it is with the society. They may agree that there are consensus values in the society, but they believe them to be the wrong values. They are the values of the rich and powerful—the ruling class, not the values of the poor and the minorities—the people. The organizations and institutions in the system are duped or coerced into perpetuating the so-called consensus values.

This raises the basic question of how it is possible for the multitudes to be duped into doing things that are not in their best interests. Marxists contend that this can happen because the masses are "coerced, or seduced by false promises."[11] Even more important, they are duped by elaborate sets of beliefs that make conformity to the system seem reasonable and the only way open. The system of beliefs are *ideologies*, or the shared values of the society. Following the functionalists, the Marxists agree that the schools play an important role in socializing students to the official ideology. Thus students may be treated to both open and hidden exhortations of the great values of the "free enterprise system," "what is good for business is good for America," "that we should all work hard and cooperate with the system," "everyone shares in the productive enterprise," and so on. Conflict is minimized in this system because the masses tend to accept these beliefs as immutable truths. The "realities" of inequality, poverty, and injustice become masked, are hidden from us, and we blindly accept the values of the ruling class as authentic values even when they work against our own best interests.

Marxists suggest that, in order for the ruling class to maintain its hold over the working class, some apparatus is needed by which to impose the ideology of the ruling class. This is where education fits into the scheme. Thus the major function of education becomes maintaining the status quo. Althusser refers to this as maintenance of the existing system of production: "the reproduction of the relations of production."[12] Althusser contends that the school reproduces the capitalist relations of exploitation. In school the children are given the ideology necessary to make them fit the role which they must play in class society. Individuals are molded and shaped into obedient subjects who fit the needs of capitalist society. Children are taught the things needed to ensure "subjection to the ruling ideology."[13]

How this can be accomplished with minimal effort and virtually no serious conflict is explained by Herbert Marcuse. In Marcuse's view, in order to maintain its domination over the working class, the ruling class must practice "organized domination."[14] According to Marcuse, the ruling class manages to control and repress the masses by utilizing the principle of scarcity. "Scarcity teaches men that they cannot freely gratify their instinctual impulses. . . . "[15] Utilizing an historical explanation, Marcuse develops the idea that men have been repressed by forcing them to work. In the early stages of civilization, men were forced into work patterns through the use of violence and threats; more recently, it has been accomplished through the rational utilization of power. Following Marx, Marcuse asserted that it is the increasing specialization of labor which provides the opportunity for rational domination. That is, as the tasks of labor become more specialized and require greater skills, men are educated to perform the necessary tasks. The working class is convinced by the ruling class that it is necessary to learn to do the tasks. Following the rules established in industrial society by the specialization of labor, the society becomes stratified according to the competitive economic performance of its members, in which those with more advanced skills gain advantages over the others. All, however, are forced to work in a structure which they do not control. As specialization increases and functions become more narrowly focused, the worker becomes more alienated toward the system and toward other workers with whom he is forced to compete.

Carrying this argument to what Marcuse believed to be its logical conclusion, work itself then becomes an alienating force. Men hate work because it fulfills not their own needs but the needs of those who control them. Work time is painful time. Moreover, there is no room for leisure. Leisure is a myth, since all the workers' time is spent either working, sleeping, or preparing for work.

Thus, workers are dominated by the ruling class in the name of scarcity. Men are driven to work because they fear starvation and death. But what if this is not a real fear? What if scarcity is a myth perpetuated by the ruling class to make domination of the working class possible? This is a possibility in Marcuse's view. He suggests that domination is understandable where real scarcity exists. But in advanced technological society, there is no "real" scarcity. How, then, is domination justified in a society in which real scarcity no longer exists? Marcuse's answer was that "the closer the real possibility of liberating the individual from the constraints once justified by scarcity and immaturity, the greater the need for maintaining and streamlining these constraints lest the established order of domination dissolve."[16]

This takes place in society by various means. The social functions of the family are co-opted. Whereas in earlier times the family was the primary socializing agent, more recently it has been replaced by economic, political, and cultural monopolies. Clearly the school is one of these monopolies. In addition, youth are prematurely socialized by a whole system of extrafamilial agents and agencies. The most important of these are peer groups and the mass media. In this kind of structure, deviations are punished not so much within the family as outside and against the family. Indeed the family can no longer compete in its socialization function with mass media and the schools.[17]

The significance of all of this is that it makes it possible for the social structure of the elites, utilizing bureaucratic forms, to dominate, and for their system to be accepted without question.

> Control is . . . administered by offices in which the controlled are the employers and the employed. The masters no longer perform an individual function. The sadistic principals, the capitalist exploiters, have been transformed into salaried members of a bureaucracy, whom their subjects meet as members of another bureaucracy. The pain, frustration, impotence of the individual derive from a highly productive and efficiently functioning system in which he makes a better living than ever before. Responsibility for the organization of his life lies with the whole, the "system," the sum total of the institutions that determine, satisfy, and control his needs. The aggressive impulse plunges into a void—or rather the hate encounters smiling colleagues, busy competitors, obedient officials, helpful social workers who are all doing their duty and who are all innocent victims.[18]

Conflict is thus effectively suppressed. Where it exists it tends to be unorganized and spontaneous. Those who are "unhappy" are avoided and branded as malcontents or asked to go somewhere else. This system of domination works, according to Marcuse, because we don't know what is going on. The overpowering machine of education and entertainment keeps us in a state of anesthesia from which all detrimental ideas tend to be excluded.[19]

The goal then is to somehow get into a position of power or at least into a position where one comes to believe he has power. Freire[20] asserts that men are shaped by the system to be "oppressors." Men tend to become identified with their oppressors. "They have no consciousness of themselves as persons or as members of an oppressed class."[21] Everyone in the system desires to become the boss. In this position they tend to become more tyrannical toward their former comrades than the original boss was. It is in this way that the oppressed individuals in society internalize the image of the oppressor. These people fear freedom, according to Freire, because freedom would require that the image of the oppressor be replaced with autonomy and responsibility. The central question asked by Freire is "How can the oppressed, . . . participate in developing the pedagogy of their liberation?"[22] Only, he says, "as they discover themselves to be the 'hosts' of the oppressor. . . . The pedagogy of the oppressed is an instrument for their critical discovery that both they and their oppressors are manifestations of dehumanization."[23]

Illich expands on the point of schools as oppressive institutions by suggesting that schools are involved largely in teaching myths: in his words, the "myth of institutionalized values," the "myth of measurement of values," the "myth of packaging values," and the "myth of self-perpetuating progress."[24] The myth of institutionalized values teaches us that schools are essential to progress within the system. Schooling tends to create the need for more schooling, and as it does, it discredits those who attempt to learn on their own, it stifles creativity, and it fosters manipulation and control by the other repressive institutions in the society. School also teaches that everything can be measured, including man himself. It teaches people to put themselves into "slots." Once we teach people that everything can be measured, they tend to accept all kinds of social rankings. The school sells a packaged curriculum. Illich characterizes the curriculum as part of the production-consumption process in which the curriculum is the packaged product; the teacher, the distributor; and the pupil, the consumer. The curriculum being sold is a bundle of "packaged values." Finally, the school teaches the myth of self-perpetuating progress by teaching that more is better, where growth is conceived as open-ended consumption.

According to Illich, the school curriculum does an excellent job of socializing students to the values of a bureaucratic and productive society as opposed to a humanistic existence. Nor is the curriculum limited to the formal packaged textbook teaching. Schools have a hidden curriculum which is also destructive of the values of humanity and creativity, or, for that matter, of real learning itself. The hidden curriculum teaches the myth that the route to a better life is in increased production. It "develops the habit of self-defeating consumption of services and alienating production, the tolerance for institutional dependence, and the recognition of institutional rankings."[25]

Bowles and Gintis in *Schooling in Capitalist America*[26] come to some of the same conclusions reached by Illich. They argue that, from the beginning, the public school system in the United States can be seen as a method of "disciplining children in the interest of producing a properly subordinate adult population."[27] Using evidence collected from the statements of educational leaders and school laws throughout United States history, they charge that the schools have been consistent in attempting to implement this single objective. For Bowles and Gintis, the major reason for producing a subordinate adult population was to serve the existing class structure. From the beginning, schools fostered prompt and "obedient response to bureaucratically sanctioned authority."[28] They were able to do this through the system of discipline, including corporal punishment, through the system of grading, and through other forms of approval and disapproval. Bowles and Gintis cite evidence that schools tended to stifle creativity, flexibility, and independent judgment. Indeed, the schools tended to punish these human values when they cropped up in students, while rewarding docility, passivity, and obedience. Progressive education which tried to change the pattern failed to do so. Bowles and Gintis characterize the progressive movement, influenced by such thinkers as Dewey, Elliot, Whitehead, James, and Hall, as "triumphant in educational theory" but a system of thought which was never given a chance in the classroom.[29] Thus the history of education in the twentieth century was not a history of progressivism, but a history of the "imposition of business values and social relationships reflecting the pyramid of authority and privilege in the burgeoning capitalist system.[30] In the words of Bowles and Gintis, "Values, beliefs, modes of personal behavior, and patterns of social and economic loyalties were formed, transformed, and reproduced in the process of bringing the individual into line with the needs of capital accumulation and the extension of the wage-labor system."

Most of the critics of capitalist schooling who have been described in the preceding pages are Marxist in their orientation. Their central thesis is that the schools tend to reflect the inequalities, racism, and class conflict which are features of the capitalist system. Most agree that humanistic education, in the sense of providing expanding freedom and creativity for the individual with the concomitant values of equality and social justice, cannot be achieved through education until the structure and values of a capitalist system are destroyed.

However, all Marxist theorists do not share this view. Antonio Gramsci had a different view of why the schools tend to neglect the working class and what should be done about it. Briefly, his arguments contend that existing schools could, in fact, educate the workers in a way that would make working-class children open to socialist revolution, but they refuse to do so.

In his *Selections from the Prison Notebooks*,[31] Gramsci made it clear that the schools in fascist Italy in the 1930s did not mold the children of the workers into anything. They merely neglected them; or worse, mistaught them. Gramsci believed that all children could and should be taught basic skills and the language and culture of the nation. He accused Italian schools under the Fascists of abdicating this responsibility. He charged that the schools were redirecting the schooling of working-class children. The children were left to their own devices or were allowed to wallow in their own ignorance and superstitions. Their working-class language and values were left more or less undisturbed by the schools. This was unfortunate, in Gramsci's view, since it caused the interests of poor children to be limited and provincial. What they needed was effective teaching in the standard language and culture so that they would develop a "universal view." In his words: "A great culture can be translated into the language of another great culture, that is to say a great national language with historic richness and complexity, can translate any other great culture and can be a world-wide means of expression. But a dialect (provincialism) cannot do this."[32]

Gramsci saw the schools promoting good skills for the privileged and accepting sloppy practices for the poor. This was tragic because without mastery of the basic skills, the poor were doomed to function at the edge of national life and outside the political mainstream. To Gramsci, cultural deprivation was not a myth; it did exist and was promoted by the schools. The subservient class was not kept subservient by the things the schools taught them but by the things the schools did not teach. The dominant classes were able to maintain themselves in power by keeping the people ignorant. It is only through a superior education that the subservient class can change the system. Gramsci argued that converts to socialism might best be found by raising their culture to that "of their professors."

SOME PROBLEMS WITH MARXIST ANALYSIS

A major problem with Marxists is that they tend to agree with most of the assumptions of the functionalists. A central assumption often accepted by Marxist theorists is the idea that society is like a natural organism which tends to seek equilibrium. The functionalists, often charged with an inadequate explanation for change, assume that the society changes as the environment changes. It must and can adjust to a changing environment. Change in this milieu tends to be slow and evolutionary in nature. This is a central problem for Marxists. They assume that change can be controlled by the ruling class, or, at the very least, the ruling class can maintain control even in a changing environment. Thus, even though the society changes and the institutions of the society—including the schools—reflect this change, control is always maintained by those in power. This constitutes a significant difference between functional and Marxist theory. Functionalists see change as natural adaptations to environmental conditions. Consensus values and the subsequent goals of the system will adapt to these changes. Whereas the functionalists assume that consensus develops naturally and is broad based by definition, the Marxists argue that in the process of evaluating change in capitalism the dominant group determines the consensus values and goals of the society.

This difference has great relevance for the manner in which social problems are viewed. Whereas the functionalists tend to view problems of racism, unemployment, poverty, delinquency, and school dropouts as dysfunctions, Marxists see these problems as evidence that the system itself is the basic culprit. The functionalists see these problems as temporary maladjustments which cause temporary disequilibrium in the system. The system will naturally tend to seek equilibrium and these problems, as they become a serious threat to the existence of the system, will be ameliorated. Since he observed a ruling class manipulating the system, Marx referred to such efforts as "sop" to the working class. Thus, efforts of the system to alleviate hunger, for example, were merely planned exercises by the ruling class to maintain themselves in power. Marxists see the social injustices as a basic fault of the system itself—often, in fact, as deliberate, caused, and encouraged by those in power. Marxists argue that these injustices can be corrected only by a change in the system.

This constitutes a serious problem for Marxists. If, indeed, the society can be improved only by dramatic change, what is to be the source of this change? Marxists advocate revolutionary change, but what is to be the source of the revolution? It is assumed by many Marxists that the masses will somehow wrest control from their elitist oppressors. Yet the Marxists seem to believe that the educational system, the knowledge and values that the masses receive, are determined by the ruling class. More than that, they insist that this socialization process is effective. Where, then, will this restless mass yearning to overthrow its oppressors come from?

Marx and Lenin, of course, had the answer. The vanguard of the revolution would be the intellectual class, presumably a group of intellectuals who had somehow avoided the socialization process of repressive institutions. The problem this raises is: what assurance do the masses have that the new consensus will include them? Is it not possible that the change will result only in a different set of consensus values promulgated by a new ruling class which will impose its own values and goals on the people and will change the institutions of the society, including the schools, in their own image?

Of the Marxist theorists reviewed here, only Gramsci deals effectively with this problem. Gramsci recognizes a good basic classical education as a necessary precondition for the end to a repressive system. Ignorant masses may not know they are being repressed; or, even if they do, they do not understand why or how it is done or who their oppressors are. Above all, they cannot be expected to create a new and enlightened society.

Another problem raised by the Marxist analysis is: who is the ruling class? Is it a relatively static group purposely and effectively guarding its privilege and power, or is it something else? If the ruling class is defined as those who are in power, how did they arrive there? These questions are addressed, at least indirectly, by Michael Young in his satirical fable, *The Rise of the Meritocracy*.[33] Young described, in some detail, the development in England of what he called "meritocracy." His position was that it was the development of meritocracy which kept conflict in check. Young referred to the term meritocracy as an "unpleasant term," a term whose origin he did not know, but which seemed to him to refer to a system in which the "cleverest people" and the talented comprised the ruling class, or at least were the class with power. According to Young, it had become possible to discover the brightest and most talented people by measuring intelligence and ability. The meritocratic system was encouraged by the growth of industry. While the traditional agricultural system in England maintained the status quo—virtually a caste system—the growth of industry encouraged the development of merit. In Young's words: "The soil grows castes; the machine makes classes."[34] This happened, according to Young, because industrial development was paralleled by the development of large organizations and the increasing specialization of skills in both industry and government.

In England, as Young described it, merit as measured by tests and performance ultimately came to dominate the entire social system. It affected the family, schools, government, and other institutions. Future leaders were selected in the schools on the basis of merit. Merit considerations were basic in the workplace and parents who benefited from merit considerations were able to pass along these benefits to their children. Major conflict was avoided in this system because, unlike hereditary advantage, merit was more widely distributed. When merit is the basis for determination of ruling class membership, even the rich are not safe. They, as well as the poor who succeed, must demonstrate ability. Stupid children of rich people cannot succeed in a merit system. The poor, a source of major social conflict in the Marxist analysis, are in a sense co-opted, because within their number there are always many who have merit and can become part of the ruling class. It is then in their interests to maintain the existing structure. In Young's words: "there are not revolutions, only the slow accretions of a ceaseless change that reproduces the past while transforming it."[35] Thus conflict is blunted or avoided, and more or less peaceful change is possible. If Young is correct, the Marxists obviously have a hopeless task.

A final assumption of both functional and Marxist theory, which may be a weakness of both, is that theory by its nature must make broad generalizations about institutions. Theory must explain classes of things, and by its nature theory tends to lump all schools together as if they all had similar characteristics. This may not be the case. In the United States, in the last quarter of the twentieth century, it is at times difficult to determine who is in charge. Consensus is certainly difficult to find on any single value, much less on a large cluster of values. Though the schools may not be serving the "real" needs of the exploited class, neither have they been universally successful in stamping on their clientele a central system of beliefs.

Whatever the case, the "new" sociology of the symbolic interactionists, the ethnomethodologists, and the phenomenologists tends to eschew global explanations for more specific examinations of social settings. The new sociology tends to derive its conclusions from in-depth observations of very restricted settings viewed with an "open mind" without the intellectual trappings of conventional social theory. The next section will deal briefly with this approach.

THE NEW SOCIOLOGY

The new sociology of education is difficult to describe and classify partly because it is so recent and partly because its practitioners tend to approach the study of society differently. As in the case of the Marxists, the reader should be aware that all new sociologists are not alike. Some are clearly Marxist in their philosophical orientation but reject the Marxian rational scientific view of society. Some are difficult to classify in terms of philosophical orientation and seem to be concerned largely with utilizing participant-observation techniques to arrive at general conclusions not only about the setting in which they are participant observers but about the nature of society generally. This work is not intended to provide the reader with a detailed account of these differences or to provide any really comprehensive review of all those who might be classified as new sociologists. A few examples will be selected to provide the reader with a general view of what has come to be called new sociology.

All "new educational sociologists" reject scientific positivism, but no single inclusive theory, such as that of the functionalists, is embraced by them. Those who are considered to be part of the new sociology group tend to agree that it includes elements of phenomenology, ethnography, and social interactionism. All of these approaches have in common a tendency to reject the "old" sociology of structural functionalism and to advocate a methodology which examines the classroom setting without the trappings of preconceived notions about the social structure and social values. The phenomenologist, for example, attempts to suspend all presuppositions and describe experiences as they are intuitively received. The phenomenologist argues that researchers should observe, describe, and analyze the structures, properties, boundaries, and interrelationships of a specific social setting as they are apprehended. The theorists of the new sociology charge orthodox social scientists with oversimplification. The functionalists, they charge, make common-sense hypotheses about human behavior which may not describe reality at all. For the old sociologists, the methods of natural science are important. They apply its methods to the study of human behavior. They classify, categorize, and label it. The new theorists reject such mechanistic interpretations of human behavior. They cannot find any predetermined psychological, social, or cultural assumptions that apply to all people. The phenomenologists, along with the ethnomethodologists and interactionists, view humanity as creative and stress the "importance of the social context of other actors in the development of mind, consciousness, and self."[36] Human behavior is not a result of predetermined factors but depends on the situation and the actors in it. The way people behave in given situations depends on a number of things which reveal themselves only through painstaking study of a given setting. In this format, understanding communication is vital. Relationships tend to be "negotiated" through various forms of communication.

Moreover, how the individual views the setting is crucial. The social consciousness of the individual is not an entity which can lend itself to scientific measurement in the same way that objects in the physical world can. This is the case because consciousness is determined in the mind, which is not a static organism and subject to predetermined assumptions, but dynamic, subjected to a myriad of forces within the immediate environment which influence the images formed, the interpretation of the environment, and individual reactions to the environment. Consciousness and the "self" are never fixed and static. Unlike other organisms, human beings are always open to socialization and modification. Thus the child might conceptualize the classroom in one way and his peer social group might conceptualize it in quite a different way. Or he may react differently in different classroom settings.

As Sharp and Green put it: "Society is a process of creative interpretations by individuals who are engaged in a vast number of concerted interactions with each other."[37] The task of the sociologists who would undertake the study of education then becomes clear. They eschew theoretical generalizations and limit themselves to specific settings. They try to determine how the actors in a specific setting see themselves; they attempt to describe the rules of the game which exist in social settings; and they look for ways by which the actors attempt to negotiate their own position in that setting and ways in which the status and role behaviors of the actors are affected by their interactions with each other.

Most orthodox social scientists gloss over this problem, according to their new sociology critics. Schutz, for example, charged the traditional social scientist with a kind of prejudicial approach to social reality. For most social scientists, social reality has a specific meaning.

> By a series of common-sense constructs they have preselected and pre-interpreted this world which they experience as the reality of their daily lives. It is these thought objects of theirs which determine their behavior by motivating it. The thought objects constructed by the social scientist, in order to grasp this social reality, have to be founded upon the thought objects constructed by the common-sense thinking of men, living their daily life within their social world.[38]

Thus the constructs of the social sciences are secondhand. They are, in a sense, inventions of the social scientist based on what he perceives to be the constructs of the actors on the social scene, "whose behavior the social scientist has to observe and to explain in accordance with the procedural rules of his science."[39]

The new sociologists argue that the functionalists' assumptions tend to accept the status quo and that the functionalists' theory is essentially a conservative one. Rejecting the knowledge and value assumptions of the functionalists, they tend to study classroom behavior with an open mind. They see such measures as IQ tests, for example, as reflecting the knowledge and values of the existing system. Empiricists do not measure intelligence, or achievement, or values, but intelligence, achievement, or values as defined by the existing system or, worse, as defined arbitrarily by the researcher.[40] The new sociologists assert that all knowledge is ideological. They suggest that

> cognitive learning in schools involves the acquisition, not of competence and rationality in some objective sense, but rather a different set of rules and procedures for interpreting the world. And if school knowledge has no inherently greater complexity or rationality than other ways of comprehending the world, . . . then there is no . . . reason why the acquisition of such knowledge should depend on variations in some general intellectual abilities or "intelligence." Explanations which assume it does are ideological.[41]

Thus, those who are outside the mainstream are sure to perform poorly on such tests which are based on mainstream or consensus value culture. When these characteristics are measured with an open mind or with an understanding of the personal and cultural characteristics of those being measured, different results are obtained. To vastly oversimplify the approach of the new sociology, researchers examine children in terms of their background and culture. Ghetto blacks or British working-class children, for example, are not examined in terms of how well they can deal with knowledge and values which are important to the white middle class, but in terms of what is important to them.

Social reality for the new sociologists does not consist of stable social structure, institutions, and roles, but is defined as a process. In Etzioni's words, "The elements out of which social reality is communally constructed and reconstructed are personal and interpersonal activities and rules that ascribe meaning to them. These rules are somewhat similar to what the consensus approach refers to as 'norms'; however . . . the new sociologists do not focus on generalized forms 'or abstract values, but on their concrete, specific, daily manifestations. . . .'"[42]

The new sociologists place a great deal of importance on interpersonal relationships. In the classroom they are interested in formal and informal rules, the manner in which the teacher views students and vice versa, and the interactions among students and between students and teachers. The study of social class structure and values as they are reflected in the classroom is not nearly so important to the new sociologists as what goes on there. The new sociologist prefers the method of participant observation or direct observation without participation.[43] Rather than testing common sense hypotheses about relationships between social class and achievement, for example, they may spend their time observing and analyzing teacher behavior as reflected in speech patterns, or in the seating arrangements of the students, or in the kind of communications which take place between students. It is out of these detailed and specific observations that they draw conclusions. Whereas the old sociologist might make predetermined hypotheses, gather data from tests administered to randomly selected groups, and test the predetermined constructs, the new sociologist collects descriptive data from direct observation.

In the task of attempting to interpret the social processes of the classroom, three areas seem to be most important. These include the teacher-student interaction, the concepts and categories used by teachers, and the curriculum. The differences between new sociology and traditional sociology have significance far greater than a mere academic argument. The differences lead researchers who are studying the same phenomenon to entirely different conclusions and thus different prescriptions. For example, the traditionalists might hypothesize that minority children do poorly in school because of cultural deficiencies. They would isolate the variables they wished to test and prove or reject their predetermined assumptions. If they find inability to cope significantly related to preschool family culture, they may then prescribe compensatory training for these children. Some of the new sociologists might agree. Other new sociologists studying the same group of children might conclude that the problem is the deficiencies not of the children but of the measures used to test them and the nature of the curriculum used to teach them. Yet even those new sociologists who agree with the prescriptions of the traditional sociologists go much farther. Some, especially the "conflict" sociologists, see basic and fundamental change in both society and the schools as necessary if school failures are to be corrected.

CLASSROOM RESEARCH

In school research the phenomenologist rejects much of the scientific study of education since it tends to ignore the views of social reality of the subjects being studied and it imposes the views of the researcher. Labov, for example, in his research on black students in Harlem, found that merely changing the situation in certain ways would lead to radically different conclusions about the intelligence of students. When individual intelligence tests were administered in the usual way, with an adult examining a student on a one-to-one basis, the student was unresponsive and appeared stupid. When the interviewer changed the setting, sat on the floor with the child and brought in the child's best friend, and carried on the interview in the language of the child, the child became very responsive and appeared interested and bright.[44] Other studies of classroom behavior by Robert McKay and Hugh Mehan support these findings.[45]

Basil Bernstein and his research group at the University of London's Institute of Education have been very active in classroom research in the British Primary Schools. Not satisfied with the results of traditional sociological research, Bernstein and his colleagues utilized the methods of the new sociology in their research. Some of the theoretical and philosophical bases of this work are summarized in an excellent essay review by Christopher Hurn in the *Harvard Educational Review*.[46]

In attempting to explain differences in school performance of working-class children and middle-class children, Bernstein's group spent a great deal of time in classrooms observing relationships between social class, language, and socialization.[47]

The sorts of questions asked by the researchers as well as the assumptions and methods of procedure utilized by the Bernstein group were quite different from those of traditional sociology. For example, in the examination of the differences in students' ability to perform in the language of the school, the Bernstein group examined students in specific settings. In a typical and much cited experiment, Peter Hawkins, assistant research officer in the sociological research unit of the University of London, constructed theory not from preconceived notions about the nature of working-class speech but from experiments designed to analyze that speech. Thus, children were given a series of four pictures and asked to tell a story about the pictures. The first picture showed boys playing football. In the second picture, the ball breaks a window in a nearby house. In the third picture, there is a woman looking out the window and a man is making a threatening gesture. The fourth picture shows the children moving away from the scene. The two stories as told by a middle class student and a working-class student were as follows:[48]

  1. Middle-class child:
     "Three boys are playing football and one boy kicks the ball and it goes through the window the ball breaks the window and the boys are looking at it and a man comes out and shouts at them because they've broken the window so they run away and then that lady looks out of her window and she tells the boys off."

2. Working-class child:

"They're playing football and he kicks it and it goes through then it breaks the window and they're looking at it and he comes out and shouts at them because they've broken it so they run away and then she looks out and she tells them off."

In their analysis of the differences, the researchers point out that the middle-class account can be understood without the pictures, that is, the frame of reference used to tell the story. The second story is tied closely to the context. Yet both accounts say essentially the same thing. The middle-class child makes the meanings explicit; the working-class child does not. The first child generated universalistic meanings in the sense that his story can be universally understood. In order to understand the working-class child's story, one would have to know the context.

Obviously the findings, at least with regard to the two children tested, have great relevance for an understanding of academic success or failure. If the stories were graded in a classroom, where the teacher values universalistic language, it is obvious that the middle-class child's story would rank much higher in quality than the account of the working-class child. Thus, even though both accounts may make sense in accurately describing the scene, the middle-class student would get a higher grade on his paper than the lower-class student.

In a similarly designed but more ambitious study, Rachel Sharp and Anthony Green seemed to find that there was little hope that the schools could accomplish much change in providing upward mobility for working-class children.[49] Theirs was a study of open education in the British Primary School. The researchers went into Mapledene Lane School in a working-class neighborhood and made detailed observations of curriculum methodology and the philosophy and practices of three teachers. The classrooms were child-centered, as was the philosophy of the school. In terms of philosophical orientation, the school followed Rousseau, Froebel, Montessori, Pestalozzi, and Dewey. From in-depth interviews, it became clear that the teachers did not fully understand the child-centered theories themselves. In practice, it became difficult to implement child-centered learning since the teachers had to deal with large numbers of students with limited space and materials. What happened in their daily teaching was that the teachers tended to be conservative and traditional in their approaches— whatever their philosophy as expressed in the interviews. There was much concern about "keeping the children busy," teaching respect for the hardware and materials in the school, and other "middle-class values." Even though it was supposedly an open school deliberately designed to ignore class distinctions, the teachers seemed unable to avoid classification of students. Teachers were influenced greatly by their knowledge of the student's family. That is, those whose parents were alcoholics, or who were in difficulty with authorities, or whose parents didn't seem to care about them had difficulty in school. Teachers tended to prejudge them. As the year progressed, teachers classified students as "bright" or "dull"; and, as in any school, the bright students seemed to get the most attention, while those classified as dull were left to their own devices so long as they did not disturb the other children. The teachers sorted their students into groups and the result was a system of social stratification within the working-class school that was not unlike that of British society. Thus, the researchers found that open schools were not unlike other schools in that the responsibility for failure was placed on the student not the system.

Although the authors of the study argue that existing sociological theory does not adequately explain their findings, their study doesn't add much. They argue, however, that sociologists cannot wait for the development of a grand social theory but should continue to examine schooling in specific contexts. They argue that their study explains how the social structuring of pupils originates, that there is a "developing hierarchy of pupils" and that the "content of education is being selectively organized and socially transmitted."[50] An observation, incidentally, which had already been made by many structural functionalists and conflict theorists.

The contribution of Sharp and Green, if there is one, is more with methodology than findings. The depth interviews, the description of the ethnic division of the school population, the detailed observations over a period of time of students and interactions between students and teachers were essentially new sociology approaches. The fact that there were serious gaps in the researchers' data[51] does detract some from its quality as a "pure" approach utilizing the methods of the new sociology. It is an interesting study methodologically, however, in that it uses ethnography (description of the school setting), phenomenology (descriptions of specific classroom happenings), and interactionism (communication and classification by teachers) in its approach.

In the United States, Cicourel[52] and others utilized the methods of the new sociology to examine language use and problems encountered by students in the classroom. Concerned about school failure in the early grades, Cicourel and his colleagues found that students were classified by their performance on classroom lessons, tests, promotion interviews, and teacher-administrator conferences. Most significantly, they found the methods used for evaluating and placing students were inadequate—one might even say stupid. Cicourel's group did its research in actual classroom settings where they were involved in direct observation of classroom teaching and testing. They also selected a number of Anglo, black, and Chicano children for observation and testing at home. In addition to extensive note taking, the group used audio and video equipment for the collection of data. Basically, they found that in classroom teaching situations and in testing situations, the children "did not always share the teacher's or tester's idea on what the lesson or test is about."[53] A few examples should illustrate both the methodology and the nature of some of the findings.

In his observations of a classroom lesson which was supposed to teach spacial relations and basic grammar, Hugh Mehan [54] found large gaps between what the teacher had in mind as the correct answer and the way the students interpreted the questions asked by the teacher. In one exercise the students drew a line on a piece of paper and were asked to draw objects on the paper in relation to that line. They were then asked to explain in a complete sentence where the objects were in relation to the line. The teacher wanted the students' responses to be factually and grammatically correct. They were asked to draw worms, trees, and a sun in relation to the line on their papers without being told why they were doing it. They were not given instructions on what it meant to put things above or below the line. When they finished, the teacher asked where they had put the sun or trees or worms. She expected them to say, "I put the sun above the line." or, "I put the worm below the line." The kids, of course, not knowing what the teacher wanted, gave all sorts of answers. For example, in response to the question, "Where did you put the tree?", they might say, "by the sun." Or, "I put the worm by the tree." Obviously, there were many correct responses from the students' point of view, but only one as far as the teacher was concerned. The teacher was operating from a different context than the students. Unfortunately, when a "wrong" answer was provided, the teacher might conclude that the student was not very bright.

David Roth[55] found the same problems with the Peabody Intelligence Test, where the correct answer depends upon the test maker's construct of the situation. Given the opportunity to explain why they selected what they did when they selected "incorrect" responses, the children gave perfectly logical reasons for their selections. Other researchers found the same problems with standardized tests and classroom tests. This research is notable not because it made revolutionary discoveries—anyone with any sense should know that one's personal interpretations of a context will influence answers given when questioned about it. In the words of Ellion Mishler: "Meaning in context: is there any other kind?"[56] Rather, it is notable because the researchers found that teachers and other school officials grouped and classified students on the basis of their performance on these impossible tasks.

The work of Ray C. Rist[57] is, methodologically at least, within the realm of the new sociology. He made twice-weekly observations of a single group of black children in an urban ghetto school during their stay in kindergarten and later during the first half of their second-grade year. Using a method labeled *microethnography*, the researcher observed classes and then made written comments on the experience after the visit. In-depth interviews were conducted with the teachers. Rist described in some detail the social stratification which took place in a kindergarten classroom. He found four major criteria used by teachers to classify children. These included physical appearance, instructional behavior, classroom language usage, and previously known (by the teacher) social factors. Children were grouped at four different tables according to these criteria. Basically, the first table seemed to get most of the teacher's attention, the second table a little less, the third table even less, while those at the fourth table were virtually ignored. The physical characteristics used to place students included such things as dress, cleanliness, skin color, personal grooming, and so on. The interactional behaviors which were most approved by the teacher were behaviors which tended to support the teacher. Group leaders who helped the teacher organize the students into teacher-directed tasks seemed to be favored. The more articulate students who displayed a greater use of standard American English were favored. Finally, such factors as family conditions, the educational level of parents, size of family, and whether or not the family was on welfare seemed to have some effect on student placement at the tables. Rist found that once the classifications had been made, they tended to continue in force through the second grade. Although the classifications were made by the teacher on purely subjective grounds, they tended to be self-fulfilling. Those who were encouraged to do well and were favored by the teacher did well and continued in their advantageous position even with different teachers in the first and second grades. Going beyond the immediate data, Rist concluded that "it appears that the public school system not only mirrors the configurations of the larger society, but also significantly contributes to maintaining them. Thus the system of public education in reality perpetuates what it is ideologically committed to eradicate—class barriers which result in inequality in the social and economic life of the citizenry."[58]

Many more illustrations of classroom studies could be provided, and certainly very important studies have been omitted from this brief discussion. However, commonalities in the methodology of the new sociologists are emerging. Accepting no basic truths, they prefer to develop general concepts from detailed observations and analysis of those observations.

SOME PROBLEMS WITH THE NEW SOCIOLOGY

A major problem with the new sociology of education is the difficulty the research has with ideology. It may be true, as many new sociologists argue, that the curriculum is ideological. Once this position is taken, however, it still leaves one with serious questions. Whose ideology does the school reflect? The new sociologists offer little that the conflict theorists have not already suggested. The studies seem to come down on the side of conflict theory in that the established ideology which the curriculum teaches is that which reflects the interests of the middle class. This is a middle-class society with middle-class values, with teachers who hold middle-class values; ergo, this is what the schools value. Of course, the middle class is manipulated by the ruling elite. Nothing new or exciting in that. Many new sociologists, in addressing the question, 'Whose ideology should the schools reflect?", seem to vaguely suggest that some other ideology would be better.

It is not always clear where the data provided by new sociologists lead one. For whatever reasons, it is true that the public school classrooms contain students who are heterogeneous, with widely ranging abilities and interests. How the school should deal with differences and problems of inequity is not made completely clear by the new sociologists. An interesting criticism of the approaches of the new sociology can be found in an article by Harry L. Miller, "Hard Realities and Soft Social Science."[59] Miller's central point is that the new sociology of education is blatantly political. He charged that the new sociologists were unhappy with hard research because its findings sometimes undermine what Miller called "liberal and radical convictions about social causation."

New sociologists seem better prepared to define problems in education than to find solutions. This is partly because of a sort of self-effacing reluctance to appear deterministic, but it is also because of basic shortcomings in the methodology itself. One cannot deny that specific in-depth studies of situations can result in reasonably accurate descriptions of the problems. Thus, one can determine, through prolonged and painstaking observation, that little George does not perceive a context in the same way as Maria or the teacher. If generalizations can't be made from such precise observations, the question arises: Why do the study at all?

Perhaps an even more serious criticism of the new sociology is the tendency for prolonged observational studies of classroom situations to reveal the obvious. Stripped of its sociological jargon, much of the new sociology reveals what everybody already knew. It seems so obvious, for example, that perception is an individual thing. Nor did we need a new sociology to inform us that perception is greatly influenced by life's experiences and that there are wide differences in students' environmental backgrounds. What is remarkable is that teachers and other school officials often seem unaware of this obvious phenomenon. Or worse, they are deliberately designing their classroom practices and school policies to assure that those who are different will most certainly fail.

These become important difficulties with the new sociology approaches since the time and expense involved in this type of research should promise more. If all the new sociologists can offer is more precise definition of problems already defined, or more specific documentation of the obvious, then the expense in time and money required with the new sociology may not be worth the effort.

Finally, there is a certain amount of naivete in the new sociology. If the language of the black ghetto is acceptable in given situations, if patterns of behavior are determined by the situation in the classroom, if all elements of all value systems must be openly and equally accepted, what happens when the child enters a society which has certain specific prerequisites for success?

One way out of this dilemma is to reject the so-called consensus values, as conflict theorists do. The new sociologist tends to accept what exists—assuming it is accurately perceived—as simply that which exists. Thus, the implication in new sociology research in education, that children's perceptions of reality should be understood in order to effectively teach them, somehow doesn't provide much direction. An understanding of children's "real" problems in a school setting and what these children need to be able to share in the benefits of the larger society is a connection not often made clear by the new sociologist. Given a society in which there is an identifiable knowledge base and a group of specific skills which need to be learned to function in that society, it would seem that schools which respected and perhaps promoted certain kinds of pluralism would do little to change the broader social system. Unless, of course, one assumes that the school can single-handedly change the society in fundamental ways. The fact that students can succeed on their own grounds means little unless that success is rewarded in the larger society. Perhaps the greatest hope for the new sociology lies in the possibility that, as it develops its data base, new and more comprehensive theory will emerge.

SOME CONCLUDING COMMENTS ON SOCIAL THEORY

Social theorists, no matter how scientific their claims, find objectivity difficult because the object of their study is society and its problems. A certain amount of subjectivity exists because values are central to any society and what "ought to be" becomes a legitimate concern of theory. The development of theory is related to the manner in which theorists perceive the real world, and assumptions are based, to some degree at least, on the values of the theorist.

If the description of social theory in this chapter demonstrates anything, it is that there is no consensus among scholars on what constitutes reality in schooling as an institution or a process. Functionalists, who like to claim scholarly detachment and objectivity, are accused of accepting and thus promoting a conservative social order, and failing somehow to clearly understand what really happens in classrooms. At the other extreme, the phenomenologists are charged with practicing soft social science, of documenting the obvious and adding little to our understanding of schooling. Marxists charge the functionalists with ideological bias. It isn't that Marxists reject ideological assumptions themselves, they simply do not agree with what they perceive as the ideological assumptions of the functionalists.

Because of these and other difficulties and since each theoretical approach has something to offer, what follows does not embrace a single theory. Rather, the approach is descriptive and eclectic, leaving to the reader the opportunity to delve more deeply into theoretical explanations of the problems outlined. This approach is taken with the hope of providing a broader understanding of schooling in American society than is possible when schooling is described from a limited set of assumptions.

More significantly, perhaps, it is possible that there is no satisfactory way to explain something as complex as schools and schooling. It is possible that there is no real consensus in America on the purpose of schooling. Even if there were, what if each school system, as an entrenched bureaucracy, had a life of its own independent of anything save the perpetuation of its own existence? Are schools like the federal bureaucracy in this sense? It doesn't seem to matter who is in residence at 1600 Pennsylvania Avenue or which party is in control of Congress—the federal bureaucracy tends to go its own way. It has a life of its own, insulated, independent, and protected from the political storms which surround it. What if this is the case with school bureaucracies? Clearly schools are influenced by society, but to what extent?

What if a significant part of what the schools do is independent of community forces, national problems, conflicts, and change? What if the schools have a life of their own, oblivious in many respects to what is happening in the larger society? These questions will reappear in many forms in the pages which follow. One of the purposes of this effort, like much of the work of social theorists, is to raise questions, not answer them.

NOTES

1. David Silverman, *The Theory of Organizations* (New York: Basic Books, 1971), pp. 54–60.
2. Madan Sarup, *Marxism and Education* (London: Routledge & Kegan Paul, 1978), p. 69.
3. Talcott Parsons, "The School Class as a Social System: Some of Its Functions in American Society," *Harvard Educational Review* 29 (Fall 1959): 297–319.
4. Robert K. Merton and Robert A. Nisbet, eds., *Contemporary Social Problems*, 3d ed. (New York: Harcourt Brace Jovanovich, 1971), pp. 1–28.
5. Robert K. Merton, *Social Theory and Social Structure* (New York: The Free Press, 1968), p. 105.
6. Christopher J. Hurn, *The Limits and Possibilities of Schooling* (Boston: Allyn & Bacon, 1978), pp. 37–43.
7. John Ogbu, *The Next Generation* (New York: Academic Press, 1974), pp. 10–11.
8. Richard A. Cloward and Lloyd E. Ohlin, *Delinquency and Opportunity: A Theory of Delinquent Gangs* (New York: Free Press, 1960).
9. Alvin Gouldner, *Patterns of Industrial Democracy* (New York: Free Press, 1954).
10. Rachel Sharp and Anthony Green, *Education and Social Control* (London: Routledge & Kegan Paul, 1975), pp. 4–9.
11. Donald A. Hansen, *An Invitation to Critical Sociology* (New York: Macmillan Publishing Co., 1976), p. 136.
12. Alex Callinicos, *Althusser's Marxism* (New York: Pluto Press, 1976), p. 66.
13. Sarup, *Marxism and Education*, p. 151.
14. Herbert Marcuse, *Eros and Civilization* (New York: Vintage, 1955), p. 30.
15. Ibid., p. 16.
16. Ibid., p. 85.
17. Ibid., p. 88.
18. Ibid., pp. 89–90.
19. Ibid., p. 94.
20. Paulo Freire, *Pedagogy of the Oppressed* (New York: Seabury Press, 1968).
21. Ibid., p. 30.
22. Ibid., p. 33.
23. Ibid.
24. Ivan Illich, *Deschooling Society* (New York: Harrow Books, 1970), pp. 55–62.
25. Ibid., p. 106.
26. Samuel Bowles and Herbert Gintis, *Schooling in Capitalist America* (New York: Basic Books, 1976).
27. Ibid., p. 37.
28. Ibid., p. 39.
29. Ibid., pp. 42–43.
30. Ibid., p. 44.
31. Antonio Gramsci, *Selections from the Prison Notebooks*, ed. and trans. by Q. Hoare and G. N. Smith (London: Lawrence & Wishart, 1971).
32. Ibid., p. 325.
33. Michael Young, *The Rise of Meritocracy* (New York: Random House, 1959).
34. Ibid., p. 21.
35. Ibid., p. 11.
36. Rachael Sharp and Anthony Green, *Education and Social Control: A Study in Progressive Primary Education* (London: Routledge & Kegan Paul, 1975), p. 19.
37. Ibid., p. 18.

38. Alfred Schutz, "Concept and Theory Formation in the Social Sciences," in collected papers, ed. Maurice Natanson (The Hague: Martinus Nijhoff, 1967), p. 56.
39. Ibid., p. 18.
40. David Gorbutt, "The New Sociology of Education," *Education for Teaching* 89 (Autumn 1972): 3–11.
41. Christopher Hurn, "Recent Trends in the Sociology of Education in Britain," *Harvard Educational Review* 46 (February 1976): 111.
42. Amitai Etzioni, *Social Problems* (Englewood Cliffs, N.J.: Prentice-Hall, 1976), p. 16.
43. Gorbutt, "The New Sociology of Education," p. 7.
44. William Labov, "The Logic of Nonstandard English," in *The Myth of Cultural Deprivation*, ed. Neil Keddie (London: Penguin Books, 1973), p. 24.
45. Aaron Cicourel et al., *Language Use and School Performance* (New York: Academic Press, 1974).
46. Hurn, *Harvard Educational Review*, pp. 105–114.
47. Basil Bernstein, "Social Class, Language and Socialization," in *Current Trends in Linguistics*, vol. 12, ed. A. S. Abramson et al. (London: Mouton, 1973).
48. Basil Bernstein, "Social Class, Language and Socialization," in *Power and Ideology in Education*, ed. Jerome Karabel and A. H. Halsey (New York: Oxford University Press, 1977), p. 479.
49. Sharp and Green, *Education and Social Control.*
50. Ibid., p. 221.
51. See Frances Schwartz' review of the study in *Harvard Educational Review* 46 (November 1976): 639–642.
52. Cicourel et al., *Language Use and School Performance.*
53. Ibid., p. 5.
54. Ibid., chap. 3.
55. Ibid., chap. 4.
56. Ellion Mishler, "Meaning in Context: Is There Any Other Kind?" *Harvard Educational Review* 49 (February 1979): 1.
57. Ray C. Rist, "Student Social Class and Teacher Expectations: The Self-Fulfilling Prophecy in Ghetto Education," *Harvard Educational Review* 40 (August 1970): 411–451.
58. Ibid., p. 415.
59. Harry L. Miller, "Hard Realities and Soft Social Science," *The Public Interest*, no. 59 (Spring 1980): 67–81.

Part II

The State and the Schools

The material in this part deals with the scope of state control over schools. In the United States, as in other nations, schools are expected to socialize students to the political values of the society and to produce citizens who are capable of assuming productive adult roles in that society.

In American society a comprehensive network of public control of public and private education has developed. If schooling is a major function of the state, one might expect a number of things to follow. If schooling is to promote the political values of the society, one should be able to determine, at least in rough outline, what the major political values are. Chapter 2 attempts to outline the efforts the schools have made to define and promote something loosely called "American ideology."

If the school does serve as an agent of the state, it is not surprising that serious efforts have been made through the years, first to make schooling compulsory, then gradually to extend this program of compulsory schooling. Chapter 3 deals with efforts to establish a comprehensive system of compulsory schooling in America.

Not every child in America attends the public schools. There is a large and growing nonpublic school movement in America. For a variety of reasons, church-related schools have always been popular in the United States. For most of our history these schools have been sponsored by the "old-line" churches, and their efforts to establish moral and religious training have met with both success and failure. More recently fundamentalist Christian schools have become a significant part of the American educational scene. These schools and other alternatives to public schooling are discussed in Chapter 4.

Finally, Chapter 5 deals with the huge bureaucracy which has grown around the public school enterprise. The emphasis in Chapter 5 is on the increasing importance of state control and the growing state bureaucracies which have developed to administer the school function on the state and local levels.

2

The Schools and the Democratic Idea

Schools exist for some purpose. At least those who pay the bills and make educational policy think they do. In any society one might assume that a central function of schooling is to socialize students to the knowledge and values considered important in that society. This assumes, of course, both that there is some consensus on which knowledge and values are most important and that the schools can teach them.

Although it may be impossible to determine if there is a national consensus on what the schools ought to do, we do have a rough notion of what schools are like. There is some evidence that schools, in their general outlines, are more alike than they are different. Generally, school buildings are built in much the same way, with halls and rooms and gyms and playgrounds. Any citizen, traveling anywhere in the country, knows a school when he sees one. From the inside they look alike. Most are organized similarly, with school boards, superintendents, principals, teachers, and pupils. An incredible number of schools use the same textbooks. Teachers are trained in very similar ways and seem to move about from state to state with only very minor adjustments. More could be said, but there does appear to be a pattern here. Such obvious similarity might lead one to believe that there is also some general agreement on the knowledge and values promoted within these look-alike settings. Alas, this is where we encounter grave difficulties in making generalizations. Schools are one thing; *schooling* may be something quite different.

What is happening in schools? Are they teaching all children an identifiable body of knowledge and values deliberately designed to somehow socialize them to something loosely called "American Democracy"?

Have they always done this? Do scholars agree on how it has been done, how it should be done, and how effective the schools have been in that socialization task? These questions are difficult since a major problem in this society is attempting to determine the meaning of the system: what the ideals are. Obviously, if one is to utilize the schools as a method of socialization to the ideals of the system, one must be able to define the ideals. If the public schools in the United States are dedicated to socializing the young to something called the American ideology, what is it? The material which follows examines this question, and, using the framework developed, describes different interpretations of the role of the schools in the process of political socialization.

IS THERE AN AMERICAN IDEOLOGY?

The existence of an ideology of democratic society has been for centuries a central theme in the development of democratic political systems. A democracy of sorts was said to exist in Athens as early as the fifth century B.C. The American and French revolutions of the eighteenth century and the Russian revolution of the twentieth are often characterized as democratic; that is, leaders in these movements claimed they were fighting tyranny and attempting to establish democratic systems. Claims from such diverse sources should perhaps discourage one from pursuing the issue further. Yet the meaning of democracy has been a central question in American education.

If any historian were truly successful in writing a "people's" history of the United States, the major theme could very well be a struggle on the part of the people or those honestly representing them to realize an ideology based on the democratic principles of equality, freedom, and social justice. History, of course, is not that story. It is much more selective; it is a story of great leaders and large movements and "progress," with the implication that everyone shared in it. In American history it is easy enough to find this thread of development. Most histories are "success stories" in which each new generation seems to be better off than the last. Yet as one looks more closely at the society, relative positions of the poor and the rich, minorities and majorities, remain basically unchanged.

It is easy enough to demonstrate that certain leading citizens, political figures, captains of industry, labor leaders, and others have from time to time championed something they called the great American democratic ideal. It is difficult, however, to determine in each case what is meant by that ideal. It seems to vary in time and place and depends in large measure on the views of its advocates. From the beginning, democratic ideology has been beset with confusion and ambiguity. The democratic concepts of equality, freedom, and individualism have never been completely clear. *Equality* as used in the Declaration of Independence and the Constitution did not really mean that *all* men are equal: slavery existed, the propertyless could not vote, and neither could women. Even Jacksonian democracy did not include everyone. The freedom and individualism of the great capitalist industrialists, from Andrew Carnegie to his present descendants, did not necessarily mean freedom and individualism for everybody. The injustices persisted into the twentieth century. Wilson's New Freedom, Roosevelt's New Deal, and Lyndon Johnson's Great Society addressed the problems of injustice and inequality, but many of these problems still await solutions.

In the American experience there can be little argument that political ideologies have existed and that political efforts have been made within ideological frameworks and in behalf of achieving broader definitions of ideology—broader in the sense that they covered more people. Even so, there have always been limits on the realization of the democratic ideals of equality, freedom, and individualism. Somehow these ideas seem to have had more relevance for the intellectuals, the educated, the powerful, and the wealthy than for the masses. Inequality has always existed and continues to be a major characteristic of American society. The rich and powerful appear to have more freedom than the poor. Thus, democratic ideology has been for the masses an elusive, even though cherished, ideal. Still, because of the central role that certain major political values have played in the minds of those who are responsible for schooling, it is a useful undertaking to attempt to outline them. Moreover, there is some evidence that the powerless in American society—the poor, women, blacks, and others—have discovered that the invocation of ideology, particularly the themes of equality and freedom, can serve their political, economic, and social ends. In a sense they have used the belief or myth of consensus democratic values as a political club. What, then, are the ideologies which have been so vital in the American system?

AMERICAN IDEOLOGY

Throughout American history those who worked in the schools or who were interested in promoting public education have tended to push their ideas for public support of education within the general context of what they viewed as American ideology. From the beginning, advocates of public education have argued that more support be given to public education because schooling was necessary for developing honest, intelligent, and democratic citizens. Regardless of differences of opinion as to what the American ideology was, public school advocates almost universally viewed the school as a major instrument to be utilized by the society to promote American ideals. That is, disagreements over definitions of American ideology or even over whether or not an ideology existed, did not get in the way of efforts to propagandize the importance of schooling.

Although there appears to be a great deal of disagreement regarding the role of ideology in relationship to the political and economic system, this disagreement seems less evident in the development of public education. In order to examine the relationship between the schools and ideology, it might be helpful to consider two general ways in which ideology has been viewed. One way of looking at ideology in relationship to the schools is to attempt to determine if the schools practiced it. Another approach is to view ideology as a system of beliefs which may or may not be acted upon by an institution such as the school.

Since it would be extremely difficult to examine precisely what the schools have or have not done throughout history to promote some well-defined ideology, a more general view will be taken. For purposes of analysis, the following definition of ideology will be used:

> The "way of life" of a people reflected in terms of their political system, economic order, social goals, and moral values. Ideology is particularly concerned with the form and role of government and the nature of a state's economic system. Ideology may also describe the ideas and views held by a party, class, or group.[1]

Given this definition of ideology, it is difficult to determine precisely if there is an ideology in the United States. There has always been much disagreement over political, economic, social, and moral values and goals. This might be why a number of social scientists in recent years have declared that America is essentially a pragmatic society without a guiding ideology. Robert L. Heilbroner in *The Future as History*[2] described the United States as primarily a pragmatic society which willy-nilly tended to follow the siren call of technology, and the result was essentially a nonplanned, albeit successful, development. Historically the system worked; there was steady though uneven growth, and that was enough for most. What disturbed Heilbroner was how long America could continue to drift aimlessly without conscious planning for the future. This point was made again in *An Inquiry into the Human Prospect*.[3] In both of these works, Heilbroner advocated greater efforts at planning, lest the society flounder hopelessly in uncharted seas. Planning for the future assumes that the society has some generalized goals toward which it strives; thus, planning very often involves some general agreement on a basic ideological framework.

Daniel Bell couldn't see any general agreement; indeed, he proclaimed the end of ideology.[4] Depression and wars and class struggles, the rise of fascism and racial imperialism, and the failure of revolutionaries from 1930 to 1950 spelled doom to ideology in Bell's view. This was true because in order to succeed, ideology had to be the road to action. Without action, without concrete accomplishment of goals, ideology failed. Bell could find little in the way of accomplishment by those who dreamed of a better society. Ideology was defeated by a combination of fear, apathy, and repression. Bell blamed the Moscow trials, the Nazi-Soviet pact, concentration camps, the modification of capitalism, and the rise of the welfare state for the end of ideology. These events and others caused men to realize that it was impossible to follow some blueprint to a new "utopia of social harmony." This does not mean that the death of ideology was total. Bell indicated that ideology was still alive and well in the developing world, but there it was an ideology of materialism, industrialization, modernization, and nationalism imposed by leaders. The old nineteenth-century ideology of humanism was dead.

This was written in 1960 and there was no way that Bell could have foreseen the movement in the decades ahead of the poor, the blacks, the students, and women. Interestingly, the unrest and activism of the disenchanted groups of recent years have been, in many ways, a return to the humanistic ideology of an earlier century. Much of the ideological base of newly organized minorities has been a classic expression of what had long been claimed as the classical concensus values. In their struggles for equality, freedom, liberty, and justice, the outsiders had suddenly discovered the ideology which the mainstream had apparently taken for granted. Yet the successes were limited. The rhetorical expression of the ideal, whatever its form, was always far ahead of concrete action. Perhaps the ideal was a myth after all. Maybe Daniel Boorstin was correct when he wrote in *The Genius of American Politics*[5] that the real genius of American politics is that it has been without a dogma.

It is possible to marshal much evidence to demonstrate the pragmatic, nonideological nature of the decision-making process in the American system. The political system and its institutions have been able, until now at least, to deal with issues which confront the society, if not to solve them. The major economic and social issues which have confronted society either have been dealt with in some manner, or, if ignored by those with formal political power, they have not proved fatal. It is as easy to demonstrate the successes of a decision-making process operating without ideological guidelines as it is to demonstrate its failures.

The manner in which the system has faced or adjusted to major economic and social issues throughout our history lends some weight to the theory that ours has been essentially a pragmatic, nonideological society. In the realm of economics, for example, the ideology of liberal capitalism has always been there in the form of the classical model of Adam Smith, which was based on the political ideology of eighteenth-century liberal thought. Yet as one economic crisis followed another, it almost seems as if the ideology came as an afterthought, a rationalization for specific solutions to specific problems, rather than as a guideline for their solution.

Ideology notwithstanding, there have been no revolutionary solutions to social problems. The problems of race, poverty, and social stratification, the educational deficiencies of the poor—the most serious continuing problems in American society have yet to be solved. Progress has been made but never in terms which bring any basic change. The progress toward racial equality is in complete conformity with the nineteenth-century liberal formulation of the ideal of equality —that is, equality of opportunity. Everyone should be provided an equal chance to succeed. If they are unsuccessful, it is their own fault, not the fault of the system. The attacks on poverty were accomplished largely through a welfare system which made no significant change in the economic system and the social structure. If anything, it hardened the system of social stratification. Welfare capitalism assumed responsibility for keeping the poor from starving, not for elevating a whole class into the main-stream.

School reform has been the concern of every generation, yet the schools continue to serve the poor and minorities inadequately. Thus, the system generally has been able to escape an ideology narrowly defined. Even so, something loosely called democratic ideology continues to provide some guidance to the system. The real question, perhaps, is not so much whether the American system is guided by an ideology, but whose ideology it is.

Perhaps more than any other institution in the society, including even political parties, the schools have been at the center of a continuing controversy over the meaning of American democracy. Educational historians from Cubberley onward have included as a significant part of their description and analysis, the efforts—or lack of them—that the schools have made to promote and extend the democratic idea, especially the idea of equality.

What has emerged from educational history, at the risk of oversimplification, are two broad views of the schools in their relationship to democratic ideology. The first, which has been labeled traditional educational history, reports the shortcomings and difficulties faced by the schools but nonetheless enthusiastically declares that the schools have promoted the democratic idea. The second view, that of the radical historians or revisionists, suggests that the schools at best have tended to serve the ruling class, and at worst have been a major obstacle to the realization of the democratic idea. Both views implicitly accept the notion that an ideology exists, however vague it might be. Thus, in a loose way, the criteria used to judge the efficacy of the schools are similar, while the conclusions drawn are much different.

THE TRADITIONAL CASE

In Cubberley's classic *Public Education in the United States*,[6] the author character-ized the growth of schools in America as the fruition of the Protestant Revolt and the "general awakening" of the European Enlightenment. Cubberley's book deals with what he elected to call the "great battles" of education in nineteenth-century America. These included the battle for tax-supported education, the battle to elim-inate the pauper school idea, the battle to eliminate tuition and make the schools completely free, the battle to provide supervision, the battle to eliminate religious influences, the battle for high schools and higher education, the battle to provide for normal schools, the evolution of a graded system of instruction, and the opening of educational opportunity for women.[7] By the beginning of the twentieth century, Cubberley and other traditional historians could boast that all of these battles had been won.

Even by nineteenth-century standards of objective historiography, it would be difficult to classify Cubberley as an objective chronicler of the schools. His enthusiasm and optimism seemed to know no bounds. Cubberley didn't appear to have much doubt about the purpose of the schools. In his conclusions in *Public Education* he declared flatly that education was and ought to be a constructive national tool. His views of the purposes of public education in the United States can be summarized in the following statement:

> We have here the makings of a great Nation, but the task before us is to make it. The raw materials—Saxon and Celt, Teuton and Slav, Latin and Hun—all are here. Our problem is to assimilate and amalgamate them all into a unified Nation, actuated by common impulses, inspired by common ideals, conscious of a moral unity and pur-pose which will be our strength, and so filled with reverence for our type of national life that our youth will feel that our form of government is worth dying for to defend.[8]

Those who followed Cubberley in the writing of educational history tended to echo these sentiments. The tradition was continued by Knight in four editions of his *Education in the United States*, spanning the years from 1929 to 1951. In his introductory chapter to the 1951 edition, Knight kept the faith. He saw the school system as necessary for the maintenance of a democratic form of govern-ment. He declared that "through proper education they [the people] learn that their obligation is to properly constituted government, which is all its citizens —rich and poor, high and low, strong and feeble, bright and dull."[9]

Following Cubberley's themes, Knight declared that the schools were built upon the "so-called democratic principles of education which have come to be accepted and are now more or less practically applied in all sections of the entire United States."[10] These principles according to Knight included: (1) universal free education paid for with public taxes, (2) public control, (3) compulsory attendance, and (4) nonsectarian schools.[11]

In fairness, Knight did see problems in the system. His history, as well as Cubberley's, focused on school problems awaiting solution, but these histories were more compendiums of progress than criticisms of shortcomings. Both seemed convinced that the people would find the answers somehow. This was because the importance of schooling was so obvious to all concerned. In Knight's words, "the doctrine of educational equality and the principles of universal, free, public, compulsory, and secular education have already been justified in the diffusion of knowledge and in the moral uplift, the heightened civic virtue, and the improved economic and social conditions of the masses."[12] There was, in Knight's view, "hope for the future."

It is difficult to fault the traditional historians for their idealism; the belief that the existence of free public schools was the most sure way to promote the democratic ideal was commonplace throughout much of the nineteenth century and well into the twentieth century. A few examples should demonstrate this unbounded faith in the schools.

In 1830 the *Report of a Committee of Philadelphia Workingmen* expected great accomplishments from the schools. In their opinion there could be

> no real liberty without a wide diffusion of real intelligence; that the members of a republic, should all be alike instructed in the nature and character of their equal rights and duties, as human beings, and as citizens; and that education, instead of being limited as in our public schools, to a simple acquaintance with words and cyphers, should tend, as far as possible, to the production of just disposition, virtuous habits, and a rational self-governing character.[13]

The *Common School Journal* echoed these sentiments a decade later in an editorial statement in support of free public schools.

> By education, I do not mean a mere capacity to read, write and cipher; but some faithful training of the power of thought...I would give every poor and friendless boy a chance to grow up a strong-minded and right-hearted man,—independent, free, able to bear himself well in the struggle of life....[14]

Some saw the common school as the great equalizer, necessary in a pluralistic and stratified society in order to break down class barriers. Horace Bushnell from Connecticut defended the public school idea as the only reasonable alternative to religious and private schools. Concerned about class biases of private schools, Bushnell commented:

> I seriously doubt whether any system of popular government can stand the shock, for any length of time, of that fierce animosity, that is certain to be gendered where the children are trained up wholly in their classes, and never brought together to feel, understand, appreciate and respect each other, on the common footing of merit and of native talent, in a common school.[15]

Those who didn't like the idea of common schools could love us or leave us: "No! take your place with us in our common schools, and consent to be Americans, or else go back to Turkey, where Mohammedans, Greeks, Armenians and Jews are walled up by the laws themselves, forbidding them ever to pass over or to change their superstitions. . . ."[16]

There was much concern in the late nineteenth and early twentieth centuries about the Americanization of millions of children of the foreign born. Many believed that the public schools should turn the children of immigrants into Americans as quickly as possible. Typical of this view was a statement by A. R. Dugmore, who was writing in *The World's Work* in 1903:

> It is a large task that schools . . . are doing, taking the raw, low-class foreign boys of many nationalities and molding them into self-supporting, self-respecting citizens of the republic. The amount of this work done by the public schools in New York is indicated by the figures of the immigration bureau, for of the great body of foreigners who come into this country, more than two-thirds come through the port of New York, beyond which most of them rarely get. There are many things in which, as a rule, the public consider that the public schools fail, but the one thing that cannot be denied—and it is the greatest—is that these boys and girls of foreign parentage catch readily the simple American ideas of independence and individual work, and, with them, social progress.[17]

Sometimes the advocates of the democratic promise of the common school tended to lump democratic values and the values of industry and business together. Many would have agreed with James Patterson, state Superintendent of Public Instruction in New Hampshire, when he wrote in 1881:

> The laws of trade and social economy, the inventive skill, the thrift and enterprise of business, the capacity for industrial production, and the accumulations of wealth, the growth of brain power, and moral stamina which brings influence and character to communities have their birth and nourishment in the schools.[18]

In deed, the notion that business values and the development of democracy were identical was common in the late nineteenth and early twentieth centuries. The main purpose of the schools for those who held these beliefs was to produce a properly disciplined work force for industrial America. The major expression of this idea was in the development of manual training programs which began to appear in the last quarter of the nineteenth century. Cubberley reported that by 1919 the idea of manual training was commonplace even in elementary schools.[19]

In the early part of the twentieth century, a great deal of interest was expressed in the idea of something called "industrial intelligence." Industrialists and some school officials were concerned about the problem of unhappy and alienated workers in the early years of the twentieth century. This was a problem since the industrial system needed workers who would be content to work at boring and repetitive tasks. The schools were called upon to train such workers not only in the minimal skills needed to man the machines but, more importantly, in the right attitudes which would make them happy with their work. Although some felt that this type of worker needed very little in the way of formal schooling, others thought that moral training and especially devotion, loyalty, the dedication to the idea of work itself were things which the common schools should teach. Always, of course, these ideas were couched in terms which extolled these ordinary virtues as important to the preservation and progress of the democratic idea. The perfect society was comprised of workers who were happy in their menial tasks—productive, obedient, and law-abiding citizens.

These values were long associated with the democratic mission of the common school. As early as 1852 the notion that the school could provide an effective training ground for factory workers was expressed by the Lowell, Massachusetts school committee. Advocating an expansion of schools into a graded system, they observed:

> The principle of the division of labor holds good in schools, as in mechanical industry. One might as justly demand that all operations of carding, spinning and weaving be carried out in the same room, and by the same hands, as insist that children of different ages and attainments should go to the same school, and be instructed by the same teacher. . . . What a school system requires is that it be systematic; that each grade, from the lowest to the highest, be distinctly marked, and afford a thorough preparation for each . . . grade.[20]

A writer in the *Massachusetts Teacher* was even more specific on the meaning of industrial intelligence and the sort of training necessary to produce it:

> That the habit of prompt action in the performance of the duty required of the boy, by the teacher at school, becomes in the man of business confirmed; thus the system and order characterize the employment of the day laborer. He must begin each half day with as much promptness as he drops his tools at the close of it; and he must meet every appointment and order during the hours of the day with no less precision. It is in this way that regularity and economy of time have become characteristic of our community, as appears on the running 'on time' of long trains . . . the strict regulations of all large manufacturing establishments; as well as the daily arrangements of our school duties . . . Thus, what has been instilled in the mind is of first importance in the transaction of business.[21]

Nor was there any doubt in the minds of some industrialists that schools could successfully turn out the sort of workers they desired. In Lowell, Massachusetts, a factory owner testified in 1841 that workers with more education posed "a higher and better state of morals, [were] more orderly and respectful in their deportment, and more ready to comply with the wholesome and necessary regulations of an establishment."[22]

By the time Cubberley's *History* was published in 1919, the idea that a major function of the common schools and the graded system of instruction was basic training for industrial work was firmly established. In his discussion of the graded system of instruction, Cubberley declared: "With such an introductory training pupils would be . . . better fitted to enter . . . the regular high school which follows, or to turn to the trade and vocational courses and become intelligent workers in our modern industrial society."[23]

One can easily overgeneralize the position of the traditionalists. If they erred in somehow confusing the ideology of democratic society with the welfare of the business enterprise, they had lots of company. The 25 years before and after 1900 were the age of big industry, big business. The whole society was caught up in it. Yet there were doubts even in the minds of the most optimistic traditionalists. In 1919 Professor Knight expressed certain reservations about the influence of industry on the schools. He was concerned that the schools were following the factory model too closely:

> Mass production and standardization are becoming as characteristic of the American school as of the American factory; volume and velocity of output are almost as conspicuous in the realm of education as in the field of machine-made materials.... the mechanical practices of the factory and the countinghouse are coming more and more to be the practices of the schools and colleges.... Education has become increasingly standardized and mechanical, graded by years, by points, by credits, by majors, by courses, and wearing the veneer of finality.[24]

In spite of these misgivings, the traditional educational historians saw the development of public education in the United States as a success story—a story of almost uninterrupted progress in which the public assumed increasing responsibility for provision of a universal system of free public education for all citizens. The idea that a central purpose of this growing system was to socialize children to fit into the industrial system as productive workers was rarely questioned. Thus, democratic education meant a school system which supported the existing political, social, and—especially—economic systems.

THE REVISIONISTS

More recently, a group of educational historians has put a different interpretation on the historical development of the schools. A number of scholars—most notable Colin Greer, Joel Spring, Samuel Bowles, Herbert Gintis, Michael Katz, David Tyack, Paul Violas, Clarence Karier, John Ogbu, and others—have studied the history of the schools in the United States and have reached the conclusion that the schools have never promoted the democratic idea. In the view of these scholars, the schools have instead promoted narrow and selfish class interests and have been instrumental in conserving what is basically an undemocratic and limited system.

Colin Greer concluded in *The Great School Legend*[25] that the schools not only failed in their great democratic promise but served as a major obstacle to the realization of the democratic ideals of equality and economic and social justice. According to Greer, the notion that the schools took the children of the poor and immigrants and minorities from their conditions of ignorance and poverty and elevated them into the mainstream of society was a myth. Greer provides data to demonstrate that the schools failed miserably in their attempts to provide even a basic education for the children of the poor and immigrants and minorities. Reviewing census data from 1920 to 1960, Greer found that "neither the schools nor society offered quite the mobility imagined."[26] Using New York and New Jersey as examples, Greer reported that in "1950 more than 80 percent of New York and New Jersey's working men of Italian, Irish, and Slavic extraction were employed in unskilled or semiskilled occupations."[27] Looking at the statistics in 1969, he discovered that the sons of fathers with fewer than eight years of education, many of whom were the children and grandchildren of immigrants from southern and eastern Europe, "have had little effective access to college, and thus even less access to upper-level jobs."[28] Rather than providing a ladder of upward mobility for these children, the schools tended to keep them in their place. In various school reports studied by Greer in cities where large numbers of immigrant children lived, such as Chicago, Boston, New York, Philadelphia, and Detroit, it was clear that the children of immigrants in the decades from 1920 to 1940 did poorly in school. School performance was poor, and dropout rates at the compulsory school-leaving age exceeded 50 percent. Many in school were over-aged for their grade level and were classified as slow learners by the school systems. Greer found that black children did even more poorly.

Greer's statistics are convincing, particularly those he cites from census data. It is possible to find, in the census data of the twentieth century, documentation of a certain lack of mobility identifiable by race and nationality. This raises an interesting question. Why did certain groups, such as Slavs, Italians, and blacks, consistently, decade after decade, continue to drop out of school early and remain in large numbers in the working class? One answer to this question is that they are somehow inferior, not as capable as native-born white children to cope with the requirements of schooling. Were this the case, the answer could lie in either cultural deficiencies or genetic inferiority. Either way one must admit cultural and racial bias. Greer concludes that the failure of the children of immigrants and blacks to succeed has been the result of a deliberate policy on the part of the schools to perpetuate bigotry, racism, and class distinction. In his words, "the school's failure has been, in fact a criterion of their social success . . . the failure of many children has been, and still is, a learning experience precisely appropriate to the place assigned them and their families in the social order. They are being taught to fail and to accept their failure."[29]

Even without the data, some support for Greer's conclusions can be found in the attitudes of even the most ardent supporters of the early common school. As early as the 1840s, Henry Barnard revealed his repulsion with the family conditions of the urban poor:

> No one at all familiar with the deficient household arrangements and deranged machinery of the domestic life, of the extreme poor, and ignorant, to say nothing of the intemperate—of the examples of rude manners, impure and profane language, and all the vicious habits of low bred idleness, which abound in certain sections of all populous districts—can doubt, that it is better for children to be removed as early and as long as possible from such scenes and examples.[30]

The solution for Barnard and many other early school advocates was to use the school to civilize these monsters. Providing children with genuine enlightenment was not seriously considered. Teaching them "gentleness, kindness and truth," values of character, and discipline always seemed to take precedence over any deeper intellectual purpose. In the words of Katz: "Barnard . . . accurately reflected the sentiment of most people promoting schools. Nearly without exception, they chose heart over the head."[31]

According to the revisionist critics, public schooling in the nineteenth century, and for that matter much of the twentieth, was not meant so much to provide for a general improvement of the intellect and culture of the society as to provide the minimal skills needed and the right attitudes necessary for the preservation and development of existing society. Hofstadter makes this point in *Anti-Intellectualism in American Life*: "The belief in mass education was not founded primarily upon a passion for the development of mind, or upon pride in learning and culture for their own sakes, but rather upon the supposed political and economic benefits of education."[32]

The early advocates, including Barnard and Mann, were interested, according to Hofstadter, in "selling" common schools. "They . . . fixed upon the American mind the idea that under popular government popular education is an absolute necessity. To the rich, . . . they presented popular education as the only alternative to public disorder, to an unskilled and ignorant labor force, to misgovernment, crime, and radicalism."[33]

It was in this vein that Joel Spring viewed the development of the common school as an instrument of social control. With the growth of the industrial system and massive immigration in the last quarter of the nineteenth century, the problems of poverty and family disorganization in 1900 were perhaps worse than those described by Barnard in the 1840s. If there was a justification in 1840 of the "civilizing" effects of compulsory free public schooling, the need had geometrically expanded by 1900. Spring suggested that by 1900 compulsory schooling had, in a sense, replaced the family and the church as the major socializing agency. Moreover, it was a simple kind of socialization, designed to conserve and perpetuate the existing social, economic, and political systems. In Spring's words: "The quest for social control turned the school into a custodial institution designed to maintain the social order. It also led to differentiating and selecting students for social roles on the basis of tests. . . ."[34]

Spring could have added a graded system of instruction, the neglect of minorities and foreign born, and authoritarian classroom practices to support his major point that the schools tended to reflect and perpetuate the existing social order.

What children learn in school has always been a difficult question to answer. Perhaps Hofstadter was correct in the kindest thing he had to say about the common schools, that "the system of common schools was meant to take a vast, heterogeneous, and mobile population . . . and forge it into a nation, make it literate, and give it . . . the minimal civic competence necessary to the operation of republican institutions."[35] It is true that the social order has been able to function and that the population has been generally supportive of it. Whether this is the result of what the schools taught or a combination of forces is not completely clear. There can be little doubt, however, that those who were responsible for deciding what was to be taught were clear, even though not always in agreement, on what they wanted to do. According to the revisionist historians, their motives were equally clear.

It is easy to find class bias in the common school movement from its beginning to the present. Katz charged school leaders with shaping a system which advocated Protestant values and social stratification. He found "a configuration of moral and cultural values" which he characterized as "mid-Victorian" which "permeated school textbooks and statements of educational objectives."[36] Katz saw the movement from small schools and what he called "democratic localism" to "incipient bureaucracy" as a more efficient way to stamp a narrow cultural bias on the entire system of schooling. Moreover, he saw this as a deliberate movement. "... the bias was central and not incidental to the standardization and administrative rationalization of public education. For, in the last analysis, the rejection of democratic localism rested only partly on its inefficiency and violation of parental prerogative. It stemmed equally from a gut fear of the cultural divisiveness inherent in the increasing religious and ethnic diversity of American life. ..." Thus, in the view of Katz, "Bureaucracy was intended to standardize far more than the conduct of public life."[37]

Although much of revisionist history deals with the development of the schools in the nineteenth century, development of the common school in this century has not escaped its attention. Paul Violas found a major theme in twentieth-century American schooling to be the impact of industrial capitalism:

> Educators found the requirements of good citizenship to be identical to those for efficient service in the modern economic system. This ... relationship fostered not only vocational training and guidance programs, but the play movement, extracurricular activities, and Americanization campaigns as well. Examination of the explicit objectives produce adults who met the requirements for an industrial work force. Modern capitalism needed employees who were punctual, accurate, and willing to act as a production team within the boundaries set by superiors.[38]

The effects on the schools of their embrace of the values of American capitalism were pervasive, according to Violas. It made the old notion of cultural and intellectual training obsolete. "Once American public education committed itself to compulsory universal schooling, the idea of education for leadership and independent decision making became dysfunctional."[39] The same education could not be provided for leaders and followers. A liberal education for the masses would surely lead to discontent and labor unrest. The development of the intellect for the masses was a dangerous doctrine and did not develop the qualities needed for production-line workers.

The industrial intelligence concept of the nineteenth century extended into the twentieth with a vengeance. It was defined by Violas as "a sense of reality or a consciousness that led children to envision themselves as industrial workers." Violas continues:

> The schools wanted to equip these children with personality structures and emotional habits suitable to the industrial workplace. Other areas of the curriculum were similarly revised to so condition children slotted for factory service. These children ... spent little time pondering the dilemma of Hamlet, or the character flaws of Oedipus, or the

creative accomplishments of Michaelangelo. They read about *Romance of Modern Electricity* or *Lives of Undistinguished Americans* ... [and learned] how to fill out job applications.[40]

In their survey of common school reform and efforts at school reform in the twentieth century, Bowles and Gintis declared: "We conclude that U.S. education is highly unequal, the chances of attaining much or little schooling being substantially dependent on one's race and parents' economic level."[41]

In agreement with other revisionists, Bowles and Gintis saw the major purpose of the public school system as producing docile workers for a capitalist system. "Values, beliefs, modes of personal behavior, and patterns of social and economic loyalties were formed, transformed and reproduced in the process of bringing the individual into line with the needs of capital accumulation and the extension of the wage-labor system."[42] Bowles and Gintis presented an impressive array of documentation which attempted to prove that the schools promoted social stratification needed in order for capitalism to function. Schools were not only unable to correct the injustices, but they were deliberately designed to maintain existing inequalities and economic injustices which Bowles and Gintis saw as basic characteristics of the capitalist system.

This theme is central to the research of John Ogbu which he reported in *Minority Education and Caste*.[43] Ogbu concentrated much of his study on the black population in the United States. Ogbu suggested that a caste system (ascription by birth) existed in the United States. He presented socioeconomic data designed to demonstrate that a "job ceiling" existed for blacks. That is, for the vast majority of blacks, income and occupational level are absolutely limited. Moreover, he claimed that black school children learn early, through direct observation and experience, that this job ceiling exists, and it has a devastating effect on their motivation and success in school. This thesis will be expanded in a later chapter.

Although it is difficult to lump all revisionists into a single school of thought, there are certain commonalities in their findings which are quite different from those of the so-called traditionalists. Whereas the traditionalists tended to glorify the mission of the schools and implied that mass education was really good for the masses, the revisionists saw serious problems. Mass education was not really for the benefit of the masses at all, but rather was a system designed to control them. Common schools did not have broad enlightenment goals but narrow vocational ones. The schools operated not in the interest of the children but in the interests of the dominant class in society. The schools did not provide a ladder of upward mobility for the masses, but fixed upon them a rigid system of stratification. More than that, it taught them that such a system was something to be admired.

WHOSE IDEALS HAVE THE SCHOOLS PROMOTED?

Which view, then, is the correct one? A major problem rests with the assumption that something called the "democratic ideal" exists, and that the schools have been able to socialize the children of the masses toward that ideal. That a single, superordinate democratic ideal ever existed is open to question. Thus it is difficult to determine whether or not the schools have promoted it.

Ideology notwithstanding, any contemporary observer of the schools, no matter how ardently he supports them, would have to admit that they are failing large numbers of children. The causes for this are not so clear. It is a simple matter to declare that school failure or the anti-intellectualism which exists in public education is deliberate and planned. Evidence can be found to support this position. Evidence can also be found to support the position that the schools have served and continue to serve many children well. What one proves with data often depends on what one sets out to prove.

Even if the weight of evidence comes down on the side of those who suggest that the schools were never really intended as places for the development of intellect, that they are nothing more than extensions of social bigotry and racism, that they exacerbate existing inequalities in capitalist society, it is difficult to prove this has been a deliberate effort on the part of school people.

If the traditionalists who found nothing but schools promoting democracy were wrong, perhaps the revisionists who found capitalist plotters deliberately designing a bad system were equally misled. It is possible that both views are based on faulty assumptions. There is, after all, agreement by traditional historians and revisionists that the search for the one best system assumed that the schools were training grounds for the world of work and the realities of existing industrial society.

In Cubberley's words:

> Our schools are in a sense, factories in which the raw materials are to be shaped and fashioned into products to meet the various demands of life. The specifications for manufacturing come from the demands of the twentieth century civilization, and it is the business of the school to build its pupils to the specifications laid down. This demands good tools, specialized machinery, continuous measurement of production . . . the elimination of waste . . . and a large variety of output.[44]

Or in the words of Bowles and Gintis: "The major characteristics of the educational system in the United States today flow directly from its role in producing a work force able and willing to staff occupational positions in the capitalist system."[45]

In reality both views are based on the same assumption; that is, the major task of the school is to develop docile and obedient servants for the workplace. It must then follow that the workplace requires docile and obedient servants. It is much easier to demonstrate that this is what the schools are like than it is to so characterize the workplace. Indeed, the workplace may be much more open than the school. In *The One Best System*, Tyack suggests this when he cites an interview made by Helen Todd. In 1909 Helen Todd asked some 500 children in Chicago whether they would rather go to school or work in a factory. Out of 500 children, 412 said they liked the factory better. The following are some of the reasons they gave:

Because it's easier to work in the factory than 'tis to learn in school.

They ain't always pickin' on you because you don't know things in a factory.

The children don't hollar at ye and call ye a Christ-killer in a factory.

They're good to you at home when you earn money.

What ye learn in school ain't no good. Ye git paid just as much in the factory if ye never was there.[46]

Any contemporary classroom teacher who has talked to dropouts who go to work will tell you they get the same sort of answers from their ex-students who work on their cars or serve them their hamburgers.

What both the traditionalists and the revisionists may have missed is the essential nature of the workplace in the United States. Although the factory was and is a large and impersonal place where many times workers are treated as extensions of the machine, people who work in factories, mines, and at low-level skill jobs know the workplace is more than that. The workers themselves tend to make it into something human. Ordinarily the workplace consists of a small group of men and women working on some common task. They may hate their work, the factory system, the working conditions, and the injustices, but they are not alienated from each other. Even in the old days, before unions and the improvement of working conditions, men in the mines and factories tended to work within a small group who came to know each other well and respect each other's common problems and needs. Thus, even within a large impersonal system, the workplace was small and of human dimensions. Men of different beliefs and cultures got along or perished. Common problems, common suffering, and the camaraderie of the workplace were essentially egalitarian and democratic.

Somehow the traditionalists and the revisionists missed this aspect of the industrial system. The school missed it. Where the schools were described as following the factory model, the democratic aspect of the workplace was strangely absent. The school never followed the factory model because children have always been, and continue to be, considered as units of production. This is unlike the factory, where the worker was never considered the basic unit of production, and where he was not a product but part of the production system. Not so in the schools. School successes were counted as the number of graduates or the number enrolled. Failures were the dropouts. Inputs and outputs in schools were children. A true factory model, as brutal as it was, would have considered learning the product.

Where children are considered the product of an enterprise, many strange things follow. Means must be devised to deal efficiently with large numbers. Tasks tend to become global and universal in nature. Everybody, with machinelike precision, does the same thing on the same grade level. There is no need for human-sized work teams engaged in group undertakings. There is, instead, a large group of children in a given classroom working not so much as a group toward the completion of a common task as individuals in competition with each other to achieve what is demanded by the system or those in immediate control. There is nothing like this in the factory, or, for that matter, anywhere else in the society.

In fairness to those who advocate the factory-school analogy, there are certain aspects of the school which are functional to the factory system. The bells, timed drills, rules and regulations, the boss-worker relationship between teacher and pupils, and grades as pay are analogous. But clearly, this analogy can be overworked.

In total, in terms of the human environment of the workplace and the schoolroom, there may be many more differences than similarities. These differences can explain how an adolescent can be alienated from school but not necessarily from work. He may be alienated from the nature of work, from meaningless, boring tasks, but he still can find a human place in the work environment. He can be accepted there as an equal among equals, all suffering some degree of alienation from the work itself. But he is accepted by his fellow workers for what he can do and the tasks he must perform. He can and does relate to his fellow workers on a human level. Distinctions of color, nationality, and race tend to blur in the environment of the workplace. Although classrooms have some of these features, they are different. Where the student is considered the basic unit of production and there is no sense of common task entered into cooperatively, differences in personality and other differences tend to remain distinct and undisturbed. Thus, both and traditionalists and the revisionists who saw the school as a melting pot and as a functional training ground for industrial workers may have been wrong.

In this context, whether one accepts traditionalist arguments or revisionist arguments concerning the nature of the content and values taught in the schools may not matter. The traditionalist might argue that the schools need to teach functional knowledge and values so that children can ultimately find a useful place in society. The revisionist might argue that such knowledge is ideological, that the content and values taught comprise the ideology of the ruling class. This argument is meaningless if the children are not learning. For a significant number of children who fail to learn much of anything in school it really doesn't matter what the school is trying to teach.[47]

NOTES

1. Jack Plano and Milton Greenberg, *The American Political Dictionary* (New York: Holt, Rinehart & Winston, 1962), p. 8.
2. Robert L. Heilbroner, *The Future as History* (New York: Harper & Row, 1960).
3. Robert L. Heilbroner, *An Inquiry into the Human Prospect* (New York: W. W. Norton, 1974).
4. Daniel Bell, *The End of Ideology* (Glencoe, Ill.: Free Press, 1960).
5. Daniel Boorstin, *The Genius of American Politics* (Chicago: University of Chicago Press, 1953).
6. Ellwood P. Cubberley, *Public Education in the United States* (Boston: Houghton Mifflin Co., 1919).
7. Ibid., p. ix.

8. Ibid., p. 503.
9. Edgar W. Knight, *Education in the United States* (Boston: Ginn & Co., 1951), p. 2.
10. Ibid., p. 3.
11. Ibid.
12. Ibid., p. 35.
13. From *Working Man's Advocate*, 6 March 1830, reprinted in John R. Commons et al., eds., *A Documentary History of American Industrial Society* (New York: Russell & Russell, 1958), p. 101.
14. From *The Common School Journal*, 15 February 1940, reprinted in Welter, *American Writings on Popular Education*, p. 79.
15. From Horace Bushnell, "Common Schools: A Discourse on the Modifications Demanded by the Roman Catholics," delivered in North Church, Hartford, 25 March 1853, reprinted in Welter, *American Writings on Popular Education*, p. 183.
16. Ibid., p. 185.
17. A. R. Dugmore, "New Citizens for the Republic," *The World's Work* (April 1903), reprinted in David B. Tyack, ed., *Turning Points in American Educational History* (Waltham, Mass.: Blaisdell Publishing Co., 1967), p. 252.
18. From United States Bureau of Education, Circulars of Information, 1881, reprinted in Welter, *American Writings on Popular Education*, p. 299.
19. Cubberley, *Public Education in the United States*, p. 325.
20. Lowell School Committee Report of 1852, cited in Samuel Bowles and Herbert Gintis, *Schooling in Capitalist America* (New York: Basic Books, 1976), p. 168.
21. Michael B. Katz, *The Irony of Early School Reform* (Cambridge, Mass.: Harvard University Press, 1968), p. 87.
22. Ibid., p. 88.
23. Cubberley, *Public Education in the United States*, p. 462.
24. Knight, *Education in the United States*, pp. 568–569.
25. Colin Greer, *The Great School Legend* (New York: Basic Books, 1972).
26. Ibid., p. 85.
27. Ibid., p. 86.
28. Ibid.
29. Ibid., p. 152.
30. Cited in Michael B. Katz, *Class, Bureaucracy and Schools* (New York: Praeger Publishers, 1971), p. 31.
31. Ibid., p. 91.
32. Richard Hofstadter, *Anti-Intellectualism in American Life* (New York: Vintage Books, 1966), p. 300.
33. Ibid., p. 305.
34. Joel Spring, "Education as a Form of Social Control," in *Roots of Crisis*, ed. Clarence Karier, Paul Violas, and Joel Spring (Chicago: Rand McNally Publishing Co., 1955), p. 39.
35. Hofstadter, *Anti-Intellectualism in American Life*, p. 305.
36. Katz, *The Irony of Early School Reforms*, p. 37.
37. Ibid., p. 39.
38. Paul Violas, *The Training of the Urban Working Class* (Chicago: Rand McNally Publishing Co., 1978), p. 230.
39. Ibid., p. 231.
40. Ibid., p. 233.
41. Samuel Bowles and Herbert Gintis, *Schooling in Capitalist America* (New York: Basic Books, 1976), p. 35.

42. Ibid., p. 47.
43. John Ogbu, *Minority Education and Caste* (New York: Academic Press, 1978).
44. Cubberley, *Public Education in the United States*, p. 503.
45. Bowles and Gintis, *Schooling in Capitalist America*, p. 265.
46. David B. Tyack, *The One Best System: A History of American Education* (Cambridge, Mass.: Harvard University Press, 1974), pp. 177–178.
47. Some of the ideas presented in this conclusion were developed in discussions with Oliver Keels, a colleague.

3

Compulsory Schooling: The School as an Agent of the State

In every state in the United States there are laws, court decisions, and administrative rules and regulations which exert some form of control over nearly every aspect of public and private schooling. Students and teachers, school administrators, school governing boards, and parents are guided in what they do by this comprehensive legal network.

The political, social, and economic development of the society have significantly influenced the character and degree of control individual states have attempted to exert over the society's schools. The economic environment, moving from agrarianism to industrialism to high technology, has had great influence over what the states have done in their attempts not only to establish public schools but also to determine their purpose and shape.

This chapter will provide a brief outline of some of the more important aspects of the nature and extent of political control of the schools. In this task, the chapter outlines the development of the idea of compulsory schooling and presents selected court cases which illustrate the nature of state control over schools. Finally, recent arguments over the validity of compulsory school laws are presented.

A central purpose of this chapter is to demonstrate that the efforts of the state to control schools have been, in part at least, a reflection of existing social realities. Universal compulsory schooling was an idea that developed slowly and was accomplished only after economic and social realities demonstrated a real need for it. Compulsion, in the sense of parents feeling compelled to send their children to school, has perhaps always been more social than legal in this country. That is, as the environment changed from agrarian-rural to urban-industrial to high technology, the idea developed that more schooling was necessary for survival. In a sense, the political agents of the state, especially the legislatures and the courts, tended to reflect the changing attitudes of the general population on the need for increasing the quantity of education. Even more significantly, as economic and social changes affected family life and what people did for a living, these changes resulted in popular demands for new and different forms of schooling.

COMPULSORY SCHOOLING

Forest C. Ensign, in his comprehensive monograph *Compulsory School Attendance and Child Labor* (1921),[1] suggested that the history of compulsory schooling can be divided roughly into three stages—roughly, because the movement was state by state, with the various stages occurring later in some states than in others, and because there were some notable gains and reverses in the movement even within certain states. The first period was characterized by an effort to provide minimal schooling for the poor; the second, by numerous state laws which established the idea of universal compulsory schooling but which were largely unenforced; and the third period, beginning near the turn of the twentieth century, by the reality of meaningful and enforceable compulsory school legislation.

It appears that in the early national period some national leaders were as interested in children's productive capacity as their schooling. Hamilton, for example, saw children as a major supply of labor for the developing textile industry in New England. He was greatly impressed with what he observed in the textile mills of England where women and children provided much of the labor. He expressed the opinion in 1791 that work by women and children in the textile mills would make them "more useful." He pointed out that in the textile mills in Great Britain "it is computed that four-sevenths, nearly, are women and children, of whom the greatest proportion are children, and many of them a tender age."[2]

This was not an uncommon view for the times, and many women and children were employed in the textile mills of New England during the early national period. Indeed, the practice was so widespread that the mill owners themselves worried about the long hours of labor and the neglect of schooling for working children. Some mill owners, notably Samuel Slater in Rhode Island and Col. David Humphreys in Connecticut, established Sunday schools for the children of the mills. In these schools morals and basic literacy were taught.

Child labor had become such an obvious social ill by the first decades of the nineteenth century that efforts were made in a number of states either to limit its use or to provide the alternative of schooling for young children. In the 1820s and 30s, efforts were made in New York, Pennsylvania, Connecticut, Massachusetts, and other states to improve working conditions in the mills, to limit the number of hours children could work, and to provide some public support for schools. Although the laws were weak and often went unenforced, it was a start.

Beginning with the Massachusetts compulsory school law in 1852, and continuing throughout the nineteenth century, many states established in their constitutions or through legislation, compulsory attendance requirements. By contemporary standards these were meager, but they were an expression of the idea of compulsory universal schooling. For the most part, the number of years required was minimal; schooling to age 14 was a common requirement in the early laws and constitutional provisions. In addition, the school year defined was short by contemporary standards. Required school attendance for three to six months was not uncommon. In almost every case serious exceptions were allowed. Characteristically, early compulsory school laws permitted parents to keep children out of school for a variety of reasons, and penalties for failure to send children to school were not severe and frequently were not enforced. Indeed, in many localities the machinery for enforcement was totally inadequate.

During most of the nineteenth century there seemed to be all sorts of reasons for not sending children to school, even for the short period legally required by most states. In the more industrialized states of the northeast, children continued to work in factories because their families needed the income. Even where attempts were made to enforce compulsory attendance laws, in some cities the school facilities necessary to implement the laws did not exist. There simply were not enough schools to accommodate all the children who were in violation of compulsory attendance laws.

While rural school facilities in the agrarian states in the midwest were sufficient to accommodate the children, it was not uncommon in this part of the country for the school year to be extremely short and for attendance to be limited to eight years. When school attendance conflicted with necessary farm work during planting and harvesting seasons, in most cases work was more important than school. The same was true in the south, except that in the case of southern black children there was no serious effort at all to see that compulsory school attendance laws were enforced. In fact, in many localities no schools existed for black children.

The picture which emerges from Ensign's study of compulsory education is one of serious educational neglect at the beginning of the twentieth century. Many children in the industrial cities of the northeast continued to enter the factory at age seven or eight and never saw the inside of a schoolroom. Black children were almost totally neglected. Even the midwestern states, which had the best overall record for school attendance, failed to take compulsory education very seriously.

By 1918 every state had some form of compulsory school law on the books. Moreover, attitudes had changed during the first two decades of the twentieth century. Better laws were passed in the sense that the periods of compulsory education were extended; in many cases significant penalties for truancy were set; and effective machinery for enforcement was established. By the time the *Pierce* case was heard by the U.S. Supreme Court in 1925, the concept of universal, state-supported public compulsory education was firmly entrenched.[3]

THE *PIERCE* CASE

A court case in Oregon in the early 1920s, *Pierce v. Society of Sisters*, provides an excellent illustration of how far the voters in a state were willing to go to provide compulsory public education for the children of their state. In 1922 the voters of Oregon, by means of an initiative petition, strengthened their compulsory education law in a way which threatened the very existence in Oregon of any alternative to public schooling. The Oregon Compulsory School Law of 1922 was a result of a burst of a narrow patriotism which was sweeping the nation after World War I.

In 1917 the Congress of the United States passed the Espionage Act, which defined almost any opposition to the war effort as treasonable. A year later Congress approved the Sedition Act, which forbade Americans to "utter, print, write, or publish any disloyal, profane, scurrilous or abusive language about the form of government of the United States, or the uniform of the Army or Navy of the United States. . . ." These were times in which a variety of patriotic groups engaged in unrestrained expressions of a narrowly defined Americanism. The newly formed American Legion (1919) was able to recruit thousands of recently released military men who had served their country in World War I. The legion eagerly promoted the patriotic fervor that was characteristic of the last years of the war. They became an important political voice in many states during the early twenties. Also during this period, the Ku Klux Klan, with its peculiar brand of patriotism which was anti-Negro, anti-foreign, anti-Semitic, and anti-Catholic, was able to gain wide support and serious political power. It is against this background that the Oregon petition was approved by the voters.

Pierce v. Society of Sisters
268 US 510 (1925)

Mr. Justice McReynolds delivered the opinion of the Court.

These appeals are from decrees, based upon undenied allegations, which granted preliminary orders restraining appellants from threatening or attempting to enforce the Compulsory Education Act adopted November 7, 1922, under the initiative provision of her Constitution by the voters of Oregon.

The challenged act, effective September 1, 1926, requires every parent, guardian, or other person having control or charge or custody of a child between eight and sixteen years to send him "to a public school for the period of time a public school shall be held during the current year" in the district where the child resides; and failure so to do is declared a misdemeanor. . . . The manifest purpose is to compel general attendance at public schools by normal children, between eight and sixteen, who have not completed the eighth grade. And without doubt enforcement of the statute would seriously impair, perhaps destroy, the profitable features of appellees' business, and greatly diminish the value of their property.

Appellee the Society of Sisters is an Oregon corporation, organized in 1880, with power to care for orphans, educate and instruct the youth, establish and maintain academies or schools, and acquire necessary real and personal property. It has long devoted its property and effort to the secular and religious education and care of children, and has acquired the valuable good will of many parents and guardians. It conducts interdependent primary and high schools and junior colleges, and maintains orphanages for the custody and control of children between eight and sixteen. In its primary schools many children between those ages are taught the subjects usually pursued in Oregon public schools during the first eight years. Systematic religious instruction and moral training according to the tenets of the Roman Catholic Church are also regularly provided. All courses of study, both temporal and religious, contemplate continuity of training under appellee's charge; the primary schools are essential to the system and the most profitable. It owns valuable buildings, especially constructed and equipped for school purposes. The business is remunerative,—the annual income from primary schools exceeds $30,000,—and the successful conduct of this requires long-time contracts with teachers and parents. The Compulsory Education Act of 1922 has already caused the withdrawal from its schools of children who would otherwise continue, and their income has steadily declined. The appellants, public officers, have proclaimed their purpose strictly to enforce the statute.

After setting out the above facts, the Society's bill alleges that the enactment conflicts with the right of parents to choose schools where their children will receive appropriate mental and religious training, the right of the child to influence the parents' choice of a school, the right of schools and teachers therein to engage in a useful business or profession, and is accordingly repugnant to the Constitution and void. And, further, that unless enforcement of the measure is enjoined, the corporation's business and property will suffer irreparable injury.

Appellee Hill Military Academy is a private corporation organized in 1908 under the laws of Oregon, engaged in owning, operating, and conducting for profit an elementary, college preparatory, and military training school for boys between the ages of five and twenty-one years. The average attendance is one hundred, and the annual fees received for each student amount to some $800. The elementary department is divided into eight grades, as in the public schools; the college preparatory department has four grades, similar to those of the public high schools; the courses of study conform to the requirements of the state board of education. Military instruction and training are also given, under the supervision of an Army officer. It owns considerable real and personal property, some useful only for school purposes. The business and incident good will are very valuable. In order to conduct its affairs long-time contracts must be made for supplies, equipment, teachers, and pupils. Appellants, law officers of the state and county, have publicly announced that the Act of November 7, 1922, is valid, and have declared their intention to enforce it. By reason of the statute and threat of enforcment, appellee's business is being destroyed and its property depreciated; parents and guardians are refusing to make contracts for the future instruction of their sons, and some are being withdrawn. . . .

No question is raised concerning the power of the state reasonably to regulate all schools, to inspect, supervise, and examine them, their teachers and pupils; to require that all children of proper age attend some school, that teachers shall be of good moral character and patriotic disposition, that certain studies plainly essential to good citizenship must be taught, and that nothing be taught which is manifestly inimical to the public welfare.

The inevitable practical result of enforcing the act under consideration would be destruction of appellees' primary schools, and perhaps all other private primary schools for normal children within the state of Oregon. Appellees are engaged in a kind of undertaking not inherently harmful, but long regarded as useful and meritorious. Certainly there is nothing in the present records to indicate that they have failed to discharge their obligations to patrons, students, or the state. And there are no peculiar circumstances or present emergencies which demand extraordinary measures relative to primary education.

Under the doctrine of *Meyer v. Nebraska*, . . . we think it entirely plain that the Act of 1922 unreasonably interferes with the liberty of parents and guardians to direct the upbringing and education of children under their control. As often heretofore pointed out, rights guaranteed by the Constitution may not be abridged by legislation which has no reasonable relation to some purpose within the competency of the state. The fundamental theory of liberty upon which all governments in the Union repose excludes any general power of the state to standardize its children by forcing them to accept instruction from public teachers only. The child is not the mere creature of the state; those who nurture him and direct his destiny have the right, coupled with the high duty, to recognize and prepare him for additional obligations.

Appellees are corporations, and therefore, it is said, they cannot claim for themselves the liberty which the 14th Amendment guarantees. Accepted in the proper sense, this is true. . . . But they have business and property for which they claim protection. These are threatened with destruction through the unwarranted compulsion which appellants are exercising over present and prospective patrons of their schools. And this court has gone very far to protect against loss threatened by such action. . . .

Generally it is entirely true, as urged by counsel, that no person in any business has such an interest in possible customers as to enable him to restrain exercise of proper power of the state upon the ground that he will be deprived of patronage. But the injunctions here sought are not against the exercise of any proper power. Appellees asked protection against arbitrary, unreasonable, and unlawful interference with their patrons, and the consequent destruction of their business and property. Their interest is clear and immediate, within the rule approved in *Truax v. Raich, Truax v. Corrigan*, and *Terrace v. Thompson*, . . . and many other cases where injunctions have been issued to protect business enterprises against interference with the freedom of patrons or customers.

The suits were not premature. The injury to appellees was present and very real, —not a mere possibility in the remote future. If no relief had been possible prior to the effective date of the act, the injury would have become irreparable. Prevention of impending injury by unlawful action is a well-recognized function of courts of equity.

SOME ISSUES RAISED BY *PIERCE*

Because it dealt with issues so basic to the state's rights to govern schooling, *Pierce* has been an important case often cited in other cases involving the rights of parents, the power of states to regulate private schools, and the nature of state-controlled public education. Although the case is short and appears to be a clear statement limiting a state's right to inhibit the development of private schools, it does contain some serious ambiguities. Stephen Arons described some of these in 1976 in his analysis of the *Pierce* case.[4] In *Pierce* one can find strong assertions on both the property rights of the Society of Sisters and Hill Military Academy and on the rights of parents to select for their children schools which reflect their own religious values. Some of the questions raised by Arons include the following: (1) Did the Court intend to merely uphold the "property" right of private schools to exist, or did it recognize the importance of allowing parents to direct the schooling of their children? (2) Was religious freedom the basis of the opinion, and if not, what "is the nature of the non-religious 'education' rights for which *Pierce* might stand?"[5] (3) How far can a state go in regulating private schools without infringing on the rights of parents outlined in the *Pierce* case?

Whatever the answers to these questions, it seems that the *Pierce* case was a compromise. The Court could have decided with the state and in effect established a completely state-controlled system of education. It could have opted for total control of educational choice by the family and significantly weakened the state's ability to regulate private schooling. The Court chose instead a position somewhere between these two extremes. The result was a decision which respected the right of parents to choose for their children and yet recognized the right of the state to provide a system of compulsory education.

One of the problems with *Pierce*, according to Arons, is that it assumes that public schools are neutral—that is, that they do not teach values. This is a myth in Arons' view, and the result is that a compulsory state school system requires parents to sacrifice First Amendment rights as a condition of receiving a free education. The effect of this condition is that the rich can send their children to schools which reflect their values, while the poor cannot. "The state has created a category of parents who, solely by reason of their economic status, must subject their children to upwards of six hours a day of state approved socialization they would not have chosen themselves."[6] The argument still leaves unanswered the issues which were raised in the preceding chapter; that is, assuming the schools are not neutral, whose values do they teach? Although this is unanswered in general terms in specific school systems, the question is one which tends to keep schools in a more or less constant state of controversy. Even the poor are not always apathetic and subservient—especially the poor with strong religious views. In many local schools, conflicts arise nearly every year over the values which schools should teach. Being poor may mean that parents have no choice other than the public schools, but it doesn't necessarily follow that they are quiescent about what goes on there. Especially where strong religious beliefs are involved, efforts are almost always made to pressure the schools to be something more than neutral on these beliefs.

Although many religious groups have openly expressed their desire to have public schools accept their views to teach Christian morality, to not teach Christian beliefs, to ignore Darwinian theories, to extol the virtues of labor or to denounce the excesses of unions, to praise the glories of free enterprise, or whatever, there are times when the differences between what the school is perceived as teaching and what parents value become so great that open resistance to public education develops. Although there are many such illustrations possible, one of the most notable is the case of the Amish.

COMPULSORY EDUCATION AND THE AMISH

Whether or not the schools actually succeed in teaching children a discernible set of values matters little when closely knit community groups believe that they do. Such has been the case with the Amish who have consistently insisted that public education, at least beyond the eighth grade, threatens to destroy their beliefs. The Amish in Pennsylvania, Iowa, Wisconsin, and elsewhere did not strenuously object to school attendance in public schools in rural areas where their children constituted an overwhelming majority of the school population and where they could hire Amish teachers. However, when the school consolidation movement in some states and the increase in compulsory attendance into the high school years threatened to force their children into schools where they would have to mix significantly with outsiders, they expressed great distress and resistance. In an article entitled, "Who Shall Educate our Children?", Joseph Stoll, a leading Amish writer and teacher, detailed Amish objections to public school for Amish children.[7]

Stoll came right to the point. "Children from other types of homes—godless, atheistic, materialistic, of false cults—have an un-Christian influence on our children."[8] The public schools, in Stoll's view, taught everything that was wrong for Amish children—not the least of which was worldly values. He was concerned lest the outsiders have undue influence on the children to get them to conform to outside values. He was especially concerned about profanity and "sex talk," which he claimed were common in the public schools. "Evolutionism, atheism, and a host of other godless 'isms' are not kept out of public school."[9] Another serious concern expressed by Stoll was that teachers were dedicated and sincere public servants, but they simply did not understand or appreciate Amish beliefs. Change worried Stoll because he felt that the changes which he saw in public schooling were "not for the better." He abhorred the trend toward centralization and the loss of individualism. He saw "the creeping evil of socialism" and "increasing control of almost every area of our lives," which could mean "only one thing, the gradual loss of our freedom."[10]

In view of such antagonism toward the values believed to be taught by public schools, it is not surprising that Old Order Amish settlements resisted attempts to have their children sent to the public schools. One of the most widely publicized resistance efforts on the part of an Amish community took place in Oelwein, Iowa in the mid-sixties. It all began in the late 1940s when, as a result of a school consolidation vote, a number of rural schools which Amish children attended were closed. The Amish community purchased some of the schools and set them up as private schools. Not satisfied that the Amish schools were meeting minimal state requirements, school officials pushed for complete consolidation of the schools. Since the Amish who lived in Oelwein did not wish their children to be transported by bus to the larger village of Hazelton, five miles away, to a school they did not control, they threatened to withdraw their children from the public schools. A compromise of sorts was reached in which the Amish were promised control over two one-room schools in the Oelwein district if they would vote in favor of unification of the two districts. Their vote was important because it could decide the outcome of the election. After the unification vote, however, local school officials forgot this promise and declared that the Amish schools would be closed in two years. The Amish retaliated by refusing to accept state-certified teachers to teach in their schools.

Since there was some feeling against the Amish in the community, pressure was brought to have local school officials enforce the compulsory school laws against the Amish. Amish parents were fined and jailed for refusal to obey the law. Efforts were then made to bus the Amish children from their one-room schools to the larger public school at Hazelton. What followed was a tragic series of events in which public school officials, who felt somehow responsible for performing their legal duties, looked like villains right out of a melodrama.

A coordinated effort was launched by school officials, the county sheriff, and the county attorney to forcibly bring the erring Amish children to the Hazelton school. A bus was dispatched to the Amish schools to bring in the children. At the first school, when the children were being led onto the bus, one of the parents shouted "Run!" The scene which followed was a comedy of errors in which school officials and deputy sheriffs attempted to run down the children who were scurrying into nearby cornfields and woods. The press was there, of course, recording the whole business. Since school officials failed in their mission at the first school, the bus journeyed on to the second one. The scene there was described by Donald Erickson in "Showdown at an Amish Schoolhouse."

> Mrs. Schwarz (the Amish teacher) and her frightened brood scurried into the schoolhouse. The entry-room was full of weeping women. A group of stern faced fathers stood outside, guarding the door. Truant Officer Snively (the principal at Hazelton) pushed his way through the men (the Plain People are pacifists), and brushed off the mothers who pulled at his clothing and begged him not to proceed. Sheriff Beier followed soon after. As Snively stepped inside, the pupils began singing, half hysterically, chorus after chorus of "Jesus Loves Me," led by a teacher who circled the room in agitation. Soon mothers entered to embrace their children protectively. Snively attempted to pry a screaming schoolboy loose from a desk. A group of girls ran into a corner to huddle and sob as Snively approached them. Fathers burst in to protest. County Attorney Lemon shouted his disgust at the way the Amish were behaving. Newsmen came in, scribbling madly. Children wailed, women whimpered, flashbulbs popped, and the tides of emotion swept the room. . . .[11]

The Amish ultimately won this skirmish when the Iowa state legislature, embarrassed by the whole affair, exempted the Amish from some of the state's school laws. The legislature gave the state superintendent discretionary power to treat Amish schools separately and to establish different minimum requirements for them.

It was such deep feelings and a background of Amish resistance to public education which led to the case of *Wisconsin v. Yoder* in 1972.

Wisconsin v. Yoder
406 US 205 (1972)

Mr. Chief Justice Burger delivered the opinion of the Court.

On petition of the State of Wisconsin, we granted the writ of certiorari in this case to review a decision of the Wisconsin Supreme Court holding that respondents' convictions for violating the State's compulsory school-attendance law were invalid under the Free Exercise Clause of the First Amendment to the United States Constitution made applicable to the States by the Fourteenth Amendment. For the reasons hereafter stated we affirmed the judgment of the Supreme Court of Wisconsin.

Respondents Jonas Yoder and Wallace Miller are members of the Old Order Amish religion, and respondent Adin Yutzy is a member of the Conservative Amish

Mennonite Church. . . . Wisconsin's compulsory school-attendance law required them to cause their children to attend public or private school until reaching age 16 but the respondents declined to send their children, ages 14 and 15, to public school after they completed the eighth grade.

On complaint of the school district administrator for the public schools, respondents were charged, tried, and convicted of violating the compulsory-attendance law in Green County Court and were fined the sum of $5 each. Respondents defended on the ground that the application of the compulsory-attendance law violated their rights under the First and Fourteenth Amendments. The trial testimony showed that respondents believed, in accordance with the tenets of Old Order Amish communities generally, that their children's attendance at high school, public or private, was contrary to the Amish religion and way of life. . . .

. . . Amish objection to formal education beyond the eighth grade is firmly grounded in . . . central religious concepts. They object to the high school, and higher education generally, because the values they teach are in marked variance with Amish values and the Amish way of life; they view secondary school education as an impermissible exposure of their children to a "worldly" influence in conflict with their beliefs. . . . Amish society emphasizes informal learning-through-doing; a life of "goodness," rather than a life of intellect; wisdom, rather than technical knowledge; community welfare, rather than competition; and separation from, rather than integration with, contemporary worldly society. . . .

On the basis of such considerations, Dr. Hostetler testified that compulsory high school attendance could not only result in great psychological harm to Amish children, because of the conflicts it would produce, but would also, in his opinion, ultimately result in the destruction of the Old Order Amish church community as it exists in the United States today. . . .

Although the trial court in its careful findings determined that the Wisconsin compulsory school-attendance law "does interfere with the freedom of the Defendants to act in accordance with their sincere religious belief" it also concluded that the requirement of high school attendance until age 16 was a "reasonable and constitutional" exercise of governmental power, and therefore denied the motion to dismiss the charges. The Wisconsin Circuit Court affirmed the convictions. The Wisconsin Supreme Court, however, sustained respondents' claim under the Free Exercise Clause of the First Amendment and reversed the convictions. A majority of the court was of the opinion that the state had failed to make an adequate showing that its interest in "establishing and maintaining an educational system overrides the defendants' right to the free exercise of their religion."

There is no doubt as to the power of a State, having a high responsibility for education of its citizens, to impose reasonable regulations for the control and duration of basic education. Providing public schools ranks at the very apex of the function of a State. Yet even this paramount responsibility was, in Pierce, made to yield to the right of parents to provide an equivalent education in a privately operated system. . . . As that case suggests, the values of parental direction of the religious upbringing and education of their children in their early and formative years have a high place in our society. Thus, a State's interest in universal education, however highly we rank it, is not totally free from a balancing process when it impinges on fundamental rights and interests, such as those specifically protected by the Free Exercise Clause of the First Amendment, and the traditional interest of parents with respect to the religious upbringing of their children so long as they, in the words of Pierce, "prepare (them) for additional obligations."

It follows that in order for Wisconsin to compel school attendance beyond the eighth grade against a claim that such attendance interferes with the practice of a legitimate religious belief, it must appear either that the State does not deny the free exercise of religious belief by its requirement, or that there is a state interest of sufficient magnitude to override the interest claiming protection under the Free Exercise Clause. . . .

We can accept it as settled, therefore, that however strong the State's interest in universal compulsory education, it is by no means absolute to the exclusion or subordination of all other interests.

We come then to the quality of the claims of the respondents concerning the alleged encroachment of Wisconsin's compulsory school-attendance statute on their rights and the rights of their children to the free exercise of the religious beliefs they and their forebears have adhered to for almost three centuries. . . . Although a determination of what is a "religious" belief or practice entitled to constitutional protection may present a most delicate question, the very concept of ordered liberty precludes allowing every person to make his own standards on matters of conduct in which society as a whole has important interests. Thus, if the Amish asserted their claims because of their subjective evaluation and rejection of the contemporary secular values accepted by the majority, much as Thoreau rejected the social values of his time and isolated himself at Walden Pond, their claims would not rest on a religious basis. Thoreau's choice was philosophical and personal rather than religious, and such belief does not rise to the demands of the Religion Clauses.

The record shows that the respondents' religious beliefs and attitude toward life, family, and home have remained constant—perhaps some would say static—in a period of unparalleled progress in human knowledge generally and great changes in education. The respondents freely concede, and indeed assert as an article of faith, that their religious beliefs and what we would today call "life style" have not altered in fundamentals for centuries. Their way of life in a church-oriented community, separated from the outside world and "worldly" influences, their attachment to nature and the soil, is a way inherently simple and uncomplicated, albeit difficult to preserve against the pressure to conform. Their rejection of telephones, automobiles, radios, and television, their mode of dress, of speech, their habits of manual work do indeed set them apart from much of contemporary society; these customs are both symbolic and practical. . . .

The impact of the compulsory-attendance law on respondents' practice of the Amish religion is not only severe, but inescapable, for the Wisconsin law affirmatively compels them, under threat of criminal sanction, to perform acts undeniably at odds with fundamental tenets of their religious beliefs. . . . As the record shows, compulsory school attendance to age 16 for Amish children carries with it a very real threat of undermining the Amish community and religious practice as they exist today; they must either abandon belief and be assimilated into society at large, or be forced to migrate to some other and more tolerant region. . . .

Wisconsin concedes that under the Religion Clauses religious beliefs are absolutely free from the State's control, but it argues that "actions," even though religiously grounded, are outside the protection of the First Amendment. But our decisions have rejected the idea that religiously grounded conduct is always outside the protection of the Free Exercise Clause. It is true that activities of individuals, even when religiously based, are often subject to regulation by the States in the exercise of their undoubted power to promote the health, safety, and general welfare, or the Federal Government in the exercise of its delegated powers. But to agree that religiously grounded conduct must often be subject to the broad police power of the State is not to deny that there are areas of conduct protected by the Free Exercise Clause of the First Amendment and thus beyond the power of the State to control, even under regulations of general applicability. . . .

The State advances two primary arguments in support of its system of compulsory education. It notes, as Thomas Jefferson pointed out early in our history, that some degree of education is necessary to prepare citizens to participate effectively and intelligently in our open political system if we are to preserve freedom and independence. Further, education prepares individuals to be self-reliant and self-sufficient participants in society. We accept these propositions.

However, the evidence adduced by the Amish in this case is persuasively to the effect that an additional one or two years of formal high school for Amish children in place of their long-established program of informal vocational education would do little to serve those interests. . . .

The State attacks respondents' position as one fostering "ignorance" from which the child must be protected by the State. No one can question the State's duty to protect children from ignorance but this argument does not square with the facts disclosed in the record. Whatever their idiosyncrasies as seen by the majority, this record strongly shows that the Amish community has been a highly successful social unit within our society, even if apart from the conventional "mainstream." Its members are productive and very law-abiding members of society; they reject public welfare in any of its usual modern forms. The Congress itself recognized their self-sufficiency by authorizing exemption of such groups as the Amish from the obligation to pay social security taxes. . . .

The State, however, supports its interest in providing an additional one or two years of compulsory high school education to Amish children because of the possibility that some such children will choose to leave the Amish community, and that if this occurs they will be ill-equipped for life. The State argues that if Amish children leave their church they should not be in the position of making their way in the world without the education available in the one or two additional years the State requires. However, on this record, that argument is highly speculative. There is no specific evidence of the loss of Amish adherents by attrition, nor is there any showing that upon leaving the Amish community Amish children, with their practical agricultural training and habits of industry and self-reliance, would become burdens on society because of educational shortcomings. . . .

There is nothing in this record to suggest that the Amish qualities of reliability, self-reliance, and dedication of work would fail to find ready markets in today's society. . . .

The Amish alternative to formal secondary school education has enabled them to function effectively in their day-to-day life under self-imposed limitations on relations with the world, and to survive and prosper in contemporary society as a separate, sharply identifiable and highly self-sufficient community for more than 200 years in this country. . . .

. . . Finally, the State, on authority of *Prince v. Massachusetts*, argues that a decision exempting Amish children from the State's requirement fails to recognize the substantive right of the Amish child to a secondary education, and fails to give due regard to the power of the State as *parens patriae* to extend the benefit of secondary education to children regardless of the wishes of their parents. . . .

The State's argument proceeds without reliance on any actual conflict between the wishes of parents and children. It appears to rest on the potential that exemption of Amish parents from the requirements of the compulsory-education law might allow some parents to act contrary to the best interests of their children by foreclosing their opportunity to make an intelligent choice between the Amish way of life and that of the outside world. The same argument could, of course, be made with respect to all church schools short of college. There is nothing in the record or in the ordinary course of human experience to suggest that non-Amish parents generally consult with children of ages 14–16 if they are placed in a church school of the parents' faith.

Indeed it seems clear that if the State is empowered, as *parens patriae*, to "save" a child from himself or his Amish parents by requiring an additional two years of compulsory formal high school education, the State will in large measure influence, if not determine, the religious future of the child. . . . The history and culture of Western civilization reflect a strong tradition of parental concern for the nurture and upbringing of their children. This primary role of the parents in the upbringing of their children is now established beyond debate as an enduring American tradition. . . .

In the face of our consistent emphasis on the central values underlying the Religion Clauses in our constitutional scheme of government, we cannot accept a parens patriae claim of such all-encompassing scope and with such sweeping potential for broad and unforeseeable application as that urged by the State.

For the reasons stated we hold, with the Supreme Court of Wisconsin, that the First and Fourteenth Amendments prevent the State from compelling respondents to cause their children to attend formal high school to age 16. Our disposition of this case, however, in no way alters our recognition of the obvious fact that courts are not school boards or legislatures, and are ill-equipped to determine the "necessity" of discrete aspects of a State's program of compulsory education. This should suggest that courts must move with great circumspection in performing the sensitive and delicate task of weighing a State's legitimate social concern when faced with religious claims for exemption from generally applicable educational requirements. It cannot be overemphasized that we are not dealing with a way of life and mode of education by a group claiming to have recently discovered some "progressive" or more enlightened process for rearing children for modern life. . . .

Nothing we hold is intended to undermine the general applicability of the State's compulsory school-attendance statutes or to limit the power of the State to promulgate reasonable standards that, while not impairing the free exercise of religion, provide for continuing agricultural vocational education under parental and church guidance by the Old Order Amish or others similarly situated. The States have had a long history of amicable and effective relationships with church-sponsored schools, and there is no basis for assuming that, in this related context, reasonable standards cannot be established concerning the content of the continuing vocational education of Amish children under parental guidance, provided always that state regulations are not inconsistent with what we have said in this opinion.

Mr. Justice Douglas, dissenting in part.

I agree with the Court that the religious scruples of the Amish are opposed to the education of their children beyond the grade schools, yet I disagree with the Court's conclusion that the matter is within the dispensation of parents alone. The Court's analysis assumes that the only interests at stake in the case are those of the Amish parents on the one hand, and those of the State on the other. The difficulty with this approach is that, despite the Court's claim, the parents are seeking to vindicate not only their own free exercise claims, but also those of their high-school-age children.

It is argued that the right of the Amish children to religious freedom is not presented by the facts of the case, as the issue before the Court involves only the Amish parents' religious freedom to defy a state criminal statute imposing upon them as affirmative duty to cause their children to attend high school.

First, respondents' motion to dismiss in the trial court expressly asserts, not only the religious liberty of the adults, but also that of the children, as a defense to the prosecutions. . . . Although the lower courts and a majority of this Court assume an identity of interest between parent and child, it is clear that they have treated the religious interest of the child as a factor in the analysis.

Second, . . . if the parents in this case are allowed a religious exemption, the inevitable effect is to impose the parents' notions of religious duty upon their children. Where the child is mature enough to express potentially conflicting desires, it would be an invasion of the child's rights to permit such an imposition without canvassing his views. . . .

Religion is an individual experience. It is not necessary, nor even appropriate, for every Amish child to express his views on the subject in a prosecution of a single adult. Crucial, however, are the views of the child whose parent is the subject of the suit. . . .

This issue has never been squarely presented before today. Our opinions are full of talk about the power of the parents over the child's education. And we have in the past analyzed similar conflicts between parent and State with little regard for the views of the child. . . . Recent cases, however, have clearly held that the children themselves have constitutionally protectible interests.

These children are "persons" within the meaning of the Bill of Rights. We have so held over and over again. In *Haley v. Ohio*, . . . we extended the protection of the Fourteenth Amendment in a state trial of a 15-year-old boy. In *In re Gault*, . . . we held that "neither the Fourteenth Amendment nor the Bill of Rights is for adults alone." In *In re Winship*, . . . we held that a 12-year-old boy, when charged with an act which would be a crime if committed by an adult, was entitled to procedural safeguards contained in the Sixth Amendment.

In *Tinker v. Des Moines School District*, . . . we dealt with 13-year-old, 15-year-old, and 16-year-old students who wore armbands to public schools and were disciplined for doing so. We gave them relief, saying that their First Amendment rights had been abridged.

"Students in school as well as out of school are 'persons' under our Constitution. They are possessed of fundamental rights which the State must respect, just as they themselves must respect their obligations to the State. . . ."

On this important and vital matter of education, I think the children should be entitled to be heard. While the parents, absent dissent, normally speak for the entire family, the education of the child is a matter on which the child will often have decided views. He may want to be a pianist or an astronaut or an oceanographer. To do so he will have to break from the Amish tradition.

It is the future of the student, not the future of the parents, that is imperiled by today's decision. If a parent keeps his child out of school beyond the grade school, then the child will be forever barred from entry into the new and amazing world of diversity that we have today. The child may decide that that is the preferred course, or he may rebel. It is the student's judgment, not his parents', that is essential if we are to give full meaning to what we have said about the Bill of Rights and of the right of students to be masters of their own destiny.[12]

SOME ISSUES RAISED BY *YODER*

In attempting to determine the sort of "religious" beliefs that were entitled to constitutional protection against state regulation, the Court viewed Amish beliefs as "religious" while it characterized the views of Thoreau as "philosophical." Is this a clear distinction?

If the schools are neutral on religious values, why would school attendance by the Amish children beyond the eighth grade cause them to "abandon their belief and be assimilated into the society . . . or be forced to migrate to some other and more tolerant region" as the Court suggested?

The Court seemed to make much of the fact that Amish people were law-abiding, that they taught their children to be good citizens, and that the values and skills learned by Amish children would not make them a burden on society. These appear to be more sociological than legal arguments. Do such sociological arguments strengthen the meaning of the First and Fourteenth Amendments?

In the dissent in *Yoder*, Justice Douglas was concerned about the rights of the children involved. He was concerned that the religious beliefs of the parents might handicap the children in the event that they decided to enter mainstream society at some later date. The issue of the welfare of children is quite common in our society, especially where the state can demonstrate that the interests of the parents are in some way harmful to the children or if the interests of the parents are in serious conflict with "compelling" interests of the state. Were standards established in the *Yoder* case to resolve these kinds of conflicts?

The majority of the *Yoder* Court implied that children aged 14, 15, and 16 were not capable of making their own decisions regarding their moral and religious beliefs. In his dissent, Douglas cited a number of authorities who suggested that children of this age are capable of making moral judgments. Who is correct? Which side of this argument has the most convincing evidence in support? Is this a key issue in the case? What evidence did the majority use in support of parental authority?

Perhaps the most serious issue raised by *Yoder* was that it brought into question in the minds of some parents the legal status of universal compulsory schooling. In a nation as large and diverse as the United States, there are always some who object to any form of legal compulsion. There were many parents in the early seventies who didn't like the public schools and were not particularly interested in a private school alternative. It was inevitable that some of these people would ask: If the Amish can avoid compulsory school laws, why not us? This was, after all, an era in which alternative "free schools" and "counter-culture" schools experienced some growth. It was an era in which critics of the schools gained a wide audience. Ivan Illich's "deschooling" was almost a household word. This is not to suggest that the decision in *Yoder* stimulated any serious flight from public education. It was a case, however, which state courts had to consider when state school officials brought parents to court for refusing to send their children to school.

The *Franz* case in New York State, which was heard in 1977, provides an illustration of this.

THE *FRANZ* CASE

In the Matter of Franz Children
390 N.Y.S. 2nd. 940

Before Hopkins, Acting P. J., and Cohalan, Shapiro and Suozzi, J. J. Cohalan, Justice.

The appellant, Barbara Franz, a widow, is the mother of three children of compulsory school attendance age. Because the youngest child John, then aged six and one-half years, was not doing well in reading and arithmetic at public school, she kept him at home with the avowed intention of teaching him herself, in seeming defiance of the provisions of article 65 of the Education Law.

A month or two later she also removed Peter and Susan, then aged 11 and 13, respectively, from school. Peter was removed for no stated reason, but Susan was indulged by her mother when she discontinued attending classes because she thought that she had had enough schooling. Again, the mother insisted that she could teach them anything else they needed to know, even though her own formal education ended upon graduation from high school.

In due course the school authorities, after trying in vain to persuade Mrs. Franz to abandon her adamant position, commenced appropriate proceedings in the Family Court to have the children declared neglected within the meaning and intent of article 10 of the Family Court Act. . . .

The appellant argues that she can teach her child as much in one and one-half hours per day as the school system can in five. To support the argument, she notes that where one teacher must deal with 25 or 30 pupils, the time differential is explained by the diffusion of information and instruction that must be imparted in dealing with fast learners and slow ones, and with the necessary diversions and distractions that occur with a great number of children, as contrasted with the channeled focus of imparting knowledge to one child. The argument does not bear scrutiny in light of the circumstance that education consists as much in the teacher's interrelation with all the other children in a classroom as it does with any individual child. In theory, at least, each child is learning from his classmates as he hears them recite—or answer questions—or ask questions that elicit a response from the instructor. We see, then, no justifiable reason for allowing home study to be limited to one and one-half hours as against the school requirement of five. In our view, the five-hour requirement is not arbitrary in nature; nor does it impinge upon any constitutional right. . . .

The appellant's second constitutional point is that the compulsory features of the Education Law impinge upon the fundamental guaranty of privacy.

The rationale of this argument is that Mrs. Franz holds a sincere moral and philosophical belief that the children can best be taught at home under her sole and individual guidance; and that she should therefore be allowed her own way. . . .

To support her point that compulsory education is an invasion of privacy, the appellant cites *Pierce v. Society of Sisters.* . . .

As in Oregon prior to the *Pierce* case there were—and perhaps still are—people in our society who read the First Amendment (as to religion) as an absolute. They read that "Congress shall make no law respecting an establishment of religion," but ignore the following clause, "or prohibiting the free exercise thereof." In *Pierce*, this type sought unsuccessfully to close the parochial schools, which concededly could, and did, impart an education equivalent to that of the public schools.

On the other hand, we have individuals, such as the appellant, who take the subjective approach that each parent can chart the destiny of her own children with respect to education, at least at the elementary and secondary levels.

Our State Education Law strikes a happy balance between the two schools of thought. There is no rigid, robotlike regimentation of children; nor, conversely, can each child step to the music that he hears, however measured or far away. The State's interest in education is, to a degree, paramount.

For, as stated in *Jacobson v. Massachusetts*, 197 U.S. 11:

> There are manifold restraints to which every person is necessarily subject for the common good. On any other basis organized society could not exist with safety to its members. Society based on the rule that each one is a law unto himself would soon be confronted with disorder and anarchy.

Appellant also cites *Wisconsin v. Yoder*, . . . and seeks to include her individual circumstance within the framework of that case. . . .

The parents in Yoder were members of the Amish sect. Their creed included a belief that attendance at high school would expose their children to the risk of censure from the church community and would endanger both their own hope of salvation and that of their children.

However we may try to fit the appellant's argument, procrustean-like, into Yoder, there is no credible analogy between the two.

Finally, the argument is advanced that in reality the compulsory feature of education has been debased to the point that it has become merely a compulsory attendance law. As such, the argument runs, it must be deemed unresponsive to the purposes and intentions of the legislators and must therefore be set aside as unconstitutional.

That argument is somewhat akin to throwing out the baby with the bathwater, or burning down the barn to get rid of the rats. . . .

We share a feeling of empathy with Mrs. Franz. We know that she desires to do what is best for her children for their betterment and for their future careers. No one could be more sincere. But we echo the sentiments of Jeremy Bentham that the morality of actions is estimated by their utility. As translated into an apothegm, it is "the greatest happiness of the greatest number."

COMPULSORY EDUCATION AND THE QUALITY OF SCHOOLING

Clearly the state has the right to require school attendance, although there have been notable exceptions. The courts have ruled that compulsory attendance might violate First and Fourteenth Amendment rights (*Pierce, Yoder*) and have allowed parents to keep children out of school when they could prove they were providing an "equivalent" education (*State v. Massa*, 95 NF Super 382). Even so, in these cases the Supreme Court and the state courts have been careful to defend and uphold the right of states to require school attendance.

A basic assumption of compulsory attendance laws is that children who are required to attend school for a specified number of years learn something from that experience. Legislatures are beginning to look at this issue. As a result of criticism that the public schools are graduating students who are functionally illiterate, state legislatures have been going beyond compulsion to requiring achievement of basic competence.

Some legislatures in recent years have attempted to require that schools be accountable in what they teach; that children are entitled, by law, to learn a certain minimum level of skills. The state of Florida was one of the first to make a functional literacy test a requirement for high school graduation. Under direction from the state legislature, the Florida state department of education developed and supervised the administration of a minimal competency exam. Passing the examination as a precondition for gaining a high school diploma was challenged in *Debra P. v. Turlington*.[13] In this case a U.S. district judge ruled that the test was a violation of the student's Fourteenth Amendment rights. Although upholding the validity of the minimal competency exam, Judge George Carr ruled that students who were then seniors had attended segregated Florida schools for their first three years, and a disproportionate failure by black students on the exam was the result of past discrimination. The court viewed the failure to grant diplomas to functionally illiterate blacks as punishment of the victims of past discrimination for "deficits created by an inferior educational environment. . . ." The court ruled that the state must provide adequate prior notice before linking a diploma with literacy exam results. In the words of Judge Carr: "The plaintiffs, after spending 10 years in schools where their attendance was compelled, were informed of a requirement concerning skills, which, if taught, should have been in grades they had long since completed."

A growing public concern with the quality of schooling provided by the public schools suggests that more such cases will find their way into the courts in future years. Of course, state legislatures have long been concerned with more than merely providing for compulsory schooling. From time to time in most states, legislatures have not been reluctant to express their views, in the form of laws, on what the schools should be doing. There are many laws mandating the teaching of certain subjects such as history or civics, the teaching of the dangers of alcohol and other drugs, the provision of minimal courses in English, and so on. It would seem that the next logical step in this process is for legislatures to provide some means of holding the schools accountable for doing some of these things.

THE DEBATE OVER COMPULSORY SCHOOLING

In the face of increasing legislative controls over schooling, it seems ironic to note that there is a growing debate over the most basic of all legislative requirements, that of compulsory schooling.

There has always been some opposition to the idea of compulsory schooling. In recent years the voices of opposition appear to be on the increase. Along with the criticism of public schools as places where children find learning difficult, there have been new concerns raised about student apathy, the use of drugs, and increasing violence, particularly in public high schools. With increasing frequency critics have been suggesting that a simple "cure" for some of the problems would be a modification of the compulsory school laws.

The criticism of Frank Brown, chairman of the National Commission on the Reform of Secondary Education, is in many ways typical of the new attack on compulsory education. Mr. Brown, in a speech before the HEW Regional Conference in Kansas City in 1975, declared that "the nation's high schools cannot continue as custodial institutions, and at the same time, excel . . . in the matter of teaching and learning." Present compulsory attendance laws, he said, only "make high schools institutions of incarceration." He suggested that students should be given the option of leaving school at age 14 to enroll in a community-based school which would prepare them for work.[14] Many teachers who have to deal daily with problems of the urban high school would probably agree with Mr. Brown. Many teachers, if given the opportunity, would be happy to go through their classes and weed out those students who they feel are "unteachable" and who create problems for the other students in class who "really want to learn." It is this sort of attitude, which is by no means isolated, which has given support to a growing debate over the educational as well as the social validity of existing compulsory school laws.

Roger Sipher, professor of history at the State University of New York at Cortland, argues that public schools are in grave difficulties, that they are no longer institutions in which learning takes place. He suggests that the root of the problem is compulsory education laws which need to be modified in order to save our schools. M. S. Katz, a professor of philosophy of education at The American University in Washington, D.C., argues that compulsory education laws perform a legitimate legal and social function and that compulsory school laws are not the basic cause of bad schools. He can find nothing to support the position that compulsory school laws by themselves create the problems which exist in the public schools. Following are excerpts which express major points of each position.

Compulsory Education
An Idea Whose Time Has Passed
Roger Sipher[15]

For the last two decades, Americans have made truly unprecedented efforts to reform and improve public elementary and secondary education. Yet in spite of these efforts, the quality of American education is steadily declining and, perhaps of greater importance, Americans in growing numbers are beginning to question the basic legitimacy of our educational system. Why, at the end of such a period of reform, should the system be worse then before? Why, after spending billions to improve the system, are Americans casting jaundiced eyes at the very schools they attended? There are very likely a number of good reasons, but the major one has to do with the students—their behavior makes a mockery of the learning environment of our public schools. Behind this reason, however, are the laws that mandate school attendance. As long as all American children have to attend school through age 16, or thereabouts, and as long as American children know they can eventually get high school diplomas with a minimum of effort, by merely "hanging on," public education and Americans' confidence in it will continue to decline, leading, perhaps, to the ultimate collapse of the system. The situation is more serious than many will allow themselves to believe. . . .

. . . compulsory attendance laws have served to pervert what might otherwise have been sound educational practice. An early solution to serving a heterogeneous student population was to offer different types of educational programs to meet the different levels of ability and interest. Students who satisfactorily completed their studies were awarded either a general diploma or an academic one. Since World War II, however, this system has been corrupted so that now there are three types of diplomas: general, academic, and something called the "attendance diploma." Within this latter group fall many of the students who are either apathetic or openly hostile to school. The unfortunate final outcome of this process is that the educational atmosphere in schools has been so polluted by these hostile and apathetic students that many who now receive either general or academic diplomas do not really deserve them. . . .

Moreover, it seems clear that the mandatory attendance laws presently serve as a massive legal barrier to taking the necessary steps to save our schools. Public school officials who want to dismiss lazy or unruly students are confronted with a public attitude, which compulsory attendance laws support, that youngsters can not be dismissed from school, for whatever reason—apathy, hostility, or open violence—until they reach the age of 16. . . .

. . . To counter these growing problems, the American public needs to develop an attitude that formal schooling, at least after the age of 10 or 11, is not for everyone. . . . Abolition of archaic attendance laws would be the beginning of the change. Such action would produce enormous, immediate dividends. First, and probably most important for the over-all improvement of American public education, it would mean that, within a short amount of time, having a high school diploma would once again be something to be proud of. . . .

Second, abolishing mandatory attendance laws would permit teachers to turn their energies away from policing hostile students and pleading with apathetic ones to educating those who want an education. . . .

Third, public esteem for schools would increase because people once again could believe that the schools were providing a sound basic education. . . .

Fourth, stripped of the need to justify passing just about everyone, teachers could again insist that grades mean what they are supposed to—how well a student is learning.

Fifth, elementary schools would change as students came to realize very early that they had better learn something or risk flunking out. Parents would reinforce this.

Sixth, the cost of trying to enforce the compulsory attendance laws would be eliminated. Despite enforcement efforts, nearly 15% of the school-age children in our largest cities are almost permanently absent from school and the figure is going up steadily in suburban areas. . . .

At long last, the time has come to distinguish between the functions of various institutions that deal with young people. Schools should be for formal education; other agencies should be for other things. Failure to recognize this simple fact will only serve to perpetuate, rather than remedy, the present mess in American education. At present, schools are only tangentially educational institutions. Have we not given the noble idea of a formal education for everyone enough time to be disproved? Must we continue to pay homage to the homily, "you can lead a horse to water but you can't make him drink," yet pretend it does not hold for education? At the very least, it is time for a public debate on this question, followed, if agreement is reached, by elimination of the public laws that require every child to attend school through adolescence.

Quite a different view of compulsory schooling is provided by Professor Katz.

Compulsion and the Discourse on Compulsory School Attendance
M. S. Katz[16]

Of various responses to the widespread skepticism over the value of public schooling one of the most serious has been an escalating debate over compulsory school attendance. Unfortunately, many of the recent writings on compulsory schooling have obscured the complex relationships between compulsion and legal rules and between attendance laws and the practices of schooling. These ideas can be stated as follows:

1. Compulsory school attendance laws are forms of coercion.
2. Compulsory school attendance makes effective teaching or creative learning impossible.

... The critical discourse on compulsory school attendance is characterized by numerous references to "compulsion" and "coercion." In many instances, authors speak of compulsion as if it were an entity separable from the sanctions attached to compulsory attendance laws, separable from the overall coercive authority of a legal system, and disconnected from the social pressures underlying laws that have been accepted as legitimate. ...

In our craving for generality, we are tempted to reduce all forms of non-optional, obligatory conduct to the categories of compulsion or coercion. However, all forms of non-optional conduct are not the same, and we ignore basic differences when they are discussed as products of compulsion. While some people will act in accordance with the laws from the standpoint of the unpleasant consequences attached to violating them, most will voluntarily accept the standard built into the law and follow the law as they would a social rule of custom that they accept. For the majority, laws should not be regarded as forms of coercion nor should normal compliance with the law be viewed as the product of compulsion. ...

To speak of school attendance laws as forms of coercion is to fail to distinguish between legal and social compulsion. Although social compulsion exerts a different kind of control over people's conduct than does legal compulsion, we must remember not to deny its subtle impact. Compulsory school attendance laws today codify an existing social norm or standard—that young people should be in school rather than at home, on the streets, or at work, at least for most of the year. Indeed, this social norm operates in a more extensive domain than does compulsory school attendance as a legal rule. Many Americans believe that they should send their children to school before they are legally compelled to do so. Moreover, since over seventy-five percent of young people are graduating from high school in the U.S. and numerous jobs that once required only a high school diploma now demand a credential from a community college, one might argue that post-secondary education is becoming socially compulsory. As long as attendance remains the chief avenue to schooling credentials and schooling credentials remain prerequisites to most jobs, social compulsion will remain a more dominant underpinning to school attendance than legal rules. Consequently, removing or lowering school attendance laws by itself would probably bring about a state of de facto rather than de jure compulsory schooling.

... In its recommendation to lower the compulsory school leaving age to fourteen, the National Commission on the Reform of Secondary Education asserted:

> Compulsory attendance laws are the dead hand on the high schools. The liberation of youth and the many freedoms which the courts have given to students within the last decade make it impossible for the school to continue as a learning institution. ...

Do compulsory attendance laws create "compulsory formats" in which "learning cannot be fostered"? Probably not. However, the question itself suggests that we examine briefly the logical relationship between compulsory attendance laws and the effects of schooling.

A logical distinction should be made between compulsory schooling as a set of diverse legal rules and the substantive practices of schooling children on a non-voluntary basis. Legal rules and substantive practices are not the same kinds of things and it is a mistake to confuse them. Moreover, it is not at all clear that one can make a substantive claim about what children can or cannot learn in schools on the grounds that there is a legal requirement for them to attend. That there is a legal rule mandating school attendance does not tell us very much about the content of schooling practices; whether those practices are classroom practices, the practices of preventing truancy, or the administrative practices governing life in the interstices of the classrooms. Individual schools may be good or bad, bureaucratic and impersonal or non-bureaucratic and personal, but we will not be able to make such appraisals by learning about the rule that makes school attendance mandatory. The substantive administrative and classroom practices of schools wherein attendance is mandatory are structured by different rules that define and govern them. It is a mistake, and not an insignificant one, to see a logical connection between compulsory school attendance and the results of schooling. If there is an empirical connection between compulsory school attendance and the results of schooling, it has not been clearly established. Moreover, it is highly doubtful that such a connection would suggest that "effective teaching" or "creative learning," however these terms are operationally defined, would be unlikely to occur in schools where children are required to attend.

The complex relationships between laws, social standards, and compulsion will not be understood by simplified references to laws as forms of compulsion; neither will the problematic relationship between school attendance and educational achievement become any less problematic through simplistic utterances about compulsory attendance laws creating failures in the schools. The discourse on compulsory schooling demands philosophical attention so that the debate over changing compulsory attendance laws can be a clear rather than a muddled one.

THE STATE AND THE SCHOOL: SOME CONCLUSIONS

In both the *Pierce* and *Yoder* cases the Supreme Court of the United States, no doubt expressing the conventional wisdom of the society, made it clear that states have a clear responsibility for providing for compulsory schooling for the purpose of political socialization of the young. Justice McReynolds, writing for the majority in *Pierce*, made it clear that "no question is raised concerning the power of the state reasonably to regulate all schools, to inspect, supervise, and examine them ... to require that all children of proper age attend some school..." Moreover, in *Pierce* the Court left little doubt about the political socialization function of the schools when it said that "teachers shall be of good moral character and patriotic disposition, that certain studies plainly essential to good citizenship must be taught, and that nothing be taught which is manifestly inimical to the public welfare."

Similarly, while ruling for the Amish, the Supreme Court pointed out in *Yoder* that "there is no doubt as to the power of a State, having a high responsibility for education of its citizens, to impose reasonable regulations for the control and duration of basic education." In *Yoder*, the Court also seemed to want to make it clear that the decision permitting the Amish to avoid compulsory school legislation should not be too broadly interpreted; that is, it was a narrow decision that did not affect others who might find compulsory schooling objectionable:

> Our disposition of this case, however, in no way alters our recognition of the obvious fact that courts are not school boards or legislatures, and are ill equipped to determine the "necessity of discrete aspects of a state's program of compulsory education. ..." It cannot be over-emphasized that we are not dealing with a way of life and mode of education by a group claiming to have recently discovered some "progressive" or more enlightened process for rearing children for modern life.

In other words, the Court was saying as clearly as possible that "self-styled counter-culture groups need not apply." Its decision was limited strictly to a centuries-old established religious group. Thus, neither the decision in *Pierce* nor the one in *Yoder* significantly altered the state's right, even duty, to provide compulsory education for all children.

Of course, this did not dissuade parents from trying. The *Franz* case cited in this chapter is just one of many in which parents, unhappy with the public schools, made efforts to flaunt the compulsory school laws of the state. Almost always the state courts, which normally hear these cases, require parents to prove that they have a legal basis for taking such action. Most state compulsory school laws have what amounts to "escape clauses" which enable parents to provide schooling at home under certain specified conditions. Usually these clauses permit parents to provide for independent schooling where they can prove that public schools are seriously damaging to their children or that the children cannot benefit from public compulsory schooling. In addition, most state laws require that, even under these circumstances, the education provided by parents must be equivalent to that provided by the public schools. Always the burden of proof is on the parents. Moreover, it is usually a heavy burden—such cases are not lightly considered by the courts. Even so, by 1980 there was a growing movement for parents to opt for this approach. Indeed, in characteristic American fashion, a national organization was in operation by 1980 which called itself the Center for Independent Education; one of its major purposes was the encouragement of parents' efforts to educate their children at home. Through a periodic newsletter titled *Inform*, it publicized such efforts on the part of parents.

In addition to these isolated efforts, public dissatisfaction with the public schools found expression in increasing calls for modification of compulsory school laws. Voices as prominent as James Coleman's raised questions about the viability of compulsory school laws. In *Youth: Transition to Adulthood*,[17] Coleman and his associates wondered if the present compulsory laws which forced children to remain in school past the age of 14 served any useful purpose for many children. Coleman and his colleagues suggested alternatives to compulsory school attendance might be considered for students who were getting nothing out of their public school attendance. In the face of high levels of functional illiteracy among certain adolescent populations, violence in high schools, disruptive students, and other problems, there appears to be increasing interest in the development of alternatives to rigid age levels for compulsory school laws.

Whether or not this debate will cause any significant change in compulsory school laws is an open question. What is more likely to happen are efforts, which are becoming national in scope, to attempt somehow to legislate the improvement of the quality of public schools. It seems unlikely that an idea so entrenched in the United States as compulsory schooling will be seriously modified in the near future. There are too many forces in our society which would lead one to believe that any basic change in the system would be difficult. The long struggle to establish universal "free" compulsory schooling, the belief that somehow compulsory schooling serves local, state, and national purposes, local pride in public schools, and an entrenched educational bureaucracy on the local, state, and national levels are all forces which tend to resist any sweeping changes.

NOTES

1. Much of this section is based on Forest Chester Ensign, *Compulsory School Attendance and Child Labor* (Iowa City, Iowa: Athens Press, 1921).
2. Ensign, *Compulsory School Attendance and Child Labor*, p. 32.
3. An interesting essay which deals with the general subject of compulsion in American society and the manner in which it affected public schools was written by Charles Burgess, "The Goddess, the School Book and Compulsion," *Harvard Educational Review* 46 (May 1976): 199–216.
4. Stephen Arons, "The Separation of School and State: Pierce Reconsidered," *Harvard Educational Review* 46 (February 1976): 76–104.
5. Ibid., p. 80.
6. Ibid., p. 101.
7. Joseph Stoll, "Who Shall Educate Our children?" in *Compulsory Education and the Amish*, Albert N. Keim (Boston: Beacon Press, 1975), pp. 16–42.
8. Ibid., p. 27.

9. Ibid., p. 34.

10. Ibid., pp. 41–42.

11. Donald A. Erickson, ed., *Public Controls for Nonpublic Schools* (Chicago: University of Chicago Press, 1969), p. 19.

12. The court below brushed aside the students' interests with the off-hand comment that "(w)hen a child reaches the age of judgment, he can choose for himself his religion." ... But there is nothing in this record to indicate that the moral and intellectual judgment demanded of the student by the question in the case is beyond his capacity. Children far younger than the 14- and 15-year-olds involved here are regularly permitted to testify in custody and other proceedings. Indeed, the failure to call the affected child in a custody hearing is often reversible error. ... Moreover, there is substantial agreement among child psychologists and sociologists that the moral and intellectual maturity of the 14-year-old approaches that of the adult. See, e.g., J. Piaget, *The Moral Judgment of the Child* (1948); D. Elkind, *Children and Adolescents*, 75–80 (1970); Kohlberg, "Moral Education in the Schools: A Developmental View," in R. Muuss, *Adolescent Behavior and Society*, 193, 199–200 (1971); W. Kay, *Moral Development*, 172–183 (1968); A. Gesell & F. Ilg, *Youth: The Years From Ten to Sixteen*, 175–182 (1956). The maturity of Amish youth, who identify with and assume adult roles from early childhood, see M. Goodman, *The Culture of Childhood*, 92–94 (1970), is certainly not less than that of children in the general population.

13. *Education Daily*, 17 July 1979, pp. 1–2.

14. *Education Daily*, 10 December 1975, p. 5.

15. From *USA Today*, September 1978, pp. 17–19.

16. From *Educational Theory* 27, no. 3 (Summer 1977): 170–185.

17. James Coleman, *Youth: Transition to Adulthood* (Chicago: University of Chicago Press, 1974).

4

Nonpublic Schools: Alternatives to Public Schooling

If one assumes that a major function of state supported and controlled public schooling is the political socialization of the children of the society, it is interesting to note that in the United States a tenth of the children escape this experience by attending nonpublic schools. This is not to say that nonpublic schools do not socialize children to national values or that they fail to promote something vaguely called "good citizenship." Whatever they do in the way of socialization of children toward political, religious, or social values apparently is different from what takes place in the public schools. At least the advocates of nonpublic education suggest that there are differences. Indeed, if nonpublic schools were not deliberately different from the public schools, there would be little reason for their existence.

Thus, as strenuously as the public schools have attempted to be all things to all people, they have stopped short of success. Millions of parents continue to opt for nonpublic schooling. This should not be surprising in a nation which claims to be democratic and in a society which is as large and diverse as the United States. This chapter provides a brief overview of the more important aspects of nonpublic schooling in the United States. In this effort, it examines some of the reasons for the persistence of nonpublic schools, the voucher system, tuition tax credits, and the relationship of the state to nonpublic schools.

WHY PARENTS CHOOSE NONPUBLIC SCHOOLS

Although the reasons parents opt for nonpublic schooling are often very personal and varied, there are certain major reasons which seem to stand out. Religious beliefs seem to head the list. Part of the reason for the existence of private religious schools can be found in tradition and tightly knit religious communities. Catholic schools have been around so long it is difficult to imagine this society without them. The long struggle of the Amish and the Orthodox Jews to promote their own religious views in the education of their children is legend. The same might be said of other groups. More recently, dissatisfaction on the part of many religious groups with the public schools has tended to strengthen their resolve to provide alternatives to public schooling. Some of the dissatisfaction is historic; some is of more recent vintage.

Although Catholic schooling had existed in America from Colonial times, the great public school movement beginning with the mid-nineteenth century created serious problems for Catholics. The working-class people from Ireland, Germany, and southern and eastern Europe, who formed the bulk of the immigrant population in the nineteenth century, were largely Catholic. They were also eager to become Americanized as quickly as possible. This created a dilemma for them in that the public school appeared to be the social institution most specifically designed to Americanize the children of the foreign born. Yet public schools at best appeared to neglect Catholic values and, at worst, were openly anti-Catholic. In the words of Neil McCluskey, "the common schools had not been designed with Roman Catholic children in mind. These schools, for whose support Catholics were taxed, smacked strongly of Protestantism, with their Protestant books, hymns, prayers, and above all, their Protestant Bible."[1] In response to what they considered to be predominantly Protestant schools, Catholics insisted that the public schools be neutral in matters of religion or, failing in that, they urged that the school taxes they paid be used to provide Catholic schools for their children. On both counts their efforts, until very recently, failed. When the Supreme Court of the United States finally did act in the 1960s—in such cases as *Engle v. Vitale*, which barred a New York State Regents official prayer in the schools, and *Abington School District v. Schempp*, which banned Bible reading—the Catholics and other non-Protestants religious groups, especially the Jews, had virtually resigned themselves to the fact that public schools were anything but neutral on religious teaching. What bothered such groups, and continues to worry them, was that the religious orientation of the schools was overwhelmingly Protestant in nature. Ironically, the position of the Court which insisted on neutrality in public schooling came so late that it may have created more problems than it solved.[2] The Catholics were not especially pleased for they were not easily convinced, after years of struggle, that the schools were forever purged of Protestant religious teachings. On the other hand, many Protestant groups were incensed that the Court had "taken God out of the schools." This was an understandable reaction in view of the fact that prayer and other religious activities in the schools had become deeply entrenched over a long period. Religious exercises, in most cases oriented toward Protestant values, had indeed been part of the public school experience from the beginning. To suddenly end this was a shock greater than some could easily bear. For many, neutrality was not a simple logical proposition. Opposition to religious neutrality for the schools has been serious and continuous for at least two decades. For many, the Court's definition of neutrality settled nothing. The central thesis of the antineutrality argument was expressed by Justice Stewart in his dissent in the *Schempp* case. Stewart dissented, in part, because he felt that there appeared to be some conflict between the two major religion clauses in the First Amendment: "Congress shall make no law respecting an establishment of religion, or prohibiting the free exercise thereof. . . ." The majority in *Schempp* felt that Bible reading which was required by the schools was a clear violation of the establishment clause. That is, an agency of the state, the school, was "establishing" a religious practice. What worried Stewart was the fact that by prohibiting the reading of verses from the King James version of the Bible, a significant number of students who wanted the exercise were being denied that opportunity. Thus they were being denied their "free exercise" First Amendment rights. In Stewart's words: "For a compulsory state educational system so structures a child's life that if religious exercises are held to be an impermissible activity in schools, religion is placed at an artificial and state-created disadvantage."[3]

The Catholics and other religious "minorities" continue to argue that free exercise has an even broader application than that suggested by Justice Stewart. They feel that millions of American children are being denied free exercise of their religion by being forced for financial reasons to attend public schools. Free exercise, as it is defined by the most ardent advocates of nonpublic religious schooling, should at least mean that the many public welfare benefits enjoyed by public school children are extended to private religious schools. Although the Court has moved somewhat in this direction by upholding free textbooks for religious schools,[4] bus transportation,[5] property tax exemptions,[6] lending texts and other materials from the public schools to private schools,[7] supplying state textbooks and tests at no cost to sectarian schools,[8] it is clear that public school students continue to have many benefits provided by tax money which are not enjoyed by private sectarian school students. In nearly every case where the Court has moved to provide state assistance to private church-related schools, it has done so on the basis that such assistance promotes the free exercise of religion without substantially eroding the establishment clause. In every case the Court has been careful in its examination of the question of whether the aid provided through state legislation is an effort of the state which promotes religious purposes.

Thus, the Court has struck a delicate balance. On the one hand, it has attempted to maintain the wall of separation between church and state which is implicit in the establishment clause of the First Amendment, while on the other hand, it has permitted in the interest of free exercise a certain amount of state aid for nonreligious purposes to private sectarian schools. In the case of free exercise, there is little doubt that without some of the aid which has been provided, some private church-related schools would be hard pressed to survive. In a sense, then, the argument for nonpublic schooling advanced by many parents, that the public schools deny them the freedom to teach their children religious values, has been supported in part by the Court.

Although the desire of parents to send their children to schools which reflect their religious values is an important reason for the continued existence of the nonpublic school sector in American education, the case can be easily overstated. There are many other reasons why parents choose nonpublic schools. Indeed, the desire to socialize children to particular religious values tends to get mixed up with a number of other motives. Otto Kraushaar's work[9] makes this point rather

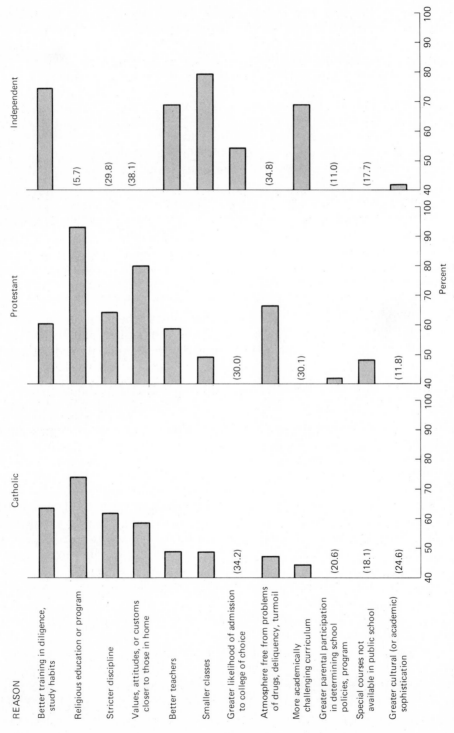

FIGURE 4.1 Why parents choose nonpublic secondary schools (reasons endorsed as important or very important by at least 40 percent of the parents).

well. In a very large sample of more than 18,000 nonpublic schools, Kraushaar asked parents why they sent their children to nonpublic schools. The answer is provided in Figure 4.1.[10]

Clearly the parents who sent children to independent schools felt their children received better academic preparation than they would have received in public schools. Indeed, if one lumps together a cluster of issues generally related to academic excellence, including better study habits, better teachers, smaller classes, and a more challenging curriculum, the independent group seems to be highly motivated by its general concern for academic excellence. Interestingly, both Catholic and Protestant parents were not greatly concerned about the likelihood of the nonpublic schools of their choice adequately preparing their children for admission to college. Even though parents who send children to nonpublic schools offer a variety of reasons for doing so, moral and religious training seems to be most important for parents who send children to church-related schools, while academic concerns seem uppermost in the minds of those who support independent schools. Certainly Kraushaar did not mean to imply that the necessarily limited number of questions included in his questionnaire encompassed all reasons for the existence of nonpublic schools. As Theodore Sizer has suggested, private schools have developed for a number of other reasons.[11]

Nonpublic schools have developed in communities where the public schools were not adequately providing for the special needs of certain parents. In some communities, private schools developed to provide for the special needs of handicapped students. Native Americans maintain nonpublic tribal schools. Black Panthers and Black Muslims have established their own schools in protest to what they believe to be the racist character of public schools. On the opposite end of the continuum, private, white, segregated academies have developed to avoid court-ordered integrated schooling.[12] Finally, hundreds of independent schools developed during the sixties and early seventies in response to parental dissatisfaction with the "system." Parents who, for one reason or another, had given up on public education, established alternative schools in hundreds of communities across the nation.[13]

There is some evidence that private schools do provide the educational experiences and environment that many parents claim for them. In a study commissioned by the National Center for Education Statistics, James Coleman and his colleagues found that private schools were superior to public schools in many respects.[14] Based on a sample taken in 1980 of 58,728 high school sophomores and 1,016 seniors in public and private schools, Coleman and his associates found, among other things, that students achieve on a higher level in private schools, which provide a safer and more disciplined environment and maintain a lower teacher-pupil ratio than do public schools. In addition, Coleman found that even though private schools are more segregated than public schools, they have less segregation within the classroom than do public schools. Although the private schools examined in the study did not provide as wide a range of educational experiences as did public schools, the students in private schools had higher self-esteem and seemed to feel that they had more control over their own destiny than did students in public schools. On the basis of his findings, Coleman urged that private schools be given more public financial support. Although Coleman's study has been widely criticized in terms of research methodology and design, it does support the views of many parents who opt for private over public education for their children. In the long run, what parents believe about public and private schooling may be more important than whether or not Coleman's research is an accurate representation of reality.

Whatever the reasons for the existence of nonpublic schools in America, it is obvious that the private education sector is an important part of the educational landscape. Table 4.1[15] illustrates the great numbers involved as well as the diversity of nonpublic school enrollment in the United States.

TABLE 4.1
Nonpublic School Enrollment Trends, 1970 to 1975[a]

Nonpublic School Group	Enrollments 1970–71	Enrollments 1975–76	% Change 1970–71 to 1975–76
Roman Catholic	4,364,000	3,415,000	–21.7
Lutheran			
Missouri Synod	163,386	165,604	+1.4
Wisconsin Synod	29,050	31,183	+7.3
American Lutheran	9,926	16,121	+62.4
Seventh-Day Adventist	(no data available)	71,539[b]	+
Calvinist (National Union of Christian Schools)	51,183	48,585	–5.1
Evangelical			
National Association of Christian Schools	50,860	23,185	–54.4
Western Association of Christian Schools	32,327	63,131	+95.3
National Christian School Educational Association[c]		38,175	+
American Association of Christian Schools[c]		94,722[d]	+
Assembly of God	7,462	21,921	+193.8
Jewish Day Schools			
National Society for Hebrew Day Schools (Orthodox)	75,000	82,200	+9.6
Solomon Schechter Day Schools (Conservative)	6,042	7,965	+31.8
Reform Jewish		373	+2.8
National Association of Independent Schools	221,216	277,406	+2.8
Episcopal Schools			
Parish Day Schools[e]	4,559[f]	5,536	+21.4
Nonparish Schools[e]	61,186[f]	71,020	+16.1

TABLE 4.1 (continued)

Nonpublic School Group	Enrollments 1970–71	Enrollments 1975–76	% Change 1970–71 to 1975–76
Friends (Quaker) Schools	13,706	13,801	+0.1
Military		13,600	–
Greek Orthodox	4,468	5,009	+12.1
Mennonite Schools	7,368	8,079	+9.6
Nonpublic Alternative (Free) Schools	13,142	23,498	+78.9

[a] These figures were gathered from nonpublic school personnel and from yearly enrollment reports. For the most part, only elementary and secondary school enrollments are reported.
[b] 1974–75
[c] Founded after 1970
[d] School enrollments of regular and affiliate schools listed in the 1975 membership listing
[e] Includes some preschool enrollments
[f] 1969–70

The data on enrollment trends are interesting in that they reveal both a serious drop in enrollment in Catholic schools and the emergence of some dramatic developments in other forms of nonpublic schooling. Lutheran schools managed to hold their own, with the exception of the American Lutheran movement which made a dramatic gain. The schools which showed the most dramatic gains were the more recently launched evangelical Christian academies. The next section will briefly examine some of the problems facing Catholic schools, the phenomenal growth of Christian academies, and the nature of the free school movement.

THE ISSUES OF RELIGION, RACE, AND FREEDOM: SOME EXAMPLES

Religion

Since this work does not attempt to provide an in-depth treatment of nonpublic schools in America, the following discussion is only a brief treatment of a few of the problems faced by Catholic schools and the phenomenon of the growth of "Christian" academies and so called "free" schools.

The Catholic school system is by far the largest private, church-related effort in the United States to provide schooling for elementary and secondary students. The most recent *Official Catholic Directory* (1975) contains some useful data on the size of the Catholic school operation. Catholic schooling during the period from 1945 to 1975 experienced some rapid growth followed by a rather serious decline. In 1945 there were 10,192 Catholic schools with an enrollment of 2,590,660 students. By 1965 the enrollment had increased by 35 percent to a little over 3.5 million students. According to the 1975 *Directory*, the schools experienced a drop of 35 percent in enrollment during the decade from 1965–75, to a total of 2,959,788 students. Most of the decline occurred at the elementary school level, which experienced a steady drop in the decade between 1965–75. Secondary school enrollment finished the 1965–75 decade with nearly a million students, about the same number as was enrolled in 1965.

In the 1970s the most serious problem facing Catholic schools was their inability to grow. This is puzzling in view of the fact that other, less well established, church-related schools experienced rapid growth. Apparently, even the officials in charge of Catholic education are not certain about the reasons for the drop in elementary school enrollments, but there is much speculation. In his comprehensive study in 1976 of Catholic education, Andrew Greeley[16] speculated that some of the decline might have been attributed to the fact that Catholics, like other middle-class Americans, were opting for smaller families. In addition, Greeley suggested that Church leaders seemed reluctant to follow their parishioners into the suburbs. That is, they continued to support inner-city parochial schools long after the populations which once supported them had moved to the suburbs. Personal reasons might also have accounted for some of the decline. In Greeley's words: "some of the decline may result from a conscious repudiation by Catholics of the idea of parochial schools or a decision that in one's own community the public schools simply offer better educational opportunities." Finally, cost was certainly a factor since inflationary forces took their toll on private schools as they did on the rest of the economy. In spite of these problems, Catholic Americans expressed strong support of the Catholic school idea, and existing schools seemed to be fulfilling their religious teaching function rather well.

In their sociological study of the status of Catholic education in the United States, Greeley and his associates attempted to determine how effective Catholic schools were in promoting support for the Church and how Catholic Church members felt about their schools. They found surprisingly strong support for Catholic schools during a time in which the Church itself was experiencing great difficulty. Great changes had occurred in the Church, the most important of which, at least for American Catholics, seemed to be the reforms of the Second Vatican Council, phased into most churches in the sixties, and the encyclical Humanae Vitae (anti-birth control) in 1967. According to the Greeley report, the Council reforms were widely accepted among the American Catholic population, while the birth control encyclical tended to get a negative reception. Whatever their views on Church reform and birth control, Catholics in the mid-seventies continued to overwhelmingly support their schools. According to Greeley, "While only about half of the American Catholics go to church every week, eighty percent would be willing to contribute more money to keep the parish school operating."[17] Indeed, Greeley and associates found support was great among all age groups and suggested that there was a reservoir of as much as two billion dollars a year which could be had for the asking if Catholic officials were interested in expanding their school operations. Moreover, the support extended beyond an expressed willingness to contribute, as important as that is. Overwhelmingly, American Catholics approved of the expansion of the curriculum in Catholic schools. New methods of religious education, the inclusion of sex education in the schools, and the addition of lay teachers for the schools all received overwhelming support from the sample polled. In the face of such support, how then does one explain the decline in enrollment of Catholic schools during the period from 1965–75? Greeley's group suggested that it was not a problem of support but one of leadership. That is, Catholic leaders were simply not interested in building new schools to meet the obvious demand which existed among rank-and-file Catholic Americans.

This attitude is even more puzzling in the face of other evidence presented in the Greeley study. The study found Catholic schools very effective in promoting Catholicism. While they found religious instruction provided by the Church outside the school setting as relatively unimportant in influencing religious attitudes, the schools were very effective. The study found that Catholic education was "second only to religiousness of spouse in predicting religious behavior."[18] In short, it seemed to the authors of *Catholic Schools in a Declining Church* that Catholic education not only was desired by American Catholics but was effective. In their summary, the authors noted the following major findings:

1. Support for Catholic schools among the American Catholic population is as strong as ever, and there is available a substantial amount of unused resources (perhaps as much as two billion dollars a year) to sustain the schools in existence.
2. Far from declining in effectiveness in the past decade, Catholic schools seem to have increased their impact. In a time of general decline of religious behavior, the rate of decline for those who have gone to Catholic schools is much slower. The correlation between Catholic school attendance and religiousness is especially strong for those under thirty.
3. In terms of the future of the organization, Catholic schools seem more important for a church in time of transition than for one in a time of peaceful stability.[19]

The decline in enrollments for Catholic schools was thus explained not by forces outside the Church, although these contributed, but by the deliberate policies set by Church leadership. The paradox of public support and declining enrollment was explained by Greeley and his associates by pointing out that the Catholic Church in America is not run by popular vote. "the decision making structure of the Catholic Church in the United States is not responsive either to popular sentiment or to empirical evidence."[20] Even more to the point: "The leadership of the American Church has only very slight information on what the reality is outside of its own meeting rooms. It tends to project into that reality its own fears and discontents."[21]

Given the large number of students attending Catholic schools and the immense investment of private capital in land and buildings, coupled with the strong attachments of Catholic people to their schools, one should be able to predict that they are not likely to close their doors anytime soon. This is important not only to Catholics but to non-Catholics as well, since Catholic schooling in the United States is rich and varied. Because it is, it meets some real needs which would be costly and difficult for the public sector to assume. The Catholic parochial schools, diocesan schools and various private schools and academies, serve a variety of purposes and clientele. Not only are many working-class and middle-class children benefiting from schools located on the fringes of the suburbs, but the inner-city schools continue to provide genuine and effective schooling alternatives for inner-city blacks, a service which the public might be reluctant to replace.

According to the 1980 statistical report on *Catholic Schools in America* made by the National Catholic Education Association, the issue of increasing the number of ethnic minorities in Catholic schools was "much discussed" during the decade of the seventies. Almost apologetically, the report pointed out that some minorities were not well served because "Catholic schools naturally tend to service those who support the school." The report stated that "Black, Indian and Oriental races have not historically embraced the Catholic religion," while the Spanish have. However, partly because the Catholics have resisted closing urban schools, the percentage of Catholic schools serving urban children increased in the decade 1969–79. The increase in urban percentage came not through expansion but as a result of the closing of rural schools at a faster rate than urban schools.[22]

During the 1970s there was an increase in black, Hispanic, and Asian American enrollments in Catholic elementary and secondary schools, as indicated in Table 4.2.[23]

TABLE 4.2
Catholic School Enrollment–by Ethnic Background, 1970–71, 1978–79, 1979–80

Ethnic group	1970–71	1978–79	1979–80
Black Americans	209,500	248,500	249,000
Hispanic Americans	216,500	245,600	248,000
Asian Americans	23,500	47,000	56,900
American Indians	20,400	8,600	10,000

The National Catholic Education Association reported that many of the new black students were non-Catholic. According to the association, the decline in percentage of Catholics in Catholic schools, from 95 percent in 1970 to about 91 percent in 1979, "is in great part due to the increased percentage of Black students in Catholic urban schools."[24] The reason for this increase is not clear. Andrew Greeley noted this development in 1981 and suggested that "something interesting was happening," but no research had been done on the phenomenon. Greeley also noted that black students were doing well in Catholic schools and he found no evidence that Catholic schools "have any religious effect on Black and Hispanic students."[25]

In summary, Catholic schools have not only a rich tradition but also a significant social and economic role. In a very real way, the prosperity of Catholic schools affects the entire society. In the words of Kraushaar: "If Catholic schools were to be phased out in large numbers, the loss to educational diversity alone would be incalculable, and the added cost to the American taxpayer would assume critical proportions."[26]

The case of diversity can be easily overstated. In many ways the private school movement in the United States was an expression of support for mainstream, middle-class American values. This is particularly true for the major established religious schools and especially true of the Catholic educational experience. No one can seriously accuse the Catholic Church in America of officially promoting racism or segregation, nor did the schools it sponsored ignore the realities of American society. Indeed, in almost any period in history, the Catholic schools seemed dedicated to teaching their charges basic knowledge and skills needed to succeed in mainstream America. Certainly with regard to their efforts with the children of immigrants in major urban areas of the country, there can be little doubt that a major goal of Catholic education was to integrate these children into the mainstream of society. Andrew Greeley provides an interesting case study on this point in an article in *The Public Interest*. The article, entitled "The Ethnic Miracle," examines conditions in the Polish ghetto in Chicago in the 1920s. Briefly, he described conditions there as the most horrible slum imaginable. Yet, by the midseventies these conditions had disappeared. Greeley gave a great deal of credit for the improvement of second generation Poles in Chicago to the Catholic schools. Expanding his study to other ethnic immigrant groups, Greeley found that "given parental educational level, the Catholic ethnics have a higher academic achievement than do British Americans; indeed it is higher than anyone else in the country save for the Jews—and the Italians have an even higher achievement than Jews."[27]

Contemporary Catholic school students, whatever their ethnic backgrounds, continue to outperform public school students in achievement. Although there is little hard evidence to demonstrate why this is the case, part of it may be due to the fact that parents who send their children there desire for their children a good basic education which will enable them to compete in mainstream America.

Fundamentalist Academies

Schools sometimes referred to as "Christian fundamentalist" schools have experienced rapid growth in recent years. Supporters of these schools make no excuses for their distaste for public schools. Some of these Christian fundamentalist schools have been labeled "segregation academies" since their inception and growth seems to have paralleled court-ordered integration and their student enrollment is totally white. Some of the early academies were clearly segregationist in purpose and secular in philosophy. Later, and with increasing frequency in the seventies, evangelical Christian schools sponsored by fundamentalist Protestant groups, with heavy emphasis on fundamentalist theological teaching, became popular. By the end of the decade, these schools outnumbered the old secular segregationist academies.[28]

Although specific data on the growth of these schools are not readily available, one group—Accelerated Christian Education, Inc., (A.C.E.) based in Garland, Texas—provides some indication of the phenomenal growth of evangelical Christian education. Accelerated Christian Education gives prospective members specific instruction on how to start a school. More than this, they provide a comprehensive set of teacher proof, self-paced curriculum materials which can be util-

II. THE SEVEN DAYS OF CREATION WEEK

"And the earth was without form, and void: and darkness was upon the face of the deep. And the Spirit of God moved upon the face of the waters." Genesis 1:2

The Bible tells us that when God created the earth it was "without *form* and *void*." This verse means that the earth *had no shape* and that it *was empty*. No living things were upon it. Great darkness was over the earth and around it. God, however, was working, and the darkness made no difference to Him. He can work in the darkness as well as in the light.

(1) Genesis 1:2 tells us that the earth was without form and ....

The First Day

"And God said, Let there be light: and there was light." Genesis 1:3

God spoke, and suddenly, there was LIGHT! Light is very wonderful. Many people feel lonely and afraid when it is dark. It is good to see the darkness go and the morning come because light comes with morning. God named the light *day* and the darkness *night.*

God made the earth to travel (TRĂV l) through space around the sun. The earth also spins on its own **axis** (ĂK sĭs). The earth's axis is a line that we make-believe goes through the earth. It helps us to learn how the earth can spin. Have you ever spun a top? A top spins around an axis. The earth does not seem to spin as a top does because it is so big. A **solar** (SŌL luhr) day is how long it takes the earth to turn around once on its axis. A day and a night are 24 hours.

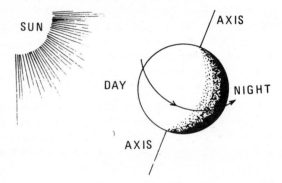

FIGURE 4.2 The text of a lesson on the "second day" of creation, from a unit for elementary school children on "The Seven Days of Creation Week," published by Accelerated Christian Education, Inc.

ized from kindergarten through the first year or so of college. Their Product Catalog 1979–80 included more than 100 pages of "curriculum materials" for use by "Christian schools." Every lesson in every subject—math, social studies, science, English, reading, and so forth—has what Accelerated Christian Education, Inc., refers to as a "character objective." All lessons in every field are based on some selection from the Bible. An entire social studies unit, for example, is based on "the Seven Days of Creation." Each lesson in the unit begins with a quotation from Genesis (see the example in Figure 4.2).[29]

The advertisements from A.C.E. claim that the number of schools in the program has grown from one school in 1970 to more than 3,000 in 1980. According to one of their publicity pamphlets: "When A.C.E. first started in 1970, there was one school; in 1971, there were 5 or 6. We put up a big map on the wall—more than five feet across. . . . That great map is without question the largest pin cushion in the state of Texas! . . . Christian schools are found not just in the South, in the East or West, but all over America . . ."[30]

Their philosophy is straightforward. "Only when combined with *learning materials* that are thoroughly CHRISTIAN, can a child learn truth from God's point of view."[31] In other sections of *Facts*, their publicity pamphlet, the authors state that A.C.E. believes in the Bible, the existence of one God, the "pre-existence," "incarnation," "virgin birth," "miracles," the "second coming," and "witnessing." They flatly state that they will not "knowingly become identified with a church . . . that holds a doctrinal position inconsistent with . . . basic principles set forth in the Scripture."[32] In total, the materials provide complete and total submersion in the Scriptures, and biblical teachings permeate every piece of material they produce.

In an article in the *Phi Delta Kappan* in February 1980, Virginia Davis Nordin and William Turner declared that the private Protestant fundamentalist schools were the "most rapidly growing segment of American elementary and secondary education. . . ."[33] According to Nordin and Turner, the majority of these schools were sponsored by four organizations: "the National Association of Christian Schools, the American Association of Christian Schools, the Association of Christian Schools International, and Christian Schools International."[34] The number of schools holding memberships in these organizations grew dramatically during the seventies. Enrollment jumped from 159,916 in 1971 to 349,679 in 1977, an increase of 118 percent.[35]

Nordin and Turner were hampered in their study by the lack of available statistics on the growth of these schools and the reluctance of such schools to make data on enrollment public. They pointed out that fundamentalist schools in several states have filed suit to prevent collection of data. Even so, some surprising hard data were presented in Turner's doctoral dissertation, in which he studied the development of these schools in Wisconsin and Kentucky. He found the phenomenon could not be explained solely on the basis of race. In Wisconsin, for example, private fundamentalist school enrollment increased by 274 percent during a nine-year period from 1969 to 1978. This figure can be misleading in that it is based on an increase in enrollment during that period from 426 students to 1,592. This small number could be accounted for by the opening of a relatively small number of schools. Yet it does make the point that this is not a purely regional phenomenon, and racism as a major motivating factor may be an oversimplification.

Nevin and Bills agree. In their words, "The reason for the success of the new schools go far beyond simple racism. Their success represents a deep conviction on the part of their supporters, which suggests a fundamental and dangerous dissatisfaction in American society."[36] In explaining the motivations of parents who send their children to these schools, Nevin and Bills suggest that parents tend to have a "pessimistic view" of society. They don't like change. They are unhappy not only with the "Godless" public schools but also with a whole panorama of values they see in modern society which they find destructive and which they label as "secular humanism." They are disturbed about the end of old-fashioned patriotism, "the new view of America's role in the world, the changing attitude toward authority and leaders, shrinking church attendance, rising divorce rates, acceptance of premarital sex, dirty movies, public nudity, foul language, ... abortion, crime, drugs, erosion of the work ethic ...," bad textbooks, the loss of discipline, and many other ills and evils extant in American society.[37] Turner's study supports these assertions. In his surveys of parents of children in evangelical schools in Madison, Wisconsin and Louisville, Kentucky, Turner found that parents withdrew their children from public schools for basically the same reasons in both cities. "Most frequently they alleged poor academic quality of public education, a perceived lack of discipline in public schools, and the fact that public schools were believed to be promulgating a philosophy of secular humanism that these parents found inimical to their religious beliefs."[38]

The analysis made by Nordin and Turner of Christian fundamentalists' views which support the idea of separate private schools is similar to the analysis made by Nevin and Bills. Nordin and Turner characterize fundamentalists as nostalgic for the old days.

> One hears frequent references to "old time religion," "old fashioned virtues," and the "faith of our fathers." ... Rock music, movies, and most television programs are forbidden, hair and clothing styles resemble those of a bygone era; textbooks stress "traditional" concepts in math, while education gets "back to basics." Sex roles are sharply defined, and school policies are enforced through the administration of corporal punishment by an authoritarian teacher or principal.[39]

Many of these schools would find the materials published by Accelerated Christian Education, Inc., very attractive.

Although Nevin and Bills do not draw a direct causal relationship between the emergence of evangelical Protestantism as a powerful force in America and the growth of private Christian schools, they do see a connection. As they correctly point out, many fundamentalist religious groups which have an evangelical mission are not uncomfortable with the public schools. They may exert pressure to get the public schools to conform to their beliefs, or attack the schools when they feel the schools are violating what they consider to be basic Christian values, but not all of the estimated 40 million Americans who are part of the evangelical Protestant movement opt for the establishment of their own schools.

However, there are in the evangelical movement, according to Nevin and Bills, certain qualities which motivate these groups to consider providing private "Christian" education for their children. The more conservative elements in the movement have "found the truth." They are inflexible in their beliefs because they feel that the truth has been revealed by God. Sharing this truth with others becomes an important part of their faith. In the words of Nevin and Bills:

> the evangelical ... is expected to be a salesman for his point of view, "to go to the ends of the earth and preach the gospel to every creature." ... Since aggressive preaching of the gospel and carrying of God's word is basic, the idea of starting schools which are infused with it follows naturally in a time when believers find that public schools are moving away from it.[40]

The dedication of the patrons of evangelical schools seems to know no bounds. An interesting anecdote revealed in Nevin and Bills' study illustrates this point. Nevin and Bills are mildly critical of some of the schools they visited because the schools appeared to have rather poor facilities. They found inadequate libraries, poor teachers, and few services. At one school they found that a good source of income was the coke machines. The school had hired a full-time person to stock the coke machines in preparation for mid-morning and lunch-time breaks. The coke machine attendant reported that many children arrived at school without breakfast since their mothers worked and left home before the children had to go to school. In response to a critical question on this situation, she replied: "It's a matter of values. If you want your child to have a good Christian education such as they get here, both parents have to work. You have to decide if you want your child to have a good breakfast or a good Christian education."[41]

The limited information on evangelical fundamentalist schools does not permit many conclusions. However, it does seem that the classification of "segregationist academies" is too simple. There is evidence that racism is at least one motive for the creation of such schools, since they are nearly as pure white as Ivory soap. Also, their growth does often parallel court desegregation orders. But these things in themselves do not explain the attraction of the schools for an increasingly large number of parents.

Finally, it should be pointed out that those who have researched these schools agree that thus far they have managed to escape much of the public control that applies to the public schools. Not that the same state agencies responsible for public schooling haven't tried. Religious fundamentalist schools have argued that state laws regulating schools do not apply to them. Recent cases in Kentucky and North Carolina illustrate different court responses to state attempts to regulate these schools.

In *Hinton v. Kentucky State Board of Education*,[42] the state board of education in Kentucky brought action against fundamentalist Christian schools because they failed to meet minimum state requirements in the schools they had established. The fundamentalist school leaders argued that their First Amendment rights to freedom of religion were being violated by state regulations. The circuit court in Kentucky agreed. The court found that the education offered by the schools was an exercise of religion and a basic part of their ministry. The state had refused accreditation because the school used noncertified teachers, refused to use state-approved texts, and violated curriculum guidelines by teaching the Bible as scientific fact.

The court admitted that the state had the right to review the adequacy of religious schools on certain standards, such as state laws on required courses, the number of school days and hours, health, safety, and immunization. Nonetheless, the court ruled for the fundamentalist schools. It did so by questioning the validity of state requirements. The court seemed more concerned with the quality of schooling provided by the fundamentalist schools than with whether or not the schools were meeting basic minimum legal requirements. In the words of the court:

The students in Plaintiffs' schools are progressing in academics at a rate at least equal to their peers in accredited schools. While the body of standards, regulations, and textbook and curriculum requirements may represent an attempt by the State to identify the conditions necessary for good education, there is no empirical, demonstrable, or reasonable causal connection to the guaranteeing of quality education, and in effect such standards, regulations, and requirements preclude diversity and may hamper the development of superior educational and pedagogical methods.

The court ruled that the approval of curriculum and certification requirements violated the free exercise and establishment clauses of the First Amendment and Section 5 of the Kentucky Constitution. They found the evidence presented by the state that the schools were inferior unconvincing. In the words of the court:

The State is unable to demonstrate that its regulatory scheme applied to the public schools has any reasonable relationship to the supposed objective of advancing educational quality; not only is that unfortunate truth apparent in this case, but more ominously, it has become apparent to the taxpaying Kentucky citizens who support the educational apparatus.

In *State of North Carolina v. Columbus Christian Academy*,[43] a North Carolina court ruled differently. In this case North Carolina officials were seeking the right to regulate nonpublic, sectarian schools as required by North Carolina Statutes. The law required an annual report by such schools. Columbus Christian Academy refused to file the report which was legally supposed to include information on teacher qualifications, curriculum, textbooks, health and safety conditions, graduation requirements, length of the school term, and school organization. The law specifically required "substantial equivalence" between public and private schools in these areas. The state argued that it not only had a legitimate interest in making the requirements, but that compliance with the regulations in no way hindered the fundamentalist school from presenting religious instruction. In this case, the court agreed with the state. Although the court was careful to point out that "parents have a constitutional right to provide a non-public education for their children," they found that state laws

on their face and as applied, do not violate the rights of the named defendants, or the class they represent, protected by the Due Process and Equal Protection Clauses of the Fourteenth Amendment to the United States Constitution and Article I, Section 19 of the North Carolina Constitution. . . . The laws, rules and regulations do not violate any rights of the defendants to transmit, express or receive ideas, under the First and Ninth Amendments to the United States Constitution, or Article I, Section 35 of the North Carolina Constitution.

The court found the laws reasonable since they did not "authorize the State Board of Education to regulate, supervise or approve nonpublic schools or to require information therefrom except in the areas of teacher certification, curriculum, length of school year, and such other areas as may be specifically referred to by statute, such as health certification and student innoculation." However, the court prohibited state officials from requesting information on anything not covered in the law. The court then required the school to comply with the legal requirement to file a report on the subjects covered in the law.

Some Issues Raised by the Court Cases

The major issue raised by these cases is the right of the state to regulate the educational enterprise within its borders versus the First Amendment rights of its citizens. Both positions can be strongly supported. It has long been recognized that the various states have "police power," that is, the right to regulate in the interest of the health, welfare, and morals of the citizens of the state. Such regulations, when applied in the area of religious education, come into conflict with the basic First Amendment right to free exercise of religious belief and the prohibition against an established religion.

Many leaders of the fundamentalist movement argue that the nature of state regulations forces all schools to teach a secular religion and that this is a violation of the rights of their children. On the other hand, the state officials can argue that there is a long tradition of regulating both public and private schools in the interest of the health, welfare, and morals of the children. Where leaders of fundamentalist schools can demonstrate to the satisfaction of the courts that state regulations clearly violate First Amendment rights, they have a very strong case. They can also argue that state regulations as applied are hypocritical in the sense that they do not result in schools which are protecting the morals of their children.

Thus, even if the states are moved by increasing litigation to rewrite their laws on the regulation of private schools, the courts can still measure the laws against the prohibitions of the First Amendment. The basic issue may be the role of the state in the education of its children. If private schools can escape the most basic minimal state regulation under the umbrella of protection of the First Amendment, this could constitute a serious threat to public education as we have known it in the United States.

The legal issue is thus clouded and can only be decided on a case-by-case basis. What is perhaps more clear is that what the courts decide may be based more on public opinion, the political strength of the adversaries, and the general condition of the public schools in the specific setting of the litigation than on any grand legal principles.

Alternative Schools

The nature and character of independent schools changed dramatically during the decade of the seventies. In the early seventies when the term *alternative schools* was used, it usually referred to the so-called free schools. These were schools which were established by parents who, for one reason or another, were unhappy with their experiences with the public schools but were not interested in sending their children to church-related schools. In a very comprehensive description of this movement, Jerry Long[44] suggested that the free school movement was the most dramatic change which took place in the educational system of the United States in the last half of the decade of the sixties. In an article in the *Harvard Educational Review* in August 1972, Allen Graubard reported that from 1967 to 1972 "the number of free schools had grown from around 25 to perhaps 600."[45] Graubard suggested that the number of such schools had peaked and was clearly in decline by 1972.

In his analysis of the free school movement, Long established two rough classifications of independent, alternative private schools. These were the free schools, which were designed to promote open inquiry, democratic and non-bureaucratic organization, and freedom for children to develop according to their needs, and counter-culture schools, which were sponsored by counter-culture groups alienated from mainstream society, with rather clear objectives on the sort of culture they wanted to pass on to their children. Prophetically, Long suggested that the free schools were doomed to failure, while counter-culture schools, where parents agreed on the culture they wanted taught, had a fair chance for survival. By the time Long had finished his work in 1972, it was becoming clear that the days of genuinely open free schools were numbered. It was difficult to get parents to agree on curriculum, methodology, teachers, and general purposes. Financial support was thin, and middle-class parents who often began such schools were concerned about the ability of these schools to properly prepare their children to enter the mainstream at some future date.

Problems which plagued the free schools were so great that even the most enthusiastic parental support was often not enough to insure the survival of many of the new schools.[46] Moreover, most parents, even if they were seriously dissatisfied with the public schools, were reluctant to make the financial and personal commitments needed to establish, then insure the continued operation of, independent free schools. Yet many parents were willing to work within the established school systems to make them more responsive to their demands. The mere existence of free schools and the great amount of publicity which often attended their opening must have had some impact on the resolve of disaffected parents to seek reform. Since criticisms of the public schools during the early seventies came from the very parents in the community who were influential, i.e., the articulate middle class, the message being sent by the opening of free schools was not lost on the public school establishment. Its reaction, beginning in the late sixties and continuing throughout the decade of the seventies, was at first to establish open classrooms and later to develop alternative and experimental schools within the public school system. In short, the public schools were able to react to the most central criticisms and co-opt many of the reforms attempted by independent, privately financed free schools.

The result, for all practical purposes, was the end of the free school movement of the late sixties as a significant alternative to the public schools. The waning of the private "free school movement" is evident to anyone who reviews the literature in the guides to periodical literature during the decade of the seventies. During the early years of the decade, one can find may entries under the heading of free schools. By the middle of the decade, this entry had begun to disappear and in its place one finds experimental schools or alternative schools. More significantly, articles written on experimental and alternative schools in the last half of the seventies are, for the most part, articles about experimental and alternative schools within the public school system. Experimental and alternative schools which have developed within the public school provide for almost every conceivable interest, ranging from special vocational training to specific academic specialities to schools designed to encourage creativity and spontaneity.

This is not to say that the free school movement of the late sixties died without a trace. Montessori schools experienced a growth during this period and appear to have rather consistent staying power where they are well supported. A few private schools patterned after A.S. Neill's Summerhill continue to survive.[47] However, the number of students involved is small and the movement hardly constitutes a threat to public schools or private sectarian schools.

Independent Schools

The nonpublic school establishment in the United States is not limited to Catholic schools, Christian academies, and alternative schools. In addition to these, there is a very large private, independent school system in the United States. Some of these schools are affiliated with religious groups and some are not. Most of the schools are represented by national organizations. Some of these include: the American Lutheran Church; the Association of Military Colleges and Schools of the United States; the Friends Council on Education; the National Association of Episcopal Schools; the National Association of Private Schools for Exceptional Children; and the National Society for Hebrew Day Schools.

A major organization representing private schools of all types is the National Association of Independent Schools (NAIS). Since the early sixties, this organization has experienced rapid growth, with a school membership of 840 schools in 1978.[48] In recent years the NAIS has been active in conducting administrative training programs, teacher workshops in many areas, programs for minority recruitment, sex education conferences, and many other activities. The organization has established a Washington offite which engages in lobbying activities in the interests of its membership. In 1978 it launched the School Effectiveness Project, designed to improve the curriculum, teaching, and organization in its member schools. The NAIS also provides assistance in organizing independent schools.

Widely diverse schools hold membership in the NAIS, including independent schools as disparate in location and size as Panahou school in the mid-Pacific with 3,600 students, and Thomas Jefferson school in the mid-western United States with just a few students.

The national office has been prolific in its publications. Its major effort, *Independent School*, is a quarterly journal which deals with major educational issues as well as specific problems facing independent private schools. Recent issues of the journal contain articles ranging from how to recruit more minority students and teachers to reports on successful lessons by teacher-members. The NAIS publishes an annual report on statistics of independent schools which surveys tuition, fees, salaries, enrollment, and other data. In addition, the organization publishes monographs and bulletins dealing with curriculum and methods in everything from Latin to social studies.

In the early 1970s the leadership of NAIS, recognizing the need for a broader organization representing private independent schools, worked with other groups to establish the Council for American Private Education (CAPE). Under the leadership of Cary Potter, who was president of NAIS, the Council for American Private Education was able to boast that its membership included a coalition "of 14 national organizations serving 15,000 schools, employing 225,000 teachers, and enrolling 4.2 million children."[49] In fact, CAPE schools enroll about 85 percent of all those attending private schools. Groups which have elected not to join CAPE include the Seventh Day Adventists, some Lutheran denominations, two Hebrew sects, the Christian Scientists, the Amish, and the Mennonites. Also outside of the CAPE organization are most of the Christian fundamentalist schools.[50] With the organization of CAPE, the private school establishment in America is prepared, organizationally at least, to make its voice heard on the national level.

VOUCHERS: THE ULTIMATE ALTERNATIVE

The idea of vouchers to replace existing systems of financing public education is relatively simple. Voucher advocates propose that instead of distributing tax money for schools directly to the school districts in a state some agency of government—state or local—should collect the taxes for school purposes and distribute them to the parents to use as they wish for the education of their children. For example, the state legislature could determine the total amount of funds available, divide this by the number of students to be served, and merely distribute vouchers in equal amounts to parents to pay the cost of schooling in any school of their choice. As the vouchers are presented to the schools, they would collect them and be reimbursed by the funding agency for the face amount of each voucher. In practice this would mean that all schools would be in competition for students.

Although economist Milton Friedman is given credit for introducing this idea in the United States when he proposed vouchers in *Capitalism and Freedom* in 1962, the basic idea had been in practice for some time in other countries. In the late sixties and early seventies, the idea gained popularity in some circles in the United States. This interest was fed by a comprehensive report on the voucher system published in March of 1970 by the Center for the Study of Public Policy in Cambridge, Massachusetts. Eager to test the system, the Center, with the cooperation of the Office of Economic Opportunity, secured funds from Congress to attempt a voucher experiment. A large-scale experiment involving some 4,600 students was conducted in the early seventies in the Alum Rock school district in San Jose, California. Six out of 24 schools in the Alum Rock district participated, and within these 6 schools, 22 mini-school programs were established.[51] Parents were given extensive brochures explaining the different programs and the goals and objectives of the experimental mini-schools. In addition, parents were informed about the nature of the curriculum, the faculty, and the organization of the school, as well as other details concerning the operation of the school. Within limits, parents were given choices as to where they wished to enroll their children. Other less ambitious voucher-type schools were established in Berkeley; Pasadena; East Lansing, Michigan; and Minneapolis. In terms of staying power and ability to attract students to alternative programs, these schools were deemed successful by their promoters. Although some of the programs later closed due to lack of interest, a number of them were still in operation by the end of the decade.

It should be noted that these experiments never really created a free market in schooling in the sense that a wide range of market alternatives was available to parents. The number of alternatives was severely limited and the experiments were undertaken only by public schools. From the beginning, the local public school systems had control of the projects at least in terms of the kinds of alternatives which would be offered. After several years of operation, the data on success of the alternatives in terms of student achievement, attitudes, parental participation, and meeting diverse needs were inconclusive. Successful or not, the experiments did not attract much attention. There continued to be much opposition from many sources to the general idea of vouchers, and there were very few school districts which expressed an interest in emulating the early experiments. Indeed, by the mid-seventies, it appeared that the idea "whose time had come" had lost much of its appeal.

Yet the idea of vouchers persisted. Although the massive public school establishment generally opposed the idea, some advocates of private education supported it. Catholic groups saw the possibility for direct public support for their students. The new evangelical Christian groups saw possibilities in certain kinds of voucher schemes. Some free market advocates saw it as a way to reduce the cost of education. Opponents charged that any voucher system proposed would violate the First Amendment prohibitions of church-state relations and that free market schools would result in unconstitutional segregation. Voucher advocates argued that these problems could be overcome if the correct system were adopted. Thus, a great variety of voucher proposals were made. Most were based on the 1970 proposals of the Center for the Study of Public Policy, or some variation thereof. In its work, the center suggested the following seven alternative voucher proposals:

Seven Alternative Education Voucher Plans

1. *Unregulated Market Model*: The value of the voucher is the same for each child. Schools are permitted to charge whatever additional tuition the traffic will bear.
2. *Unregulated Compensatory Model*: The value of the voucher is higher for poor children. Schools are permitted to charge whatever additional tuition they wish.
3. *Compulsory Private Scholarship Model*: Schools may charge as much tuition as they like, provided they give scholarships to those children unable to pay full tuition. Eligibility and size of scholarships are determined by the Education Voucher Authority, which establishes a formula showing how much families with certain incomes can be charged.

4. *The Effort Voucher*: This model establishes several different possible levels of per pupil expenditure and allows a school to choose its own level. Parents who choose high-expenditure schools are then charged more tuition (or tax) than parents who choose low-expenditure schools. Tuition (or tax) is also related to income; in theory the "effort" demanded of a low-income family attending a high-expenditure school is the same as the "effort" demanded of a high-income family in the same school.

5. *"Egalitarian" Model*: The value of the voucher is the same for each child. No school is permitted to charge any additional tuition.

6. *Achievement Model*: The value of the voucher is based on the progress made by the child during the year. In this model, the school is paid according to the gains on achievement scores of its students.

7. *Regulated Compensatory Model*: Schools may not charge tuition beyond the value of the voucher. They may "earn" extra funds by accepting children from poor families or educationally disadvantaged children. (A variant of this model permits privately managed voucher schools to charge affluent families according to their ability to pay.)[52]

One of the best known advocates of the voucher system is John Coons, a law professor at the University of California at Berkeley. He is so enthusiastic about vouchers that he, along with others, has sponsored a referendum in the state of California which would establish a state voucher system. Coons' arguments are summarized in an article he wrote for *Newsweek* magazine in 1980.[53] Coons charged that the public schools were basically undemocratic because they varied so much in quality. Only the rich could afford to live in school districts with good schools, according to Coons. The private schools, on the other hand, were characterized as more democratic since they "take kids who live anywhere." He claimed that the private schools wanted to admit more poor and minority children but were unable to do so because of the costs involved.

Without bothering to document his argument, Coons charged that children who attend public and private schools picked by their parents "do better" academically. Meanwhile, the children who attend what he called "government" schools "turn stupid," become hostile, drop out and flunk out. This difference existed, in Coons' view, because public schools were a monopoly. "The school is not your servant but your master."

Coons appears to believe that the solution to this problem is the introduction of a voucher system. If all schools were financed through a voucher system, they "would be free to set their own curricula, choose facilities" and otherwise free themselves from crushing governmental regulations. He advocates taking the state out of schooling, including the regulation of hiring, curriculum, and school facilities. "The only regulators would be the family and the school, not the state bureaucracy."

Coons claimed many advantages for such a system, including the freedom to teach religion. He said that a voucher system which provided funds for children attending religious schools could easily be validated by the Supreme Court. In addition to religious freedom, Coons claimed a voucher system would "give new

hope for racial integration." He predicted that voluntary integration would proceed rapidly under the system. "The biggest winners" under the system would
be teachers, since private schools emphasize teaching rather than administration
and somehow, according to Coons, teachers under a voucher system would
greatly improve their economic rewards.

No doubt Coons' arguments have great appeal to a public which is concerned
about low-quality schools, violence in the schools, poor teaching, and busing for
integration. How a voucher system would solve these problems is not completely
clear. Although there is some evidence that private school students do better
academically, it is by no means clear what the reasons for this are. Even Professor
Coleman's study which compares public and private school achievement admits
that the poorer showing of public schools may be due in large parts to forces
outside the school—especially family conditions. One can't compare existing private and public schools with an untried voucher system. If private schools were
forced to accept the children from poor homes where there is little support for
schooling, perhaps they might face the same achievement problems confronting
the public schools.

Coons' claim that a voucher system in which taxes are used to support religious schools would be validated by the Supreme Court is pure speculation. Indeed, the weight of historical evidence is on the other side. The Supreme Court
has been extremely cautious in its interpretation of First Amendment rights. It has
ruled consistently that tax money cannot be used for religious purposes. There
have been very few exceptions to this position.

Regarding the integration argument, it seems unlikely that private schools
which in some cases have developed to avoid integration would suddenly become
interested in promoting it. There is nothing inherent in the voucher system which
would encourage schools to do anything but reflect the racial and economic segregation that presently exists in the society. Even many public school officials,
who must accept everyone, have had to be dragged reluctantly into integrating
their schools.

The voucher system has many opponents. An editorial in *Church and State*[54]
summarized most of the arguments against a voucher system. The editorial
claimed that the voucher system would clearly violate the First Amendment. It
pointed out that the Supreme Court had made this clear in a series of rulings on
"state parochial aid plans . . . since 1971." The editorial stated that "over 90 percent" of existing nonpublic schools have student bodies which approach 100 percent religious homogeneity. It claimed that a voucher system would result not
only in racial segregation but in religious segregation as well. In the long run, a
voucher system would cost more and would lead to the "fragmenting and balkan-
izing of education into narrow sectarian, political, ideological, racial, sexist,
academic level, class and possibly ethnic enclaves," according to the editorial.

One can only speculate on whether the voucher system is the wave of the
future or merely a passing educational fad. Certain forces, such as the growing
private school segment, seem to portend at least the continued advocacy of
voucher plans. On the other hand, the force of tradition in public education is
strong. Wherever voucher plans or some form of them are seriously considered,

however, one can be sure that they will be tested in court. The major case on voucher-type plans is *Committee for Public Education and Religious Liberty v. Nyquist* (413 U.S. 756, 1973). In this case the Supreme Court of the United States struck down a voucher-type plan in the state of New York. The New York legislature, concerned with the complaints of parents of Catholic school children that they were paying their share of taxes for public schools but not benefiting directly from them, attempted to give Catholic parents some relief. In brief, the legislature provided a $50-per-child grant to the parents of each elementary school child enrolled in a nonpublic school. Parents of high school students were awarded $100. In addition, nonpublic schools were allotted funds for building maintenance, and parents were given tax allowances for children enrolled in nonpublic schools. State education officials argued that since these funds were not presented directly to nonpublic schools, they did not violate the establishment clause of the First Amendment. The Court didn't agree. Referring to what it called the "well-defined three-part test" which developed out of religion education precedents, the Supreme Court found that the New York law did not meet the test. The test, according to the reasoning of the Court, was first, that the law in question must reflect "a clearly secular legislative purpose"; second, "must have a primary effect that neither advances nor inhibits religion"; and third, "must avoid excessive government entanglement with religion."

With regard to the first test, the Court declared that tuition grants and the state assistance for maintenance of private school buildings were efforts designed to advance religion. On the funding of maintenance, the Court found this to be a direct subsidy which supported the "religious activities of sectarian elementary and secondary schools." Finally, the Court found that the New York law did involve the state in excessive entanglement with religion. The Court said: "A proper respect for both the free exercise and establishment clauses compels the state to pursue a course of 'neutrality' toward religion." Special tax benefits, such as those provided in the New York law, "cannot be squared with the principle of neutrality," said the Court. Benefits "which render assistance to parents who send their children to sectarian schools" have the "inevitable effect" of aiding and advancing religious institutions.

The state argued that the law was, in principle, no different than the practice of granting churches exemptions from state property tax. On this point the Court argued that such exemptions were an indirect benefit, and their purpose was to keep the government out of religion. In a sense, the Court was arguing that the supporters of government aid to private school children could not have it both ways. On the one hand, they could not expect the Constitution to protect churches from governmental regulation in the form of taxation, while at the same time providing direct tax funds which would benefit churches.

TUITION CREDITS

Apparently undaunted by the ruling in *Nyquist*, supporters of tuition credits for nonpublic school parents continued their efforts on the national level. The most notable effort in recent years was the so-called Packwood-Moynihan Bill first introduced in Congress in 1978. In general terms, this legislation would have granted tax credits to parents of nonpublic elementary, secondary, and college students. Although the bill failed to gain approval in 1978, it is by no means a dead issue. In an article in the *Kappan* in 1978, Senator Moynihan summarized some of the arguments used in favor of the bill.[55] Moynihan was concerned that nonpublic schools were facing grave financial difficulties. So much so, in fact, that they were in danger of disappearing. This was unfortunate, in Moynihan's view, because "a historic manifestation of American pluralism and diversity is at stake." Moynihan dismissed arguments that tuition tax credits benefited only the middle-class white majority. He pointed out that "four hundred thousand black and other minority group members now attend nongovernment schools." He felt that with tuition help from the national government, this role could be vastly expanded by private schools. Moynihan claimed that his bill would not aid private schools which supported segregation, since the proposal included a provision which would not allow the tax credit for segregated schools. With regard to the constitutional issue, Moynihan simply observed: "It has been said that our proposal would be struck down by the Supreme Court. If so, that will be the end of it." All he wanted, he said, was "our day in court."

Opposing tuition tax credits, Senator Hollings argued that the Packwood-Moynihan Bill would wreck American education. In Hollings' words:

> Careful study convinced me that this proposal would turn our nation's education policy on its head, benefit the few at the expense of the many, proliferate substandard segregation academies, add a sea of red ink to the federal deficit, violate the clear meaning of the First Amendment . . . and destroy the diversity and genius of our system of public education.[56]

Hollings was particularly worried about the encouragement the credits would give to "segregation academies." He also argued that the bill would be another form of aid to the rich. He pointed out that schools such as Exeter, with an endowment of $60 million, as well as other well-financed schools, would benefit from tax credits. He felt that tuition tax credits would not help the poor but would motivate the rich schools to raise their tuition even higher to gain greater tax write-off benefits for wealthy parents. Also, the way Hollings viewed the bill, it would create another gigantic bureaucracy. This would happen because, as Hollings put it: "Claiming a tax credit means authenticating the tax return; authenticating the return means commandeering the records of both the citizen and the school; commandeering records means another new bureaucracy. . . ." Finally, Hollings cited *Nyquist* to support his claim that tuition tax credits would violate the First Amendment.

Given the size of the nonpublic school sector, plus the fact that it is well organized, plus the financial difficulties facing many nonpublic schools, it is unlikely that the debate over some form of national public assistance will end soon.

CONCLUSIONS

Although the next chapter deals with government regulation of schools, a chapter on nonpublic schools would not be complete without a note on the extensive controls exercised by state authority over private schools. In his conclusions in a lengthy discussion of state regulation of nonpublic schools, John Elson[57] declared that nonpublic school regulations are intended "to promote five main policies." First, private as well as public schools are subject to state laws providing for minimum curriculum offerings and teacher certification. Second, states have legislated to protect students from ideas which are considered socially dangerous. Third, many states have laws designed to promote cultural unity, such as the required teaching of American history or citizenship education. Fourth, most state legislatures have delegated to state educational agencies powers to accredit schools. Finally, states have clearly established the power to regulate nonpublic schools in the interest of protecting the health, welfare, and morals of minor children.

Taken together, these major areas of regulation concentrate a great deal of power in state authority to supervise educational establishments and practices in nonpublic schools. Although it is true that the Supreme Court in a number of important cases (*Pierce, Farrington, Meyer, Yoder*) has curbed overzealous state attempts to regulate nonpublic schools, in none of these cases did the Supreme Court deny the right of the state to regulate nonpublic schools.[58]

Every state has an extensive school code regulating everything from pupil transportation and school lunches to the number of courses an accredited high school must offer. All states have a large and well-established bureaucracy to administer and implement the laws. In nearly every case, the codes and the rules and regulations designed to implement them apply to nonpublic as well as public schools. Yet nonpublic schools do operate in states in clear violation of these codes. There are private free schools in some places which fail to meet many minimum state standards. At the height of the free school movement, there were schools in many states which did not offer the minimum required curriculum, which employed teachers who were not state certified, which did not meet minimum building regulations established by the state for schools, and in which a myriad of other violations of the state school code could be documented. This condition continues to exist. Generally, violations are permitted for two major reasons. First, in some cases certain loopholes exist in state school codes. That is, many school codes have what amounts to an escape clause which is in the form of a general statement that permits exceptions for certain reasons. Exceptions are permitted in some instances where the population is so sparse that the observance of the code would be difficult. Exceptions are permitted where parents and school officials on the local or state level agree that children who are not attending state-accredited schools might not benefit from such attendance.

The second major reason that school codes are selectively enforced is blatantly political. Whether or not the codes are enforced depends on who is violating them. For example, in most instances, the established church-related schools, especially the Catholic schools which exist in predominantly Protestant communities, find that the school codes are very important—and serious efforts are made by these groups to meet state minimum accreditation standards; indeed, where private religious education is unpopular, school codes can be enforced with a vengeance. In some communities, on the other hand, local school authorities and the state educational bureaucracy wink at almost total disregard for school codes. This happens in cases where disgruntled parents who are viewed as trouble-makers for the local school establish their own schools. The most extreme cases of this nature are local counter culture schools where the parents teach their children values which are in serious opposition to mainstream culture. Nobody objects when such children are removed from the public schools. Indeed, the reaction could be characterized by the statement: "Good riddance, let them have their own schools." On the other end of the scale, failure by the so-called Christian schools to meet minimum standards is sometimes overlooked because of the fervor of support for them, the potential political power of the evangelical Christian move-ment in some communities, and the reluctance for political reasons on the part of state agencies to become embroiled in controversy. Finally, it should be noted that in some cases parents simply do not care about state accreditation.

Even though the number of children attending nonpublic schools remains relatively small in the United States, it is a growing movement and the issues raised by nonpublic education are significant. A major issue related to the matter of state regulation of nonpublic schools is financial. If the most rapidly growing nonpublic school movement in the country, that of the evangelical Christian schools, is per-mitted to develop with disregard for minimum requirements established in school codes, they are, in effect, being encouraged by official neglect. Although this may encourage pluralism, its effect in some school districts could be disastrous. As the private schools grow and more middle-class students are recruited into the sys-tem, the very element of the population whose support the public schools most need tends to decline. The result for some school districts could be a serious loss of revenue caused by indifference or even opposition to increased local taxes for support of local schools. The bottom line in this scenario would be a public school system for the poor and a private system for the middle classes.

The broader issue for public schools is an issue which has always existed in the United States. That is, how can a pluralistic, democratic society balance the legitimate interest of the state in establishing schools against the basic right to individual freedom? The society has struggled with this issue from the beginning. The issue has appeared in the courts in many forms. It is not easily resolved, for the legitimate interests of the state are immensely complicated by the need to promote social purposes. It is obvious to even the casual student of American educational development that the schools have become involved in much more than teaching basic skills. From the beginning, public schools have had political and social purposes, and the list has become longer each time a new social prob-lem has been identified. With increasing frequency, the public schools have been called upon to solve the ills of the society. An important part of this mission has always been to promote good citizenship—whatever that is. As the years passed, they were called upon to deal with more specific issues. When racism was identified as a problem, the schools were ordered to find a cure. Juvenile crime? Let the schools hire more counselors. Are the churches and the family failing children? Have the schools fill the vacuum. Are drugs a problem? Institute drug education. Unwed mothers? Offer sex education in the schools. Unemployed youth? Dump the problem on the schools. The list is endless.

Burdened with this impossible list of social ills needing attention, coupled with inadequate resources to deal with the problems, the public schools in the future, as in the past, will continue to grope with their assigned tasks. When they are unsuccessful, the society loses because the problems continue unchecked. The public schools lose credibility and, in some cases, students, to the nonpublic schools. Barring a very significant increase in funding, it is unlikely that these problems will be solved.

NOTES

1. Neil G. McCluskey, S. J., ed., *Catholic Education in America: A Documentary History* (New York: Teachers College, Columbia University, 1964), p. 13.
2. For an analysis of the long hesitancy of the Court to ideal with religion in the public schools, see James M. Powell, "Public Schools and the First Amendment," *America*, 9 (July 1978): 5–9.
3. *Abington School District v. Schempp*, 374 US 203 (1963).
4. *Cochran v. Louisiana State Board of Education*, 281 US 370 (1930).
5. *Everson v. Board of Education*, 330 US 1 (1947).
6. *Walz v. Tax Commission*, 397 US 664 (1970).
7. *Meek v. Pittenger*, 421 US 349 (1975).
8. *Wolman v. Walter*, 45 USLW 4861 (June 24, 1977).
9. Otto F. Kraushaar, *American Nonpublic Schools: Patterns of Diversity* (Baltimore: Johns Hopkins University Press, 1972).
10. Ibid., p. 105.
11. Theodore R. Sizer, "Why the Public School?" *National Elementary School Principal* 56 (July–August 1977): 6–11.
12. David Nevin and Robert Bills, *The Schools That Fear Built* (Washington, D.C.: Acropolis Books, 1976).
13. Jerry C. Long, "The Free School Movement" (Ph.D. dissertation, Oklahoma State University, 1972).
14. James Coleman et al., *High School and Beyond* (National Center for Education Statistics, U.S. Government Printing Office 1981).
15. Richard Nault, Donald A. Erickson, and Bruce S. Cooper, "Hard Times for Nonpublic Schools," *National Elementary School Principal* 56 (July–August 1977): 18.
16. Andrew Greeley, William C. McCready, and Kathleen McCourt, *Catholic Schools in a Declining Church* (Kansas City: Sheed & Ward, 1976).
17. Ibid., p. 305.
18. Ibid., p. 306.
19. Ibid., p. 310.
20. Ibid., p. 311.
21. Ibid.

22. National Catholic Education Association, *Catholic Schools in America* (Englewood, Colo.: Fisher Publishing Co., 1980), p. xiv.

23. Ibid., p. xv.

24. Ibid., p. xiv.

25. Andrew Greeley, "Minority Students in Catholic Secondary Schools" (Unpublished report, April 1981).

26. Kraushaar, *American Nonpublic Schools*, p. 29.

27. Andrew Greeley, "The Ethnic Miracle," *The Public Interest* 45 (Fall 1976): 27.

28. David Nevin and Robert Bills, "The Schools That Fear Built," *Just Schools*, A Special Issue of *Southern Exposure* (Chapel Hill: Institute for Southern Studies, May 1979), p. 110.

29. Virginia Ford and Donald von Dohlen, Jr., "Social Studies Unit: *God's Creation*," 2d ed. (Garland, Tex.: Accelerated Christian Education, P.O. Box 2205, Garland, Tex., 1974), p. 3.

30. *Facts about Accelerated Christian Education* (Garland, Tex.: Accelerated Christian Education, 1979), p. 30.

31. Ibid., p. 10.

32. Ibid., p. 24.

33. Virginia Nordin and William Turner, "More Than Segregation Academies: The Growing Protestant Fundamentalist School," *Phi Delta Kappan* 61 (February 1980): 391.

34. Ibid.

35. Nordin and Turner presented this figure based on a telephone interview with Herman Van Schuyver, Executive Director of the National Association of Christian Schools.

36. Nevin and Bills, "The Schools That Fear Built," p. 110.

37. Ibid., p. 110.

38. Nordin and Turner, "More Than Segregation Academies," p. 392.

39. Ibid., p. 393.

40. Nevin and Bills, "The Schools That Fear Built," p. 112.

41. Ibid., p. 113.

42. *Hinton v. Kentucky State Board of Education*, C.A. No. 88314. (Clearing House #26, 482, A, B.), 4 October 1978.

43. *State of North Carolina v. Columbus Christian Academy*, C.A. No. 78. (Clearing House #26 481 A), 5 September 1978.

44. Long, "The Free School Movement."

45. Allen Graubard, "The Free Schools Movement," *Harvard Educational Review* 42 (August 1972): 352.

46. An interesting research study which reports some of the problems of the free school is "Xanadu: A Study of the Structure of Crisis in an Alternative School," by Steven Singleton, David Boyer, and Paul Dorsey in *The Review of Educational Research* 42 (March 1972): 521–531. A personal and detailed account of what went on in a free school can be found in "Konoma—A Free School," by W. M. Fred Stoker, in *Educational Forum* 36 (January 1972): 189–91. For an excellent typology of "educational ideologies" represented within the alternative public school movement, see Terrance E. Deal and Robert R. Nolan, "Alternative Schools: A Conceptual Map," *School Review* 87 (November 1978): 29–137.

47. For a brief description of some of these schools, see Kraushaar, *American Nonpublic Schools*, pp. 83–88.

48. *Independent School* 37 (May 1978): 9.

49. Ibid., p. 10.

50. Robert Lamborn, "The Case for Diversity," *National Elementary School Principal* 56 (July–August 1977): 14.

51. Margaret A. Thomas, *Analysis of Multiple Options in Education: A Working Note.* (Washington, D.C.: National Institute of Education, 1976).

52. Condensed from Center for the Study of Public Policy, Cambridge, Mass., *Education Vouchers: A Preliminary Report on Financing Education by Payments to Parents*, March 1970, p. 20.

53. John E. Coons, "The Public School Monopoly," *Newsweek*, 9 June 1980, p. 21.

54. Editorial, "The Voucher Plan: Blueprint for Disaster," *Church and State*, February 1978, pp. 7–11.

55. Daniel P. Moynihan, "The Case for Tuition Tax Credits," *Phi Delta Kappan* 59 (December 1978): 274–276.

56. Ernest F. Hollings, "The Case Against Tuition Tax Credits," *Phi Delta Kappan* 59 December 1978): 277–279.

57. John Elson, "State Regulation of Nonpublic Schools," in *Public Controls for Nonpublic Schools*, ed. Donald Ericson (Chicago: University of Chicago Press, 1969), p. 133.

58. For a review and summary of these cases, see Donald Ericson, "Legal Impediments to Private Educational Options," in *The Courts and Education*, ed. Clifford P. Hooker (Chicago: University of Chicago Press, 1978), pp. 116–140.

5

Government and Schooling: The Scope of Control

Governmental control of schools in American society is extensive and pervasive. A myriad of agencies—from the local school board to the Congress of the United States—is involved in the function of schooling. It would take several volumes merely to list the state constitutional provisions, state and national laws, and rules and regulations which govern schools. The bureaucracy which has grown to administer this extensive code is huge and still growing. There are many reasons for the size and complexity of this relationship between schools and local, state, and national levels of government. Foremost among these would be tradition and economic and political reasons.

Historically, schools have been rather simple operations, established in many localities as enterprises with local financial support and local control. As the idea of public schooling grew, the scope of governmental control grew. As taxes were levied to pay for expanded schooling, those who paid wanted to exercise control.

On the local level, school committees were elected to see that schools were organized and that schooling was conducted in a manner that had the approval of taxpayers. As the functions of schooling grew and states became involved in helping to pay the costs, state legislatures exercised control over expenditures of state money. Compulsory schooling laws were a beginning, followed by teacher certification laws, regulation of school buildings, supervision of school curricula, and provisions for special programs—in a word, nearly everything schools do is in some way regulated by legal provisions and by some local, state, or national agency with legal standing.

In recent years several forces have emerged which raise the possibility that the focus of control on local public schools is undergoing some subtle changes. Reacting to public concern about poor schooling and pressured by organized and politicized teachers, state legislatures have become very active in providing their own specific and often detailed solutions to school problems. Paralleling this force are teachers, who, as they gain more power through organization on the local and state levels, are becoming increasingly involved in decision making on policy that was once the exclusive domain of boards of education, parents, and state departments of education. Finally, the courts have become involved in very specific ways in the government of local schools. This chapter will deal briefly with the scope of this control and some issues raised by efforts to control schooling.

LOCAL CONTROL

On the local level the function of education is organized on a district basis theoretically governed by a school board which has broad powers over local administration and policy making.

School districts are much the same wherever they are found. A school district has been defined as "the basic governmental unit through which the exercise of local control of schools is effected."[1] As governmental units, all school districts have quasi-corporate powers, which include the power to tax, the right to make contracts, and the right to sue and be sued.

There are a large number of school districts in the United States. In the early 1980s there were approximately 16,000 including about 15,700 operating school districts and 300 nonoperating districts. Nonoperating districts do not maintain schools but elect school boards to raise taxes for tuition so that they can send their children to school outside the district on a tuition basis. It appears that nonoperating school districts are being gradually phased out of existence. In the early sixties there were several thousand. From 1971 to 1977, the number declined from 451 to 322.[2] These districts generally exist in areas which are isolated, or where most of the children attend private schools, or where there are so few pupils that it is cheaper to send the children to neighboring districts than to provide a school for them.

School districts vary greatly in size both in terms of school population and geographic area. In some of the nonoperating school districts there may be no school-age children at all, while in other districts there are thousands of students. In 1977, 187 school systems in the nation enrolled 25,000 or more students each, while at the other extreme, 278 systems enrolled fewer than 300 students each.[3] In terms of area, some school districts in the west cover areas as large as some eastern states. The Elko County, Nevada school district, for example, covers an area larger than that of Massachusetts, Connecticut, and Rhode Island combined.[4]

School districts vary in other ways as well. As might be expected, school districts vary widely in wealth and in their ability to tax for educational purposes. They vary in the kinds of schooling provided. In some districts there may be a few dilapidated rural schools housing a few students in terribly poor facilities, while in others there are huge building complexes with excellent facilities and the latest equipment. Some districts provide a cornucopia of educational experiences, while others are hard pressed to support minimal basic schooling. Some districts provide elementary schooling only, while others provide programs through the junior college level.

Legally, school districts are creatures of the state legislature. Under most state constitutions, the legislature has complete control over the creation and organization of school districts within the state. In nearly every state, at some time in the past, legislatures established classification schemes for school districts for almost any purpose they deemed necessary. This process continues to the present. A recent example is the state of Michigan where, in 1969, the legislature, anticipating a major desegregation suit in Detroit, mandated the decentralization of any first-class school district with more than 100,000 pupils. The law divided the district into eight regions with a 13-member board. The law specified how the district was to be organized and how each region was to be represented on the board, and instructed that the regions be drawn as compact, "contiguous and nearly equal in population." This legislation, as comprehensive and detailed as it was, applied to only one school district in the state—that of Detroit. Not only did the legislature detail the organization of the new school district for Detroit, but it spelled out in some detail the powers of the new board of education. Nor is this sort of legislation peculiar to Michigan. Many states have established special districts in recent years, and they have outlined the functions which must be performed by the districts they have created. Legislatures may require local governmental units to establish school systems, they may create independent districts or divide large districts into smaller ones, or they may create special districts for special purposes.

Finally, a discussion of school district organization would not be complete without some reference to the power of the federal courts to determine whether or not the organization and powers of local school districts are in conformity with the U.S Constitution. Indeed, the courts have been so active in recent years regarding the organization and powers of school districts that it might not be an overstatement to suggest that the federal courts have become almost as important as the state legislatures in determining the legal responsibilities of school districts in this country. On the matter of segregation, beginning with the *Brown* case in 1954 and continuing to the present, federal courts have directed school districts to integrate students, have ordered busing and integration of faculties, have mandated special training programs for faculties, have redrawn attendance boundaries within school districts, have ordered buildings constructed in specified locations, have established racial quotas within schools, and have changed grade configurations within established schools. This is only a partial list. Some of these issues will be discussed in a later chapter, so it is sufficient only to note these activities in this context.

More to the point, in several cases the courts have considered the power of the state legislature to organize and finance schools. Generally, the U.S. Supreme Court has upheld the broad powers assumed by state legislatures in the matter of organization and finance of local school districts. In *Springfield v. Quick*,[5] the Court upheld the power of state legislatures to collect and disburse taxes for educational purposes. In *Attorney General of Michigan ex rel. Kies v. Lowrey*,[6] the Court upheld the right of the legislature to make and change school district boundary lines. In more recent cases, the Court has ruled that an election system for school board members which was not based on population was a permissible legislative activity,[7] and that the Illinois and Texas state systems of school finance which resulted in unequal expenditures were not a violation of the U.S. Constitution.[8] However, in a New York case[9] the Supreme Court ruled that a New York statute which prohibited from voting in school elections those residents who did not pay property taxes but who were otherwise qualified to vote, was a violation of the equal protection clause of the Fourteenth Amendment. Also, the Court found that a Georgia law which required that members of county boards of education be landowners was an unconstitutional denial of equal protection of the laws.[10] Although this is a small sampling of court cases involving the organization and functions of school districts, it does illustrate that the federal court system has long been involved in the legal aspects of their organization and powers.

Whether or not the school district can survive in its present form is an open question. The ability of the school district to perform the basic educational functions on the local level is being attacked from all quarters. The tendency on the part of state legislatures to move toward more centralized control of education is growing. Still, there is a parallel tendency in opposition to this which is variously called the "community control" or "decentralization" movement. The issue of desegregation will continue to create problems for local school districts. Add to this the problems created by teachers demanding an increasing voice in local school governance, the pressure to equalize school finance within states—and it becomes difficult to speculate on the future of school districts.

For years the state legislatures have acted to consolidate school districts. The reasons were clear enough. Legislatures in every state sought to increase the tax base of school districts in the interest of providing a better school program. Better facilities, better teachers, and a more comprehensive program were always claimed when school district consolidation was mandated by the state legislatures. Typically, legally constituted school districts were described by legislation in terms of minimal numbers of students enrolled or the ability to maintain a K-12 program; a minimum number of "state certified" programs was established; or other means were used to legally mandate consolidation of small or "inadequate" school districts. Usually an office or agency was created in the state department of education with the sole function of promoting school consolidation and implementing state legislation on minimally acceptable school districts. The movement was greatly successful, at least in terms of the reduction of the number of school districts in the United States.

School administrators generally supported the idea of consolidation in the interests of better schools, which usually meant that larger school districts had stronger tax bases and could offer more comprehensive and specialized programs. In most localities, teachers approved of consolidation since larger administrative units tended to encourage the organization of teachers and gave them a stronger voice in local school policies. Also, larger school districts tended to enable teachers to practice their own specialties and to reduce the number of preparations they were required to make.

There was, of course, opposition to the idea of consolidation. Much of the early opposition came from isolated areas where local patrons agonized over the loss of their local schools. Later, beginning in the mid-sixties, another form of opposition developed which came to be known as the "community control" or "decentralization" movement. Although both community control and decentralization often got their impetus from local school patrons who wanted more control over their local schools, the terms do not mean the same thing. Decentralization, as it developed, usually meant that while the school district was changed administratively, very little change occurred in the policy-making powers of the central board. Community control involved a basic restructing of the governance of schools with major alterations in the distribution of policy-making power to neighborhoods or local communities.

Perhaps the best single illustration of the decentralization movement was in New York City beginning in the late sixties. The New York legislature, pressed by demands from black and Puerto Rican groups in New York City, passed a decentralization law in 1969 which divided the city into 31 school districts with separate boards. These boards were given substantial control over the operation of elementary, intermediate, and junior high schools. They could hire administrators and teachers, select materials for use in the schools, submit budgets to the central administration, and in other ways influence the policy and operation of the schools in their districts.

After several years of operation, no one seemed to be particularly enthusiastic about decentralization. Unlike the earlier opposition to rural school consolidation, the urban decentralization movement developed after large school bureaucracies with central control had already been established. The New York City effort at decentralization began in 1966 when groups of black and Puerto Rican parents occupied the office of the city board of education[11] where they demanded local control of their schools. They were concerned about the lack of black and Puerto Rican administrators and teachers and felt that the central school board didn't understand their needs. They felt that more local control would better meet the needs of their children. There doesn't seem to be much evidence that this happened. As early as 1972, Dr. Kenneth Clark, who was an early advocate of decentralization, suggested that it had become a "disastrous" experiment in which children's interests in good schooling had become subordinated to racial politics.[12]

Other communities—including Detroit, Boston, Los Angeles, Washington, D.C., Chicago, Philadelphia, and many others—were involved in decentralization or community control in one form or another in the late sixties and early seventies. Increasing opposition to large impersonal bureaucracies coupled with real school problems, including poor teaching of basic skills, school discipline problems, and the general inability of some large school systems to meet local needs and demands, make it unlikely that the decentralization-community control movement will disappear. Whether decentralization can solve many school problems has yet to be demonstrated.

Central to the decentralization-community control movement is the issue of desegregation. From the beginning, the cries in urban areas for decentralization and community control have had a racial tone. Minorities seemed to have lost faith in genuinely equal integrated schools. Having failed in that, it seemed logical to demand minority control of predominantly minority schools. Of course, this must have come as a pleasant surprise to those whites who were not seriously interested in integration anyway. Where there are racial motivations, demands for local control tend to fly in the face of the court-ordered integration attempts of the last 30 years. If the ultimate goal of court-ordered integration is a single, unified, nonracial school system—as the courts have declared in case after case, it would seem that community control based on race has little hope for success. Indeed, if desegregation is to be pursued with enthusiasm, the ultimate result, as far as school district organization is concerned, would seem to be ever larger districts. This would have to be the case in the many areas of the country where central cities are predominantly black in population, and suburban rings, with their separate school districts, are predominantly white. Barring a radical shift in the federal court system's interpretation of what constitutes a constitutionally defensible racial mix in the schools, it seems unlikely that decentralization or community control has a great future. The Supreme Court and the federal district courts have tended to follow the *Swan* (*Swan v. Charlotte-Mecklenburg* 1971) logic which calls for busing and, if necessary, the manipulation of district boundary lines to provide for racially balanced schools. As desirable as the idea of local control may be, it is difficult to see how any large national movement for local control, even with enthusiastic support from predominantly white legislatures, could be made to conform with the interpretations of the Fourteenth Amendment's equal protection clause which have been made by the courts in the last three decades.

Even if the constitutional problems could be overcome, there are other serious obstacles working against any movement to reduce the size of school districts. Teachers not only have learned to live with large educational bureaucracies, they have almost come to depend upon them. In the New York decentralization battle, as elsewhere, teachers unions have opposed any move to break up the large school districts. This is understandable from a group which has spent many decades attempting to organize and consolidate its power based on existing administrative arrangements. Teachers have learned that, all things considered, large organizations tend to wield more effective power than small isolated groups. After decades of struggle to organize teachers in large cities, it is inconceivable that the leadership of teachers groups in these cities would support the dismemberment of their organizational base. Indeed, in New York City, the advocates of decentralization pointed to the opposition of the teachers union and the opposition of the union's leader, Albert Shanker, as the single most serious obstacle to effective decentralization. From the beginning, Shanker vehemently opposed decentralization. In other cities where teachers have finally found an effective collective voice in negotiations with central city school boards, they tend to view local control as a threat to their newly found power.

Finally, decentralization and movements for local control tend to cloud an already complicated school finance situation. Although this issue as well as issues related to teacher power will be dealt with more thoroughly in later chapters, it should be pointed out here that financial support for local schools is moving in the direction of more, not less, centralized control. An early major reason for expanding the size of the school district was financial. As the function of schooling became more comprehensive, a broader financial base was needed. That problem has not diminished; if anything, it has become more severe. Nearly every state in the Union is facing a *Serrano*-type decision. In *Serrano*, the California Supreme Court (*Serrano v. Priest* 1971) found the California system of school finance to be a violation of the equal protection clauses of the California and the U.S. constitutions. In California, as elsewhere, a large share of the financial support for education was the local property tax. The problem with the property tax is that it is based on taxable wealth which exists in the local school district, and this wealth varies greatly from one district to the next in virtually every state. In practice this means that wealth-poor districts can make a much greater tax effort and raise less money per pupil than wealth-rich districts. The California court and about half of the other state supreme courts have found fault with this system. Cases are pending in most of the other states.

What this means in California and elsewhere is that the local school districts and the state legislature must take action to correct the inequities. As a practical matter, it means that a broader base than the local school district must be utilized to finance schools. Thus there is a movement to provide more state support to equalize school per pupil expenditure among local school districts throughout the country. What effect this movement will have on local school districts is anybody's guess. In the past, increases in state support have tended to be followed by increasing state control. Although it does not necessarily follow that dramatic changes in school district size, organization, and powers will occur in the future, the possibilities certainly exist.

THE SCHOOL BOARD

If the future of school districts is uncertain, the viability of the local board of education as the basic governing unit for local schools may be even more uncertain. The forces operating which threaten the traditional role of the school board are many. The various programs of the national government which provide aid to local schools require school boards to do many things over which they have little control. Federal as well as state courts have ordered school boards to cease certain practices or to take specific action in many areas. In most places, boards cannot deal with teachers as they wish. The newly discovered powers of collective negotiations, arbitration, and the threat of teacher strikes have tended to place many school boards in adversary relationships with teachers, definitely a nontraditional role for school boards. As state legislatures and state agencies become more concerned with local education, school boards must attend to increasing legal direction from these sources. Finally, well-organized local pressure groups and individual parents willing to take their concerns to court have whittled away at the school board's power.

Even more significant, perhaps, is the apparently growing apathy on the part of the public toward the role of the local school board. A recent survey (1975) made by the National School Board Association discovered that the public didn't seem really to know much about their local school boards. The National School Board Association, reporting on the results of a national sample of public opinion on school boards, found that on overwhelming majority (63 percent) could not name anything their local board had done in the last year. Sixty-two percent did not think their local board was responsible for public representation within the school system. Fifty-eight percent felt that during school disputes school boards catered to special interest groups rather than acted in the best interests of the students. An incredible 44 percent did not think their school boards had authority over school administrators. Those surveyed apparently didn't care much about what the board did, since only 7 percent of the national sample had attended a school board meeting in the previous three-year period. A full 25 percent didn't even have a general opinion on their school board, although half of the respondents rated school boards favorably.

These results are surprising in a nation which seems to put so much stock in local control. The lack of knowledge about what local boards do is remarkable in itself. Yet many of those who know little about the powers and duties of local boards and appear apathetic about them will argue vehemently against increasing state and federal control of schools.

Whatever the views of local school patrons toward their local boards, there can be little doubt that the powers of local boards have been seriously eroded. Many of the powers exercised by the school board are defined in some way by agents and agencies outside the local school district. Although they have the power to decide whether or not they should build new schools, this function is guided and directed by state building codes, by state provisions on capital improvements in local school districts, and by courts which order racially balanced schools. Boards can hire the superintendent and administrative staff as well as teachers, but this is not an absolute power. State certification requirements provide clear guidelines on the minimum qualifications for these positions. School boards also have the power to fire those whom they hire, but they are limited and controlled in this power by local teachers organizations as well as state laws on tenure and court decisions on due process for teachers. Additionally, the laws and court activities on affirmative action have further limited the local board's decision-making power in the area of school personnel.

State compulsory school laws must be enforced by the boards, and they must observe state laws on required courses and programs. Thus, school boards have the local authority to fix the local school curriculum, but they may be required by state law to provide for instruction in English or history or to have a drug education program in the schools. State laws on minimum competency and school accountability have made further incursions into the power of local boards to determine curriculum.

School boards can fix the school calendar, but this may be limited to determining the date of school opening and setting vacation periods, since state laws in nearly every state determine the actual number of days children must attend school.

Even something like extracurricular activities—which might appear to be primarily local in nature—are not completely controlled by the local board. Although the board can set local policy on the nature and quantity of extracurricular activities, there often are comprehensive state guidelines on competitive sports; courts have ordered school boards to provide opportunities for girls in competitive sports; and teachers have negotiated with school boards over their duties and responsibilities in extracurricular activities.

Although the local school board assumes basic responsibility for providing for auxiliary services such as school lunches and school transportation, state and national laws and programs often strictly limit the school board's autonomy in these areas. The school lunch programs are greatly influenced by state and national funds and regulations. The local school board can set policy on transportation of students, but state rules and regulations on bus safety and the qualifications of bus drivers must be observed. Also, the federal courts have ordered student busing in some districts where it was necessary to achieve integrated schools, even though the local board may have been strongly opposed.

The local board can also initiate special programs, such as special classes for the handicapped or special programs for the gifted. However, national laws, particularly Public Law 94–142 (The Education For All Handicapped Children Act of 1976) and the Rehabilitation Act of 1973, not only have pretty well directed what the school board can do, but, through federal guidelines, they have spelled out in some detail what local school boards *must* do to be in compliance with the laws. To a lesser extent the same is true with programs for the gifted student. Federal and state assistance is provided for local school districts in these areas, and local school boards must follow their guidelines in order to qualify for funds.

Even though the school board may have seen better days, it still plays an important role. Indeed, in some ways the increased attention which the state and national governments have focused on local schools has vastly extended educational functions. If it didn't exist, something like it would have to be created to locally implement school policy which is made on the state and national levels. It should also be noted that local school boards sometimes act as if they had extensive powers. They may be ignorant of state and federal regulations or they may choose to ignore them as long as possible. Thus the school board, even though its powers in many areas are determined for it, continues to be a very significant agency in school governance. Perhaps this is why people continue to run for school board positions and why school boards attract the sort of people they do.

Most school board members who were serving in the 1970s were elected (92 percent).[13] However, the appointive system is not uncommon in the south, where a survey conducted for the *American School Board Journal* in the early seventies found 34.2 percent had been appointed to their positions.[14] In a comprehensive study of school boards published in the mid-seventies, Harmon Zeigler and his associates found a pattern of apprenticeship for prospective school board members. They found that many school board members had been active in education-related services before election to the board. The major vehicles utilized to gain community recognition as potential board members included work or leadership in parent-teacher organizations, educational "citizens advisory committees," or local service organizations such as the Lions, Chamber of Commerce, Rotary, and Kiwanis.[15] An interesting characteristic of those who run for school board positions is that few of them seem to have political ambitions beyond the school board. That is, the school board seems to be a political dead end.[16]

Although it is difficult to describe the typical school board member, they do tend to be Protestant, mature, middle-class males. Recently more female members have been elected or appointed to school board positions. Whereas in 1972 an *American School Board Journal* survey found only 11.9 percent of school board members to be female, by 1978 this had increased to 26 percent.[17] In the mid-seventies school board members were characteristically middle-aged, with 65.6 percent over 40. Only 2.4 percent were under 30 years of age.[18]

The typical school board member is relatively affluent. One-fourth of school board members polled in 1978 reported incomes above $40,000 per year. A little over 18 percent reported incomes from $20,000–$30,000, while approximately one-fourth listed their incomes as less than $20,000.[19]

More than half of the school board members had a college degree in 1978, while 20 percent more had completed some college work. Only 23 percent had 12 or fewer years of schooling. The vast majority were Protestant (71 percent), with a sprinkling of Catholics (16 percent) and Jews (2.2 percent).[20]

Men and women school board members apparently agree on the major issues facing the schools, and both tend to be rather conservative on school issues. The *American School Board Journal* survey in 1978 found men to be concerned about the following issues (in order of importance): (1) collective bargaining; (2) declining enrollment; (3) discipline; (4) curriculum reform; and (5) in a tie for fifth place, cutting programs and public apathy. The women's list was only slightly different; all of the concerns which appeared on the men's list of the top ten problems were also identified by the women.[21]

A serious complaint leveled against local school boards is that they do not represent the typical American community, that they cater to small elites and special interests. There isn't much evidence that the typical board, given the power to represent the needs of all the children in its local school district, would be interested in doing so. Harmon Zeigler's study, conducted during the sixties, concluded that "when measured against the yardstick of a classic democratic theory of leadership selection, school district governance hardly comes through with flying colors."[22] This conclusion is based on data which demonstrate that school board candidates were not genuinely representative of the population in the district in terms of income, educational level, sex, or political orientations. Moreover, the recruitment of persons to run for school board elections was severely limited, often to the extent that new school board members tended to be from the same socioeconomic and community "elitist" group as the outgoing members. Incumbents were rarely challenged and "more rarely still defeated."[23] Moreover, once elected, school board members did not appear to be the protectors and clarions of local interest that some claimed to be. School board members seemed to be most influenced in their policy making by close friends rather than mass opinion. Boards even tended to ignore the advice of pressure groups unless these groups were assertive and militant on specific issues.[24] In short, the most significant influences on the board seemed to be their own views and those of their close associates, unfettered by the concerns of the general public.

It is obviously clear that when some school board members cry out for local control, they have a very limited view of what that means. Ironically, those they often accuse of usurping their power—including state legislators and members of Congress—seem much more attuned to mass opinion on political issues. In reality, the paradoxical situation may exist where those policy makers on the state and national level, who are often accused of taking the schools away from the people on the local level, may be much more representative of local public interests than the local school board itself.

THE INTERMEDIATE UNIT

In most states there is a unit of school administration which lies between the state organization and the local school district.[25] In 13 states[26] the county is the intermediate unit. The intermediate unit began as a basic administrative unit to perform functions mandated by state legislatures and state-level educational agencies. In many states, the intermediate unit is a confederation of local school districts, which sometimes follows county boundaries but which often combines counties or divides them for administrative purposes. Like the old county superintendency, the intermediate unit performs administrative and supervisory functions and provides state educational services in an area composed of more than one school district.

Given the great variety of educational functions which exists from state to state, the intermediate units vary in their duties and responsibilities. In some states the intermediate units perform a wide range of activities, while in others they perform very few. In many states where the intermediate units are important, they have come to be called "regional education service agencies" or "centers." The services provided in the active regional agencies can include organization and administration of adult education programs; the maintenance of a central audiovisual library; multidistrict school purchasing; perhaps the maintenance of a centralized curriculum laboratory; provision of specialized services for exceptional children; financial services including accounting and reporting; inservice education for all school personnel; legal services; pupil transportation planning; research; special consultants; and trade and industrial education, to mention a few possibilities. The range of services is long and appears to be growing.

STATE CONTROL

In the American system of schooling, the state plays the central role in governance of schools. In spite of the claim that local control is all-important or the cries that the federal government is taking over the local schools, the real power lies with the state. Moreover, in most states, the state's power to control local education appears to be increasing. State control of education is provided for in most state constitutions, very often in great detail. Generally, state control in both policy and administration of schooling rests with the legislature, the governor, and a state education department or agency.

It is difficult to generalize about the extent of state control over schooling, since the amount and scope of state control varies from state to state. In a systematic investigation of the relationship of state governments to local school districts, Frederick M. Wirt[27] presented an interesting analysis of patterns of state control. His analysis is useful in that it presents data on both the amount of state control in various states and the variety of school functions which are controlled by states.

Wirt and his associates did a content analysis of the laws on education policy of the 50 states. The study was made in the early seventies. The research involved an analysis of each state's constitution, statutes, court decisions, and administrative regulations. They reviewed the data on each state in 36 policy areas and rated each state on a "school centralization score" ranging from 0.00 (no state control) to 6.00 (complete state control). The highest state control existed in five major policy areas. These are listed in Table 5.1.[28]

TABLE 5.1
Policies of Highest State Control

Policy	50-state score	Number of states with total control
Certification	5.50	33
Vocational education	4.89	15
Attendance	4.64	12
Accreditation	4.50	27
Financial records	4.27	16

The median score for all states on a 6.0 scale was 4.64 in these five areas. On these issues, the state clearly exercised extensive control. Indeed, many states exercised complete control over local school districts in all of these areas. Wirt suggested that these were significant powers. In his words: "Embodied in this set are the key, 'gate-keeping' state reforms of another era. ... Here lie control over personnel, compulsory attendance, financial records, requirements, and—the ultimate control—accreditation of the LEA" (Local Education Agency).[29]

In another set of policies, the states exercised extensive control which Wirt characterized as "high state control." These policies along with their corresponding 50-state "score" are listed in Table 5.2.[30]

TABLE 5.2
Policies in Which There Is High State Control

Policy	50-state score (Scale: 0.00–6.00)
Special education	5.09
Curriculum	4.41
Safety-health	4.37
Textbooks	4.35
Transportation	4.34
Teacher employment	4.17
Calendar	4.09
Graduation	4.06
Admissions	3.82
Construction	3.76
Records	3.71
Adult education	3.63
Revenue	3.57

Wirt notes that in the case of high state control, the "gatekeeping function is seen again in teacher employment, calendar, records and revenue controls."[31]

Even policies which are often believed to be matters of local discretion involve moderate state control, according to Wirt's analysis. In many states there are laws or constitutional provisions relating to school district organization, the school library, counseling services, and the physical plant. There is "moderate" state control over policies on equal educational opportunities and salaries of school personnel. States exercise moderate control over such local activities as educational objectives and grading standards.[32]

Finally, Wirt and his associates found a group of policies which had "bimodal

TABLE 5.3
Policies of Bimodal State Control Patterns

Policy	Number of states with requirements	
	Absent	High
State accounting	21	27
Evaluation	22	23
Teacher-pupil ratios	22	21
Extracurricular activities	14	11
Expenditures	27	20
Experimental programs	25	15
Personnel training	24	12

control patterns." These were policies in which some states had very high state regulation while others had no state requirements. This group is presented in Table 5.3.[33]

It can thus be seen that extensive local control over most educational policies is a myth. State constitutions, statutes, court decisions, and administrative rules and regulations emanating from state departments of education have in most states invaded nearly every aspect of schooling. There is very little that local school officials can do in providing for local schooling that is not in some way influenced by the state. What this means, according to Wirt, is that little in the way of change can be expected to come from the local level. "Systemic reform will begin and be implemented only through victory in state or federal areas. That has been the lesson recently in changes involving desegregation, finance reform, teacher power, student rights, and accountability. Significant change in these areas has come only with success in state legislatures and state courts, in Congress and the Supreme Court."[34] Although the cries for local control may be popular and a "rallying symbol" for school reform, they are, according to Wirt, an empty symbol. Not only do states exercise a high degree of control over what the local schools do as a general proposition, but very often the nature of that control is very specific in its content. For example, in the matter of curriculum policy, which Wirt scores "high," states can and do exercise very specific control. In an article on the status of state-legislated curricula in the United States, Earl J. Ogletree not only found extensive state control of the local school curriculum, but declared that there is considerable "national uniformity" in such controls.[35] Ogletree found a total of 116 subjects which had been legislated by the states. In a summary of school laws in the 50 states, he discovered that all states had some laws dealing with state-required curriculum. Some subjects have been very popular with state legislatures. A significant number of states prescribe subjects dealing with the three Rs—"reading (40%), writing (30%), grammar (24%), spelling (30%), arithmetic or mathematics (28%). Physical and health education (66% and 58%, respectively), alcohol and narcotics (68%), hygiene (40%), safety (36%), and physiology (30%)."[36]

Ogletree suggested that there were many influences in this extension of state control into curriculum areas and the developing national pattern. He listed the increasing influence of the federal government, the growth of state departments of education, state legislatures abdicating their educational obligations to state departments of education, and the influence of national assessment of educational progress as forces which were causing a decline in local control. He concluded that "these and other factors suggest that control of the schools will increasingly center in state departments of education, not in local school districts. In turn, the state departments will come under the influence of the federal government through funding of categorical programs and court decisions."[37] Although it is true that state departments of education have vastly increased influence, the governor and legislature continue to play an important role.

In a sense, the governor of each state is at the apex of the state educational bureaucracy. In recent years in most states, education has been at or near the top of the list vying with roads and social welfare programs as the most important single function of the state. Additionally, teachers in every state have become organized politically and constitute a powerful political pressure group in every state. Also, the public has become sensitive to the needs and problems of schooling and is concerned with the manner in which its school taxes are appropriated and spent. In view of these facts, it is not surprising that in every state every potential candidate for governor must give some attention to the needs and problems of the schools. Proposals for salary increases for school personnel, school reform, taxation as it relates to education, and the quality of schooling often become major political issues in gubernatorial campaigns. No aspiring candidate to the governor's office can ignore the subject. Once elected, the governor must present to the legislature his or her views regarding programs and budgets for education.

The legislature also gets into the act—in much the same way as the governors do. No one running for a legislative post from any district can ignore the politics of education. Organized teachers, taxpayers groups, pressure groups with specific school interests, and ordinary unorganized citizens want to know the candidates' positions on educational policy issues on the legislative district level. In view of the power of the typical state legislature over school matters, appointment to an educational committee of the legislature is an important assignment. What the legislature does regarding education can have direct and significant effect on hundreds of thousands of school children and parents and on thousands of school employees.

In recent years state legislatures have tended to pass comprehensive school reform measures affecting the manner in which taxes are raised and distributed, the pupil-teacher ratio, teacher accountability, the organization and administration of the schools, and countless other matters. Below are the "stated purposes" of House Bill 1706, which was passed by the legislature of Oklahoma in 1980. Although the bill is 23 pages in length, the stated purposes provide an illustration of the scope of legislative concerns. Moreover, the Oklahoma bill is typical of the manner in which state legislatures have been attempting recently to address a large number of educational problems in a single comprehensive piece of legislation.

AN ACT RELATING TO SCHOOLS: AMENDING 70 O.S. 1971, SECTIONS 1–116, AS AMENDED BY SECTION 1, CHAPTER 193, O.S.L. 1973, 6–125 AND 18–114, AS LAST AMENDED BY SECTION 24, CHAPTER 282, O.S.L. 1979.
Stating purposes: Providing for allocation of funds for in-service teacher training programs; modifying schedule for minimum salaries for teachers; requiring proposed yearly compensation schedule for staff development programs; providing for teacher improvement programs . . . requiring expertise and experience; providing teacher education requirements and reports; providing criteria for student admission to college education programs; providing for teacher education faculty development committee; including directly involved college of education faculty members; providing for faculty development plans and alternatives; requiring teaching certificates; . . . setting certain requirements; establishing an entry-year program; providing certain requirements

and procedures for the entry-year assistance program; requesting legislative review committee; establishing examinations; providing procedures for temporary certificates; requiring continuing education programs; providing penalties for noncompliance with staff development programs; authorizing a job availability program; establishing a teacher register; creating a continuing revolving fund and prescribing procedure for expenditure of funds; creating the Oklahoma citizens commission on education; defining certain positions; providing for inter-district cooperation; providing responsibilities of the professional standards board; providing for student application, certification and licensing procedures; providing for review of rules and regulations. . . .

Nor is the Oklahoma law merely a restatement of past legislative control over public schools and teacher education. It contains much that is new. For example, it establishes a totally new system of teacher certification. Under the old system, teacher education colleges in the state recommended students for certification to the state Department of Education. Under House Bill 1706, colleges and universities issue a "license" to graduates. Committees formed in local school districts are given the power to recommend teachers for certification after they have had a year of experience.

The bill is specific in intent. For example, it requires that every prospective teacher, after 90 semester hours of college work, be given competency exams in his or her subject area as well as English usage. It also makes specific requirements of college and university professors who teach education courses. For example, Section 6, Paragraph 4, mandates "programs whereby all full-time college of education faculty members, including the Dean of the College of Education, are required once every five (5) years to serve in a state accredited public school the equivalent of at least one-half day per week for one semester in responsibilities related to their respective college of education teaching fields."

The Oklahoma bill illustrates the responsiveness of a state legislature to organized pressure within the state. In Oklahoma, as in many other states, organized classroom teachers have become an effective political force. At least two provisions of the bill illustrate this: first, its provision for a substantial salary increase for teachers, and second—and by far the most important—its assignment to classroom teachers of a significant voice in the certification of teachers. Of secondary importance, but significant nonetheless, is the "reform" tone of the bill. Apparently legislators in Oklahoma, as elsewhere, were attuned to public criticism of the poor quality of education in the state.

Oklahoma's House Bill 1706 also illustrates the point made by Ogletree. The state legislature did expand the authority and control of a state department of education. The Oklahoma Department of Education is given broad powers to implement the general provisions of the legislation. For example, the state department is charged with developing and administering the competency tests for prospective teachers. It is charged with assisting local school districts in developing in-service programs. The Department of Education is given the responsibility for developing guidelines for the "entry-year assistance program" for beginning teachers. In short, a single act of the legislature not only provided for sweeping changes in teacher training and certification, but also delegated vastly increased powers of administration and supervision to the state Department of Education.

This is one way that state departments of education have expanded their activities; it is not the only way. State education departments were greatly enhanced by Title V of the Elementary and Secondary Education Act of 1965. In this act, Congress recognized that the success of federally mandated programs depended upon adequate organization within the states in order to carry them out. Title V enabled state departments of education to add personnel in order to efficiently administer the programs funded under ESEA. As federal support for programs has grown, there has been an infusion of federal funds into state departments to provide for the administration of the federal support funds.

According to Sam Harris, another source of growth for state departments was their expertise. "People have not been willing to place educational control fully in the hands of the executive or legislative branches of State governments. Educators have felt that education is a matter which the legislative and executive branches of State government should support, but with which they should not interfere."[38] Because of this feeling, Harris suggested that state legislatures tended to deal with broad policy, as did state boards of education. Rules and regulations and actual administration fell to the chief state school officer and his staff.

In view of the increasing role of state departments of education, their traditional functions have become more important. These functions generally have included: (1) general management, including establishing goals and developing policies; (2) planning, research, and evaluation; (3) consulting services; (4) regulation of existing policies and programs; (5) seeking public support and cooperation. Nearly every new program mandated by the state legislature or by the federal government requires an expansion of one or more of these activities by the state department of education.

Finally, it should be noted that bureaucracy tends to breed more bureaucracy. As the duties and responsibilities of the state department increase and the organization becomes larger, it tends to build on itself. Each section and division within the state department of education, as it goes about its appointed tasks, discovers problems and new needs. The law doesn't work the way it should. There is inadequate staffing to perform the legally mandated function. Gaps are discovered in the program which need funding and administrative supervision. And so it goes. In the normal political process, as each agency is working on its annual budget to submit to the state legislature, or as the people who work with federal programs are asked to file reports, there is always an opportunity (seldom overlooked) to ask for expansion of programs and an increase in staff to administer them. As these requests are channeled through appropriate legislative and congressional committees or through the budgetary process in the governor's office or through the U.S. Department of Education, they have a way of appearing as requests for increases in programs and budgets. Thus the educational bureaucracies, perhaps especially the state-level bureaucracies, have a way of initiating legislation for new programs.

SOME ISSUES RAISED BY STATE CONTROL

Studies of state control of education leave little doubt that localism in American education is rapidly becoming a myth. This comes through very clearly in Wirt's study.[39] Wirt demonstrates that even in the most decentralized states and regions, the state still has rigid control over what he calls "major gatekeeping" functions of accreditation, certification, and attendance. Moreover, on matters relating to administration, personnel, and school finance, locals have very little real control.

Wirt concludes that school reform cannot come from the bottom up since his studies demonstrate that most change is dictated from the top down. No matter how much it is desired, local policy cannot operate independent of the state educational structure. Even if local reforms are achieved, they rarely change the structure above. Wirt characterizes local school politics as "marginal politics," a struggle over things "at the fringe." The major decisions about schooling are made at other than the local level, and even more significant, these decisions cannot be locally affected.

If local school board members and superintendents don't know this, they soon discover it. Indeed, this fact of educational life is often used by local school authorities as an excuse for not doing what a local public or pressure group is demanding. In many cases in recent years, locals have become violent in their opposition to court orders to integrate schools. While advocating resistance and "local control," local school authorities must know that the battle is lost before it is undertaken. Less heated but similar situations exist when school authorities are directed to provide special education programs mandated by state or national law. The laws are cursed, but the responsible officials know there is no escaping them. Affirmative action guidelines, state-mandated curricula, in-service requirements for teachers, building codes and standards, school calendars, and state regulation of extracurricular activities—all could be included, along with many other issues, in this group.

A note of caution is necessary regarding the increasing power and role in education of state-level bureaucracies. Although state-level control of local schools has been increasing, this does not necessarily mean that power at the state level is concentrated in some monolithic form. As Jerome Murphy points out, [40] in many states the increased power at the state level is not so much concentrated as it is diffuse. Murphy suggests that as states have become more involved in policy making and have increased the functions they perform in education, local power has also grown. In Murphy's view, this has happened because the new functions have often been delegated to local authorities for implementation. Murphy argues that increasing educational power within states has not resulted in a "pyramid" of power, with most of the power resting at the top. He compares the expansion of educational functions to a modern shopping center with specialty shops, "each catering to a small segment of the populace." He points out that "specialty shops" now exist on the state level to serve such special groups as the handicapped, the bicultural, the gifted, girls, blacks, and Native Americans, as well as others. In this environment of pressure groups with special interests, state educational bureaucracies are fragmented, with various agencies serving special interests. Each of these "shops" or agencies is in competition with the others to get a larger share of the available state funds. Thus, even though the real center of power in education may be at the state level, it is not necessarily a centralized power unresponsive to local pressures.

THE FEDERAL GOVERNMENT AND SCHOOLS

In the words of Skee Smith, writing in *American Education*, the official journal of the U.S. Department of Education: "It has taken two centuries, but the federal commitment to education now has been finally raised to the level of agriculture, defense, commerce, and other cabinet level departments of the U.S. Government."[41] Of course, Smith was referring to the establishment on October 17, 1979, of a cabinet-level Department of Education. This occurred in the face of serious opposition from the American Federation of Teachers and opposition from conservative forces in Congress which expressed concern about the creation of yet another large bureaucracy. The idea was supported by President Carter who was not ungrateful for the support given him by the National Education Association, which had long urged the creation of a separate Department of Education. Pressure was also being applied on the president and Congress by the federal educational bureaucracy itself which, by 1979, had become a huge system. In that year, the U.S. Office of Education, then located in the Department of Health, Education, and Welfare, was responsible for administering nearly 100 programs which provided funds, materials, teachers and other staff, training activities, and technical staff for all levels of public and private education in the country. In 1979 the Office of Education had spent more than $12 billion and had 3,300 employees in Washington and at its 10 regional offices.[42]

The new department experienced an immediate expansion of functions over the old Office of Education under HEW. Many educational functions which had previously been administered under other departments and agencies were transferred to the new, enlarged cabinet department. For example, the new department assumed responsibility for the Defense Department's overseas dependents' schools with their more than 10,000 employees and an annual budget of $346 million. HEW's Rehabilitation Services Administration, with a budget of $872 million in 1979 and 445 employees, was shifted to the new department. Additionally, the education functions of the Office for Civil Rights were immediately transferred to the new department. Four major functions of HEW were placed under the supervision of the new department: the National Center for Education Statistics, the Fund for the Improvement of Postsecondary Education, the Institute for Museum Services, and program direction and support services. Finally, four "special" institutions with a total budget of more than $178 million in 1979 moved from HEW to the new department. These included Howard University, Gallaudet College for the hearing-impaired, the National Technical Institute for the Deaf in Rochester, New York, and the American Printing House for the Blind in Louisville, Kentucky.[43]

Thus, the move was more than an empty symbolic gesture, for the creation of a new Department of Education extended the influence and authority of an already large bureaucracy. The new department, which struggled for its own identity under Health and Welfare, was given its own single-purpose voice which officials in the old U.S. Office of Education had so long desired.

Unfortunately for the political supporters of a cabinet-level Department of Education, it soon became clear that the new department might have a short life. President Reagan seemed determined to dismantle the educational bureaucracy and appointed a secretary of education whose major purpose seemed to be to reverse the trend toward centralization of educational policy making and administration. By late 1981 it was clear that continued cabinet status for the Department of Education was questionable. Secretary Bell had recommended that education's departmental status be ended, with many of the functions of the department seriously curtailed and many of the new responsibilities which had been centralized within the department placed in other agencies of the federal government.

Even allowing for serious retrenchment, the federal government will continue to be deeply involved in education. Regardless of who has controlled the White House, the federal government has had a long history of involvement in education. In the Ordinance of 1785, Congress provided for the sixteenth section in each township to be set aside for the support of education. Two years later, in a more comprehensive manner, Congress enacted another ordinance which provided for the Northwest Territory to be divided into not fewer than three nor more than five states. The third article of the Ordinance in 1787 stated that "religion, morality and knowledge being necessary to good government and the happiness of mankind, schools and the means of education shall forever be encouraged." Again, as in the earlier ordinance, every sixteenth section was set aside for the support of schools. In 1826 the land which was acquired as a result of the Louisiana Purchase was brought under the same general principle.

Congress again concerned itself with a program of national education after the Civil War. Some kind of a program had to be established to provide for the newly freed blacks. The immediate needs of food, clothing, and shelter were provided for in an act passed in March of 1865, which established the Bureau of Refugees and the so-called Freedman's Bureau. Not only were the freed slaves given some of the bare essentials of life under the provisions of this legislation, but in some places the bureau provided a kind of rudimentary education for all ages.

In this same period Congress passed the Morrill Act (1862), under which each state was granted 30 thousand acres of public land (or its equivalent in money) for each of its congressmen. The proceeds were to be used to establish colleges of agriculture and mechanical arts. The Hatch Experiment Station Act in 1887 extended the idea of the Morrill Act by providing some $15 thousand annually to each state to establish agricultural experiment stations at the land-grant colleges. The Second Morrill Act of 1890 extended the program and provided for increased funds.[44]

In terms of the national government's future development in education, the creation of the Department of Education in 1867 was very significant. The original act stated the purpose of the department to be that of "collecting such statistics and facts as shall show the condition and progress of education in the several States and Territories and of diffusing such information respecting the organization and management of schools and school systems, and methods of teaching as shall aid the people of the United States in the establishment and maintenance of efficient school systems, and otherwise promote the cause of education throughout the country." Heading the new department was the commissioner of education, with very little authority, funds, or responsibilities.

In the early twentieth century, programs which had already been established were expanded. The Smith Lever Act of 1914 provided that the national government would match the contributions of those states which wanted to provide programs in agricultural extension. A few years later, the Smith-Hughes Act made funds available on a matching basis for industrial, commercial, and domestic science subjects for the secondary schools. The teaching of agricultural and vocational subjects was further encouraged by Congress in the George-Reed Act in 1929, the George-Ellzey Act in 1934, and the George-Deen Act in 1936. In addition to these efforts, the New Deal programs of the Great Depression brought the national government into many education activities. The National Youth Association employed students in secondary schools and colleges; the Civilian Conservation Corps had more than a quarter of a million young men at work on a variety of projects; a national school lunch program was launched; and the national government became directly involved in training the handicapped under the Social Security Act. In addition, the Public Works Administration and the Works Project Administration of the 1930s assisted the states and local communities in building schools and providing for adult education, citizenship education, and certain kinds of vocational education. Finally, during World War II the Servicemen's Readjustment Act (1944), popularly known as the G.I. Bill, provided varying amounts of education for more than eight million World War II veterans at a total cost of $15 billion.

Thus it is misleading to declare simply that the interest of the national government in education is of recent vintage. This argument is often made by those who insist that since the Constitution of the United States does not mention education, it is a power reserved to the states and a principle that for years the national Congress respected. This obviously is not the case. From the beginning, Congress has been directly involved in education in one way or another. Indeed, a good case might be made that the national government has been as deeply involved in this area as in some others which are sometimes taken for granted. The history of national involvement in education is, in fact, quite similar to its involvement in agriculture, commerce, labor, and other areas.

As in other areas, the national presence in education expanded geometrically after World War II. As with so many other aspects of our national life, our concern for national defense opened the door for massive participation of the national government in education. In a way, the National Science Foundation Act of 1950 grew out of a concern that our enemies were moving ahead of us in the math and science areas. The Impacted Areas programs in 1950 were directly related to national defense in that they recognized the need for federal help to local school districts which had to deal with large populations of students whose parents were employed in federal installations or military bases. The really big breakthrough came with the National Defense Education Act of 1958, which was at the time the most extensive federal aid program in the field of education. In direct reaction to Sputnik and what was thought to be a superior system of Soviet education, Congress provided funds for the improvement of the teaching of math, science, and modern foreign language. It was a direct effort by the national government to influence the curriculum and organization of schools.[45]

This seemed to open the floodgates for national involvement in education. The following, from the *Congressional Digest*,[46] is a summary of major federal programs in education in 1978:

Aid to Institutions & Agencies

Twenty-one such programs are directed at the area of elementary and secondary education:

Arts in Education—to encourage establishment of arts education programs; fiscal 1978 appropriation $2 million.

Bilingual education basic programs—to meet special needs of children of limited English-speaking ability; 1978 appropriation $93.9 million.

Bilingual education support services—to operate regional centers to assist bilingual programs; $18 million.

Community education program—to establish and improve community school programs; $3.5 million.

Educational innovation and support—to improve leadership resources of state and local education agencies and support nutrition and health services, dropout prevention, and other exemplary projects; $177.8 million.

Four programs directed at educationally-deprived children, with total 1978 funding $2.1 billion.

Ethnic Heritage Studies, $2.3 million.

Follow Through—to extend into primary grades educational gains made by deprived children in Head Start; $59 million.

Incentive grants—to encourage greater state and local expenditures for education, $24.5 million.

Indian education—for supplemental programs to meet special needs of Indian students (3 programs); $53.2 million.

Impact aid for Federally affected areas—$770 million.

Metric education—to encourage education agencies to prepare for U.S. metrication; $2 million.

Packaging & dissemination—to promote wide dissemination of exemplary education programs; $10 million.

Right to Read—to stimulate expansion of reading-related activities for children, youth, and adults; $27 million.

Teacher centers—to assist local education agencies operate teacher centers; $8.2 million.

Women's educational equity—to support programs contributing to women's educational equity; $8 million.

An additional ten programs of institutional aid are directed at strengthening organizational resources:

Alcohol and drug abuse education programs—$2 million.

Bilingual education technical assistance coordination—$4.3 million.

Educational television & radio (2 programs)—$24 million.

Environmental education—$3.5 million.

Interlibrary cooperative services, library and learning resources, and public library services—$227.7 million.

State student financial assistance training—$467,000.

Teacher Corps—$37.5 million.

A third group of 24 programs in the "aid to institutions" category is targeted at postsecondary education:

Institutional development (basic and advanced—2 programs)—to assist new and developing institutions to enter the mainstream of higher education; $120 million, which includes funding for an additional program of national teaching fellowships for developing institutions.

Bilingual education—for training stipends and institutional assistance; $16 million.

College library resources—$9.9 million.

College work-study—to promote part-time employment for needy postsecondary students; $382.3 million.

Community service and continuing education—$18 million.

Cooperative education programs—to integrate periods of academic study with gainful employment; $15 million.

Educational information centers—$2 million.

Educational opportunity centers—$5 million.

Graduate and professional opportunities program—$3.2 million.

Improvement of postsecondary education—$12 million.

Job location and development program—$33.4 million.

Law school clinical experience programs—$1 million.

National direct student loan program—for direct tuition loans for qualified students through the institution they are attending; $325.5 million.

State planning commissions—$3.5 million.

State student incentive grants—to encourage increase in state aid for needy students; $63.7 million.

Student special services—to help low-income and handicapped students complete higher education; $1 million.

Supplemental education opportunity grants—to aid students of exceptional financial need; $269.9 million.

Talent Search—to identify and encourage promising students to pursue postsecondary education; $11 million.

Training for higher education personnel—$8.2 million.

Undergraduate instructional equipment—$7.5 million.

Upward Bound—to motivate young people from low-income backgrounds with inadequate high school preparation to enter and succeed in postsecondary education; $44 million.

Veterans cost of instruction—to encourage recruitment and counseling of veterans; $23.7 million.

Sixteen additional programs are directed at education of the exceptional and the handicapped:

Centers and services for deaf-blind children—$16 million.

Early education for handicapped children—$22 million.

Gifted and talented children—$2.6 million.

Handicapped regional resource centers—$9.7 million.

Information and recruitment—to encourage recruitment of educational personnel for special education—$1 million.

Media services and captioned film loan program (3 separate programs)—$19 million.

Personnel training for the education of the handicapped—$45.3 million, which includes funding for an additional but related program of training physical education and recreational personnel for handicapped children.

Preschool incentive grants—to stimulate state activity to serve needs of handicapped preschool children; $15 million.

Regional education programs for the handicapped—$2.4 million.

Severely handicapped projects—$5 million.

State aid for programs for the handicapped—$465 million.

State-supported school programs for the handicapped—$121.6 million.

Supplementary educational centers and services, guidance, counseling, and testing for handicapped—$19.7 million.

An additional five programs are directed at developing and strengthening international studies programs:

Consultant services of foreign curriculum specialists—$325,000.

Foreign language and area studies research—$1 million.

Group projects abroad for non-Western language and area studies—$919,710.

International studies centers—$8 million.

International studies programs, graduate and undergraduate—$1.4 million.

Ten institutionally targeted programs are directed at occupational, adult, vocational and career education:

Adult education—for basic adult education programs up to 12th grade competency; $90.7 million.

Career education—for development and demonstration of techniques and modes; $10 million.

Consumer and homemaking education—$40.9 million.

Indian education—$4.4 million.

Vocational education (2 programs)—basic programs and contract programs for Indian tribes and organizations; $430.3 million.

Vocational programs for persons with special needs—$20 million.

Vocational education: state advisory councils—$5 million.

An additional ten programs provide funds for education desegregation assistance:

Grants to nonprofit organizations—$17.2 million.

Basic grants—to provide aid to desegregating school districts; $137.6 million.

Pilot programs—$32.3 million.

Educational television—$6.5 million.

Special programs and projects—$51.3 million.

Civil rights training and advisory services—$34.7 million.

ESSA evaluation—to evaluate programs and projects under the Emergency School Aid Act; $2.2 million.

Magnet schools and neutral site planning (2 programs)—$20 million.

Aid to Individuals

A second major group of OE-funded programs consists of individual aid for teacher and other professional training and for student assistance, and is carried out through 25 distinct programs (in fiscal 1978):

Basic educational opportunity grants to provide financial assistance to undergraduate postsecondary students; $2,140 million.

Bilingual education graduate fellowships—$5 million.

Bilingual vocational instructor training—$2.8 million, which includes funds for three additional programs, two of institutional aid and one for research.

College Work-Study and direct student loan programs are a form of individual aid enumerated in the foregoing summary of aid to institutions because of their funding through such institutions.

Domestic mining and mineral-fuel conservation fellowships—$4.5 million.

Education for the Public Service—to attract and prepare students for entrance into state, local, or Federal service; $4 million.

Ellender fellowships—to increase understanding of the Federal Government among secondary school students and their communities; $750,000.

Fellowships abroad for doctoral dissertation research in foreign language and area studies—$1.09 million.

Fellowships abroad for faculty in foreign language and area studies—$640,000.

Foreign language and area studies fellowships—$4.56 million.

Guaranteed student loan program (private capital used for the actual loans, with federal guaranty).

Indian education—$1.3 million.

Librarian training—$2 million.

Funds for individuals are available under seven additional programs included in the foregoing listing of institutional aid: media services and captioned films training grants; national teaching fellowships; personnel training for the education of the handicapped; state student incentive grants; supplemental educational opportunity grants; Teacher Corps project grants; and training of physical education and recreation personnel for handicapped children.

Teacher Exchange—operated with transfer funds from the Department of State.

Training for the disadvantaged—$1 million.

Vocational education graduate leadership development awards—$1.65 million.

Vocational education certification fellowship program—$1.85 million.

Educational Aid for Research

A third major grouping of OE educational aid programs consists of those providing aid for research:

Bilingual education research, demonstration and evaluation activities—$2 million. An additional bilingual program for vocational instruction materials, methods and techniques is listed above under individual aid.

Consumer education—$4.09 million.

Library research and demonstration—$1 million.

Research and demonstration for the handicapped—$20 million.

Strengthening research library resources—$5 million.

Vocational education program improvement and supportive services—$107.6 million.

Construction Aid

Two programs of construction aid for education are directed at:

Public schools—to aid school districts in Federally impacted areas provide minimum school facilities and to aid school districts suffering disaster emergencies—$30 million.

Vocational facilities—to construct area vocational education facilities in the Appalachian region; operated with transfer funds from the Appalachian Regional Commission.

The manner in which the national government became so deeply involved in education is a long and complex story. However, there have been certain major forces operating which should be briefly noted. Over the years the central focus of the struggle over federal aid has been the issue of states' rights. Those who opposed federal aid generally argued that since education was not mentioned in the Constitution, it was not a proper area for national government action. As demands grew for a more comprehensive system, as special needs were identified, and as it became clear by the 1950s that the national government was increasing its interest in education, the argument shifted. Unable to hold the line on the position that the national government should play no role at all in education, the opposition seemed to grudgingly accept the idea that federal aid was all right so long as it was general aid distributed to the states to do with as they wished. Unfortunately for the "states' rights" position, this is not the way in which federal aid has developed. In the field of education, dating back at least to the creation of the Freedmen's Bureau, Congress has had specific purposes in mind. In the twentieth century, beginning with the Smith-Lever Act in 1914 and continuing to the present, the Congress has tended to provide what has come to be called "categorical aid," that is, federal money for specific categories or purposes. This is understandable in view of the forces which promoted and encouraged increasing national activity in education. Generally there have been two major forces operating which have encouraged the vast expansion of national activity in education. These forces tended to favor categorical aid over general aid.

First, the very nature of educational needs as viewed by the Congress tended to encourage the categorical aid approach. Congress has tended to concentrate its efforts in education around specific needs and problems. As suggested above, the needs of national defense in the fifties stimulated the development by the national government of specific curricula and teacher education activities. Beginning in the sixties and continuing to the present, efforts to combat poverty stimulated congressional interest in the schools. A basic assumption of antipoverty programs has been that a major cause of poverty was a lack of marketable skills and low educational levels for large numbers of poor people. Beginning with the decisions on integration in the late forties and early fifties and continuing until the present, the issue of civil rights of minorities has been closely related to the education of minorities. As Congress considered national problems such as unemployment and underemployment, manpower needs—especially the need for skilled workers, crime and delinquency in the inner cities, the need for retraining, environmental problems, and more, specific educational programs were offered as solutions.

A second force operating in this environment was that of organized pressure groups. For years certain established pressure groups had expressed an interest in education. The NEA had always been interested, and by the fifties it was pushing hard for increasing the national role in education. The American Federation of Teachers and other labor unions had worked for years to increase funding for education. So had many school-related groups such as the Parent-Teacher Association and the National School Boards Association, although these groups certainly could not be characterized as favoring categorical aid by the national government. Groups interested in civil rights, particularly the National Association for the Advancement of Colored People, had long been interested in education for blacks and other minorities and worked hard for an extension of national activity in this area. Some of the activities of these groups will be discussed in a later chapter.

As Congress responded to national problems with educational solutions, a new kind of pressure developed—pressure from within the growing educational bureaucracy itself. Every new program and every new agency created by Congress became, in effect, its own lobbying group. By the end of the sixties, the federal educational bureaucracy had become the most important and effective educational pressure group working for the expansion of national efforts in education.

With the advent of the Reagan administration, a new debate has developed over the relative merits of "block grants" versus categorical aid. The Reagan administration, in the interests of greater state and local control of education, has taken the position that block grants would better serve the purpose of states' rights and increased local control. In theory, block grants to the states would reduce bureaucratic red tape and allow educational officials on the state and local levels greater discretion in the use of federal funds. Yet no one has seriously proposed that federal funds be deposited with the states without any controls. Given the nature of state bureaucracies in education, it is unlikely that they will allocate funds to local agencies with no strings attached. Thus, in terms of bureaucratic control, it seems unlikely that block grants will result in many dramatic changes. It is possible, however, that block grants could result in some shifting of available funds to different purposes on the state and local levels. Of course, President Reagan will have to get the approval of Congress for a shift from categorical aid to block grants. In the process, each categorical aid program will be examined by Congress and will be subjected to intensive and, in some cases, prolonged, political debate. Whatever its merits, or lack of them, the block grant idea faces a difficult struggle.

A NOTE ON BUREAUCRACY

As the size of local school districts has grown following consolidation of school districts, and as the state and national interest in education has grown, the educational bureaucracy has grown. Webster defines a bureaucracy as "a system of carrying on the business of government by means of bureaus, each controlled by a chief; also, government by bureau heads and their superior administrative officers. Hence, officialism in government; rigid, formal measures or routine procedure in administration. . . ."

Max Weber, the German sociologist, is often credited with the first serious analysis of bureaucratic structure. In his *Essays in Sociology* (1958), Weber described the following characteristics of bureaucracy:

1. A bureaucracy is a structure of offices each having specific responsibilities and duties.
2. Authority rests with the office rather than the person and the division of authority and competence tend to be specified.
3. Bureaucracy tends to encourage specialization of duties, tasks and functions.
4. The organization is governed by rules of procedure which tend to routinize and categorize activities.
5. Functions and procedures in bureaucracies tend to be formal and impersonal.
6. Bureaucratic organizations are stratified and hierarchical.[47]

Even very small schools are bureaucratically organized into hierarchical patterns with more or less clearly defined duties and responsibilities for each task. Specialization exists both on the administrative level and, of course, in teaching. Vacancies or "slots" in the organization are filled according to specialized competence or expertise. There are rules and regulations to be followed by students, teachers, administrators, and even members of the school board. A "picture" of a school bureaucracy is provided in Figure 5.1.

A serious study of this organizational chart might lead one to believe that this is an organizational chart for a rather large school system. Not so. This chart represents the organization of a school system with 800 pupils. The chart provides an instant view of the complex nature of schooling even in a relatively small school district. It also illustrates how state and federal laws, rules and regulations, and bureaucracies have impacted on the schooling function on the local level. In this small school system several functions are mandated at the state level, requiring the establishment of local offices to perform the functions. In this typical small school system, most of the salary of the assistant superintendent for special education is paid from federal funds. Part of the cost for the operation of the office of the assistant superintendent of instruction is carried by federal programs. This is also true of some of the activities of the assistant superintendent of finance and business affairs.

Another picture of bureaucracy is provided in Figure 5.2. This chart depicts the major activities and offices of the old U.S. Office of Education when it was located in the Department of Health, Education, and Welfare. A look at this chart makes it difficult to realize that this was a serious effort to capture the organizational arrangements of the U.S. Office of Education. One would almost think it was done in a spirit of levity.

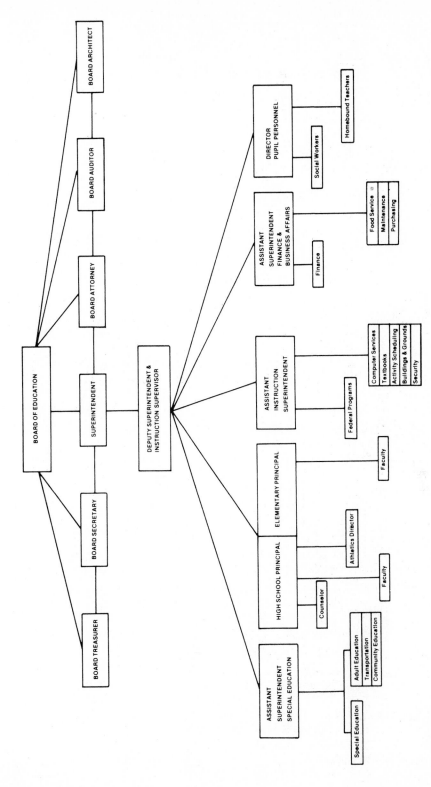

FIGURE 5.1

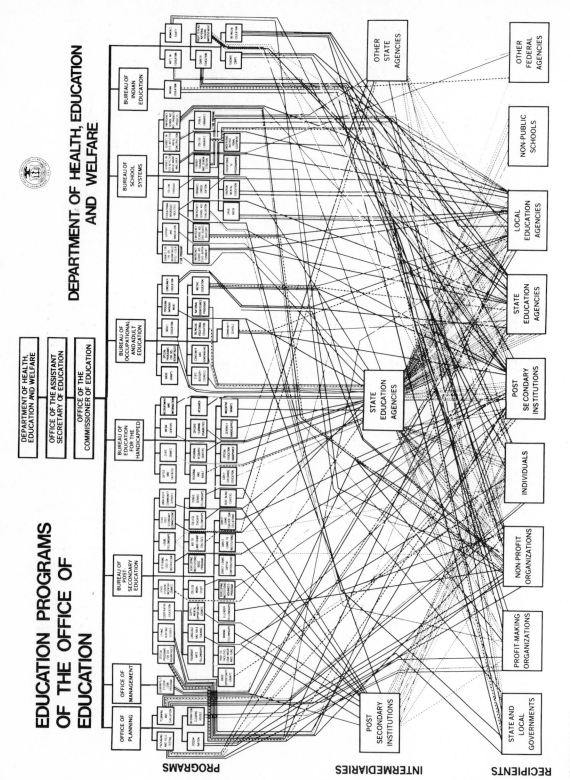

FIGURE 5.2

As bureaucracies in education have grown, so has criticism of them; and though the criticisms are legion, a few serious complaints are consistently made by those who have to deal with the bureaucracies. Most commonly heard are criticisms that bureaucratic organizations in education have become so large and unwieldy that it is difficult to get decisions. No one seems to be in charge. Large bureaucracies are said to be a good hiding place for incompetents. Hardly a year passes that someone doesn't blow the whistle on some highly paid bureaucrat who heads an office which no longer has anything to do. Another often heard criticism is that bureaucracies grow so large that they tend to lose sight of the purposes for which they were originally created. They become so involved in the rules and regulations that individual bureaucrats become functionaries who seem to be more interested in filing reports and shuffling papers than in serving the real needs of clients. Finally, most antibureaucrats scorn the irrational growth of the system. Life in a federal bureaucracy is described in a light vein in the following article.

Down the Bureaucracy!
Matthew P. Dumont[48]

There has been a certain tension among the people of our federal city lately. I am not talking about the black population of the district, which becomes visible to the rest of the world only when its rage boils over. I am referring to the public servants who ooze across the Maryland and Virginia lines each day to manipulate the machinery of government. . . .

They are good people, which is to say that they are no less good than anyone else, which is to say that we are all pretty much cut from the same material and most of it is pretty rotten. . . .

I have been and will be more sober and precise about this issue in other writings, but what I am attempting to convey is a conviction that the great evils of mankind, the genocides and holy wars, the monstrous exploitations and negligences and injustices of societies have less to do with the malice of individuals than with unexamined and unquestioned institutional practices.

I am talking about the Eichmannism—a syndrome wherein individual motives, consciences or goals become irrelevant in the context of organizational behaviors. This can be seen in pure culture in the federal government. There are a host of written rules for behavior for the federal civil servants, but these are rarely salient. It is the unwritten rules, tacit but ever present, subtle but overwhelming, unarticulated but commanding, that determine the behavior of the men and women who buzz out their lives in the spaces defined by the United States government.

These rules are few in number. Rule number one is to maintain your tenure. This is at the same time the most significant and the easiest rule to abide by. If you desire to keep a job for several decades and retire from it with an adequate pension, and if you have the capacity to appear at once occupied and inconspicuous, then you can be satisfied as a "fed."

Appearing occupied means walking briskly at all times. It means looking down at your desk rather than up into the distance when thinking. It means always having papers in your hands. Above all, it means, when asked how things are, responding "very hectic" rather than "terrific" or "lousy."

Being inconspicuous means that your competence in appearing occupied should be expressed quietly and without affect. The most intolerable behavior in a civil servant is psychotic behavior. Being psychotic in the federal government is looking people directly in the eye for a moment too long. It is walking around on a weekday without a tie. It is kissing a girl in an elevator. (It doesn't matter whether she is a wife, mistress, secretary or daughter.) It is writing a memo that is excessively detailed, or refusing to write memos. It is laughing too loud or too long at a conference. It is taking a clandestine gulp of wine in a locker room rather than ordering two martinis over lunch. (This explains why there are more suspensions for alcoholism among lower level workers than higher level ones.)

In short, there is no more sensitive indicator of deviant behavior than personnel records of the federal government. . . .

The second rule of behavior in the government, and clearly related to the sustenance of your own tenure, is to keep the boss from getting embarrassed. That is the single, most important standard of competence for a federal official. The man who runs interference effectively, who can anticipate and obviate impertinent, urgent or obvious demands from the boss's boss, or from the press, or from the public, or from Congress, will be treasured and rewarded. This is so pervasive a desideratum in a civil servant that the distinction between line and staff activities becomes thin and artificial in the face of it. Your primary function in the hierarchy (after the protection of your own tenure) is the protection of your superior's tenure rather than the fulfillment of assigned responsibilities. . . .

The third unwritten rule of federal behavior is to make sure that all appropriated funds are spent by the end of the fiscal year. Much of the paper that stuffs the orifices of executive desks has to do with justifications for requests for more money. For money to be returned after such justifications are approved is to imply that the requester, his supervisor and Congress itself were improvident in their demands on the taxpayer's money. It would be like a bum asking for a handout for a cup of coffee. A passerby offers a quarter and the bum returns 15¢ saying, "Coffee is only a dime, schmuck." . . .

The only effective way to evaluate a federal program is the rapidity with which money is spent. Federal agencies, no less than purveyors of situation comedies, cigarettes and medical care, are dominated by a marketplace mentality which assumes that you have a good product if the demand exceeds the supply.

The fourth unwritten rule of behavior in government is to keep the program alive. It is not appropriate to question the original purposes of the program. Nor is it appropriate to ask if the program has any consonance with its original purposes. It is certainly not appropriate to assume that its purposes have been served. It is only appropriate to assume that once a program has been legislated, funded and staffed it must endure. An unstated and probably unconscious blessing of immortality is bestowed upon the titles that clutter organizational charts in federal agencies. . . .

The fifth and final unwritten rule of federal behavior is to maintain a stable and well-circumscribed constituency. With so great a concern for survival in the government, it is necessary to have friends outside of it. One's equity within an agency and a program's equity in Congress are a function of equity with vested interests outside. The most visible and articulate vestedness is best to cultivate. Every agency and every department knows this, as does every successful executive. The constituency not only represents survival credits but has the quality of a significant reference group. The values, purposes and rewards of the federal agent must mesh with those of his program's constituents. ...

... One other feature of the Washington scene must be described before we can say we know enough of it to elaborate a strategy of assault. This has to do with power.

There is a lot of nonsense about power in the government. One sees a black Chrysler with a vinyl top speeding by. A liveried chauffeur, determined and grim, operates the vehicle. In the rear, a gooseneck, high-intensity lamp arched over his shoulder, sits a man studying the Washington Post. One is tempted to say, "There goes a man of power."

It is a vain temptation. Power in the government does not reside within gray eminences in black Chryslers. It is a soft, pluralistic business shared by a large number of middle managers. Organizational charts in federal agencies read as if there is a rigid line of authority and control from the top down. It would appear that the secretary of each department with his designated assistants and deputies would control the behavior of the entire establishment. In fact, there is a huge permanent government that watches with covert bemusement as the political appointees at the top come and go, attempting in their turn to control the behavior of the agencies "responsible to them."

This does not mean that there is not a good deal of respect and deference paid by middle managers to their superiors. But, as in many organizations, this deference can have an empty and superficial quality to it that amounts to mockery. In most hospitals, for example, it is not the doctors who determine what happens to patients, but nurses. Nurses may appear as subordinate to physicians as slaves to their masters, but as soon as the doctor has left the ward the nurse does what she wants to do anyway.

Similarly, in federal agencies, it is the great army of middle managers that controls the show. There is not even the built-in accountability of a dead patient for the boss to see.

Power in the government resides less in position and funds than it does in information, which is the medium of exchange. The flow of information is controlled not at the top, but at the middle. There is very little horizontal flow between agencies because of the constant competition for funds, and all vertical flow must be mediated by the GS 14 to GS 17 bureaucrats who make up the permanent government.

This concentration of power in the middle, controlled by masses of managers who subscribe to the unwritten code of behavior described above, is the reason why the national government is essentially unresponsive. It does not respond to the top or the bottom; it does not respond to ideology. It is a great, indestructible mollusk that absorbs kicks and taunts and seductions and does nothing but grow.

But it's worse than that. The government is righteous. The people who man the bastions of the executive branch (like the rest of us) have the capacity to invest their personal identities. Because it is theirs, their function must be defended. Their roles become, in the language of psychiatry, egosyntonic. Their sense of personal integrity, their consciences, their self-esteem begin to grow into the positions they hold. It is as if their very identities partake of the same definition as their organizationally defined function.

Can you imagine trying to fight a revolution against a huge, righteous marshmallow? Even if you had enough troops not to be suffocated by it, the best you can hope for is to eat it. And, as you all know, you become what you eat. And that is the point. For a revolution to be meaningful it must take into account the nature of organizational life. It must assume that the ideologically pure and the ideologically impure are subject to the same Eichmannesque forces. If a revolution harbors the illusion that a reign of terror will purify a bureaucracy of scoundrels and exploiters, it will fail. It matters little whether bureaucrats are Royalist or Republican, Czarist or Bolshevik, Conservative or Liberal, or what have you. It is the built-in forces of life in a bureaucracy that result in the bureaucracy being so indifferent to suffering and aspiration. . . .

Of course, there are defenders of bureaucracy. Writing in the *Nation* magazine, Peter Woll and Rochelle Jones saw bureaucracy as a protection against a weak Congress or a "bad" president.[49] They saw it as a "fourth branch" of government which could act independent of the Congress, the president, and the courts. Bureaucracy gets its power from "independent constituencies," that is, from the clients it serves. According to Woll and Jones, this has its good points, since bureaucracy can curb the desire of a president to change seriously the direction of major governmental programs. They cited Nixon's abortive attempts to influence the federal bureaucracy, even to the point of appointing a "super-Cabinet to attempt to centralize power in the executive office." They asserted that the "Watergate affair clearly reveals the value of a semi-autonomous bureaucracy."[50] Woll and Jones felt that if Nixon had been able to manipulate the bureaucracy as he wished, certain basic constitutional rights might have been violated. Professional bureaucrats in the Nixon administration balked at his attempted exercise of power.

Political considerations notwithstanding, certain other strengths can be claimed for bureaucracy. Bureaucracies are, or can be, efficient. It would be difficult to imagine how without them we could provide schooling for more than 40 million children in our vast educational system. The educational bureaucracy also provides a basic kind of equality. It has, to some extent, resulted in a kind of standardization of the curriculum, teachers' qualifications, administrators' qualifications, as well as books and materials. This may be positive in the sense that it makes possible a great deal of mobility, the existence of "interchangeable parts," as it were, in educational personnel. It also brings order to what might otherwise be chaos in curriculum development and the publication of texts and other materials. It supports a kind of egalitarianism. Because of its impersonal nature, bureaucracy tends to operate according to a standard pattern of rules; and at least in their initial contacts with it, people tend to be treated alike.

Bureaucracy is also a relatively inexpensive way to perform important functions. Not only has government learned this lesson, but private enterprise has as well. Given the experience of the private economic sector, it seems unlikely that if education were turned over to private enterprise, bureaucracies would be eliminated. Economies of size have been a feature of school bureaucracies for some time. Related to this, large bureaucratic organizations do permit specialization and expertise which would be impossible in small personal organizations. Finally, from the point of view of workers within the bureaucratic system, a certain amount of anonymity and protection is assured. This can be particularly important in teaching, where rules and regulations, rather than circumscribing the worker, can provide security and freedom to operate within known parameters.

SOME ISSUES AND PROBLEMS IN SCHOOL GOVERNANCE

A major problem with bureaucratic and hierarchical organizations is the difficulty in effecting change from outside the organization or from the rank and file within the organization. Changes in highly structured bureaucracies tend to flow from the top down. How have recent changes in schooling reflected this problem? What would have to happen to the governing system in education in order for local citizens to exercise effective policy controls over their schools?

Without question, a major aspect of American education in the last several decades has been increasing centralization. State governments and their agencies have exercised increasing control, as has the national government. Perhaps the time has come, as Robert Hutchins suggested as early as 1969, for a national system of education. In Hutchins' words:

> I suggest that the whole idea of state control of education is outmoded. It runs counter to everything that is going on in the world. The advance of transportation and communication, the high mobility of our population, the irrelevance of state boundaries, and the importance to the nation as a whole of the education conducted in any part of it all support the proposition that education has to be a national enterprise.[51]

Hutchins' reasons for making this statement were straightforward:

> It is important to devise means of equalizing educational opportunity within each state. It is far more important to equalize educational opportunity among the states. The differences in resources and the number of children in the states are too great to permit anything like equal educational opportunity. ...[52]

Hutchins was worried about not only economic inequality but other forms of inequality as well:

> ... the trend of litigation suggests that the states cannot be relied on to rid their schools of bigotry and prejudice or to establish satisfactory standards of fair treatment for teachers and students. ...[53]

Hutchins argued that education was too important to be left to the states since "... schooling is now a prerequisite to 'success' in life." He saw education as a basic right because "it is indispensable to the development of human beings. The chance to become a human being is too important to be defined by state lines."

Finally, Hutchins suggested that legal and constitutional problems could be overcome if we wished to establish a national system of education:

> The "necessary and proper" and "General Welfare" clauses [of the Constitution] seem to supply adequate constitutional sanction for a national program of education. Other provisions offer additional support. For example, the Equal Protection Clause of the Fourteenth Amendment applies only to the states. But the Fifth Amendment, which operates against both the federal and the state governments, prohibits deprivation of life, liberty, or property without due process of law, and the Supreme Court ... has said that though equal protection and due process are not interchangeable phrases, discrimination may be so unjustifiable as to be violative of due process.
>
> The due-process clause of the Fifth Amendment might, then, at least in extreme cases, authorize the federal government to equalize educational opportunity among the states.[54]

Are we, in fact, moving in the direction of a national system of education? One of the fears often expressed in connection with expanding state and national control is that the local citizen is losing his voice in educational matters. Is this true? Assuming school boards still possess significant powers, how representative of the voters are they? Are U.S. representatives and senators as representative of the "will of the people" as local school board members? Has anything happened since Dr. Hutchins' article appeared in 1969 either to weaken or strengthen his arguments?

NOTES

1. Roald F. Campbell et al., *The Organization and Control of American Schools*, 3d ed. (Columbus, Ohio: Charles E. Merrill Publishing Co., 1975), p. 75.
2. *Digest of Education Statistics*, 1979 (Washington, D.C.: U.S. Government Printing Office, 1979), p. 60
3. Ibid., p. 61.
4. Campbell et al., *The Organization and Control of American Schools*, p. 92.
5. *Springfield v. Quick*, 63 U.S. 56 (1859).
6. *Attorney General of Michigan ex rel. Kies v. Lowrey*, 1999 U.S. 233 (1905).
7. *Sailor v. Board of Education*, 387 U.S. 105 (1967).
8. *McInnis v. Ogilvie*, 394 U.S. 322 (1969), and *San Antonio Independent School District v. Rodriguez*, 411 U.S. 1 (1973).
9. *Kramer v. Union Free School District No. 15*, 395 U.S. 621 (1969).
10. *Turner v. Fouche*, 396 U.S. 346 (1970).
11. Helen B. Shaffer, "Community Control of Public Schools," *Editorial Research Reports* (Washington, D.C.: Congressional Quarterly, 1968), p. 946.
12. Michael Knight, "School-Decentralization Backers Dismayed by Clark's Criticism," *New York Times*, 1 December 1972, p. 12.
13. Kenneth E. Underwood, Lawrence McCluskey, and George R. Umberger, "A Profile of the School Board Member," *The American School Board Journal* 165 (October 1978): 23.
14. Ibid.
15. Harmon L. Zeigler, M. Kent Jennings, and G. Wayne Peak, *Governing American Schools* (North Scituate, Mass.: Duxbury Press, 1974), pp. 31–32.
16. Ibid., pp. 39–41.
17. Underwood et al., "A Profile of the School Board Member," p. 23.
18. Ibid., p. 24.
19. Ibid.
20. Ibid.
21. Ibid., p. 25.
22. Zeigler et al., *Governing American Schools*, p. 244.
23. Ibid.
24. Ibid., p. 245.
25. For a complete discussion of this unit of school administration, see W. J. Emerson, "Intermediate School Dsitrict," *Journal on State School Systems* 1 (Spring 1967): 34–45; and E. Robert Stephens, "A Profile of Exemplary Regional Educational Service Agencies," *Planning and Change: A Journal for School Administrators* 14 (Fall 1972): 33–40.
26. Alabama, Florida, Georgia, Kentucky, Louisiana, Maryland, Nevada, New Mexico, North Carolina, Tennessee, Utah, Virginia, and West Virginia.

27. Frederick M. Wirt, "What State Laws Say about Local Control," *Phi Delta Kappan* 58 (April 1978): 517–520. For a more extensive treatment, see Frederick M. Wirt, "School Policy Culture and State Decentralization," in "The Politics of Education," *The Seventy-sixth Yearbook of the National Society for the Study of Education, Part II*, ed. Jay D. Scribner (Chicago: University of Chicago Press, 1977).

28. Adopted from a chart by Wirt, "What State Laws Say about Local Control," p. 519.

29. Ibid.

30. Adopted from Wirt, "What State Laws Say about Local Control," p. 519.

31. Ibid.

32. Ibid.

33. Adopted from a chart provided by Wirt, "What State Laws Say about Local Control," p. 520.

34. Ibid.

35. Earl J. Ogletree, "The Status of State-Legislated Curricula in the U.S.," *Phi Delta Kappan* 59 (October 1979): 133–135.

36. Ibid., p. 133.

37. Ibid., p. 135.

38. Sam P. Harris, *State Department of Education, State School Boards and Chief State School Officers* (Washington, D.C.: Government Printing Office, for the U.S. Department of Health, Education, and Welfare, 1973), p. 26.

39. Wirt, "School Policy Culture and State Decentralization," pp. 164–187.

40. Jerome T. Murphy, "The Paradox of State Government Reform," *The Public Interest* 64 (Summer 1981): 124–140.

41. Skee Smith, "The U.S. Department of Education," *American Education* 15 (November 1979), p. 6.

42. U.S. Department of Health, Education, and Welfare, Office of Education, Annual Evaluation Report on Programs Administered by the U.S. Office of Education, Fiscal Year 1979 (Washington, D.C.: U.S. Office of Education, 1979), p. 5.

43. Smith, "The U.S. Department of Education," p. 8.

44. Butts and Cremin, *A History of Education in American Culture*, pp. 426–428.

45. Joel Spring, *American Education* (New York: Longman, 1978), p. 141.

46. *Congressional Digest*, November 1978, pp. 262, 288.

47. Paraphrased from Max Weber, *Essays in Sociology* (New York: Oxford University Press, 1958), ch. 8.

48. Matthew P. Dumont, "Down the Bureaucracy," *Transaction* 8 (October 1970): 10–14.

49. Peter Woll and Rochelle Jones, "Bureaucratic Defense in Depth," *The Nation*, 17 September 1973, pp. 229–232.

50. Ibid., p. 232.

51. Robert M. Hutchins, "Public Education, Who's Responsible?" *The Center Magazine*, November 1969, p. 89.

52. Ibid.

53. Ibid., p. 90.

54. Ibid.

Part III

The School as a Reflection of Society

In the chapters which follow in this part, an effort is made to describe the manner in which the schools tend to reflect the goals and values of society. A basic assumption of the chapters is that tax-supported education can do little else than support the values and goals of the communities in which the schools operate. Through a variety of means, students are socialized to the existing values within the society. Thus, schools are not revolutionary agents of change but tend to support the political, religious, and economic values which exist in the society.

Even on the matter of social class, the schools may be more reflective of existing class structure than agents of change. Although schooling is often promoted as the most certain avenue of upward mobility in democratic capitalism, minorities and the most desperately poor have experienced difficulty in exploiting their school experience as a path for upward mobility.

School officials and teachers often find it difficult to do new and different things. When they depart from traditional roles, they are subject to attack from organized pressure groups—and those who work in schools are easy targets for such groups. Local and national pressure groups, especially those with extreme views on educational issues, have been very active in recent years. Thus, teachers are not a major source of change. Although teachers have clearly become more powerful politically, they are by no means the power center in American schooling. Indeed, teachers have had an uphill battle in establishing their professionalism and finding an effective voice in policy matters in education.

These realities and other forces make the schools unlikely agents of change in American society.

The Socialization of Students

There once was a time when the schools were not the major instrument of socialization in America. In a chapter entitled "The Unmaking of the American Child" Urie Bronfenbrenner suggests that at some time in our past "children used to be brought up by their parents."[1] When this was true, families were larger—many were extended families, few mothers worked, communities were small, and adults in the community took more responsibility for the children.

These conditions existed in many rural areas and small towns in America until World War II. People living on farms and in small towns often lived close to relatives or with them. They knew many relatives and visited them on a regular basis. In small town America, as Bronfenbrenner correctly points out, "everybody in the neighborhood minded your business." If one went to the corner grocery or the nearest country store, almost everyone there was a familiar face. The proprietor knew all the children and their parents. If a child had earned a little extra money and decided to treat his school chums to an ice cream soda at the local drug store, everybody in town, including his parents, would know about it before he got home. Childhood experiments with dishonesty, such as shoplifting, were in most instances reported to the parents, not to the police or some social agency. In such instances the punishments were often quick and harsh. There were many opportunities in the "old America" for communication between adults and children in small community settings. Adults seemed to have time for children. They showed them how to do things; they talked with them. People could borrow a neighbor's tools or use his shop or ask how to make something. Adults would tell the children stories about all sorts of things, often related to moral values, and keep an eye on them when their parents were not around. Teachers were not reluctant to call parents and did not hesitate to report on progress or deviancies. Thus, in the America of the last generation, the entire community, including the school, was a socializing agency.

This situation has changed radically in recent years. With the growth of cities and suburbs, not only has the extended family disappeared, but in many places viable neighborhoods and communities have disappeared with them. In Bronfenbrenner's words:

Urbanization has reduced the extended family to a nuclear one with only two adults; and the functioning neighborhood—where it has not decayed into an urban or rural slum—has withered to a small circle of friends, most of them accessible only by car or telephone. . . . Whereas, before, the world in which the child lived consisted of a diversity of people in a diversity of settings, now for millions of American children the neighborhood is nothing but row upon row of buildings where 'other people' live.[2]

Neighborhood experiences for children are severely limited. Everything must be planned. If a child wants to play baseball, he must join the Little League to be coached by strange adults. Going to a movie, bowling, swimming—or whatever— have become organized activities. There isn't much to do at home either. Home time is often spent before the TV set. Children get up earlier to go to school, stay longer, and come home later. Even when they are home, they are often alone. Both parents work and no one is there to hear about the adventures of the school day or to provide guidance for leisure time. For small children, there is often the institutionalized and formal world of the day care center or an over-burdened "professional" baby sitter, the most successful of whom have developed baby-sitting "factories." As Bronfenbrenner observed: "It is a pretty bland world."[3]

In this kind of world, much of the socialization process has been transferred from the family and the community to other institutions. These include day care centers, nursery schools, Little Leagues, city recreation departments, juvenile officers, jails, and of course schools. This is not a new role for the schools, but because of the decline of other socialization forces, the school has become much more significant as an agent of socialization.

THE SCHOOL AS A GENERAL SOCIALIZING AGENT

In 1925, Emile Durkheim observed that the major duty of the school was to teach the values of society. He suggested that the "school has, above all, the function of linking the child to his society." The teacher, in Durkheim's analysis, was "society's agent, the critical link in cultural transmission. . . . "[4] Thus, Durkheim was following a long tradition and a deeply held belief that a major purpose of schooling was to socialize children to the norms and values of society. In what appeared to be simpler times, during much of the nineteenth century and the first three or four decades of the twentieth, those who wrote about public schooling in America certainly shared Durkheim's views. Even curriculum materials appeared to be deliberately designed not only to teach the basic fundamentals of the three Rs, but included, along with the reading, writing, and math assignments, heavy doses of morality and character building. The old McGuffey readers with their lessons in Christian morality provide the most obvious illustration. Nor was socialization to basic Christian moral standards limited to the elementary school. Secondary school courses in civics and American history were often deliberately designed to teach patriotism and to socialize students to the "American way of life."

This is not to say that there was always complete agreement on this function of the schools. Parents sometimes objected when they felt that the schools were not supporting the values taught in the home and in the churches. Generally, however, the schools tended to support and reinforce the values parents thought were important for their children. In an earlier era, even those parents whose values did not conform with the Protestant Christian values which were characteristic of the schools did not raise voices of protest. For example, non-Protestant immigrants were often convinced that the schools were a major vehicle of Americanization of their children, and they were, above all, new American "patriots." Even though they may have felt discomfort with some of the "American values" being taught in the schools, there appears to have been no serious organized voice of protest. Perhaps they felt that the teachers knew best what was good for their children, or they felt secure that what was taught in the homes and in the church could not easily be shaken by the schools.

Regardless of how parents felt, the school has become a major agent of socialization. In his analysis of the school class as a social system, Talcott Parsons suggested that from the first grade until marriage or entry into the labor force, "the school class may be regarded as the focal socializing agency."[5] He defined this school socialization as "the development in individuals of the commitments and capacities which are essential prerequisites of their future role performance."[6] Parsons saw two major components in the commitments made by individuals: commitment to the broad values of the society and commitment to the performance of a specific role within the structure of society. He suggested that one could be committed to one's role as an honest, hard-working citizen without internalizing the general values of the society. He regarded the school class as a primary agency which attempts to socialize individuals to both roles, that of a "good citizen" in society as well as a responsible worker. The schools are an "agency of manpower allocation" since the level of schooling is closely related to occupational status. Since schooling is so important in determining future occupational roles, what happens to children in elementary school is vital. Parsons suggested that the child's success or failure in elementary school greatly influences future success in school and thus directly influences one's status in later life. The question this raises is: "What determines 'success' in the elementary school?" It could be a number of things, depending upon the demands of the society in which one lives or the specific requirements of the social setting of the classroom itself. In some societies, it might be merit or basic intellectual ability; in others, a willingness to follow the rules and work hard; in still others, it could be family connections or ascribed status. In American schools these are all predeterminants of success, but ability to conform to the social system of the classroom and to accept the assigned roles which identify "good" students are very important. In a word, success in pleasing the teacher seems to be vital. A child can be very intelligent and creative and do poorly in many elementary school classrooms. Even a child from a high status family who will not follow the rules can find himself in serious difficulty. "Good families" do not always mean high status families but often mean that the child has parents, from whatever social class, who give the school and teacher support in their efforts to socialize the child. It is the child who gets along well in school who has the best chance of success. Getting along means supporting the teacher, doing what one is told, socializing with the other children, and performing according to the teacher's expectations. In the words of Phillip Jackson: "The point is simply that in schools as in prisons, good behavior pays off. . . ."[7]

Obviously, there are other forms of socialization. Since complete analysis of socialization in the school setting would require much more than a single chapter, what follows is a brief discussion of some of the blatantly obvious efforts of the school to socialize political and religious values. The material which follows also deals with the impact of the formal and hidden curriculum and extra-class activities. In addition, a brief analysis is made of the influence of peers in the socialization process. Finally, the chapter deals with the limits of socialization.

POLITICAL SOCIALIZATION

Political socialization, simply defined, is the manner in which a society attempts to induct new members (children and immigrants) into the system and provide them with the information and attitudes necessary for support of the system. A major assumption underlying political socialization is that those who are properly socialized will behave in certain acceptable ways. That is, they will exhibit "appropriate" behaviors including observing the laws, paying taxes, voting, and submitting to military conscription.[8] Although many forces and institutions are important in this process, the schools clearly assume a major responsibility in political socialization. In an autocratic society, political socialization is a fairly straightforward process, since an "official" political ideology exists and the schools as well as other institutions in the society have rather clear responsibilities. In a pluralistic democratic society, the process is more difficult and the effects are infinitely harder to measure, since there is always a certain amount of disagreement over basic political values. In spite of these difficulties, there is little doubt that the schools in the United States are deeply involved in political socialization.

The Curriculum

Significantly, it seems that much of the political socialization that occurs in the United States takes place at the elementary school level. Studies of political socialization which have concentrated on the development of political attitudes in children have indicated that values and attitudes in political learning are well established by the age of 14 and correspond closely to the political attitudes of adults.[9] Although there are many curricular patterns in the elementary school, most children are presented with materials and experiences which are designed to help them develop information on how the system works as well as to promote positive attitudes about the system. Where a planned and articulated social studies curriculum exists, it often follows a spiral pattern where young children are first introduced to the roles of various members of the family; then units are taught on "community helpers," in which the most idealistic aspects of these roles are presented. Governors and lawmakers typically are not criticized, nor is the substance of what they do critically analyzed. Rather, idealized models of governors and legislators are presented to the children. Leaders from the past or present are more often than not depicted as important people who have done or are doing important and significant things. Given this format, it would be unlikely that children who made it through the elementary grades would have anything but a positive attitude about the political system.[10] Indeed, it is possible that the manner in which formal political socialization of elementary school children is conducted may be responsible for at least some of the cynicism about the political system which is evident in many secondary school students.

Classroom Rituals

The school curriculum is not the only vehicle in the process of political socialization. In an excellent essay on political socialization, Dawson and Prewitt suggest that classroom rituals and the teacher are important instruments in political socialization.[11] Classroom rituals include the flag salute, patriotic songs, observance of national holidays and heroes' birthdays. The fact that these are group activities make them even more important. According to Dawson and Prewitt the classroom "approximates the 'we' feeling that is an important part of political culture." They suggest that national pride is "more meaningful when experienced as part of a collectivity."

The Teacher

The teacher is a central figure in political socialization. This is true according to Dawson and Prewitt since "the teacher is the first model of political authority the beginning student encounters. They compare the teacher to political authority in the community. "The teacher, like the policeman, president or mayor, is part of an institutional pattern, a constitutional order. . . ." The teacher is in a particularly powerful position since he or she decides what will be taught and the manner in which it will be presented. Yet the political values which are taught are predictable since the teacher is limited by the community on what "should" be taught. In the words of Dawson and Prewitt:

> Teachers should not, and generally do not use the classroom as a forum for discussion of partisan values and controversial positions. Democracy, the two-party system, free enterprise, basic freedoms, and so forth, are not only permissible subjects in the classroom; the teacher is expected to urge these beliefs on his students. Liberal or conservative positions, foreign policy views, party allegiances, on the other hand, are seen as partisan values; and the teacher generally is expected to avoid particular interpretations of such issues.[12]

The teacher also influences the political development of the student by establishing a "social system" in the classroom. They do this with classroom rules and by supporting the rules of the school. On a more specific level, in their thousands of exchanges with students during the course of a school day, they have opportunities to transmit political values. Dawson and Prewitt illustrate this by examining two major areas of politically relevant learning: obedience and competitiveness. In their words:

> Evidence from American elementary school children links the "lesson of obedience" more closely with political learning. Elementary teachers place more emphasis on compliance to rules and authority than any other "political" topic. Second and third grade teachers consider the obligation of the child to conform to school rules and laws of the community a more important lesson than reading and arithmetic. This concern with compliance appears to be characteristic of teachers of all elementary grades. At the same time that teachers emphasize compliance, they underemphasize the right of citizens to participate in government. . . .
>
> Competitiveness is another politically meaningful orientation learned in the classroom. The authors of a leading text book on education in the United States write: "The child learns that it is serious to fail, important to succeed, that the society disapproves of slow people and rewards fast ones." A simple fourth grade spelling contest conveys this lesson. Whether the student masters the intricacies of spelling or not he internalizes the cultural values of competitiveness and success. . . . [13]

The "conserving" nature of the teachers' role may be acceptable to most teachers. Harmon Zeigler's study of the *Political Life of American Teachers*,[14] confirms this. Zeigler sampled the political opinions of teachers in Oregon. He reported that teachers tended to be conservative in their political views. Zeigler also found that teachers who considered themselves conservative were very reluctant to express their own political values in the classroom. Teachers also seemed reluctant to deal with controversial political issues in the classroom. On the whole, Zeigler's conclusions depict teachers as being almost apolitical, reluctant to become involved in politics, not very active on the community level, and silent on political issues in the classroom. Some of this may have changed since Zeigler's study was conducted. The obvious political efforts of teachers at all levels of government and recent successes in local, state, and national politics may indicate that teachers' attitudes about political involvement are changing.

There is some evidence, however, that in spite of the fact that teachers are becoming more active politically, the way they view their classroom roles hasn't been seriously affected. In a study reported in *The High School Journal*, Stuart Palonsky[15] concluded that teachers continue to be very cautious in the classroom. He found that teachers "rarely discussed controversial political issues among themselves" and they repeatedly warned student teachers under their supervision to avoid dealing with political controversies in the classroom. It is possible, of course, that a sort of double standard exists. That is, teachers may be active within their own professional groups and, under the cloak of anonymity, within the teachers unions, as they work as a group for the election of candidates who will support the position of their organizations, but they may be extremely reluctant to use the classroom as a podium for expression of their own political views.

Student Government

Student government has long been justified by school administrators and teachers as an effective means for political socialization. Many claims have been made for it. Its warmest advocates claim that student government helps students learn about how the political process operates and that it provides students with an opportunity to learn how to function as active citizens in the political arena. Efforts have been made to make the process of student government as much like idealized representative democracy as possible, including secret ballots, democratic elections and democratic decision making.

Unfortunately student government does not work this way and the students know it. Instead of learning citizenship roles which might serve them as adults, what students learn is that they have little power. In the worst cases student government is little more than a tool of the school administration. In the best cases, decisions, democratically made, are not implemented. In his book, *Suburban Youth in Cultural Crisis*[16] Ralph Larkin titles a chapter on student government "The Politics of Meaninglessness." Larkin's study is made of a relatively trouble-free, middle-class suburban high school where he spent a great deal of time observing and discussing school with the students. As far as student government is concerned the school may be typical of most high schools in America.

In the school studied by Larkin, students had very little interest in or respect for student government. It was difficult to get students to participate. Few students voted. Students were apathetic about what the student council did. Those who served on the student council expressed frustration at their powerlessness— their lack of ability to do anything for the betterment of student conditions in the school. Those who served on the student council felt that they were controlled by outside forces. Not only did the school administration maintain control over their agenda, but conservative interest groups within the community kept them in check. Thus, what students learned in student government was not leadership and democratic decision making, but the powerlessness of students in the school setting. As a political socialization process, student government may be more an exercise in implementing administration policies and acting in conformity with influential community pressures than anything else. In most places student government continues to be what James Farber said it was in the sixties: "toy government."

A question one could ask about the role of the school in political socialization is: "How effective is it?" No clear answer to this question may be possible. There are too many variables involved. If one could specifically define the political socialization efforts of the school and somehow isolate what the school does from other forces, administer pretests and posttests on political attitudes to students who go through the system, some meaningful conclusions might be drawn. The difficulties in doing this are probably insurmountable. One can speculate, however, on the impact schooling has on political attitudes. For whatever reasons, the political system in the United States has been relatively stable. Illustrations of massive shifts in political opinion from what is popularly viewed as conservatism to liberalism and back again can be cited from the past. The phenomenon could be observed in the sixties and seventies. The decade of the sixties has been characterized as "liberal." Beginning with the late sixties and continuing through the early years of the eighties, the basic "conservatism" of the masses was heralded in the media. What the schools have to do with these pendulum swings is open to question. Efforts have been made by both conservative and liberal pressure groups to influence the schools to do things which depict their political views in a favorable light. Because of the bureaucratic nature of the schools and the general conservatism of school boards and school administrators, it has been easier for conservative groups to get a hearing. Viewing the wave of conservatism in America in the early eighties on the local, state, and national levels, it is tempting to conclude that these forces have been effective in their efforts. However, if the past can provide any guidance for the future, it is unlikely that either conservatism or liberalism is in any way a permanent feature of our society. Political opinions seem to be influenced more by national and international problems—and to a great extent by the treatment of these problems in the media—than they are by the schools.

Thus, although the schools may have very little to do with socialization in the direction of political activism, or political orientations on a liberal/conservative continuum on specific issues at specific times, they still may exert great influence in socializing children to support the basic system. One cannot avoid the conclusion that the schools have played some role in the stability of the system. That is, they have socialized citizens to the values of a "democratic" system. Americans say they believe in individualism, justice, freedom, equality, the Constitution, and the party system, even though they may have widely differing views of what these things mean.

RELIGIOUS SOCIALIZATION

Although the Supreme Court, in a number of cases, has decreed that there should be a "wall of separation" between church and state and that the public schools should be free of specific denominational religious influences, it has been difficult in this society to eliminate religious socialization from the public schools. From the beginning, the public schools appeared to accept the idea that one of their central purposes was the moral training of the young. Throughout most of our history, parents have assumed that it was proper for the schools to be involved in moral training, and this usually has meant that teachers who socialized children to accept the ideals of Christian morality received in most communities the overwhelming support of parents.

Beginning with the Massachusetts School Law of 1647, which expressed the fear that "ye old deluder, Satan" would get control of the children of the colony through the "clever device of keeping children ignorant of the words of the Scripture," and continuing until very recently, the schools seemed to have a clear mandate for religious socialization. This tradition has continued throughout much of our history. Ruth Elson, in her comprehensive analysis of American school-books in the nineteenth century, flatly states: "The purpose of nineteenth century American public schools was to train citizens in character and proper principles."[17] Elson observes that school textbook writers were "much more concerned with the child's moral development than with the development of his mind."[18] She declares that secular books for school children simply didn't exist in the nineteenth century. A "sense of God permeates all books" regardless of the subject matter. Spelling books used the Bible for basic reading material—indeed, Webster's popular "Speller" included at least one sentence on religion in every group of practice sentences. Even geography books warmly advocated Protestant Christianity, insisting in one case that "there can be only one true belief." Elson cites the following from Woodbridge's Geography (1866): "[True religion] . . . is found in its truth and purity only where it is derived from divine revelation. This was given to our first parents, and again to Noah. . . . It was renewed in the Mosaic or Jewish religion, and was developed in its perfect form in the Christian religion."[19] Similar illustrations can be found in other nineteenth-century school-books.

Moreover, it was not simply religion which was taught by the schoolbooks, but Protestantism. "Catholicism is depicted not only as a false religion, but as a positive danger to the state; it subverts good government, sound morals, and education."[20] Catholicism was blamed in some books for the Fall of the Roman Empire and for the "superstition" of the Middle Ages. The Roman Catholic popes were universally condemned.

Nor were textbooks the only way in which children were socialized to a specific Protestant Christian morality. Well into the twentieth century, teachers who were employed in local schools were expected to support mainstream religious beliefs. Often their contracts stipulated that they teach a Sunday School class. Their religious views and practices were open to scrutiny by administrators and school board members.

In addition to teachers and textbooks, other forms of religious socialization have been common in the public schools. Bible reading and school prayers, in spite of court decisions banning them, continue to exist in some public schools. Singing religious hymns, offering courses on the Bible, employing ministers as teachers, and observing and celebrating Christian holy days and baccalaureate exercises were long-established practices in many public schools.

Of course, minority religious groups protested, and all of these efforts at religious socialization found their way into the courts. Although the decisions of the U.S. Supreme Court on issues involving religious practices in the schools have been highly publicized, state courts have a long history of action in this area. In many states, the state constitutions are more restrictive than the U.S. Constitution. A sample of these cases should give the reader some idea of the extensive nature of religious practices in the schools and the long, intensive efforts to free the schools of these practices. In Florida and New Jersey, the courts have ruled that Gideon Bibles could not be distributed in the schools.[21] Long before the Supreme Court became involved in the issue, state courts in several states ruled, as early as 1890, that Bible reading and school prayers were violations of state laws and constitutional provisions.[22] In 1902 the Nebraska Supreme Court ruled that public school teachers could not sing religious hymns in the classrooms.[23] In 1918 the Washington State Supreme Court would not allow a public high school to give academic credit to students who took a Bible course outside of school.[24] However, in Indiana, New York, and New Mexico, the courts have ruled that it was all right for the schools to employ ministers, nuns, and other religious officials as public school teachers.[25] On the observances of holy days and baccalaureate exercises, the courts have a mixed record, sometimes allowing them and at other times prohibiting them.[26]

The Supreme Court of the United States has dealt with the issue of religion in schools in a large number of cases and has been fairly consistent in its view that specific religious teaching and practices designed to promote denominational religious views are a violation of the First Amendment clause that "Congress shall make no law respecting an establishment of religion or prohibiting the free exercise thereof." Although this amendment clearly applies to a limitation on the national government only, it has been applied to the states through the use of the Fourteenth Amendment's due process clause. Although many cases could be cited to illustrate the manner in which the Court has applied the religious clause of the First Amendment, *Abington School District v. Schempp* (1963) is especially important since it is comprehensive in its analysis of the issue of religious practices in schools and since the dissent by Justice Stewart neatly summarizes some of the more serious objections to the Court's interpretation of the First Amendment as it applies to religion and the schools:

Abington School District v. Schempp
374 US 203 (1963)

Mr. Justice Clark delivered the opinion of the Court.

Once again we are called upon to consider the scope of the provision of the First Amendment to the United States Constitution which declares that "Congress shall make no law respecting an establishment of religion, or prohibiting the free exercise thereof." ... These companion cases present the issues in the context of state action requiring that schools begin each day with readings from the Bible. ... In light of the history of the First Amendment and of our cases interpreting and applying its requirements, we hold that the practices at issue and the laws requiring them are unconstitutional under the establishment clause, as applied to the states through the Fourteenth Amendment.

The Facts in Each Case: ... The Commonwealth of Pennsylvania by law, ... requires that "At least ten verses from the Holy Bible shall be read, without comment, at the opening of each public school on each school day. Any child shall be excused from such Bible reading, or attending such Bible reading, upon the written request of his parent or guardian." The Schempp family, husband and wife and two of their three children, brought suit to enjoin enforcement of the statute, contending that their rights under the Fourteenth Amendment of the Constitution of the United States are, have been, and will continue to be violated unless this statute be declared unconstitutional as violative of the provisions of the First Amendment. . . .

On each school day at the Abington Senior High School between 8:15 and 8:30 a.m., while the pupils are attending their home rooms or advisory sections, opening exercises are conducted pursuant to the statute. The exercises are broadcast into each room in the school building through an intercommunications system and are conducted under the supervision of a teacher by students attending the school's radio and television workshop. Selected students from this course gather each morning in the school's workshop studio for the exercises, which include reading by one of the students of ten verses of the Holy Bible, broadcast to each room in the building. This is followed by the recitation of the Lord's Prayer, likewise over the intercommunications system, but also by the students in the various classrooms, who are asked to stand and join in repeating the prayer in unison. The exercises are closed with the flag salute and such pertinent announcements as are of interest to the students. Participation in the opening exercises, as directed by the statute, is voluntary. The student reading the verses from the Bible may select the passages and read from any version he chooses, although the only copies furnished by the school are the King James version, copies of which were circulated to each teacher by the school district. . . . The students and parents are advised that the student may absent himself from the classroom or, should he elect to remain, not participate in the exercises. . . .

At the first trial Edward Schempp and the children testified as to specific religious doctrines purveyed by the literal reading of the Bible "which were contrary to the religious beliefs which they held and to their familial teaching." . . . The children testified that all of the doctrines to which they referred were read to them at various times as part of the exercises. Edward Schempp testified at the second trial that he had considered having Roger and Donna excused from attendance at the exercises but decided against it for several reasons, including his belief that the children's relationship with their teachers and classmates would be adversely affected. . . .

In 1905 the Board of School Commissioners of Baltimore City adopted a rule pursuant to Act 77, section 202 of the Annotated Code of Maryland. The rule provided for the holding of opening exercises in the schools of the city, consisting primarily of the "reading, without comment, of a chapter in the Holy Bible and/or the use of the Lord's Prayer." The petitioners, Mrs. Madalyn Murray and her son, William J. Murray III, are both professed atheists. Following unsuccessful attempts to have the respondent school board rescind the rule, this suit was filed for mandamus to compel its rescission and cancellation. It was alleged that William was a student in a public school of the city and Mrs. Murray, his mother, was a taxpayer therein; that it was the practice under the rule to have a reading on each school morning from the King James version of the Bible; that at petitioners' insistence the rule was amended to permit children to be excused pursuant thereto; that nevertheless the rule as amended was in violation of the petitioners' rights "to freedom of religion under the First and Fourteenth Amendments" and in violation of "the principle of separation between church and state, contained therein . . ." The petition particularized the petitioners' atheistic beliefs and stated that the rule, as practiced, violated their rights

> in that it threatens their religious liberty by placing a premium on belief as against nonbelief and subjects their freedom of conscience to the rule of the majority; it pronounces belief in God as the source of all moral and spiritual values, equating

these values with religious values, and thereby renders sinister, alien and suspect the beliefs and ideals of your petitioners, promoting doubt and question of their morality, good citizenship and good faith. . . .

In *Everson v. Board of Educ.* . . . this court, through Mr. Justice Black, stated that the "scope of the First Amendment . . . was designed forever to suppress" the establishment of religion or the prohibition of the free exercise thereof. In short, the court held that the amendment "requires the state to be neutral in its relations with groups of religious believers and nonbelievers; it does not require the state to be their adversary. State power is no more to be used so as to handicap religions than it is to favor them . . ."

Finally, in *Engel v. Vitale*, only last year, these principles were so universally recognized that the court, without the citation of a single case and over the sole dissent of Mr. Justice Stewart, reaffirmed them. . . . It held that "it is no part of the business of government to compose official prayers for any groups of the American people to recite as a part of a religious program carried on by government."

In both cases the laws require religious exercises and such exercises are being conducted in direct violation of the rights of the appellees and petitioners. Nor are these required exercises mitigated by the fact that individual students may absent themselves upon parental request, for that fact furnishes no defense to a claim of unconstitutionality under the establishment clause. . . . Further, it is no defense to urge that the religious practices here may be relatively minor encroachments on the First Amendment. The breach of neutrality that is today a trickling stream may all too soon become a raging torrent and, in the words of Madison, "it is proper to take alarm at the first experiment on our liberties. . . ."

It is insisted that unless these religious exercises are permitted a "religion of secularism" is established in the schools. We agree of course that the state may not establish a "religion of secularism" in the sense of affirmatively opposing or showing hostility to religion, thus "preferring those who believe in no religion over those who do believe." . . . We do not agree, however, that this decision in any sense has that effect. In addition, it might well be said that one's education is not complete without a study of comparative religion or the history of religion and its relationship to the advancement of civilization. It certainly may be said that the Bible is worthy of study for its literary and historic qualities. Nothing we have said here indicates that such study of the Bible or of religion, when presented objectively as part of a secular program of education, may not be effected consistently with the First Amendment. But the exercises here do not fall into those categories. They are religious exercises, required by the states in violation of the command of the First Amendment that the government maintain strict neutrality, neither aiding nor opposing religion.

Finally, we cannot accept that the concept of neutrality, which does not permit a state to require a religious exercise even with the consent of the majority of those affected, collides with the majority's right to free exercise of religion. While the free exercise clause clearly prohibits the use of state action to deny the rights of free exercise to anyone, it has never meant that a majority could use the machinery of the state to practice its beliefs.

The place of religion in our society is an exalted one, achieved through a long tradition of reliance on the home, the church and the inviolable citadel of the individual heart and mind. We have come to recognize through bitter experience that it is not within the power of government to invade that citadel, whether its purpose or effect be to aid or oppose, to advance or retard. In the relationship between man and religion, the state is firmly committed to a position of neutrality.

[Concurring opinions by Justices Douglas, Goldberg, and Brennan are omitted.]

Mr. Justice Stewart, dissenting.

I think the records in the two cases before us are so fundamentally deficient as to make impossible an informed or responsible determination of the constitutional issues presented. Specifically, I cannot agree that on these records we can say that the establishment clause has necessarily been violated. But I think there exist serious questions under both that provision and the free exercise clause—insofar as each is imbedded in the Fourteenth Amendment—which require the remand of these cases for the taking of additional evidence.

The First Amendment declares that "Congress shall make no law respecting an establishment of religion, or prohibiting the free exercise thereof. ..." It is, I think, a fallacious oversimplification to regard these two provisions as establishing a single constitutional standard of "separation of church and state," which can be mechanically applied in every case to delineate the required boundaries between government and religion. ...

Unlike other First Amendment guarantees, there is an inherent limitation upon the applicability of the establishment clause's ban on state support to religion. That limitation was succinctly put in ... "State power is no more to be used so as to handicap religions than it is to favor them." And in a later case, this court recognized that the limitation was one which was itself compelled by the free exercise guarantee. ...

It might be argued here that parents who wanted their children to be exposed to religious influences in school could ... send their children to private or parochial schools. But the consideration which renders this contention too facile to be determinative has already been recognized by the court: "Freedom of speech, freedom of the press, freedom of religion are available to all, not merely to those who can pay their own way."

It might also be argued that parents who want their children exposed to religious influences can adequately fulfill that wish off school property and outside school time. With all its surface persuasiveness, however, this argument seriously misconceives the basic constitutional justification for permitting the exercises at issue in these cases. For a compulsory state educational system so structures a child's life that if religious exercises are held to be an impermissible activity in schools, religion is placed at an artificial and state-created disadvantage. Viewed in this light, permission of such exercises for those who want them is necessary if the schools are truly to be neutral in the matter of religion. And a refusal to permit religious exercises thus is seen, not as the realization of state neutrality, but rather as the establishment of a religion of secularism, or at the least, as government support of the beliefs of those who think that religious exercises should be conducted only in private.

In *Abington v. Schempp*, the Court was careful to point out that it was not ruling against the study of religion in the schools but only against specific religious practices which were a violation of the First Amendment. The majority opinion emphasized that the schools must be neutral in matters of religion, while it pointed out that their decision in no way affected the use of the Bible or the study of religion as part of a "secular program of education" which was permissible in the schools. The Court insisted that the First Amendment meant that the government should "maintain strict neutrality, neither aiding nor opposing religion."

"Secular" education and "strict neutrality" for the schools were, and continue to be in many communities, ideas which had not occurred to teachers and school officials. Even in the *Schempp* dissent, Justice Stewart was concerned about what he saw as a conflict between the "establishment" and "free exercise" clauses of the First Amendment. In Stewart's view, denying religious practices for the majority on the grounds that it violated the establishment clause got in the way of their free exercise of religious beliefs. He felt that compulsory state education "so structures a child's life that if religious exercises are held to be impermissible activity in the schools, religion is placed at an artificial and state-created disadvantage."

Which view is correct depends, of course, upon who is arguing the issue. The majority decision is clear enough. Religious exercises of any kind which are sponsored by the school, and thus have the official stamp of state approval upon them, are a violation of the First Amendment. Although many schools observe the Court decisions, there are many who refuse to accept them, and years after *Schempp*, it is not difficult to find schools in which religious practices continue to be part of the school day. This is understandable in view of the fact that moral training in the schools often meant specific religious teaching, and the schools have been engaged in these activities for more than a century. Moreover, in many local communities people take their religion very seriously, and the schools continue to socialize to narrow and specific religious views. For some, "secularism" is a religion in itself.

Even where religious education has been thrown out of the schools by the courts, moral education has not. Indeed, after the court decisions of the early sixties, the schools seemed to experience a boom in something variously called "moral education" or "values education." Where religious education was eliminated, a genuine gap existed. In a sense, the court decisions opened the door for a new wave of moral training which became, ironically in many cases, more comprehensive in its socialization efforts than the old programs in religion were. To fill the gap left by the elimination of religious practices and to ameliorate dissatisfied parents, new programs on religious studies have been developed. Almost universally, these programs claim objectivity—they give "equal time" to Christians, Jews, and Buddhists.[27]

In addition, new programs on moral education and values analysis have been introduced. Many of these programs rely heavily on the work of Lawrence Kohlberg and Erik Erikson,[28] both of whom were greatly concerned with the development of moral character in school children and claimed "objectivity" in their approaches. Although it is not the intent of this chapter to detail the work of Kohlberg and Erikson, both make basic assumptions about "consensus moral values" which exist in society. Of course, when one engages in a deep search for "consensus" values in a predominantly Christian society, the results tend to reflect something very similar to Christian morality. Although the reader might disagree, the same might be said of other specific approaches to "values education." The early efforts were so popular with public school people that they had many imitators. A wide range of choices exists for materials which teach about morals and values.[29] Thus, the notion that the schools should be involved in the development of honest and just and fair-minded citizens is still very much alive.

Although morals education, character education, and values education are not religious education, they tend toward the same general goal. There is, of course, a great deal of difference in practice between the socialization of children toward a narrow and specific denomination and an attempt to get children to examine their own beliefs in terms of the teachings of the great religions. There is a great difference between attempting to teach children that the Bible contains the "truth," and leading children in the study of man's search for universal principles. However, at the risk of stretching a point too far, both are generally concerned with socializing children to "acceptable" behavior. Both are concerned with attempting to get children to understand that in civilized society there are limits and restrictions on human behavior. Few would question that the schools have a role in developing civilized human beings. How the schools approach this problem has become an important and controversial issue.

THE HIDDEN CURRICULUM

Overt, planned, and official efforts of the schools to socialize students may have much less impact on the socialization of students than the so-called hidden curriculum—the unofficial curriculum of every school. It is made up of the rules and regulations and classroom practices which often comprise the real world of the student. Very often it is the student's ability to conform to or simply to learn what is expected of him from teachers and other school officials which spells success or failure in school—not his ability to perform well in the official curriculum.[30]

Jules Henry illustrated the direct relationship between the formal curriculum and the hidden curriculum in the story of Boris, who was participating in a fifth-grade oral math lesson:

> At last, when Boris is unable to solve the problem the teacher turns to the class and says: "Well, who can tell Boris what the number is?" There is a forest of hands and the teacher calls on Peggy who says that 4 should be divided into both the numerator and denominator. It is obvious that Boris's failure made it possible for Peggy to succeed, and, since the excited handwaving of the children indicated that they wanted to exploit Boris' predicament or succeed where he was failing, it appears that at least some of these children were learning how to hope (covertly) for the failure of a fellow student.[31]

Henry provides us with several other illustrations of the manner in which the hidden curriculum operates in the elementary school. He is particularly harsh in his description of classroom singing. He suggests that most classroom teachers who have "song periods" teach children to "sing off key." He describes one classroom he visited where children were singing songs of Ireland and her neighbors. Children were asked to pick songs they wanted to sing, and they competed with each other for the teacher's attention so that, through the teacher, they could get the rest of the class to sing the songs they wanted to sing. Henry didn't think the exercise had anything to do with learning to sing, or, for that matter, with learning anything about the songs of Ireland. Instead, in Henry's words: "The net result was to activate the competitive, achievement, and dominance drives of the children, as they strove with one another for the teacher's attention, and through her, to get the class to do what they wanted it to do."[32] Those who were called upon were those who were quick to raise their hands and waved them enthusiastically for the teacher's attention. Henry observes: "In the first and second grades teachers constantly scold children because they do not raise their hands enough —the prime symbol of having learned what school is all about."[33] What this teaches children, according to Henry, is to extort the "maximal benefit for the Self from *any* situation."

In another illustration, the teacher, rather than asking someone in class to please hang up a visitor's coat, instead asks: "Who will hang up the visitor's coat?" Every hand in class goes up. The lesson this taught, according to Henry, was that every child in class be given an opportunity to "communicate to the teacher his eagerness to please her in front of company."[34]

Classroom games also teach strange things, according to Henry. He observed the game "spelling baseball," in which the two best spellers in the room choose up sides and a word is "pitched" to each "batter." If the "batter" spells the word correctly, he has a safe hit; if he fails to spell the word, he has a strike. The winning team is the one which scores the most "runs." Henry observes that baseball is "bizarrely *irrelevant* to spelling." He suggests that words become detached from their "real significance and become assimilated to baseballs." But according to Henry, it teaches important lessons because the game promotes absurd associations and provides an "indispensable bridge between the larger culture where doubletalk is supreme." It provides also an introduction to those "associations of mutually irrelevant ideas so well known to us from advertising—girls and vodka gimlets, people and billiard balls, lipstick and tree-houses, et cetera. . . . "[35] It also teaches a number of other "valuable lessons": competition and approval among peers, approval of authority, and teamwork.

Henry observes that in many classrooms noise is more important than the curriculum. He explains that "progressive" and enlightened teachers seem to feel that a quiet classroom can be achieved only through placing restraint on the natural impulses of students. Such teachers are reluctant to maintain "old fashioned" order and discipline in the classroom. They assume the role of an affectionate and benevolent parent and achieve control by withholding affection from the student. Although written two decades ago, Henry's observations of classroom climate are still valid in many classrooms.

> Today our emphasis on impulse release, spontaneity, and creativity goes hand in hand
> with culture-weariness, a certain tiredness and disillusionment with impulse restraint,

and a feeling that the Self has been sold down the river. In these circumstances permissiveness has invaded many phases of work with children, so that in some schools there is a great relaxation of controls, the essential nightmare is impaired, and the teacher most highly regarded is the one who lets children be free. Of course, it is the *adult* Self that is really straining to be free. . . .[36]

Dispensing affection and withholding it as a means of classroom control has its limits, which both the teacher and the students understand. The teacher cannot become too attached to the students or vice versa, since their stay in any classroom is limited. According to Henry, the classroom climate of affection is "a kind of mutual conspiracy of affectivity in which children and teacher hold themselves aloof, neither giving nor demanding more than the tacit rules permit." If this were not so, children would have to be "dragged shrieking from grade to grade, for they would become too deeply attached to teachers." This is one of the first lessons a child has to learn in kindergarten or the first grade. "From this regular replacement-in-affection they learn that the affection-giving figure, the teacher, is replaceable also."[37] Henry suggests that this is the way in which children learn "uninvolvement": they are effectively weaned from the social system. Additionally, they "learn the symbols of affectivity; that they can be used ambiguously, and that they are not binding—that they can be scattered upon the world without commitment." This, Henry observes, is functional because it provides "indispensable training . . . for the release of impulse for the buddy-buddy relations of contemporary business, government, and university."[38]

Not only is there a relationship between the hidden curriculum and the adult world, but there is an important relationship between the hidden curriculum and the formal curriculum of the school. Phillip Jackson describes that relationship:

> Two or three important observations might be made about the relationship between these two curriculums. One is that the reward system of the school is tied to both. Indeed, many of the rewards and punishments that sound as if they are being dispensed on the basis of academic success and failure are really more closely related to the mastery of the hidden curriculum. Consider, for instance, the common teaching practice of giving a student credit for trying. What do teachers mean when they say a student tries to do his work?
>
> They mean, in essence, that he complies with the procedural expectations of the institution. He does his homework . . . , he raises his hand during class discussion (though he usually comes up with the wrong answer), he keeps his nose in his book during free study period (though he does not turn the page very often), he is, in other words, a "model" student, though not necessarily a good one. . . .[39]

Jackson points out that there is another side to this coin. The student not only can succeed in the hidden curriculum, he also can fail. According to Jackson, when the student is having serious academic problems, the "demands of the hidden curriculum lurk in the shadows." In Jackson's words:

> When Johnny's parents are summoned to school because their son is not doing too well in arithmetic, what explanation will be given for their son's poor performance? More than likely blame will be placed on motivational deficiencies in Johnny rather than on his intellectual shortcomings. The teacher may even go so far as to say that

Johnny is unmotivated during arithmetic period. But what does this mean? It means, in essence, that Johnny does not even try, and not trying ... often boils down to a failure to comply with the institutional expectations, a failure to master the hidden curriculum.[40]

Most students and perhaps many teachers would agree with Jackson that:

As the student learns to live in school, he learns to subjugate his own desires to the will of the teacher and to subdue his own actions in the interest of the common good. He learns to be passive and to acquiesce to the network of rules, regulations, and routines in which he is imbedded. He learns to tolerate petty frustrations and to accept the plans and policies of higher authorities, even when their rationale is unexplained and their meaning unclear.[41]

What this means to the student in an extreme case is eloquently expressed in the following poem:

About School

He always wanted to say things. But no one understood.
He always wanted to explain things. But no one cared.
So he drew.

Sometimes he would just draw and it wasn't anything. He wanted to carve it in stone or write it in the sky.
He would lie out on the grass and look up in the sky and it would be only him and the sky and the things inside that needed saying.

And it was after that, that he drew the picture. It was a beautiful picture. He kept it under the pillow and would let no one see it.
And he would look at it every night and think about it. And when it was dark, and his eyes were closed, he could still see it.
And it was all of him. And he loved it.

When he started school he brought it with him. Not to show anyone, but just to have with him like a friend.

It was funny about school.
He sat in a square, brown desk like all the other square, brown desks and he thought it should be red.
And his room was a square, brown room. Like all the other rooms. And it was tight and close. And stiff.

He hated to hold the pencil and the chalk, with his arm stiff and his feet flat on the floor, stiff, with the teacher watching and watching.
And then he had to write numbers. And they weren't anything. They were worse than the letters that could be something if you put them together.
And the numbers were tight and square and he hated the whole thing.

The teacher came and spoke to him. She told him to wear a tie like all the other boys. He said he didn't like them and she said it didn't matter.
After that they drew. And he drew all yellow and it was the way he felt about morning. And it was beautiful.

The teacher came and smiled at him. "What's this?" she said. "Why don't you draw
    something like Ken's drawing?
Isn't that beautiful?"
It was all questions.

After that his mother bought him a tie and he always drew airplanes and rocket ships
    like everyone else.
And he threw the old picture away.
And when he lay out alone looking at the sky, it was big and blue and all of everything,
    but he wasn't anymore.
He was square inside and brown, and his hands were stiff, and he was like anyone else.
    And the thing inside him that needed saying didn't need saying anymore.

It had stopped pushing. It was crushed. Stiff.
Like everything else.

—Anonymous[42]

Much of what has been written in recent years is critical of the hidden curriculum. Indeed, much of the criticism comes from the Marxists, who charge that the hidden curriculum is really a reflection of the capitalist goals and ideology which they find oppressive. They charge that what the hidden curriculum really teaches is the values of corporate society. Thus, Giroux and Penna argue that since schooling is "a function of dominant socio-economic values" and those values reflect the values of corporate America, schools cannot be judged independent of those values.[43]

> What the hidden curriculum teaches is subordination to authority, where the child views the teacher as the boss who in turn sees the principal as the boss. It is in the school where the working class student learns his role in society. They learn they are powerless and that they don't know anything. The graded system teaches them about the hierarchy and keeps them in their place. Teachers reward students who conform to beliefs and values which support the system. The classroom is like a miniature factory system where rewards are extrinsic and "all social interactions between teachers and students are mediated by hierarchically organized structures.[44]

A discussion of the hidden curriculum would not be complete without a word on competitive sports. Although the competitive sports program in the secondary schools has been institutionalized and formalized, the values taught by the program and the manner in which competitive athletics are conducted may be a major socializing force in most secondary schools. Not much has changed since Jules Henry wrote the following about athletics in "Rome High School" in 1963:

> the athletic complex is the natural pivot of social life, school politics, and the competitive sexual ritual, where a girl measures her success by the athletes she dates.[45]

If anything, the deification of sports through the vehicle of television has intensified their importance throughout the society and especially in the schools. Many school districts have built incredible monuments to organized athletics in the form of huge gyms and football stadiums. Rarely do requests for expansion of these facilities and programs go unanswered. Much of the school week is devoted in some manner or other to the sports program. It is not difficult to find schools where the major topic of discussion in class and in the halls is the feats of the athletes during the previous Friday night game. As the week progresses, attention is turned to the upcoming rivalry. Activities are planned around Friday night's game. Teachers are organized to perform duties at the game; students meet to consider ways in which they can support their team. Athletes are excused from class to spend time nursing their injuries in the whirlpools. If the game is really important, the entire team may leave class early for extra practice. Teachers and students understand sympathetically why Friday night's "stars" do not have their homework. By game day, interest and enthusiasm have reached a fever pitch. The entire school is caught up in it. There are cheerleaders roaming the halls in uniform; there is always a "pep assembly" for which classes are dismissed. During this ritual the coaches and players are given special and often worshipful recognition. There is nothing like it in any other program the schools offer. Every aspect of the school program is affected. Pep clubs are organized; student government is often liberally sprinkled with sports "stars"; teachers and parents are solicited to help with the big show.

What this teaches is obvious. Competition builds character, winning is important, being on the team is more important than learning anything, teachers who support this madness are more popular than those who don't, and the ultimate success is a college sports scholarship where the whole process begins anew.[46] Finally, the lad who makes it as a regular on the Dallas Cowboys would be as widely acclaimed as some local medical student who found a cure for cancer. This is the world of the hidden curriculum, obviously as important as the regular curriculum—if not more so—in the socialization process.

THE PEER GROUP

The peer group may very well be the most important single institution in the socialization of children. The peer group may be defined as a specific circle of friends which develops its own rules—implicit or explicit—and has "its own organization; and its own expectations for group members."[47] From a very early age children develop friendship patterns which constitute social groupings within the classroom and the school. Usually by the time children reach the sixth or seventh grade, these groups are fairly well defined and they constitute a sort of subculture within the school, with each group having its own rites of initiation, often its own language, and its own acceptable pattern of behavior.

Much research has been done on factors which account for peer selection and association, and, as one might expect, researchers have found that group association patterns have been based on similar attitudes, personalities, abilities, family economic status, age, and physical attractiveness.[48]

Studies of peer groups in the early sixties suggested that there was a kind of duality in peer groups, with most groups being sensitive to some direction and a certain respect for adult authority. Parsons suggested this in *Social Structure and*

Personality, in which he claimed that "the most conspicuous feature of the youth peer group is a duality of orientation."[49] Parsons saw a duality in which there was a "compulsive independence in relation to certain adult expectations," but "on the other hand, within the group, there tends to be a fiercely compulsive conformity, a sharp loyalty to the group, an insistence on the literal observance of its norms, and punishment of deviance."[50] To some extent this duality continues to exist. Some groups are, in fact, formed by adults, and members conform to adult expectations. In this category Havighurst lists neighborhood play groups "under the watchful eyes of mothers," organized boys clubs, or Hi-Y groups under the leadership of a teacher.[51]

There is some evidence, however, that these groups have become less important in recent years. Even as Parsons was making his observations as long ago as the early sixties, Bowerman and Kinch, in a study of Seattle school children, reported that the seventh grade was a turning point for most children. Before the seventh grade, children looked mainly to their parents as models, companions, and guides to behavior; after that, their peers had a much greater influence.[52] Ten years later, Condry and Siman found that this turning away from parents took place at an even earlier age, in some cases as early as the fifth grade.[53] In her study of a single middle school in 1975, Judy Love found that there wasn't a high correlation between parental peer associations and groupings found in seventh-grade children.[54] Apparently the increase in working mothers and single-parent families and the heralded "breakdown of the American family" as a socializing agent have tended to increase in the United States the influence of peer groups as a major instrument in socialization.

Havighurst suggests that most peer groups are characterized as groups in which each member is substantially equal, relationships tend to be transitory, and the group's influence increases with age.[55] Within the peer group there exists a sort of rough equality. There are leaders, to be sure, but the group tends to be open and possesses common views on dress, language, and attitudes about school, teachers, administrators, and other students inside and outside the group. As Havighurst points out, these relationships may be intense but also transitory in nature. It is not uncommon for young children, especially, to change groups as their interests change and develop. As the child matures, the peer group tends to become more important as a socializing agency, to the point where the desire to belong or to "be like other kids" becomes almost an obsession. In Havighurst's words: "In adolescence, the peer group takes a certain precedence in many ways over any other group that influences the individual."

Not only are peer groups important in adolescence, but in large schools the adolescent has a wide range of choices among these groups. Every high school student and most experienced teachers know this, even though researchers have had difficulty determining this basic fact of life in large high schools. As Jere Cohen points out: "Voluminous analysis of adolescence has failed to generate consensus on a very basic fact—the number of adolescent subcultures."[56] He points out that a number of researchers have found a single adolescent subculture, while others have insisted that there are several. Clark found three major subcultures in the high school, which he characterized as the "fun" subculture of dates, cars, drinking, and athletics; an "academic" subculture of serious students; and a "delinquent subculture" which rebels against the system and is associated with "negativism, hedonism and violence."[57] Although Clark's general model may encompass a large number of students in a large high school, it may not be adequate for most contemporary American high schools. There appears to be many more groups than this.

In the late seventies and early eighties, the author of this book asked several hundred college sophomores in a large lecture class in *School and American Society* to name the groups they could remember from their high school experience. Those who had attended small schools and rural schools generally listed three or four groups which had very specific characteristics and great influence over the lives of the membership, but those from larger schools (500 or more students) had much longer lists. Interestingly, the small town and rural students agreed that the three or four groups they listed tended to reflect the socioeconomic divisions within the community. Those from larger schools agreed that not only were there many more subcultures within their schools, but there were many more groups in the school than they perceived in the community. Students who had experienced life in the larger schools felt that membership within the groups did not reflect the adult groupings within the community. That is, the criteria for admission and retention within the adolescent groups were different than those for the parent groups. For example, the "jocks" or the "drug freaks" might include membership from the country club crowd and the ghetto. The following list includes some of the high school groups identified by the college sophomores and a rough definition of each:

The "Soshes" or "Snobs"	Kids who think they are "better than anybody else."
The "Jocks"	School athletes or those who "run around with them."
The "Cheerleaders"	The cheerleaders and their circle of friends—"those who want to be cheerleaders."
The "Academics," called variously: "Brains," "Bookworms," "Teachers' Pets" (depending on the group naming them)	Kids who study all the time and get "A's."
Farm kids or "Cowboys," variously called "Goat Ropers," "Red Necks," or "Kickers"	Kids who wear cowboy hats and boots and chew "skoal" and drive pick-ups.
"Band Freaks"	Kids who play in the school band.

"Hot Rods" or "greasers"	Kids who would like to drive expensive cars but have junkers and are always under them.
"Nerds" or "Nobodys"	Those who don't seem to belong anywhere—"loners."
"Hippies," "Freaks," or "Druggers"	The drug subculture.
"Ethnics"	Blacks and other minorities.

This is only a partial list, but it provides an illustration of the great variety of peer groups which can exist in a large high school. Although these groups were not considered totally exclusive since there was some dual membership and some inter-relationships among them, many were fairly exclusive. A "sosh" would not be caught dead associating with a "greaser" and vice versa.

Although it may be difficult to generalize about the character and number of peer groups which exist in any school, there can be little doubt about their importance to students. In very many cases, the need to belong to an identifiable group is the most important thing in the student's life. The group tends to give meaning to existence. It is doubtful that many adolescents arise in the morning and look forward with great enthusiasm to their English Lit class. They are excited about meeting their friends, however. Peer groups tend to have a life of their own, related to the school experience but in many ways independent of it—certainly independent of the adults within the school setting. Each group develops its own meeting place which is eagerly sought out by members upon their arrival at school. The structure of the group is informal, and the substance of interaction is spontaneous and essentially disorganized. Leadership tends to be floating; however, certain members may be admired more or have more clout than other members. When group action is undertaken (varying from wandering aimlessly through the halls to some direct activity such as disrupting a teacher's class), it is often spontaneous or planned on the "spur of the moment." Planned or spontaneous activity shared by the peer group very often extends beyond the school day. Incredibly, in most schools teachers and school officials take little note of these groups unless they are engaged in an activity which somehow violates school rules—incredible, because the groups are so vital to the students.

Peer groups are important to students not only because they provide the students' major form of human association, but also because of their socialization function. In most schools, it is to the peer group that students look for direction and approval, at least during adolescence. Being disapproved of by teachers or principals can be survived. Being rejected by one's peers is a fate worse than death. Indeed, in some of the peer groups, a condition of acceptance may very well be gaining the disapproval of teachers or other school officials.

This explains why some individuals who are in fact alienated from school continue to attend. An excellent insight into how such alienated groups feel and operate is provided in a study of the Hammertown Grammar School in England, reported by Paul Willis. The following poem cited by Willis illustrates the group's values and the extent of their alienation from society:

On a night we go out on
the street
Troubling other people,
I suppose we're anti-social,
But we enjoy it.
The older generation
They don't like our hair,
Or the clothes we wear
They seem to like running
us down,
I don't know what I would
do if I didn't have the gang.[58]

Willis was studying a group of working class "lads" who found school a crashing bore, but who nonetheless attended (when they weren't skipping) more because it was a gathering place than for any other reason. The importance of the group and its values are further revealed in the following discussion recorded by Willis:

Will: . . . we see each other every day, don't we, at school . . .

Joey: That's it, we've developed certain ways of talking, certain ways of acting, and we developed disregards for Pakis, Jamaicans and all different . . . for all the scrubs and the fucking ear'oles (Teachers) and all that . . . We're getting to know it now, like we're getting to know all the cracks, like, how to get out of lessons and things, and we know where to have a crafty smoke. You can come over here to the youth wing and do summat, and er'm . . . all your friends are here, you know, it's sort of what's there, what's always going to be there for next year, like, and you know you have to come to school today, if you're feeling bad, your mate'll soon cheer yer up like, 'cos you couldn't go without ten minutes in this school without having a laff at something or other.[59]

Although this is a description of English "working class lads" who are clearly alienated from the system, its message is pretty universal. Although the substance of the group activity and the subject of its discussions may vary, the form probably does not. Even groups which support the system have the need to belong, to "have a laff," to know that there is someone around who shares interests and values.

Thus, the function and importance of the peer group become clear. The peer group teaches members what is important; it provides an informal but often rigid code of conduct for its members; it provides basic human association and support; it is, in short, the single most important socializing force in the school. Lest too much importance be attached to the peer group, the reader is reminded that allegiances tend to change radically for those who graduate from high school. Adolescent peer associations are vitally important, but they often fade quickly after high school.

THE LIMITS OF SOCIALIZATION

The forces which operate to socialize students are not always successful. Large numbers of school dropouts are affected to a lesser extent than are those who stay in school. Even those who are habitual truants are missing a large part of the informal and formal socialization of the school setting. For those who are in school, legal limits increasingly are being placed on the lengths to which teachers and school administrators can go in their efforts to socialize students.

The Dropouts

As pointed out in the previous section, there are many students in junior high schools and secondary schools who may be alienated from the curriculum, the teachers, and the formal rules and regulations of the school. Although some of these students attach themselves to sympathetic groups and continue in school, many simply leave. In cases where students cannot find success in the curriculum, where they are ignored or harassed by teachers and administrators, where they fail to receive peer support, they leave school at the first opportunity. For them, an important part of the socialization process has failed.

There are large numbers of such children in America. During the decade of the 1970s, 25 percent of the school population failed to graduate from high school.[60] In terms of numbers, this means that more than a million students a year drop out of school before they get their diploma. Moreover, this was a stable figure during the 1970s—virtually no progress was made to prevent this drain.

A particularly depressing aspect of the school dropout picture is that those who are in most desperate need of a high school diploma are the ones who are most apt to leave school. These are the students who come from the lowest socioeconomic classes in the society and can expect little support from their families. They often are the functional illiterates who were unsuccessful in school; perhaps even worse, they were unable to function in the informal social groupings of the school and did not benefit from even this type of socialization. This is not intended to suggest, of course, that school dropouts are social isolates in the world outside the school, or that *all* the efforts the school made to socialize them failed. It merely means that there was no longer anything in the school setting to hold them there. The extent to which socialization failed and the length of time they had been alienated would vary in each case.

Although the reasons for dropping out of school are many and varied and it would be difficult to generalize about them, the general character of the dropout population is clear enough. Dropout rates are higher for blacks and Hispanics than for whites, and dropout rates are highest in the inner city. Poor whites also drop out in large numbers. In fact, the dropout rate for low-income whites is higher than that for blacks and almost as high as the dropout rate for Hispanics.[61] In 1977, for example, the percentage of whites aged 14 to 17 who were not in school was 13.7, compared with 6.7 for blacks and 13.7 for Hispanics. In terms of numbers, this meant that 304,000 whites, 81,000 blacks, and 59,000 Hispanics under 18 years of age were not enrolled in school.

In addition to the dropouts, chronic absenteeism is a serious problem. It has been estimated that the average rate of absenteeism in major urban centers hovers around 20 percent.[62] It should be pointed out that truancy and dropping out are not always voluntary. That is, many children are pushed out, expelled, or encouraged to stay away by teachers and school administrators.

The Legal Limits of Socialization

For the majority who are enrolled in schools and who ultimately graduate, there are limits on the extent to which the schools can exercise control. With increasing frequency, parents are challenging the authority of the school to control the lives of their children. Moreover, recent legal restrictions in the form of laws and court decisions have tended to limit the schools in their efforts to control students.

Since some of these restrictions will be considered in later chapters, only a brief overview of some of the most important developments relating specifically to limitations on socialization will be presented here. Since the mid-sixties, Congress has acted in a number of areas which directly affect local schools' discretion in dealing with students. Although its general intent was to protect civil rights, especially of minority groups, certain provisions of the Civil Rights Act of 1964 can limit certain socialization practices of the public schools. Section 2000c–6 in Title IV of the Civil Rights Act of 1964 gives parents the right to petition the attorney general's office if they feel that their children, as members of a class of persons, "are being deprived by a school board of equal protection of the laws." What this has come to mean in practice is that if a school board allows practices in the school which discriminate against children because of their race, the parents have standing in the courts to challenge such practices. Thus, under Title IV, parents can challenge segregative practices. Even in schools which are integrated but which engage in grouping that results in predominantly black or predominantly white groups, parents who can demonstrate that this results in inferior programs for their children have a good case. In addition, Title V (1970) of the Civil Rights Act states: "No person in the United States shall, on the ground of race, color, or national origin be excluded from participation in, be denied the benefits of, or be subjected to discrimination under any program or activity receiving federal financial assistance." This applies to almost all public schools, since most receive some federal assistance. Under this title, many have challenged socialization practices of the schools.

Although the problems faced by females in the educational system will be treated at length in a separate chapter, it should be noted here that girls have special problems created by the socialization efforts of schools. It is not uncommon for schools to attempt to socialize girls to stereotyped feminine roles. The laws—and court decisions based on them—have caused some of these practices to be challenged. In Title VII of the Civil Rights Act of 1964, Congress declared that "no employer, labor union, or other organization subject to the provisions of the act shall discriminate against any individual on the basis of race, color, religion, sex or national origin." Schools which accept federal funds belong, of course, under the category of "other organizations" subject to the provisions of the act. Public Law 92–318, Title IX of the Education Amendments of 1972, is even more specific. Section 901 states: "No person in the United States shall, on the basis of sex, be excluded from participation in, be denied the benefits of, or be subjected to discrimination under any education program or activity receiving federal financial assistance. . . ." Title IX defines an educational institution as any "public or private preschool, elementary, or secondary school, or any institution of vocational, professional, or higher education. . . ." Under Title IX, hundreds of cases have been brought against schools at all levels where blatant as well as subtle efforts at sex-role stereotyping existed. Separate and unequal sports facilities and programs, counseling efforts which appeared prejudicial toward girls, courses and course materials, separate programs for boys and girls, and many other such programs and activities have been challenged under Title IX. Although inequality and stereotyped socialization efforts continue to exist, there have been enough challenges to make teachers and school officials wary. There can be little doubt that the law and the court challenges have changed sex-role socialization practices and attitudes in the schools. There are specific limits on what schools can legally do in this area.

In addition to civil rights legislation and the efforts to provide equality of educational opportunity for women, Congress has acted to provide greater educational opportunity for the handicapped. For years the schools had either neglected the educational needs of the handicapped or had provided them with special and often unequal treatment. Congress directed its attention to this problem in the Rehabilitation Act of 1973 when it declared that "no otherwise qualified handicapped individual . . . shall, on the basis of his handicap, be excluded from the participation in, be denied the benefits of, or be subject to discrimination under any program or activity receiving federal assistance." The legislation was strengthened by the passage in 1976 of the Education for All Handicapped Children Act (P.L. 94–142) which provided funds for the education of handicapped children, directed states to develop plans including "due process" hearings for handicapped children, ordered handicapped children to be placed in "the least restrictive environment," and mandated that an individualized written educational program be developed for each handicapped child. In a sence, this act has served to bring handicapped children out of the closet. For several million handicapped children in the United States and the school population generally, the socialization implications of this program are immense. Previous policies of neglect, deliberate or not, contained the implied message for both handicapped and nonhandicapped alike that handicapped persons were somehow inferior, destined for the scrap heap of humanity. Even where the schools attempted to deal with the problems of the handicapped, they often did so on a segregated basis. This not only failed to meet the needs of many handicapped children, but it tended to label them as inferior, in some cases almost as a subhuman class of persons. The intent of Public Law 94–142 is clearly to put an end to these practices. However one might view socialization to the mainstream of the society, handicapped persons are now part of that process.

Finally, no better illustration could be given of the recent legal limitations which have been placed on the process of socialization than the Family Educational Rights and Privacy Act of 1974, popularly called the "Buckley Amendment." Clear in its intent, the act states:

> No funds shall be made available under any applicable program to any educational agency or institution which has a policy of denying, or which effectively prevents, the parents of students who are or have been in attendance at a school of such an agency or at such institution, as the case may be, the right to inspect and review the education records of their children.

Perhaps no act is more effective in preventing school officials and teachers from treating students in careless and arbitrary ways. Before the legislation, teachers could and often did classify students as "troublemakers," and dossiers were compiled on students which contained damaging information on them, ranging from teachers' opinions of their ability and behavior to the results of test batteries on intelligence, achievement, personality, and vocational interests. Moreover, it had become common practice in schools for these "dossiers" to become widely used by teachers for the purpose of making all sorts of prejudgments about students. Although the Buckley Amendment has not stopped these practices, it has caused some of the more flagrant abuses to be discontinued. At least, any parent who feels his child is being personally damaged by things which might be in the child's folder can see the folder and insist that damaging information be expunged from the record.

This is merely a sampling of the most important legislation which has an impact on school socialization. The samples should illustrate that there are serious limitations on what schools can do. There is also an extensive legal framework developing in the area of students' rights which tends to limit the schools in their efforts to socialize students. Parents have challenged the use of corporal punishment in the schools,[63] using grades and withholding diplomas as punishment for behavior,[64] and expulsion for pregnancy.[65] Although there is a mixed record on the use of corporal punishment, the mere fact that parents can and do take teachers and principals to court for using corporal punishment has caused them to think twice before using physical punishment as a means of classroom control. The courts have ruled that punishment in the form of lowering grades or withholding diplomas as a means of attempting to impose the school's own definition of good citizenship is a violation of students' rights. In general, it seems difficult to convince a court that teachers and school administrators are always right in their views of what constitutes good citizenship.

Students and their parents have also taken their teachers, and administrators to court on their constitutional right of free expression and the right of assembly. On basic constitutional rights, the big breakthrough for students was the case of *Tinker v. Des Moines*, in which the Supreme Court of the United States declared in 1969 that minor students were "persons" under the Constitution and were protected by it. Before *Tinker*, teachers and school officials assumed that they had almost total authority to control students in any way they deemed appropriate. Unhindered by any legal restraints, they assumed that they could determine what was appropriate in matters of student speech, dress, and school conduct. In a word, they were free to socialize students to any set of standards they felt appropriate. If students objected, if they broke the rules, school officials could arbitrarily remove them from school. Due process for students was unheard of. *Tinker* and *Goss v. Lopez* (1975) changed all that.

Excerpts of the cases which follow—*West Virginia v. Barnette* (1945), *Tinker v. Des Moines*, and *Goss v. Lopez*— are not intended as a comprehensive review of students' legal rights but merely as illustrations of the manner in which major decisions of the Supreme Court of the United States have dealt with efforts of the schools to socialize students. The *Barnette* case is included because it illustrates the efforts of a school district to impose a form both of religious and political socialization on school children. *Tinker* illustrates the manner in which students were given standing as citizens under the Constitution, and *Lopez* illustrates the lengths to which the Court was willing to go to change specific practices of the school in dealing with discipline problems. Each of these cases has had far-reaching implications which have placed genuine limitations on school authorities in the process of socialization.

West Virginia State Board of Education v. Barnette
319 US 624 (1943)

Mr. Justice Jackson delivered the opinion of the Court.

Following the decision by this court on June 3, 1940, in *Minersville School Dist. v. Gobitis* 310 US 485, the West Virginia legislature amended its statutes to require all schools therein to conduct courses of instruction in history, civics, and in the Constitutions of the United States and of the state "for the purpose of teaching, fostering and perpetuating the ideals, principles and spirit of Americanism, and increasing the knowledge of the organization and machinery of the government." ...

The board education on January 9, 1942, adopted a resolution containing recitals taken largely from the court's *Gobitis* opinion and ordering that the salute to the flag become "a regular part of the program of activities in the public schools," that all teachers and pupils "shall be required to participate in the salute honoring the nation represented by the flag; provided, however, that refusal to salute the flag be regarded as an act of insubordination, and shall be dealt with accordingly." ...

Appellees, citizen of the United States and of West Virginia, brought suit in the United States District Court for themselves and others similarly situated asking its injunction to restrain enforcement of these laws and regulations against Jehovah's Witnesses. The Witnesses are an unincorporated body teaching that the obligation imposed by law of God is superior to that of laws enacted by temporal government. Their religious beliefs include a literal version of Exodus, chapter 20, verses 4 and 5, which says: "Thou shalt not make unto thee any graven image, or any likeness of anything that is in heaven above, or that is in the earth beneath, or that is in the water under the earth; thou shalt not bow down thyself to them nor serve them." They consider that the flag is an "image" within this command. For this reason they refuse to salute it. . . .

As the present Chief Justice said in dissent in the Gobitis case, the state may "require teaching by instruction and study of all in our history and in the structure and organization of our government, including the guaranties of civil liberty, which tend to inspire patriotism and love of country." . . . Here, however, we are dealing with a compulsion of students to declare a belief. They are not merely made acquainted with the flag salute so that they may be informed as to what it is or even what it means. The issue here is whether this slow and easily neglected route to aroused loyalties constitutionally may be short-cut by substituting a compulsory salute and slogan. . . .

Whether the First Amendment to the Constitution will permit officials to order observance of ritual of this nature does not depend upon whether as a voluntary exercise we would think it to be good, bad or merely innocuous. Any credo of nationalism is likely to include what some disapprove or to omit what others think essential, and to give off different overtones as it takes on different accents or interpretations. If official power exists to coerce acceptance of any patriotic creed, what it shall contain cannot be decided by courts, but must be largely discretionary with the ordaining authority, whose power to prescribe would no doubt include power to amend. Hence validity of the asserted power to force an American citizen publicly to profess any statement of belief or to engage in any ceremony of assent to one, presents questions of power that must be considered independently of any idea we may have as to the utility of the ceremony in question.

The question which underlies the flag salute controversy is whether such a ceremony so touching matters of opinion and political attitude may be imposed upon the individual by official authority under powers committed to any political organization under our Constitution. . . .

The *Fourteenth Amendment, as now applied to the states, protects the citizen against the state itself and all of its creatures—boards of education not excepted* (emphasis added). These have, of course, important, delicate, and highly discretionary functions, but none that they may not perform within the limits of the Bill of Rights. That they are educating the young for citizenship is reason for scrupulous protection of Constitutional freedoms of the individual, if we are not to strangle the free mind at its source and teach youth to discount important principles of our government as mere platitudes.

Such boards are numerous and their territorial jurisdiction often small. But small and local authority may feel less sense of responsibility to the Constitution, and agencies of publicity may be less vigilant in calling it to account. The action of Congress in making flag observance voluntary and respecting the conscience of the objector is a matter relatively trivial to the welfare of the nation. There are village tyrants as well as village Hampdens, but none who acts under color of law is beyond reach of the Constitution. . . .

The very purpose of a Bill of Rights was to withdraw certain subjects from the vicissitudes of political controversy, to place them beyond the reach of majorities and officials and to establish them as legal principles to be applied by the courts. One's right to life, liberty, and property, to free speech, a free press, freedom of worship and assembly, and other fundamental rights may not be submitted to vote; they depend on the outcome of no elections. . . .

Lastly, and this is the very heart of the Gobitis opinion, it reasons that "National unity is the basis of national security," that the authorities have "the right to select appropriate means for its attainment," and hence reaches the conclusion that such compulsory measures toward "national unity" are constitutional. . . . Upon the verity of this assumption depends our answer in this case.

If there is any fixed star in our constitutional constellation it is that no official, high or petty, can prescribe what shall be orthodox in politics, nationalism, religion, or other matters of opinion or force citizens to confess by word or act their faith therein. If there are any circumstances which permit an exception, they do not now occur to us.

We think the action of the local authorities in compelling the flag salute and pledge transcends constitutional limitations on their power and invades the sphere of intellect and spirit which it is the purpose of the First Amendment to our Constitution to reserve from all official control.

Affirmed.

[Concurring opinions of Justices Black, Douglas, and Murphy are omitted.]

Mr. Justice Frankfurter, dissenting.

The constitutional protection of religious freedom terminated disabilities, it did not create new privileges. It gave religious equality, not civil immunity. Its essence is freedom from conformity to religious dogma, not freedom from conformity to law because of religious dogma. Religious loyalties may be exercised without hindrance from the state, not the state may not exercise that which except by leave of religious loyalties is within the domain of temporal power. Otherwise each individual could set up his own censor against obedience to laws conscientiously deemed for the public good by those whose business it is to make laws.

The essence of the religious freedom guaranteed by our Constitution is therefore this: no religion shall either receive the state's support or incur its hostility. Religion is outside the sphere of political government. This does not mean that all matters on which religious organizations or beliefs may pronounce are outside the sphere of government. Were this so, instead of the separation of church and state, there would be the subordination of the state on any matter deemed within the sovereignty of the religious conscience. The validity of secular laws cannot be measured by their conformity to religious doctrines. It is only in a theocratic state that ecclesiastical doctrines measure legal right and wrong.

An act compelling profession of allegiance to a religion, no matter how subtly or tenuously promoted, is bad. But an act promoting good citizenship and national allegiance is within the domain of governmental authority and is therefore to be judged by the same considerations of power and of constitutionality as those involved in the many claims of immunity from civil obedience because of religious scruples. . . .

In *Barnette*, the Court not only dealt with the plaintiffs' religious beliefs but also commented on the role of the school in political socialization. What did the Court say about political socialization? Is political socialization acceptable if it does not interfere with religious beliefs? Are there limits to political socialization of school children? In an issue in which national unity and matters of conscience are in conflict, the Court seemed to be saying that conscience was a higher value. Does this mean that any parent could succeed in getting his child excused from any school activity if it violated the right of "conscience"? Under the logic of

Barnette, could students refuse, for example, to attend school assemblies which featured speakers who took positions with which they disagreed? In his dissent, Frankfurter argued that the Court had gone too far. Why?

Tinker v. Des Moines Independent Community School District
393 US 503 (1969)

Mr. Justice Fortas delivered the opinion of the Court.

Petitioner John F. Tinker, fifteen years old, and petitioner Christopher Eckhardt, sixteen years old, attended high school.

In December 1965, a group of adults and students in Des Moines held a meeting at the Eckhardt home. The group determined to publicize their objections to the hostilities in Vietnam and their support for a truce by wearing black armbands during the holiday season and by fasting on December 16 and New Year's Eve. Petitioners and their parents had previously engaged in similar activities, and they decided to participate in the program.

The principals of the Des Moines schools became aware of the plan to wear armbands. On December 14, 1965, they met and adopted a policy that any student wearing an armband to school would be asked to remove it, and if he refused he would be suspended until he returned without the armband. Petitioners were aware of the regulation that the school authorities adopted.

On December 16, Mary Beth and Christopher wore black armbands to their schools. John Tinker wore his armband the next day. They were all sent home and suspended from school until they would come back without their armbands. They did not return to school until after the planned period for wearing armbands had expired—that is, until after New Year's Day. . . .

First Amendment rights, applied in light of the special characteristics of the school environment, are available to teachers and students. It can hardly be argued that either students or teachers shed their constitutional rights to freedom of speech or expression at the schoolhouse gate. This has been the unmistakable holding of this court for almost fifty years. . . . On the other hand, the court has repeatedly emphasized the need for affirming the comprehensive authority of the states and of school officials, consistent with fundamental constitutional safeguards, to prescribe and control conduct in the schools. Our problem lies in the area where students in the exercise of First Amendment rights collide with the rules of the school authorities.

The problem posed by the present case does not relate to regulation of the length of skirts or the type of clothing, to hair style, or deportment. It does not concern aggressive, disruptive action or even group demonstrations. Our problem involves direct, primary First Amendment rights akin to "pure speech."

The school officials banned and sought to punish petitioners for a silent, passive expression of opinion, unaccompanied by any disorder or disturbance on the part of petitioners. There is here no evidence whatever of petitioners' interference, actual or nascent, with the schools' work or of collision with the rights of other students to be secure and to be let alone. Accordingly, this case does not concern speech or action that intrudes upon the work of the schools or the rights of other students. . . .

The district court concluded that the action of the school authorities was reasonable because it was based upon their fear of a disturbance from the wearing of the armbands. But, in our system, undifferentiated fear or apprehension of disturbance is

not enough to overcome the right to freedom of expression. Any departure from absolute regimentation may cause trouble. Any variation from the majority's opinion may
inspire fear. Any word spoken, in class, in the lunchroom, or on the campus, that
deviates from the views of another person may start an argument or cause a disturbance. But our Constitution says we must take this risk, and our history says that it is
this sort of hazardous freedom—this kind of openness—that is the basis of our national strength and of the independence and vigor of Americans who grow up and live in
this relatively permissive, often disputatious, society.

In order for the state in the person of school officials to justify prohibition of a
particular expression of opinion, it must be able to show that its action was caused by
something more than a mere desire to avoid the discomfort and unpleasantness that
always accompany an unpopular viewpoint. Certainly where there is no finding and
no showing that engaging in the forbidden conduct would "materially and substantially interfere with the requirements of appropriate discipline in the operation of the
school," the prohibition cannot be sustained. . . .

In our system, state-operated schools may not be enclaves of totalitarianism.
School officials do not possess absolute authority over their students. Students in
school as well as out of school are "persons" under our Constitution. They are possessed
of fundamental rights which the state must respect, just as they themselves must
respect their obligations to the state. In our system, students may not be regarded as
closed-circuit recipients of only that which the state chooses to communicate. They
may not be confined to the expression of those sentiments that are officially approved.
In the absence of a specific showing of constitutionally valid reasons to regulate their
speech, students are entitled to freedom of expression of their views. . . .

In *Keyishian v. Board of Regents* . . . Mr. Justice Brennan, speaking for the court said:
"The vigilant protection of constitutional freedoms is nowhere more vital than in the
community of American schools. . . . The classroom is peculiarly the marketplace of
ideas. The nation's future depends upon leaders trained through wide exposure to
that robust exchange of ideas which discovers truth out of a multitude of tongues,
(rather) than through any kind of authoritative selection."

The principle of these cases is not confined to the supervised and ordained discussion which takes place in the classroom. The principal use to which the schools are
dedicated is to accommodate students during prescribed hours for the purpose of certain types of activities. Among those activities is personal intercommunication among
the students. This is not only an inevitable part of the process of attending school; it is
also an important part of the educational process. A student's rights, therefore, do not
embrace merely the classroom hours. When he is in the cafeteria, or on the playing
field, or on the campus during the authorized hours, he may express his opinions,
even on controversial subjects like the conflict in Vietnam, if he does so without
"materially and substantially interfer(ing) with the requirements of appropriate discipline in the operation of the school" and without colliding with the rights of others.
But conduct by the student, in class or out of it, which for any reason—whether it
stems from time, place, or type of behavior—materially disrupts classwork or involves
substantial disorder or invasion of the rights of others is, of course, not immunized by
the constitutional guarantee of freedom of speech. . . .

We express no opinion as to the form of relief which should be granted, this being
a matter for the lower courts to determine. We reverse and remand for further proceedings consistent with this opinion. . . .

Mr. Justice Black dissenting.

... Assuming that the court is correct in holding that the conduct of wearing armbands for the purpose of conveying political ideas is protected by the First Amendment, the crucial remaining questions are whether students and teachers may use the schools at their whim as a platform for the exercise of free speech—"symbolic" or "pure"—and whether the courts will allocate to themselves the function of deciding how the pupils' school day will be spent. While I have always believed that under the First and Fourteenth Amendments neither the state nor the federal government has any authority to regulate or censor the content of speech, I have never believed that any person has a right to give speeches or engage in demonstrations where he pleases and when he pleases.

While the record does not show that any of these armband students shouted, used profane language, or were violent in any manner, detailed testimony by some of them shows their armbands caused comments, warnings by other students, the poking of fun at them, and a warning by an older football player that other nonprotesting students had better let them alone. There is also evidence that a teacher of mathematics had his lesson period practically "wrecked" chiefly by disputes with Mary Beth Tinker, who wore her armband for her "demonstration." Even a casual reading of the record shows that this armband did divert students' minds from their regular lessons, and that talk, comments, etc., made John Tinker "self-conscious" in attending school with his armband. While the absence of obscene remarks or boisterous and loud disorder perhaps justifies the court's statement that the few armband students did not actually "disrupt" the classwork, I think the record overwhelmingly shows that the armbands did exactly what the elected school officials and principals foresaw they would, that is, took the students' minds off their classwork and diverted them to thoughts about the highly emotional subject of the Vietnam War. And I repeat that if the time has come when pupils of state-supported schools, kindergartens, grammer schools, or high schools, can defy and flout orders of school officials to keep their minds on their own schoolwork, it is the beginning of a new revolutionary era of permissiveness in this country fostered by the judiciary. The next logical step, it appears to me, would be to hold unconstitutional laws that bar pupils under twenty-one or eighteen from voting, or from being elected members of the boards of education.

I deny, therefore, that it has been the "unmistakable holding of this court for almost fifty years" that "students" and "teachers" take with them into the "schoolhouse gate" constitutional rights to "freedom of speech or expression." Even Meyer did not hold that. It makes no reference to "symbolic speech," at all; what it did was to strike down as "unreasonable" and therefore unconstitutional a Nebraska law barring the teaching of the German language before the children reached the eighth grade. One can well agree with Mr. Justice Holmes and Mr. Justice Sutherland, as I do, that such a law was no more unreasonable than it would be to bar the teaching of Latin and Greek to pupils who have not reached the eighth grade. In fact, I think the majority's reason for invalidating the Nebraska law was that it did not like it or in legal jargon that it "shocked the court's conscience," "offended its sense of justice, or" was "contrary to fundamental concepts of the English-speaking world," as the court has sometimes said. ...

In my view, teachers in state-controlled public schools are hired to teach there. Although Mr. Justice McReynolds may have intimated to the contrary in *Meyer v.*

Nebraska, . . . certainly a teacher is not paid to go into school and teach subjects the state does not hire him to teach as a part of its selected curriculum. Nor are public school students sent to the schools at public expense to broadcast political or any other views to educate and inform the public. The original idea of schools, which I do not believe is yet abandoned as worthless or out of date, was that children had not yet reached the point of experience and wisdom which enabled them to teach all of their elders. It may be that the nation has outgrown the old-fashioned slogan that "children are to be seen not heard," but one may, I hope, be permitted to harbor the thought that taxpayers send children to school on the premise that at their age they need to learn, not teach. . . .

Change has been said to be truly the law of life but sometimes the old and the tried and true are worth holding. The schools of this nation have undoubtedly contributed to giving us tranquility and to making us a more law-abiding people. Uncontrolled and uncontrollable liberty is an enemy to domestic peace. We cannot close our eyes to the fact that some of the country's greatest problems are crimes committed by the youth, too many of school age. School discipline, like parental discipline, is an integral and important part of training our children to be good citizens—to be better citizens. Here a very small number of students have crisply and summarily refused to obey a school order designed to give pupils who want to learn the opportunity to do so. One does not need to be a prophet or the son of a prophet to know that after the court's holding today some students in Iowa schools and indeed in all schools will be ready, able, and willing to defy their teachers on practically all orders. This is the more unfortunate for the schools since groups of students all over the land are already running loose, conducting break-ins, sit-ins, lie-ins, and smash-ins. Many of these student groups, as is all too familiar to all who read the newspapers and watch the television news programs, have already engaged in rioting, property seizures, and destruction. They have picketed schools to force students not to cross their picket lines and have too often violently attacked earnest but frightened students who wanted an education that the pickets did not want them to get. Students engaged in such activities are apparently confident that they know far more about how to operate public school systems than do their parents, teachers, and elected school officials. It is no answer to say that the particular students here have not yet reached such high points in their demands to attend classes in order to exercise their political pressures. Turned loose with lawsuits for damages and injunctions against their teachers as they are here, it is nothing but wishful thinking to imagine that young, immature students will not soon believe it is their right to control the schools rather than the right of the states that collect the taxes to hire the teachers for the benefit of the pupils. This case, therefore, wholly without constitutional reasons in my judgment, subjects all the public schools in the country to the whims and caprices of their loudest-mouthed, but maybe not their brightest, students. I, for one, am not fully persuaded that school pupils are wise enough, even with this court's expert help from Washington, to run the 23,390 public school systems in our fifty states. I wish, therefore, wholly to disclaim any purpose on my part to hold that the federal Constitution compels the teachers, parents, and elected school officials to surrender control of the American public school system to public school students . . . I dissent. . . .

In *Tinker,* the Court made the point that students are "persons" under the Constitution. Does this mean that students in school generally have the same basic rights as adults in the community? If so, are there any restrictions which school officials can place on students' First Amendment rights? Does the finding in *Tinker* imply that school officials have no right to control the student newspaper or student organizations and associations? Obviously, even after *Tinker*, school rules relative to freedom of speech and press within the school environment have continued to be in force. Does *Tinker* provide guidelines for school officials which enable them to determine which regulations are permissible and which are not? How does Black in his dissent deal with the issue of the socialization function of the school?

Goss v. Lopez

In *Goss*, the Supreme Court placed some specific limitations on the power of school officials to punish what they claimed to be deviant behavior. The ruling in *Goss* has had far-reaching effects on certain disciplinary practices which had developed in the schools. Following are excerpts from the case.

Norval Goss et al., Appellants v. Eileen Lopez et al.
95 S. Ct. 729 (1975)

Mr. Justice White delivered the opinion of the Court.

This appeal by various administrators of the Columbus, Ohio, Public School System ("CPSS") challenges the judgment of a three-judge federal court, declaring that appellees—various high school students in the CPSS—were denied due process of law contrary to the command of the Fourteenth Amendment in that they were temporarily suspended from their high schools without a hearing either prior to suspension or within a reasonable time thereafter, and enjoining the administrators to remove all references to such suspensions from the students' records. . . .

The nine named appellees, each of whom alleged that he or she had been suspended from public high school in Columbus for up to 10 days without a hearing, filed an action against the Columbus Board of Education and various administrators of the CPSS. The complaint sought a declaration that (An Ohio Law permitting suspension) was unconstitutional in that it permitted public school administrators to deprive plaintiffs of their right to an education without a hearing of any kind, in violation of the procedural due process component of the Fourteenth Amendment. It also sought to enjoin the public school officials from issuing future suspensions and to require them to remove reference to the past suspensions from the records of the students in question.

The proof below established that the suspensions in question arose out of a period of widespread student unrest in the CPSS during February and March in 1971. Six of the named plaintiffs, Rudolph Sutton, Tyrone Washington, Susan Cooper, Deborah Fox, Clarence Byars and Bruce Harris, were students at the Marion-Franklin High School and were each suspended for 10 days on account of disruptive or disobedient conduct committed in the presence of the school administrator who ordered the suspension. One of these, Tyrone Washington, was among a group of students demonstrating in the school auditorium while a class was being conducted there. He was ordered by the school principal to leave, refused to do so and was suspended. Rudolph Sutton, in the presence of the principal, physically attacked a police officer who was attempting to remove Tyrone Washington from the auditorium. He was immediately suspended. The other four Marion-Franklin students were suspended for similar conduct. None was given a hearing to determine the operative facts underlying the suspension, but each, together with his or her parents, was offered the opportunity to attend a conference, subsequent to the effective date of the suspension, to discuss the student's future.

Two named plaintiffs, Dwight Lopez and Betty Crome, were students at the Central High School, and McGuffey Junior High School, respectively. The former was suspended in connection with a disturbance in the lunchroom which involved some physical damage to school property. Lopez testified that at least 74 other students were suspended from his school on the same day. He also testified below that he was not a party to the destructive conduct but was instead an innocent bystander. Because no one from the school testified with regard to this incident there is no evidence in the record indicating the official basis for concluding otherwise. Lopez never had a hearing.

Betty Crome was present at a demonstration at a high school different from the one she was attending. There she was arrested together with others, taken to the police station, and released without being formally charged. Before she went to school on the following day, she was notified that she had been suspended for a 10-day period. Because no one from the school testified with respect to this incident, the record does not disclose how the McGuffey Junior High School principal went about making the decision to suspend Betty Crome nor does it disclose on what information the decision was based. It is clear from the record that no hearing was ever held. . . .

At the outset, appellants contend that because there is no constitutional right to an education at public expenses, the Due Process Clause does not protect against expulsions from the public school system. This position misconceives the nature of the issue and is refuted by prior decisions. The Fourteenth Amendment forbids the State to deprive any person of life, liberty or property without due process of law. Protected interests in property are normally "not created by the Constitution." Rather, they are created and their dimensions are defined by an independent source such as state statutes or rules entitling the citizen to certain benefits.

Here, on the basis of state law, appellees plainly had legitimate claims of entitlement to a public education. Ohio Rev. Code 3313.48 and 3313.64 direct local authorities to provide a free education to all residents between six and 21 years of age, and a compulsory attendance law requires attendance for a school year of not less than 32 weeks. It is true that the code permits school principals to suspend students for up to two weeks; but suspensions may not be imposed without any grounds whatsoever. All of the schools had their own rules specifying the grounds for expulsion or suspension. Having chosen to extend the right to an education to people of appellees' class generally, Ohio may not withdraw that right on grounds of misconduct absent fundamentally fair procedures to determine whether the misconduct has occurred.

The Due Process Clause also forbids arbitrary deprivations of liberty. "Where a person's good name, reputation, honor, or integrity is at stake because of what the government is doing to him," the minimal requirements of the clause must be satisfied. School authorities here suspended appellees from school for periods of up to 10 days based on charges of misconduct. If sustained and recorded, those charges could seriously damage the students' standing with their fellow pupils and their teachers as well as interfere with later opportunities for higher education and employment. It is apparent that the claimed right of the State to determine unilaterally and without due process whether that misconduct has occurred immediately collides with the requirements of the Constitution. . . .

A 10-day suspension from school is not de minimis in our view and may not be imposed in complete disregard of the Due Process Clause.

A short suspension is of course a far milder deprivation than expulsion. But, "education is perhaps the most important function of state and local governments." The total exclusion from the educational process for more than a trivial period, and certainly if the suspension is for 10 days, is a serious event in the life of the suspended child. Neither the property interest in educational benefits temporarily denied nor the liberty interest in reputation, which is also implicated, is so insubstantial that suspensions may constitutionally be imposed by any procedure the school chooses, no matter how arbitrary.

"Once it is determined that due process applies, the question remains what process is due." We turn to that question, fully realizing as our cases regularly do that the interpretation and application of the Due Process Clause are intensely practical matters and that "the very nature of due process negates any concepts of inflexible procedures universally applicable to every imaginable situation."

. . . The student's interest is to avoid unfair or mistaken exclusion from the educational process, with all of its unfortunate consequences. The Due Process Clause will not shield him from suspensions properly imposed, but it deserves both his interest and the interest of the State if his suspension is in fact unwarranted. The concern would be mostly academic if the disciplinary process were a totally accurate, unerring process, never mistaken and never unfair. Unfortunately, that is not the case, and no one suggests that it is. Disciplinarians, although proceeding in utmost good faith, frequently act on the reports and advice of others; and the controlling facts and the nature of the conduct under challenge are often disputed. The risk of error is not at all trivial, and it should be guarded against if that may be done without prohibitive cost or interference with the educational process. . . .

We do not believe that school authorities must be totally free from notice and hearing requirements if their schools are to operate with acceptable efficiency. Students facing temporary suspension have interests qualifying for protection of the Due Process Clause, and due process requires, in connection with a suspension of 10 days or less, that the student be given oral or written notice of the charges against him and, if he denies them, an explanation of the evidence the authorities have and an opportunity to present his side of the story. The clause requires at least these rudimentary precautions against unfair or mistaken findings of misconduct and arbitrary exclusion from school. . . .

There need be no delay between the time "notice" is given and the time of the hearing. In the great majority of cases the disciplinarian may informally discuss the alleged misconduct with the student minutes after it has occurred. We hold only that, in being given an opportunity to explain his version of the facts at this discussion, the student first be told what he is accused of doing and what the basis of the accusation is. Since the hearing may occur almost immediately following the misconduct, it follows that as a general rule notice and hearing should precede removal of the student from school. We agree with the District Court, however, that there are recurring situations in which prior notice and hearing cannot be insisted upon. Students whose presence poses a continuing danger to persons or property or an ongoing threat of disrupting the academic process may be immediately removed from school. In such cases, the necessary notice and rudimentary hearing should follow as soon as practicable, as the District Court indicated. . . .

We stop short of construing the Due Process Clause to require, countrywide, that hearings in connection with short suspensions must afford the student the opportunity to secure counsel, to confront and cross-examine witnesses supporting the charge or to call his own witnesses to verify his version of the incident. Brief disciplinary suspensions are almost countless. To impose in each such case even truncated trial type procedures might well overwhelm administrative facilities in many places and, by diverting resources, cost more than it would save in educational effectiveness. Moreover, further formalizing the suspension process and escalating its formality and adversary nature may not only make it too costly as a regular disciplinary tool but also destroy its effectiveness as part of the teaching process.

On the other hand, requiring effective notice and informal hearing permitting the student to give his version of the events will provide a meaningful hedge against erroneous action. At least the disciplinarian will be alerted to the existence of disputes about facts and arguments about cause and effect. He may then determine himself to summon the accuser, permit cross-examination and allow the student to present his own witnesses. In more difficult cases, he may permit counsel. In any event, his discretion will be more informed and we think the risk of error substantially reduced.

Mr. Justice Powell, with whom The Chief Justice, Mr. Justice Blackmun, and Mr. Justice Rehnquist join, dissenting.

The Court today invalidates an Ohio statute that permits student suspensions from school without a hearing "for not more than ten days." The decision unnecessarily opens avenues for judicial intervention in the operation of our public school that may affect adversely the quality of education. The Court holds for the first time that the federal courts, rather than educational officials and state legislatures, have the authority to determine the rules applicable to routine classroom discipline of children and teenagers in the public schools. It justifies this unprecedented intrusion into the process of elementary and secondary education by identifying a new constitutional right: the right of a student not to be suspended for as much as a single day without notice and a due process hearing either before or promptly following the suspension. . . .

In my view, a student's interest in education is not infringed by a suspension within the limited period prescribed by Ohio law. Moreover, to the extent that there may be some arguable infringement, it is too speculative, transitory and insubstantial to justify imposition of a constitutional rule.

The Ohio suspension statute allows no serious or significant infringement of education. It authorizes only a maximum suspension of eight school days, less than 5% of the normal 180-day school year. Absences of such limited duration will rarely affect a pupil's opportunity to learn or his scholastic performance. Indeed, the record in this case reflects no educational injury to appellees. Each completed the semester in which the suspension occurred and performed at least as well as he or she had in previous years. Despite the Court's unsupported speculation that a suspended student could be "seriously damaged" . . . there is no factual showing of any such damage to appellees. . . .

The State's interest, broadly put, is in the proper functioning of its public school system for the benefit of all pupils and the public generally. Few rulings would interfere more extensively in the daily functioning of schools than subjecting routine discipline to the formalities and judicial oversight of due process. Suspensions are one of the traditional means—ranging from keeping a student after class to permanent expulsion—used to maintain discipline in the schools. It is common knowledge that maintaining order and reasonable decorum in school buildings and classrooms is a major educational problem, and one which has increased significantly in magnitude in recent years. Often the teacher, in protecting the rights of other children to an education (if not his or their safety), is compelled to rely on the power to suspend.

The lesson of discipline is not merely a matter of the student's self-interest in the shaping of his own character and personality; it provides an early understanding of the relevance to the social compact of respect for the rights of others. The classroom is the laboratory in which this lesson of life is best learned.

In assessing in constitutional terms the need to protect pupils from unfair minor discipline by school authorities, the Court ignores the commonality of interest of the State and pupils in the public school system. Rather, it thinks in traditional judicial terms of an adversary situation. To be sure, there will be the occasional pupil innocent of any rule infringement who is mistakenly suspended or whose infraction is too minor to justify suspension. But, while there is no evidence indicating the frequency of unjust suspensions, common sense suggests that they will not be numerous in relation to the total number, and that mistakes or injustices will usually be righted by informal means.

One of the more disturbing aspects of today's decision is its indiscriminate reliance upon the judiciary, and the adversary process, as the means of resolving many of the most routine problems arising in the classroom. In mandating due process procedures the Court misapprehends the reality of the normal teacher-pupil relationship. There is an ongoing relationship, one in which the teacher must occupy many roles —educator, adviser, friend and, at times, parent-substitute. It is rarely adversary in nature except with respect to the chronically disruptive or insubordinate pupils whom the teacher must be free to discipline without frustrating formalities.

In my view, the constitutionalizing of routine classroom decisions not only represents a significant and unwise extension of the Due Process Clause; it also was quite unnecessary in view of the safeguards prescribed by the Ohio statute. . . .

No one can foresee the ultimate frontiers of the new "thicket" the Court now enters. Today's ruling appears to sweep within the protected interest in education a multitude of discretionary decisions in the educational process. . . .

If, as seems apparent, the Court will now require due process procedures whenever such routine school decisions are challenged, the impact upon public education will be serious indeed. The discretion and judgment of federal courts across the land often will be substituted for that of the 50 state legislatures, the 14,000 school boards and the 2,000,000 teachers who heretofore have been responsible for the administration of the American public school system. If the Court perceives a rational and analytically sound distinction between the discretionary decision by school authorities to suspend a pupil for a brief period, and the types of discretionary school decisions described above, it would be prudent to articulate it in today's opinion. Otherwise, the federal courts should prepare themselves for a vast new role in society. . . .

In *Lopez*, the Court appeared to be lecturing the school system on its disciplinary procedures. What did the Court have to say about the "proper" role of discipline in a school? What guidelines were suggested by the Court as minimal guarantees of the right of due process? In *Lopez*, the Court admitted that due process for students might not be as comprehensive as it is for adults. Why did they stop short of demanding the whole range of due process rights for students?

In general the dissent argued that the Court was invading an area where state and local agencies should have control. What points were made to support that argument? How did the view of the discipline presented by the minority of the Court differ from that of the majority? The dissent suggested that the decision would open a Pandora's box of cases in which students felt that they were being denied due process in many decisions made by school authorities. In the years since *Lopez*, has this fear been justified?

SOCIALIZATION—WHO IS SERVED BY IT?

Schools are socializing agents. The way they do it and the general nature of their socialization process are clear enough. Schools do attempt to develop in children positive attitudes toward the political system, and, through the formal curriculum and the hidden curriculum, they tend to teach support for the existing system. Because of the long tradition of religious teaching in the schools and the strong feeling in local communities about the need for moral training, the schools continue a certain amount of religious socialization. The hidden curriculum can be more or less accurately described, and it is basically much the same from one school to the next anywhere in the country. A good case can also be made that the values it teaches are important to obedient and well-trained citizens who will accept the requirements of the work-place and support mainstream values. Peer groups in the school have many of the same characteristics as peer groups in the larger society and, except in the case of the alienated groups, they tend to be supportive of conditions which exist in the "real" world.

If all this is true, it is tempting to conclude that schools are deliberately engaged in preparing docile and uncritical citizens who accept the existing socioeconomic system without question. This is essentially the position of some Marxist critics of the system. However, this analysis may be oversimplified. It assumes, as functionalists do, that what happens in school is functional for existing capitalist society. Through the socialization process—which emphasizes competition; acceptance of superior-inferior roles; role placement through testing, grouping, and other classroom practices; and the inculcation of existing economic, social, and political values through formal and informal means, the school supports the existing system of economic, social, and political values and arrangements. The functionalists tend merely to describe this process without comment, while the Marxists find fault with it. It may be that both these views are incorrect.

A clear implication of the basic assumption that the schools support the socioeconomic system is that those who are in charge—the school boards, the principals, and the teachers—know a great deal about the system. Obviously they would have to understand quite clearly the demands of large corporate capitalism in order to design formal programs of instruction and establish the rules and procedures which make up the hidden curriculum which would deliberately promote the goals of the socioeconomic system. This is giving a great deal of credit to the level of understanding of school people. It is doubtful that many school administrators are this sophisticated in their knowledge of the system. Few elementary school teachers could demonstrate even the most rudimentary understanding of the political and economic complexities of the system. Yet they are charged with promoting it.

The efforts of the school in the socialization process might be more sensibly explained by tradition and by the day-to-day operational needs of the school. Thus, administrators and teachers may do what they do in the classrooms because they have more or less always done it that way. School principals may be more interested in running a tight ship, where everyone understands and follows the rules, simply because they abhor controversy and desire a low profile in the community. They do "what works" in order to keep the organization operating as smoothly as possible. What works may closely parallel bureaucratic organization or factory organization. What works may have very little to do with a studied effort to have the schools replicate institutions in the larger society. It may have very little to do with socializing children to their roles in the larger society. What it may have to do with most is meeting the perceived need to have an orderly and more or less controlled population within the school setting. This may be even more true of teachers. Their classroom rules, required behavior, and the techniques they use to control classroom populations may be based more on the desire to maintain order and organization within the classroom than on anything else. Both administrators and teachers may be more interested in making their lives at school easy and conflict free than in making the school a place where children learn specific adult roles. Thus, the socialization process may have more to do with the demands of the school setting itself than with the demands of the capitalist corporate state. The goals of school socialization may be the self-preservation of those in control, which becomes translated in practice into a well-ordered and more or less controlled population which is crowded into a very limited space.

What the laws and the courts, as well as other outside agencies, have done from time to time is remind those who run the schools—the school boards, administrators, and teachers—that they do not have a completely free hand. Congress, state legislatures, and the courts appear interested not so much in changing the traditional practices of the schools as in reminding those in charge that they are part of a larger system in which individuals, including students, do have certain rights.

Thus, the answer to the question "who is served by school socialization?" might be simple: those who work in the schools.

NOTES

1. Urie Bronfenbrenner, *Two Worlds of Childhood: U.S. and U.S.S.R.* (New York: Russell Sage Foundation, 1970), p. 95.
2. Ibid.. p. 97.
3. Ibid.

4. Emile Durkheim, *Moral Education* (New York: Free Press, 1925), p. 32.

5. Talcott Parsons, *Social Structure and Personality* (Glencoe, Ill.: Free Press, 1964), p. 130.

6. Ibid.

7. Phillip Jackson, "The Student's World," *Elementary School Journal* 67 (April 1966): 350.

8. Stuart B. Palonsky, "Political Socialization and Organizational Restraint in Secondary Schools," *The High School Journal* 62 (October 1978): p. 3.

9. See David Easton and Jack Dennis, *Children in the Political System* (New York: McGraw-Hill Book Co., 1968); Robert D. Hess and Judith V. Torney, *The Development of Political Attitudes in Children* (Chicago: Aldine Publishing Co., 1967); Fred I. Greenstein, *Children and Politics* (New Haven: Yale University Press, 1965); Robert D. Hess and David Easton, "The Child's Changing Image of the President," *Public Opinion Quarterly* 24(Spring 1960): 237–238; Helen F. Durio, "Taxonomy of Democratic Development," *Human Development* 19 (Fall 1976): 197–219.

10. For a more complete analysis of the impact of the school curriculum on political socialization of children, see: Gwyneth E. Britton and Margaret C. Pumpkin, "For Sale: Subliminal Bias in Textbooks," *The Reading Teacher* 31 (October 1977): 40–45; William C. Miller, "Examining the School Curriculum," *Educational Leadership* 37 (October 1978): 60–62; Michael W. Apple, "Politics and National Curriculum Policy," *Curriculum Inquiry* 7 (1977): 355–361; Carol R. Foster, "The School's Influence and Responsibility for the Socialization of the Young Child," *Journal of Research and Development in Education* 13 (1979): 13–19; Frederic W. Wirt and Michael W. Kirst, *The Political Web of American Schools* (Boston: Little, Brown & Company, 1972), pp. 27–31; Jean Anyon, "Ideology and United States History Textbooks," *Harvard Educational Review* 49 (August 1979): 361–387; Francis Fitzgerald, *America Revised* (Boston: Little, Brown & Company, 1979).

11. Richard E. Dawson and Kenneth Prewitt, *Political Socialization* (Boston: Little, Brown & Company, 1969), pp. 147–167.

12. Ibid., p. 149.

13. Ibid., p. 162.

14. Harmon Zeigler, *The Political Life of American Teachers* (Englewood Cliffs, N.J.: Prentice-Hall, 1967).

15. Palonsky, "Political Socialization and Organizational Restraint in Secondary Schools," pp. 3–6.

16. Ralph Larkin, *Suburban Youth in Cultural Crisis* (New York: Oxford University Press, 1971), Ch. 5.

17. Ruth Miller Elson, *Guardians of Tradition* (Lincoln, Neb.: University of Nebraska Press, 1964), p. 1.

18. Ibid.

19. Ibid., p. 45.

20. Ibid., p. 47.

21. *Brown v. Orange Co. Board of Public Instruction*, 128 So. 2nd 181 Fla. (1960); *Tudor v. Board of Education*, 14 N.J. 31 100A 2nd 857 (1954).

22. Wisconsin in 1890; Nebraska in 1902; Illinois in 1910; Louisiana in 1915.

23. *State v. Scheve*, 55 Neb. 853 91 N.W. 846 (1902).

24. *State ex rel Dearle v. Frazier*, 102 Wash. 369 (1918).

25. *State ex rel Johnson v. Boyd*, 217 Ind. 348 28 N.E. 2nd 256 (1940); *O'Connor v. Hendrick*, 184 N.Y. 421 77 N.E. 612 (1906); *Zellers v. Huff*, 55 N.M. 501 P. 2nd 949 (1951).

26. For a comprehensive treatment of this subject, see: Chester James Antieau, Phillip M. Carrol, and Thomas C. Burke, *Religion under the State Constitutions* (Brooklyn, N.Y.: Central Book Co., 1965), ch. 3.

27. For an example of a suggested program, see: Philip H. Phenix, "Religion in Public Education: Principles and Issues," *Religious Education* 67. (July-August 1972). For some sample programs, see: David Engel, ed., *Religion in Public Education* (New York: Paulist Press, 1974), pp. 87–170.

28. See Erik Erikson, *Identity, Youth and Crisis* (New York: W. W. Norton & Company, 1968), and Lawrence Kohlberg, "Development of Children's Orientations Toward a Moral Order," in *Educational Psychology*, eds. Richard C. Sprinthall and Norman Sprinthall (New York: Van Nostrand-Reinhold Co., 1969).

29. See especially, Louis E. Raths, Merrill Marmin, and Sidney B. Simon, *Values and Teaching* (Columbus, Ohio: Charles E. Merrill Books, 1966).

30. Henry Giroux and Anthony Penna, "The Dialectic of the Hidden Curriculum," *Edcentric* (Spring-Summer 1977), p. 40.

31. Jules Henry, *On Education* (New York: Vintage Books, 1972), p. 172.

32. Jules Henry, *Culture Against Man* (New York: Random House, 1963), p. 291.

33. Ibid.

34. Ibid., p. 294.

35. Ibid., p. 300.

36. Ibid., pp. 317–318.

37. Ibid., p. 318.

38. Ibid., p. 319.

39. Jackson, "The Student's World," p. 345.

40. Ibid., p. 354.

41. Ibid., p. 355.

42. *Colloquy*, January 1970. Copyright United Church Press.

43. Giroux and Penna, "The Dialectic of the Hidden Curriculum," p. 41.

44. Giroux and Penna utilize the work of Bowles and Gintis, *Schooling in Capitalist America*; Paulo Freire, *Cultural Action and Freedom*; Ivan Illich, *Deschooling Society*; and William Domhoff, *Who Rules America*, to support some of their arguments. For an excellent discussion of conflict theory as it relates to the hidden curriculum, see Michael Apple, *Ideology and the Curriculum* (London: Routledge & Kegan Paul, 1979), ch. 5.

45. Henry, *Culture Against Man*, p. 190.

46. For a good description of the preferential treatment of athletes, see John Underwood, "Student Athletes: The Sham and the Shame," *Sports Illustrated*, May 1980.

47. Robert J. Havighurst and Daniel U. Levine, *Society and Education*, 5th ed. (Boston: Allyn & Bacon, 1979), p. 245.

48. See J. R. Barclay et al., "The Influence of Paternal Occupation on Social Interaction Measures in Elementary School Children," ERIC ED 062–393 (1972); D. Byrne, *The Attraction Paradigm* (New York: Academic Press, 1971); J. S. Coleman et al., *Equality of Educational Opportunity* (Washington, D.C.: Government Printing Office, 1965); D. Whittaker, "Student Subcultures Revisited," ERIC ED 026–003 (1968).

49. Parsons, *Social Structure and Personality*, p. 174

50. Ibid., p. 174.

51. Havighurst and Levine, *Society and Education*, p. 245.

52. Charles E. Bowerman and John W. Kinch, "Changes in Family and Peer Orientation of Children Between the 4th and 10th Grades," *Social Forces* 37 (April 1959), p. 210.

53. John C. Condry, Jr., and Michael L. Siman, "An Experimental Study of Adult Versus Peer Orientation," Department of Child Development, Cornell University, 1968. (Unpublished manuscript).

54. Judy C. Love, "Demographic Characteristics of Interpersonal Attraction of Seventh-Grade Students" (Ed.D. dissertation, Oklahoma State University, 1975).

55. Havighurst and Levine, *Society and Education*, p. 246.

56. Jere Cohen, "High School Subcultures and the Adult World," *Adolescence* 14 (Fall 1979): 491.

57. Burton Clark, *Educating the Expert Society* (San Francisco: Chandler Publishing Co., 1962).

58. Paul E. Willis, *Learning to Labour* (London: Saxon House, 1977), p. 22.

59. Ibid., p. 23.

60. *Digest of Educational Statistics* (Washington, D.C.: U.S. Government Printing Office, 1979).

61. U.S., Department of Commerce, Bureau of the Census, 1979b, table 14.

62. Carnegie Council on Policy Studies in Higher Education, *Giving Youth a Better Chance* (Washington, D.C.: Jossey Bass, 1979), p. 53.

63. See National Institute of Education, *Proceedings: Conference on Corporal Punishment in the Schools: A National Debate* (Washington, D.C.: Government Printing Office, 1977).

64. *Brooks v. Geneseo Community School District no. 228* (Clearinghouse #21.337A). *In Re Wilson*, Commissioner of Education State of New York, No. 8421 (1972).

65. *Ordway v. Hargraves*, 323 F. Supp 1155 (D Mass 1971) and *Hill v. A. B. Johnson*, C.A. No. 77–51MAC, M.D. Ga. (1977), Clearinghouse numbers 22, 612A, B.

7

Social Class and the Schools

The nature of social class in the United States depends, in large measure, on one's ideological views. Traditional sociologists have recognized that there are several social classes and subclasses and they have attempted to identify and explain them. The traditional sociologist often claims ideological neutrality; that is, they claim that they examine social class without ideological bias. They are more concerned with what they view as accurate definitions and explanations than they are with criticism of the system. Indeed, many sociologists who study social class see the American system as a rather loose system in which upward mobility exists and they attempt to find reasons for it. After finding what they are looking for—that is, upward mobility—they tend to explain it in terms of merit or one's training, ability, ambitions, and natural talent.

Marxists view social class differently. Marx characterized capitalism as comprised of a two-class system—the ruling class and the working class. This has been a problem for contemporary Marxists since this seems to be an oversimplication of what exists in modern capitalist states. In the classical Marxian definition of class, it was assumed that surplus or profit was extracted from the worker through his exploitation in the workplace. Marx wrote about the early industrial era, before the appearance of large corporations. He assumed that a "free" market system existed. More recently Marxists suggest that in corporate capitalist society profit from labor is only one form of exploitation. Workers can also be exploited by administered pricing and through taxes. That is, the free market can be manipulated so that any losses incurred from labor shortages, for example, which drive the cost of labor up, can be passed on to the consumer. Taxes can also be levied and used in clever ways not only to regulate the income of workers but to provide support for the ruling elite.

Rigid division of society into a two-class system causes serious problems for contemporary Marxists since it is obvious that there are degrees of exploitation. Those who are unemployed are easily explained in classical Marxism as the pool of surplus workers needed to keep wages depressed. Those who are working, however, do not all appear to be similarly oppressed. Some, who are not part of the elite, seem to be living quite well. This is why some contemporary Marxists have developed a "new class theory" in which they admit that merit can operate in capitalism. What constitutes merit and opportunities for its achievement is controlled by the ruling elite. A few can be permitted to prosper without seriously endangering the system of control. For Marxists the opportunity for merit is greatly influenced by family ties, political power, and wealth.

Because of these ideological differences the concepts of social class, stratification, and status are beset with confusion. These introductory remarks are designed to caution the reader concerning the difficulty in defining these concepts and the reasons different sociologists utilize them in different ways. At the risk of oversimplification social class and social stratification will be used in this chapter to refer to inequalities which exist among individuals and groups in society (with apologies to sophisticated social theorists who may read this work).

However they are defined, stratification and social class are central concerns of American sociologists. In the words of Peter Rossi, in referring to the scholarly activities of sociologists: "If we have anything close to a legitimate monopoly on a substantive area, social stratification is it."[1] This observation is more than substantiated in the pages of recent issues of major journals in sociology which are filled with studies of social stratification and social class.

It isn't difficult to understand why this theme attracts so much interest, not only from sociologists but from ordinary mortals as well. First, the existence of social inequality may be the most obvious feature of any large society. Some form of inequality exists in every large society. Simply stated, some people have more than others. Second, at least in the United States, the existence of wide differences in wealth and living style among groups and individuals is a violation of a cherished belief in equality. A central theme in American ideology, if there is one, is the belief in equality of opportunity. Popularly expressed, it means at the least that individuals are limited only by their lack of ambition or drive and that everyone has a more or less equal chance to succeed. Ideally, success should depend more on individual effort than on family, sex, color of skin, place of birth, or any other factor which the individual cannot control. A third reason why the existence of social inequality has been important to Americans is because of its relation to the ideological struggle between Marxism and capitalism. Marxists argue that even equality of opportunity is a myth in a capitalist society, because the ruling class will not willingly relinquish its power.

A fourth reason why social inequality is important, especially to school people, is the belief that somehow there is a relationship between social class and values people hold. This has been considered important because of observed differences in behavior of students in the classroom. Experienced teachers observed that some students placed a higher value than others on achievement in school. They also observed that some students were pliable and easy to discipline while others were not. They observed that some students had the necessary language skills to deal with the school curriculum and others didn't. These observations were studied at length by researchers in education who found that, in many cases, the observed differences were related to social class. That is, students, especially those from the lower class, had different backgrounds, different value systems, and different language patterns, and viewed school differently than did students from the middle class. Since middle-class students seemed to achieve better in most school settings, a major task of teachers became one of attempting to somehow manage to get students to accept the values and learn the skills necessary to succeed in the schools. If school could not make everyone equal, it could at least provide individuals with the opportunity for upward mobility.

Finally, inequality has been studied at great length in America because it is something of a mystery. Once it is admitted that inequality exists, scholars become interested in why it exists. In the words of Peter Rossi: "As a distributional phenomenon, stratification attracts attention because the processes of allocation are not totally clear. It is obvious ... that life chances are unequally distributed at birth, but the paths to ultimate status destinations are not clearly marked and certainly not direct."[2]

Although many more reasons could be given for the importance of the study of inequality, including the psychological, political, and economic effects of the phenomenon, the above reasons are justification enough for a brief description and analysis of the phenomenon as it relates to the schools.

THE DIMENSIONS OF SOCIAL CLASS

Studying social class in America was a fairly simple undertaking for sociologists of an earlier generation. They began with the assumption that class existed within the social structure and could be rather clearly described. Methods utilized to determine the patterns of social class which existed in communities were relatively simple. The method employed by Warner,[3] for example, called for the social scientist to move into the community, get to know the community and its people, and ask them to rank their neighbors on a social class scale. This came to be known as the "reputational" approach. Another approach was to simply ask individuals to rank themselves on a social class scale. In other studies, the researcher first defined the important variables which were related to social class, such as income, prestige, wealth, power, values, and others, and then, through the use of data collected from questionnaires and other means, determined the class structure in a given community. Although each of the early researchers who published work on social class in America developed his or her own definition of social class, many traditional sociologists would have been willing to accept the definition provided by Robert MacIver:

> A social class is any portion of a community marked off from the rest by social status. A system of structure of social class involves: first, a hierarchy of status groups; second, the recognition of the superior-inferior stratification; and finally, some degree of permanency of the structure.[4]

It should be noted here that this is not a definition with which Marxists would agree. Marxists view class in relation to the means of production, with class membership determined by the control, or the lack of control, of these means.

The manner in which persons in communities were placed into a specific class varied, but most traditional studies relied upon the variables of income, prestige, occupation, values, and power. In addition, self-perception and race were prominent variables in some of the early studies. These studies, led by such distinguished scholars as Warner,[5] Hollingshead,[6] Havighurst,[7] and others, tended to agree, with slight differences, on the basic social class composition of American society. Reisman's description of class in "Hometown" is not an untypical example of what was found:

1. An upper class whose status was determined by old family ties—the descendants of the founders of "Hometown." The only way one could get into this group was to be born into it.

2. The lower-upper class was comprised of those who achieved some of the symbols of status including wealth, education, and a "good" home. They were either newcomers or old residents without the "proper" family ties to entitle them to upper-class status.

3. The middle class consisted of two segments, based principally on wealth. The upper-middle class was ready to "approach the next hurdle into the upper class," while the lower segment of the middle class "includes those individuals of solid respectability with a steady, sober life pattern." These were the "average citizens of Hometown."

4. The lower class included those who by income, occupation, and education stood near the bottom of the hierarchy. They were the skilled and semi-skilled workers. Their incomes were modest and socially they were "the most invisible class." At the very bottom were the lower-lowers. These were the unskilled workers who "didn't amount to much of anything" according to Hometowners. In Reisman's words: "If the upper-uppers are the contemporary versions of aristocracy, then the lower-lowers are the American version of the untouchables rejected by a caste system."[8]

Although the classification system varied with the community studied and the sociologist doing the study, most found three major classes, including the upper class, middle class, and lower class. Within these groupings there were often subgroups, with as many as three subgroups within each major classification.

As useful as these studies were, they were plagued with difficulties. A central problem had to do with the definition of social class itself. Local respondents did not always have a clear understanding of social classes in their community. A central problem for researchers was attempting to determine which variables were the most important determinants of social class. Different variables were selected by different researchers. Many concentrated on social status, which was variously determined and often included a number of indexes of superiority including education, income, and occupation. This constituted a problem since it was difficult to determine where to place individuals who, for example, had a high income but a low educational level. It was also difficult to draw precise boundaries or divisions between classes. It was not always clear how one moved up or down the social structure. Finally, since community studies often differed in their findings, it was difficult to generalize from them about the nature of social class in the society as a whole.

Although contemporary research on social class is much more sophisticated, problems still haunt the researcher. Peter Rossi outlined some unsolved problems in an article in *Contemporary Sociology*.[9] Rossi suggested that most mobility and status studies focused exclusively on males. "Children and women have derivative stratification position, if any."

A second problem was the failure of the studies to determine why social class exists. Social class research reveals a basic disagreement on this issue. Rossi referred to the differences between meritocratic theories of structural functionalists and Marxist class conflict theories. He stated the argument succinctly: "On the one side there are those who note . . . that those who garner the most also tend to contribute more," clearly a meritocratic theme. "An equally astute observation is that those who are on top like it there and not only are reluctant to reduce their share . . . but are actively seeking to augment their share." This observation supports the ruling class theory of Marx.

A third problem noted by Rossi was what he called the "local-global contrast." This was the tendency to confuse local class structure with societal structure. He correctly pointed out that the society was very interdependent in its economic activities and that national economic policy tended to have great influence on jobs, income, and lifestyle. Moreover, local communities tended to vary greatly in their perceptions of variables such as occupational prestige. He pointed out that in some communities a college professor might be ranked higher than local businessmen, while in others the reverse might be true.

Finally, Rossi pointed out that "there is more to a man or woman's concrete social position than can be indexed by his or her occupational or ethnic ties." For example "an alcoholic doctor may be despised for his wife abuse, just as a plumber may be elevated to a deaconship in recognition of his unusual piety."

A problem with research methodology related to clear classification of social class groups was suggested by Peter Blau.[10] He felt the complexity and heterogeneity of industrial societies make accurate findings difficult. In such societies every person tends to belong to a variety of groups and has a variety of roles. This creates problems of measurement of social structure and mobility because in complex societies "so many roles are important that people often must set aside ingrained ingroup prejudices for the sake of other roles." Blau suggested that in the workplace, for example, even divisions along racial lines tend to break down. This complexity extends to institutions in the society. Blau pointed out that "different group affiliations are most salient in different contexts—sometimes the people's union, sometimes their church, sometimes their neighborhood—and the changing ingroup preferences, depending on the situation, undermine social norms that would preserve certain ingroup preferences." These phenomena make rigid classifications exceedingly difficult.

In view of these difficulties, hard conclusions on the nature and effects of social structure in the United States are not possible. Even something which seems as obvious as the relationship between years of schooling and social mobility is not as clear as one might expect. Indeed, there are large differences of opinion among sociologists who have attempted to pin down this relationship. In spite of these difficulties, an examination of the relationship between social class and schooling is not an exercise in futility. In the first place, even if the researchers have substantially failed to provide an accurate picture of the realities of social class, what people believe on this subject may be as important as reality. If enough people believe that there is a relationship between social class and years of schooling, for example, that belief alone tends to take on the character of self-fulfilling prophecy. Secondly, we can be reasonably certain that large numbers of people recognize that this society includes within it a large segment of the population which is considered poor. Poverty is a reality that can be accurately described in that the number of poor people can be counted.

The existence of large numbers of poor people has great implications for the schools and for policy decisions relating to the schooling of the poor. Whereas the findings of research studies on social class relate only indirectly to the poor, the fact that many children of the poor occupy places in the schools and that they have special problems relates directly to everything the school does. The same might be said of governmental policy. While studies on social class provide data for policy makers, a major concern of educational policy on both the national and state levels in recent years has been with the existence of a single group in the schools—the poor.

SOCIAL CLASS AND THE SCHOOLS

The relationship between social class and the schools has been studied extensively. Most educational sociologists who have examined this relationship agree that schooling has some effect on mobility in the social system. Relationships have been discovered between social class and achievement in school, the type and level of education and jobs, years of schooling and income level, and educational attainment and life chances. In *Education and Inequality*,[11] Caroline Persell suggested that the three most prevalent explanations of the relationship between standing and education "suggest a deficit in the principal participants in the educational setting: the children, the parents or the teachers."

Educational sociologists seem to be in general agreement that children in low-income families do not do as well as children from affluent homes, but that is where the agreement ends. There is a division of opinion on why this phenomenon exists. Generally, the theorists who follow the Marxist model expect the schools to reflect the conditions which exist in the society. Thus they see in American capitalism a society which has sharp class divisions and schools operated in the interests of the "ruling class." The Marxists' view of the relationship between social class and the schools is that schools not only reflect the class divisions within the society, but do everything they can to perpetuate them. They point to the failures of lower-class children to succeed in elementary and secondary schools, increased dropout rates of lower-class children, and a low level of college

attendance by the children of the poor as evidence that the school system deliberately neglects the lower class. Following Marx, they see a basic system of class
conflict within the socioeconomic system in which the schools serve the rich and
the powerful. Moreover, the class conflict theorists see this as a deliberate effort
on the part of the schools to keep the lower class in its place. It is the basic
structure of class society, not the schools per se, which is the root of the problem.

At the other extreme, some traditional sociologists have considered the
socioeconomic system as essentially meritocratic. That is, they recognize the existence of social class but see the class system not as rigid and unchangeable but as
fluid and with a great deal of social mobility. Mobility, that is, movement up or
down, is based on individual merit. Thus anyone, from any social class, can rise in
the system. This has come to be called the *meritocratic hypothesis*. Meritocratic theorists tend to agree that school achievement and years of schooling can make significant contributions to upward mobility of groups and individuals. Stated simply,
the better one's achievement in school and the further one progresses in years of
schooling, the better one's life chances.

Ideally, for the meritocratic theorists, if everyone is given equal educational
opportunity, everyone will have equal life chances. For the Marxists, equal educational opportunity is a myth in a capitalistic society which is based on the preservation of the privileges of the ruling elite, since it is the ruling elite which
effectively controls the schools.

It should be noted that meritocratic theorists are not so naive as to believe that
in reality everyone does have an equal chance. They simply do not believe that
the socioeconomic system is the major culprit. Equality of opportunity could be
thwarted in the case of some individuals and groups because they are genetically
inferior. Another cause might be that family backgrounds are so poor that children cannot compete with more affluent peers. Finally, something in the organization of the school and the manner in which teachers and school officials treat
the children of the poor and minorities could keep the children from succeeding
in school. These are all in the nature of social problems, to be sure, but for those
who support the idea of merit, there is nothing in the social structure itself which
makes school success for the children of the poor and minorities impossible.
Given these differences in basic assumptions, there are serious differences in the
solutions proposed by the Marxists and the meritocratic theorists to the school
problems of the children of the poor. The Marxists see no real school solution to
the problems until the basic nature of the society is changed. The meritocratic
theorists seem to believe that adjustments can be made in the society and the
school which would lead to greater equality of opportunity. Thus, for the Marxists, the outlook is pessimistic. The disadvantages of class cannot be overcome in
the schools—classes themselves must be eliminated. For the meritocratic theorists, family environments can be improved, greater attention can be given to the
problems of the lower-class children in the school setting, and the school can
become a major instrument in upward social mobility.

Whatever terms one uses to describe different schools of thought, the relationship between the schools and social class is of central importance in the study

of any society. Whether the schools promote social mobility or fail to do so has become, perhaps, the central question in the study of schooling in America. The question has tremendous implications for the school and society.

THE MERITOCRATIC POSITION

One of the clearest statements on the role of merit was made by Kingsley Davis and Wilbert Moore.[12] Davis and Moore find some kind of stratification in every society. It exists, in their words, because of the "requirement faced by any society of placing and motivating individuals in the social structure." As a functioning mechanism, a society must somehow distribute its members in social positions and induce them to perform the duties of these positions. Davis and Moore point out that if the various positions which existed in a society were all of equal importance and "all equally in need of the same ability and talent," it would make no difference who got into the positions and "the problem of social placement would be greatly reduced." However, it does make a difference, and some kind of a reward system has to be devised to see that the positions are adequately filled. This, according to Davis and Moore, is the reason for stratification. In their words: "The rewards and their distribution become part of the social order, and thus give rise to stratification." These rewards take the form of rights and perquisites. "If the rights and perquisites of different positions in a society must be unequal, then the society must be stratified. . . . Hence every society, no matter how simple or complex must differentiate persons in terms of both prestige and esteem, and must therefore possess a certain amount of institutionalized inequality."

According to Davis and Moore, "there are two major determinants of positional rank in any society. In general, the positions which receive the greatest reward and have the highest rank are positions which (a) have the greatest importance for the society and (b) require the greatest training or talent."[13] Basically, there are only two ways that one's qualifications for any position can be established: through inherent capacity or through training. If the skills required for the position are scarce because they require a rare talent or a long period of training, the position is apt to be high on the social scale. Davis and Moore suggest that "a position does not bring power and prestige *because* it draws a high income. Rather, it draws a high income because it is functionally important and the available personnel is for one reason or another scarce."

In discussing the role that schooling or training plays in the process of stratification, Davis and Moore take the position of the nineteenth-century classical supply and demand economic theory of Ricardo, Smith, Mill, and others. They argue that interpretations which hold that high status technical positions can be economically determined, or limited only to the rich, are wrong. In their words, "the acquisition of knowledge and skill cannot be accomplished by purchase, although the opportunity to learn may be." Where certain families or elites controlled the avenues of training, this would result in the creation of an artificial scarcity of persons trained for certain positions. The opposite situation could just as easily exist. That is, an acute shortage of trained persons for important positions could have the effect of driving up the rewards. This could result in an oversupply leading to a "devaluation of the rewards." Davis and Moore argued that such adjustments were constantly occurring in changing society.

Thus, over the long run, a system of merit is in operation in stratified societies. No group, whether an elite based on religious beliefs, powerful politicians, or the owners of property, can maintain a completely stable social structure indefinitely. However, the system will never rid itself of social inequality, since there will always be "functionally important" positions in society for which there is a scarcity of personnel, and those who fill these positions will obtain the greatest rewards.

This analysis seemed to describe with some accuracy the United States of the nineteenth and much of the twentieth centuries. It also coincided with nineteenth century classical liberal economic and political philosophy in the sense that there was a market place in social position as well as in goods and services. It was not a powerful and scheming elite guiding the system but what Adam Smith called the "unseen hand" of the market place. Through a system of rewards, this "unseen hand" assured that there would be at least an adequate supply of goods and services as well as trained or talented people to fill the important positions in the society. Oversupply was controlled impersonally by the market. Scarcity, diligence, and sacrifice were rewarded. Above all, it was a system which, for the most part, rewarded merit. The incompetent and lazy would fail. Even the property rich could not maintain their position indefinitely without being able to demonstrate that what they did was functionally important to the society.

Although the relationship between schooling or training and social class was difficult to demonstrate during the nineteenth century and during the first three decades of the twentieth century in America, in recent years the relationship has become direct for most meritocratic theorists. Until very recently it was possible to attain high status without much schooling. This happened because it was possible to gain high rewards in positions which required little training and a very narrowly defined talent. School dropouts could "strike it rich" through luck, the exploitation of an invention, shrewdness in the market, inheritance, or some other means requiring very little formal schooling. This condition has changed in recent years. There aren't many people left who would not agree that there is a close relationship between success and years of schooling. The notion that high technology demands highly trained workers, whether true or not, has become part of the popular imagination. This notion has created its own demands for increased schooling. As schooling for the masses increases, it tends to create demands for even more schooling, since those who employ workers can adjust their requirements upward as the overwhelming majority of the population becomes schooled for a longer number of years. Thus the idea becomes fixed on the population that the more time one spends in school, the better one's chances are for success and mobility in the system.

This phenomenon, sometimes called "credentialism," perhaps as much as anything else, is basic to the contemporary theory of merit. Perhaps foremost among those who believed in a theory of merit was Talcott Parsons. In a discussion of the growth of higher education in the United States, Parsons observed: "there would seem to be no doubt about one major trend: that entrance to the higher occupational role-levels has been becoming increasingly dependent on educational qualifications."[14] Parsons saw the development of meritocracy in this trend when he pointed out: "This development . . . of the connection between education and occupational status is clearly complemented by the decreasing importance of ascriptive bases of higher occupational status, at least standing alone."[15] This argument clearly supports the position of Davis and Moore cited earlier, since they suggested that high status positions could not be held indefinitely by birth or family connections (ascription) because the rewards of such positions would create competition for them. Although Parsons admitted that it was nice to have family connections, this alone was not enough. Even children of the rich had to go through the "educational channel" in the contemporary world, whereas in earlier eras this was unnecessary. The importance of schooling as the most certain means to upward mobility is perhaps best illustrated by the incredible increase in recent years in college attendance. Between 1940 and 1960, the number of 18 to 21 year olds enrolled in college doubled. By the late seventies, before it began to level off, it had reached 45 percent of all high school graduates.

Other researchers have agreed with Parsons' major conclusions. In describing studies made in *River City* and *Prairie City* in the 1960s, Robert Havighurst and Daniel Levine concluded that schooling played a central role in upward mobility.[16] In the River City study, the authors estimated that 20 percent of upwardly mobile youth were relying primarily "upon intellectual ability and intellectual training."[17] Fifty percent of the upwardly mobile relied primarily on social skills or on drive and ambition. In *River City*, the authors concluded that their study "showed clearly two main paths of social mobility. Men, and some women, will climb the social ladder by making use of superior intelligence and superior social effectiveness to succeed in school and college and on the job. The more frequent path for women was by marrying a relatively successful young man."[18] In this study and in their analysis of others, Havighurst and Levine seem to conclude that schooling is a central key to upward mobility. In fairness it must be pointed out that Havighurst and Levine qualified their position. They cautioned that although "many young people use education to become upwardly mobile . . . many lower-status students are disadvantaged before they ever enter school and are not able to achieve much success through the schools. . . ."[19]

However, they pointed out that "there is no logical reason to believe that the schools cannot function *both* as a route to mobility for some students and a barrier for others . . . nor is there a logical contradiction in the conclusion that the schools are becoming more of a force for upward mobility than they have been in the past and at the same time becoming more of a barrier to the mobility of some segments of the population."[20]

In a study of changes in rates of mobility over generations, Peter Blau and Otis Duncan[21] were able to conclude that "there is a grain of truth in the Horatio

Alger myth," that is, the traditional "rags to riches" story, where success comes through hard work, thrift, or sheer luck. They observed that nearly 10 percent of the sons of manual workers achieve elite status in the United States. The data for their research came from a large national sample of males from the Census reports of 1960, in which respondents were asked to describe the occupational status of their parents and grandparents. In reviewing earlier studies made by Jackson and Crockett, which supported meritocratic assumptions about upward mobility, Blau and Duncan concluded that their study supported the major findings of earlier studies. Jackson and Crockett reported that "the rate of occupational mobility in the United States has increased somewhat since the end of World War II."[22] In reviewing the data from the 1960 Census and their own data, Blau and Duncan flatly stated: "We are still in the position of Jackson and Crockett."[23]

In their analysis of the data from the years 1952 to 1962 they concluded:

(1) a decreasing proportion of men with farm origins remained on farms, whereas an increasing proportion achieved manual status; (2) an increasing proportion from manual origins moved up into white-collar positions; (3) yet there was no compensatory increase in downward mobility from white-collar origins; on the contrary, increasing proportions of those originating at this level remained there.[24]

Blau and Duncan claimed that their study revealed that upward mobility had been enchanced by "rapidly expanding higher salaried positions," and they reported that the fears "current in the sociological fraternity a decade or two ago —that the 'land of opportunity' was giving way to a society with rigid classes —were ill-founded, or at least premature."[25]

The difficulties faced by minorities in their struggle to enter the mainstream of society have attracted a great deal of attention on the part of sociologists interested in social class. Much of the research has concentrated on the mobility of the black population. Researchers have obviously been interested in attempting to determine if the long struggle on the part of blacks for civil rights and equal educational opportunity has had any impact on social mobility. Some have positive results to report. In a study spanning the decade from 1962–1973, which involved more than 20,000 men aged 20 to 64, David Featherman and Robert Hauser reported that "at every age, black men enjoyed larger absolute and relative upward shifts in current occupational status than did whites."[26] The gain for black men aged 25 to 63 was "almost two and one half times the gain for whites, and it represented an improvement equal to 53% of the black standard deviation in 1962."[27] Although blacks gained at every age, the largest gains took place among young workers. Blacks also made gains in educational level. Indeed, the educational gains made by blacks were so impressive to Featherman and Hauser that they announced that "racial differentials in educational attainment seem to be disappearing."[28] This cheerful view was based on the advance in years of schooling. In 1962 the mean difference in education for black and white men aged 25 to 64 was 3.0 years; the gap had narrowed to two years by 1973. Among younger men (25 to 34), the mean difference dropped from 2.3 years in 1962 to 1.2

years in 1973. By 1979 the gap had virtually disappeared. For that year, the Bureau of the Census reported that the median school years completed for all white males was 12.6, and for blacks, 11.9. However, there continued to be a wide gap between white males (17.2 percent) and blacks (7.9 percent) who completed four years or more of college. For females, 13.3 percent of all white females had four or more years of college; the figure for black females was 7.5 percent.

The increasing concern for equal rights for women, plus the fact that women were marrying later and were developing careers independent of their husbands, created an interest in mobility studies on women. In view of the limited economic opportunities for women and their traditional roles in families, it was expected that studies on women would tend to show less mobility for women than men. However, some studies which included women tended to support the position of upward mobility based on merit. In a study by DeJong, Brawer, and Robin, it was discovered that mobility among women generally paralleled that found in the studies of men.[29] It should be pointed out that this study was widely criticized —critics didn't like the design of the study and generally charged that sex differences were not adequately isolated.

Hauser and Featherman reported that "women appear to be more mobile than men."[30] However, Hauser and Featherman's study on the mobility of women is not a model of clarity. They found it difficult to separate married couples in their attempts to assess upward mobility among women. Other researchers have experienced difficulty in applying to women the traditional models for the study of upward social mobility. Using a modified form of the Blau-Duncan basic model of the stratification process, Michael Hout and William Morgan[31] found that it was difficult to estimate the educational and occupational expectations of women. They found that the variables which affected school achievement were different for males and females. For white females, grades were "solely a function of measured intelligence," whereas for white males, parental encouragement was as important as intelligence. They also found differences in the influence of peers on the educational and occupational expectation of males and females. The influence of the educational and occupational aspirations of friends appeared to be much more important to boys than girls. They also found that black females could not be measured on expected attainment models in the same way as white or black males. They concluded, in part, that existing research models on attainment fit white males better than either white or black females. They attributed the difficulty of measurement of female educational and occupational aspirations in part, at least, to "differential positions of whites and blacks, males and females, in the American stratification system and of the complex socialization processes which help to maintain that system."

Alexander and Eckland[32] found significant differences between the sexes on variables which influenced educational attainment. They found that the variables which affected male educational and occupational attainment did not affect females in the same way. Being female was an "unmediated depressant" on actual educational attainment. Sex was discovered to be more important than academic ability, status background, performance, educational goal orientations, academic self-concept, and influences of parents, teachers, and peers. Alexander and Eckland offered no explanation for this, but they did suggest that new research models had to be developed for females which would include factors typically not considered in the study of males.

For years, sociologists noted the apparent anomaly that girls made better grades in high school and tended to drop out less than boys but were grossly underrepresented in college. There is evidence that this is no longer true. Rehberg and Rosenthal reported some interesting developments in this area. In a discussion of "gender and school outcomes," they found that while the long-standing female advantage in graduation from high school had "just about disappeared, the gap between male and female enrollments in four-year colleges had narrowed." They found that 35 percent of the men and 29 percent of the women in their sample were enrolled in four-year colleges one year after high school graduation.[33] This study was based on data from 1970. The authors did not report earlier enrollment figures. In summarizing their findings, Rehberg and Rosenthal observed that by 1970 the total effect of sex on post-high school educational activity was "trivial." Moreover, girls continued as in the past to make better grades in school. They also had a slight advantage in curriculum location in that they tended to be found more often than boys in academic programs. Females were more likely to graduate from high school, and, even though fewer enrolled in four-year colleges, they were more likely than males to enter two-year colleges. Rehberg and Rosenthal concluded that if one controlled "for ability and social class, the female advantage in ambition offset each other and result in an educational stratification order very similar by sex one year after high school."[34] For both boys and girls, Rehberg and Rosenthal present a rather strong argument for merit. "Ability certainly outweighs social-class background in total effects on educational decisions and college entry for both boys and girls. . . ."[35] Although ability seemed to be a strong factor in social mobility for women, Rehberg and Rosenthal hedged with the statement" . . . in total effects neither ability nor class predict college entry as strongly for women as for men."[36]

For whatever reasons, females have closed the educational gap with males. According to Census data for 1979, white and black females over 25 years of age were about equal in the number of years of college they had completed. The percentage of black males who had some college was 11.3; for black females, the percentage was 11.6. For whites who had some college attendance, the figures were 15.0 for males and 15.8 for females. The percentage of black females who had four or more years of college was 7.5; for black males it was 8.3. For white males who had completed four or more years of college by 1979, the percentage was 17.2; for white females, the figure was 21.4. A more complete analysis of sex differences in education and income will be presented in a later chapter.

The research on the relationship of academic achievement and class appears to provide more substantial conclusions. This relationship was often avoided by early research involved in generational studies because of the difficulty in measuring the contribution of academic achievement. It was virtually impossible to compare school achievement between fathers and sons. This problem left researchers with school attainment rather than school achievement as the basic measure of educational success when comparing generations.

More recently, relationships between school achievement and social mobility have been observed. In a way, the Coleman Report[37] dealt with this relationship when Coleman and his associates reported that school children varied on verbal achievement tests from school to school and within schools where educational resources were substantially equal. This finding became important for later researchers, for example Jencks, who observed that standardized achievement tests are good predictors of grades in school or college, number of years of schooling attained, and later occupational status.[38]

In their study of class and merit in high school, Rehberg and Rosenthal observed: "Achievements inside the school . . . mirrors . . . achievement in the real world . . . because high school grades have so much to do with access to post-secondary education and hence to jobs and earnings. . . . "[39] In their data on achievement they found strong support for merit as expressed by school grades. Moreover, they found that course grades achieved by students were not strongly affected by student social class.

In the research based on the meritocratic model of society discussed here, there seems to be general agreement that there is a relationship between schooling and social mobility. Most would agree with Blau and Duncan when they noted:

> The achieved status of a man, what he has accomplished in terms of some objective criteria, becomes more important than his ascribed status, who he is in the sense of what family he comes from. This does not mean that family background no longer influences careers. What it does imply is that superior status cannot any more be directly inherited but must be legitimated by actual achievements that are socially acknowledged. Education assumes increasing significance for social status in general and for the transmission of social standing from fathers to sons in particular.[40]

In a comprehensive analysis of research findings, Brent Shea reported that "high status occupations have been found to demand educational attainment beyond secondary school" and high incomes have been shown to be associated with advanced education. He concluded that social status is affected more by the classroom than by any other factor. In his words, "occupational status attainment criteria" increasingly reside "in schools, where certification requirements are increasingly determining employment and promotion."[41]

In their widely quoted study of changes in socioeconomic stratification of races from 1962 to 1972, Featherman and Hauser appeared to be convinced that there was great merit in educational attainment. They found that "schooling mediates much of the influence of socioeconomic background on occupational status among men of both races throughout the economically active years."[42] In comparing their results to those found by Duncan 10 years earlier, they found that each additional year of schooling had increased the occupational status of whites aged 25 to 64 by 18 percent. During the same 10-year period, even though blacks still lagged behind whites in occupational status, an additional year of schooling meant even more. The return on one year of schooling for blacks increased their occupational status by 63 percent. Featherman and Hauser announced that "schooling remains the single most important element of status allocation" even though "whites were unable to convert their educational attainments into occupational statuses at the same level as did men of equivalent schooling in 1962."[43] The authors speculated that the reason for this may have been the increasing level of schooling for the entire population. Even considering this factor, blacks seemed to be more dependent upon years of schooling for social mobility. Their pattern in 1973 was similar to the pattern for whites of a decade earlier. That is, although school attainment was important to both blacks and whites in the 1963 study and the 1973 study, years of schooling was more important for the social mobility of blacks in 1973 than it was for whites.

Although many other studies could be cited, they generally reach the same conclusions as those reported here. That is, there is a close relationship between years of schooling and occupational status. Thus the meritocratic theorists suggest that schools do much more than mirror the social class structure of existing society. Schooling is important, indeed perhaps the most important single factor, in upward social mobility in American society. If this is true, it is a comforting view for ambitious and capable youngsters who come from impoverished family backgrounds, since these are obstacles which can be overcome by personal individual effort in school.

THE CRITICS OF MERITOCRACY

Not everyone agrees with such an optimistic view of the role of schooling in upward social mobility. There is a growing body of criticism of this view. Ironically, without the criticism there might have been a decline in social mobility research. The criticism seems to encourage more research. After all, it does seem obvious in a society which puts so much stock in democracy and individual achievement and which is becoming increasingly technological, that the more years of schooling the better. The notion that there is a cause and effect relationship between schooling and occupational mobility seems so self-evident that it hardly is worth proving. Certainly for school people and students of social mobility, it would be convenient merely to accept the fact that school pays and go on from there. Unfortunately, it isn't that simple.

The revisionist historians, the varieties of Marxists, the "human capitalists" and others who looked at the society and the social stratification within it felt uneasy about the conclusions of meritocratic research. They weren't at all certain that upward social mobility existed in the society and that which could be documented might be largely an illusion.

Ivan Illich thought that the poor did not have an equal chance to succeed. According to Illich, "poor children lack most of the educational opportunities which are casually available to the middle-class child. These advantages range from conversation and books in the home to vacation travel and a different sense of oneself. . . . So the poorer student will generally fall behind so long as he depends on school for advancement of learning."[44]

In Illich's view, the schools do not teach students what is needed to climb the ladder of socioeconomic success. They teach the myths which support the capitalist system. The schools teach the "myth of unending consumption," which is the notion that schools themselves produce the demand for schooling.[45] According to Illich, schools also instill the "myth of measurement of values," the notion that everything can be measured. This tends to produce a population that is willing to accept the strict structure of the existing capitalist system. In Illich's words: "Once people have the idea schooled into them that values can be produced and measured, they tend to accept all kinds of rankings."[46] The school also "sells curriculum," according to Illich. He called this the "myth of packaging values." He compared the curriculum to other marketable products. The curriculum itself and the delivery system are analogous to the capitalist market system. The curriculum is the product; the teacher, the distributor; and the pupil, the consumer. Finally, the school teaches the "myth of self-perpetuating progress"—that is, that more is better. As per-pupil cost increases and the number of years of school required increases, the consumers of the product internalize the notion that, as is true with anything else in the market, what takes more time and costs more must be worth more. In Illich's words: "If it teaches nothing else, the school teaches the value of escalation: the value of the American way of doing things."[47]

Perhaps the clearest statement of Marxist theory may be found in Samuel Bowles and Herbert Gintis' *Schooling in Capitalist America*.[48] They give the schools little credit as an agent of upward social mobility. In their work they attempt to support the assertion that this is basically a society in which there is a fairly rigid social structure, and the roots of inequality "are to be found in the class structure and the system of sexual and racial power relationships."[49] In the United States, the school is but one of several institutions which serve to perpetuate a structure of privilege. In Bowles and Gintis' view, "education is relatively powerless to correct economic inequality. The class, sex, and race biases in schooling do not produce, but rather reflect, the structure of privilege in society at large."[50] In order for the schools to make a basic contribution to equality or to provide a means for upward mobility, the economic system would have to change. This is so, according to Bowles and Gintis, because it is the economic system which demands inequality and promotes a more or less static social system. The schools are controlled by this system, support and correspond to it, and are a functionally integral part of it.

Writing in *Contemporary Sociology*, Herbert Gintis finds serious fault with Featherman and Hauser's replication of Blau and Duncan's well-known study of *The American Occupational Structure*. Blau and Duncan reported their findings in 1967. Eleven years later, in *Opportunity and Change*, Featherman and Hauser replicated the Blau and Duncan study and reached many of the same conclusions. Like Blau and Duncan before them, Featherman and Hauser found a strong relationship between educational and occupational status. They were, in a word, optimistic about their findings regarding upward social mobility in the society. Gintis was upset because Featherman and Hauser included school attainment as an important variable in upward mobility. If years of schooling were rewarded by the system in the form of higher income and better occupational status, Gintis wondered how one could account for the inferior position of blacks, other minorities, and women whose educational attainment level was relatively high. He charged that Featherman and Hauser's findings on blacks were misleading. Because Featherman and Hauser's study dealt only with blacks in the labor force, Gintis was critical of the finding that blacks had made great gains. The problem of unemployment was inadequately treated in the study, and Gintis pointed out that this oversight could seriously distort the findings, since Featherman and Hauser reported in the youngest cohort (25 to 29 years of age) a very sharp decline in racial deficit for occupational status, from 10.5 to 3.4 on the Duncan scale, "while unemployment rates for young blacks are notoriously high and variable."[51]

Another sharp criticism made by Gintis concerned his observation that 11 years was too short a period to permit hard conclusions. He pointed out that the seventies provided special problems in the labor market, including business cycles, "war, structural unevenness in the growth of occupational categories, specific governmental policies, and the like . . ."[52] and that conclusions based on this period would be open to serious question.

Perhaps an even more serious criticism of the work of the meritocratic theorists was made by Gregory D. Squires.[53] Squires examined what he called the "techno-democratic model" of social stratification. This model assumes that the increasing of skill requirements for jobs leads to an increasing educational level. That educational levels among the population increase with each succeeding decade cannot be questioned. What Squires questioned was whether, in fact, available jobs were demanding higher levels of education because of their increasing complexity. If this were true, it would appear to have some influence on educational decisions. Individuals would choose to get more schooling to meet increasing skill demands. What Squires found was that although educational levels were increasing, the jobs were becoming less, not more, complex. He pointed out that "shifts in the occupational structure from farm laborer to operative or from blue-collar to white-collar occupations are often misinterpreted as representing an upgrading of skill requirements."[54] A different view was offered by Squires. The introduction of new technology into the production process often results in the fragmentation of skilled occupations into unskilled tasks. What the most productive enterprise seeks from technology is not to make the jobs more complex, but to make them more simple. This process is apparent even to the most casual observer of large factories. For years, the work in large factories—the automobile and steel industries, for example—has been broken down into smaller and smaller segments requiring the learning of very few skills on the part of each worker. Of course, the ultimate simplification of specific tasks is reached at the point where the tasks can be performed by industrial robots, which is precisely what is happening. Squires points out that "an assembly line worker may use more sophisticated machinery than the small family farmer, but operatives are not therefore more highly skilled workers."[55] Also, while it is true that white-collar jobs have been expanding, it does not always follow that they are more complex or require a higher level of skills. Although Squires admits that technology does create some jobs that require a high level of skills, the net effect of the application of advanced technology to the production process is to lessen the need for high level skills. From the evidence which he reviewed, Squires concluded that "skill requirements of jobs throughout the occupational structure have not undergone massive upgrading. When changes have occurred, they have not resulted in a demand for extensive formal retraining or educational programs."[56]

Another view of this issue was reported by Kenneth Spenner in 1979 in the *American Sociological Review*.[57] Using a sample of job descriptions from two editions of the *Dictionary of Occupational Titles*, Spenner attempted to determine if skills required for jobs had been upgraded, downgraded, or had remained unchanged over the last quarter-century. Spenner defined skills as the degree of "mental, interpersonal, and manipulative complexity inherent in a job." Spenner concluded that his study suggested "very little change, if any a slight upgrading, in the actual skill content of work over the last quarter century." Spenner admitted that his conceptualization of skills was arbitrary and that there existed the possibility of serious problems with the comparability of data from editions of the *Dictionary of Occupational Titles*.

Even if Spenner's conclusions are accurate, it seems unlikely that a slight increase in skill content of work would justify the tremendous increase in educational level in the last quarter-century. For example, the National Center for Educational Statistics reported that 376,973 bachelor's degrees were conferred in 1955, while the figure for 1979 was 1,347,000.

How does one explain this phenomenon? Put simply: Why are so many people spending more time in school to qualify for jobs which require at most only slightly higher skills? If Squires' analysis is correct, the answer to this question has nothing to do with merit. Illich may have been right. Schooling creates demand for more schooling. As the number of years of schooling of the masses increases, employers can demand more schooling as a condition of employment. Thus, the schools have not necessarily contributed to upward social mobility; they have merely created a situation in which more schooling is required for any employment. This reasoning has to lead to the conclusion that if there is genuine upward mobility in the system, it is a function not of the schools but of the economic system. As technology is introduced and production increased, some of the economic benefits find their way into the pockets of the workers. Although this process may lead to higher incomes and new job descriptions, the social class configuration remains basically unchanged. Large numbers of workers may be better off than their fathers, but their relative position in the social structure has not changed.

For the critics of meritocracy, schools support the existing system of social stratification in many ways: by classifying students on the basis of test scores, grouping them by race, counseling them into dead-end careers, and in general doing things which will insure the existence of the present class structure. Space does not permit a full treatment of these topics. For an excellent case study on some of these problems the reader should see the case of *Hobson v. Hansen* (408 F2d 175,1969).[58]

A NOTE ON THE AMERICAN UNDERCLASS

Public schools are not for the poor. The children of the poor do not do well there. These are the children who are economically, socially, and educationally disadvantaged from the time they enter kindergarten until they drop out or, more rarely, graduate. The children of the poor are not prepared to cope with the formal or informal curriculum. From the beginning, they fail to develop basic skills, and, as the years progress, they get further behind. In many localities, the children of the poor in urban and rural slums tend to go to school with children very much like themselves. Often their schools are poor in any way one wishes to measure them. When schools serving the poor are located in urban and rural poverty ghettos where there is a low tax base, the schools tend to match the poverty of the communities they serve. Characteristically, the buildings are old and dilapidated. Science labs and good libraries are rare. The buildings are uncomfortable, often cold in winter months. Teachers don't like to teach there and often the teachers are the most poorly qualified in the district. Those who get their first jobs there don't stay long.

Although they tend to be concentrated in rural and urban slums, there are so many poor children in America that they can be found anywhere. According to 1980 Census data, approximately 29 million people were officially designated as poor. Most of them were white. There were approximately two white poor persons for every poor nonwhite in 1980, although being black, native American, or Hispanic gave one a better chance of being poor. Only about 10 percent of the white population was classified as poor in 1980, while the figure for blacks and other minority races approached 30 percent. Although they can be found in every state in large numbers, the states with large cities are clearly the leaders. New York, California, and Texas led the list in absolute numbers, with Florida, Ohio, Pennsylvania, and Illinois not far behind. Even with its remarkable gains in economic development, the South, with its large black population, continued in 1980 to be a region in which poverty was a serious problem. Even with the war on poverty, social welfare programs, food stamps, and a myriad of other federal and state programs, poverty has not been eliminated in America.

The children of the poor continue, as always, to have difficult problems in school. Many come from backgrounds that are so horrendous that the schools seem unable to cope. Homes characterized by one-parent families are a growing problem, especially among black families. The homes of the poor are homes where cultural enrichment is virtually nonexistent. The children of the poor, due to their lack of success and the difficult circumstances of their environment—including hunger, poor health care, survival values, and others—find themselves isolated and alienated in school. Their home surroundings and school experiences tend to give them a low self-image, and many eventually come to believe that they are victims of society and that their life chances are nil.

If these generalizations about the poor seem harsh, the specific conditions of large urban ghettos are even worse. Youth in the ghetto comprise what has been called an underclass in American society. Stuck in the bottom of the social structure with no obvious chance to escape, they find upward mobility difficult. The social agencies established to assist the poor often measure success in terms of their own productivity—how many cases they handle, not in terms of how many escape. Welfare workers, teachers, and others tend to become custodial in their approach to the problem. Helping those who want to achieve in terms of mainstream America is difficult. There may be no school solution to this problem. The situation for many underclass children may be so hopeless that only massive and imaginative programs of assistance can provide the environment in which schooling might have a chance.

Of course, not everyone agrees on precisely what the problems are, much less what the solutions should be. In a published debate over the issues of race and class in the black community, Carl Gershman, a white scholar and long-time civil rights advocate, and Kenneth B. Clark, a distinguished black psychologist,[59] presented their ideas on the nature of the problem. The debate was stimulated in part by the futile efforts of well-known and highly respected black leaders to cool the riots of blacks in Miami, Florida, in the summer of 1980. Shocked by the rejection of these leaders by the "street people," Clark and Gershman, among others, have attempted an analysis of the problem.

Both Clark and Gershman recognized the existence of a large black underclass. Clark worried about the growing class divisions within black society itself; he was concerned that racism was still a major problem for blacks and a major reason for the existence of a black underclass. He noted that the civil rights movement had shifted from the southern states to northern urban centers and he observed that a new "intellectual leadership has emerged as a major factor in blocking further racial progress."[60] According to Clark, northern advocates of the racial status quo, advocating a policy of benign neglect, reject the excesses of the old southern racist but at the same time "extol the virtues of ethnic isolation and protection of white groups from black 'invasion.'"[61] Clark contends that public officials and even black civil rights leaders have contributed "by omission" to a retreat on issues of racial equality. In his words:

> Black middle class leaders, in confusion . . . have lost the initiative to define the issues and to counter the new semantics of racism. They have yet to present an effective rebuttal against such racial code words as "busing," "quotas," "reverse discrimination," "meritocracy," "maintaining standards"—the shorthand terms implying that remedies for racial injustice will weaken the fiber of society as a whole and lead to a new racism.[62]

Critical of the black separatist movement, Clark considered it a failure—a retreat, as it were, to the old Plessy doctrine of "separate but equal." According to Clark, racism was increasing in America, and black leadership, for a number of reasons, was experiencing increasing difficulty in coping with it. The great leaders of the past were gone. Some had been killed, while others had retired from the struggle. Most ironic was that the very success of the civil rights movement "deprived it of many of its potential leaders." Clark pointed out that many of these potential leaders had, in effect, become part of the establishment. However, he was careful to point out that their positions there were precarious. They tended to be in fringe jobs where they might "jeopardize what little power they have if they seek to exercise it too aggressively in behalf of other blacks."[63]

Like Clark, Gershman recognized the unfinished nature of the battle for black equality in American society. Gershman also argued that growing class divisions within black society itself were a major obstacle to progress for the large mass of underclass blacks. Gershman felt that the major cause for the existence of a black underclass was not racism but economics, and he charged that various programs designed to help blacks during the sixties did nothing to help the large black ghetto underclass. What the programs did was to help economically a few blacks at the expense of most of them. In his words: "the new approach both rationalized and subsidized the underclass's continued existence. It appealed to many whites by offering them a convenient excuse to evade the whole problem while, at the same time, allowing them to show proper 'concern' for the disadvantaged by submitting to 'black demands.'"[64] Finally, it appealed to a new class of black political leaders and federally funded antipoverty workers "who became, in effect, the power brokers between Government and the black poor."[65] These new leaders, according to Gershman "had a stake in preserving the underclass as a political base from which they could threaten—and extract concessions from—white society."[66]

To support his thesis, Gershman cited data which demonstrated that some blacks did benefit from programs to help blacks. He cited the phenomenal increase in college attendance between 1965 and 1977—"from 274,000 to 1.1 million." Due to higher educational achievement and a decline in job-market discrimination, Gershman noted that the number of blacks "in professional and managerial jobs nearly doubled during the 1970s to 1.9 million."[67] Even more encouraging, the income gap was closing. Young college-educated blacks made about the same income as their white counterparts. Gershman was optimistic about earnings ratios for all fully employed blacks, noting that black males earned "77 percent as much as white males in 1975, up from 63 percent in 1955." For females, the situation was even better. By 1975, income for black females was 98.6 percent of white female earnings. Unfortunately, this upward movement affected only about two-thirds of the black population. "The bottom third has not only failed to participate in the progress of the last 15 years but its social and economic position has deteriorated to an alarming extent."[68] In support of this argument, he cited a black unemployment level of nearly 40 percent for young blacks, and a slowly but steadily increasing female-headed black family, up from 23.2 percent of all black families in 1962 to 40.5 percent in 1979.[69] Agreeing with William Julius Wilson's argument in *The Declining Significance of Race* (1978), Gershman suggested that the real problem was not race but the existence of the black economic underclass. Wilson made the point that blacks with education and skills could now advance economically, while the underclass could not.

Whatever the cause for the existence of a black underclass—race or the economics of class, the fact upon which everyone can agree is that there is a large number of ghetto blacks who are virtually immobile, and, without some radical

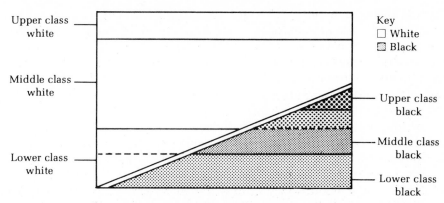

FIGURE 7.1 Contiguous systems of the black and white castes in the United States. (Note that this illustration is not drawn according to scale.)

changes in social and economic policy, there may be little hope for them. The implications for policy decisions on the problem of black poverty are important. So long as there exists a large black ghetto underclass with all of its potential for social unrest, policy makers can be convinced that something should be done. Whatever is done is sure to benefit a few. For those who are directly employed in programs designed to benefit poor ghetto blacks, there is an obvious vested interest in seeing that the problem continues to exist. Carried to an extreme, antiracism could not exist without racism. If one believes that racism continues to be the major problem for blacks in America, then social policies designed to attack that illness are indicated. This would mean a rededication to past policies which favor integration in all institutions, and affirmative action and education programs designed to combat racism. If one believes that poverty is the basic problem, then attention of policy makers must be more directly focused on the specific economic problems of the poorest of the poor and on programs to directly assist the ghetto underclass.

Whatever the cause, everybody must agree that one can find serious inequality between blacks and whites. Even recent data which demonstrate that blacks are closing the income as well as the educational gap are not encouraging—for the fact that a gap can be found is tragic enough. Moreover, it may be a bit misleading to consider black class stratification in isolation. That is, one gets quite a different picture of social stratification when blacks are compared to whites. John Ogbu did this in *Minority Education and Caste.*[70] Figure 7.1, based on data in the early seventies, supports both class and race arguments. The diagram shows how Ogbu depicted what he called the "caste" system* in America.

Ogbu maintains that each caste has its own classes but that the two class systems are not equal. Members of the two castes have "unequal access to education, occupation, income, and other attributes that determine social class mem-

---

* Caste system may be defined as a system in which an individual is born into a given social category where he remains for life.

bership for a given individual."[71] Ogbu suggests that members of the black caste are restricted from competing for the most important jobs in the society. Very few ever make it to the top in white terms. If, indeed, a caste system does exist, the implications for schooling are great. In Ogbu's words: "The caste organization of black-white stratification leads to divergent development in the education of the two groups." According to Ogbu, "blacks and whites have tended to occupy two different worlds which require different attitudes, values, personalities, skills, and behavioral patterns. In order to produce the kind of people who will adapt to such different worlds, the caste system requires different modes of training the young members of both groups, including the institutionalization of differences in their formal education."[72]

Whether or not Ogbu is correct in his analysis of caste in America, what he has to say about school practices—"the subtle mechanisms of inferior education" —is so well documented that it is difficult to challenge. At the top of the list are continued efforts to segregate blacks, accompanied by inadequate funding of predominantly black schools. There is no serious reason to be cheered by progress made in this area. A later chapter will deal specifically with this problem. Even where there is integration, Ogbu correctly points out that teacher attitudes and expectations can be racist, in the sense that some teachers regard black children as intellectually inferior. Ogbu also listed the misuse of IQ tests, misclassification based on standardized achievement tests, tracking, biased texts, misconceptions about black families, bad counseling, and deliberately inferior teaching, as well as other mechanisms for delivering inferior education to blacks. The closing of the education gap between blacks and whites is misleading because it says nothing about the kind of schooling blacks get or the curriculum they follow. The increase in the number of blacks in professional and managerial positions is misleading because the total is still very small, even though percentages have increased dramatically. Although progress has been made, there is still a large gap between fully employed black males and white males. The female gains were irrelevant because a large gap existed between all females and males with equal qualifications.

The most central criticism made by Ogbu, however, was that a job ceiling existed for blacks. Ogbu provides data which demonstrate that regardless of level of educational attainment, blacks cannot expect to acquire a job which has equal status with whites at the same level of educational attainment nor can they expect the same level of income.[73] Although his data ends with 1970, he makes a convincing case. Even with later data, viewed in the most optimistic light, his case is still strong, since any difference which can be observed which is based on race supports his point.

SOME CONCLUSIONS

What conclusions, then, can one draw from the debate between meritocratic theorists and their critics? If one accepts the critics' view a number of things follow. Most central, perhaps, is the sense that nothing the schools do, or can do, matters much. That is, if the schools only reflect existing social arrangements, it doesn't matter what they do—social classes remain basically unchanged. Indeed, as in the case of the black underclass, it might even be argued that the schools have a negative impact in that they encourage and perpetuate a pathological condition. The school takes on the character of a holding or custodial institution where what is learned, how teachers go about their business, the bureaucratic rules, or whatever is done, is irrelevant in the long run.

If, on the other hand, one accepts the meritocratic hypothesis—that the schools can and do make a significant contribution to upward social mobility, a number of different things follow. School becomes vitally important: what teachers do, the curriculum, the successes of school are important in the lives of millions of students.

Perhaps neither side is totally correct. There are strong arguments and research findings which support each side. In terms of large groups in the society, the evidence seems rather clear that mass upward movement has not taken place. At least it is very difficult to demonstrate that whole groups have moved up the ladder. Granted that the working class is more prosperous than at any past date, this movement was a sliding one in which whole classes improved their absolute advantage. But this was an advantage over time, not over contemporary class competitors. There is no good evidence that whole classes of persons were involved in mobility in the sense that they moved out of the class into which they were born. There is movement within classes but very little documented movement out of them. However, the meritocratic theorists might be correct if their arguments are limited to individuals. Only the most close minded would fail to admit that many individuals, perhaps millions in the course of a generation or two, have moved up the socioeconomic ladder. What is not so clear is what caused this. Certainly, generalizations are hazardous. In many cases it might have been schooling; in just as many, it could have been luck[74] or some other outside influence. This does not mean that one who is convinced that the critics are correct need give up on the schools. If for no other reason, schooling is essential just to keep even in the rat race. Also, even the critics understand that though class structure may not change much through the years, society does change. This is a different society than it was a generation ago or even a decade ago. Schools do contribute to the change in some ways. The direction of change and the role schools play in it may not be clear. What is clear, or should be, even for Marxists, is that neither success in a capitalist class society nor the enlightened citizenry needed for revolutionary change of the system is possible without schooling.

NOTES

1. Peter H. Rossi, "The Ups and Downs of Social Class in America," *Contemporary Sociology* 9 (January 1980), p. 40.
2. Ibid.
3. Lloyd Warner and Paul S. Lunt, *The Social Life of a Modern Community* (New Haven, Conn.: Yale University Press, 1942).

4. Robert M. MacIver and Charles H. Page, *Society: An Introductory Analysis* (New York: Holt, Rinehart & Winston, 1949), p. 348.
5. Lloyd Warner et al., *Social Class in America* (New York: Harper & Row, 1960).
6. August B. Hollingshead, *Elmstown's Youth* (New York: John Wiley & Sons, 1949).
7. Robert J. Havighurst et al., *Growing Up in River City* (New York: John Wiley & Sons, 1962).
8. Leonard Reisman, *Class in American Society* (New York: Free Press of Glencoe, 1959), p. 83.
9. Peter H. Rossi, "The Ups and Downs of Social Class in America," pp. 41–42.
10. Peter M. Blau, "Presidential Address: Parameters of Social Structure," *American Sociological Review* 39 (October 1974): 615–635.
11. Caroline Nodges Persell, *Education and Inequality* (New York: Free Press, 1977), p. 1.
12. Kingsley Davis and Wilbert Moore, "Some Principles of Stratification," in *Class Status and Power*, ed. Reinhard Bendix and Seymour Lipset, 2d ed. (New York: Free Press, 1966), pp. 47–53.
13. Ibid., p. 48.
14. Talcott Parsons, *Social Structure and Personality* (London: Collier-Macmillan, 1964), p. 210.
15. Ibid.
16. Robert J. Havighurst and Daniel U. Levine, *Society and Education*, 5th ed. (Boston: Allyn & Bacon, 1979), chs. 4 and 5.
17. Ibid., p. 93.
18. Ibid.
19. Ibid., p. 116.
20. Ibid.
21. Peter Blau and Otis Dudley Duncan, *The American Occupational Structure* (New York: John Wiley & Sons, 1967).
22. Elton F. Jackson and Harry J. Crockett, Jr., "Occupational Mobility in the United States," *American Sociological Review* 29 (1964): 15.
23. Blau and Duncan, *The American Occupational Structure*, p. 98.
24. Ibid., p. 103.
25. Ibid., p. 113.
26. David L. Featherman and Robert M. Hauser, "Changes in Socioeconomic Stratification of the Races, 1962–73," *American Journal of Sociology* 82 (1976): 627.
27. Ibid.
28. Ibid., p. 631.
29. Peter DeJong, Y. Milton, J. Brawer, and Stanley S. Robin, "Patterns of Female Intergenerational Occupational Mobility: A Comparison with Male Patterns of Intergenerational Occupational Mobility," *American Sociological Review* 36 (December 1971): 1033–1041.
30. Robert M. Hauser and David L. Featherman, *The Process of Stratification* (New York: Academic Press, 1977), p. 208.
31. Michael Hout and William Morgan, "Race and Sex Variations in the Causes of Expected Attainments of High School Seniors," *American Journal of Sociology* 81 (September 1975): 364–384.
32. Karl Alexander and Bruce Eckland, "Sex Differences in the Educational Attainment Process," *American Sociological Review* 39 (October 1974): 668–682.
33. Richard A. Rehberg and Evelyn R. Rosenthal, *Class and Merit in the American High School* (New York: Longman, 1978), p. 235.

34. Ibid., p. 236.

35. Ibid., p. 245.

36. Ibid., p. 244.

37. James S. Coleman et al., *Equality of Educational Opportunity* (Washington, D.C.: U.S. Government Printing Office, 1966).

38. Christopher Jencks, "The Quality of the Data Collected by the Equality of Educational Opportunity Survey," in *On Equality of Educational Opportunity*, ed. F. Nosteller and D. P. Moynihan (New York: Vintage, 1972), pp. 437–512.

39. Rehberg and Rosenthal, *Class and Merit in the American High School*, p. 168.

40. Blau and Duncan, *The American Occupational Structure*, p. 430.

41. Brent Mack Shea, "Schooling and Its Antecedents: Substantive and Methodological Issues in the Status Attainment Process," *Review of Educational Research* 46 (Fall 1976): 513.

42. Featherman and Hauser, "Socioeconomic Stratification of the Races," p. 638.

43. Ibid., p. 646.

44. Ivan Illich, *Deschooling Society* (New York: Harper & Row, 1970), p. 6.

45. Ibid., p. 38.

46. Ibid.

47. Ibid., p. 42.

48. Samuel Bowles and Herbert Gintis, *Schooling in Capitalist America* (New York: Basic Books, 1976).

49. Ibid., p. 85.

50. Ibid.

51. Herbert Gintis, "The American Occupational Structure Eleven Years Later," *Contemporary Sociology* 9 (January 1980): 13.

52. Ibid., p. 14.

53. Gregory D. Squires, "Education, Jobs and Inequality: Functional and Conflict Models of Social Stratification in the United States," *Social Problems* 24 (April 1977): 436–450.

54. Ibid., p. 438.

55. Ibid.

56. Ibid., p. 439.

57. Kenneth Spenner, "Temporal Changes in the Work Content," *American Sociological Review* 44 (November 1979): 968–975.

58. Also useful in this context is Joel Spring, *American Education* (New York: Longman, 1978), pp. 28–29. For a different view based on research, see Karl Alexander et al., "Curriculum Tracking and Educational Stratification: Some Further Evidence," *American Sociological Review* 46 (February 1981): 47–66. See also James Rosenbaum, *Making Inequality: The Hidden Curriculum of High School Tracking* (New York: John Wiley & Sons, 1976).

59. Kenneth B. Clark and Carl Gershman, "The Black Plight: Race or Class?" *New York Times Magazine*, 5 October 1980, pp. 22–37, 90–109.

60. Ibid., p. 25.

61. Ibid.

62. Ibid., p. 26.

63. Ibid., p. 30.

64. Ibid., p. 94.

65. Ibid.

66. Ibid.

67. Ibid., p. 95.

68. Ibid., p. 96.
69. Ibid.
70. John Ogbu, *Minority Education and Caste* (New York: Academic Press, 1978), p. 104.
71. Ibid., p. 103.
72. Ibid., p. 104.
73. Ibid., chap. 5.
74. See Christopher Jencks, *Who Gets Ahead?* (New York: Basic Books, 1977), pp. 306–307.

Community Pressures and the Schools

"Aroused Parents Declare War on the System" according to a headline in an article in the *U.S. News and World Report*.[1] Such declarations have been common in recent years in hundreds of communities across the country. In describing parent activism on school matters in the late seventies, the *U.S. News* article related that parents were "fed up and frustrated" and "are using . . . combative tactics to express disillusionment with schools and to regain a role in decisions that affect their children's education." Moreover, the article suggested that parental concerns were broad and deep. "Today's militant and controversial parent groups are a far cry from the old-fashioned, amiable parent organizations that often worked hand in hand with the school boards. Now parents are influencing textbook selection, curriculum, teacher hiring, school budgets, collective bargaining, school consolidation and busing."[2]

Although the *U.S. News* article suggests that such parent involvement with their local schools is something new, it really isn't. Throughout history the local school has been particularly susceptible to all sorts of pressure from a variety of interests. Although the pressure varies, it seems always to be there, sometimes dramatically exploding into open community conflict. What follows in this chapter is a brief description of the major sources of pressure, an historical overview of pressure, some examples of organized radical efforts to change the schools, a look at the nature and character of pressure, and a brief analysis of why schools are subjected to pressure.

MAJOR SOURCES OF SCHOOL PRESSURE

Community pressures on schooling are wide ranging. Religious concerns have always been a major source of pressure. In many communities, certain interests want the schools to provide children with basic and fundamental Christian education. Opposing these interests are those who feel just as strongly that the school should be neutral on religion. Economic interests span a scale from extreme conservatism to radical liberalism. Conservative groups may pressure the schools to

provide materials which indoctrinate the students in the philosophy of the benefits of the free enterprise system, while liberal groups may advocate more governmental regulation. Conservative political groups may insist that students learn
the values of good citizenship as they define it, while more liberal groups may
object to this definition. Local business groups have applied pressure to have the
schools extol the virtues of business, while labor organizations have sought to
have the schools present in a favorable light the struggle of labor to organize.

Added to this list are various minority special interest groups which consider
the school to be a major target. Thus, in some communities, Mexican Americans
may be pushing for expansion of bilingual programs, blacks for black studies, and
native Americans for attention to the special needs of their children. More recently, parents of children with mental and physical handicaps have found strength
in organization and have successfully brought pressure on groups ranging from
the local school district to Congress to address school problems faced by their
children. In short, every group with a special interest, as well as individuals who
feel they are somehow being shortchanged by the schools, becomes a potential
source of pressure.

As if this weren't enough, there are many sources of in-school pressure. Students have been known to go to great lengths to make their special demands felt.
In recent years students have organized school walkouts and strikes and have
published underground newspapers to make their demands known. Teachers
have petitioned, struck, and publicized in local and national news media their
complaints against school administrators. State and regional accrediting associations, in their efforts to maintain minimal standards, are a constant source of
pressure on local schools as they hire teachers, develop curriculum and libraries,
provide services for students, and attempt to enforce a myriad of other standards.
Finally, a major source of pressure on local schools in recent years has been
the various agencies of government—from the local to the national level. Local
governmental agencies are interested in cost-efficient programs and the level of
taxation. State agencies bring pressure on local schools to provide minimal state-
required programs, such as certified teachers, state-mandated curriculum, testing
programs, minimum transportation standards, building and playground safety,
and literally hundreds of other programs and procedures in the local school.
National agencies are interested in programs for the poor and minorities, education of the handicapped, and the proper expenditure of federal funds in scores of
programs funded by the national government. The courts have become involved
in virtually every aspect of local schooling. Court action or the threat of court action
on racial balance, treatment of minorities and the handicapped, busing, and the
rights of students and teachers, to mention just a few, constitutes a real and
continuing pressure on public school personnel. It has reached the point where
everyone connected with the schools, from the janitor to the president of the
school board, must function with the ever-present threat of organized pressure
ready to challenge everything they do. A brief review of the history of school
pressure might provide some perspective.

A BRIEF HISTORY OF PRESSURE

Historically, pressure on the schools as a national problem has been cyclical. That is, there have been periods when, in the nation as a whole, the schools have been able to go about their business rather quietly with a minimum of public criticism, while at other times the schools have appeared to be at the center of public controversy. These cycles appear to follow the political destinies and fortunes of the nation. In peaceful and relatively prosperous times, when there appear to be no serious domestic or foreign crises, pressures on schools have tended to be minimal. During periods of domestic or international crises, the schools come in for what appears to be more than their share of public interest.

There was no problem with community consensus in the colonial period. Schools were established with the express purpose of promoting the religious views of the community. Even so, there were pressures to see that the religious views were adequately presented by the teachers. Nor was the religious concern limited to the township elementary schools. An early and notorious example of religious pressure on education was the dismissal of the first president of Harvard College after he announced that he didn't believe in infant baptism.

During the American revolutionary period, a demand for political conformity was added to the demand for religious conformity. All states established some form of oath for government officials as well as teachers.[3] Massachusetts enacted a loyalty oath for teachers in 1776, followed a year later by New Jersey. The New Jersey oath contained a self-enforcing provision which made it the citizen's responsibility to discover and bring suit against any teacher who might not have taken the oath. As an added inducement, the law imposed a fine of six pounds on the offending teacher, half of which could be claimed by the informant.[4]

A major source of pressure on public schools during the early years was from those who felt that schooling was an unnecessary waste of time and money. Many might have agreed with the viewpoint in an editorial in the *Philadelphia National Gazette* on July 10, 1830, which argued that education was wasted on most people. The "peasant," said the editor, "must labor during those hours of the day, which his wealthy neighbor can give to the...culture of his mind; otherwise, the earth would not yield enough subsistence for all."[5]

Even in those early years, it was difficult to find consensus. A Philadelphia union, The Workingmen, had a different view of schooling for the children of working people. The Workingmen charged that schooling in Pennsylvania was handled as a charity. They were upset with the attitude that public schools should exist primarily for paupers, and they expressed the opinion that "all who receive the limited knowledge imparted by the present system of public education are looked upon as paupers."[6] They insisted that public schools were consistent with the spirit of free institutions which was a central part of the American character.

Beginning in the late 1830s and continuing until the present, a different kind of pressure developed. The developing conflict between the North and South found its way into the classrooms of America. Even before the Civil War, some

southerners were concerned with the inadequacy of the system of higher education in the South. Some didn't like the idea of having to send southern scholars to
northern colleges and universities where students were exposed to ideas that
were foreign to southern culture. In the limited number of schools which existed
in the South before the Civil War, it was dangerous for teachers to advocate abolition, and there were instances in which teachers were dismissed and sometimes
driven from the community for taking an abolitionist position.[7]

After the war, the issues which divided North and South were still strongly
felt, and this feeling found its way into the schools. Militant patriotic groups in
both the North and the South often became the self-appointed watchdogs of the
materials and texts used in the schools. The Grand Army of the Republic, an
organization of ex-Union soldiers in the North, and the Sons and Daughters of
the Confederacy in the South expressed direct interest in what their local schools
were doing. They attacked teachers and texts and did whatever they could to
influence the curriculum in a direction which would be favorable to their interests. This battle continued throughout the nineteenth century. The southern
groups were especially vocal in their criticism of history textbooks which had
been published in the North and which appeared to the Southerners to be critical
of the South. A major tactic of the patriotic southern groups was to bring pressure
on school officials not to use texts which contained materials prejudicial to the
southern cause. Moreover, they were successful. By the turn of the century, publishers had succumbed to the pressure and were turning out materials which
were "neutral" on the war. By 1899, General Lee, head of the United Confeder-
ate Veterans historical committee, could announce: "The style of historical authors has become less sectional and controversial and much more liberal and
patriotic."[8]

Great nationalistic fervor accompanied the entry of the United States into
World War I. A major thrust of this period was a concern on the part of many
self-appointed guardians of liberty with the loyalty of teachers. Caught up in the
spirit, teachers themselves often demanded the dismissal of teachers whom they
considered disloyal. Loyalty, of course, was rather loosely defined. During the
World War I years there were periodic outbursts of fear and hysteria, and if one
couldn't engage the enemy on the war front, there were plenty of enemies at
home. Loyalty oaths for teachers became a universal requirement in the states,
and hundreds of teachers were reprimanded or fired for being pro-German, un-
American, or otherwise subversive. Teachers were harassed and sometimes jailed
for what local patriotic groups considered unpatriotic statements or criticism of
the conduct of the war.

The period between World War I and World War II continued to provide an
atmosphere in which patriotic pressure on the schools thrived. The patriotic fervor of the war years continued into the decade of the 1920s. The American Legion
was formed in Paris in 1919, and in every national convention in the 1920s, it
pressed its demand on the schools for patriotic education. The Ku Klux Klan's
brand of patriotism preached hatred of Catholics, Communists, Jews, and for-
eigners. Favorite targets of these groups were textbooks and teachers, and in many

states this form of pressure found expression in state legislation which attempted to ban books which were unpatriotic or which tended to degrade national heroes. During the decade, many states legislated against the teaching of evolution and passed "pure history laws," which had the effect of dictating content in courses in science and history.

The advent of the Great Depression and the New Deal created many problems for the schools.[9] The attacks of the thirties centered on free public education, certain topics, the textbook loyalty oaths, the "red scare," and political liberalism.

Even as recently as the 1930s, some Americans were not yet convinced that free public schooling was essential or desirable. Tax money was hard to come by during the Depression, and the arguments for tax-saving measures had a great deal of appeal. Critics of the schools in the 1930s opposed what they called "fads and frills" in the schools and suggested that the state was trying to do too much in the area of education. For example, in Tennessee, the *Memphis Commercial Appeal*, concerned with a legislative cut in normal school appropriations so that the state could provide more funds for working with what it called "subnormals" in the state's elementary schools, editorialized:

> Will the state continue to save money to half educate those best capacitated to receive it and then try to waste money on expensive but futile methods by trying to educate those incapable of being educated? In other words, will we keep the frills and discard the essentials to a real education?[10]

The New York Daily News said much the same thing in a March 18, 1932 editorial. The *News* editor objected to such frills as child guidance, homemaking, music, sewing, speech, and kindergartens, adding that "it is a question, we think, whether our schools aren't turning out too many white collar workers for the nation to absorb."[11] There were instances when the critics of the schools in the 1930s identified "free" education with the dole. Clearly, the desire to reduce spending for schools was a major source of school pressure. In tabulating editorial criticism of education from 1930 to 1935, Foster found that the cost of education exceeded all topics in percentage of criticism which was negative.[12]

World War II and the Cold War which followed in the the forties and the fifties created special problems for the schools. The spirit of patriotism was abroad in the land, and the schools appeared to be a major target. By far the most active groups in the period between 1945 and 1960 were conservative and right-wing patriotic groups. Robert MacIver, in *Academic Freedom in Our Time*, summarized these activities:

> Minute Women are out to purge the libraries, American Legion Posts are at work to prevent unorthodox speakers from being heard, members of a post of Veterans of Foreign Wars hunt for subversives in their locality, textbook committees find subversives in unexpected places—perhaps the most notable discovery being that of a member of the Indiana Textbook Commission who revealed the communist line in Robin Hood. This is something different from the older but still sufficiently vigorous censorship carried on in the name of morals and religion. It doesn't usually go as far as the book-burning affair that occurred in a town in Oklahoma, but it exhibits the same

spirit. The favorite charge is that of being subversive—an accommodating label to stick on any doctrine that deviates to the left.[13]

This was the period in which the Senate Committee on Un-American Activities, under the chairmanship of Senator Joseph McCarthy, seemed to get the undivided attention of the country. McCarthy's committee found alleged communists and their sympathizers everywhere: in government, the army, churches, colleges, and of course in the public schools. McCarthy's efforts on the national level were replicated on state and local levels. State legislative committees were formed to ferret out disloyal citizens. State attorney generals were active in developing lists of "subversive" organizations. State loyalty oaths were required by numerous legislatures to protect citizens from subversives. On the local level, self-styled patriotic groups were active in seeking out local people, especially classroom teachers, whose loyalty was questionable. It was an era of fear, which enabled right-wing extremists to launch what amounted to a national campaign to promote their views.

Their views were easy enough to describe. Defenders of states' rights, they were consistently critical of what they saw as a dangerous expansion of the power of the national government. Many right-wing spokesmen seemed to believe that the expansion of the functions of the national government was a deliberate attempt to lead the nation down the road to socialism. They preached the doctrines of nineteenth-century capitalism and limited government. Any departure from nineteenth-century economic and political values was labeled as subversive of the American ideal. Many right-wing extremists opposed foreign aid and were enraged with any effort to compromise with socialist nations. The world was viewed as a struggle between socialism-communism on the one hand and capitalism on the other.

The schools were affected by these developments in the fifties because local as well as national extremist groups felt that their ideas should be taught there. Many saw the schools as communistic, and they even blamed the communistic teaching in the schools for the incidence of "turncoats" in the Korean War in the early fifties. The turncoats were American soldiers who were captured and tortured by the enemy and forced to renounce the United States—merely another convincing piece of evidence, in the view of the right-wing extremists, that the schools were failing to inculcate capitalist and democratic values in their students.

On the local level, when groups such as the John Birch Society found text materials or teachers who did not teach their political values, the text authors and the teachers were accused of deliberate efforts to lead the students into communism. Many local schools found themselves under serious attack by right-wing groups. In keeping with their conservative views, the local extremist groups argued that the schools should teach the fundamentals. They charged that allowing classroom discussions of significant contemporary problems in which many views were aired tended only to confuse the students, and that if such discussions were not openly led by teachers who were communist sympathizers, then they were the work of teachers who were at least dupes of the communists. This was true, they argued, because open discussions tend to leave students without the ideals and values which could be used to oppose communism.

Their tactics were effective and widely publicized. A major tactic was to examine texts and other materials in an effort to discover the communist party line. Somehow they always seemed to find what they were looking for. Of course, if a "communist" text was discovered, the loyalty of the teacher was brought into question. Where teachers resisted, they were subjected to attacks in letters to the editor and "investigations" by a local committee or even a state investigating committee. When administrators or school boards attempted to come to the defense of a teacher, they were also accused of subversive leanings.

Local schools found it difficult to resist this kind of pressure, and in many ways the groups were successful. Many legislatures succumbed to extreme conservative pressure in the fifties by mandating curriculum units in Americanism, anticommunism, or the values of free enterprise. In some communities, the fear of attack was enough to bring liberal teachers into line. In other places, objectionable texts and other materials were expunged from the classroom.

FROM 1960 TO 1980—A STUDY IN CONTRASTS

Perhaps no two decades in history demonstrate the pendulum-like nature of school pressure better than the years from 1960 to 1980. Although the right-wing extremists did not disappear in the sixties, they were overshadowed by a different kind of pressure, that from the so-called New Left. As the sixties came to a close, there was a resurgence of conservative pressure which was then clearly in the spotlight by the end of the seventies.

Domestic and international conditions reflected in the mood of the country were dramatically different in the two decades. The sixties were the decade of the Great Society, when political leadership on the national level, at least, appeared to have faith that government—especially the national government—could solve the worst of our problems. The election of President Nixon in 1968 reflected a change in mood in the country. Not only was there some disillusionment with the notion that the government could solve domestic problems, but there appeared to be a new wave of conservatism in the sense that the problems of the society were deemed to be better left to the states and local agencies.

In keeping with its philosophy that government could solve problems, President Johnson's Great Society tackled a number of domestic problems. With the help of Congress, it declared war on poverty, passed a massive civil rights bill, and, in the Elementary and Secondary Education Act of 1965, it made the greatest effort in history to provide federal funds for the improvement of schools. Its position created a new awareness among the poor and minorities that genuine reform was a possibility. Encouraged by this possibility, liberal extremists, particularly minorities and some student groups, discovered the value of confrontation with what they liked to call "the establishment." The most convenient establishment for many of these groups was the educational establishment. Black militants, middle-class white college students, Chicano groups, and others seized the initiative in the sixties. Many groups saw the schools and colleges as oppressive institutions, destructive of human values. They staged sit-ins in university administrative offices, refused to attend class, presented school authorities with lists of "nonnegotiable" demands, held protest meetings, and utilized other means of resistance to authority to call attention to their demands. In 1964 the public got its first look at a large campus demonstration in the form of the Free Speech Movement at the University of California at Berkeley. A year later a group of students was able to close the University of Chicago for a time.[14]

The period from 1965 to 1972 was characterized by increasing militance on the part of students and blacks. New groups sprouted, and established groups such as the Students for a Democratic Society became progressively more active and radical in their position and tactics. The most radical of these groups were calling for total destruction of the school system as well as of the social, economic, and political system. Students in all parts of the country and on all levels, from junior high through college, utilized the tactic of confrontation with authority to protest the war in Vietnam, the draft, and what they considered to be repressive schools, irrelevant curricula, and prejudiced teachers. The confrontation was not always peaceful, as illustrated by the following:

> the ambassador of South Viet Nam visited New York University as an invited guest speaker. At a given signal, members of the Students for a Democratic Society . . . stormed the stage, physically assaulted the ambassador and completely disrupted the meeting. Thereupon, they proceeded to another floor, battered down the doors leading to the podium of a meeting-hall where James Reston, executive editor of the New York Times, was about to deliver the annual Homer Watts Lecture. . . . The rampaging students spurned an invitation from Mr. Reston to state their objections to what they thought he was going to say, and by threats of violence forced the cancellation of the meeting.[15]

Nor did the students always initiate the violence, as illustrated by the following description of an incident at San Francisco State College in 1968:

> A few of the several hundred white students gathered nearby for lunch shouted taunts at the cops, but most were more puzzled than anything else, since nothing had happened in that part of the campus (San Francisco State College) to warrant police presence.
>
> Suddenly for no apparent reason, the cops broke formation, raised their clubs and started after the black students. Two of them jammed (Nelson) Crutchfield (a member of the Black Student Union) against the wall. . . . One hit him in the midsection, then when he doubled over, he was clubbed to the ground with repeated blows. One of the cops jammed his knee into Crutchfield's back, while the other continued to club him. . . . He was dragged off, to be charged with assaulting a police officer.[16]

Skirmishes between students and police were common in the late sixties and early seventies. Strikes, protests, and resistance to authority were prolonged on several campuses. The efforts of the Third World Liberation Front at San Francisco State College provide a good example of many of the demands which were being made by students of the period. The Third World called for a nonwhite faculty, an improved black studies program, a more relevant curriculum, and a clear student voice in the administration of the college.

The battle in the college was not lost on high school students. The Montgomery County Student Alliance made a plea for what it called a "humane education" for students of Montgomery County, Maryland, and found a receptive audience in other schools around the country. In 1969, the Student Alliance accused the Montgomery County school system of dishonesty; of placing a premium on conformity; of destroying eagerness to learn; and of alienating large numbers of students through a repressive administrative system, an archaic testing and grading system, and a curriculum which was not in any way responsive to student needs.[17]

By the early seventies, the radical message was being circulated throughout the country. *Outside the Net*, which labeled itself a magazine in radical education, provided instruction on how to disrupt a public school. They listed specific ways students could make life miserable for administrators and teachers. Some of these suggestions included:

1. In hallways during class breaks, have massive searches for "lost" contact lenses so that no one can walk through the hall.
2. If your school has a dress code, "protest it by doing something disruptive that does not violate the . . . code" such as "dye your hair green with food coloring."
3. Conduct "giant coughing and sneezing epidemics in class. . . ."
4. Scatter marbles in hallways.
5. Impersonate parents' voices and make irate telephone calls to the office.
6. "Have everybody take out hundreds and hundreds of library books over a period of a week then return them at the same time."
7. Since teachers leave gradebooks and attendance records unguarded . . . "help yourself."
8. "On a given day, everyone chew gum all day and spit it on the floor."
9. "Start wailing in the halls."
10. Get the entire class to "forget to sign their names on a homework assignment."[18]

This is only a partial list; altogether, 61 items were suggested, but even a partial list indicates the pandemonium which could be created by a determined group of students.

Fortunately for the schools, this sort of advice was not taken seriously, and even the more serious and determined efforts of radical student groups on college campuses were relatively short lived. Indeed, the radical student pressure appears to have had little significant impact on public schools and colleges.

The conservative movement of the late seventies was another matter. There are many possible reasons for a resurgence of conservatism. In part, the interest expressed in the schools by extreme conservatives in the latter years of the decade of the seventies was a continuation of the conservatism of earlier years. However, fundamentalist religious groups seemed to be more active in the late seventies.

Unlike the earlier conservative critics of the schools, who were largely interested in protecting children from subversives and various forms of un-Americanism, the new conservatives appeared to have much broader goals. A favorite criticism of the new conservatives was their expressed concern that the public schools were neglecting the moral training of children. Added to this criticism was a general dissatisfaction with the much heralded "decline" in student achievement, increasing worry about permissiveness in the society and the schools, the loss of local control of schools to state and federal agencies, teachers who were militant or didn't seem to care about teaching basic values, and domestic and international crises over which local citizens had little voice and little control. Thus, in addition to expressing a concern with the neglect in the schools of "fundamentals" and the teaching of "correct" economic and political values, the new conservatives launched attacks on the mortality of the schools. Such a broadside can include almost anything the schools do.

Much of the support for the new wave of conservatism came via the television and radio pulpit. According to an article in the *U.S. News and World Report*: "Conservative ministers and lobbyists are out to arouse the 'sleeping giant' of American politics—millions of evangelical Christians who say they have enough votes to change the course of U.S. history in the 1980's."[19] Written on the eve of the November elections of 1980, the *U.S. News* article implied that the new religious conservatives were effectively organized for political action. This group, which came to be known as the "Moral Majority," did claim significant successes in the elections of 1980. They claimed a major role in the election of President Reagan and admitted freely that they were successful in congressional elections where they had developed a "hit list" of "liberal" congressmen whom they were out to defeat. Defeating so-called liberal politicians was only one of their goals. They were opposed to the Equal Rights Amendment, in favor of protecting church-related schools, and opposed to candidates in local elections who would not subscribe to their views.

They raised huge sums for their political efforts, largely through direct appeals from the pulpit on religious radio and television programs. They were well organized to do this. Their broadcasts were beamed to almost every corner of the nation. By 1979 the evangelical broadcast network included 36 religious TV channels, 1,300 radio stations, and dozens of gospel TV shows that were able to buy time on commercial television. *U.S. News* estimated that they reached some 50 million viewers weekly just with their TV efforts. Many more were reached with their radio shows and publications. In describing what it called a typical appeal, the *U.S. News* reported that TV evangelist Jerry Falwell called for "12,000 followers to the U.S. Capitol for a 'Clean Up America' rally. . . ."[20] The Baptist from Lynchburg, Virginia, and host of the "Old Time Gospel Hour," set up a new pressure group called the "Moral Majority" and declared: "We need more Christians in politics."[21] Falwell's aims were clearly stated. He called for restrictions on abortion, "an end to pornography, defeat of the proposed SALT treaty and rejection of the equal rights amendment," which he called "a vicious attack on the monogamous Christian home."[22]

Although the Moral Majority was concerned mainly with the election of "Christian" politicians, it was a short step away from the schools. According to Charles Park, writing in the *Phi Delta Kappan*, "the renewed strength of the political right has serious implications for the future of public education."[23] Park believed that the political successes of the right-wing religious groups would encourage them to focus on public education. According to Park, the New Right owed much of its success to the fund-raising genius of Richard A. Viguerie, who had developed a computerized list of 25 million supporters of right-wing causes. Groups such as the Conservative Caucus, the Committee for Survival of a Free Congress, and the National Conservative Political Action Committee all found Viguerie's lists and consultation useful. They were unified in their philosophy. In Park's words, the New Right argued that "the ills of society . . . are traceable to taxes, big government, liberalism, progressivism, and Godlessness."[24]

The schools offered an attractive target. A fund-raising letter sent out by the National Conservative Political Action Committee, signed by Jesse Helms, said: "your tax dollars are being used to pay for grade school courses that teach our children that cannibalism, wife swapping, and murder of infants and the elderly are acceptable behavior."[25] This occurred during the heat of the debate over the elementary school program, *Man a Course of Study.*

The leaders of the New Right were directly interested in the public schools. In 1979, in his Clean Up America Campaign, Falwell announced that "there can be no real Holy Spirit conviction until there is a national awareness of sin."[26] In the view of Falwell, schoolbooks contributed to sin. "Textbooks have become absolutely obscene and vulgar. Many of them are openly attacking the integrity of the Bible. Humanism is the main thrust of the public school textbook. Darwinian evolution is taught from kindergarten age right through high school. . . . For our nation this is a life-and-death struggle, and the battle line for this struggle is the textbooks."[27]

Another organization, Education Research Analysts, run by Norma and Mel Gabler out of their office in Longview, Texas, was thriving in its review of school textbooks. They sent interested citizens reviews of school textbooks which they found to be obscene, immoral, or Godless. Even more, their service provided instructions on how to combat such books on the local and state levels. Other groups listed by Park, which have been active in screening texts and curriculum materials, include the Heritage Foundation, established by Joseph Coors of the Coors Brewing Corporation, and the Movement to Restore Decency (MOTOREDE), a John Birch Society front group.[28]

Park suggested that the Kanawha County textbook controversy of the mid-1970s had gone national. Clearly the most heated of such controversies, perhaps in history, the Kanawha controversy in the mid-seventies provides an excellent case study of the views of right-wing fundamentalists as well as of the tactics used by such groups on a local level. A summary description of that controversy might prove useful. After the heat of the controversy had somewhat subsided, a National Education Association panel assembled to investigate the incident. The panel seemed to take great pains in providing an "objective" report, yet the basic nature of the controversy comes through clearly. Excerpts from the report follow.[29]

Kanawha County, West Virginia
A Textbook Study in Cultural Conflict

. . . A question that the NEA Panel asked of Kanawha County school personnel and other citizens, and a question that many of them still seemed to be asking of themselves, was why did it happen here? . . .

One answer, on which there seemed to be general agreement, was that for a number of years the school system has failed to communicate effectively with its diverse communities—most particularly with its rural communities—and to involve them sufficiently in the development of educational objectives and programs. The selection of textbooks, traditionally, has been a routine affair, previous boards of education having accepted without challenge the recommendations of the superintendent and textbook selection committees. . . .

But when the recommendations of this committee were made to the Board of Education in 1974, one member—an individual who had been elected to the Board in 1970 on an anti-sex education platform—did challenge and did communicate her concerns most effectively to all who had reason to feel resentful of, or alienated from, the public school establishment.

The English Language Arts text and supplementary book recommendations—a product of hundreds of hours of volunteer work by the five-member Textbook Selection Committee and its elementary and secondary curriculum study subcommittees— were first submitted to the Board at its regular meeting on March 12, 1974, a meeting not attended by the Board member who would later challenge the recommendations. Following the March meeting, the books were displayed in the Kanawha County Public Library for examination by the public. . . .

Between May 15, 1974, when the Textbook Selection Committee attempted to present to the Board of Education the rationale for its recommendations, and June 27, when the Board was to make its final decision regarding purchase of the books, the Board member who had challenged the materials launched a communications campaign that would soon involve Kanawha County parents in their public schools as they had never been involved before. She appeared frequently at meetings of church and community groups, informing them of her objections to the books, reading, and circulating printed excerpts from the materials that she deemed offensive. She taped excerpts from a "listening library cassette" for advanced secondary students, which she then played back with her own commentary to her various audiences. . . .

Copies of the books were made available for examination by concerned citizens, and petitions were circulated to parents, churches, and other groups, asking that materials be prohibited in the schools.

These petitions, bearing 12,000 signatures, were presented to the Board of Education at the stormy meeting of June 27 when the members voted 3–2 to purchase all of the disputed materials except for eight supplemental texts. . . .

Before the June 27 meeting, there had been public condemnation of the books by 27 ministers; and the Executive Board of Kanawha County Council of Parents and Teachers had expressed opposition to the several volumes that its members had read. There had also been public endorsement of the books by the West Virginia Human

Relations Commission, the Vice-President of the Charleston Branch of the NAACP, and by ten clergy.

Following the June 27 vote, various anti-textbook groups were formed; a minister leader of the protest announced plans for establishment of a private church school; and excerpted "objectionable" materials from the books were widely circulated. During the months of controversy, school personnel stated, out-of-context passages from secondary level materials have been represented as passages from elementary books; other materials—for example, sex education information from a junior high school library and excerpts from a copy of Kate Millett's *Sexual Politics* taken from a teacher's desk—have been portrayed as excerpts from the textbook adoptions.

Escalation of Protest

It was not until school opened on September 3 that the full intensity of the protest became evident. During the first two weeks of September, the schools were boycotted and picketed. Picket lines went up around businesses, industrial plants, and coal mines in the Upper Kanawha Valley. On September 4, an estimated 3,500 miners walked off the job on a wildcat strike, ostensibly in sympathy with the protesters. Local efforts to obtain assistance from the state police were unsuccessful. On September 7, a citizens group—the Kanawha Coalition for Quality Education—formed in support of the books. On September 10, the protesters shut down the city bus system; and on September 11, the Board voted to remove the disputed books from the school system pending their examination by a Citizens Review Committee, to be composed of 18 members—three members appointed by each of the five Board members and three appointed by the Board-member elect, who would also chair the Review Committee.

This compromise on the part of the Board was at first accepted and then rejected by the protesters. The Board's move also prompted protests from the Kanawha County Education Association, the Schoolmaster's Club, and Kanawha County Association of Classroom Teachers, who urged that teacher members be placed on the Review Committee and questioned the Board's right to remove the legally adopted books.

During the following weeks, public education in Kanawha County was halted by the politics of violent confrontation. There were exchanges of gunfire. School buses were shot at, cars and homes firebombed, anti-book picketers arrested and released. Schools were vandalized and dynamited. Between September 12 and 16, the Kanawha County Schools were closed and all extracurricular activities cancelled. At book protest rallies, dissension became evident among the ministers leading the anti-book movement, some of them urging continuance of the school boycott and others favoring a return to school and work. Demands were made for resignation of the Superintendent and the three board members who had voted for adoption of the books.

Appointments, Resignation, and Recommendations

All members of the Textbook Review Committee were appointed on September 24. But, on October 9, six members and one alternate—all of anti-book persuasion—withdrew from the committee and proceeded to conduct their own textbook review, the product of which was to be a 500-page document recommending removal of 184 of the 254 titles they had been assigned to review.

On October 9, the President of the Board of Education, whose term would have expired on December 31, announced his early resignation. . . . The Board-member elect, resigning his chairmanship of the Textbook Review Committee, was appointed to the Board, effective immediately; and on the following day, October 11, the superintendent of schools announced that he was looking for another job.

During this period, as protest rallies, boycotts, and sporadic violence continued, the Kanawha Coalition for Quality Education attempted to counter the impact of the anti-book movement by holding meetings with citizens, discussing the textbook adoption and responding to criticism and questions concerning the books.

The report of the Textbook Review Committee's majority members, completed on October 15, recommended return to the school system of all basal texts and all of the supplemental texts that they had reviewed, with provision that no student would be required to use any book containing material offensive to the religious beliefs of the student or his or her parents. The Committee majority further recommended that the return of other unreviewed supplementary materials be delayed pending thorough review "without the pressure of a Board-imposed time limit."

Board Decisions

The Board, on November 8, 1974, voted 4–1 to return all of the books to the schools with the following exceptions: (1) the D.C. Heath Communicating series, textbooks for grades 1–6, would be removed from the classroom and placed in the school libraries for use as supplementary reading; a form furnished by the school system would "give parental authority on who is to use or not use" the supplemental books; and an additional series of books would be adopted from the state multiple listing for use by children whose parents did not want them to use the D.C. Heath texts as a supplement to the basal elementary textbooks. (2) The level four Interaction series (Houghton-Mifflin) including the teacher's manual, would be placed in the library and no additional books in this series would be purchased.

On a 4–1 vote, the Board further adopted two additional motions:

These decisions, although accepted by the teachers, and hailed by the press and most pro-textbook groups as a reasonable and responsible compromise, did not halt the protest. Anti-book rallies and marches continued; school buses were hit by gunshot blasts; a car owned by parents who continued to send their children to school was firebombed, the driver escaping injury only by leaping from the car; and protesters continued the pressure of phone threats to intimidate other parents to keep their children home from school.

On November 16, while attending a meeting with protest leaders that had been called by a Methodist Bishop who has acted as mediator to the conflict, the superintendent and three Board members were served with arrest warrants. The warrants, filed by the Upper Kanawha Valley Mayors' Association, charged the school officials . . . with contributing to the delinquency of minors by permitting use of un-American and un-Christian textbooks. The men were released on bond after brief court appearances.

> That no student be required to use a book that is objectionable to that student's parents on either moral or religious grounds. The parents of each student shall have the opportunity to present a written signed statement to the principal of the school, listing the books that are objectionable for that parent's child. That no teacher is authorized to indoctrinate a student to follow either moral values or religious beliefs which are objectionable to either the student or the student's parents.

Guidelines and Procedures for Future Textbook Adoptions

By their action on November 21, 1974, the members of the Kanawha County Board of Education moved from a position of conciliation to one of near capitulation to the anti-textbook forces. On that date, the Board of Education adopted a set of guidelines for future textbook adoptions . . . that, if given the interpretation obviously meant by their proponent—the anti-book Board member—would not only bar the disputed books from Kanawha County classrooms, but would proscribe the use of any language arts books, including the McGuffey's Readers, and would permit very little learning.

At meetings in December 1974, the Board of Education reached tentative agreement on a set of policies . . . under which a proliferation of committees would be established, involving parents—not only as advisors, but as censors—in the processes of textbook selection and adoption for the Kanawha County Public Schools. At the time of the NEA hearings in Charleston, Board members were announcing their appointments of lay citizens who would comprise 75% majorities on screening committees to review instructional materials to be selected in four subject areas—Social Studies, Music, Business Education, and Home Economics—and to set aside any materials that, in their judgment, failed to meet satisfactorily the Board of Education guidelines for textbook adoption.

On December 12, 1974, the Kanawha Coalition for Quality Education issued a public statement urging the Board of Education to rescind the new guidelines and procedures for textbook adoption. But on that same day, the Board moved to refine and approve the new policies. Even this action failed to bring immediate peace to Kanawha County. The meeting of December 12 was heavily attended by citizens against the books, some of whom carried placards announcing "We are KKK members." Following the business portion of the meeting, the superintendent, the assistant superintendent, and two Board members were physically attacked by protesters. The newest member of the Board, according to press reports, was hit repeatedly and denounced by some protesters as "nigger lover, Jew lover and Hitler lover." The superintendent, in attempting to defend the Board member, was also assaulted and sprayed with mace by a female member of the audience. . . .

In its analysis of the West Virginia controversy, the NEA panel found national right-wing influences very prominent. In its discussion of outside influences, the panel reported:

. . . Without question, some of the imported funding of the Kanawha County anti-book movement has come from individual donors who have sincerely supported the movement's purposes. Other sources of legal, organizational, and financial assistance have been extreme right-wing organizations, either directly associated or in apparently close sympathy with the John Birch Society. Among these organizations have been Citizens for Decency through Law, whose public relations representative, Robert Dornan, has been in Kanawha County helping to organize the protest movement; the American Opinion Book Store in Reedy, West Virginia, one of the outlets for John Birch Society materials, whose manager has printed excerpts from the books and other handouts for the protesters; the Heritage Foundation, Inc., of Washington, D.C., one of whose attorneys, James McKenna, has acted as counsel to the anti-book leaders in the preparation of legal suits; Mr. & Mrs. Mel Gabler, self-appointed textbook censors of Longview, Texas; and the National Parents League, an Oregon-based organization dedicated to the proposition that to protect their children from the moral corruption of the schools, Christian parents should teach them in their own homes. . . . A more recent entrant into the Kanawha County protest has been the Ku Klux Klan, whose Imperial Wizard, James R. Venable, has charged that the objectionable books "are part of a Communist plot." As this report was being written, announcement had been made that a group of klansmen from five or six states would conduct an investigation of the controversy in order "to expose those textbooks. . . ."

THE NATURE OF PRESSURE

From the foregoing discussion, certain characteristics of effective pressure on public schooling seem to stand out in sharp relief. Perhaps most obvious is the cyclical nature of pressure on schools. The period from 1960 to 1980 is particularly revealing since the schools were attacked in turn by the Left and the Right. The philosophy and goals of these groups are so divergent, it is difficult to imagine that they exist in the same country. The tactics, however, are quite similar.

The cry of the New Left was for a more humanistic school system. Student groups and minority groups protested that the schools were "killing" the students. They wanted textbooks and curriculum materials that were more humanistic, that valued human life and gave adequate treatment to different beliefs and cultures. They demanded courses and units on birth control. They wanted students to have a voice in curriculum decisions. They wanted teachers and administrators who were sympathetic with their views. They wanted power at the local school district level to make policy decisions which affected the lives of students and the things they were asked to learn. Their tactics were protest and confrontation, sometimes violent. They used the media in every way they could to publicize their views. In some places the pressure was so intense that school officials bowed, at least partially, to their demands. Some new courses and units were introduced. Textbook publishers responded by including more material on minority groups and real problems and conflicts in the society.

The right-wing resurgence of the late seventies demanded almost a completely opposite response from the schools. Right-wing groups wanted to purge the schools of multicultural education materials; they demanded a return to the fundamentals and the elimination of humanistic teaching and materials. They were enraged at the successes of earlier student groups in their efforts to get sex education units and courses into the schools. They charged the schools with being almost totally antagonistic toward their basic Christian values. Like the New Left, the New Right engaged in tactics of protest and confrontation with school authorities. Neither side seemed reluctant to resort to violence to achieve its goals.

The ideological base of the New Left was never totally clear. Although certain groups tended to have a Marxist orientation, the New Left of the sixties for the most part rejected the Old Left ideologues. The movement among students seemed to be more spontaneous than ideological. The issues were contemporary and changing. Major radicalizing forces were the war in Vietnam and the draft, which tended to spill over into other areas including concern with schools. There was a religious theme in some of the confrontation. Malcolm X introduced it into his protests, as did Boyd Harvey Cox ("The Secular City"). Certainly Rev. William Sloane Coffin, the Berrigan brothers, and of course Martin Luther King used religious themes in their struggles. When the war and the draft ended, much of the student activism evaporated. The minorities were more ideological, but theirs tended to be an ideology that was at least partially system supporting. That is, their demands were based on what they viewed as basic rights under the system. They were interested in pressuring the schools to recognize their rights as citizens, to end the neglect of minority needs, rather than in effecting deep changes in the system.

The New Right, like the Old Right, has clear ideological goals. It is essentially the ideology of political and economic conservatism with a generous sprinkling of fundamentalist Christianity. Unlike those of the New Left, the goals of the New Right have been fairly consistent. Reading the demands of the New Right today is a familiar experience for anyone who understands the right-wing movement of the period from 1920 to 1960. What has changed for the New Right is its improved organization and its closer tie with fundamentalist religious views. It has also become much more successful in raising huge sums and in utilizing the media.

From the point of view of those who must struggle in the schools in an attempt to meet the needs of as many students and as many views as possible, each cycle of protest from the left and right extremes must seem to be more severe. Perhaps they learn from past efforts and past mistakes. To be sure, the past efforts of such organized pressure groups were bothersome, but in most cases reason prevailed, and in the most extreme cases school leaders were able to mobilize the forces of reason within the community to combat the worst of the extremists. Given the improved organization of the extremists, their ability to raise funds, and their skill in utilizing propaganda, there may be some cause for concern in the future.

School pressure tends to be not only cyclical but also issue oriented. Very often pressure on the local school begins with a single issue, but, as the conflict grows, the issues have a way of multiplying. Thus, as in the case of Kanawha County, the original issue appeared to be the objection of a single school board member to certain texts. As more people became involved and organized groups joined the fray, the conflict broadened to the whole textbook selection process, sex education, racially mixed schools, and finally to the larger issue of who was going to control the schools. In another community, a single set of parents may object to posting the Ten Commandments on the bulletin board in the classroom. This starts a debate in the community. Liberals and civil rights groups line up on one side of the issue and Christian fundamentalists on the other, and the dispute grows. As more people become involved, the issues multiply on the one hand to criticism of all real and fancied religious exercises in the school and on the other to a cry for more such activities. What might begin as a simple request can result in the polarization of the community on a whole range of school issues, sometimes unrelated to the original dispute.

Another characteristic of school pressure is that the most effective pressure is organized. Individuals can and do bring pressure on teachers and school administrators, and they often may appear before school boards. Without organized support, however, they are easily put off. When the American Civil Liberties Union, the John Birch Society, or any organized pressure group becomes involved in an individual case, it is difficult to disregard them. Groups can organize petition drives, make sure that regular and sustained pressure is brought at board meetings, secure funds for publicizing their grievances, hire legal counsel, and involve the local media in the dispute. Moreover, school people have discovered, much to their discomfort, that almost any issue felt strongly by a single set of parents can find champions without too much difficulty.

Finally, at the risk of being charged with a lack of objectivity, it appears to this writer that conservative pressure groups seem to have greater impact than liberal ones. School officials seem to succumb more readily to right-wing pressure than to pressure from the left wing. Compare, for example, the reaction of established authority to the violence surrounding the efforts of militant students at Columbia and San Francisco State in the 1960s with the Kanawha County incident. At first disorganized and willing to negotiate as the militant students pressed for ever greater power, school authorities at Columbia and San Francisco eventually called upon outside forces to help in their battle to maintain control. Local police called upon to disperse students were very cooperative. The police were on the side of school officials. In Kanawha County, this was not the case. Local police were often on the side of the protesters, even to the point of arresting school officials for "corrupting the minds of youths."

There are all kinds of reasons for this phenomenon. In most communities where the right wing has been well organized, it has been able to elicit a broad base of support in the community. Even though it may not be a majority, it is a significant number of citizens. The left wing, on the other hand, has been singularly unsuccessful in such attempts. The determined efforts of the New Left to gain worker support in places like Chicago, New York City, and San Francisco met with disaster. The experience of the sixties indicates that the most extreme of the left-wing militants never had a broad base of community support in specific communities, even though their national sympathizers might have constituted a large number. Even Martin Luther King had to struggle for public support and was able to achieve it not so much by the legitimacy of his cause as by the excesses of his extremist and establishment enemies. Dr. King's message for human rights was never so clear as it was when his totally peaceful followers were being brutally attacked by local police with their dogs, clubs, and shotguns.

Perhaps an equally important reason why the right wing has been more successful is that it is often able to identify itself with "American" values and "Christian" principles. The flag and the Bible are used without restraint by many right-wing groups. These symbols are such a basic part of the American experience that it is difficult to attack them. It is much easier, in most communities, to convince people that God-fearing anticommunists are really good people who have the best interests of the children at heart than it is to convince them that school people are somehow violating basic humanitarian and constitutional rights of students.

Left-wing critics seem somehow foreign to the American experience. In past struggles, left-wing leadership has decried American capitalism as an unmitigated evil. Many have called for the destruction of capitalism and have advocated utilizing the schools as a revolutionary instrument for change. The right wing, on the other hand, has a familiar message. Always supportive of free enterprise, American capitalism, and individual freedom, its message has a familiar and decidedly American ring. The change they advocate is not so much revolutionary as it is reactionary. They recall the "good old days" when the society had strong moral values and purpose. The fact that such good old days may never have existed is beside the point. People are more easily convinced that it is better to base change on traditional values than they are that it should be based on some vague promises of future utopia.

THE SUSCEPTIBILITY OF SCHOOLS TO POLITICAL PRESSURE

If the school activities of extremists demonstrate anything clearly, it is that the schools are very sensitive to pressure. Scarcely a community in the country has not been subjected to some kind of organized pressure in the last quarter-century. It has had many forms. In some communities there are groups out to get the superintendent or certain members of the school board. In others, teachers become the target. In other places, schools are called to task for neglecting minorities, the handicapped, or any one of a hundred different things.

Although there are many reasons for the susceptibility of the schools to these kinds of pressure, a few seem to be most prominent. These include: (1) local community control of schools; (2) the belief by many patrons that the schools influence attitudes, beliefs, and values and subsequent citizen behavior; (3) the absence of any general agreement on the role of schooling in American society; and (4) the inability of school professionals to provide an adequate and clear statement of purpose.

Schools in the United States have always been close to the public. In the early years of our history, schooling was a simple matter, paid for and controlled by local citizens. Local citizens were elected to run the schools, and for more than a century, in a predominantly rural and small-town America, schools were often the center of community activity. Local patrons had a real voice in running their schools. As schooling expanded and schools became larger, more of the day-to-day decision making was in the hands of the professionals. Even so, the heritage of local control remained strong, and in most communities, right up to the present, citizens often feel that it is not only their right but also their duty to take a direct interest in the affairs of their local schools. Moreover, local communities have fought desperately to maintain control of the schools at the local level. Of course, local control makes the schools particularly susceptible to pressure. Purely as a matter of logistics, it is much easier to bring pressure on a local school board than on a state legislature or Congress.

The belief that schools influence attitudes, beliefs, and values is an open invitation to pressure. Every group that has an ax to grind somehow manages to try to influence what the schools are doing. The local school, which has a captive audience of impressionable young minds, is an attractive target. Any organized pressure group which has long-range political goals assumes that its interests can be greatly served if it can succeed in getting its own views adopted by the schools as a regular part of the curriculum. Thus, in every community, there are groups of every political hue anxious to get their views incorporated into the school curriculum.

Local school people are often hard pressed to resist this kind of pressure partly because there doesn't appear to be any really clear general agreement on the role of schooling in American society. Although professionals have attempted through the years to articulate this role, there has never been a complete consensus on the general philosophy and values which should be promoted by the schools. What the schools should do in their efforts to provide good citizenship training provides an excellent illustration of this lack of consensus. Although nearly every study of public education places citizenship training high on the list of priorities, no one seems to know what this means. The right wing has one definition, the left wing quite another. Any citizenship education goal which finds general acceptance is often so broad that it is meaningless. Such goals as "education for democracy" or "developing appreciations of the American heritage," and so on, present the same problems. This is not meant to be critical of the lack of a dogma in American schools. Only a totalitarian state can be certain of the purposes of schooling. The danger exists, however, that such looseness of purposes leaves the schools open to all sorts of pressure. On balance, however, the cure for this problem might be worse than the disease.

A final reason why pressures have a good chance of success in the local school is the inability of school people to provide the necessary guidance in terms which can be understood by the public. Related to the absence of a general professional agreement on the role of the school, this is more than mere lack of agreement. The professionalization of schooling has created a communications gap between citizens and the professionals. The field of education is befogged with "educationese" or the peculiar and mystifying language of the professional educator. Grades and test scores become "learning outcomes," special tutoring becomes "compensatory education," the children of the poor are called "low socioeconomic status students," a poor reader may be said to have "learning deficits," and so it goes. In practice, a curriculum expert may be found explaining the mysteries of role theory, structure, a new and exciting "taxonomy," and the nature of "idiosyncratic" material to a lay group from which he or she may expect unflagging support. Added to this is the fear on the part of many parents that professionals like to experiment with their children without regard for how the experiments are meeting the educational needs of the children.

Thus the schools offer an open invitation to pressure. Yet if the schools are to be democratic institutions, there may be no solution to this problem. One can only hope that the forces of light and reason prevail. The special problem discussed in these pages is the problem of extremism—which is anything but light and reason. The real threat of extremists is summarized in the NEA's *Inquiry Report* of the Kanawha County, West Virginia, controversy:[3]

> Without questioning the right of the extremists to enter into the public school controversy in Kanawha County, or any other area of the country, the NEA Panel considers it vitally important for citizens of such communities to recognize that the charges these groups make are groundless and irrational . . . and that their methods of incitement are violative of democratic principles of this nation, which they purport to defend. It is also essential that citizens recognize that the tactics of extremism—right or left—are the tactics of exploitation. . . . And whatever that intent may be, the forces of extremism in this country are destructive of every advance toward social justice that this nation has made over the past twenty years. . . .

NOTES

1. *U.S. News and World Report*, 10 September 1979, p. 33.
2. Ibid.
3. Howard K. Beale, "Teacher as Rebel: His War for Freedom," *The Nation* 176 (May 1953), p. 412.
4. Edgar W. Knight and Clifton L: Hall, eds., *Readings in American Educational History* (New York: Appleton-Century-Crofts, 1951), p. 37.
5. Ibid., p. 148.
6. Ibid., p. 342.
7. Beale, "Teacher as Rebel: His War for Freedom," p. 413.
8. Wallace E. Davies, *Patriotism on Parade* (Cambridge, Mass.: Harvard University Press, 1955), p. 230.
9. For a more complete treatment of this period, see Daniel Selakovich, "The Techniques of Certain Pressure Groups Attempting to Influence the Teaching of American History and Government in the Secondary School" (Ed.D. dissertation, University of Colorado, 1962).
10. Charles R. Foster, *Editorial Treatment of Education in the American Press* (Cambridge, Mass.: Harvard University Press, 1938), p. 39.
11. Ibid., p. 57.
12. Ibid.
13. Robert M. MacIver, *Academic Freedom in Our Time* (New York: Columbia University Press, 1955), p. 35.
14. For an excellent description of student activism in the 1960s, see Jerome H. Skolnick, *The Politics of Protest* (New York: Ballantine Books, 1969).
15. Sidney Hook, "Violence and Responsibility in the Academy," *Human Events*, 10 May 1969, pp. 3–4.
16. Gene Marine and Reese Erhlich, "Schools Out," *Ramparts*, 14 December 1968, p. 24.
17. Montgomery County Student Alliance, *Wanted: A Humane Education* (Bethesda, Md.: Montgomery School Alliance, 1969).
18. From: *Outside the Net*, no. 4 (Winter/Spring 1979): pp. 38–39.
19. *U.S. News and World Report*, 24 September 1979, p. 37.
20. Ibid., p. 39.
21. Ibid.

22. Ibid.
23. J. Charles Park, "Preachers, Politics, and Public Education: A Review of Right-Wing Pressures Against Public Schooling in America," *Phi Delta Kappan* 62 (May 1980), p. 608.
24. Ibid.
25. Senator Jesse Helms, Fund Raising Letter, The National Conservative Political Action Committee, 8 March 1976.
26. Cited by Park, "Preachers, Politics, and Public Education," p. 609.
27. Ibid.
28. Ibid., p. 610.
29. Excerpted from: National Education Association, *Inquiry Report, Kanawha County, West Virginia: A Textbook Study in Cultural Conflict* (Washington, D.C.: National Education Association, Teacher Rights Division, 1975). For a more analytical account, see George Hillocks, Jr., "Books and Bombs: Ideological Conflict and the Schools—A Case Study of the Kanawha County Book Protest," *School Review* 86 (August 1978): 632–654. Mr. Hillocks is critical of the NEA report, suggesting that the NEA panel oversimplified the conflict.
30. National Education Association, *Inquiry Report*, p. 52.

Teachers and Teaching

The role and the status of teachers have been greatly influenced by community values. The function of teaching and the role of teachers in community schools have always been affected by the manner in which the public views its schools. This has created some problems for teachers, especially as they have worked to gain recognition as professionals. Since teaching is such a visible public function, teachers have found it difficult to establish their own standards and to define their role as teachers independent of the publics they serve. The teachers' clients—the students and their parents—have always had their own beliefs about the manner in which teachers should conduct themselves, what good teaching is, and the social role of teachers in the community. That is, teachers have an ascribed[1] role in most communities. Considering the variety of communities, the large number of school districts, the large number of teachers in American society, and the phenomenon of almost constant change in most communities, it is difficult to describe accurately the social role of American teachers.

In an insightful description of the anomalies of teaching, Dan Lortie said:

> It is honored and disdained, praised as "dedicated service" and lampooned as "easy work." It is permeated with the rhetoric of professionalism, yet features incomes below those earned by workers with considerably less education. It is middle-class work in which more and more participants use bargaining strategies developed by wage-earners in factories. . . .[2]

Lortie suggests that teaching in America has always occupied a "special but shadowed social standing." That is, while teachers have always been held in high esteem by the community, they somehow have never achieved the high status of other professions.

This shadowed position was clearly described by Willard Waller more than a generation ago in his discussion of the peculiar treatment of the teacher in the community. Waller suggested that the community isolated the teacher. "The community can never know the teacher because it insists upon regarding him as something more than a god and something less than a man." This is what Waller called the "teacher stereotype."[3]

Lortie suggests that in spite of the growth of teacher power and militance, the shadowed position of the teacher in the community has not changed all that much. In the early years teachers were overshadowed, as it were, by the clergy, which stood "at the center of things." Teachers were expected to hold and teach high moral values, but they were always "almost-but-not-quite a minister, . . . off to the side."[4] Supporting Waller's theme, Lortie suggests that as urbanization, secularization, and school expansion changed the roles of schools, teachers continued to lead a shadowed existence. "Whereas earlier teachers were symbolically and literally outranked by preachers, later teachers have found themselves in a similar position vis-à-vis school administrators and professors, both within their immediate field and in the disciplines." He suggests that "those teaching particular subjects at the secondary level were placed in a less expert position than those teaching the same subjects in institutions of 'higher' learning. Thus teachers never did gain control of any area of practice where they were clearly in charge and most expert; day-to-day operations, pedagogical theory, and substantive expertise have been dominated by persons in other roles."[5]

Certainly part of the contemporary image of the teacher has been created by what might be called a bad press. As Allen Ornstein pointed out: "The traditional teacher stereotype we inherited was mainly based on novels and is reinforced by television and the movies."[6] Ornstein charged that "teachers are often shown as silly, authoritative, rigid, and unmarried as in Washington Irving's creation of Ichabod Crane, run out of town by the virile men of the community with a pumpkin smashed over his head." The image continues, according to Ornstein, with J. D. Salinger's Old Spencer, the history teacher, dressed in "ratty old clothes" and "picking his nose . . . getting his thumb right in there" while scolding Holden Crawford in *Catcher in the Rye*. Ornstein reminds us of the mass media's contribution with movies such as "The Nutty Professor," TVs "Professor Backward," the cartoon "Professor," Whimple's "Crossword Zoo," and Pat Paulsen's "Laugh-In" version.[7] Other image makers mentioned by Ornstein include the simplistic "Our Miss Brooks," "Mr. Peepers," and, to a great extent, the mindlessness of Mr. Kotter's "warthogs" (which Ornstein thought presented a positive image). This image seems somehow much more lasting than the sincere and professional efforts of Mr. Novak in "Room 222" and Sidney Poitier's moving performance in "To Sir With Love."

There can be little doubt, however, that the image of the teacher is changing. This is dramatically illustrated by two profiles presented by Myron Brenton—one of the "typical" teacher of 35 years ago and another of the contemporary teacher:

> Decidedly a "she" . . . thirty-one years old . . . and had been teaching for a decade. She was not married. Her educational background consisted of from two to four years worth of college. She earned $1500 a year.
>
> People generally ascribed a fierce sense of dedication to her, believing that this prompted her to go into the profession. A love for children and a pride in teaching may well have nourished her professional ambitions.[8]

And the contemporary image:

the most distinguishing feature of today's teacher is his militancy. Where's the spinster lady devoted to her boys and girls? Where's the Mr. Chips who used to teach when I was a boy? rhetorically demanded a father (whose son was affected by a teacher strike). The men talk aggressively, the women wear miniskirts. They parade around in front of schools they've closed, with picket signs. . . .[9]

A CONTEMPORARY VIEW OF TEACHING

Whatever the contemporary image of the teacher, there can be little doubt that teachers are a much-studied group and that teaching in America is a huge enterprise. There were more than 2 million teachers employed in public and private education in 1982. If one adds to this the total number of people employed in supervisory and support positions, the number was well over 3 million.

Since it is such a large enterprise, the characteristics of the people who work in it tend to be subjected to major changes from decade to decade, and it may not be possible to characterize the typical teacher. However, it should be useful to describe how the teaching work force changed from the mid-sixties to the mid-seventies. Some interesting and significant facts about teachers were presented in a survey by the National Education Association in its report on the *Status of the American Public School Teacher, 1975–76*.[10]

In the 10-year period between 1966 and 1976, NEA found that the median age of teachers had declined from 35 in 1966 to 33 in 1976. The NEA survey discovered that the proportion of teachers under age 40 had increased significantly while the proportion of those over 50 had declined significantly. The change had taken place among women and elementary teachers, since the median age of men and secondary teachers showed no change during the decade. However, women age 50 or older had decreased from 33 to 17 percent during the 1966–1976 decade.

In 1976 the typical teacher was white (90.8 percent) with a mixed social background. In terms of family background, there was some change in the composition of the teaching force in the United States during the decade of the sixties. The data below indicate these changes:[11]

	Percentages	
	1961	1971
Farmer	26.5	19.3
Unskilled worker	6.5	8.4
Skilled or semiskilled worker	23.4	25.7
Clerical or sales worker	7.1	5.5
Managerial worker or self-employed	22.0	22.1
Professional or semiprofessional worker	14.5	18.9

As is evident from the data on family background, teachers are a heterogeneous lot. Simple classifications which label teachers as predominantly middle class in terms of family background are obviously not accurate.

TABLE 9.1
Salaries of Classroom Teachers

School Year Ending		Average Annual Salary	
		Current Dollars	Constant (1978–79) Dollars
1969		$ 8,260	$15,885
1970		8,944	16,232
1971		9,695	16,744
1972		10,342	17,237
1973		10,530	16,848
1974		11,223	16,504
1975		12,291	16,258
1976		13,177	16,268
1977		14,134	16,512
1978		15,027	16,441
1979		15,867	15,887
1980			15,435
1981			15,160
1982			15,346
1983			15,488
1984			15,621
1985			15,791
1986			16,107
1987			16,497
1988			16,850
1989			17,115

As a whole, teaching was a female occupation in 1976. Elementary teachers overwhelmingly were female. During the last three decades, however, the proportion of men in teaching has been gradually increasing. The National Center for Education Statistics reported that, during the 30-year period from 1947 to 1977, men teachers in all schools had increased from 18.8 percent in 1948 to 33.9 percent in 1978. In elementary schools during the same period, the number of men teachers increased from 7.1 percent to 17.1 percent. On the secondary level, the figures for men were 40 percent in 1948 and 54 percent in 1978.[12] In total numbers, there were 745,000 men and 1,455,000 women teachers in 1978.

In 1976, 71.3 percent of the classroom teachers were married, and approximately two-thirds of those reported that their spouse worked full or part time. Significantly, nearly twice as many women as men reported their spouses worked full time.[13]

Although teachers may not be easily classified as middle class in terms of family background, they may have achieved at least lower-middle class status in terms of property ownership and income. In 1976 most teachers (92.8 percent) owned one or more cars, and 71 percent owned or were buying a home.[14] In terms of income, at least during the decade of the seventies, teachers could be classified as lower-middle class as indicated in Table 9.1.[15]

TEACHER SUPPLY AND DEMAND

A significant development relating to the status of teaching in recent years has been the existence of a surplus of teachers in most areas of teaching. This is not a unique phenomenon, for there have been times in the past when teacher over-supply existed, at least in certain areas. In the thirties, of course, teachers often had difficulty finding employment. Generally, beginning with World War II and continuing until the mid-sixties, there always appeared to be a shortage of teachers. Even during these years, however, there were periods, such as the early fifties, when there were surpluses in certain areas, principally in the secondary school in the social sciences and the humanities.

On the whole, however, teachers who were seeking employment from 1940 to 1965 fared well. By the late sixties, however, a large surplus of teachers had developed. There were many reasons for this. A major one was the fact that the birth rate began to decline sharply in 1960. This led to a significantly reduced elementary school population which had progressed through the high-school level by the end of the seventies. Meanwhile, the decline in the supply of new teachers was not as great as the decline in population. Teachers' organizations, in spite of their increasing power, have been singularly unsuccessful in their attempts to control supply. In economic terms, teacher supply is fairly inelastic; that is, training institutions continue to turn out certified teachers long after the demand has been met. This is due, in part at least, to the relatively long period of preparation. Unlike the unskilled and semiskilled labor markets, adjustments in supply and demand in skilled markets are not quickly achieved. In addition to this problem, teacher training has unique problems which are not typical of the labor market generally. The big bulge in oversupply occurred during the mid-sixties and resulted, in part at least, from the psychological mood of that period. Large numbers of college students who were caught up in the antiwar movement appeared to be interested in what they termed "socially useful" careers. Teaching was one of these. In addition, with a genuine teacher shortage in the early sixties, various government programs were provided for retraining of teachers who had left the classroom, and crash programs were initiated, most notably the Teacher Corps program, designed to turn arts and sciences graduates into certified teachers in a relatively short period of time. These programs continued even after it was becoming obvious that the need for them no longer existed. In addition to this, recessions, such as the ones which took place in the seventies when there were large numbers of students enrolled in college, tended to cause students to seek out programs where there was at least an employment possibility. Certification for teaching was one of these areas. College students enrolled in such "soft" areas as the humanities and the social sciences, sensing the possibility of unemployment upon graduation, could rather easily earn a teaching certificate.

Finally, and perhaps most important, enrollments in colleges and universities were growing most rapidly at the very time that enrollments in elementary and secondary schools were declining. This enrollment bulge was felt in colleges of teacher education as it was in other areas of preparation.

Ultimately, college students began to recognize the problem of teacher surplus and to react accordingly. The decline in enrollments in teacher education has been severe in recent years. Figure 9.1[16] graphically illustrates the recent history of the supply and demand problem in teacher education. It also demonstrates the future impact of declining supply. Apparently, the market system works in the teacher labor force, albeit somewhat slowly and imperfectly.

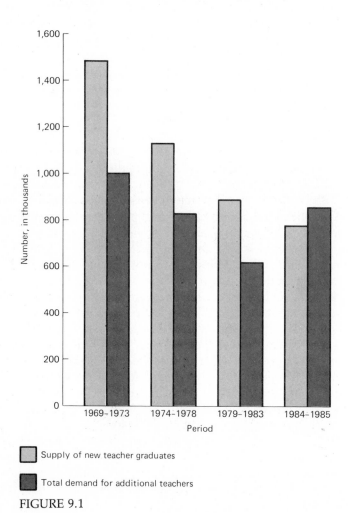

FIGURE 9.1

Such global representations can be misleading. Even during times of "surplus," there were teaching fields that were in high demand. It should also be noted that during times when there is an overall shortage of teachers, there are often areas which are in oversupply. These kinds of maladjustments in teacher supply tend to be more responsive to teacher demand. That is, supply tends to adjust itself more quickly in specific teaching fields than in teaching as a whole. The reason for this may be that it is simply much easier for prospective teachers in teacher training programs to change teaching fields than it is to opt for another career.

THE NATURE OF TEACHING AND TEACHER EFFECTIVENESS

Teaching is virtually impossible to describe. It seems to be all things to all people. It would seem that each teacher has his or her own definition of teaching, as does each authority in pedagogy. Waller was probably right when he observed: "It would be incorrect to assume that teaching inevitably develops the same character traits in all teachers. The adjustments of personality which different teachers make to the conditions of school life differ as radically as the personalities of those who enter teaching."[17] More than 40 years later, reporting on the extensive research they had done on teaching, Michael Dunkin and Bruce Biddle came to the same general conclusion.[18] After dealing with such issues as "teaching as an art," "teaching as obvious," "teaching as ineffective," "teaching as a reflection of learning," "teaching skills," and "performance criteria," along with other topics, Dunkin and Biddle concluded that these were merely ideological beliefs about teaching. They suggested that most of the writing on the nature of teaching was lacking in scientific knowledge of teaching. Dunkin and Biddle advocated "tentativeness with respect to all systems of belief concerning teaching until they are based on evidence."[19]

For Dunkin and Biddle, teaching was a complex problem influenced by an incredible number of variables which they attempted to outline in the model shown in Figure 9.2.[20]

Although the variables listed by Dunkin and Biddle are more or less self-explanatory, the complexity of the model as a whole is striking. The model should discourage one from drawing generalized conclusions about the nature of teaching. It obviously involves a great number of variables, perhaps many not included in the model, which are probably beyond the ability of a single researcher or classroom observer, however competent, to grasp. Thus, much of the recent research on the nature of teaching tends to deal with isolated aspects of teaching. This research is extensive, and volumes have been written reporting it. Although it would be impossible to present here a comprehensive review of this literature, a few examples should give the reader some idea of its nature.

Research on classroom climate and teacher behavior has been popular in recent years. Old assumptions about teacher-controlled classrooms have been questioned. No longer is the classroom conceived of as the relatively simple setting described by Waller in 1932:

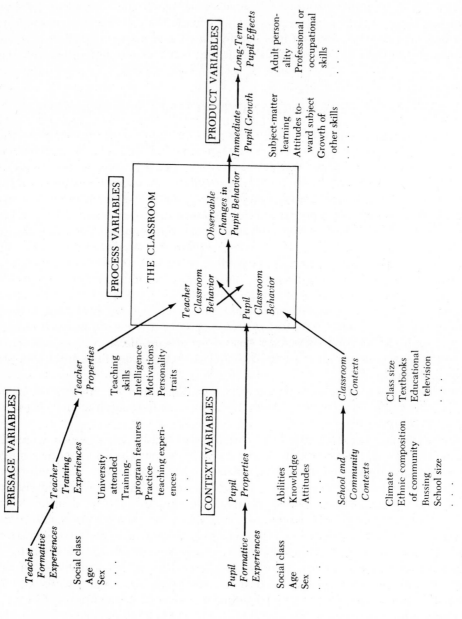

FIGURE 9.2

The teacher-pupil relationship is a form of institutionalized dominance and subordination. . . . The teacher represents the adult group, ever the enemy of the spontaneous life of . . . children.[21]

Waller characterized the classroom as an arena of conflict in which the teacher "represents the formal curriculum, and his interest is in imposing that curriculum upon the children in the form of tasks. . . ." On the other hand, "pupils are much more interested in life in their own world than in the dissociable bits of adult life which teachers have to offer." Waller suggested that "teacher and pupil confront each other with attitudes from which the underlying hostility can never be altogether removed."[22]

In recent years a number of researchers have assumed that "warm and responsive" classrooms provided a more effective learning environment than cold and authoritarian ones. Such researchers visit classrooms and, by studying the interaction between pupils and teachers, attempt to determine the effectiveness of the teacher. One aspect of classroom climate which has been measured is something called "indirectness." In a review of this research, Dunkin and Biddle noted that indirectness is associated with greater freedom of the students to make their feelings known. They concluded that, from the findings reported, the existence of indirectness in the classroom was a "good thing." However, they found many of the studies poorly designed and concluded that indirectness "is not associated with more pupil responses, the cognitive level of the classroom discourse, greater pupil achievement, and more positive pupil attitudes."[23]

Dunkin and Biddle found problems with other research on various aspects of classroom climate. It might be assumed that teacher praise or approval should contribute to pupil morale and achievement. The research in this area claims that praise enhances pupils' achievement, that it is associated with more positive self-concepts on the part of students, and that it is positively related to effective teaching. However, when teachers have been measured on the Flanders Interaction Analysis Categories, or other such instruments, the research has produced ambiguous results with regard to praise. Dunkin and Biddle reported that "the majority of studies have found praise unrelated to pupil achievement and pupil attitudes. . . ." They concluded that "unmitigated teacher praise, or approval, is not a particularly good thing to encourage in teachers."[24]

The findings in other aspects of classroom climate offer little encouragement. On teachers' acceptance of pupils' ideas, the research reported finds most classrooms clearly lacking in this quality (although some of the studies show encouraging results—that is, where teachers have more humanistic attitudes toward pupils and teachers accept pupils' ideas, there is greater pupil creativity and lower pupil anxiety). After reviewing this research, Dunkin and Biddle conclude: "although teachers can be trained to provide greater acceptance to pupils' ideas, only poor evidence has yet been advanced to indicate pupils would benefit if this were done."[25]

Many other variables which have been tested which are related to classroom climate provide little valuable assistance to the teacher who is interested in creating a more effective learning environment. In terms of student achievement, it doesn't seem to matter if the teacher talks a lot or a little, if the teacher questions frequently or lectures most of the time, if the teacher spends an undue amount of time on giving directions, if the pupils sit in silence or talk a lot, or if the pupils or the teacher initiate the classroom discussions.

Some studies make no effort to relate classroom climate or teacher effectiveness to student results as measured by achievement tests. Many researchers are content to determine teacher effectiveness by comparing certain teacher characteristics with the opinions of supervisors or objective observers. David G. Ryans has done a great deal of research in this area. In one study, Ryans defined good teachers through the use of classroom observations and assessments by trained observers. The Ryans group found three prominent patterns of observable classroom behavior: "Pattern X—friendly, understanding, sympathetic teacher behavior; Pattern Y—responsible, businesslike, systematic teacher behavior, and Pattern Z—stimulating, imaginative teacher behavior."[26] They then selected large groups of teachers who were "high," "low," and "average" in these categories and attempted to isolate the characteristics within each classification that applied commonly to all the teachers within each category. They found that the high teacher group almost uniformly expressed satisfaction with personal contacts with other people. The teachers in the high group reported few behavioral problems with children, seemed not to be jealous of others' success, and were willing to assume extra duties in school. They were middle-aged and married. They had achieved better than average grades in college. They were active in high school and college and were avid readers and adult learners. The low group, on the other hand, were self-centered, anxious, and restricted. They thought a large proportion of teachers suffered from ulcers and classroom tensions; they viewed the parents as enemies of the school and believed that people were influenced in their opinions of others by feelings of jealousy. They were older than the high group, read less, and participated much less in community activities. Whether these characteristics measure teacher effectiveness or personality type is open to question. It should also be obvious that the characteristics of the high group would probably be more highly valued than those of the low group in any work situation. In fairness, Ryans does not attempt to make judgments about the success of high or low groups in the achievement of pupils. His research—and it is impressive in terms of quantity and sophistication of design—merely suggests that there are identifiable characteristics which result in teachers being labeled as good or poor teachers by adult and trained observers.

Unlike Dunkin and Biddle, Rosenshine, after reviewing some 50 studies of classroom behavior, was able to find 11 "constellations" in teacher behavior which he thought offered promise. These included:

1. Clarity.
2. Variability.
3. Enthusiasm.
4. Task oriented and/or businesslike.

5. Student opportunity to learn criterion material.
6. Use of student ideas and teacher indirectness.
7. Teacher's use of criticism.
8. Use of structuring comments.
9. Good questioning skills.
10. Probing.
11. Appropriate level of instruction.

Each of these, according to Rosenshine, was positively related to pupil achievement.[27]

Some studies of the classroom behavior of teachers have isolated very specific variables and tested them against student achievement. One of the most comprehensive examples of such studies is the *Beginning Teacher Evaluation Study* (BTES) in California.[28] Through interviews with teachers and classroom observations of time allocated to learning specific tasks, the researchers sought to discover relationships between academic learning time and student achievement, classroom environment and student achievement, and teaching processes and student achievement. Not surprisingly, they found that there were positive relationships between the amount of time spent on instruction and student learning. They found also that student time spent without successful progress in the subject was negatively associated with learning. (Thus, the math student who is not having success with his assignment does poorly.)

On teaching processes, these researchers discovered that students achieved better when they had teachers who could properly diagnose their students' level of ability and prescribe appropriate tasks for them. This—along with the finding that the more time the teacher spent with the student, the higher his or her achievement—should come as no surprise. Among other things, the *Beginning Teacher Evaluation Study* found that feedback, structuring, clear explanations, and teacher emphasis on academic goals were positively related to student success. Perhaps it is research of this nature and quality which has caused others to look differently at teacher behavior and effectiveness.

Dissatisfied with the inconclusive nature of research on the teaching-learning process and on the teacher characteristics and behaviors related to student achievement, some researchers have concentrated on the teacher's philosophy, values, and beliefs. In a comprehensive review of research on teacher values and beliefs, Dobson and Dobson state: "teacher effectiveness is a personal matter of the effective use of a unique self."[29] The Dobsons argue that it is the teacher's feelings, self-concept, and personality which determine teacher behavior. They opt for teachers who are humanistic and respect the worth of the child; teachers who encourage open communication of feelings in the classroom; teachers who, in a word, act as warm and receptive human beings. They urge that teachers be freed from playing stereotyped roles in the classroom and merely try to be human in their interactions with students.

Those who emphasize what they like to call "humaneness" in the classroom generally cite research to demonstrate that many teachers lack these qualities, but they tend to disdain research which would measure the effectiveness of the humane teacher. Indeed, many would consider such research to be a violation of human principles. The sensitive and humane teacher is unique; the qualities which make up such a personality cannot be quantified and subjected to the tests of empirical research. The concept of humaneness is more philosophical than technical. Sensitivity and humaneness are not skills to be learned; they are traits to be developed with long periods of study, experience, and introspection. This is not to say that teachers are "born not made," but rather that skill-specific and training approaches are futile and, to an extent, dysfunctional in the development of people who are effective in dealing with children's needs.

Whatever the quality of usefulness of the research on teacher effectiveness, any experienced teacher would have to agree that teaching is a complex activity and that somehow teacher training falls short of adequately preparing teachers to cope. Nor can the practicing teacher look to peers or to supervisors for much help. Lortie[30] suggested that because of what he called the cellular nature of teaching, help from peers on specific classroom problems is seldom sought and seldom offered. (Cellular as used by Lortie can be roughly defined as the practical workplace isolation of the teacher.) Nor are supervisors much help. Few teachers seek them out, perhaps from fear of being considered "weak." In most places, supervision, even of first-year teachers, is done sporadically and often unsystematically. It may be just as well—for in view of the state of the art of research on teacher effectiveness, supervisors may have a very limited knowledge base from which to offer good assistance to struggling teachers.

What many teachers also know is that they need help. Teaching is a *pressured* undertaking. Phillip Jackson reported that in a single day a teacher might engage in more than one thousand interpersonal exchanges with students.[31] Even in the best of schools the job is difficult. In some schools, where some of these exchanges can be violent, the job can be impossible. Such pressure has led to a phenomenon among teachers which has come to be called teacher burnout. Burnout has been defined as "physical, emotional, and attitudinal exhaustion."[32] No one knows how many teachers are affected by it and it has many causes. Teachers who have large teaching loads and a number of students in each class who don't seem to care about learning can begin to develop symptoms of the disease. Teachers who feel they are being used by an uncaring community develop symptoms. Teachers who are constantly called upon for extra duties and seem trapped in an endless cycle of meetings and paperwork face the danger of teacher burnout. Teachers who are abused by students and parents are prime candidates. In a word, the realization that somehow teaching is much less than a high professional calling leads to a general disillusionment among teachers.

THE TEACHER AS A PROFESSIONAL

Whether or not teaching is a profession depends upon how one defines a profession. There are many definitions. Webster's *New World Dictionary* defines a profession as:

A vocation or occupation requiring advanced training in some liberal art or science, and usually involving mental rather than manual work, as teaching, engineering, writing, etc.; especially medicine, law, or theology. . . .

Ronald Corwin, in *Militant Professionalism*, defined a "mature profession" as "an organized work group that has a legal monopoly to establish procedures for recruiting and policing members and for maximizing control over a body of theoretical knowledge and applying it to the solution of social problems."[33]

A generation ago, the National Education Association suggested that a profession should embrace the following criteria:

1. Involves activities essentially intellectual.
2. Commands a body of specialized knowledge.
3. Requires extended professional preparation.
4. Demands continuous inservice growth.
5. Affords a life career and permanent membership.
6. Sets up its own standards.
7. Exalts service above personal gain.
8. Has a strong, closely knit professional organization.[34]

In the years since this list was developed, other characteristics have been added. For example, Allen Ornstein's list of the characteristics of a profession included the following in addition to the list above:

9. Application of research and theory to practice. . . .
10. Autonomy in making decisions about selected spheres of work.
11. Administrators facilitate work of professionals; administrators' functions are considered secondary and their work is considered undesirable.
12. There is a code of ethics to help clarify ambiguous matters or doubtful points related to services rendered.
13. High prestige and economic standing.[35]

If one arbitrarily uses these characteristics as the criteria for determining if teaching is a profession, it obviously falls far short. Even more significantly, if these are the standards of a profession, teaching seems to be moving away from these standards rather than toward their achievement. Although the number of specialized courses in something loosely called "professional education" has increased, we are no closer today to a clear definition of what should comprise that essential core of specialized knowledge in teaching than we were a generation ago. Indeed, a generation ago most teachers were among that small group of individuals within the society who had earned a bachelor's degree. With the growth of higher education in the past two decades, this accomplishment is no longer limited to a small elite group.

Although teaching does require a certain amount of professional preparation, teaching certificates are relatively easy to earn. Few students find it difficult to meet admission standards in most colleges of education. Once in a program, failure rates are not notoriously high. Almost anyone who can earn a bachelor's degree should experience little difficulty in getting a teaching certificate in most programs. In most states, teachers who earn certificates upon completion of a bachelor's degree have such a loose collection of undergraduate courses that they are often woefully unprepared in any specific discipline.

Although many school districts require a certain amount of in-service work, teachers themselves have lobbied on the local and state levels to assure that these demands are easily met. The most popular in-service growth efforts in recent years have been those offered through teacher centers and other teacher-controlled activities which have little quality control. Teacher workshops, beginning school conferences, and teacher center activities are not noted for their rigor. Indeed, in most cases, the physical presence of teachers is about all that is required.

Although teaching does provide a life career and permanent membership, the ease of entry coupled with meager financial rewards tends to make this meaningless. It is still not uncommon to hear the tragic view expressed that people teach because they can't do anything else. Moreover, movement in and out of teaching is a common phenomenon. Nor is it uncommon to find the attitude among teacher education candidates that they "want to teach awhile until they decide what they want to do."

Largely through lobbying efforts by their organizations, teachers do make an effort to set up their own standards for entry and continuation in the field. Unfortunately, these efforts are not noted for their high level of professionalism. Tenured teachers whom the organizations represent are not interested in any significant increase in standards for themselves. Few teachers appear interested in lobbying for higher standards that would force them back into the classrooms for expensive and time-consuming in-service work. Although most would like to make entry requirements more rigorous, this is difficult to accomplish without creating additional requirements for in-service work. The interest on the part of working teachers in higher standards for entry into teaching seems to be motivated as much by a desire to reduce the supply of teachers as to increase the professional level of teaching.

Surely some teachers exalt service above personal gain, but it is difficult to characterize teaching as a whole in this way when each school year teachers in hundreds of school districts strike or threaten to do so in order to get more favorable contracts on working conditions and salaries. This appears to be the major goal of teachers' organizations also. The major organizations which represent them, the National Education Association and the American Federation of Teachers, seem much more interested in "bread and butter" issues than in professionalism. More than half of all teachers belong to these groups, while only a tiny fraction of teachers are active in the professional associations, such as the National Council for Teachers of English or the National Council for the Social Studies, which are primarily concerned with the improvement of teaching and the curriculum in these areas.

Research and theory are not held in high esteem by teachers. Anyone who has worked with in-service teachers can testify that they want "practical stuff" they can "use in the classroom"; they don't want theory and research. In fairness to teachers, research and theory in education have not been areas noted for their contribution to the professionalization of the field.

In the matter of autonomy and relationships with supervisors and administrators, teachers fall far short of professional standards in other fields. The contemporary teacher may have less control over how his or her time is spent than the teacher of a generation ago. It is becoming increasingly difficult for classroom teachers to "close the classroom door and do as they please." Increasingly, outside influences impact on the teacher's time. As schools have grown in size and as they have experienced greater control by state and national agencies, the teacher has become less, not more, autonomous. There are reports to file, meetings to attend, guidelines to be observed, and a myriad of bureaucratic tasks to be done that were unknown to the teacher of the last generation. Although through their organizations teachers have gained some independence from administrative control, administrators continue to exercise a great deal of authority. There is no comparison, for example, between the administrative staff in a hospital and the administrative staff in the school. Whereas the administrative staff in hospitals is controlled by professionals, almost the opposite situation prevails in most schools. Administrators in schools continue to hire and fire teachers; they supervise and evaluate and establish rules and regulations for the teachers.

As a practical matter in most schools, it is the administration, acting for the school board, which determines the ethical code for the school—not the teachers. Nor is the ethical code necessarily professional in character. More often the ethical code for teachers is based on community standards of ethical behavior. When there is an alleged breach in the code and it is challenged by the teacher who had no part in its composition, the challenge is settled not by a group of professional teachers but often by the courts. Finally, prestige, particularly as it relates to economic status in the community, is so obviously lacking in teaching that it hardly deserves comment.

Although there are many reasons why teaching falls far short of the characteristics normally associated with a profession, it is most distressing that teachers as a group have not been able to move in that direction. Indeed, as pointed out in the beginning of this section, teaching seems to be moving away from this goal. Perhaps a major reason for this phenomenon is the increasing bureaucratization of teaching. Bureaucratization of schooling, according to Corwin, has caused teaching to develop a "split personality as it attempts to accommodate simultaneously to the demands of bureaucratization and professionalism."[36]

Corwin suggested that the growth of educational television, large class sizes, the growth of required courses, and the standardization and centralization of education have worked against professional goals. As the work of teaching becomes more standardized and centralized and as bureaucratic rules and regulations proliferate, teachers have less control over their professional activities. Growth in size and functions and increasing impersonalization of the schooling function have had their effects on teachers. The response of teachers to increasing size and centralization of functions has been the growth of large organizations to represent teachers. Thus, not only has the schooling function itself been bureaucratized, but teachers, in order to protect themselves from large impersonal bureaucracies, have developed their own large organizations. Adversary relationships have developed in which professional concerns have been overshadowed by the more pressing personal interests of job protection, working conditions, and compensation. This is not to say that teachers' organizations are unprofessional. The leadership in teachers' organizations argues that good working conditions and high salaries are professional goals. Their general position seems to be that if the rewards were good enough, other professional goals could be met. As true as this may be, the probability of its achievement is remote. Because efforts to achieve professional income for teachers have fallen so far short of this goal, compromises are often made. Thus, if there is a conflict between spending available resources on the improvement of classroom teaching by reducing class size or providing better instructional materials and giving teachers a raise, the organizations representing teachers will almost always opt for the raise.[37] This doesn't do much for the professional image of the teacher. In view of all these problems, one must conclude that teaching cannot be classified as a profession.

TEACHER POWER

Even though teaching may not be a profession, there can be little doubt that teachers, as a group, have made serious efforts to increase their power over nearly every aspect of their working lives. What follows is a brief description of teacher power, how it is expressed, and some of the results which have been achieved through the use of organized power.

Teacher power may be described as the collective efforts of teachers to gain more control over teaching as an occupation. Through organization and collective efforts, teachers have sought to influence the standards for entry into teaching, state laws which affect teachers, tenure and promotions, freedom in the classroom and community, and of course working conditions, salaries, and fringe benefits. Although the motivations for collective action are complex, the reasons why teachers elected to organize to enhance their power are similar in many ways to the efforts of industrial workers to organize. In the first place, the size and bureaucratization in schools, as in industry, made it apparent that isolated individuals attempting to bargain with superiors placed the teacher and the worker at a distinct disadvantage. In teaching, as in industry, as the system became large and impersonal, it became obvious that some sort of collective action was needed in order for demands to be taken seriously.

Other analogies can be drawn between industrial workers in a large enterprise and teachers in a large school system. Workers tended to be exploited in large systems where they were unorganized. This was also true of teachers. When all the power rested with the "bosses," i.e., the school board and its administrators, it was sometimes abused. Before teacher power, teachers could be dismissed at will. Faculty meetings were not discussions of mutual problems; they were held to tell teachers what they must do. Teachers were told what to teach and how to teach it. When they asked for better materials, working conditions, or an increase in salary, they could be told simply: "We don't have the money." School administrators were feared, and one learned to follow orders without question.

A parallel can also be drawn between early industrial worker organization and teacher organization. Both were dominated by management. Industrial workers' early experiences were with company unions, and, until very recently, the major teachers' organization, the National Education Association, was, on the local school district level, little more than a company union. It tended to be dominated by administrators who, if they were not officers of the local organization, often determined who would be. The obvious advantage for school administrators of the existence of such organizations on the local level was simply that it was easier to deal with an organization one could control than with the demands of large numbers of individual teachers. Of course, it was a short step from this kind of organization to the more effective organization controlled by teachers which is now characteristic of the Classroom Teachers Association of the National Education Association, and the American Federation of Teachers.

Teacher power on the contemporary scene is expressed largely through the NEA and the AFT. The NEA, founded in 1886 and chartered by an act of Congress in 1906, has nearly two million members. The presence of school administrators in the organization tended to create a conflict of interests within the organization. On many issues, classroom teachers were in an adversary position vis-à-vis the school board; this was an untenable position for school administrators. It wasn't until 1962, however, as its annual meeting in Denver, that the NEA took steps to separate administrators from teachers in the organization. This was partly a reaction to the success of its rival, the American Federation of Teachers, in gaining recognition in 1961 as the bargaining agent for New York City teachers, and partly a realization on the part of the teacher-members of NEA that the company union character of the organization was ineffective.

The American Federation of Teachers, founded in Chicago in 1916, could never be charged with being a company union. From the beginning it billed itself as a classroom teachers' organization and made much of the fact that it was the only organization which truly represented teachers. In the early years the AFT grew rapidly. Indeed, by 1920 it had more members than the NEA. For the next three decades it experienced very slow growth, and by 1960 it was completely overshadowed by the NEA. Its efforts in the sixties and seventies to organize teachers in the large cities were very successful, and by 1980 the AFT was claiming a membership of more than half a million teachers.

As these organizations gained membership, they also gained power and experience in its exercise. In terms of expression of power, there is very little difference between the two organizations—with a single exception. The AFT is affiliated with the AFL-CIO while the NEA is an independent organization. Both organizations express their power in much the same manner. Their major efforts are political pressure and activity and job actions of various kinds. Both groups exercise political pressure from the precinct to the national level. Both groups seem to understand the importance of political activism. Recognizing the importance of the state legislature in school funding as well as other matters which directly affect teachers, both groups have been politically active on the local level. They have worked hard to get candidates favorable to their causes elected to the state legislature. On the local level, both organizations have been not at all reluctant to work for their own candidates for school board positions. Recognizing the increasing importance of the national government in matters relating to education, both groups have actively supported or opposed candidates for Congress. The NEA even became deeply involved in presidential politics, supporting Mr. Carter in 1976 and 1980. Local and state NEA unit representatives were a powerful presence in the National Democratic Convention in 1980. In addition to this activity, both groups have engaged in serious lobbying activities in state legislatures and in Congress in an effort to get increased funding and other favorable legislation.

Finally, teachers, with the support of their organizations, have engaged in a variety of job actions in recent years. For a time in the 1960s, sanctions were popular with the NEA. Borrowing a chapter from the American Association of University Professors, sanctions were merely efforts to publicize a state or local school district's lack of concern for the professional demands of teachers. The sanction consisted of urging teachers not to seek employment in those states or school districts which had been sanctioned. Beyond this, a popular job action in the sixties was something called a "professional holiday." Essentially, it was a one-day strike in which teachers refused to report to work. By far the most popular and most common form of job action is the old-fashioned strike and picket line. Both the NEA and the AFT have engaged in this action. It has clearly become the most commonly utilized expression of teacher power in the United States.

The results of the exercise of teacher power may be impossible to measure. However, some of the more notable achievements can be described. The major achievements of teachers in their struggle for power seem to be collective bargaining, the development of teacher centers, and greater influence generally on legislation which affects the welfare of teachers.

Collective bargaining for teachers is now permitted by law in a little over half the states. It is a procedure borrowed from the industrial labor force. Organized labor gained the right to collective bargaining as a result of the National Labor Relations Act (the Wagner Act) passed by Congress in July of 1935. Collective bargaining is a simple process. Workers elect an organization to represent them and the organization selects a bargaining committee to present their demands in contract negotiations. For years after the Wagner Act was passed, the American Federation of Teachers pushed for collective bargaining while the National Education Association was cool toward the idea. The difference in views can be explained by the fact that the basic philosophies of the two groups were different. The AFT, following the industrial union model, was an organization of "workers": classroom teachers who saw themselves in an adversary relationship with what they liked to call "management"—that is, the school board and the administrators who served the board. The NEA, which counted many administrators in its membership, saw things differently. After the early sixties, when the classroom teachers split from the administrators within NEA, it too began to push for collective bargaining. Since then, the movement has grown rapidly.

At the risk of oversimplification, the process can be described as follows. When teachers bargain collectively, their elected negotiating team presents their demands to the school board's representatives. The board's negotiators, representing the public and the taxpayers, and the teachers, representing themselves, sit in an adversary relationship just as management and unions do in contract negotiations. A contract is negotiated for all the teachers in the district. Each year the teachers decide the specific items they would like to have in their contract and the representatives of the school board present what they feel they can offer. The differences are negotiated. It is at this point that the industrial union analogy breaks down. If an industrial union and management are unable to reach an agreement, the union has a legal right to withhold services—that is, to call a strike. Since most states make teacher strikes illegal, in some places strong teachers' unions have been pressing for compulsory arbitration. Compulsory arbitration occurs when the parties to a contract negotiation cannot reach an agreement and a third, presumably neutral, party is called in to arbitrarily resolve the differences. In compulsory arbitration, both parties agree at the outset of negotiations that they will abide by the decisions of the arbitrator in the event that arbitration is needed. Industrial unions have avoided this course of action since they feel that it might interfere with their major sanction—that is, their right to strike. They generally feel that they can gain more through the strike or the threat of a strike than they can from arbitration.

Another achievement of teachers' organized power has been the establishment of teacher centers. With the help of federal funding, teacher centers became popular in the 1970s. Most teacher centers are organized and controlled by teachers. Although teacher centers come in many shapes and forms, most of them provide a variety of support and services for classroom teachers. A major function of most teacher centers is to provide in-service opportunities for teachers. This is a major change and a genuine expression of teacher power. Before teacher centers were created, the initiative as well as most of the authority for requiring in-service experiences for teachers rested with the school board and its administrative representatives. Although there were local variations, a common requirement for in-service work was that teachers take regular university courses as a condition of employment or promotion. As teachers gained power, they began to demand that they, not the school board or administration, decide what in-service activities would be appropriate. A major result of this demand was the development of teacher centers. The movement has grown rapidly, and by 1981 teacher centers were involved in a number of activities, including such things as providing workshops, courses, curriculum development, community involvement in the school program, action research, and preservice training, to mention a few.[38] Indeed, the possible services which can be performed by teacher centers seem almost unlimited.

The growth of teacher centers could dramatically change the nature of in-service education for teachers. Whereas traditionally, the graduate colleges of education provided in-service work for teachers in the form of courses, extension work, and workshops, teacher centers can ignore regular academic programs. In some places, teacher centers can seriously threaten the very existence of graduate colleges of education. The temptation is great to bypass graduate colleges with their bureaucratic organizations and standards of performance. Why should teachers spend time and money and effort taking regular courses in a graduate college when they can meet the requirements for in-service training locally, without cost, with a minimal expenditure of time, and under no pressure to achieve at any level of competence? There can be no question that teacher power as expressed through the development of teacher centers has been of great personal benefit to many teachers. It should be pointed out here that all of this has been possible because teachers in most places now have the power to establish their own standards for in-service requirements. Although the Reagan administration has recommended that teacher center funding be placed under the block grant system, it is probable, given the political power of teachers on the state level, that even with reduced federal funding the programs will continue in some form.

Finally, although impossible to measure, the new political activism of teachers has made itself felt in the various state legislatures and their legislation on schools. Teachers have been successful in gaining increased appropriations for schools, making entry requirements into the profession more stringent, reducing class size, establishing collective bargaining laws, gaining greater control over preservice education, defining teachers' rights, establishing new tenure provisions and comprehensive retirement programs, and affecting a myriad of other educational matters.

If any significant conclusion can be drawn from the exercise of teacher power, it is that teachers apparently have learned their lessons well from the experience of other organized workers in the society. They have tended to follow the well-worn path of other organized groups in their quest for power. There is really nothing new in the organizational efforts and demands of teachers. It had all been done before by organized labor. Thus, teachers in their quest for power were not so much innovative as reactive. They were reacting to the forces of size and the bureaucratization of schooling. They were reacting to a sense of powerlessness in the same sense that organized labor before them had reacted. They established effective organizations and their demands have been as much personal as professional.

TEACHER RIGHTS

Another expression of the growing awareness of power on the part of teachers is their concern for their rights as citizens. The scene of this battle has been the courtroom. Although not as determined as students and their parents in seeking to establish constitutional rights, teachers have been active. Reflecting the movement in society toward a more comprehensive definition of civil rights, teachers have gone to the courts in an effort to protect their rights in a number of areas. In recent years they have attempted to get definitions of academic freedom and freedom of expression inside and outside the classroom, tenure and due process, and the rights of teacher organizations to operate openly on the local level. Although this is only a partial list and there have been hundreds of cases brought by teachers which have never gotten beyond state courts, the illustrative cases which follow should present the reader with some idea of the nature of the struggle on the part of teachers to protect their constitutional rights.

Over the years, because of the very nature of teaching, teachers have faced difficulties in the matter of academic freedom. In 1923 the Supreme Court of the United States ruled that a Nebraska law which prohibited the teaching of a modern foreign language to school children was unconstitutional.[39] In this case a teacher was convicted under the Nebraska law for teaching German to a child in a private school. In overturning the conviction, the Court ruled that the right to practice the profession of teaching is a right protected by the Fourteenth Amendment. It found the Nebraska law "unconstitutionally unreasonable and arbitrary."

In a more recent case, *Epperson v. Arkansas*, the Supreme Court challenged the right of a state legislature to decide which view of evolution should be taught in the classroom. It is cited in part below.

Epperson v. Arkansas
393 US 97 (1968)

Mr. Justice Fortas delivered the opinion of the Court.

This appeal challenges the constitutionality of the "anti-evolution" statute which the state of Arkansas adopted in 1928 to prohibit the teaching in its public schools and universities of the theory that man evolved from other species of life. The statute was a product of the up-surge of "fundamentalist" religious fervor of the twenties. The Arkansas statute was an adaptation of the famous Tennessee "monkey law" which that state adopted in 1925. . . . The constitutionality of the Tennessee law was upheld by the Tennessee Supreme Court in the celebrated Scopes case in 1927.

The Arkansas law makes it unlawful for a teacher in any state-supported school or university "to teach the theory or doctrine that mankind ascended or descended from a lower order of animals," or "to adopt or use in any such institution a textbook that teaches" this theory. Violation is a misdemeanor and subjects the violator to dismissal from his position. . . .

The Chancery Court . . . held that the statute violated the Fourteenth Amendment to the United States Constitution. The court noted that this amendment encompasses the prohibitions upon state interference with freedom of speech and thought which are contained in the First Amendment. Accordingly, it held that the challenged statute is unconstitutional because, in violation of the First Amendment, it "tends to hinder the quest for knowledge, restrict the freedom to learn, and restrain the freedom to teach." In this perspective, the act, it held, was an unconstitutional and void restraint upon the freedom of speech guaranteed by the Constitution.

On appeal, the Supreme Court of Arkansas reversed. . . . It sustained the statute as an exercise of the state's power to specify the curriculum in public schools. It did not address itself to the competing constitutional considerations. . . .

(T)he law must be stricken because of its conflict with the constitutional prohibition of state laws respecting an establishment of religion or prohibiting the free exercise thereof. The overriding fact is that Arkansas' law selects from the body of knowledge a particular segment which it proscribes for the sole reason that it is deemed to conflict with a particular religious doctrine; that is, with a particular interpretation of the Book of Genesis by a particular religious group. . . .

While the study of religions and of the Bible from a literary and historic viewpoint, presented objectively as part of a secular program of education, need not collide with the First Amendment's prohibition, the state may not adopt programs or practices in its public schools or colleges which "aid or oppose" any religion. . . . This prohibition is absolute. It forbids alike the preference of a religious doctrine or the prohibition of theory which is deemed antagonistic to a particular dogma. As Mr. Justice Clark stated in *Joseph Burstyn, Inc. v. Wilson*, "the state has no legitimate interest in protecting any or all religions from views distasteful to them. . . ." The test was stated as follows in *Abington School Dist v. Schempp* 374 US at 222, "(W)hat are the purpose and the primary effect of the enactment? If neither is the advancement or inhibition of religion then the enactment exceeds the scope of legislative power as circumscribed by the Constitution."

These precedents inevitably determine the result in the present case. The state's undoubted right to prescribe the curriculum for its public schools does not carry with it the right to prohibit, on pain of criminal penalty, the teaching of a scientific theory or doctrine where that prohibition is based upon reasons that violate the First Amendment. It is much too late to argue that the state may impose upon the teachers in its schools any conditions that is chooses, however restrictive they may be of constitutional guarantees. . . .

In view of the many divisions in our society, it is not surprising that teachers frequently find themselves in difficulty over what they are teaching in the classroom and the manner in which they teach it. Teachers have been challenged for teaching materials which are not considered appropriate for students. Although few of these cases ever find their way into the courts, in some instances the teacher challenges the right of community groups or administrators to determine which materials and methods are appropriate. Such was the case in Texas in *Kingsville Independent School District v. Cooper* (1980). In this case, which was appealed to the US 5th District Court, Janet Cooper used a racial role-playing exercise in teaching post-Civil War American history. The parents complained, and Ms. Cooper was fired. In ruling for Ms. Cooper, the district court said that "classroom activity is a protected activity" under the First Amendment. Ms. Cooper was reinstated in her position and awarded seven years back pay.

In the same year that *Epperson* was decided, the Supreme Court dealt with freedom of expression by a teacher outside the classroom. In *Pickering v. Board of Education*, the Court had a great deal to say about the First Amendment rights of teachers when they are not so much acting as teachers but are exercising their rights as citizens. This is a particularly important case for teachers because it deals with the limitations which might reasonably be placed on school officials in controlling the actions of the teachers whom they employ. In part, this is what the Supreme Court had to say.

Pickering v. Board of Education
391 US 563 (1968)

Mr. Justice Marshall delivered the opinion of the Court.

Appellant Marvin L. Pickering, a teacher in Township High School District 205, Will County, Illinois, was dismissed from his position by the appellee board of education for sending a letter to a local newspaper in connection with a recently proposed tax increase that was critical of the way in which the board and the district superintendent of schools had handled past proposals to raise new revenue for the schools. Appellant's dismissal resulted from a determination by the board, after a full hearing, that the publication of the letter was "detrimental to the efficient operation and administration of the schools of the district" and hence, under the relevant Illinois statute ... that "interests of the school require his dismissal. ..."

The letter constituted, basically, an attack on the school board's handling of the 1961 bond issue proposals and its subsequent allocation of financial resources between the schools' educational and athletic programs. It also charged the superintendent of schools with attempting to prevent teachers in the district from opposing or criticizing the proposed bond issue.

The board dismissed Pickering for writing and publishing the letter. Pursuant to Illinois law, the board was then required to hold a hearing on the dismissal. At the hearing the board charged that numerous statements in the letter were false and that the publication of the statements unjustifiably impugned the "motives, honesty, integrity, truthfulness, responsibility and competence" of both the board and the school administration. The board also charged that the false statements damaged the professional reputations of its members and of the school administrators, would be disruptive of faculty discipline, would tend to foment "controversy, conflict and dissension" among teachers, administrators, the board of education, and the residents of the district ...

The board contends that "the teacher by virtue of his public employment has a duty of loyalty to support his superiors in attaining the generally accepted goal of education and that, if he must speak out publicly, he would do so factually and accurately, commensurate with his education and experience." Appellant, on the other hand, argues that the test applicable to defamatory statements directed against public officials by persons having no occupationl relationship with them, namely, that statements to be legally actionable must be made "with knowledge that (they were) ... false or with reckless disregard of whether (they were) ... false or not" (*New York Times Co v. Sullivan* 376 US 254, 180 [1964]), should also be applied to public statements made by teachers. ...

An examination of the statements in appellant's letter objected to by the board reveals that they, like the letter as a whole, consist essentially of criticism of the board's allocation of school funds between educational and athletic programs and of both the board's and the superintendent's methods of informing, or preventing the informing of, the district's taxpayers of the real reasons why additional tax revenues were being sought for the schools. The statements are in no way directed toward any person with whom appellant would normally be in contact in the course of his daily work as a teacher. Thus no question of maintaining either discipline by immediate superiors or harmony among coworkers is presented here. Appellant's employment relationships with the board and, to a somewhat lesser extent, with the superintendent are not the kind of close working relationships for which it can persuasively be claimed that personal loyalty and confidence are necessary to their proper functioning. Accordingly, to the extent that the board's position here can be taken to suggest that even comments on matters of public concern that are substantially correct, . . . may furnish grounds for dismissal if they are sufficiently critical in tone, we unequivocally reject it.

We next consider the statements in appellant's letter which we agree to be false. The board's original charges included allegations that the publication of the letter damaged the professional reputations of the board and the superintendent and would foment controversy and conflict among the board, teachers, administrators, and the residents of the district. However, no evidence to support these allegations was introduced at the hearing. So far as the record reveals, Pickering's letter was greeted by everyone but its main target, the board, with massive apathy and total disbelief. The board must, therefore, have decided, perhaps by analogy with the law of libel, that the statements were per se harmful to the operation of the schools.

However, the only way in which the board could conclude, absent any evidence of the actual effect of the letter, that the statements contained therein were per se detrimental to the interest of the schools was to equate the board members' own interests with that of the schools. Certainly an accusation that too much money is being spent on athletics by the administrators of the school system . . . cannot reasonably be regarded as per se detrimental to the district schools. . . .

In addition, the fact that particular illustrations of the board's claimed undesirable emphasis on athletic programs were false would not normally have any necessary impact on the actual operation of the schools, beyond its tendency to anger the board. For example, Pickering's letter was written after the defeat at the polls of the second proposed tax increase. It could, therefore, have no effect on the ability of the school district to raise necessary revenue, since there was no showing that there was any proposal to increase taxes pending when the letter was written.

More importantly, the question whether a school system requires additional funds is a matter of legitimate public concern on which the judgment of the school administration, including the school board, cannot, in a society that leaves such questions to popular vote, be taken as conclusive. On such a question free and open debate is vital to informed decision making by the electorate. Teachers are, as a class, the members of a community most likely to have informed and definite opinions as to how funds allotted to the operation of the schools should be spent. Accordingly, it is essential that they be able to speak out freely on such questions without fear of retaliatory dismissal.

In addition, the amounts expended on athletics which Pickering reported erroneously were matters of public record on which his position as a teacher in the district did not qualify him to speak with any greater authority than any other taxpayer. The board could easily have rebutted appellant's errors by publishing the accurate figures itself, either via a letter to the same newspaper or otherwise. We are thus not presented with a situation in which a teacher has carelessly made false statements about matters so closely related to the day-to-day operations of the schools that any harmful impact on the public would be difficult to counter because of the teacher's presumed greater access to the real facts. Accordingly, we have no occasion to consider at this time whether under such circumstances a school board could reasonably require that a teacher made substantial efforts to verify the accuracy of his charges before publishing them.

What we do have before us is a case in which a teacher has made erroneous public statements upon issues then currently the subject of public attention, which are critical of his ultimate employer but which are neither shown nor can be presumed to have in any way either impeded the teacher's proper performance of his daily duties in the classroom or to have interfered with the regular operation of the school generally. In these circumstances we conclude that the interest of the school administration in limiting teachers' opportunities to contribute to public debate is not significantly greater than its interest in limiting a similar contribution by any member of the general public.
. . .

In sum, we hold that, in a case such as this, absent proof or false statements knowingly or recklessly made by him, a teacher's exercise of his right to speak on issues of public importance may not furnish the basis for his dismissal from public employment. Since no such showing has been made in this case regarding appellant's letter . . . his dismissal for writing it cannot be upheld and the judgment of the Illinois Supreme Court must, accordingly, be reversed and the case remanded for further proceedings not inconsistent with this opinion. . . .

In *Pickering*, the Court makes some comments about the relationship between employers and employees. It deals specifically with the question of loyalty to the system. Does the fact that Pickering was a teacher distinguish him from other citizens who might be working in a large organization? Although the Court found that the expectation that teachers should express the same views as administration on issues which vitally affected the school was unreasonable, is that same expectation common in private corporations? What might happen if an employee of a private corporation publicly disagreed with the policies established by his company? Would an employee of a private firm have a good case? Are there basic differences in the rights of public and private employees?

As teachers gained political effectiveness, they worked diligently to get state legislatures to enact tenure laws. This movement has been very successful, and most states have developed some sort of tenure for teachers. Some of these laws are strong in the sense that they include very specific provisions on due process which make it very difficult to dismiss an experienced teacher without specific cause. In most strong tenure laws, the burden of proof for incompetence or ethical violations is placed on those bringing the charges. Even though tenure has been well established in law and practice in most states, teachers continue to experience difficulty in defending this right. Many cases have been brought to court in which the courts have been asked to clarify and interpret state laws and practices on tenure. Even in states where there are no tenure laws, the principle of tenure has become so well established in practice that the courts often assume that tenure exists. *Perry v. Sindermann* was such a case, and even though it is a college case, it provides a very comprehensive discussion of the meaning of tenure, for all teachers. The case also deals with issues closely related to tenure, including an extensive discussion of due process hearings for teachers who are dismissed from their jobs.

Perry v. Sindermann
408 US 593 (1974)

Mr. Justice Stewart delivered the opinion of the Court.

From 1959 to 1969 the respondent, Robert Sindermann, was a teacher in the state college system of the state of Texas. After teaching for two years at the University of Texas and four years at San Antonio Junior College, he became a professor of government and social science at Odessa Junior College in 1965. He was employed at the college for four successive years, under a series of one-year contracts. He was successful enough to be appointed, for a time, the cochairman of his department.

During the 1968–69 academic year, however, controversy arose between the respondent and the college administration. The respondent was elected president of the Texas Junior College Teachers Association. In this capacity, he left his teaching duties on several occasions to testify before committees of the Texas legislature, and he became involved in public disagreements with the policies of the college's board of regents. In particular, he aligned himself with a group advocating the elevation of the college to four-year status—a change opposed by the regents. And, on one occasion, a newspaper advertisement appeared over his name that was highly critical of the regents.

Finally, in May 1969, the respondent's one-year employment contract terminated and the board of regents voted not to offer him a new contract for the next academic year. The regents issued a press release setting forth allegations of the respondent's insubordination. But they provided him no official statement of the reasons for the nonrenewal of his contract. And they allowed him no opportunity for a hearing to challenge the basis of the nonrenewal.

The respondent then brought this action in federal district court. He alleged primarily that the regents' decision not to rehire him was based on his public criticism of the policies of the college administration and thus infringed his right to freedom of speech. He also alleged that their failure to provide him an opportunity for a hearing violated the Fourteenth Amendment's guarantee of procedural due process. The petitioners—members of the board of regents and the president of the college—denied that their decision was made in retaliation for the respondent's public criticism and argued that they had no obligation to provide a hearing. On the basis of these bare pleadings and three brief affidavits filed by the respondent, the district court granted summary judgment for the petitioners. It concluded that the respondent had "no cause of action against the (petitioners) since his contract of employment terminated May 31, 1969, and Odessa Junior College has not adopted the tenure system." . . .

The court of appeals reversed the judgment of the district court. . . .

The first question presented is whether the respondent's lack of a contractual or tenure right to reemployment, taken alone, defeats his claim that the nonrenewal of his contract violated the First and Fourteenth Amendments. We hold that it does not.

For at least a quarter century, this court has made clear that even though a person has no "right" to a valuable governmental benefit and even though the government may deny him the benefit for any number of reasons, there are some reasons upon which the government may not rely. It may not deny a benefit to a person on a basis that infringes his constitutionally protected interests—especially, his interest in freedom of speech. For if the government could deny a benefit to a person because of his constitutionally protected speech or associations, his exercise of those freedoms would in effect be penalized and inhibited. This would allow the government to "produce a result which (it) could not command directly." . . . Such interference with constitutional rights is impermissible. . . .

The respondent's lack of formal contractual or tenure security in continued employment at Odessa Junior College, though irrelevant to his free speech claim, is highly relevant to his procedural due process claim. But it may not be entirely dispositive.

We have held today in *Board of Regents v. Roth* 408 US 564, that the Constitution does not require opportunity for a hearing before the nonrenewal of a nontenured teacher's contract, unless he can show that the decision not to rehire him somehow deprived him of an interest in "liberty" or that he had a "property" interest in continued employment, despite the lack of tenure or a formal contract. In Roth the teacher had not made a showing on either point to justify summary judgment in his favor.

Similarly, the respondent here has yet to show that he has been deprived of an interest that could invoke procedural due process protection. As in Roth, the mere showing that he was not rehired in one particular job, without more, did not amount to a showing of a loss of liberty. Nor did it amount to a showing of a loss of property.

But the respondent's allegations—which we must construe most favorably to the respondent at this stage of the litigation—do raise a genuine issue as to his interest in continued employment at Odessa Junior College. He alleged that this interest, though not secured by a formal contractual tenure provision, was secured by a no less binding understanding fostered by the college administration. In particular, the respondent alleged that the college had a de facto tenure program, and that he had tenure under that program. He claimed that he and others legitimately relied upon an unusual provision that had been in the college's official faculty guide for many years:

> Teacher Tenure: Odessa College has no tenure system. The administration of the college wishes the faculty member to feel that he has permanent tenure as long as his teaching services are satisfactory and as long as he displays a cooperative attitude toward his coworkers and his superiors, and as long as he is happy in his work.

Moreover, the respondent claimed legitimate reliance upon guidelines promulgated by the Coordinating Board of the Texas College and University System that provided that a person, like himself, who had been employed as a teacher in the state college and university system for seven years or more has some form of job tenure. Thus the respondent offered to prove that a teacher, with his long period of service, at this particular state college had no less a "property" interest in continued employment than a formally tenured teacher at other colleges, and had no less a procedural due process right to a statement of reasons and a hearing before college officials upon their decision not to retain him. . . .

A written contract with an explicit tenure provision clearly is evidence of a formal understanding that supports a teacher's claim of entitlement to continued employment unless sufficient "cause" is shown. Yet absence of such an explicit contractual provision may not always foreclose the possibility that a teacher has a "property" interest in reemployment. . . .

A teacher, like the respondent, who has held his position for a number of years, might be able to show from the circumstances of this service—and from other relevant facts—that he has a legitimate claim of entitlement to job tenure. . . . This is particularly likely in a college or university, like Odessa Junior College, that has no explicit tenure system even for senior members of its faculty, but that nonetheless may have created such a system in practice. . . .

In this case, the respondent has alleged the existence of rules and understandings, promulgated and fostered by state officials, that may justify his legitimate claim of entitlement to continued employment absent "sufficient cause." ... Proof of such a property interest would not, of course, entitle him to reinstatement. But such proof would obligate college officials to grant a hearing at his request, where he could be informed of the grounds for his nonretention and challenge their sufficiency.

Therefore, while we do not wholly agree with the opinion of the court of appeals, its judgment remanding this case to the district court is affirmed.

In *Sindermann*, the Court was concerned about the property right of teachers who were entitled to tenure. In what way does this strengthen the concept of tenure? The *Sindermann* Court considered the matter of due process in the dismissal of tenured teachers. What are minimal due process guarantees for teachers? A major point made by teachers in their defense of tenure is that it is needed to protect academic freedom. That is, a tenured teacher is somewhat protected from pressures to conform. On the other hand, those who oppose tenure claim that it provides a refuge for the incompetent. Which, in your view, is the best argument?

Beginning with the first World War, teachers have been in a very sensitive position regarding loyalty. During every war in the twentieth century, as indicated in the previous chapter of this work, "patriotic" pressure groups have been active in their efforts to protect citizens from subversive or "disloyal" citizens. State legislatures as well as Congress have responded from time to time with legislation demanding loyalty from public employees. The early fifties was a particularly trying time for teachers. The wave of anticommunism epitomized by Senator Joseph McCarthy's Un-American Activities Committee found expression in state loyalty oaths for teachers. Many of these were challenged by teachers who felt that their civil rights were being violated. *Adler v. Board of Education*[40] dealt with a New York City civil service statute which held that membership in any organization which advocated the overthrow of the government of the United States made one ineligible for public school employment. A list of organizations was drawn up and membership in any of the listed organizations was prima facie evidence that the individual who belonged was ineligible for a teaching position. However, the law did require that a hearing be held to determine the nature and purposes of the organization. A hearing was also required before a member of any of the listed groups could be dismissed. If an employee could demonstrate that, despite membership in the organization, he or she was fit to be a teacher, the employee could not be dismissed. Teachers who were dismissed under the law claimed that their First and Fourteenth Amendment rights had been violated. The Supreme Court disagreed, holding that the law was constitutional in that it required a hearing and afforded sufficient protection for the employee from false charges. Given the opportunity that teachers have to influence their students, the Court felt that efforts to keep subversives out of the ranks of teaching was a legitimate state interest.

In the same year the Court ruled differently in *Wieman v. Updegraff*.[41] This case is distinguished from *Adler* in that the Oklahoma loyalty oath did not provide adequate protection to those who were charged with being disloyal. The Oklahoma loyalty oath required that all state employees, as a condition of employment, sign a statement that they were not, and had not been for the preceding five years, a member of any organization listed by the United States Attorney General as a "communist front" or "subversive" organization. Two professors at Oklahoma A and M College argued that being forced to sign such an oath was a violation of their First and Fourteenth Amendment rights. The Supreme Court agreed, holding that the law was overbroad in its application. They reasoned that the oath was so inclusive that it applied to those who might have innocently joined a subversive organization as well as to those who knowingly did so. The Court held that the law constituted "indiscriminate classification of innocent as well as knowing activity" and that this course of action "must fall as an assertion of arbitrary power" on the part of the state. The Court also found the oath to be an impermissible interference with the First Amendment freedom of association.

The Supreme Court handed down a similar decision on an Arkansas loyalty oath which was challenged by public school teachers in Arkansas in 1960.[42] In 1964 a Washington state loyalty oath was struck down on the grounds that it was so vague that it could lead to prosecution for legally or constitutionally protected behavior. The loyalty oath in Washington required teachers to swear that they would by "precept and example . . . promote respect for the flag and the institutions of the United States . . . and the State of Washington, reverence for law and order, and undivided allegiance to the government of the United States." It barred from employment those who refused to swear that they were not members of "the Communist Party or any other subversive organization."[43]

In the *Elfbrandt* case in Arizona, a teacher challenged the Arizona loyalty oath, claiming that its meaning was unclear and that she could not get a hearing in order to have the meaning clarified. In this case the Court ruled that the Arizona oath was unconstitutional because it attached sanctions to membership in organizations without determination of specific intent of the organization to pursue illegal goals. The Court did not deny the right of a state to protect itself against subversives in the schools, but it held that it was the state's responsibility to demonstrate that such restrictions of freedom could be justified only in cases in which there was a "clear and present danger" to the interests of the state.[44] However, in *Cole*, in 1972, the Court ruled that a Massachusetts loyalty oath did not violate the rights of public employees.[45]

Thus, the status of loyalty oaths is not completely clear. What is clear is that states can require loyalty oaths. Whether or not they meet constitutional tests may depend more on the composition of the Court and the conditions prevailing in the society than on the wording of the oath.

The courts have also ruled on teacher strikes, the right to organize, and collective bargaining. In a Wisconsin case,[46] the Supreme Court ruled that a school board could legally fire teachers who were on strike and refused to return to work. In this case teachers were violating state laws which forbade teacher strikes. The board held a hearing for striking teachers and voted to terminate their employment. Teachers charged that the action violated their Fourteenth Amendment due process rights since the board could not conduct an impartial hearing. The Court disagreed with the teachers, since it could find no basis in fact that the board acted in a manner which showed personal, financial, or antiunion bias. Perhaps most significantly, the Court was influenced by the fact that the teachers were engaged in an illegal action and the law which prohibited strikes was well within the realm of state authority.

The record of the courts with regard to organized efforts of teachers to improve their position has not been totally unfriendly. The Seventh Circuit Court ruled in *McLaughlin v. Tilendis*[47] that union organizing activity was a constitutionally protected right. In Oklahoma, when a local of the AFT, which was the elected bargaining agent for the teachers in Oklahoma City, went on strike in 1979, a state court took away its bargaining rights until the end of the year. This was done because the teachers were in violation of state laws prohibiting strikes by public employees. Oklahoma City District Judge Carmon Harris reasoned that an organization engaged in an illegal strike could not legally serve as the representative of Oklahoma teachers. On appeal, the Supreme Court of Oklahoma, in reversing the decision of the district court, ruled that nonrecognition of the union could apply only so long as the strike continued.

Although the preceding discussion of teachers' rights provides only a fleeting view of the problem, it does illustrate the scope of teachers' interests in their constitutional rights. It should also illustrate that the process for resolution of conflict over teachers' rights within the local school setting leaves much to be desired. Even with increasingly strong and powerful organizations, it appears that teachers have a long way to go before they can look to their organizations for support on issues involving their freedom within the classroom and their freedom as citizens outside the classroom. Taking these issues to court is always a last resort; it is prima facie evidence that the issues could not be resolved in any other way. Moreover, teachers can find little solace in the fact that the courts can be relied upon to hear the most serious of their conflicts with school administrators and school boards. The record of the courts on teachers' rights has, at best, been a mixed one. Even in the courts, teachers have experienced some of the "special but shadowed" existence Lortie wrote about. The courts have considered teachers as a special class of citizens with an exalted role in the society. They are not ordinary citizens in terms of rights relating to the First and Fourteenth Amendments. They are special in the sense that they work in the sensitive area of value transmission to the younger generation. The courts have considered this an awesome power and have tended to deal with teachers differently than they would with nonteachers. On balance, however, teachers can take some comfort in the fact that the courts have defined some very basic issues. Even though they are "special," teachers are citizens under the Constitution, and blatant attempts to restrict their rights have been successfully challenged. Finally, those who might be inclined to violate teachers' basic rights understand that teachers are not reluctant to challenge this action in the courts.

CONCLUSION: THE SOCIALIZATION OF TEACHERS

It is difficult to discuss the socialization of teachers in any universal sense. Difficulties arise if one defines the socialization of teachers as the induction of the teacher into the role of teaching, because teachers play many roles. In a sense this entire chapter has been about the socialization of teachers. Their many roles are defined by the community, their own efforts to achieve professional status, their struggle for legal rights, and their relationships with students, peers, and administrators.

Thus, certain roles are often assumed for teachers regardless of whether one is attempting to describe the student teaching experience or the teaching experience of the teacher with many years of tenure. The manner in which these roles are described depends to a large extent on those who are making the description. The functionalists, for example, look at the structure of the school system and the various elements in it and make assumptions about the teacher's roles in the system. In the functionalist view of the socialization process, the system makes certain demands and the teacher conforms to those demands. It is as if the beginning teacher is an empty vessel to be filled with the values and practices of the system he or she enters.[48] Forces outside the teacher become important socializing agents. These forces include: persons who have evaluative or supervisory power over the teacher; the pupils in the classroom and their expectations of what teachers should be; the hierarchical structure of the system itself; and the teacher subculture within the school. Thus, the teacher is expected to fit into the bureaucratic mold; to be able to get along with students and peers; to do the things the administration believes to be important; and to follow the rules and regulations established by outside agencies.

The functionalists merely accept this structure without praise or criticism. Not everyone agrees. The critics of functionalism, even though they might accept the functionalist description of the school as a social system, find fault with the system. The more extreme critics of functionalist models argue that individuals who are interested in teaching tend to be supportive of the school as a reproductive agent in the society. What the schools reproduce is the dominant culture. In the United States, that is the culture of bureaucratic capitalism. The school setting is influenced by dominant capitalist values and the teacher then becomes socialized to the role of a functionary of that system.[49] In citing the work of Bowles and Gintis,[50] Bourdieu and Passeron,[51] and Jencks,[52] Henry Giroux charges that teacher education programs in the United States "exist within a constellation of economic, social, and political institutions that make them a fundamental part of the power structure" and they operate in a way which demonstrates their "functional allegiance to the conditions of capitalism."[53]

Thus, when teachers are faced with conflicting roles, the overwhelming pressure is to play the role which is least likely to get them into difficulty with established authority. Translated into classroom practice, this means that they are socialized to neglect the poor and attend to the needs of the more affluent students. It means that they must do in their classrooms those things which please those who have power—including students, the school hierarchy, and affluent and articulate parents. This can be a very convincing argument, since one can find many practical illustrations of this kind of behavior among teachers. This system-serving attitude is expressed by teachers who claim that they "can't waste their time with kids who are not motivated or who will not learn." It is expressed in the out-of-class activities by teachers who are expected to work with student government, student clubs, and other student groups which are generally supportive of the system. Little time may be spent with students who are negative toward the system or alienated from it. In a word, it is the "good" students, defined as those who support the system, who are the ones who get most of the attention of the teacher.

Either the functionalist position or that of its critics can be overworked. There may be some truth in both positions, but socialization as a process may not be so simple. The socialization of teachers may be very much more specific and individualized than the functionalists or the antifunctionalists are willing to admit. In practice, the personality of the teacher and the setting in which he or she works may be so individually specific that any general descriptions of the socialization process are naive.

In practice, every teacher brings his or her own personality and view of what a teacher should be into the classroom setting. Personality develops from experiences and belief systems as well as from reactions to the specific settings in which one finds oneself, as well as from many other factors. In a society which is so large and diverse, it is unlikely that every teacher can be easily classified as having internalized the major values which support the power structure. Thus, the socialization process for teachers must work imperfectly at best. Moreover, this process cannot be readily defined. After all, the educational system did produce the functionalists as well as their critics. In their general and professional education, prospective teachers are not universally channelled into the classrooms of system-supporting professors. A few mavericks must get through the system.

Even if this were not the case, the demands of the setting vary greatly. The rules and regulations of all systems are not the same. Schools vary greatly, from fairly open systems which are strongly student oriented to closed systems which appear to cater more to the convenience of teachers and administrators. Administrators and supervisors are not all the same. Groups of students differ. Although it may be true that students have certain expectations of their teachers, these can vary widely. In some schools, teachers may be expected to be "good old boys and good old girls" who participate freely in student activities, while in others a high degree of aloofness is expected. In some schools, the teachers may appear to run the school; in others, the principal; or in others, a few students and their parents. There are many other variations on this theme. Expectations of the faculty vary, community expectations differ, and the very basic, essential nature of the school differs from place to place.

Perhaps teachers become socialized by learning to get along in whatever setting they find themselves. Those who are successfully socialized may behave in ways which cause them the least difficulty. What this behavior is, is anybody's guess. What is required in one setting may be inappropriate in another. Teachers may learn to conform to whatever setting they find, but within this general setting, they usually find much room for diversity in dealing with children, parents, administrators, and other teachers.

NOTES

1. See Robert J. Havighurst and Daniel Levine, *Society and Education* (Boston: Allyn & Bacon, 1978), p. 533.
2. Dan C. Lortie, *Schoolteacher: A Sociological Study* (Chicago: The University of Chicago Press, 1975), p. 10.
3. Willard Waller, *The Sociology of Teaching* (New York: John Wiley & Sons, 1932), p. 49.
4. Lortie, *Schoolteacher: A Sociological Study*, p. 12.
5. Ibid.
6. Allen Ornstein, *Education and Social Inquiry* (Itasca, Ill.: F. E. Peacock Publishers, 1978), p. 219.
7. Ibid.
8. Myron Brenton, *What's Happened to Teacher?* (New York: Coward-McCann, 1970), p. 31.
9. Ibid., p. 117.
10. National Education Association, Research Division, *Status of the American Public School Teacher, 1975–1976* (Washington, D.C.: National Education Association, 1977).
11. Ibid., p. 50.
12. U.S. Department of Health, Education, and Welfare, National Center for Education Statistics, *Digest of Educational Statistics* (Washington, D.C.: U.S. Government Printing Office, 1980).
13. National Education Association, *Status of the American Public School Teacher, 1975–1976*, p. 53.
14. Ibid., p. 55.
15. Adapted from data from the U.S. Department of Health, Education, and Welfare, National Center for Education Statistics, *Projections of Education Statistics to 1988–89* (Washington, D.C.: U.S. Government Printing Office, 1980), p. 76.
16. Ibid., p. 73.
17. Waller, *The Sociology of Teaching*, p. 410.
18. Michael J. Dunkin and Bruce J. Biddle, *The Study of Teaching* (New York: Holt, Rinehart & Winston, 1974), ch. 2.
19. Ibid., p. 29.
20. Ibid., p. 38.
21. Waller, *The Sociology of Teaching*, p. 195.
22. Ibid., p. 296.
23. Dunkin and Biddle, *The Study of Teaching*, p. 364.
24. Ibid., p. 366.
25. Ibid., p. 367.
26. David G. Ryans, "Teacher Behavior Can Be Evaluated," in *Teaching Effectiveness: Its Meaning, Assessment, and Improvement*, ed. Madan Mohan and Ronald E. Hull (Englewood Cliffs, N.J.: Educational Technology Publications, 1975), p. 59.
27. Berak Rosenshine and N. Furst, "Current and Future Research on Teacher Perfor-

mance Criteria," in *Research on Teacher Education*, ed. B. O. Smith (Englewood Cliffs, N.J.: Prentice-Hall, 1971), ch. 2.

28. Carolyn Denham and Ann Lieverman, *Time to Learn* (Washington, D.C.: National Institute of Education, 1980).

29. Judith Dobson and Russell Dobson, "School Climate and the Person of the Teacher," *The Networker* (California Teacher Corps Network) 7 (Fall/Spring 1979–80): 24.

30. Lortie, *Schoolteacher: A Sociological Study*, pp. 13–17.

31. Phillip Jackson, *Life in Classrooms* (New York: Holt, Rinehart & Winston, 1968).

32. Robert Scrivens, "The Big Click," *Today's Education* 68 (November/December 1979): 5.

33. Ronald G. Corwin, *Militant Professionalism: A Study of Organized Conflict in High Schools* (New York: Appleton-Century-Crofts, 1970), p. 43.

34. National Education Association, "The Yardstick of a Profession," *Institutes on Professional and Public Relations* (Washington, D.C.: National Education Association, Division of Field Services, 1948), p. 8.

35. Ornstein, *Education and Social Inquiry*, p. 290.

36. Corwin, *Militant Professionalism*, p. 44.

37. For an opposing view, see Donald Myers, *Teacher Power: Professionalization and Collective Bargaining* (Lexington, Mass.: D.C. Heath and Co., 1973), ch. 10.

38. For a description of teacher centers, see Harry Bell and John Peightel, *Teacher Centers and Inservice Education* (Phi Delta Kappa Educational Foundation, 1976). For a serious criticism of teacher centers, see Susan Staub, "Teacher Centers: Forced Unionism Vehicle," *RECAPS* 6 (Fall 1981): 8.

39. *Meyer v. Nebraska*, 262 US 390 (1923).

40. *Adler v. Board of Education*, 342 US 485 (1952).

41. *Wieman v. Updegraff*, 344 US 183 (1952).

42. *Shelton v. Tucker*, 364 US 479 (1960).

43. *Bagett v. Bullitt*, 377 US 360 (1964).

44. *Elfbrandt v. Russell*, 384 US 11 (1966).

45. *Cole v. Richardson*, 405 US 676 (1972).

46. *Hortonville Joint School District No. 1 v. Hortonville Education Association*, 426 US 482 (1976).

47. *McLaughlin v. Tilendis*, 398 F2nd 287 (7th Cir 1968).

48. Kenneth M. Zeichner, "The Dialectics of Teacher Socialization," paper presented at the annual meeting of the Association of Teacher Educators, Orlando, Fla., February 1979, p. 3.

49. Henry A. Giroux, "Teacher Education and the Ideology of Social Control," *Journal of Education* 162 (Winter 1980): 5–27.

50. Samuel Bowles and Herbert Gintis, *Schooling in Capitalist America: Educational Reform and the Contradictions of Economic Life* (New York: Basic Books, 1976).

51. P. Bourdieu and J. Passeron, *Reproduction in Education, Society and Culture* (Beverly Hills, Calif.: Sage, 1977).

52. Christopher Jencks, *Who Gets Ahead?* (New York: Basic Books, 1979).

53. Giroux, "Teacher Education and the Ideology of Social Control," p. 5.

Part IV
Expanding Educational Opportunity

The chapters which follow examine the long struggle of minorities for equal educational opportunity. They also deal with the struggle on the part of women and the handicapped for the improvement of their treatment by the schools.

The struggle on the part of blacks for equal rights under the Constitution has been an epic one, waged in the schoolrooms of America and in the courts. In spite of some serious efforts to give up on the struggle and to seek solutions in separatism, the general historical thrust of the movement has been the efforts on the part of blacks to join the educational mainstream of American society. Much more recent is the new militancy of the Hispanic population. With many of the same economic, social, and educational problems of blacks, the Hispanic community has special linguistic and cultural problems which are considered in the material which follows. Although native Americans have experienced many of the same problems as blacks and Mexican Americans, their struggle has progressed somewhat differently because of their long association with the national government.

Generally, women who have been members of minority groups have had the same kind of school problems as their male counterparts—although perhaps even more severe since they seem to have been laboring under a dual handicap. Even favored majority white women, however, have experienced serious problems. While they have always been able to achieve in school, they have experienced difficulty in turning school achievement into economic success.

In recent years, we have discovered the handicapped in our schools. Their special problems have been addressed in national legislation which promises some sweeping and significant changes in the schooling of children with mental and physical problems.

Finally, this part deals with a topic which cuts across all of these problems —that is, the problem in the United States of unequal school finance. It should be clear from the material which follows that, although some progress has been made in providing equal educational opportunity for Americans, we still have a long way to go.

10

The Drive for Equality: Minorities and the Schools

THE BLACK STRUGGLE

The black struggle for decent schools has been a long and difficult one. Progress has been made, but it has been painfully slow. Although there is much current evidence that racism continues to exist, one doesn't have to go far back in history to appreciate recent progress. This is what it was like in Clarendon County, South Carolina in the late forties:

> In Clarendon County, there were then 61 Negro schools, more than half of them ramshackle or plain falling-down shanties that accommodated one or two teachers and their charges, and 12 schools for whites. The total value of the 61 black schools attended by 6,531 pupils was officially listed as $194,575. The value of the white schools, attended by 2,375 youngsters, was put at $673,850.
>
> In charge of this dual school system was a slender, gray-haired clergyman named L. B. McCord, who three years after winning election as county superintendent of schools in 1940 was also named pastor of the Manning Presbyterian Church, the pillar of Christendom in those parts. Given the place of honor accorded to education and religion in small American communities, his dual occupation made L. B. McCord a powerful citizen indeed in Clarendon County. "He is a capable man," wrote the *Manning Times*, the county weekly, "with a keen perception of fairness to all, and the best interests of the school children of Clarendon are close to his heart."
>
> This, though, was not the unanimous estimate of L. B. McCord. Views of him tended to diverge along racial lines. "He was a white-supremacist, is all," says Billie S. Fleming, . . . perhaps the most successful black businessman in the county. "As a minister, he was fond of saying that God had intended things to be this way, and if you doubted it, he'd point to the sky and say, 'Now if you just look up at the birds, you'll see that the buzzards don't mingle with the crows, and down here dogs don't mingle with cats.' " Other blacks say he cared nothing for the caliber of the teachers in the Negro schools or the condition of the schoolhouses. "He was always shortchanging us," a former black teacher recalls. "When you come in and asked for money for say, window sashes, he'd say something like, 'Look, you fellas do it yourselves—we can't hardly pay the teachers. Go get some boards.' "
>
> And they did. That was how it was with Superintendent McCord. If you crossed

him, you were in trouble. If you were black and you crossed him, you were in worse trouble and not long for a place on the Clarendon County public-school payroll. . . .

There were 30 school buses for the white children. There was none for the black children. A muscular, soft-spoken farmer named James Gibson remembers what the chairman of the school board said when they asked for the bus. His name was Elliott, R. W. Elliott, he ran a sawmill, and he was white. Everyone who ran anything in the county was white. What he said was: "We ain't got no money to buy a bus for your nigger children." But there was always money for buses for the white children. "And you'd know it," farmer Gibson recalls, "Because they was always muddyin' you up."[1]

Even though Clarendon County is a different place today largely because of the efforts of blacks themselves, the heritage of racism dies hard. A brief history of the struggle of blacks for better schools for their children can place contemporary educational problems faced by the black community in some perspective.

The Struggle for Educational Opportunity

Given the political and economic suppression of blacks during the nineteenth century and into the first decades of the twentieth century, it is remarkable that there is any record of educational attainment to report. As a group, blacks were almost universally denied access even to basic literacy during the period of slavery. As Carter Woodson pointed out, the slaveowners feared education because they believed that "slaves could not be enlightened without developing in them a longing for liberty."[2] About the only sort of schooling allowed for plantation blacks was oral religious instruction provided by the plantation owner.

This is not to say that the system designed to keep slaves in ignorance was universally applied. Individual blacks were trained by their masters in some of the skilled trades needed on the plantation, such as carpentry, bricklaying, blacksmithing, tailoring, and weaving. In addition, there were a few mission schools which engaged in teaching household blacks and the growing number of free blacks who lived in the South. Henry Bullock referred to these limited educational opportunities as "a hidden passage"[3] which laid the groundwork for the development of a potential black middle class. In the North, before the Civil War, blacks could be found in segregated private schools which existed in some places as a result of the generosity of philanthropists.

After the Civil War, the Freedman's Bureau provided some schooling for the newly freed blacks. These schools ministered to all ages and the teachers were usually Northerners who had been trained in northern colleges. The close of the radical Reconstruction period in 1876 brought an end to these activities.

While the efforts of the Freedman's Bureau were in the direction of providing a basic classical liberal arts education to southern blacks, a different system, which was to become a more or less permanent feature of black schooling in the South, began to grow in this period. The Hampton Institute, which provided industrial education for blacks, was founded in 1868. Unlike the efforts of the Freedman's Bureau, General Armstrong's Hampton Institute emphasized narrow vocational training along with a heavy dose of moral education. Booker T.

Washington opened Tuskegee Institute in 1881 based on the same principles. This sort of schooling found support in the South, for not only was it segregated schooling, but it provided for blacks a special kind of schooling which helped them adjust to an inferior status in the system.

By 1890 the school situation for blacks in much of the country, and especially in the South, was one of very limited opportunity. Indeed, even Booker T. Washington, who was enthusiastic in his praise of black education in the South, was able to report a literacy rate among American blacks of only 44.5 percent by 1904.[4] Thus, a generation after the Civil War, a majority of the black population was not in school. Those who were attending were in all-black schools.

In view of the political, social, and economic isolation of blacks, it is surprising that educational leaders of the stature of Booker T. Washington appeared to support any schooling for blacks, even schooling which might have been segregated and inferior to that provided for whites. It is difficult for one viewing this period nearly 100 years later to fully appreciate the pervasive nature of the racist system which existed. Perhaps nothing illustrates this mind-set better than the case of *Plessy v. Ferguson* in 1896. In this case a Louisiana statute which provided for separate facilities on railroads for blacks and whites was challenged. In the view of the majority of the Court, this practice was not a violation of the equal protection of the laws clause of the Fourteenth Amendment so long as the facilities provided were substantially equal. This ruling gave the stamp of legality to a wide range of local and state ordinances which provided for separation of blacks and whites. The *Plessy* case legitimatized the practice of separate schools for blacks and whites which was already commonplace by design in the South and by discriminatory housing practices in the urban areas of the North. This policy continued substantially unchanged until 1954. *Plessy* is cited in part below.

Plessy v. Ferguson
163 US 537 (1896)

Mr. Justice Brown, after stating the case, delivered the opinion of the court. This case turns upon the constitutionality of an act of the general assembly of the state of Louisiana, passed in 1890, providing for separate railway carriages for the white and colored races....

The information filed in the criminal district court charged in substance that Plessy, being a passenger between two stations within the state of Louisiana, was assigned by officers of the company to the coach used for the race to which he belonged, but he insisted upon going into a coach used by the race to which he did not belong. Neither in the information nor plea was his particular race or color averred.

The petition for the writ of prohibition averred that petitioner was seven-eighths Caucasian and one-eighth African blood; that the mixture of colored blood was not discernible in him, and that he was entitled to every right, privilege and immunity secured to citizens of the United States of the white race; and that, upon such theory, he took possession of a vacant seat in a coach where passengers of the white race were accommodated, and was ordered by the conductor to vacate said coach and take a seat in another assigned to persons of the colored race, and having refused to comply with such demand he was forcibly ejected with the aid of a police officer, and imprisoned in the parish jail to answer a charge of having violated the above act.

The constitutionality of this act is attacked upon the ground that it conflicts both with the Thirteenth Amendment of the Constitution, abolishing slavery, and the Fourteenth Amendment, which prohibits certain restrictive legislation on the part of the states.

1. That it does not conflict with the Thirteenth Amendment, which abolished slavery and involuntary servitude, except as a punishment for crime is too clear for argument. Slavery implies involuntary servitude—a state of bondage; the ownership of mankind as a chattel, or at least the control of the labor and services of one man for the benefit of another, and the absence of a legal right to the disposal of his own person, property and services. . . .

A statute which implies merely a legal distinction between the white and colored races—a distinction which is founded in the color of the two races, and which must always exist so long as white men are distinguished from the other race by color—has no tendency to destroy the legal equality of the two races, or reestablish a state of involuntary servitude. Indeed, we do not understand that the Thirteenth Amendment is strenuously relied upon by the plaintiff in error in this connection.

2. By the Fourteenth Amendment, all persons born or naturalized in the United States, and subject to the jurisdiction thereof, are made citizens of the United States and of the state wherein they reside; and the states are forbidden from making or enforcing any law which shall abridge the privileges or immunities of citizens of the United States, or shall deprive any person of life, liberty or property without due process of law, or deny to any person within their jurisdiction the equal protection of the laws. . . .

The object of the amendment was undoubtedly to enforce the absolute equality of the two races before the law, but in the nature of things it could not have been intended to abolish distinctions based upon color, or to enforce social, as distinguished from political equality, or a commingling of the two races upon terms unsatisfactory to either. Laws permitting, and even requiring, their separation in places where they are liable to be brought into contact do not necessarily imply the inferiority of either race to the other, and have been generally, if not universally recognized as within the competency of the state legislatures in the exercise of their police power. The most common instance of this is connected with the establishment of separate schools for white and colored children, which has been held to be a valid exercise of the legislative power even by courts of states where the political rights of the colored race have been longest and most earnestly enforced.

One of the earliest of these cases is that of *Robert v. City of Boston*, in which the Supreme Judicial Court of Massachusetts held that the general school committee of Boston had power to make provision for the instruction of colored children in separate schools established exclusively for them, and to prohibit their attendance upon the other schools. . . . It was held that the powers of the committee extended to the establishment of separate schools for children of different ages, sexes and colors, and that they might also establish special schools for poor and neglected children, who have become too old to attend the primary school, and yet have not acquired the rudiments of learning, to enable them to enter the ordinary schools. Similar laws have been enacted by Congress under its general power of legislation over the District of Columbia, . . . as well as by the legislatures of many of the states, and have been generally, if not uniformly, sustained by the courts. . . .

So far, then, as conflict with the Fourteenth Amendment is concerned, the case reduces itself to the question whether the statute of Louisiana is a reasonable regulation, and with respect to this there must necessarily be a large discretion on the part of the legislature. In determining the question of reasonableness it is at liberty to act with reference to the established usages, customs and traditions of the people, and with a view to the promotion of their comfort, and the preservation of the public peace and good order. Gauged by this standard, we cannot say that a law which authorizes or even requires the separation of the two races in public conveyances is unreasonable, or more obnoxious to the Fourteenth Amendment than the acts of Congress requiring separate schools for colored children in the District of Columbia, the constitutionality of which does not seem to have been questioned, or the corresponding acts of state legislatures.

We consider the underlying fallacy of the plaintiff's argument to consist in the assumption that the enforced separation of the two races stamps the colored race with a badge of inferiority. If this be so, it is not by reason of anything found in the act, but solely because the colored race chooses to put that construction upon it. The argument necessarily assumes that if, as has been more than once the case, and is not unlikely to be so again, the colored race should become the dominant power in the state legislature, and should enact a law in precisely similar terms, it would thereby relegate the white race to an inferior position. We imagine that the white race, at least, would not acquiesce in this assumption. The argument also assumes that social prejudices may be overcome by legislation, and that equal rights cannot be secured to the negro except by an enforced commingling of the two races. We cannot accept this proposition. If the two races are to meet upon terms of social equality, it must be the result of natural affinities, a mutual appreciation of each other's merits and a voluntary consent of individuals. . . .

The judgment of the court below is therefore, *affirmed*.

Although Justice Harlan did not agree for constitutional reasons with the majority of the Court, his dissent provided little comfort for blacks. It is, perhaps, an even more detailed statement of white superiority than the majority opinion.

Mr. Justice Harlan dissenting:

. . . It was said in argument that the state of Louisiana does not discriminate against either race but prescribes a rule applicable alike to white and colored citizens. But this argument does not meet the difficulty. Everyone knows that the statute in question had its origin in the purpose, not so much to exclude white persons from railroad cars occupied by blacks, as to exclude colored people from coaches occupied by or assigned to white persons. . . . The fundamental objection, therefore, to the statute is that it interferes with the personal freedom of citizens. . . . If a white man and a black man choose to occupy the same public conveyance on a public highway, it is their right to do so, and no government, proceeding alone on grounds of race, can prevent it without infringing the personal liberty of each. . . .

The white race deems itself to be the dominant race in this country. And so it is, in prestige, in achievements, in education, in wealth and in power. So, I doubt not, it will continue to be for all time, if it remains true to its great heritage and holds fast to the principles of constitutional liberty. But in view of the Constitution, in the eye of the law, there is in this country no superior, dominant, ruling class of citizens. There is no caste here. Our Constitution is color-blind, and neither knows nor tolerates classes among citizens. In respect of civil rights, all citizens are equal before the law. The humblest is the peer of the most powerful. The law regards man as man, and takes no account of his surroundings or of his color when his civil rights as guaranteed by the supreme law of the land are involved. It is, therefore, to be regretted that this tribunal, the final expositor of the fundamental law of the land, has reached the conclusion that it is competent for a state to regulate the enjoyment by citizens of their civil rights solely upon the basis of race. . . .

The destinies of the two races, in this country, are indissolubly linked together, and the interests of both require that the common government of all shall not permit the seeds of race hate to be planted under the sanction of law. . . .

This question is not met by the suggestion that social equality cannot exist between the white and black races in this country. That argument, if it can be properly regarded as one, is scarcely worthy of consideration; for social equality no more exists between two races when traveling in a passenger coach or a public highway than when members of the same races sit by each other in a street car or in the jury box, or stand or sit with each other in a political assembly, or when they use in common the streets of a city or town, or when they are in the same room for the purpose of having their names placed on the registry of voters, or when they approach the ballot box in order to exercise the high privilege of voting. . . .

For the reasons stated, I am constrained to withhold my assent from the opinion and judgment of the majority. . . .

The Desegregation Battle: The Courts

Blacks of course challenged the *Plessy* decision. In 1899, in *Cumming v. Richmond County*, a group of blacks from Augusta, Georgia, demanded an end to public support for two white high schools after the only black high school was closed. The Court heard their appeal but ruled against them. In effect, the decision meant that blacks in Richmond County were deprived of obtaining a high school education while whites were not. In 1899, ''substantial equality'' had a very loose meaning. The Court upheld the segregationist view when it ruled against integrated education in the *Berea College* case in Kentucky in 1908. Berea, a privately financed college, was defying legal mandatory segregation in Kentucky by admitting both blacks and whites. In this case the Court upheld a state law providing for segregation. In *Gong Lum v. Rice* in 1927, the Court upheld the Mississippi law on segregation by ruling that a Chinese girl could be required by the state to attend an all-black school.

The first signs of change in the interpretation of the equal protection of the laws clause of the Fourteenth Amendment came in 1937 in *State of Missouri ex. rel. Gaines v. Canada, Sweatt v. Painter*, a Texas case, and the *Sipuel* and *McLaurin* cases in Oklahoma in 1948 and 1949. In *Gaines*, the Court ruled that Gaines was entitled to enter the law school at the University of Missouri since there was no law school for blacks in Missouri. The state wanted to send Gaines out of Missouri to an all-black law school in another state. This had been customary practice at the time. Indeed, this practice continued in other states long after the Gaines case. In the *Sweatt* case, the Court ruled that Texas did not provide separate, equal graduate facilities in Negro education and that they must either do so or permit Mr. Sweatt to enter the university graduate school. In *Sipuel*, the Supreme Court ruled that the law school at the University of Oklahoma was in violation of the Fourteenth Amendment in its refusal to admit Ada Lois Sipuel solely on the basis of her color. The McLaurin case followed when the legislature of Oklahoma attempted to maintain segregation on the campus by providing that blacks be segregated from white students on the campus—in the classrooms, dining hall, and library. McLaurin challenged this segregation and the Supreme Court supported his challenge. In the words of the majority: "The Appellant, having been admitted to a state-supported school, must receive the same treatment at the hands of the state as students of other races." Thus, half-a-century after the *Plessy* case, blacks managed to crack open the segregated school door. What followed in 1954 in *Brown v. Board of Education of Topeka* brought an end to the legality of the separate but equal doctrine in education.

The *Brown* case was considered along with similar cases from South Carolina, Virginia, and Delaware. In each case, blacks were seeking the aid of the courts in obtaining admission to the schools on a nonsegregated basis. In each case, the blacks had been denied admission by laws which established segregated school systems. The blacks claimed that such laws denied them equal protection of the law under the Fourteenth Amendment. In this series of cases, the Court decided to look at the general effect of segregation on public education. *Brown* is cited in part below.

Brown v. Board of Education
347 US 483 (1954)

Mr. Justice Warren delivered the opinion of the Court.

... In each of the cases, minors of the Negro race, through their legal representatives, seek the aid of the courts in obtaining admission to the public schools of their community on a nonsegregated basis. In each instance, they have been denied admission to schools attended by white children under laws requiring or permitting segregation according to race. This segregation was alleged to deprive the plaintiffs of the equal protection of the laws under the Fourteenth Amendment. In each of the cases other than the Delaware case, a three-judge federal district court denied relief to the plaintiffs on the so-called separate but equal doctrine announced by this court in *Plessy v. Ferguson*. ...

The plaintiffs contend that segregated public schools are not "equal" and cannot be made "equal" and that hence they are deprived of the equal protection of the laws. ...

In the first cases in this court construing the Fourteenth Amendment, decided shortly after its adoption, the court interpreted it as proscribing all state-imposed discriminations against the Negro race. The doctrine of separate but equal did not make its appearance in this court until 1896 in the case of *Plessy v. Ferguson*, involving not education but transportation. American courts have since labored with the doctrine for over half a century. In this court, there have been six cases involving the separate but equal doctrine in the field of public education.

In *Cumming v. Board of Educ. of Richmond County* and *Gong Lum v. Rice* ... the validity of the doctrine itself was not challenged. In more recent cases, all on the graduate school level, inequality was found in that specific benefits enjoyed by white students were denied to Negro students of the same educational qualifications. *State of Mo ex rel Gaines v. Canada* ... *Sipuel v. Board of Regents of Univ. of Oklahoma* ... *Sweatt v. Painter* ... *McLaurin v. Oklahoma State Regents* .... In none of these cases was it necessary to reexamine the doctrine to grant relief to the Negro plaintiff. And in *Sweatt v. Painter*, the court expressly reserved decision of the question whether *Plessy v. Ferguson* should be held inapplicable to public education.

In the instant cases, that question is directly presented. Here, unlike *Sweatt v. Painter*, there are findings below that the Negro and white schools involved have been equalized, or are being equalized, with respect to buildings, curricula, qualifications and salaries of teachers, and other "tangible" factors. Our decision, therefore, cannot turn on merely a comparison of these tangible factors in the Negro and white schools involved in each of the cases. We must look instead to the effect of segregation itself on public education.

In approaching this problem, we cannot turn the clock back to 1868 when the amendment was adopted, or even to 1896 when *Plessy v. Ferguson* was written. We must consider public education in the light of its full development and its present place in American life throughout the nation. Only in this way can it be determined if segregation in public schools deprives these plaintiffs of the equal protection of the laws.

Today, education is perhaps the most important function of state and local governments. Compulsory school attendance laws and the great expenditures for education both demonstrate our recognition of the importance of education to our democratic society. It is required in the performance of our most basic public responsibilities, even service in the armed forces. It is the very foundation of good citizenship. Today it is a principal instrument in awakening the child to cultural values, in preparing him for later professional training, and in helping him to adjust normally to his environment. In these days, it is doubtful that any child may reasonably be expected to succeed in life if he is denied the opportunity of an education. Such an opportunity, where the state has undertaken to provide it, is a right which must be made available to all on equal terms.

We come then to the question presented: Does segregation of children in public schools solely on the basis of race, even though the physical facilities and other "tangible" factors may be equal, deprive the children of the minority group of equal educational opportunities? We believe that it does.

In *Sweatt v. Painter*, in finding that a segregated law school for Negroes could not provide them equal educational opportunities, this court relied in large part on "those qualities which are incapable of objective measurement but which make for greatness in a law school." In *McLaurin v. Oklahoma State Regents*, the court, in requiring that a Negro admitted to a white graduate school be treated like all other students, again resorted to intangible considerations: "his ability to study, to engage in discussions and exchange views with other students, and, in general, to learn his profession." Such considerations apply with added force to children in grade and high schools. To separate them from others of similar age and qualifications solely because of their race generates a feeling of inferiority as to their status in the community that may affect their hearts and minds in a way unlikely ever to be undone. The effect of this separation on their educational opportunities was well stated by a finding in the Kansas case by a court which nevertheless felt compelled to rule against the Negro plaintiffs:

> Segregation of white and colored children in public schools has a detrimental effect upon the colored children. The impact is greater when it has the sanction of the law; for the policy of separating the races is usually interpreted as denoting the inferiority of the Negro group. A sense of inferiority affects the motivation of a child to learn. Segregation with the sanction of law, therefore, has a tendency to retard the educational and mental development of Negro children and to deprive them of some of the benefits they would receive in a racial[ly] integrated school system.

Whatever may have been the extent of psychological knowledge at the time of *Plessy v. Ferguson*, this finding is amply supported by modern authority. Any language in *Plessy v. Ferguson* contrary to this finding is rejected.

We conclude that in the field of public education the doctrine of separate but equal has no place. Separated educational facilities are inherently unequal. Therefore, we hold that the plaintiffs and others situated for whom the actions have been brought are, by reason of the segregation complained of, deprived of the equal protection of the laws guaranteed by the Fourteenth Amendment. This disposition makes unnecessary any discussion whether such segregation also violates the due process clause of the Fourteenth Amendment. . . .

In 1955, *Brown v. Board of Education* came back to the Supreme Court. Popularly known as Brown II, the second *Brown* case supplemented the decision in Brown I. This was necessary since Brown I left a major question unanswered. Since the first *Brown* case was such a sweeping indictment of segregated schools and there were thousands of local school districts which were affected, there was some concern about how soon the local school districts would be required to end the practice of segregation. Although the Court expressed an understanding of the difficulties involved in eliminating the dual school systems which had developed, it ruled in Brown II that school districts "make a prompt and reasonable start toward full compliance" with Brown I. The Court admitted that "once a start has been made, the courts may find that additional time is necessary to carry out the ruling in an effective manner." However, the Court placed the burden on the school district officials to demonstrate, in cases where integration was delayed, that they needed time to comply with the mandate in Brown I. They had to demonstrate "good faith" in compliance with the principles of Brown I. Finally, the Court ordered district courts which were handling desegregation cases to order school officials to proceed with the admission of students to public schools "on a racially nondiscriminatory basis with all deliberate speed. . . ."

Even Brown II, however, did not result in a speedy elimination of dual school systems. Since it was decided in 1955, there have been hundreds of cases in which the courts have had to deal with school districts which were attempting to avoid implementing the Brown I decision.

Although some of the border states in the South made serious efforts to comply with the *Brown* decision, many southern states resisted. Moreover, much of this resistance was officially sanctioned. As Laughlin McDonald observed: "Within three years of *Brown*, seven Southern states passed 'interposition' or 'nullification' resolutions calling for defiance of the Supreme Court's order."[5] The reaction of southern senators and representatives in Congress gave support to the resistance movement. It came in the form of the "Southern Manifesto," authored by Sam J. Ervin, Jr., U.S. senator from North Carolina, and signed by 17 senators and 77 representatives. Critical of the decision in *Brown*, the manifesto stated in part: "the Supreme Court of the United States, with no legal basis for such action, undertook to exercise their naked judicial power and substituted their personal political and social ideas for the established law of the land."[6] The signers of the manifesto pledged to use all lawful means to prevent the implementation of the *Brown* decision. Judging from the long struggle in several states and hundreds of school districts, there can be little doubt that many took the spirit of the manifesto seriously.

Cases since Brown

Soon after the *Brown* case, it became apparent that there would be difficulties in applying the decision. The most dramatic early illustration of these difficulties came in Little Rock, Arkansas, where the *Brown* decision was being resisted by state and local authorities and it was necessary for President Eisenhower to dispatch federal troops to protect the lives of black children who wanted to attend formerly all-white schools. In Little Rock, the school board appealed to the Supreme Court to give it time to work out the difficulties surrounding integration. The Court refused, placing the blame for the hostility and disorder accompanying efforts to integrate the Little Rock schools squarely on the shoulders of state and local officials who had resisted the implementation of the *Brown* decision. The Court said that constitutional rights "are not to be sacrificed or yielded to the violence and disorder which have followed upon the action of the Governor and the Legislature."[7]

It wasn't until almost 10 years after the *Brown* case, however, that the Court began to concern itself with specific implementation of the decision. In 1963, the Court ruled against a transfer plan which had been devised in Knoxville, Tennessee.[8] In some cities, such as Knoxville, it became necessary in order to accomplish integration to redraw school district boundary lines in a way that would permit some mixture of the races in the schools. In Knoxville, the boundaries were drawn in a manner designed to avoid major mixing. In order to soften the implementation even further, the school board provided a system wherein any student who was relocated in a new school could request transfer back to his old school. In effect, the board was attempting to make integration almost wholly voluntary. The Court invalidated the plan since it appeared to be based completely on racial factors and would have left the schools effectively segregated.

In a case involving Prince Edward County, Virginia, the Court was more specific in its definition of the principle of equality established in *Brown* as well as in explaining the meaning of "all deliberate speed." Most whites in Prince Edward County seemed to be opposed to integration, and so they chose the expedient of merely eliminating the public schools. The white citizens of Prince Edward County immediately proceeded to establish a number of all-white private schools. The legislature of Virginia cooperated by providing financial assistance to private segregated schools. The Court saw this as merely another means of avoiding the implementation of the "equal protection of the laws" of the Fourteenth Amendment and it invalidated the practice.[9] This case, however, gave the Court an opportunity to more clearly define equal protection of the laws as far as the schools were concerned. In the Prince Edward County case, the Court said: "The time for mere 'deliberate speed' has run out and that phrase can no longer justify denying these Prince Edward County school children their constitutional right to an education equal to that afforded by the public schools in other parts of Virginia." Thus, for the first time since the *Brown* case 10 years earlier, there was a more specific indication of what all deliberate speed meant. Consistent with the decision in the *Griffin* case, the Court decided the following year (1965) that a one-grade-a-year plan adopted in Fort Smith, Arkansas was not "deliberate speed."[10]

The Supreme Court dealt with the issue of freedom of choice in 1968 in a Virginia case.[11] Although this case could be interpreted as a mere technical application of the principle of negating segregation laid down in *Brown*, it goes beyond *Brown* in that it is positive and precise in its definition of what constitutes an integrated school system. In this case, the Court held that a "freedom of choice" plan which allowed a pupil to choose his own public school was not in compliance with the principle of integrated education.

In reviewing the facts of the case, the Court observed that under the operation of the freedom of choice plan in New Kent County, Virginia, not a single white child had chosen to attend the Negro school and so few Negro children had elected to attend the white school that 85 percent of the Negro children in the system were in the all-black school. In this case, the Court explained at some length the meaning of the *Brown* case. In the process, it defined more clearly what was intended by the *Brown* decision. The Court explained that the immediate effect of *Brown* was to obtain "for those Negro children courageous enough to break with tradition a place in the 'white' schools." The Court pointed out, however, that this was intended as only a first step. The ultimate end was to be a "transition to a unitary, nonracial system of public education." The *Brown* case provided for all deliberate speed because of the "complexities arising from the transition to a system of public education freed of racial discrimination." There was the tacit admission in *Brown* that various school districts would find a variety of ways to solve their own problems in their own communities. However, in the *Green* case, the Court assumed the obligation to determine whether school boards such as the one in New Kent County had accepted "the affirmative duty to take whatever steps might be necessary to convert to a unitary system in which racial discrimination would be eliminated root and branch."[12] This case was an interpretation not so much of the Fourteenth Amendment as of the meaning set forth in general principle in the *Brown* case. That meaning, as it was defined in *Green*, was a clear and affirmative movement toward the elimination of a dual school system. Mr. Justice Brennan, speaking for a unanimous Court in the *Green* case, cited the wording of the *Griffin* case: "The time for mere 'deliberate speed' has run out"; and he added: "The burden on the school board today is to come forward with a plan that promises realistically to work, and promises realistically to work *now*."[13] Significantly, the Court was not opposed to freedom of choice plans; these were not in themselves unconstitutional. What made them constitutional or unconstitutional was whether or not they resulted in a unitary nonracial system. If they did not, they were invalid.

Finally, the positive nature of the definition of equality in the *Green* case is perhaps no better illustrated than in one of the footnotes in the case, in which the Court suggested that New Kent County might achieve a unitary system by dividing the county into two school districts, sending half the children to one school and the other half to the other. This was an appropriate solution in the view of the majority of the Court, since the white and black populations were not residentially segregated in the country but rather were evenly distributed geographically.[14] The details of the Court's suggested plan for the establishment of a unitary system are not nearly so important as the fact they offered them. There was nothing in previous cases or in the law which required such a gesture. Indeed, most of the previous decisions on equality in education seemed to put great faith in local authorities to solve their own problems.

A year after the *Green* case, blacks finally got the definition of all deliberate speed for which they had waited since 1954. In a Mississippi case, the Supreme Court refused to clarify further the meaning of all deliberate speed and merely stated that "all deliberate speed for desegregation is no longer constitutionally permissible. . . . The obligation of every school district is to terminate dual systems at once."[15] In the words of Justice Black, "there is no longer any excuse for permitting the 'all deliberate speed' phrase to delay the time when Negro children and white children will sit together and learn together in the same public schools."[16] In even more direct language, Justice Black said: "In my opinion there is no reason why such wholesale deprivation of constitutional rights should be tolerated another minute. I fear that this long denial of constitutional rights is due in large part to the phrase 'with all deliberate speed.' I would do away with that phrase completely."[17]

In April 1971, the Court delivered a unanimous opinion on several cases involving the issue of segregated schools.[18] The major issue involved the busing of students in order to achieve racial balance. The cases affected students in several southern communities. In general, the Court ruled that the school districts involved must do everything possible to achieve racial balance. It supported busing as a means for desegregation and gave its stamp of approval to desegregation plans which gerrymandered or paired school districts to achieve a racial mix. It did this in spite of the fact that a great deal of political opposition had developed toward busing as a means for integration. (The discussion of the *Green* and *Holmes* cases closely parallels the discussion of these cases found in Daniel Selakovich, *Ethnicity and the Schools*, Danville Ill.: Interstate Publishers, Inc., 1978, pp. 50–52.)

Although much of the court action on desegregation during the early years took place in southern school districts, by the early 1970s the courts had discovered the problem of segregated schools in northern cities. In *Kelly v. Guinn*,[19] a federal district court found that elementary schools in Clark County, Nevada were racially segregated. In the city of Las Vegas, the black population was concentrated on the west side where student enrollment in the elementary schools was 97 percent black. When the complaint was filed, there was a total of 1,359 teachers in the system, 102 of whom were black. Eighty-three of these black teachers were assigned to west side schools. The school board built new schools in the predominantly black neighborhood and in the white suburbs while it closed schools in fringe areas where there would be a mixed racial school population. In this case the court found the board guilty of policies which promoted and encouraged segregated schools, and it ordered the board to provide integration of faculty and students within the system.

In Denver, Colorado, in the *Keyes* case,[20] the U.S. Supreme Court found evidence of deliberate segregative practices in the Denver school system. In Denver, the black and Hispanic populations were concentrated in the central core city, and the district had developed a system of neighborhood schools. The result was a number of schools which were predominantly black and Hispanic. The school board argued that the segregation which resulted was not caused by deliberate policies of the school board but was the result of demographic problems over which they had no control. That is, in their desire to provide neighborhood schools, the board could not avoid the concentration of black and Hispanic school populations in certain neighborhoods. However, in *Keyes*, the Court found that the board had engaged in practices which encouraged segregated schools. It had built new schools in the middle of the black community and had drawn school district attendance zones in a manner to insure the segregation of Hispanic and black students. The district court had found the school system innocent of deliberate segregative policies, but that decision was based in part on the fact that Hispanos were considered as part of the majority population. Thus, schools with a mixture of Hispanos and blacks were considered integrated. The Supreme Court was not satisfied, and for the first time in a school case it defined Hispanos as a minority class with Constitutional standing. In the words of the Court:

> We conclude . . . that the district court erred in separating Negroes and Hispanos for purposes of defining a "segregated" school. We have held that Hispanos constitute an identifiable class for purposes of the Fourteenth Amendment. (Citing *Hernandez v. Texas* 347 US 475 [1954]).

The Supreme Court found that Hispanos and blacks had many similar school problems in the southwest. They noted that "Negroes and Hispanos in Denver suffer identical discrimination in treatment when compared with the treatment afforded Anglo students." They concluded that: "petitioners are entitled to have schools with a combined predominance of Negroes and Hispanos included in the category of 'segregated' schools." The Denver school officials were ordered to institute policies which would result in integrated schools.

However, there was a significant dissent to the majority opinion in the *Keyes* case. Concurring in part and dissenting in part from the majority opinion, Justice Powell had serious questions about the reasoning of the majority. Although he agreed with the majority that Denver was operating a segregated system in violation of the Constitution, he was concerned about the remedy of busing. In Powell's words:

> In the commendable national concern of alleviating public schools segregation, courts may have overlooked the fact that the rights and interests of children affected by a desegregation program also are entitled to consideration. Any child, white or black, who is compelled to leave his neighborhood and spend significant time each day being transported to a distant school suffers an impairment of his liberty and his privacy. . . .
>
> The argument for student transportation also overlooks the fact that the remedy exceeds that which may be necessary to redress the constitutional evil. Let us use Denver as an example. The Denver School Board, by its action and nonaction, may be legally responsible for some of the segregation that exists. But if one assumes a maximum discharge of constitutional duty by the Denver Board over the past decades, the fundamental problem of residential segregation would persist. It is indeed a novel application of equitable power—not to mention a dubious extension of constitutional doctrine—to require so much greater a degree of forced school integration than would have resulted from purely natural and neutral nonstate causes.
>
> The compulsory transportation of students carries a further infirmity as a constitutional remedy. With most constitutional violations, the major burden of remedial action falls on offending state officials. Public officials who act to infringe personal rights of speech, voting, or religious exercise, for example, are obliged to cease the offending act or practice and, where necessary, institute corrective measures. It is they who bear the brunt of remedial action, though other citizens will to varying degrees feel its effects. School authorities responsible for segregation must, at the very minimum, discontinue segregatory acts. But when the obligation further extends to the transportation of students, the full burden of the affirmative remedial action is borne by children and parents who did not participate in any constitutional violation.
>
> Finally, courts in requiring so far-reaching a remedy as student transportation solely to maximize integration, risk setting in motion unpredictable and unmanageable social consequences. No one can estimate the extent to which dismantling neighborhood education will hasten an exodus to private schools, leaving public school systems the preserve of the disadvantaged of both races. Or guess how much impetus such dismantlement gives the movement from inner city to suburb, and the further geographical separation of the races. Nor do we know to what degree this remedy may cause deterioration of community and parental support of public schools, or divert attention from the paramount goal of quality in education to a perennially divisive debate over who is to be transported where. . . .
>
> It is time to return to a more balanced evaluation of the recognized interests of our society in achieving desegregation with other educational and societal interests a community may legitimately assert. This will help assure that integrated school systems will be established and maintained by rational action, will be better understood and supported by parents and children of both races, and will promote the enduring qualities of an integrated society so essential to its genuine success.

The reasoning of Justice Powell was dramatically different from the unanimous opinion in *Swan v. Charlotte-Mecklenburg Board of Education* just two years earlier. In *Swan*, the Court had this to say about busing:

> Absent a constitutional violation there would be no basis for judicially ordering assignment of students on a racial basis. All things being equal, with no history of discrimination, it might well be desirable to assign pupils to schools nearest their homes. But all things are not equal in a system that has been deliberately constructed and maintained to enforce racial segregation. The remedy for such segregation may be administratively awkward, inconvenient, and even bizarre in some situations and may impose burdens on some; but all awkwardness and inconvenience cannot be avoided in the interim period when remedial adjustments are being made to eliminate the dual school systems.[21]

With increasing political pressure against busing and a more conservative Court, blacks were concerned about losing some of their hard-earned gains. This concern was justified in *Milliken v. Bradley* in 1974.[22] This case reached the Supreme Court when the Detroit school district appealed a district court ruling which ordered a metropolitan busing plan for Detroit and its suburbs. In many ways the problem in Detroit was similar to that of many large northern cities. Detroit did not have a history of efforts on the part of the state or the city to provide for a dual school system. However, there was a long history of white flight from the central city and private as well as public discrimination in housing that encouraged residential segregation. By 1970, the inner city in Detroit was overwhelmingly black, and the suburbs overwhelmingly white. Detroit, with the assistance of the state legislature, developed a decentralized school system based on a neighborhood school concept which provided for some school desegregation.

Unfortunately, significant integration of students could not be achieved in Detroit without a great amount of interdistrict busing. Thus, the real issue in the case was whether interdistrict busing was necessary in order for the Detroit metropolitan schools to be in compliance with the Constitution. Blacks claimed that the Detroit plan was unconstitutional, not only because it failed to provide significant integration of the metropolitan Detroit area schools, but also because the school board had engaged in unconstitutional practices in their drawing of school attendance zones, in their neglect of fringe area school buildings, and in the creation of optional attendance zones. The district court agreed with the blacks and ordered the adoption of a plan which would have required interdistrict busing in order to achieve racially balanced schools. On appeal, the Supreme Court did not question the fact that unconstitutional segregation existed in Detroit. What it questioned was the comprehensive plan for desegregation ordered by the district court.

In the words of the Court:

> Before the boundaries of separate and autonomous school districts may be set aside by consolidating the separate units for remedial purposes or by imposing a cross-district remedy, it must first be shown that there has been a constitutional violation within one district that produces a significant segregative effect in another district. Specifically, it must be shown that racially discriminatory acts of the state or local school districts, or of a single school district, have been a substantial cause of inter-

district segregation. Thus, an inter-district remedy might be in order where the racially discriminatory acts of one or more school districts caused racial segregation in an adjacent district, or where district lines have been deliberately drawn on the basis of race.[23]

The black plaintiffs argued that since the outlying school districts were subdivisions of the state, the state had given its official stamp of approval to the segregation which existed. The Court rejected this argument:

> There were no findings that the differing racial composition between schools in the city and in the outlying suburbs was caused by official activity of any sort. It follows that the decision to include in the desegregation plan pupils from school districts outside Detroit was not predicated upon any constitutional violation involving those school districts. By approving a remedy that would reach beyond the limits of the city of Detroit to correct a constitutional violation found to have occurred solely within that city the Court of Appeals thus went beyond the governing equitable principles established in this Court's decisions.[24]

The case was sent back to the district court for reconsideration. In effect, the district court was ordered to formulate a new plan which would include only the city of Detroit. The Supreme Court thus rejected an interdistrict busing remedy for Detroit.

One cannot conclude, however, that the Detroit case ended interdistrict busing as a solution to racially segregated schools in the North. The Court's record since the Detroit case is mixed. In the case of Louisville, Kentucky, the Supreme Court in 1977 refused to review a court of appeals decision which had the effect of approving large-scale busing in the Louisville metropolitan area. In this case, the district court in 1975 ordered a school desegregation plan which included transportation of students to schools outside their regular districts. The court of appeals, after hearing the case, instructed the district court to implement a plan eliminating "all vestiges of state-imposed segregation," and held that "state-created school district lines shall impose no barrier." However, an interdistrict busing solution was not necessary in this case, since the Kentucky State Board of Education consolidated the county and city schools in Louisville and they were able to develop a desegregation plan which did not necessitate interdistrict busing. In effect, they gerrymandered school attendance boundaries in the new larger district, thus significantly reducing the amount of busing needed to achieve integrated schools.

By 1980 the Supreme Court's position on desegregation suits was by no means clear. In *Dayton Board of Education v. Brinkman*, the Supreme Court reversed a district court systemwide desegregation order because it found that the actions of the school board resulted in only an "incremental" increase in segregation. They ruled, therefore, that the solution should be "incremental" rather than systemwide. This was in direct contradiction to the finding in *Keyes*, wherein the Court held that if discriminatory practices existed in part of a school district, systemwide desegregation could properly be required. The case was remanded to the district court for reconsideration. On rehearing, the district court found the Dayton school system in violation of the *Brown* decision and ordered large-scale busing in order to achieve racially balanced schools. After a second look at the facts, the Supreme Court found the new remedy ordered by the district court to be justified.[25]

In *Evans v. Buchanon*,[26] which involved the Wilmington, Delaware school system, the Supreme Court refused to hear a case in which the lower court had ordered interdistrict busing, thereby leaving a metropolitan remedy in effect.

In its 1980 term, the Supreme Court refused to hear any major desegregation cases. It seemed content to let the decisions of the district and appeals courts stand. This created some confusion, since some district and appellate court decisions followed principles in *Swan* (which mandated interdistrict busing because a long history of segregation existed) and *Keyes* (which found discriminatory intent even though there was no such history), while other district and appellate courts applied the *Milliken* principle, where an interdistrict busing solution was not imposed when neither a long history nor segregative intent could be found.

The busing issue had not been resolved by the Court by its 1982 term. In narrow decisions in the States of Washington and California the Court upheld restrictions on busing in one case and overruled it in another. In *Washington v. Seattle School District* the Court found an antibusing referendum passed by the voters of the State of Washington an "intervention into the affairs of local school boards." The effect of this decision was to let stand local plans for integration which involved busing. In *Crawford v. Board of Education of the City of Los Angeles*, a statewide referendum which limited busing was upheld. The referendum amended the state constitution, forbidding state courts to order mandatory busing remedies unless intentional segregation is proven. The Court thought this was permissible since it did "not inhibit enforcement of any federal law or constitutional requirement."

Even so, the trend continues to be in the direction of enforcement of the principle in the *Brown* case. This principle continues to guide district court judges where most of the decisions are made. That principle, simply stated, is that there must be unitary and integrated school systems in the United States.

A Note on Busing

Perhaps growing public opinion adverse to busing children for integration purposes, coupled with the negative sentiment in Congress toward busing, will continue to influence the courts. Justice Powell in his lengthy dissent in the *Keyes* case no doubt spoke for many white and black Americans when he observed that the burden of desegregation fell upon the children of America, who were innocent victims of segregative practices. As busing became a hot political issue, leaders in Congress were quick to jump on the antibusing bandwagon. In addition, presidents since Nixon have seen the political risks involved in its advocacy. Even some academics have been quick to condemn the practice as being educationally unsound.[27]

Much of the public and political criticism of busing has revolved around arguments in which the critic attempts to demonstrate the great hardships which are visited upon young children where busing is mandated as a solution to the problem of segregated schools. Horror stories are told of how very young elementary students are bused far from their homes into strange neighborhoods on long and dangerous routes. The antibusing scholars have set out to demonstrate that busing for the purpose of desegregation results in a lowering of the quality of education for both black and white children. However, research does not appear to support this position. Summarizing a nine-volume report submitted to the National Institute of Education, Vanderbilt University Professor Willis Hawley suggested that the research which had been collected and reviewed over a seven-year period showed that minority children's achievement improved when desegregation was imposed early, while white student achievement "at least is not harmed." Moreover, he pointed out that desegregation has "cut racial isolation and students' test scores have improved in the most desegregated part of the country, the southeast. . . ."[28]

Neighborhood schools has become the euphemism for racially segregated schools. In most communities, busing solutions would not impose great hardships. A study made by the Lambda Corporation found that elimination of segregation would be possible without exceeding practical limits for student travel time, nor would busing have to be massive in order to achieve maximum desegregation.[29] Eleanor Blumenberg pointed out that "if busing were increased only 3 percent and school attendance areas rearranged to promote integration, even in the largest cities the number of black pupils attending majority-white schools would increase over 70 percent."[30] In fact, total busing mileage has decreased in many southern states as desegregation was implemented, since segregation required extensive busing of both black and white students to separate schools.[31] One might think, from the furor over busing which makes the evening television news, that millions of school children are bused as a result of court orders. Yet, at the peak of the busing controversy in the early seventies, less than 4 percent of all pupils were bused for purposes of desegregation. The increased cost of busing for desegregation can also be misleading. In 1972, a peak year for busing for purposes of desegregation, some 43.5 percent of all school children rode buses to school. During that year only 3.7 percent of all educational expenditures were allocated for transportation and less than 1 percent of the rise in busing costs was due to desegregation.[32]

The Federal Bureaucracy and Desegregation

A discussion of the struggle to provide a unitary, desegregated school system would not be complete without some reference to bureaucratic efforts in the area of desegregation. Ten years after *Brown*, Congress passed a comprehensive civil rights law which not only strengthened the legal position of the courts in cases involving the desegregation of schools but also mobilized the federal bureaucracy in the battle.

Section 200c in Title IV of the Civil Rights Act of 1964 gave the commissioner of education broad powers to assist schools in their desegregation efforts:

The commissioner is authorized, upon the application of any school board, state, municipality, school district, or other governmental unit legally responsible for operating a public school or schools, to render technical assistance to such applicant in the preparation, adoption, and implementation of plans for the desegregation of public schools.

In addition to technical assistance, Title IV provided funds for in-service training of teachers who were involved in dealing with problems incident to desegregation.

Perhaps the most significant provisions in Title IV were the ones which gave citizens an avenue to pursue desegregation actions through the attorney general's office as well as through the courts. Under Title IV, any parent or group of parents could initiate an investigation of a school district by presenting a written complaint to the attorney general stipulating that they were being deprived by a school board of equal protection of the laws. If, in the language of Title IV, the attorney general:

> believes the complaint is meritorious and certifies that the signer or signers of such complaint are unable in his judgement, to initiate and maintain appropriate legal proceedings for relief and that the institution of an action will materially further the orderly achievement of desegregation in public education, the attorney general is authorized, after giving notice of such complaint to the appropriate school board or college authority and after certifying that he is satisfied that such board or authority has had a reasonable time to adjust the conditions alleged in such complaint, to institute for or in the name of the United States a civil action in any appropriate district court of the United States against such parties and for such relief as may be appropriate, and such court shall have and shall exercise jurisdiction of proceedings instituted pursuant to this section, provided that nothing herein shall empower any official or court of the United States to issue any order seeking to achieve a racial balance in any school by requiring the transportation of pupils or students from one school district to another in order to achieve such racial balance, or otherwise enlarge the existing power of the court to insure compliance with constitutional standards. . . .

Title VI put teeth into the enforcement process by giving federal agencies the expressed power to withhold funds from school districts which failed to comply:

> No person in the United States shall, on the ground of race, color, or national origin, be excluded from participation in, be denied the benefits of, or be subjected to discrimination under any program or activity receiving federal financial assistance.

Thus, all federal funds could be withheld from school districts which were not in compliance with court-ordered desegregation plans or with plans which were drawn up by the office of the commissioner of education in conformity with court orders.

Titles IV and VI of the Civil Rights Act of 1964 were implemented by Executive Order No. 11247 issued by President Johnson in 1965. This order directed the attorney general to assist federal departments and agencies to coordinate their programs and activities and to adopt procedures and practices needed to enforce Title VI.

According to Gary Orfield,[33] "the results were phenomenal." During the first year of enforcement, desegregation began in nearly every rural school district in the South. This was followed the next year by faculty desegregation, and by 1968, "the schools of the rural South were on notice that they must finish desegregation by fall 1969." By 1969, the staff which had been developed to investigate and help implement desegregation in the Department of Health, Education, and Welfare (HEW) had moved into several middle-sized cities, and the Justice Department had filed four lawsuits against northern urban school districts. Although the progress was slow in these cases, by the time Johnson left office local school officials had become resigned to the fact that if they wanted to receive any federal funds they were going to have to come up with a satisfactory desegregation plan.

Under the mandate from Title VI, HEW developed guidelines in the late sixties which set standards for desegregation. Although the first guidelines set only minimal standards, as the agency got involved in local investigations field workers pressed for more stringent standards. By 1968, HEW's work in the desegregation of local communities involved serious efforts on the part of the communities, including significant busing of students.

Unfortunately for minorities, congressional and administrative solutions change with the political winds. Enforcement changed with Nixon, again with the election of Carter, and again with the election of President Reagan. In his campaign for the presidency, candidate Nixon assured prospective voters that busing was not necessary, and he gave them every reason to believe that he would be less enthusiastic than his predecessor in enforcing the provisions of Title VI. Nixon was able to keep his promise since, according to the way the program of enforcement had been designed, decisions to actually withhold federal funds from school districts which were not in compliance had to be signed by the secretary of HEW. It soon became clear that, without support form the White House, administrative solutions to the problem of desegregation were not effective. In the words of Orfield:

> By the mid-1970's the Office for Civil Rights had almost totally redefined its basic objective, giving only passing attention to the old goal of eliminating dual school systems. . . .[34]

Even so, the Office of Civil Rights continued to grow. In the mid-seventies, Congress gave the office added responsibility for ending discrimination against women and the handicapped. The Supreme Court upheld its activities in developing regulations against linguistic discrimination. During the same period, however, Congress limited HEW's powers to desegregate schools.

According to Orfield, "the result was ironic":

> An agency that had carried out perhaps the most effective drive against racial discrimination in American history grew in size and resources under a hostile administration but had less impact on the problem it was designed to solve. By the mid-1970's its principal civil rights goal was to make separate institutions more nearly equal. The vision of the 1954 Supreme Court decision had given way to the doctrine of the 1896 Plessy decision. The Carter administration inherited an agency that would have been unrecognizable to its founders.[35]

Those who were interested in continuing the struggle for desegregated schools must have been heartened by President Carter's words in early 1977 when he told the employees of HEW that:

> I'm committed . . . to complete equality of opportunity in our Nation, to the elimination of discrimination in our schools, and to the rigid enforcement of all Federal laws. There will never be any attempt made while I'm President to weaken the basic provisions or the detailed provisions of the great civil rights acts that have been passed in years gone by.[36]

Moreover, Carter seemed determined to reinstitute the rigorous enforcement of Title VI when he wrote:

> the government of all the people should not support programs which discriminate on the grounds of race, color, or national origin. There are no exceptions to this rule; no matter how important a program, no matter how urgent the goals, they do not excuse violating any of our laws—including the laws against discrimination. This Administration will enforce Title VI.[37]

Following this memo, the Department of Justice was directed by the President to coordinate the Title VI enforcement efforts; conferences were held and efforts were made to enforce Title VI provisions within governmental agencies themselves.

The Title IV program was strengthened by increased funding, and new emphasis was placed on sex and language discrimination. A major thrust of the late seventies was to provide greater assistance to local school districts in coping with problems of court-ordered desegregation under Title IV. When the new Department of Education was created in 1980, the civil rights functions of HEW related to educational problems were transferred to that department. By early 1981, however, it had become apparent that the Reagan administration was dedicated to the elimination of the Department of Education.

The Future of Desegregation

Desegregation of the public schools is clearly an unfinished task. We are not much closer to an integrated unified school system in the early eighties than we were when *Brown* was decided in 1954. The laws are clear; Title VI and the Fourteenth Amendment upon which it is based are not difficult to understand. The recent decisions of the Supreme Court, while they tend to be less sweeping and more technical than in the past, continue to consistently support desegregation. What seems to be missing is public support. Although pollsters tell us that an overwhelming majority of the public supports integrated schools, they just as overwhelmingly reject busing as a solution. Given this situation, the progress made in desegregation in the future will depend to a great extent upon the resolve and courage of our political leadership.

Whatever the reason for an apparent retreat on the issue of desegregation by the public, the political leaders, and perhaps the courts, that retreat can only insure that the desegregation issue will haunt American education for many years. What was apparently settled in principle in *Brown v. Topeka*, and implemented in a sweeping manner in *Swan*, is far from settled. Nor can any long-range solution be expected unless the implementation of busing in *Swan* is given wide application. Indeed, because of population movements, even school systems which were once racially balanced are no longer so. As long as white flight continues for whatever reasons, as long as there is economic discrimination in jobs and housing, and as long as social discrimination continues to exist, the school problem is unlikely to be solved on any permanent basis. If the schools, by themselves, are expected to achieve an integrated society, metropolitanwide solutions must be imposed upon them. In effect, if whites are fleeing to avoid integrated schools (which is an assumption open to serious question),[38] then that avenue of escape would have to be closed. Clearly this solution has certain physical limitations, and it is unlikely that any fixed racial mix can ever be permanently achieved. Greater success might be expected from a multifaceted attack on segregation. This would require a massive effort to eliminate ghettos, improve job opportunities, provide subsidies for integrated housing—all of which may be more difficult to implement than school solutions.

A Footnote on the Sociology of Desegregation

The preceding descriptive account of the battle to desegregate the schools omits detailed references to the large body of research which has been undertaken on the various social and academic effects of racially mixed schools. This has been a deliberate oversight. In view of the mandate of the Fourteenth Amendment, court decisions since *Brown*, and the Civil Rights Act of 1964 and its many amendments, the research on the social and educational effects of racially mixed schools seems irrelevant. The moral and legal obligations which require a unitary, racially balanced school system are well established. Arguments over whether busing, for example, increases the academic achievement of blacks, or raises or lowers aspiration levels, or improves or deteriorates race relations, as well as other similar problems which have been extensively researched, are purely academic. Social science research can be used to "prove" that desegregation is "good" or "bad." Quality education can be provided in a segregated or an integrated system. Poor education can be provided in either system. This is irrelevant. What is relevant is that our legal system mandates a desegregated system. Ultimately, research may convince us that the Constitution and the laws need to be changed, but it would have to be much more convincing than it presently is to support changing the basic moral and philosophical assumptions of existing law.

Affirmative Action

Obviously one of the most serious consequences of the long history of discrimination was the fact that large numbers of minority children received an inferior education. In most of the desegregation cases, facts were usually presented which demonstrated virtually beyond question that separate schools were not equal. In a sense, that is what the desegregation battle was all about. Minority groups were concerned about inferior education, and they assumed not only that integrated schools were morally and legally correct but also that their children would have better educational opportunities in integrated schools. As the struggle for integration proceeded, its advocates did not miss the opportunity to go beyond demands for equality of educational opportunity to a concern for equality of result. They were concerned, and properly so, that being black or native American or Hispanic meant that one's achievement in school tended to be lower than that of the majority white population. Hundreds of studies have demonstrated that the children of major minority groups in the society score lower on IQ and achievement tests and are significantly behind their white, mainstream, same-age peers in their achievement of basic skills.

Although a few scholars attributed at least some of this retardation to hereditary factors,[39] overwhelmingly sociologists and psychologists have suggested that the differences are accounted for by environmental factors, such as poverty, poor home conditions, family conditions, and poor schools. All of these conditions can be related to discrimination against minorities. Since efforts to end discrimination were less than successful, some means had to be devised to enable the victims to escape. Affirmative action programs offered one solution.

Put simply, affirmative action has come to mean that it is somehow the responsibility of government to redress past wrongs. That is, the agencies and agents of government have a clear duty to take positive steps to assist minorities to become full participating citizens in the system. Where it can be demonstrated that minorities have suffered in the system as a result of past, officially sanctioned discrimination, they are entitled to special treatment designed to offset its negative effects.

Given the fact that inequities can be identified on the basis of race and/or minority status, it is not surprising that the courts have addressed the issue. The three major cases on affirmative action in the seventies—*DeFunis v. Odegard, University of California Regents v. Bakke,* and *United Steel Workers of America v. Weber* — were all challenges to what had become a well-established affirmative action program in education and employment. In each of these cases, whites felt that they were being deprived of their rights under Title VI of the Civil Rights Act and under the equal protection clause of the Fourteenth Amendment. Title VI bars discrimination in any program receiving federal financial assistance and prohibits the setting of racial quotas, while the Fourteenth Amendment states that no state may "deprive any person of life, liberty, or property, without due process of law; nor deny to any person within its jurisdiction the equal protection of the laws."

DeFunis, who was white, claimed that the affirmative action program of the University of Washington denied him his Fourteenth Amendment rights. DeFunis was denied admission to the law school while less qualified minority students were accepted. In upholding the constitutionality of the University of Washington's affirmative action program, the Supreme Court of the state of Washington said in part:

It can hardly be gainsaid that the minorities have been, and are, grossly underrepresented in the law schools—and consequently in the legal profession—of this state and this nation. We believe the state has an overriding interest in promoting integration in public education. In light of the serious underrepresentation of minority groups in the law schools, and considering that minority groups participate on an equal basis in the tax support of the law school, we find the state interest in eliminating racial imbalance within public legal education to be compelling.

In a statement which goes right to the heart of the philosophy of affirmative action, the Washington State Supreme Court added:

It has been suggested that the minority admissions policy is not necessary, since the same objective could be accomplished by improving the elementary and secondary education of minority students to a point where they could secure equal representation in law schools through direct competition with non-minority applicants on the basis of the same academic criteria. This would be highly desirable, but eighteen years have passed since the decision in *Brown v. Board of Education* . . . and minority groups are still grossly underrepresented in law schools. If the law school is forbidden from taking affirmative action, this underrepresentation may be perpetuated indefinitely. . . .

This case was heard by the Washington State Supreme Court and reached the Supreme Court of the United States on appeal in 1974. The Supreme Court found the case moot, since DeFunis had finally been admitted and was scheduled to graduate from the law school in 1974.

In 1978, however, in a 5–4 decision, the Supreme Court struck down a quota system established by the medical school at the University of California at Davis. In this case, Allan Bakke was denied admission to the medical school although blacks who were less qualified were admitted. Like DeFunis, Bakke claimed that the system violated his Fourteenth Amendment rights. Although the Court's decision found the quota system at Davis in violation of Title VI, it was a very narrow decision. That is, it did not rule against all quota systems. The Court referred to the Davis program as "explicit racial classification." Such classifications, the Court noted, were not always unconstitutional, "but when a state's distribution of benefits or imposition of burdens hinges on . . . the color of a person's skin or ancestry, that individual is entitled to a demonstration that the challenged classification is necessary to promote a substantial state interest." In this case, the Court could find no substantial state interest to justify the particular program at Davis.

It is difficult to draw any hard conclusions from *Bakke* since the Court was seriously split on the issue. No sweeping principles were established, nor were all afirmative action programs negated. There were three principal opinions in *Bakke*: one by Justice Powell; one by Justices Brennan, White, Marshall, and Blackmun; and one by Justice Stevens, joined by Justices Stewart and Rehnquist. The Stevens group decided only that the university program had violated Title VI. The Brennan group found that neither Title VI nor the Fourteenth Amendment prohibited the adoption of an admission program that reserved a specific number of places for qualified members of minority groups. The Stevens group concluded that Davis had illegally excluded Bakke. Thus, although a majority of the Court (five justices) found the Davis program unconstitutional, they did so for different reasons, and even this majority held that there are circumstances under which a properly constructed race-conscious admission program is valid.

The *Weber* case provided a clearer expression of the Court's understanding of the meaning of affirmative action. The *Weber* case did not raise the issue of equal protection under the Fourteenth Amendment. It was limited to a consideration of whether Title VII of the Civil Rights Act barred an employer from establishing an affirmative action program that gave preference to minorities. In 1974, Kaiser Aluminium and the United Steelworkers Union had negotiated an affirmative action plan which reserved 50 percent of all training slots for minorities. Weber, who was white and had more seniority than most blacks accepted for the training, was rejected. He charged that he had been a victim of reverse discrimination. The district court and the court of appeals supported his claim. The Supreme Court reversed, indicating that the intent of Title VII could not have been to prohibit private employers from establishing affirmative action programs for blacks. In the words of the Court:

> It would be ironic indeed if a law triggered by a Nation's concern over centuries of racial injustice and intended to improve the lot of those who had been excluded from the American dream so long . . . constituted the first legislative prohibition of all voluntary, private, race-conscious efforts to abolish traditional patterns of racial segregation and hierarchy. . . .

Since the decision was inconsistent with *Bakke*, the Court found it necessary to distinguish what it saw as differences in intent between Title VI and Title VII of the Civil Rights Act. The majority of the Court reasoned that the purpose of Title VI, as applied in *Bakke*, was to assure that federal funds were not used in an improper manner. On the other hand, Title VII was designed to regulate purely private decision making and was not intended to incorporate the protections of the Fifth and Fourteenth Amendments. Such technical manipulation of Titles VI and VII bothered the dissenting justices. Rehnquist, in his dissent, charged that the majority had contorted the language of Title VII. The majority opinion, he observed, is "reminiscent not of jurists . . . but of escape artists. . . ." The majority opinion, in Rehnquist's view, "eludes clear statutory language, uncontradicted in legislative history, and uniform precedent in concluding that employers are, after all, permitted to consider race in making employment decisions."

The status of affirmative action on the part of government as well as private employers seems to have been affected little by the three cases. Although the Washington State Supreme Court in *DeFunis* provided a clear philosophical and legal statement with consistent reasoning in support, the Supreme Court in both *Bakke* and *Weber* leaves serious questions unanswered. The massive affirmative action program of the federal government, which of course directly affects employment practices in public schools, colleges, universities, state agencies which receive federal funds, and all federal government employment, appears to be untouched by the decisions. It is possible, however, that individual public and private programs which provide for affirmative action will be subject to review on an individual basis. The Court did very little in either *Bakke* or *Weber* to provide a clear working definition of Titles VI or VII, or, for that matter, the Fourteenth Amendment, as they apply to the process of affirmative action.

HISPANICS AND THE SCHOOLS

Who are we? Some call us the forgotten people; others call us chili snappers, tacos, spics, mexs, or greasers. Some just wish that we would go away. The late U.S. Senator Chavez from New Mexico once said: "At the time of war we are called 'the great patriotic Americans,' and during elections politicals call us 'the great Spanish-speaking community of America.' When we ask for jobs, we are called 'those damn Mexicans.'"

Who am I? I'm a human being, I have the same hopes that you have, the same fears, the same drives, the same desires, same concerns, and same abilities. I want the same chance that you have to be an individual. Who am I? In reality, I am who you want me to be.[40]

Those who have been sympathetic with the problems of Mexican-American children in American schools have variously referred to them as "forgotten Americans," "strangers in their own land," and the "invisible minority." George Sanchez, in a paper presented at a symposium at the University of California in 1971, said with some digust: "I said it in print over thirty years ago; I've said it repeatedly through the years: my people are still forgotten people."[41]

The problems of the Hispanic minority in the United States are perhaps even more severe than the problems which are faced by the black minority. In almost every community where they are found in large numbers, they live in conditions of permanent depression. In many places they are part of a more or less permanent underclass—poorly educated, economically depressed, possessing few skills, and, in many cases, suffering from the additional handicap of a serious language problem.

Although it is difficult to determine how many Hispanics live in the United States, if one includes all groups—Mexicans, Puerto Ricans, Cubans, Central and South Americans, and others of Spanish descent, they would number at least 11 or 12 million. Moreover, this figure includes only those who are citizens or who are legal aliens. If illegal aliens were included, another three to five million persons could be added to the total. Unless dramatic and positive action is taken to curb the influx of illegal immigrants, it is possible that by the year 1990 the total number of Hispanic people in the United States could easily surpass 20 million. The Hispanic population is rapidly becoming the largest minority group in the United States.

Like other minority populations, the Hispanic minority tends to be concentrated in urban and rural ghettos. Although most of the Mexican-American population is concentrated in seven states in the West and Southwest, a large number of Hispanics can be found in several large cities of the Northeast and in Florida. In the mid-seventies, nearly half of the population was urban (49 percent), while the remainder was scattered in suburban (32 percent) and rural (19 percent) areas.[42]

Every group of Hispanic students has its own problems with prejudice, unemployment, cultural conflict, and schooling. However, since dealing with each group separately would require volumes, the brief discussion which follows describes the largest group: the Mexican-American population of the United States.

School Problems: A Brief History

When the Anglo-American population from the United States began to move into Mexican territory in California, Texas, and the Southwest before the Mexican War in 1848, they found a Mexican population already there.[43] It was largely an unschooled population. Although the Mexican Constitution of 1824 gave the power to control education to the Mexican Congress, no public schools were established. Even after the annexation of California and the Southwest following the Mexican War of 1848, little progress was made in developing schools for the Mexican population there. In New Mexico, the most populous of the new territories, the first public school was not organized until 1871.[44] By the mid-1870s, New Mexico had a total of 133 schools which enrolled 5,624 pupils. Most of these schools (83 percent) conducted classes wholly in Spanish, while the remainder were conducted in both Spanish and English or only in English. This pattern continued, and by 1908 the territory's 41,000 elementary school students were almost "evenly distributed among English and Spanish-language schools."[45] A similar pattern developed in Texas during the nineteenth century.

In California and the Southwest, the prejudice which existed among the Anglo population toward Mexican Americans created genuine problems of school neglect for the children of Mexican Americans. Even well into the twentieth century, Anglos didn't want Mexican children in their schools, and they found ways to keep them out.[46] In the words of a West Texas county superintendent: "I have already learned that there are Mexicans in two or three districts who really wanted to send their children to school, but the 'whites' scare them out of it. They tell them if they send their children to school, they will be out of a job."[47]

The Anglos who were in charge of public education seemed to feel that Mexican children had to "learn their place" in the economic system, and this didn't include schooling. In the words of another Texas superintendent:

> Most of our Mexicans are of the lower class. They transplant onions, harvest them, etc. The less they know about everything else, the better contented they are. You have doubtless heard that ignorance is bliss; it seems that it is so when one has to transplant onions. . . . If a man has very much sense or education either, he is not going to stick to this kind of work. So you see it is up to the white population to keep the Mexican on his knees in an onion patch. . . . This does not mix well with education.[48]

Nor was this attitude limited to the last generation. In the late sixties, a Neuces County, Texas school board member and farmer declared: "I don't believe in mixing. They are filthy and lousy—not all, but most of them. . . ."[49] Another school official said: "We segregate for the same reason that southerners [sic] segregate the Negro. They are an inferior race, that is all. . . ."[50] In Weinberg's words: "In the Southwest, patterns of discrimination, segregation, and financial deprivation dominated the education of Mexican-American children throughout the second and third quarters of the century as it had the first quarter. The consequences were, predictably, underachievement and alienation."[51]

Weinberg presented much evidence to support his point. He reported that it was not uncommon, until very recently, for the schools in Texas to automatically retain Mexican-American children in the first grade for two or three years. In addition, the schools seemed very willing to accommodate employers of Mexican-American children. School for such children was held on a half-day basis in some localities, and work excuses allowing students to leave school during the fall harvest and spring planting seasons were easy to obtain. Weinberg reported that it was rare in the 1920s and 1930s for Mexican-American children to get as far as the eighth grade: the schools didn't seem to want to encourage them to stay; employers were more concerned with having a large labor pool available than they were with the schooling of Mexican-American children; and Anglo taxpayers didn't want to waste their tax dollars on the schooling of these children. Added to this tragic condition was the fact that many Mexican-American families, caught in the deep rut of poverty, needed the income of working children in order to survive.

This long heritage of prejudice and neglect has its contemporary forms. Mexican-American children continue to experience great difficulty in school. Although a complete accounting of these school problems is not possible here, a few illustrations should make the point. Mexican-American children tend to drop out of school early; they lag in school achievement; they are victimized and segregated by ability grouping; and they are often mistreated by teachers.

The dropout rate for Mexican-American children is incredibly high. In the mid-seventies, Mexican Americans of any age were six times more apt than the population as a whole to have fewer than five years of elementary school.[52] Compared to the total adult American population, fewer than half as many Mexican Americans graduated from high school. At least part of the reason for this was the fact that Mexican Americans appeared to have difficulty succeeding in school. In the southwestern United States, according to a 1974 report of the U.S. Civil Rights Commission, 74.7 percent of Anglos and 48.7 percent of Mexican Americans in the fourth grade read at grade level. By the time they reached the eighth grade, the percentages were 71.8 for Anglos and 35.8 for Mexican Americans. In the twelfth grade, even though many had already been pushed out, a wide gap continued to exist. Only 37.4 percent of the Mexican-American high school seniors were reading at twelfth-grade level, while the percentage for Anglos was 66.3.[53]

From the beginning of public schools in the West and Southwest, except in the very small communities, Mexican-American children have been effectively segregated. Even in small towns there developed barrios, where Mexican-American populations were effectively segregated from Anglos. Neighborhood elementary schools, and high schools in the larger cities, reflected residential patterns. Thus, in many communities in the West and Southwest, there developed schools which were predominantly Mexican American or predominantly Anglo. In rural areas, the school consolidation movement provided for a time a limited amount of integration of Mexican and Anglo students. However, even where there was some integration, the use of ability grouping based on IQ or achievement or reading tests tended to segregate students within the schools. More recently, bilingual educational programs have made these divisions within schools even more pronounced.

Where the Anglo majority, for one reason or another, has been unable to segregate the Mexican-American student, serious problems exist. In classrooms where there is a large Mexican-American minority student population, it is not difficult to find illustrations of neglect and open mistreatment of Mexican-American children. Many such illustrations have been reported in the literature by scholars who have made detailed observations of classroom practices.[54] These researchers report examples of prejudice and mistreatment which occur in the classrooms every day. Teachers tend systematically to ignore the raised hands of Mexican-American children while calling on Anglo students repeatedly. Mexican-American children are interrupted by the teacher during classroom recitation so that the teacher can listen to what an Anglo student has to say on the subject. Numerous illustrations have been provided which demonstrate that teachers tend to be more strict with Mexican-American children than with Anglos. Teachers frequently praise Anglo children and much more frequently criticize Mexican-American children. In sum, the Mexican-American children learn in class that they are less intelligent and somehow less worthy than Anglos. Evidence gathered by the Commission on Civil Rights indicates that this treatment is picked up by Anglo students, who treat the Mexican-American children outside of class in much the same way as teachers treat them in class.

Clearly, the most serious single problem of any minority in the United States is the problem of illegal aliens who can be found in a condition of virtual slavery. These are the hopelessly poor, largely from Mexico, who enter the United States by the thousands each year, and in the words of John Crewdson, "are bought and sold on sophisticated underground labor exchanges. They are trucked around the country in consignments by self-described labor contractors who deliver them to farmers and growers for hundreds of dollars a head."[55] Crewdson, writing in the *New York Times*, described in detail the horrors experienced by many such illegal aliens. Crewdson found work crews who were kept as virtual prisoners by farmers; they were kept on bare subsistence diets and their pay was withheld by farmers to compensate for the fees paid to the contractor for delivering the workers to the fields. They were poorly housed and were required to work for virtually nothing, and they had no medical care and inadequate food. Although the plight of these farm workers may be even worse than conditions on the slave plantations in the nineteenth century, many others who are illegal aliens are not much better off. These are the thousands of workers in cities across the country who are working illegally in factories and assembly plants. These workers include adults of both sexes, as well as minor children, who are reliving the horrors of the early industrial era. They, too, are virtual prisoners. They have spent every cent they have to get into the United States, and they are completely at the mercy of their employers. Since the workers are illegals, the employers do not have to concern themselves with the minimum wage scale, health and insurance benefits, social security, or, for that matter, any laws which are designed to protect the worker from exploitation. The workers can't protest because they have no alternative to their present situation. If they are discovered and returned to Mexico, they know that they may face starvation. Many of these workers have brought their families with them. There is no way of knowing how many children are involved. What is known is that the children face neglect and serious educational deprivation.

In Texas during the late seventies, several school districts simply refused to provide any schooling at all for the children of illegal aliens. The legislature of Texas, apparently concerned with the influx of large numbers of alien children, passed a law in 1975 denying free education to illegal aliens. The law was challenged in 1978, and a district court declared that aliens had Fourteenth Amendment rights and that the law was an attempt to regulate immigration, a power which did not legally reside in the states. The case, along with those of 17 other school districts, was heard by the Supreme Court in 1980. Justice Powell, speaking for the Court, upheld the district court ruling. In its review of the facts of the case, the district court noted that the "plight of an uneducated, illegal alien approaches a state of serfdom," confining the individual to "the lowest socioeconomic level of modern society." Although Texas argued that its law would have the effect of reducing illegal entry into this country, Powell rejected that argument. Justice Powell pointed out that Texas had "declined to . . . prohibit employers from employing illegal aliens,"[56] which would have been a more reasonable method of limiting immigration. He seemed to be saying that the Texas legislature didn't seem concerned about cheap illegal labor but was reluctant to assume responsibility for educating the children of the workers. In *Doe v. Tyler* (1982), the Court declared that the Tyler, Texas school district could not require alien children to pay tuition. They found the policy in violation of equal protection in the Fourteenth Amendment. In these cases, the Court has made it clear that alien children are protected by the Constitution.

Hispanic Demands for Equal Educational Opportunity

In view of these horrendous conditions, the Hispanic population has not been idle. Efforts have been made to provide better educational opportunities for Hispanic children. Unfortunately, the struggle has had only limited success.

From the end of the Mexican war to the present, Mexican-American leaders have been aware of the school problems of their children. The early form of the struggle was an effort on the part of the Mexican population in the West and Southwest to remain separate from the United States. For many, the war didn't really end in 1848. For many years after the war, Mexican guerrillas continued the struggle against American forces. This limited warfare didn't really end until after the Civil War, when large numbers of Anglos moved into the Southwest and

California and secured the territory for the United States. Finally resigned to defeat, the Mexican-American population in the Southwest formed mutual aid societies after 1890 to help Mexican Americans adjust to the Anglo ways. The goals of these groups appeared to be accommodation and assimilation into the American mainstream. The Order of the Sons of America was typical of these mutual aid societies. According to Meier and Rivera: "The basic objectives of this organization were to enable Mexican Americans to achieve acculturation and integration, principally through political action. Ultimately, the Order sought to end prejudice, . . . to achieve equality before the law, to acquire political representation at all levels and to obtain greater educational opportunities. . . ."[57]

More militant groups were formed in later years. In 1919 in Arizona, the Liga Protectora Latina (Latin Protective Association) submitted a petition complaining of the treatment of Mexican laborers by the Arizona Cotton Growers Association. In the 1920s, R. M. Sanchez and E. M. Flores attempted to organize the farm workers in the cotton fields. These attempts met with disaster.[58] There were other brief encounters in the truck farming regions of the West and in the coal mining camps. Most of these efforts were brutally suppressed by the local establishment.

As in the case of blacks, the Mexican-American school battle was fought in the courts. In 1921 in Coryell County, Texas, the school board refused to permit an eight-year-old child of Mexican nationals to attend the public school. His parents appealed to the state superintendent who asked for a ruling from the attorney general of Texas. The attorney general held for the parents, stating that "every child in this state, of scholastic age, shall be permitted to attend the public free schools of the district. . . ."[59]

In the 1920s, segregated schools for Mexican Americans were common practice in Texas. This practice was challenged in 1928 by Felipe Vela, who had been turned away when he tried to enroll his daughter in the "American" school in Atascosa County, Texas. The school board defended its practice of providing separate schools for Anglos and Mexican Americans on the grounds that separate schools were justified since Mexican Americans had poor school attendance records and serious language difficulties. Vela appealed to the state superintendent who directed the board to admit the girl "because she was a good student and could keep up with American [sic] students."[60]

Many school battles were fought by the League of United Latin American Citizens (LULAC), which was formed in 1929. From the beginning, this organization was opposed to segregated schools for Mexican-American children. In 1930 LULAC challenged segregation in the Del Rio school system. In Del Rio, Mexican-American children were segregated for the first three years of elementary school. Although LULAC got a local court injunction prohibiting the practice, the board appealed. In *Independent School District v. Salvatierra*,[61] a U.S. district court could find no intent to segregate on the basis of race and upheld the practice of segregation. In effect, the decision approved segregation for educational reasons so long as race was not an issue. In practice, however, the segregation which existed was largely along racial lines.

In California, Mexican-American children became "Indians." California had no law segregating Mexican-American children from Anglos in the schools. California law provided that school "trustees shall have the power to establish separate schools for Indian children and for children of Mongolian descent." In January 1930, the California attorney general ruled that Mexican-American children were included in this legislation. He stated: "It is well known that the greater portion of the population of Mexico are Indians, and when such Indians migrate to the United States they are subject to the laws applicable generally to other Indians."[62] Although this law was modified in 1935, care was taken, according to Weinberg, "not to disturb the newfound Indianism of Mexican-Americans."[63] The new law read in part:

> The governing board of the school district shall have power to establish separate schools for Indian children . . . and children of all other Indians who are descendants of the original American Indians of the United States. . . .[64]

The segregation issue was finally challenged successfully in the *Mendez* case.[65] In *Mendez*, the ninth circuit court upheld a district court ruling that segregation of Mexican-American children in the Orange County, California schools was a violation of equal protection of the laws. Other cases followed. In *Delgado*, a district court held that segregation in three Texas counties was a violation of the Fourteenth Amendment.[66]

Getting a favorable court decision is one thing; ending the practice of segregating Mexican-American children seemed to be quite another. Weinberg reports that many school districts simply ignored the decisions. Even worse, at least for purposes of integration, schools in Texas and elsewhere where there was a large Mexican-American population decided, after *Brown* in 1954, that Mexican Americans were "white" after all, and they attempted to meet the demands of *Brown* by mixing Mexican Americans and blacks, thus eliminating the need to integrate white Anglo students with either blacks or Mexican Americans.[67] Strangely, the Supreme Court did not really confront this issue until the *Keyes* case in Denver in 1973. This decision was based in part on the *Hernandez* case of 1954. Trying to decide if Mexican Americans were black, white, or Indian was settled, at least legally, in 1954. Although the case did not involve the schools, it had great implications for the school integration struggle. In the *Hernandez* case,[68] the Supreme Court recognized that Mexican Americans had class standing under the Constitution. The case was brought in behalf of Pete Hernandez who had been convicted of murder in Texas. In reviewing the facts, the Supreme Court found that Mexican Americans had been systematically excluded from juries in Texas, including the one which heard the *Hernandez* case. The Court reversed Hernandez' conviction on the grounds that he had been denied a trial by a jury of his peers, since Mexican Americans are a distinct and identifiable ethnic group.

Even with the *Hernandez* principle behind them, Mexican Americans were much less active than blacks in their attacks on segregation in the fifties and sixties. Many of the efforts of Mexican-American groups in the sixties were directed toward militant protests, often in the form of public school and university strikes, to publicize their educational needs and the prejudicial treatment they felt they were being subjected to in schools and colleges. Mexican Americans had worked, along with blacks and others, for the passage of the Civil Rights Act of 1964, but by the end of the decade they had made little progress toward desegregation of the schools. Of course, Title VI of the Civil Rights Act provided the legal base needed to combat segregation since it outlawed the discriminatory use of federal funds on the grounds of national origin as well as race and color. Yet challenges to school practices came more from the federal bureaucracy than from the Mexican-American militants. In 1969 the Office of Civil Rights in HEW began an in-depth study of the educational problems of Mexican Americans.[69] There can be little question that the activism of militant Chicano groups was a factor in stimulating the commission to undertake this study.

By 1970 the courts were finally beginning to recognize the problem of segregation. In *Cisneros*, U.S. District Judge Woodrow Seals ruled that Mexican Americans constituted an "identifiable ethnic minority with a past pattern of discrimination" in Corpus Christi, Texas.[70] In *United States v. Texas Education Agency*, the fifth circuit court declared: "We see no reason to believe that ethnic segregation is any less detrimental than racial segregation."[71] On a rehearing of the case in 1978, the Court cited *Keyes* in finding that intentional segregation "against one minority group raises the presumption that any segregation suffered by the second minority group was intentional."[72] The petition for rehearing was based on the Austin school district's claim that residential patterns and population movements made it difficult to provide for schools with balanced minority populations. The Court didn't agree, since it found that the Austin school officials had built schools with segregative intent, had gerrymandered districts in ways which grouped Mexican Americans and blacks in predominantly minority schools, and had operated under policies which resulted in faculty segregation.

Other cases could be cited, but these few should demonstrate that serious problems of segregation exist and that the Mexican-American minority has been working to eliminate such practices. Unfortunately, the practices continue, and in most places where there is a large concentration of Mexican Americans, schools with predominantly Mexican-American populations may be more the rule than the exception. Like the black struggle, the Mexican-American struggle for integrated educational opportunity has a long way to go.

The Bilingual/Bicultural Battle

In recent years, paralleling the struggle for integrated education and sometimes in contradiction to the principle of integrated education, the bilingual/bicultural movement has been a major concern for Mexican Americans. Perhaps out of frustration because of their failure to achieve significant results in the integration struggle, perhaps for other reasons, Mexican Americans interested in improving the school experience for their children have worked for recognition of their language and culture in the public schools.

By the mid-seventies, efforts to include Mexican-American history and Mexican culture in the public school curriculum had met with some success. In 1974, the Commission on Civil Rights announced that nearly half the schools in the Southwest reported that one or more units of Mexican-American history were being offered in the elementary and secondary schools. There have also been sporadic efforts to introduce Mexican-American studies into the teacher education curriculum. This has met with only limited success even in areas where there are large numbers of Mexican-American students.

Perhaps the greatest thrust has been in the direction of providing bilingual education programs in schools with large numbers of Mexican-American students. This effort was given a large push by HEW in 1970 when that agency developed guidelines for providing equal services to schools with a 5 percent or more minority enrollment. A memorandum entitled "Identification of Discrimination and Denial of Services on the Basis of National Origin" set forth the following requirements for compliance with Title VI of the Civil Rights Act of 1964:

1. Where inability to speak and understand the English language excludes national-origin minority group children from effective participation in the educational program offered by a school district, the district must take affirmative steps to rectify the language deficiency in order to open its instructional program to these students.
2. School districts must not assign national-origin minority group students to classes for the mentally retarded on the basis of criteria which measure . . . English language skills; nor may school districts deny national-origin minority group children access to college preparatory courses on a basis directly related to the failure of the school system to inculcate English language skills.
3. Any ability grouping or tracking system employed by the school to deal with special language skill needs of national-origin minority group children must be designed to meet such language skill needs as soon as possible. . . .
4. School districts have the responsibility to notify national-origin minority group parents of school activities which are called to the attention of other parents. Such notice . . . may have to be provided in a language other than English.[73]

The language of this memorandum attempted not only to correct school problems but also to provide a rather comprehensive description of the kinds of problems which existed for Mexican-American children. Of course, the major problem, and the one which is most directly addressed, is the language problem. In terms of numbers alone, it is a huge problem. It has been estimated that approximately 3.5 million children in the United States speak a language other than English at home. Added to this is another large number whose primary language may be English but who have great difficulty with the standard American English used in the schools.

On August 4, 1980, the U.S. Department of Education issued new regulations designed to direct local school districts to comply with the major provisions of Title VI of the Civil Rights Act of 1964. The new guidelines were much more specific than those offered in the 1970 memorandum. In part, at least, the new guidelines grew out of the *Lau v. Nichols* case decided by the Supreme Court in 1974. In *Lau*, the Court held that minority children in San Francisco were being denied equal educational opportunity under Title VI. The case involved non-

English-speaking Chinese children who were nonetheless required to attend classes conducted in the English language. The Court ruled that the school district must take affirmative steps to assist children of limited English-speaking ability who were not benefiting from an English-only curriculum. It did not specify what steps were to be taken. In 1975, HEW developed a set of guidelines which became known as the "Lau Remedies" to assist the Office for Civil Rights and local schools in complying with the decision in *Lau*. Under these guidelines many schools developed bilingual programs, but there was a great deal of confusion over precisely what was required. The Court decision was not clear in its mandate for the implementation of specific programs, and the guidelines were criticized as cumbersome and contradictory.

Partly because of the criticism, new guidelines were proposed in 1980. In brief, the new guidelines provided:

1. Identification of students whose primary language is other than English.
2. Assessment of their level of language proficiency and a determination of whether such standards are superior in English, their primary language, or limited in both languages.
3. Children through grade eight who are superior in their primary language are to receive bilingual services.
4. Children who are superior in English are to receive no bilingual services.
5. Children who do get bilingual services may be "exited" from the programs if they achieve sufficient English language skills after two years in the program to score at the 30th percentile on reading achievement tests.[74]

As might be expected, a flood of criticism followed the publication of the new guidelines. Teachers' unions criticized them on the grounds that there weren't enough qualified teachers to handle the thousands of new programs that would have to be instituted. They feared that noncertified teachers would have to be employed. Minority groups were critical because they felt that limited-English students would be neglected under the programs established. School officials were angry because they claimed that they didn't have the resources to fund the programs. As always, local taxpayers complained because they saw the new guidelines as just another example of the federal government taking over the local schools.

The end of 1980 brought much more criticism than praise. In regional hearings in the fall of 1980, the Department of Education heard mostly complaints from those who were to be affected by the guidelines. Early in 1981, President Reagan ordered HEW to rescind the guidelines. Although this order did not end local efforts to provide bilingual programs, it put an end to federal supervision of the programs. The future of bilingual education is probably limited, since local communities have been reluctant to establish such programs. Whatever happens, it is unlikely that the school problems of the large Hispanic population in the United States will soon be solved. The problems seem almost too large for even a dedicated federal bureaucracy to solve anytime soon. In 1980, the dropout rate of

Hispanics was double that of white students. Nearly 25 percent who were enrolled in school were below grade level for their age. Home factors such as large family size, low income, and non-English background are endemic among the Hispanic population. School achievement scores trail significantly behind those of whites.[75]

If the goal of educational policy is to prepare Mexican-American students to enter the mainstream of society, it might require much more than even the best program in bilingual education can provide. After all, New Mexico and, to some extent, Texas had more than a quarter of a century of experience with bilingual education in the last part of the nineteenth and early part of the twentieth century. Unfortunately, there is no evidence that these programs were any more successful than harsh efforts to impose standard American English upon Spanish-speaking students. What was lacking and is perhaps still lacking is any real spirit or desire to effectively teach these children. If that spirit existed, any program might work. Without that spirit, nothing will. Unfortunately for Hispanic children, the solutions to these problems may rest with political rather than educational decision makers.

AMERICAN INDIANS

American Indians have had a unique school experience because of their special relationship to the federal government. It has not been a good experience. In the words of Diane Ravitch: "Where educational oppression of a minority was blatant and purposeful, as in the case of the American Indian, the policy was a disaster which neither educated nor assimilated."[76]

From the beginning, the special concerns on the part of the national government for the schooling of American Indians have been fraught with tragedy and disaster. The agency in the federal government which has been most responsible for the schooling of American Indians has been the Bureau of Indian Affairs (BIA). Established in 1832, it has a record on Indian education which Delores Huff, admittedly not a completely objective source, described as "horrendous." As she correctly pointed out:

> It doesn't make a bit of difference whether the facility itself was a mission school, or a reservation school, the literacy rate, the drop-out rate, and the poverty level are below those of any minority group in this country, and considerably below the average population. For centuries, Indians have told Bureau personnel what was needed . . . yet the objective of the Bureau has always been to assimilate the Indian into the non-Indian society, using the education system, while the Indian has resisted assimilation, and therefore education, in order to maintain some semblance of cultural integrity.[77]

The Mythical American Indian

According to Robert Faherty, writing in *Current History*,[78] many of the problems facing American Indians are due to the myths about them which are held by the white majority. Briefly, these myths embrace the following stereotypes: (1) all

Indians are uncivilized savages; (2) Indians are a vanishing race; (3) all Indians are alike; and (4) Indians do not change.

From the image of Indians as savages came the policy that they must be either eliminated, segregated from the rest of the society on a reservation, or assimilated into the society. Faherty accuses even the community of scholars of contributing to the "savage" stereotype by concentrating their study on dramatic but miniscule aspects of tribal culture and publicizing the strange and the bizarre—at least in white man's terms—rather than looking at Indian cultures as "dynamic, living and changing." For example, the use of peyote in certain religious ceremonies becomes more significant than the contemporary social and economic problems facing a particular Indian tribe. Faherty charges that the popular media and literature contributed to this myth by depicting the Indian in primitive settings and by labeling the Indian as "someone who is not quite able to survive on his own."

Another misconception about the American Indian population is that it is a vanishing race. The most famous depiction of this is James Fraser's classic statue of a "bent and battered Indian sitting on an equally forlorn horse," both of whom have reached "The End of the Trail." This myth hurts the Indians because it lowers their already low level of visibility in the society. What is really happening is that the Indian population is growing, not vanishing. The year 1900 was the low point, with a population of 237,196. In 1980, the Census Bureau counted 1,418,000 native Americans, including Eskimos, living in the United States.

Perhaps the greatest myth of all is that all Indians are alike. Faherty suggests that "there is no such creature as *the* American Indian." There is no "Indian" culture, no "Indian" language, no "Indian" value system, and no "Indian" religion. There never has been. From the first contact between Indians and Europeans, it was recognized that there was greater linguistic and cultural diversity among Indians than among Europeans. As Faherty points out, anthropologists' estimates of the number of separate languages among American Indians range from 200 to between 600 and 800. In addition to language, each tribe had its own separate and distinct religion, philosophy, and institutions. Even within tribes, there is great diversity. Obviously when the pluralism of American Indians is ignored and they are all treated as if they are alike, many things follow. Thus, for example, a standard educational policy for all American Indians is certain to end in disaster, at least for some.

Finally, the myth that American Indian tribal culture does not change creates serious difficulties in policy making. It blinds policy makers to a clear understanding of what the problems are and how to deal with them. Whole tribes, as well as individuals who count themselves as members, have changed in ways necessary for survival. The idea that all American Indians are clinging to ancient cultural values, unchanged and unchanging, is a false one.

Economic and Social Conditions

Whatever the myths, the realities of life for most American Indians are harsh. They include poverty, illness, poor education, and an early death. Agonizingly for the Indians, the popular media continue to misrepresent them. We are more often treated to stories of the unbounded wealth of Indian lands[79] and Indian tribes suing the national government and individual states for millions of dollars than we are to stories about the disease, poverty, and unemployment which are much more typical of the real conditions on and off the reservations. In reality, American Indians are trapped on reservations scattered throughout the country, in rural and urban pockets of poverty from the Olympic Peninsula to the urban ghettos of New York City. They are trapped because most are desperately poor, uneducated, and almost completely dependent upon a government which barely keeps them alive.

Although American Indians can be found almost anywhere in the country, about half of the population tends to be concentrated in a few areas. The state with the largest population is California (201,300), followed by Oklahoma (169,000), Arizona (152,900), New Mexico (104,800), and Alaska (64,000). Moreover, it is misleading to assume that American Indians are an overwhelming rural population. In 1980, approximately 40 percent lived in metropolitan areas.[80]

Wherever they live, they are among the poorest of the poor. Even though they are the most governmentally supervised of all populations in the United States, statistics on Indian poverty are difficult to find. Gerald Nagel reported that, in 1973, 40 percent of all Indians lived in poverty.[81] A Bureau of the Census report in 1973 indicated that the median family income for American Indians in 1969 was $5,832, compared to $9,590 for the general population and $6,191 for all minorities.

A major cause of Indian poverty is unemployment and underemployment. The BIA estimates that, at any given time, 40 percent of American Indians on reservations are out of work. Rates of unemployment among specific tribes have been as high as 80 or 90 percent in the 1970s. Major causes of such horrendous unemployment include lack of education and skills and the fact that Indians are too far removed from the places where jobs exist.

Poverty and unemployment lead to other problems. The most noticeable is housing. To the outsider, the Indian pueblo on the reservation may be colorful, an excellent subject for a photograph. To the poor Indian who has to live in one, it is smoke-filled, cold in winter, and dirty. For many rural and reservation Indians, plumbing does not exist and water supplies are unreliable, often a long distance from where they live. Electricity is an unknown luxury. Things most Americans take for granted are unavailable.

In 1972, the Indian Health Service reported some unbelievable conditions among the Indian populations in South Dakota and Arizona. On the Pine Ridge Reservation in South Dakota, it was found that 40 percent of the children below the age of five were chronically ill. At Tuba City Hospital in Arizona, of 676 Indian children below the age of four who were discharged during a 10-month period in 1967, 44 suffered from malnutrition, 38 had iron deficiency anemia, 13 under one year manifested marasmus and 8 had incurred kwashiorkor. The death rate for Indian children under 14 years of age is nearly two-and-one-half times that for all American children under 14. Indian life expectancy is 44 years, the lowest of any group in the United States.

School Conditions

In 1978 there were some 275,000 American Indian children between the ages of 6 and 17 in the United States. Of this number, approximately 60,000 were enrolled in predominantly Indian population schools, including about 50,000 in BIA-operated or -controlled schools and 9,000 in mission or other private schools. More than 200,000 were enrolled in the public schools.[82] According to Havighurst and Levine: "Practically all Native Americans between the ages of 6 and 17 inclusive have access to schools and attend schools almost as fully, in terms of proportions attending school by age, as do the Anglos, the Spanish descent groups, and the blacks."[83] Havighurst and Levine point out that the dropout rate for American Indians is greater than that for American students as a whole, but they conclude that this is more a matter of socioeconomic status than of ethnicity, since the proportion of American Indians who graduate from high school is "approximately the same as the proportions of other ethnic groups which have a similar socio-economic or income composition."[84]

This may overstate the case. Although their socioeconomic condition probably is an important reason, American Indians do have special problems in school which are different from those of other groups. Or, put another way, many Indian children have all the problems of both black ghetto children and Mexican-American children in addition to some of their own specific problems. The U.S. Civil Rights Commission reported in 1973 that both the BIA schools and the public school systems were "failing Indian children." In the words of the report:

> Their educational attainment is two to three years below the general population's. The drop-out rate of Indian children, particularly toward the end of high school, far exceeds that of the general population.[85]

Bilingual and bicultural education for American Indians has been virtually non-existent in most school districts until very recently—unlike the situation with Mexican-American children. Until recently, according to the Civil Rights Commission, "the entire educational effort was aimed at teaching Indians the English language and 'American' behavioral patterns." The report continued:

> Indian children are in a classroom environment controlled and dominated by non-Indians. Many Indian children must learn English as a second language if he or she is to survive.[86]

It should be noted that about two-thirds of all Indian children attend the public schools, with an increasing number attending those in urban areas. Their situation in these schools is described by Mary Klein:

> In these schools, Indian children often encounter unfamiliar customs and values, teachers who may be insensitive to the needs of Indian students, textbooks that say their Indian ancestors were savages and a conspicuous lack of Indian teachers. Under such conditions, it is not surprising that one Indian educator says Indian students are "emotional dropouts by the third grade."[87]

Certainly part of the reason for the massive failure of American Indian children in the public as well as BIA schools is the fact that they have the same handicaps that poverty creates for all poor people's children. Added to these problems, which are severe enough, is the peculiar history of Indian education and the contemporary problems related to prejudice which were created, in part, by that history.

The early attitude toward the American Indian population is revealed in the position of King James I of England, who asked the clergy of England to raise money "for the erecting of some churches and schools for ye education of ye children of these Barbarians in Virginia."[88] Dartmouth College began as a training school for American Indians. In the early years, Indians wanted a practical education. They wanted to learn to read and write, to farm, and to build houses. Instead, they got training in the white man's religion. Mission schools dominated Indian education through most of the nineteenth century. These schools were encouraged and subsidized by the federal government and often were feared and hated by Indians. In their zeal to Christianize and Americanize the children of American Indians, the missionaries literally kidnapped them. In the words of Delores Huff: "There is hardly an Indian today who can't remember horror stories told him by his grandparents of how the school agents used to come out to the reservation and round up the kids, in spite of parental and tribal objections. Children were taught to hide."[89]

Children were often abused in these schools. They were whipped for speaking tribal languages. They were sent hundreds of miles from home to prevent contact with their parents or to remove the temptation to run away. The boarding school model was Carlisle Indian School, founded in Pennsylvania in 1879. It was run in strict military fashion. Its curriculum was mainstream Anglo with emphasis on vocational and job training. Its mission was to obliterate totally any sign of Indian culture.[90] Thus, the early effort in Indian education were unique—there is nothing else like it in the American educational experience.

Before the turn of the century, many schools—including boarding schools and day schools—were founded on the Carlisle philosophy. By the mid-twenties, Indian children were attending public schools, federally controlled boarding and day schools, and some mission schools. None of it worked. In the words of Diane Ravitch: "Not until 1926 did government officials begin to question the effectiveness of their Indian education policies."[91]

The Census of 1920 revealed that 36 percent of all American Indians were illiterate. Such shocking data stimulated the government to undertake in the twenties a study of Indian education. The result was the so-called "Meriam Report," named for its director, Lewis Meriam. Published in 1928, the Meriam Report was a repudiation of the previous half-century's educational policies for American Indians. It urged the government "to renounce coercive assimilation and . . . to respect the rights of the Indian . . . as a human being living in a free country."[92]

The Meriam Report, with its strong recommendations for the reorganization of education for Indian children, was taken seriously by Roosevelt's New Deal. Under the direction of John Collier, Commissioner of Indian Affairs from 1933 until 1945, some significant changes were made. Collier encouraged the development of programs in bilingualism, the employment of Indian teachers, and the establishment of new programs in adult education, and he appeared to be genuinely dedicated to the preservation of native American culture.[93]

Funds for these ambitious projects were made available during the New Deal. The money came in the form of the Johnson-O'Malley Act which stated in its opening paragraph:

> the Secretary of the Interior is hereby authorized in his discretion, to enter into a contract or contracts with any State or Territory . . . for the education, medical attention, agricultural assistance and social welfare . . . of Indians in such State or Territory, through the qualified agencies of such State or Territory, and to expand under such contract or contracts moneys appropriated by Congress for the education, medical attention, agricultural assistance, and social welfare, including relief of distress, of Indians in such state.[94]

Under this legislation, the Secretary of the Interior was given the responsibility for negotiating with states and territories for the improvement of the conditions of Indians and for developing rules and regulations for putting the intent of the law into effect.

Under the law, the states were reimbursed for programs designed to provide improved schooling for Indian children. Unfortunately, there was nothing in the law which gave Indians control over their own education. It was still controlled by whites. In the words of Delores Huff: "Now it was not only the missionaries who exploited Indian education, and the BIA with its boarding schools and reservation schools; the public school systems had their fingers in the till."[95]

In spite of this, Commissioner Collier tried. The direction of his administration of Indian affairs was clearly a de-emphasis on assimilation and an emphasis on the preservation of Indian cultures. His greatest enemies proved to be World War II and Congress. The war diverted attention away from domestic problems while creating a surge of patriotism which was damaging to the Collier program. Congress, influenced by these conditions and by a more conservative mood after the war, shifted its emphasis back to the old boarding school idea. In spite of the Meriam Report, the Johnson-O'Malley Act, and the heroics of Collier, by the mid-fifties the education of American Indians seemed to be about where it was in 1920—inadequate, underfinanced, poorly organized, ineffective, and in many ways anti-Indian.

This review of the unique and peculiar history of the role of government in Indian education, although brief, should demonstrate that, in many respects, the manner in which Indian education was undertaken is partly responsible for their contemporary educational problems. Certainly it has contributed to the contemporary neglect and prejudicial attitudes which exist.

In a discussion of more recent problems of Indian education, Will Antell,[96] Assistant Commissioner of Education for the state of Minnesota, outlined four major factors which he felt contributed significantly to the notorious lack of school success on the part of Indian children: (1) the polarization of the school community and the Indian community; (2) the media impact; (3) teachers who don't understand Indian problems; and (4) the issue of Indian control of the schools. Antell reported that in many school districts with which he was familiar, school personnel had a very negative view of Indian parents. From the point of view of the teachers, Indian parents appeared apathetic—they didn't push their children to attend school, much less to achieve while they were there. The way the parents viewed it, the schools were not interested in their children—they discriminated against them and tried to push them out of school at an early age. Antell charged that the media depicted the native American in a bad light, which created even more disrespect of Indians as people. This had an impact on teachers as well as children. He felt that most Anglo teachers disliked Indian children and preferred not to teach them. He charged that the value systems of most non-Indian teachers made them poor teachers of Indian children, and that teacher training institutions were doing little or nothing to provide training that would help teachers overcome their prejudices. Finally, he sympathized with Indian parents who complained that in most places they were such a small minority that they had no effective voice in their local public schools.

In view of the problems facing Indian children in BIA and public schools, it is not surprising that Congress has acted in an effort to improve conditions. The greatest gains in history, at least legally, were made during the decade of the seventies. Two major pieces of legislation were passed by Congress in the seventies: Public Law 92–318 (1972), better known as the "Indian Education Act" of 1972, and Public Law 93–638 (1975), better known as the "Indian Self-Determination Educational Assistance Act" of 1975. Excerpts from these laws follow.

Indian Education Act

Sec. 810. (a) The Commissioner shall carry out a program of making grants for the improvement of educational opportunities for Indian children—

(1) to support planning, pilot, and demonstration projects . . . which are designed to test and demonstrate the effectiveness of programs for improving educational opportunities for Indian children;

(2) to assist in the establishment and operation of programs . . . which are designed to stimulate (A) the provision of educational services not available to Indian children in sufficient quantity or quality, and (B) the development and establishment of exemplary educational programs to serve as models for regular school programs in which Indian children are educated;

(3) to assist in the establishment and operation of preservice and inservice training programs . . . for persons serving Indian children as educational personnel; and

(4) to encourage the dissemination of information and materials relating to, and the evaluation of the effectiveness of, educational programs which may offer educational opportunities to Indian children. . . .

In addition grants were to be made for:

(1) innovative programs related to the educational needs of educationally deprived children;

(2) bilingual and bicultural education programs and projects;

(3) special health and nutrition services, and other related activities, which meet the special health, social, and psychological problems of Indian children. . . .

Also the Act provided grants for:

(1) remedial and compensatory instruction, school health, physical education, psychological, and other services designed to assist and encourage Indian children to enter, remain in, or reenter elementary or secondary school;

(2) comprehensive academic and vocational instruction;

(3) instructional materials (such as library books, textbooks, and other printed or published or audiovisual materials) and equipment;

(4) comprehensive guidance, counseling, and testing services;

(5) special education programs for handicapped;

(6) preschool programs;

(7) bilingual and bicultural education programs. . . .

In higher education the Act provided funds:

(1) to prepare persons to serve Indian children as teachers, teacher aides, social workers, and ancillary educational personnel; and

(2) to improve the qualifications of such persons who are serving Indian children in such capacities. Grants for the purposes of this subsection may be used for the establishment of fellowship programs leading to an advanced degree, for institutes and, as part of a continuing program, for seminars, symposia, workshops, and conferences. In carrying out the programs authorized by this subsection, preference shall be given to the training of Indians. . . .[97]

Indian Self-Determination Educational Assistance Act

To provide maximum Indian participation in the Government and education of the Indian people; to provide for the full participation of Indian tribes in programs and services conducted by the Federal Government for Indians and to encourage the development of human resources of the Indian people; to establish a program of assistance to upgrade Indian education; to support the right of Indian citizens to control their own educational activities; and for other purposes. . . .

CONGRESSIONAL FINDINGS

Sec. 2. (a) The Congress, after careful review of the Federal Government's historical and special legal relationship with, and resulting responsibilities to, American Indian people, finds that—

(1) the prolonged Federal domination of Indian service programs has served to retard rather than enhance the progress of Indian people and their communities by depriving Indians of the full opportunity to develop leadership skills crucial to the realization of self-government, and has denied to the Indian people an effective voice in the planning and implementation of programs for the benefit of Indians which are responsive to the true needs of Indian communities; and

(2) the Indian people will never surrender their desire to control their relationships both among themselves and with non-Indian governments, organizations, and persons.

(b) The Congress further finds that—

(1) true self-determination in any society of people is dependent upon an educational process which will insure the development of qualified people to fulfill meaningful leadership roles;

(2) the Federal responsibility for and assistance to education of Indian children has not effected the desired level of educational achievement or created the diverse opportunities and personal satisfaction which education can and should provide; and

(3) parental and community control of the educational process is of crucial importance to the Indian people. . . .

Part A—Education of Indians in Public Schools

Sec. 5. (a) Whenever a school district affected by a contract or contracts for the education of Indians pursuant to this Act has a local school board not composed of a majority of Indians, the parents of the Indian children enrolled in the school or schools affected by such contract or contracts shall elect a local committee from among their number. Such committee shall fully participate in the development of, and shall have the authority to approve or disapprove programs to be conducted under such contract or contracts, and shall carry out such other duties, and be so structured, as the Secretary of the Interior shall by regulation provide. . . .

Sec. 6. Any school district educating Indian students who are members of recognized Indian tribes, who do not normally reside in the State in which such school district is located, and who are residing in Federal boarding facilities for the purposes of attending public schools within such district may, in the discretion of the Secretary of the Interior, be reimbursed by him for the full per capita costs of educating such Indian students. . . .

Part B—School Construction

Sec. 204. (a) The Secretary is authorized to enter into a contract or contracts with any State education agency or school district for the purpose of assisting such agency or district in the acquisition of sites for, or the construction, acquisition, or renovation of facilities (including all necessary equipment) in school districts on or adjacent to or in close proximity to any Indian reservation or other lands held in trust by the United States for Indians, if such facilities are necessary for the education of Indians residing on any such reservation or lands. . . .

(d) Any contract entered into by the Secretary pursuant to this section shall contain provisions requiring the relevant State educational agency to—

(1) provide Indian students attending any such facilities constructed, acquired, or renovated, in whole or in part, from funds made available pursuant to this section with standards of education not less than those provided non-Indian students in the school district in which the facilities are situated. . . .[98]

Many of the educational functions of these laws are administered in the Office of Indian Education. The creation of the Department of Education did not alter the organization of the Office of Indian Education. The major divisions within the Office of Indian Education are the Division of Local Education Agency Assistance and the Division of Special Projects and Programs. In 1979 Congress appropriated $72 million for Indian education and it was distributed to more than 1,000 school districts in 42 states. Grants were provided to support bilingual education, special tutors, field trips, and other activities. Some 34,000 children in Indian-controlled schools received similar services. In addition, 10,000 adults attended programs in basic literacy, high school equivalency, and job training, as well as other programs. Under the Indian fellowship program, 260 students received tuition and other support. As specified in the 1972 act, all these activities now require the active participation of Indian and Alaska native parents in planning and operating school programs.[99]

Thus, federal funds, in varying amounts, seem to be finding their way into the schools, and most American Indian children who are enrolled in school are benefiting to some extent from funds provided by the federal government through its various programs. Perhaps what is most significant is that the old approach of assimilation of the Indian population has been seriously attacked. The new official philosophy of the government is one of respect for native American cultural differences. Whether this will greatly improve the educational opportunities and educational results for Indian children remains to be seen.

SCHOOLING FOR MINORITIES—A CONTINUING STRUGGLE

What is most striking in any survey of the problems of minorities in American education is the long history of emotional resistance on the part of the white majority and the unresponsiveness of the political institutions of the society to the demands of minorities. It is striking because these have not, by and large, been revolutionary demands. Minorities have not been seeking to destroy the system; they have merely been demanding their rights within it. Even the most militant blacks, Mexican Americans, and native Americans, while critical of the system, seemed somehow content to make small gains. Yet even small gains were grudgingly offered.

Most of the success has come through liberal legislation and court decisions. Yet even the most comprehensive legislation could not be labeled radical, for in every case the legislation providing for expanded educational opportunities for minorities was more system-serving than anything else. In every case, the law sought to bring minorities into the mainstream of American society, and in many cases the law was merely a more specific restatement of basic constitutional protections and guarantees.

Clearly the explanation for resistance to full constitutional rights for minority children has nothing to do with revolutionary change in the system. It has to do with prejudice. Moreover, the prejudices seem to surface most violently when the majority white population is most personally affected. Thus, for example, whites who are not directly affected by the busing of black children to achieve integration are not greatly concerned with the problem. However, in school systems where the children of whites are personally involved, personal prejudices and personal inconveniences tend to take precedence over legal and moral principles. The reactions are so consistent that they are easy to predict. Anglos seem relatively unconcerned about bilingual education for Mexican-American children until it impacts upon them in some personal way. If bilingual education results in the separation of Mexican Americans from the Anglo population (no matter how socially damaging this segregation might be) and if it can proceed without much additional cost, few Anglos complain. If, on the other hand, Anglo children are expected in some way to pay the cost of years of prejudice or if the new programs increase taxes significantly, there are heated objections.

The Anglo problem with Indians is a little different in that there appears to be serious guilt associated with the past mistreatment of American Indians. Even in this case, however, solutions which threaten to take away from whites so that Indians might fare better are met with cries of anguish. In instances where the law attempts to redress past grievances, where special programs are provided and there is a large and necessary expenditure of funds, the white majority sees the specter of reverse discrimination.

Yet if the minorities dealt with here are ever to become full participating citizens in the mainstream of American society, the public school experience must undergo vast improvement for them. The logical goal of any effective school program should be equality of result at some time in the future. This is not to say that everyone would be equal—an impossible goal—but that we could no longer identify minorities on the basis of IQ, or educational achievement or attainment. In the society at large, it would mean that we could no longer identify minorities on the basis of occupation or income or place of residence. Yet, realistically, the goal is probably a utopian one—unless serious efforts are made in the larger society to reduce the socioeconomic problems and the prejudices which contribute to the school problems. Poor, hungry, and sick children will never be able to compete on equal terms with those who are not in that condition. Until some genuine progress is made against poverty and everything that poverty represents—poor housing, inadequate diets, unemployment, substandard health care—the schools may not be able to cope; not even with strong public support for improving the school experience. And strong public support is not likely. What is more probable is that the battles will continue. There will be progress followed by retreat. Perhaps the best that can be hoped for is that the gains will be incremental and that at some future date we will look back and, as a society, wonder how we could have been so stupid.

NOTES

1. Excerpted from Richard Kluger, "The Quest for Simple Justice," *Just Schools*, A Special Issue of *Southern Exposure*, Summer 1979, pp. 7–8.
2. Carter G. Woodson, *The Education of the Negro Prior to 1861* (Washington, D.C.: Associated Publishers, 1919), p. 1.
3. Henry Allen Bullock, *A History of Negro Education in the South: From 1619 to the Present* (Cambridge, Mass.: Harvard University Press, 1976), p. 15.
4. Booker T. Washington, *Working with the Hands* (New York: Doubleday, Page & Co., 1904), p. 233.
5. Laughlin McDonald, "The Legal Barriers Crumble," *Southern Exposure*, May 1979, p. 5.
6. Ibid., p. 25.
7. *Cooper v. Aaron*, 358 US 1 (1958).
8. *Goss v. Board of Education*, 373 US 683 (1963).

9. *Griffin v. County School Board of Prince Edward County*, 377 US 218 (1964).

10. *Rogers v. Paul*, 382 US 198 (1965).

11. *Charles C. Green et al. v. County School Board of New Kent County Virginia*, 391 US 430 (1968).

12. Ibid., pp. 437–438.

13. Ibid., p. 439.

14. Ibid., p. 442.

15. *Alexander et al. v. Holmes County Board of Education*, 90 S.Ct. 21 (1969).

16. Ibid., p. 15.

17. Ibid., p. 17.

18. *Swan v. Mecklenburg Board of Education*, 402 US 1 (1971).

19. *Kelly v. Guinn*, 456 F2nd. 100 (9th Cir. 1972).

20. *Keyes v. School District No. 1*, 93 S.Ct. 2686 (1973).

21. *Swan v. Mecklenburg*, 402 US 1 (1971).

22. *Milliken v. Bradley*, 418 US 717 (1974).

23. Ibid., pp. 744–745.

24. Ibid., p. 757.

25. *Dayton Board of Education v. Brinkman*, US 99 S.Ct. 2971 (1979).

26. *Evans v. Buchanon*, US 98 S.Ct. 235 (1977).

27. See D. Armor, "The Evidence on Busing," *The Public Interest* No. 29 (Summer 1972): 90–126, and Nathan Glazer, "Is Busing Necessary?", *Commentary* (March 1972): 39.

28. *Education Daily*, 1 October 1981, pp. 1–2.

29. Lamda Corporation, "School Desegregation with Minimum Busing," report submitted to the Department of Health, Education, and Welfare, December 10, 1971; reprinted in U.S., Congress, House, *Equal Education Opportunities Act Hearings*, p. 653.

30. Eleanor Blumenberg, "The New Yellow Peril: Facts and Fictions about School Busing," *Journal of Intergroup Relations* (Summer 1973): 37.

31. Leonard Levine and Kitty Griffiths, "The Busing Myth: Segregated Academies Bus More Children, and Further," *South Today*, November 1973.

32. Blumenberg, "The New Yellow Peril," p. 38.

33. Gary Orfield, *Must We Bus? Segregated Schools and National Policy* (Washington, D.C.: The Brookings Institution, 1978), p. 279.

34. Ibid., p. 281.

35. Ibid.

36. *Weekly Compilation of Presidential Documents, Addresses and Remarks*, 21 February 1977, p. 203.

37. *Weekly Compilation of Presidential Documents, Memorandums to Federal Agencies*, 25 July 1977, p. 1047.

38. See Thomas F. Pettigrew and Robert L. Green, "School Desegregation in Large Cities: A Critique of the Coleman 'White Flight' Thesis," *Harvard Educational Review* (February 1976): 1–54. See also US., Congress, House, Judiciary Committee, *Testimony of Christine Rossell, Hearings Before a Subcommittee on Civil and Constitutional Rights of the House Judiciary Committee*, 23 September 1981.

39. See Arthur R. Jensen, *Genetics and Education* (New York: Harper & Row, 1972), and William Shockley, "Dysgenics, Geneticity, Raceology: A Challenge to the Intellectual Responsibility of Educators," *Phi Delta Kappan* 54 (January 1972): 297–307.

40. Anonymous, from an essay written by a student in the seventh grade. The essay may be found in Henry S. Johnson and William J. Hernandez, eds., *Educating the Mexican-American* (Valley Forge, Pa.: Judson Press, 1970), p. 19.

41. George I. Sanchez, "Educational Change and Historical Perspective," in *Mexican-*

Americans and Educational Change, ed. Alfredo Casteneda et al. (New York: Arno Press, 1974), pp. 14–15.

42. U.S., Department of Commerce, Bureau of the Census, Series P–20, No. 31, December 1977.

43. For a more complete treatment of this topic, see Daniel Selakovich, *Ethnicity and the Schools* (Danville, Ill.: Interstate Press, 1978), ch. 4.

44. Meyer Weinberg, *A Chance to Learn: The History of Race Education in the United States* (Cambridge: Cambridge University Press, 1977), p. 142.

45. Ibid., p. 143.

46. Herschel T. Manuel, *The Education of Mexican and Spanish-Speaking Children in Texas* (Austin: Fund for Research in the Social Sciences, University of Texas, 1930).

47. Ibid., p. 72.

48. Ibid., p. 79.

49. U.S. Commission on Civil Rights, *Ethnic Isolation of Mexican-Americans in the Southwest*, Mexican-American Education Study, Report I (Washington, D.C.: The Commission, 1971), p. 12.

50. Ibid.

51. Weinberg, *A Chance to Learn*, p. 146.

52. Ibid., p. 151.

53. U.S. Commission on Civil Rights, *Ethnic Isolation of Mexican-Americans in the Southwest*, p. 84.

54. See Theodore W. Parsons, Jr., "Ethnic Cleavage in a California School" (doctoral dissertation, Stanford University, 1965); also, U.S. Commission on Civil Rights, *Teachers and Students: Differences in Teacher Interaction with Mexican-American and Anglo Students*, Mexican-American Education Study, Report V (Washington, D.C.: The Commission, 1973).

55. John M. Crewdson, "Thousands Held in Virtual Slavery," *New York Times*, 19 October 1980, p. 1.

56. *Certain Named and Unnamed Non-Citizen Children v. State*, 101 S.Ct.12 (1980)

57. Matt S. Meier and Feliciano Rivera, *The Chicanos: A History of Mexican-Americans* (New York: Hill & Wang, Inc., Division of Farrar, Straus & Giroux, 1972), p. 143.

58. For a complete account of the Mexican-American difficulties in Arizona in the 1920s, see Herbert B. Peterson, "Twentieth Century Search for Cibola: Post-World War I Mexican Labor Exploitation in Arizona," in *An Awakened Minority: The Mexican Americans*, 2d ed., ed. Manual P. Servin (Beverly Hills, Calif.: Glencoe Press, 1974).

59. Weinberg, *A Chance to Learn*, p. 166.

60. Ibid., p. 165.

61. *Independent School District v. Salvatierra*, 284 US 580 (1931).

62. Weinberg, *A Chance to Learn*, p. 166.

63. Ibid.

64. School Code of the State of California (Sacramento: California Department of Public Instruction, 1937), quoted in Weinberg, *A Chance to Learn*, p. 166.

65. *Westminster School District of Orange County et al. v. Mendez et al.*, 64 F. Supp. 544 (1946).

66. *Delgado v. Bastrop County*, cited in *Gonzalez v. Sheely*, 96 F. Supp. 1004 (1951).

67. Weinberg, *A Chance to Learn*, p. 169.

68. *Hernandez v. Texas*, 347 US 475 (1954).

69. The results of this study may be found in the following four reports made by the U. S. Commission on Civil Rights from 1971 to 1974: *Ethnic Isolation of Mexican-Americans in the Public Schools of the Southwest; The Excluded Student: Educational Practices Affecting*

Mexican-Americans in the Southwest; Teachers and Students: Differences in Teacher Interaction with Mexican-American and Anglo Students; and *Toward Quality Education for Mexican-Americans.* These reports are all published as part of the Mexican-American Education Study by the U.S. Commission on Civil Rights, Washington, D.C., 1971–1974.

70. *Cisneros v. Corpus Christi Independent School District,* 324 F. Sup. 599 (1970).
71. *U.S. v. Texas Education Agency,* 467 F. 2nd. 848 (1972).
72. *U.S. v. Texas Education Agency,* 579 F. 2nd. 910 (1978).
73. Department of Health, Education, and Welfare, Memorandum of 25 May 1970, *Federal Register* 35, p. 11595.
74. *Federal Register* 45, 5 August 1980.
75. National Center for Education Statistics, *The Condition of Education for Hispanic Americans* (Washington, D.C.: Statistical Information Office, 1980).
76. Diane Ravitch, "On the History of Minority Group Education in the United States," *Teachers College Record* 78 (December 1976): 219.
77. Delores Huff, "Educational Colonialism: The American Indian Experience," *Harvard Graduate School of Education Association Bulletin* 42 (Spring/Summer 1976): 3.
78. Robert L. Faherty, "The American Indian: An Overview," *Current History* 67 (December 1974): 241–244.
79. See, for example, Howell Raines, "Struggling for Power and Identity," *The New York Times Magazine,* 11 February 1979. pp. 21–29.
80. Statistical Abstract of the United States (Washington, D.C.: U.S. Dept. of Commerce, 1981), p. 32
81. Gerald S. Nagel, "Economics of the Reservation," *Current History* 67 (December 1974): 246.
82. Robert J. Havighurst and Daniel U. Levine, *Society and Education,* 5th ed. (Boston: Allyn & Bacon, 1979), pp. 466–67.
83. Ibid., p. 467.
84. Ibid.
85. U.S., Congress, Senate, "Neglect and Exploitation of American Indians," 10 July 1973, *Congressional Record* 119, pt. 18 22925.
86. Ibid., p. 22925.
87. U.S., Congress, Senate, Mary Klein, "Projects Bring Indian Concerns to Public Schools," 12 May 1976, Extension of Remarks, *Congressional Record* 122, pt. 213730.
88. Huff, "Educational Colonialism: The American Indian Experience," p. 3.
89. Ibid., p. 4.
90. Ibid.
91. Ravitch, "On the History of Minority Group Education in the United States," p. 221.
92. Ibid.
93. Huff, "Educational Colonialism: The American Indian Experience," p. 222.
94. Public Law No. 167, 73rd Cong., 2d sess., chs. 146–148 (16 April 1934).
95. Huff, "Educational Colonialism: The American Indian Experience," p. 5.
96. Will Antell, "Education of the American Indians," *Current History* 67 (December 1974): 267–279.
97. Public Law 92–318, 86 US Stat. 334 (23 June 1972).
98. Public Law 93–638, US Stat. 2203 (4 January 1975).
99. *Native American News,* September 1980.

11

Women in Education

For a number of years, the schools have been at the center of a controversy over sex discrimination. At times, the controversy has been heated. During the 1960s, militant women burned their bras, picketed employers, disrupted beauty pageants, marched for equal rights, and unleashed a barrage of literature which was deeply critical of an America which they often characterized as "male chauvinist." Since the mid-sixties, demands from organized women's groups have ranged from a relatively mild insistence on reform to a call for revolution.

In spite of the petitions, acts of defiance, and millions of words of protest, real discrimination continues. Women have gained little ground on the major issue which concerns them—a society in which women have equal rights. Women have experienced only partial success in changing stereotyped sexual roles and have so far failed in their efforts to amend the Constitution to include equal rights for women. In terms which can be measured—that is, equal pay, equal job opportunities, equal representation in the professions, and equal educational opportunities—women continue to be treated as somehow separate and unequal.

Part of this failure is surely due to the traditional roles of women in American society. The historical roles of women have stubbornly resisted change in spite of the organized and determined efforts of some women. History alone, however, cannot explain the roles of women in American society. There are deep cultural obstacles to the achievement of sexual equality. Perhaps the most central obstacle to full equality of the sexes in the United States is economic; that is, the economic system—whatever it is—would require fundamental change in order for women to gain equality with men. An end to exploitation and the achievement of full equality would require fundamental changes in the system—changes which are not likely to happen.

The major thesis of this chapter is that women are in an inferior position in the system and the schools have contributed to this. The solution to the problem cannot rest solely with the schools because they are not the sole cause of sex discrimination. Women can be as well schooled as men and gaps in employment and income continue to exist. It is not the schools but the economic and social systems which are the root of the problem.

In developing this thesis, the material in this chapter attempts to demonstrate how the historical struggle has led to only minor gains. It outlines the contemporary forms of sexual inequality in income, education, and employment; notes some special problems in schooling for women; and surveys the legal struggle for equality. The material which follows is intended to be illustrative rather than comprehensive.

THE STRUGGLE AGAINST TRADITIONAL ROLES — A BRIEF HISTORY OF WOMEN'S RIGHTS

Perhaps the first notable case in which a woman got into difficulties with established authority was that of Ann Hutchinson. Not that Mrs. Hutchinson was pleading anyone's cause but her own—her right to her own interpretation of church dogma. Nonetheless, her pointed questioning of church authority led to her trial and banishment from Massachusetts Bay. The case of Ann Hutchinson was by no means unique in the colonial experience. Certainly not a radical, Ann Hutchinson and a handful of others like her in colonial America were questioning the dictation of conscience and belief by a male theocracy. Although her religious views had a great deal to do with her difficulties, the very fact that a woman would demonstrate such independence might have been enough to get Ann Hutchinson in serious difficulty with the ruling male elite.

The discrimination against women in education can be traced to antiquity. Even the philosophy of classical liberals was a philosophy which applied to only half the population. Locke, Rousseau, John Stuart Mill and other liberal democratic philosophers were not referring to women in their definitions of liberty, equality, social justice, and democracy. Rousseau, one of the most enlightened liberals of his period, informs the reader in *Emile* that

> The whole education of women should be relative to men. To please them, to be useful to them, to win their love and esteem, to bring them up when young, to tend them when grown, to advise and console them, and to make life sweet and pleasant to them; these are the duties of women at all times, and what they ought to learn from infancy.[1]

With this tradition, one would not expect women to have played a great role in the American Revolution. Indeed, they played *no* significant role, at least as they are treated in the history books. The Revolution was a male Revolution. Perhaps more significant, the heroes of the American Revolution, as they are presented to school children, are largely male. The females of the revolutionary period and the critical early years of the Republic are cast in traditional feminine roles. Few students read about Judith Murray, who presented logical and reasoned criticisms of male superiority during the revolutionary period, but all school children read about Betsy Ross and her needle and thread and old grey head, and that very caricature of feminism, Dolly Madison.

Feminists have charged, with some validity, that the Constitution of the United States was an exercise in male chauvinism. Given the status of women in the United States in 1787, it would have been inconceivable that any of the found-ing fathers would have considered inviting female delegates to the Philadelphia convention, and certainly women were not singled out in the Constitution as re-cipients of specific rights as democratic citizens—an oversight which to this day has not been corrected. Political liberalism of the eighteenth century was for men only. Women had to wait for the day when deeper economic and social forces moved them to action. The stirrings of industrialization, the growth of the factory system, and a developing concern for mass education were forces which moved women to speak out more openly against discrimination.

In the two decades after 1820, a few women did voice their opinions on the need for education for girls and women. It was not a strong voice, but some progress was made in the establishment of girls' schools. Women became directly involved in the antislavery movement. Several American women managed to get to the World Antislavery Convention in London in 1840, and many worked for years in the abolition movemnent in this country. Armed with some experience in political activism gained from the abolitionist movement, women turned in 1848 to other interests. In that year the first women's rights convention was held at Seneca Falls, New York. At Seneca, they managed to rewrite the Declaration of Independence to include women, but, more significantly, they pushed the door of female political consciousness open just a crack. From 1848 to the Civil War, women became more active in educational reform efforts, continued their aboli-tionist struggles, and worked for equal political rights on state and local levels. There were some gains—a few educational opportunities were opened, increas-ing numbers of women moved into the labor market, some of the most oppres-sive and discriminatory state legislation was repealed or amended; but, for the most part, there continued to be a large gap in American society between male and female rights.

The first genuine success for women in their struggle for equal rights grew out of the suffrage movement. Not that it was an easy success. Leaders such as Elizabeth Stanton and Susan Anthony were hopeful that their chances were good when the Fifteenth Amendment was being considered in 1866. It read: "The right of the citizens of the United States to vote shall not be denied or abridged by the United States or any State, on account of race, color, or previous condition of servitude." For the advocates of women suffrage, it seemed a simple matter to insert the word "sex" into the amendment, yet women had to wait more than 50 years to accomplish this.

Undaunted, but bitterly disappointed, women suffrage leaders carried their battle to the states. They were more successful there, for by 1870 Wyoming and Utah territories opened their ballot boxes to women. Wyoming was admitted to the Union in 1890 with women suffrage in its constitution, as was Utah in 1896. Col-orado voters approved women suffrage in 1893, and Idaho in 1896. Encouraged by these early successes, women continued to push for an amendment to the Con-stitution extending the suffrage to women. For more than two decades, the tactics used by women in this effort were the traditional political methods of lobbying and pamphleteering. In 1917 they began their struggle in earnest when members of the Congressional Union and Women's Party picketed the White House in behalf of suffrage. Women were willing to risk jeers, insults, and even jail for the cause. They were finally successful in August 1920 when the necessary three-fourths of the state legislatures ratified the Nineteenth Amendment.[2]

The century of struggle culminating in the Nineteenth Amendment and the invasion of the work force by women during World War I set the stage for a more liberated woman in America. However, women were still a long way from anything approaching equality. They had gained the ballot, but social, economic, and political restrictions continued to exist. Although there were no large feminist movements in the twenties or thirties which would compare with the suffrage movement, a small minority of women kept the battle alive. Radical feminists continued to demand equal employment and income, the right to the same kind of social life as men, divorce laws which were more favorable to women, "liberated" sexual life, and a host of other advantages which their male counterparts enjoyed. Some gains were made, but for the most part they were either token gains or benefits which accrued to women as a result of broad social programs.

For example, Roosevelt claimed the distinction of being the first president to appoint a woman to a cabinet post, in the person of Frances Perkins as secretary of labor. For the most part, the social and economic legislation of the New Deal gave equal treatment to women who were in a position to take advantage of it. The Wagner Act benefited women who were in a position to join unions and work for their own welfare. Various public assistance programs aided women and children as well as men. The social security system applied to qualified women workers as it did to men and also provided a measure of security to widows of covered workers.

There were no great triumphs specifically for women, however. Even World War II did not prove to be a boon to the cause of women's rights. Women entered the armed forces, but not in significant numbers. True, many women entered the labor market, and the working wife became a more common feature of our culture, but "Rosie the Riveter" was soon replaced by a returning veteran and she had to seek more feminine employment or get out of the labor market. Millions of male veterans took advantage of the GI Bill and entered college, while millions of "Rosies" returned to the kitchen stove and the dirty laundry.

The fifties were relatively quiet, characterized by the phenomenon of increasing numbers of women entering the labor force and larger numbers of women entering college and the professions. The sixties were a decade of increasing unrest and dissatisfaction on the part of women and the emergence of a new feminism.

THE NEW FEMINISTS: GROUPS, GOALS, AND TACTICS

Clearly the largest and most prestigious organization representing the new feminism in the sixties was the National Organization for Women (NOW). By the end of the decade, NOW could count nearly 200,000 members in 255 chapters in 48 states.[3] In addition, hundreds of other feminist groups with varying goals and viewpoints blossomed during the late sixties. In an article written for *The Movement Toward a New America*, Karen Durbin presented an overview of the movement in which she described six groups "whose differences of style and concentration" would present "a rough measure of the movement as a whole."[4] The six discussed included the following:

1. Citywide Women's Liberation Coalition
2. The Feminists
3. National Organization for Women (NOW)
4. Redstockings
5. The Stanton-Anthony Brigade of Radical Feminists
6. Women's International Terrorist Conspiracy for Hell (WITCH)

With the exception of NOW, which was largely dedicated to working within the system for legislative reform of discriminatory practices, all of these groups were militant and revolutionary in nature. For the most part, their spokeswomen saw very little hope that reform of existing institutions would solve the problems. Most called for destruction of the system, for revolutionary change. Although working for short-range goals such as the elimination of abortion laws and discrimination in employment and the establishment of day care centers, most of these groups were radical in their long-range goals. Some, like the Feminists and WITCH, declared that the institution of the family was oppressive and should be eliminated. Others, such as the Redstockings and the Stanton-Anthony Brigade, advocated consciousness-raising activities. Most had little use for men, blaming much of the oppressed condition of women on males. The Redstockings, for example, placed men at the top of their list of enemies. In the words of their *Manifesto*: "All other forms of exploitation and oppression (racism, capitalism, imperialism, etc.) are extensions of male supremacy: men dominate women, a few men dominate the rest."[5]

Even though the radical fringe of the new feminist movement called for revolutionary change, most women who were interested in the movement and took an active part in it tended to support the National Organization for Women. The demands of NOW posed no serious threat to the system. From its beginning, it has advocated equal rights on the state and national levels. Leadership in NOW has pushed hard for an equal rights amendment to the national Constitution and has been at the forefront of efforts for equal rights amendments and legislation on the state level. Willing to work within the system, they have pushed for legislation which prohibits discrimination in employment and in job promotion policies. In addition, the reform element in the feminist movement has been working for equality in education, more liberal abortion laws, and child care centers for working mothers.

Although the tactics of feminist groups varied according to their immediate and long-range goals, every group was involved in protest and confrontation. Some of the radical feminist groups attached themselves to radical left groups, such as the Panthers, the Weathermen, and the SDS, and held their own demonstrations in conjunction or cooperation with these groups. During the waning years of the sixties, many large cities experienced women's demonstrations which featured various acts of defiance along with speeches condemning the restrictions of a male-dominated society. State legislatures were occasional targets of marches by women demanding specific reforms. In March 1970, the movement was able to put together a march on Washington designed as a symbolic protest to sex discrimination in all its forms.

Perhaps the most widely used tactic of the feminist movement was an active pamphleteering effort. Various manifestos, lists of demands, and pointed criticisms of "male chauvinism" rolled off the presses after the mid-sixties. Again, the nature and tone of the pamphleteering was mixed, depending on the views of the organization or individuals sponsoring it. Moderate groups attempted to emphasize the hypocrisy and injustice in such practices as unequal employment and educational opportunities, and violations of the principle of equality in law and practice wherever they occurred. Radical groups launched a more strident attack. For example, a WITCH pamphlet distributed at New York's Bridal Fair in 1969 declared:

> Women were the first slaves, the first barter items way back when the monied economy and the patriarchical structure were just beginning. Ever since then, the pressure has been on women to marry ... or face rejection. ... An unmarried girl is considered a freak—a lesbian, a castrating career girl, a fallen woman, a bitch, unnatural, a frustrated old maid, sick.[6]

As one would expect, feminist leaders who were active in the field had a rather optimistic view of the future. In the words of Robin Morgan: "Radical feminism is digging in for the long haul, trying to build on women's needs in terms of women's anger. ... The movement is there and is growing very organically and logically and strongly."[7] Or Gloria Steinem, who stated:

> I believe the movement will surpass the civil rights movement—fundamentally—in bringing societal change. Black and white women have already made coalitions with each other because of it. SDS girls have made coalitions with lower middle class suburban women.[8]

Steinem saw great hope in the signs of change in the family structure:

> Engels said the nineteenth century paternalistic family system was the model for capitalism—that the father owned the wife, the means of production, and the children were the labor, and that society would never change until the family system changed. It has changed somewhat ... but we don't want to admit it and this makes for hypocrisy and tension. Women's Liberation is also man's liberation: from alimony, from childlike boring women, from unfair responsibility for another adult's life. When women really take responsibility for their own lives, it will be a very revolutionary change and a very good one.[9]

In spite of the feminist movement's hope for the future, perhaps no movement in history has been so seriously plagued with ambiguities, divisions, and indecisions. If there were serious differences in immediate and long-range goals *within* the feminist movement, the general population which was outside the movement—both male and female—was even more ambivalent. Militant feminism, if anything, encouraged mixed and ambivalent feelings concerning the role of women in American society. Even though the strident militancy has cooled some, it has left a legacy of concern and ambivalence on the part of many women who were involved in the heat of the struggle.

THE STATUS OF WOMEN—INCOME, EDUCATION, AND EMPLOYMENT

Although the traditional forms of political pressure and the activist tactics of radicals called attention to the problems of women in American society, there was little basic change in the role of women in that society. It was almost as if the feminist movement did not exist; it was a nonrevolution. The basic structure or institutions of the society—the family, marriage, social class, the labor market, the church and its practices, the school and its practices—would all have to be radically changed in order for full equality of the sexes to be realized. There is no existing force, nor any visible on the horizon, which would be strong enough to accomplish such sweeping change. This is not meant to imply that change has not taken place. There has been change. But the nature of the change has not been revolutionary; rather, it has been functionally system serving, as Table 11.1[10] illustrates.

One could conclude, from a cursory view of this profile, that women made great progress from 1920 to 1970. However, there is another way to interpret the change. Obviously, more women are working; they begin working earlier and stay in the labor force longer than was true a generation ago. Also, the kind of work women do has changed significantly. One could view these statistics as an indication that women have achieved more freedom and greatly expanded opportunities. On the other hand, one could view these developments more as a reflection of some rather basic changes in the occupational structure, which are not prima facie liberating forces for women. One could conclude from this changed profile not so much that women have been liberated as that they have become the new working underclass in a high technology economy.

Clearly, the nature of work changed dramatically from 1920 to 1970. Whereas the old working class of the 1920s was very largely comprised of immigrant male laborers and their sons who held industrial jobs, the new working class—which includes a large contingent of women workers—is more likely to be clerical and semitechnical in nature. The most rapidly expanding job opportunities in the new technology of the third quarter of the twentieth century were in services and retail trade. These are jobs which require minimal skills and little training—in offices, in the rapidly expanding retail enterprises, and in the food services and health services industries. Large numbers of women have entered the labor force in these jobs. For the most part, the pay is at the minimum wage level. The workers

TABLE 11.1
Profile of the Woman Worker

1970	*1920*
Age	
39 years old.	28 years old.
Marital Status	
Married and living with husband.	Single.
Occupation	
Most likely clerical. In the labor force outside the home, in factories, and in professional technical work. Five-hundred occupations open to women.	Most likely to be a factory worker. Clerical, private household, and farm work. Extremely limited occupations.
Education	
High school graduate with some college.	Not a high school graduate.
Participation in Labor Force	
Half of the adult women in the labor force.	Less than one-fourth the adult women in labor force.
Participation in labor force dropping at age 25 and rising again at age 35.	Participation rate dropping at age 25 and decreasing to old age.
Can expect to remain in labor force until retirement.	Tends to move out of labor force before middle-age.

are unorganized, and many are in dead-end jobs. The millions of women who operate the computers and the office machines and who work in fast food places and nursing homes could be viewed as the new working class in America. Ironically, the new jobs held by women may be more secure than the better-paying industrial jobs traditionally held by men. In recent years, industrial jobs have been disappearing at an alarming rate. However, the fact that change has occurred in the sexual composition of the work force does not necessarily mean that the women who worked in 1970 were relatively any better off than those who worked in 1920. Indeed, there is much evidence that women have not improved their condition relative to men in the work force.

Table 11.2[11] illustrates that women with the same number of years of schooling lag significantly behind men in income. Even more to the point, it illustrates that, at least during the 10-year period from 1967 to 1977, the gap in incomes remained fairly constant.

TABLE 11.2
Annual Median Income (Current Dollars) of Year-Round Full-Time Workers, 25 Years Old and Over by Sex and Educational Attainment: 1967–1977

	Male		Female	
Year	4 years of high school	4 years or more of college	4 years of high school	4 years or more of college
1967	$ 7,732	$11,571	$4,499	$ 6,796
1969	9,100	13,323	5,280	7,931
1971	9,996	14,351	5,808	9,162
1973	12,017	16,576	6,623	9,771
1975	13,542	18,450	7,777	11,359
1977	15,434	20,625	8,894	12,656

Women who worked full time over the 10-year period from 1967 to 1977 earned only about half as much as men at the same educational level who were employed full time. Remarkably, men with only four years of high school could be expected to earn more than women who had four years of college.

As the aggregate numbers seem to indicate, women have not benefited greatly, in terms of income, from their movement into new areas in the labor force. That is, it doesn't seem to matter much where one finds women in terms of occupation—their income is always significantly lower than males in the same occupation. Table 11.3[12] illustrates this phenomenon over a 10-year period.

TABLE 11.3
Median Earnings of Female Full-Time Workers as Percent of Males by Selected Occupational Groups: 1967–1977

Occupational Group	1967	1971	1975	1977
Professional/technical	66.2	68.6	65.9	65.8
Manager/administrator	54.4	56.2	56.7	54.2
Clerical	67.1	62.4	62.2	61.6
Sales	42.4	43.0	38.9	42.2
Operative	57.8	60.8	56.1	58.3
Service	56.5	59.5	57.1	61.2

As might be expected, women who find themselves in professional or technical occupations are closer to equity with men than are women in other groups. Even in professional and technical occupations, however, the differential is a large one. The remarkable thing about these data is their consistency. Even fluctuations in the economic system seem to have little impact on them. Whether the economy is booming or in recession, the income of women relative to men in the same occupational group tends to remain relatively stable.

Below the college level, educational attainment has not been a problem for women in this century. From 1899 to the present, more girls than boys completed high school. However, males were more apt than females to attend and graduate from college. In 1977, for example, 14.2 percent of all males over the age of 25 had achieved one to three years of college. The percentage for females was 12.7. In that same year, 19.2 percent of all males had completed four or more years of college, while only 12.0 percent of the female population had done so. There is some indication that this gap between men and women is narrowing at the bachelor's and master's levels. In 1977, for example, slightly more than 46 percent of the bachelor's degrees and 47 percent of the master's degrees were earned by women. However, in that same year, only 24.4 percent of the doctoral degrees and 18.7 percent of the first-professional degrees were awarded to women.[13]

In view of the hypothesis presented above, that women tend to be employed in minimal skill, "new technology" jobs at low pay, one would expect their unemployment rate to be not significantly greater than men's. This has been generally true in recent years. For example, during the decade of the seventies, the rate of unemployment for all women over 20 was consistently between one to two percentage points above that of men. Thus, in 1970, the unemployment rate for men was 4.4, for women, 5.9. In 1973, the figures were 4.1 for men and 6.1 for women. In 1977, 6.2 for men and 8.2 for women. For black females, the situation was much worse, with unemployment in the 1970s ranging from a low of 11 percent to a high of nearly 15 percent. As unemployment became more severe in the early 1980s, the gap between men and women closed. In mid-1982 the unemployment rate for white women over 20 stood at 7.3 percent. For white males over 20 it was 7.5 percent. For black males over 20 the figure was 15.5 percent, for black women 14.5 percent.

SPECIAL SCHOOL PROBLEMS

The schools have been criticized, and justly so, for perpetuating myths about women and for role stereotyping. In a culture where schools tend to reflect the society, this should come as no surprise. It isn't that the schools create problems for women; they merely reflect the norms of a society which seems to cherish traditional, and in some ways inferior, roles for women. The schools, after all, are functional, in the sense that they attempt to socialize children to existing roles. As suggested in the chapter on the socialization of students, schools often make serious efforts to support the existing social arrangements in the communities they serve. Very often these efforts include different treatment for girls and boys in the elementary and secondary schools.

The differences in treatment take many forms, and although sexism in the schools has been widely criticized, the practices have existed for many years and reform of the system is difficult— nor is the discrimination always against girls. In the elementary schools, it is the boys who often find themselves at a disadvantage. It has been suggested that the elementary school environment tends to favor girls. Neatness, good manners, and docility are often rewarded in the elementary school classroom. In the words of Patricia Sexton:

> Boys and the schools seem locked in a deadly and ancient conflict that may eventually inflict mortal wounds on both. .... The problem is not just that teachers are too often women. It is that the school is too much a woman's world, governed by women's rules and standards. The school code is that of propriety, obedience, decorum, cleanliness, physical and ... mental passivity.[14]

In the elementary school classroom, girls tend to make better grades and have fewer disciplinary problems than boys, and researchers have observed that girls tend to get more positive reinforcement from teachers than do boys.

However, as Frazier and Sadker point out,[15] elementary teachers who reward the characteristics of passivity are not doing girls any favors. Frazier and Sadker charge that by rewarding and reinforcing a passive approach the school "runs the risk of decreasing the female student's ability." Thus, the discrimination against girls, although more subtle, may be more harmful in the long run. Frazier and Sadker point out that in spite of the fact that girls may have an easier time of it in the elementary classroom setting the cards are stacked against them. Even with the push for affirmative action, men still outnumber women as elementary school principals. Thus, the male boss, in the form of the principal, tends to handle the problems which are too difficult for the classroom teacher (usually female). It is an environment in which the teacher is the "boss of the class; the principal is boss of the teacher." When the female teacher takes orders from a man, "the image of female inferiority and subservience does come across. ...."

There are many other ways in which the schools reflect the sex-role stereotypes of the society. In most schools, in spite of the existence of Title IX of the Education Amendments of 1972, sex-role stereotyping continues to exist. Physical education programs separate and treat boys and girls differently. In most cases, boys are given many more opportunities in this area. In her book *Born Female*, Caroline Bird observed that in many school counseling programs females are encouraged to seek out traditional female occupations.[16]

Much has been written in recent years of sexism in the curriculum.[17] It has been charged that in some texts females are depicted in undesirable and demeaning roles. In some texts boys are portrayed as heroic and brave while girls are seen as passive, fearful, and incompetent. In the words of Frazier and Sadker, if a girl

> wishes to read a biography about a famous American, she can turn for inspiration to Henry Hudson, Lewis and Clark, Robert Peary, Kit Carson, Davy Crockett, Buffalo Bill, Abraham Lincoln. ... If for any reason she would like to read about a woman, she also has a choice: Annie Oakley, Amelia Earhart, and more recently Shirley Chisholm.[18]

Although other biographies about women do exist, according to Frazier and Sadker one has to look a great deal harder to find them. In texts, "boys are portrayed as being able to do so many things; they play with bats and balls, they work with chemistry sets, they do magic tricks that amaze their sisters, they show initiative and independence. ..." Girls, on the other hand, "help with the housework, bake cookies and sit and watch their brothers—that is, assuming that they are present."[19]

To some extent, sex-role stereotyping has yielded to pressure from organized women's groups. In 1972, Scott, Foresman and Company was the first publisher to take action by providing "guidelines for improving the image of women in textbooks." By 1978, according to Bernice Neugarten, the National Education Association reported "that almost all major textbook publishers, nearly 40, had issued such guidelines."[20] Even so, many unrevised textbooks continue to be used.

Neugarten suggested that the schools continue to reinforce sex-role stereotypes in many other ways: "in the arrangement of physical space, as when kindergartens have a corner for the dollhouse which girls are expected to use; in music activities, when boys are offered the drums to play, and girls are offered the triangles; in social studies, when only traditional family roles are portrayed."[21] Of course, many other illustrations could be provided: in vocational education programs where woman are discouraged from enrolling in traditionally male areas; in math and science programs where girls, who were the best students on the elementary level, suddenly become incompetent on the secondary level; in vocational interest testing programs, where girls tend to do less well than boys in traditional male interest areas; and so on. This sort of sex-role stereotyping has been so well decumented in recent years that it has become common knowledge.

LEGAL GAINS

By almost any measure, women who claim discrimination on the basis of sex have a valid argument. This is true in spite of the fact that women have made some legal gains in recent years. Although Title IX of the Education Amendments of 1972 is clearly the most important piece of legislation for women, the struggle for equality has a long history.

The Fair Labor Standards Act of 1938, passed during the New Deal years, applied to both men and women in occupations which involved interstate commerce. For these workers, Congress was able to set minimum wages, provide for overtime pay, and limit hours of work. However, the Fair Labor Standards Act applied only to occupations involved in interstate commerce. Many jobs typically held by females—such as those in hotels and restaurants, laundries, offices, and retail stores—were exempted from the original provisions of the act.

An even more central issue, that of equal pay, was one which interested women's rights advocates for several decades. Partly as a result of pressure brought by women, several states enacted equal pay laws in the decade following

World War I. Few such laws were very effective, however, and those who were concerned about the issue of equal pay for equal work were able to find plenty of examples of discriminatory treatment. It wasn't until 1963 that Congress finally amended the Fair Labor Standards Act to require equal pay for equal work. Unfortunately, this provision covered little more than one-fourth of the total number of workers in the country and fewer than one in ten working women.

Women have this same problem in other areas where the national government has acted to provide benefits to workers. Although women as well as men are included in the federal-state system of unemployment, more women than men are employed in situations which are not covered by the program. That is, they are employed by small firms, by nonprofit organizations, in private households, or in certain positions in state and local government which are not covered by unemployment provisions. Women have faced problems with regard to sick leave and workmen's compensation. The major reason for women being absent from their jobs—childbearing—typically has not been covered by any kind of insurance against income loss.

Because of these problems and others, the "new feminism" of the sixties made serious efforts to improve the lot of the working woman. A major breakthrough came in Title VII of the Civil Rights Act of 1964, which simply provides that discrimination based on race, color, religion, national origin, or sex is prohibited. This title was administered by the Equal Employment Opportunity Commission (EEOC), which was fairly active in the sixties and early seventies in investigating complaints brought under the provisions of the act. The complaints charging discrimination brought by women after 1964 presented the commission with opportunities to define the law. Generally, the commission has ruled that an employer cannot refuse to hire women because of his own preferences or those of his customers, clients, or other employees.[22] Nor can women be denied employment because of stereotypes about women, or because the job would require supervision over men, late night work, heavy lifting, or other strenuous physical activity.

The commission has also ruled on the terms, conditions, and privileges of employment. Generally, Title VII has come to mean that employees are entitled to equality of treatment in wages and salaries. Promotion and seniority rules which discrimination have been ruled in violation of the act. Employment policies which discriminate against married women or women with children of any age have been struck down by the commission. Nor may an employer discriminate on the basis of sex with regard to hospital, accident, medical, or life insurance coverage. The commission has ruled that maternity leaves of up to six months can be taken without jeopardizing the worker's right to reinstatement without loss of seniority or other benefits.

The Equal Employment Opportunity Commission has also prohibited the advertising of positions on the basis of sex unless sex is a bona fide occupational qualification (for example, attendants in women's rest rooms or salespersons in women's dress shops). Thus, the various guidelines and rulings of the EEOC have provided a detailed and specific list of discriminatory practices which, in its opinion, violate the provisions of Title VII of the Civil Rights Act. Some of these rulings have been tested in the courts by employers who objected for some reason, but the track record of the rulings of the EEOC has been very good. The overwhelming majority of its decisions have been upheld by the courts.

In addition, women have gained legal rights in the form of an executive order. Executive Order 11246 (Equal Employment Opportunity), issued by President Johnson in 1967, merely implemented the provisions of congressional action. The order forbade companies holding federal contracts to discriminate on the basis of sex. Of course, this gave the enforcement agency, the EEOC, a more certain legal basis for its actions. It was from this order that the EEOC was able to issue guidelines forbidding discrimination against women with children, and it was this order which enabled the commission in 1972 to spell out the steps which any employer who benefited from federal contracts or federal funds had to take to become an equal opportunity employer with regard to women. These steps were very specific: an employer who benefited from federal funds of $50,000 or more and who had 50 or more employees was given 120 days in early 1972 to adopt programs with "specific goals and timetables for increasing and upgrading employment of women."[23]

The legal position of women was strengthened significantly by the passage of Title IX of the Education Amendments of 1972. Although patterned after Title VI of the Civil Rights Act of 1964, Title IX is much more specific. Its prohibits discrimination in federally assisted education programs against students and employees on the basis of sex. The major provision of Title IX reads: "No person in the United States shall, on the basis of sex, be excluded from participation in, be denied the benefits of, or be subjected to discrimination under any education program or activity receiving Federal financial assistance." Both Title VI and Title IX were enforced by the Office for Civil Rights in the Department of Health, Education, and Welfare. When the new Department of Education was created in 1980, the education functions of the Office for Civil Rights were transferred to the new department.

In the early seventies, aided by HEW guidelines which identified discriminatory practices, the Office for Civil rights enthusiastically worked for an end to discrimination in schools and colleges on the basis of sex. The Office for Civil Rights was busy examining a number of practices, largely in higher education, which appeared to discriminate on the basis of sex. These included practices in the recruitment of students, admissions to programs, and awarding of financial aid, as well as rules and regulations directed specifically against women—for example, restricting pregnant girls to certain activities, discriminatory housing rules, separate health care provisions for pregnant women, unequal employment opportunities for male and female students, discrimination in athletic programs, and a host of other areas.

Moreover, there can be little doubt that Title IX resulted in some significant changes. Rules which restricted participation of pregnant girls in school activities were changed, different standards of conduct for men and women in college dormitories were successfully attacked, more favorable loan programs for men became suspect—in a word, almost any distinction based on sex was open to challenge. The changes which occurred in sports provided a good illustration of the impact of Title IX on schools and colleges. Title IX had the effect of increasing rather dramatically girls' participation in sports. For example, in 1971, only 7 percent of high school athletes were girls. By 1978, this had increased to 30 percent. On the college level, Title IX resulted in a massive increase in athletic scholarships. Whereas in 1974 only 60 colleges offered women's athletic scholarships, in 1978 more than 500 offered them.[24]

The Women's Educational Equity Act, enacted by Congress in 1974 and extended and amended in 1976 and 1978, was designed to promote women's educational equality by permitting the secretary of education to encourage programs which benefited women. Although the act was poorly funded ($10 million in 1981), the Department of Education has collected and produced teaching resources, such as tapes and film strips, and has established the Sports Project Referral and Information Network, which has been active in assisting in the development of sports programs for women on all levels of schooling.

Although the courts have supported women in their struggle for equal treatment under the Constitution and the laws, they have tended in recent years to follow what has been termed a "meandering course."[25] In Reed v. Reed,[26] while striking down an Idaho law giving preference to males in the administration of estates, the Court said that sex classifications "must be reasonable, not arbitrary, and must rest upon some ground of difference having a fair and substantial relationship to the object of the legislation." In Frontiero v. Richardson,[27] the Supreme Court came close to defining sex as a "suspect classification" under the Fourteenth Amendment. In this case, the military services attempted to defend a policy under which males were permitted automatically to claim their wives as dependents, while females had to show that their husbands were actually financially dependent upon them. Although four justices held that sex is an inherently suspect classification, this did not constitute a majority of the Court. However, the Court did invalidate the practice as an "inherently invidious" form of sex discrimination. In Gedulig v. Aiello,[28] however, the same Court ruled that a California law which did not include coverage of normal pregnancy disability under its disability insurance system was not an "invidious discrimination" in violation of the Fourteenth Amendment. The Court declared that the policy did not discriminate against any definable class. In the Court's words:

> While it is true that only women can become pregnant, it does not follow that every legislative classification concerning pregnancy is a sex-based classification.

The Court had an interesting view of pregnancy:

> Normal pregnancy is an objectively identifiable physical condition with unique characteristics.

In upholding the California law, the Court agreed with California officials who were concerned that the inclusion of pregnancy coverage would either end the program's self-supporting nature or require a large increase in rates. The Court said:

> Absent a showing that distinctions involving pregnancy are mere pretexts designed to effect an invidious discrimination against the members of one sex or the other, lawmakers are constitutionally free to include or exclude pregnancy from the coverage . . . on any reasonable basis, just as with respect to any other physical condition.

Thus, the Court, in this case as in others, seemed to be searching for a way to avoid making sex a suspect classification under all conditions. What it seemed to be arguing was that sex might or might not be suspect. It appears that sex is a suspect classification only if it cannot be demonstrated that such a classification is necessary for some compelling state interest. Thus, sexual classifications meet constitutional tests where they are rational or where they are used in the legitimate interests of the state. What is rational or legitimate depends on how the courts define these terms in specific cases. Such vagueness gives little comfort to those who seek a clear definition of equal rights for women under the Constitution.

In cases involving local school practices and regulations which clearly discriminate against females, the courts have generally supported students who could make a good case. Many of these cases have involved alleged discrimination in sports programs, and the courts have tended to be sympathetic in cases where there have been blatant inequalities in programs for males and females. However, there is no landmark case to report in this area.

The courts have provided little comfort for women who are seeking equality through litigation. Even the meaning of Title IX was thrown into confusion in 1979, when a dispute arose over whether it was the intent of Congress to make Title IX apply to sex discrimination in all employment or merely student employment in educational institutions receiving federal money. HEW assumed that Title IX was intended to cover all employment and issued detailed regulations on sex discrimination covering all employment in such institutions. There followed a number of cases brought into the district courts by faculty women who charged the institution with sex discrimination. Several appeals courts held that HEW exceeded its authority when it issued regulations addressing sex discrimination for all employees. In November of 1979, the Supreme Court refused to review the lower court rulings, in effect supporting the limitations imposed by the lower courts.

In its 1980–81 term, the Court heard two important cases related to women's rights. In *Rostker v. Golberg*, the Court decided 6 to 3 that women could be constitutionally excluded from registering for the draft. Using the test established in *Craig v. Boren* (1976), the Court decided that registration for men only did not constitute sexual discrimination. In *Craig*, the Court required the government to show (1) that an important governmental interest was served by the law in question and (2) that the sex-based distinction was "substantially related" to achieving that governmental interest. In this case, which involved an Oklahoma law permitting 18-year-old females to purchase beer while establishing the legal age for men at 21, the Court found that these tests were not met. In other words, the law discriminated for no good reason. The Court found that good reason existed in the draft registration case because women could not reasonably be expected to serve in combat. Thus, even though the law was discriminatory, the discrimination was justified.

In a potentially more important case, *County of Washington v. Gunther* (1981), the Supreme Court dealt with the issue of comparable pay. Federal law prohibits wage discrimination between women and men doing equal work. Federal law does not require equal pay for comparable work. *County of Washington v. Gunther* was a case in which female jail guards argued that the fact that they were paid less than male guards was a violation of Title VII of the 1964 Civil Rights Act. In this case, the jobs were not equal. The duties of female guards were different from those of male guards. Even so, five justices agreed with the women guards. Justice Brennan, writing for the majority, argued that the intent of Title VII was to "strike at the entire spectrum of disparate treatment of men and women resulting from sex stereotypes." He felt that Title VII protected women even if their jobs were not exactly equal with men's. In his words: "The failure of the county to pay [women] the full evaluated worth of their jobs can be proven to be attributable to intentional sex discrimination."

Does this mean that women whose jobs are comparable to men's—even though not equal—are entitled to equal pay under Title VII? Not necessarily. Both the majority and the minority in this case agreed that the desicion did not mean that the principle of equal pay for comparable work was being established. Such a broadly based principle would mean, of course, that pay rates in virtually every job in the country would be open to legal challenge. Even so, feminist leaders were happy with the decision in that it did, however narrowly, expand the meaning of equal pay.

Perhaps the best that can be said of the legal standing of women is that it is unclear. The following words of Ginsburg are as true in the early eighties as they were in the seventies:

> constitutional law in this area, like the public debate on the roles of men and women, is in mid-passage state. Ratification of the Equal Rights Amendment would give the Supreme Court a clear signal—a more secure handle for its rulings than the fifth and fourteenth amendments. In the meantime, doctrine is evolving, but the Court is sharply divided and its future course is uncertain. As one district judge put it: lower court judges searching for guidance in the 1970's Supreme Court sex discrimination precedent have an "uncomfortable feeling"—like players at a shell game who are not "absolutely sure there is a pea."[29]

In spite of the confusion which surrounds the legal rights of women, progress has been made. Even though the courts have been unable to define clearly women's status under the Constitution, and even though many of the regulations which developed under Title IX are no longer valid, women are clearly in a stronger legal position than at any time in history. At least some forms of sex discrimination are illegal, and even though HEW may be out of the business of investigating most employment-related sex discrimination complaints against schools and colleges, there are many other avenues open to women who feel that they are being discriminated against. As Thomas Flygare suggested: "it must be recognized that these same complaints may be filed with other state and federal agencies for investigation and enforcement."[30]

THE "CAUSES" OF SEX DISCRIMINATION

Although it may be true that "women have never had it so good," it is also true that the genuine and documented discrimination against women is a major feature of American society. Women are working in increasing numbers; in the last decade they have made inroads into professional and technical jobs; as a group they have increased their educational level; new laws have been passed which provided them with a greater measure of equality. However, the income gap between men and women continues; many top positions are still effectively closed to women; there continues to be open discrimination in employment and pay; millions continue to be underemployed in terms of their educational and technical qualifications; and there has been only a sporadic effort on the part of women to use the law to challenge discriminatory practices.

Thus, the story of women in American society, particularly regarding their progress in the sixties and seventies in their struggle for equal rights, has been ambiguous and contradictory. At least part of the problem may be due to a lack of understanding of the problem or to the nature of the problem itself. The nature of the problem might be stated in the following proposition: The advocates of equal rights for women have had limited success because changes in existing practices and institutions are least likely to occur when contradictions between ideology and practice are poorly defined and there is no general consensus that a contradiction exists. Moreover, in the case of women, there may be no general agreement on who or what the enemy is.

On the issue of sex equality, there is a long tradition in America of contradictions between belief and practice which have never been clarified and on which there is no general consensus of belief. In direct terms, the contradiction in belief which exists may be expressed: "The sexes are equal but woman's place is in the home." The remarkable thing about this expression is that it contains a dual contradiction. It is a contradiction between two beliefs (equality and the "proper" role of women) and between belief and practice (women should have equal rights, but some practices which deny them are good practices). Nothing better illustrates this than the conflict among women over the Equal Rights Amendment. Lerner stated the problem nicely in *America as a Civilization:*

> Rarely in historic civilizations have women been as free, expressive, and powerful as in America; yet rarely also has the burden of being a woman, and trying to be a fulfilled one, been as heavy to carry. . . . She is torn between trying to vie with men in jobs, careers, business, and government, and at the same time find her identity as wife, mother, and woman. The tussle between them accounts in great measure for the ambiguous place she holds in American society. . . .[31]

Perhaps part of the explanation for the ambiguity regarding the role of the American woman lies in some generalized image of her which is deeply ingrained in the American system of beliefs. This image contains many contradictions between fact and belief which are promoted by the system, taught in the home and schools, and practiced in the society. In an article in *Trans-Action* in 1970, Marijean Suelzle outlined the dimensions of eight myths which surround the American woman and which point up some of the contradictions:

1. Women naturally don't want careers, they are only interested in jobs.
2. Women are more interested in personal development than in their careers.
3. There is greater turnover and absenteeism among women workers than men.
4. Women are not really working for essentials but for extras.
5. Women control most of the wealth and power in this country.
6. Women are a disruptive force on the job when they are mixed with men.
7. Woman are better than men at boring, tedious, and repetitive tasks and are more human oriented and less mechanical than men.
8. Women are smaller and need to be protected by men.[32]

The first five of these myths are generally related to economics and the way some people view women's attitudes toward working and careers. As Suelzle points out, it would be difficult to find factual support for any of these statements. It does seem unlikely that women who must work to support either themselves or their families would not be interested in a career. The interest in personal development refers to the popular image of the working woman who intends to get married, have children, and move out of the labor market. Although this may be true for some, it is by no means universally true. Indeed, as Suelzle points out, a significant number (10 percent) of all women remain single. Many others who work are widowed, separated, or divorced. It is unlikely that all women in this category are (1) solely interested in marriage and (2) therefore not interested in careers. Even for those who are married and employed, particularly in the professional and technical fields, it would be an oversimplification to declare that they are not interested in careers or that they are working not because they enjoy the experience but because they want a new rug for the living room. The notion about greater absenteeism for women is based on the feeling that women really are the weaker sex; that they are subject to more problems with their health; that they have to stay home to take care of sick children; or that they must take time off for childbearing. The facts are that women tend to be more stable than men in the same positions, and the differences between men and women for time lost for illness are insignificant.[33] Nor, according to Suelzle, do women control most of the wealth in American society. They do not own as many stocks as men, they are not dominant on corporate boards of directors, and they do not necessarily make the decisions about major expenditures on the family level.

The last three myths are directed at certain social and psychological conditions attributed to women by many in American society. The fact that some women constitute a disruptive force in a sexually integrated work situation is no more evident than the fact that some men do. The fact that some women make poor supervisors is no more a legitimate complaint against women than against men. The difficulty lies more in the long history of discrimination and resultant attitudes than in any hard data. The fact that women often work without complaint at tedious, boring, and repetitive tasks may be due more to prejudice and differences in educational background and training than to any innate differences between the sexes. And the need for protection is more a cultural bias than anything else, according to Suelzle.[34]

Finally, to some extent at least, there is no consensus among women themselves on who or what the real enemy is. The more conservative groups seem content to work within the system, to change the institutional practices of the society so that they at least do not work against women. The more radical element in the women's movement continues to insist that in some cases the enemy is a male-dominated society and the traditional institutions of that society which must be seriously modified before change can occur. Ironically, a major institution in the society, which both groups seem to agree needs to be changed most significantly is the family. As Betty Friedan points out in *A New Feminist Manifesto*,[35] both groups may be beating a dead horse. She claims that criticism of the traditional family as an obstacle to full equality for women may be misdirected. She bases this claim on the observation that the traditional family may no longer exist if it is defined in terms of the traditional roles of mother-homemaker, father-breadwinner, and children all living under the same roof. Friedan argues that the family of the past no longer exists. Only 17 percent of the households in the United States include a breadwinner-father and a homemaker-mother. Twenty-eight percent have two breadwinners; 32.4 percent consist of one person living alone; and the rest are various forms of single-parent households. Thus, to oppose women's rights arguments on the basis that what they propose will devastate the traditional American family is to engage in fantasy.

Nonetheless, Friedan argues that the family as it realistically (not nostalgically) exists should be a genuine women's rights issue. The real issues, according to Friedan, do not center around the existence of some nostalgic notion of the family but are issues around which all women can rally. These include equal representation in existing political and economic institutions, equal pay, equal pensions, health care for women and children, the specific problems of two-worker families, and, of course, the quality of life for children.

For whatever reasons, women continue to be second-class citizens. They continue to be subject to serious discrimination in many areas of life; they continue to suffer because of ambiguities in belief and contradictions between belief and practice; and they continue to find it difficult to reach agreement, even among themselves, on what their problems are.

But perhaps Suelzle and others miss the major point. In many ways, the myths are functional to the existing economic and social system. They justify discrimination which may be necessary to maintain the prevailing system. Thus, when one begins to come to grips with the cold statistics of discrimination, one finds that the data say as much about the condition and nature of the society as they do about the condition of women in that society. One could easily read from the statistics that an overwhelming majority of women work because they really have no other choice. For many this means that they have no other means of support—often they are single, widowed, or divorced women with children to support. In fact, nearly 40 percent of working women are in this situation. Many of those who are married and work are married to husbands who are unable to earn enough to provide even a minimum decent standard of living. Worse yet, such husbands have no way to improve their positions, for they are in such a marginal economic position that they can't return to school. Life is anything but easy for such working wives, for they must not only work a full week, often at dull and tiring jobs, but also must return to the home after a hard day and spend many more hours in the traditional role of homemaker. The overwhelming majority of working women may be more enslaved than liberated by their increasing opportunity to find employment.

Although clearly there is serious discrimination in education, jobs, and pay directed against all women in society, this discrimination is most vicious in its operation against those who have no choice but to accept it—those who must work. Nor are those who often are desperately insecure in their positions likely to be the ones who are in the forefront of a protest movement or litigants in a court case.

It does not require any deep insight to find the major causes for the conditions of sexual discrimination in education, jobs, and pay. The ambiguity about the role of women in American society mentioned above certainly has contributed to the educational, employment, and income problems faced by women. The educational experience itself is an ambiguous one, in which girls are encouraged to be feminine on the one hand but to be prepared to support themselves on the other. Women who succeed in professional careers are often envied, admired, and hated by their more domesticated sisters. Working women are willing to express deep dissatisfaction in situations where they are doing the same work as men for significantly less pay, but they often are unwilling to engage in any organized action to protest the situation.

Except on rare occasions and for special purposes, such as the suffrage movement and the more recent equal rights movement, women have been notoriously difficult to organize. In recent years, even the largest organization working for equal rights, the National Organization for Women, has been unable to gain more than a fraction of its potential membership. Even in fields which have an overwhelming number of women workers, such as elementary school teaching, existing organizations such as the American Federation of Teachers have had a ficult time organizing. The Classroom Teachers Association, which is an affiliate of the National Education Association, seems to have a greater attraction for female teachers. Although a few women teachers have participated in some militant activities as members of either the AFT or the CTA, these kinds of activities have been limited. Thus, even in organizations where it is possible for women to constitute a majority, they have acted not so much as women working for women's rights but more as professionals working for the improvement of the profession. In the cases of the AFT and the CTA, the militance has been clearly much more restrained than that of other organizations whose memberships have been overwhelmingly male. In other fields of work, the efforts of the AFL-CIO to organize white-collar workers, among whom there are large numbers of women, have been singularly unsuccessful.

Although the reasons for the reluctance of women to become actively involved in organizing for their own welfare or in working within exisiting organizations for the same purpose are not completely clear, a few observations can be made. Given the employment status of women—their low pay, the fact that large numbers of females are overtrained for the positions they hold, the consistently high rate of unemployment among women—it is possible that they are insecure in their positions and certainly open to intimidation by supervisors and employers. In addition, the centuries-long stereotypes of women as meek and subservient to men serve this situation admirably.

Although the problems of ambiguity concerning women's role and their inability to organize for their own welfare are serious enough, perhaps there is an even deeper reason for continued discrimination. Discrimination based on sex may very well be extremely functional to the existing social and economic system.[36] Sex discrimination in education, income, and employment is very functional to the existing system of social stratification. Educational and economic discrimination against women tends to encourage a kind of stability in American class structure. As Randall Collins put it: "There is a system of stratification by sex which is different from familiar forms of stratification by economic, political, or status group position, although it interacts with these other stratification systems."[37] For example, men with low educational attainment and low earning potential tend to marry women who are in the same situation or in an even worse position. It becomes necessary for both partners to work in order to avoid poverty. Often there is no escape from this situation without outside help, for it is extremely difficult for either partner to take time from work to improve skills or increase educational levels. The offspring of such marriages tend to follow the pattern of their parents. For the daughters, opportunities for upward mobility through marriage exist but are extremely limited. Even here, the customs and folkways of the system have an insidious way of underlining a most gross sort of inequality. It is obvious from the popular media that the most certain means to upward mobility for girls is a good marriage, and the most certain route to success in this endeavor is a stereotype of feminine beauty. Thus, the female in the society is bombarded from early life with the message that success comes not from work and education but from clear skin, white teeth, and the right measurements. Those who are not endowed by nature with such qualities and who fail in their attempts to fake them are destined to a life of tragic loneliness. The real tragedy in this image of the American girl is that she is distracted, from very early life, from much more deeply meaningful statistics, such as years of schooling, preparation for employment, and income.

Parents accept the beautiful but stupid female image, especially if they are poor and cannot afford lengthy and costly educational programs for their daughters. Without skills, the daughter finds it difficult to accomplish this on her own. For most, education provides the best opportunity for gaining a marketable skill as quickly as possible. In practical terms, this usually means some vocational program in high school or a short post-high school period of training in such skills as those required for white-collar office work or for sales work in retail establishments. This is not an unrealistic assumption in view of the fact that recent data indicate that an overwhelming number (64 percent) of young working women in metropolitan areas are classified as white-collar workers. This assumption is also supported by the data on incomes cited above, which indicate that median earnings for all full-time women workers have been consistently about 55 to 60 percent of the earnings for men with identical educational attainment.

Thus, the major hope of the daughters of the poor for removing themselves from the particular social class into which they were born is through a good marriage. Admittedly, most are better off than their mothers in an absolute material sense; but relative to the population, their chances of remaining in the bottom strata of society are very high. Moreover, this more or less rigid stability is functional to the economic system. In the first place, it is a smoothly operating system in the sense that it does not permit a rapid or radical modification of the system of social stratification. More importantly, in economic terms, the system insures that large numbers of low-income workers are available to do some of the important work of the system. Nothing could better illustrate this point than the outcry of the business community as a result of the decision in *County of Washington v. Gunther*. In response to the decision of the Supreme Court, which appeared to suggest that even comparable work should be guided by the principle of equal pay, the editors of *Fortune* insisted that the marketplace, not the Court, should determine wages. Not just the business community but also school counselors and teachers and even husbands and fathers contribute (perhaps unwittingly) to the perpetuation of the system in the advice and counsel they give to wives and daughters and in the educational opportunities which are provided for them.

This is not meant to imply that women are totally trapped or that as a group they have made no gains. Indeed, women have made some gains that are dramatic. The most dramatic gains have been in changes in the law—earlier with regard to the legal right to vote and more recently with regard to the equal rights movement. Even though serious discrimination exists, it is true that women have been able to vote since ratification of the Nineteenth Amendment. It is also true that the Civil Rights Act of 1964 prohibited discrimination on the basis of sex and that this provision was measurably strengthened by the executive order of President Johnson in 1967 and by guidelines provided by the Equal Employment Opportunity Commission. Women have made some progress through the EEOC guidelines and in the courts in invalidating many state laws which provided for discrimination in employment and education. Finally, Title IX has provided a measure of equality. However, there still remains a serious gap between what is fact and what is law. Serious sex discrimination in the country exists as a fact, and the legal framework which has developed to combat it flies in the face of years of practice and a social and economic structure which, to some extent at least, depends on the continuation of such discrimination.

Thus, the advocates of equal rights for women have had extremely limited success. Existing practices and institutions are slow to change, in no small part because they are dependent upon maintenance of the status quo. They are slow to change in a situation where an overwhelming majority of the population sees no real problem, where attitudes toward women are ambiguous and contradictory, and where there is no consensus on what should be done.

NOTES

1. Diana Reiche, ed., "Women and Society," *The Reference Shelf* (New York: H. H. Wilson Co., 1972), p. 109.
2. For a thorough description of the history of American feminists from the colonial period to 1920, see Eleanor Flexner, *Century of Struggle: The Women's Rights Movement in the United States* (Cambridge, Mass.: Harvard University Press, 1959).
3. *Time*, 20 March 1972, p. 29.
4. Karen Durbin, "Alphabet Soup," in *The Movement Toward a New America*, ed. Michael Goodman (New York: Alfred A. Knopt, 1970), p. 65.
5. Ibid., p. 67.
6. Marie Stamberg, "Marry or Die—The New Feminism," in *The Movement Toward a New Feminism*, ed. Michael Goodman (New York: Alfred A. Knopf, 1970), p. 48.
7. Reiche, *Women and Society*, p. 41.
8. Ibid., p. 51.
9. Ibid., p. 52.
10. Adapted from the U.S. Department of Labor, Women's Bureau, April 1970. Published in U.S., Congress, House, Special Sub-Committee on Education Hearings, 91st Cong., 2nd sess., Pt. 2, July 1970, p. 1042.
11. Source: U.S. Department of Commerce, Bureau of the Census, Consumer Income, Report P–20 (Washington, D.C.: U.S. Government Printing Office, 1977).
12. Source: U.S. Department of Commerce, Bureau of the Census, Consumer Income, Money Income and Poverty Status of Families and Persons in the United States (Washington, D.C.: U.S. Government Printing Office , 1977), p. 60.
13. National Center for Education Statistics, *The Condition of Education* (Washington, D.C.: U.S. Government Printing Office, 1979), p. 230.
14. Patricia Sexton, "Are Schools Emasculating Our Boys?" *Saturday Review*, 19 June 1967, p. 57.
15. Nancy Frazier and Myra Sadker, *Sexism and Society* (New York: Harper & Row, 1973), pp. 86–106.
16. Caroline Bird, *Born Female: The High Cost of Keeping Women Down* (New York: Pocket Books, 1969).
17. See Jerry Lynch, "Equal Opportunity or Lip Service? Sex Role Stereotyping in the Schools," *Elementary School Journal* 76 (October 1975): 20–23.
18. Frazier and Sadker, *Sexism and Society*, p. 104.
19. Ibid., p. 105.

20. Bernice L. Neugarten, "Women in Education," chapter 18 in *Society and Education*, 5th ed., ed. Robert J. Havighurst and Daniel U. Levine (Boston: Allyn & Bacon, 1979), p. 497.

21. Ibid.

22. A summary of the activities of the Equal Employment Opportunity Commission in the sixties is condensed from the testimony of Sonia Pressman, Senior Attorney, EEOC, before the Special Sub-Committee on Education of the Committee on Education and Labor of the House of Representatives, 91st Cong., 2nd sess., Pt. 2, July 1970, pp. 1037–1041.

23. *Congressional Quarterly*, 18 March 1972, p. 599.

24. Mariann Pogge, "From Cheerleader to Competitor," *Update on Law Related Education* (No. 4, June 1978: American Bar Association), p 18. For a less optimistic view of gains achieved through legislation, see Kathryn G. Heath, "Educational Equality: How Long Must Women Wait?" *Educational Studies* 12 (Spring 1981): 1–21.

25. Ruth B. Ginsburg, "Sex Equality and the Constitution: The State of the Art," *Women's Rights Law Reporter* 4 (Spring 1978): 143.

26. *Reed v. Reed*, 404 US 71 (1971).

27. *Frontiero v. Richardson*, 411 US 677 (1973).

28. *Gedulig v. Aiello*, 417 US 484 (1974).

29. Ginsburg, "Sex Equality and the Constitution," p. 147.

30. Thomas J. Flygare, "Schools and the Law," *Phi Delta Kappan* 62 (February 1980): 419.

31. Max Lerner, *America as a Civilization* (New York: Simon & Schuster, 1957), p. 599.

32. Marijean Suelzle, "Women in Labor," *Trans-Action* 7 (November/December 1970): 50–58.

33. Ibid., p. 55.

34. Ibid., p. 58.

35. Betty Friedan, *A New Feminist Manifesto* (New York: Summit Books, 1981).

36. For an analysis of this position, see Randall Collins, "A Conflict Theory of Sexual Stratification," *Social Problems* 19 (Summer 1971): 3–21.

37. Ibid., p. 5.

12

Mainstreaming: The Handicapped and the Schools

In recent years a new group of parents has entered the struggle for equality of educational opportunity for their children. Parents whose children have mental and physical handicaps have become vocal in their demands for adequate educational opportunities. In many ways, their struggle has been even more difficult than that of minorities and women, for they have been ignored and neglected by the society and the schools to a greater extent than perhaps any group in society. Added to the burden of many handicapped individuals is the fact that there are many in their number who are members of minority groups.

The problem of schooling for the estimated 4 to 6 million handicapped children in the United States has been plagued with many difficulties. No one knows exactly how many there are, since there is a serious problem of definition. Even the more obvious handicaps have been difficult to classify. For example, legal definitions of deafness and blindness have been arbitrary and tend to lump people who have a wide range of problems into a single group. Classifications such as mentally retarded or emotionally disturbed pose even more difficult problems. Mental and personality tests which have been used by schools to help classify children with learning or personality problems are crude measures at best. Although teachers' judgments may be a bit more reliable, they too are very subjective and prone to error.

One classified, however crudely, what to do with children who have handicaps has been a problem which the schools have been unable to deal with in any satisfactory manner. The schools have tended to reflect the attitudes of the general society toward handicapped people. Unfortunately, until very recently, those attitudes have been characterized by apathy, ignorance, and prejudice. Historically, school officials would reject the worst cases, that is, send the severely handicapped children home. The schools' position was that they had no responsibility for these children. The less severely handicapped who were accepted by the schools were sometimes even worse off than those who were rejected. In the past, such children were often expected to perform in competition with their nonhandicapped peers in classrooms where they were given no special consideration. For many handicapped children, this was a system designed for failure.

Recognizing these problems, some schools and some entire state school systems established special programs for the handicapped. When a state legislature or a concerned local school board mandated educational programs for handicapped children, programs were developed which were not always in the best educational interests of the handicapped. There were many abuses, since the mandated programs often left to school officials the identification and classification of students as well as the development of educational programs. Given the imperfections of diagnosis and testing, it was not uncommon to find programs which had normal children enrolled in classes for the mentally retarded; children with vastly different problems treated as if they had the same problem; and the segregation and isolation of handicapped children from the rest of the school population. Added to these problems was the use of culturally biased IQ tests, which resulted in many minority children being misclassified as mentally retarded. Perhaps the most serious abuse of all was the misuse of special education programs by classroom teachers who, when they were unable for whatever reason to cope with children in their classrooms, recommended that the children be removed from the class and placed in special education classes. This situation became so bad in some schools that special education classes for the mentally handicapped in fact became dumping grounds for the school's discipline problems.

This sad chapter in the treatment of handicapped children was in the process of coming to an end by the close of the 1970s. The sixties and seventies saw the emergence of a comprehensive legal framework for the protection and assistance of handicapped adults and children. What follows outlines this legal framework and presents some illustrative cases brought by parents and friends of the handicapped in the interest of protecting and defining their rights. Since there are hundreds of such cases brought in state and federal courts each year, the cases presented are merely illustrative of the nature and scope of the problem. The cases selected do demonstrate, however, the determination of parents of handicapped children to overcome the traditional inequities which were visited upon their children, and a continued effort on the part of schools to reflect the general attitudes of neglect and apathy found in the society.

THE LEGAL FRAMEWORK

Legal protection of the handicapped has a relatively short history. Briefly, four major national laws have applied to the issue of education for the handicapped. These include: (1) The Rehabilitation Act of 1973; (2) Title VI of the Civil Rights Act of 1964; (3) The Education For All Handicapped Children Act (Public Law 94–142, 1975); and (4) The Educational Rights and Privacy Act of 1974.

Section 504 of the Rehabilitation Act can be applied to any school receiving federal funds. It provides that "no otherwise qualified handicapped individual . . . shall, on the basis of his handicap, be excluded from the participation in, be denied the benefits of, or be subject to discrimination under any program or activity receiving federal financial assistance." Discrimination is prohibited in employment, program accessibility, health, welfare, social services, and education. The act provides that every recipient of federal funds which operates a public elementary or secondary education program shall provide, either directly or through referral, a free and appropriate public education to each qualified handicapped person regardless of the nature or severity of the person's handicap. The act further provides that all educational placement shall be in "the least restrictive educational environment with the maximum degree of integration with the non-handicapped as is appropriate for the handicapped student." The regulations describe evaluation and placement procedures and establish procedural safeguards for the handicapped. The act insures the handicapped of equal access to extracurricular services, counseling services, physical education, and athletics.

Title VI of the Civil Rights Act of 1964, as amended in 1970, states that "No person shall . . . on the ground of race, color, or national origin, be excluded from participation in, be denied the benefits of, or be subjected to discrimination under any program or activity receiving federal financial assistance." Section 200d applies to handicapped children or those so identified who are in the minorities named in this act.

The major provisions of the Education for All Handicapped Children Act of 1975 (P.L. 94–142) include:

1. A formula for providing funds for handicapped school children.
2. The submission by each state of a plan which assures complete due process, nondiscriminatory testing and evaluation, and the "least restrictive" educational environment.
3. The development of an individualized written program for each handicapped child.
4. The empowering of the U.S. Commissioner of Education to cut off all federal funds if noncompliance is found.

The Educational Rights and Privacy Act of 1974 has been almost completely restated in section 121.1 15 of the Education For All Handicapped Children Act. Data confidentiality is spelled out in great detail, as are policies and procedures of records keeping and the use of records. Briefly, records cannot be kept and used without written consent of parents; parents must be informed, in their own language, of what procedures are being followed and what things are in the records; parents are to be notified of their rights under the law and they must understand that they have the right to inspect their child's record and to remove materials from the record.

THE COURTS AND THE HANDICAPPED

As pointed out in Chapter 10, in *Lau v. Nichols* (1974), the U.S. Supreme Court ruled that San Francisco's failure to take affirmative steps to address the language difficulties of non-English-speaking Chinese students constituted a violation of

Title VI of the Civil Rights Act of 1964. The Court said: "Basic English skills are at the very core of what these public schools teach. Imposition of a requirement that, before a child can effectively participate in the educational program, he must already have acquired those basic skills is to make a mockery of public education. We know that those who do not understand English are certain to find their classroom experiences wholly incomprehensive and in no way meaningful."

Lau is important to the issue of equal educational opportunity for the handicapped even though it did not deal specifically with legislation on the handicapped, since its findings have been applied to alleged discrimination by schools against a variety of handicaps in addition to language.

Hundreds of cases have been brought in federal district courts since the passage of the Rehabilitation Act of 1973 and P. L. 94–142. Most of these have been civil actions in which plaintiffs or defendants have asked the courts to clarify or define the law or to determine if existing state programs were in compliance with recent national law. This latter situation has created a blizzard of litigation in federal courts, since both those identified as handicapped and school officials were eager to determine the constitutional standing of their own state laws for special education as well as to determine the impact of P.L. 94–142 on their programs. Ironically, the states which were most progressive in developing their own programs of special education over the last decade or two found themselves with the greatest legal tangles. This problem existed largely because the Rehabilitation Act of 1973 and P.L. 94–142 constitute a radical departure from what was the conventional wisdom on special education. For several decades, schools had assumed that the best way to deal with special educational problems was through separate and special treatment. The major concern seemed to be dealing with the educational problems of handicapped students; little thought was given to the Fourteenth Amendment provisions of "equal protection of the laws" or "due process of law." With the enactment of the Rehabilitation Act and P.L. 94–142, every program in the country became legally suspect. Indeed, the philosophy of the statutes was a reversal of nearly everything that had been done in the interest of the education of the handicapped for three decades or more.

In hundreds of cases since 1975, courts have been called upon to decide technical legal issues. Although the cases cover a wide range of problems, many of them can be grouped under a small number of headings. These include: identification and evaluation, placement and programming, due process, and accessibility. The cases which follow are grouped under these headings even though most of them involve more than a single legal issue. The classifications are arbitrary and are made for the convenience of the discussion. It should be noted that the cases reported here comprise only a small fraction of the total number of cases. They do, however, illustrate the scope and nature of the problem.[1]

IDENTIFICATION AND EVALUATION

If there is a definitive case dealing with legislation on the handicapped it would have to be *Mattie T. v. Holladay*.[2] The plaintiffs in this case challenged the entire educational system in the state of Mississippi, charging that no program was available that would meet the special needs of children in that state. The case involved 40,000 children in Mississippi and more than 4 million children nationally. In this class action on behalf of 26 handicapped children in Mississippi, the plaintiffs charged that state and local school officials failed to meet the federal statutory and constitutional duties created by the Education For All Handicapped Children Act, the Rehabilitation Act of 1973, the Elementary and Secondary Education Act of 1965, the Fourteenth Amendment, and Section 1983 of the Civil Rights Act of 1875. Specifically, they charged that the state failed to: (1) provide any services for handicapped children; (2) provide adequate educational services to many other children; (3) provide fundamental procedural safeguards in decisions involving the identification, evaluation, and placement of handicapped children; and (4) eliminate racially discriminatory tests and evaluation procedures to identify and place children in special education classes. The court found for the plaintiffs on all counts and ordered the state, under the Education For All Handicapped Children Act of 1975, to file a statewide program for fiscal year 1978 for the approval of the court.

On February 22, 1979, the United States district court defined several provisions of Public Law 94–142. In effect, the court ordered Mississippi to provide adequate programs for all children between the ages of 6 and 20 who were considered to be handicapped by the school officials in the schools they attended. The court established specific criteria for determining when the school could place students in special programs separate from the main body of students. The court decreed that outside experts should be used in the testing of students to assess the extent of their handicaps and to determine how students should be classified and placed. Local schools in the state system were ordered to provide compensatory education programs for children who had been misclassified and damaged educationally from such misclassification. Due process was defined, in that the court prohibited schools from expelling students for more than three days and required each three-day dismissal to be accompanied by a hearing. Finally, parents were to be notified of the rights of handicapped children and the state department of education was established as the monitoring and enforcement agent.

In New York City, the District Court for the Eastern District of New York heard a case[3] involving the evaluation and placement of handicapped children living in New York City. The case was in behalf of all handicapped children between the ages of 5 and 21 living in New York City who, it was charged, had not been promptly evaluated and placed in appropriate educational programs. Action was brought under Public Law 94–142 and Section 504 of the Rehabilitation Act of 1973. The court ruled in favor of the plaintiffs, finding that the defendant school district had not provided a free and appropriate public education in the least restrictive environment as required by law. The school district was ordered by the court to provide an educational evaluation within 30 days and to establish an appropriate educational program within 30 days after the evaluation. The New York City schools were ordered to conduct a district-by-district census of all handicapped children under 12 and to set up a program to aid in their proper placement. The school system was further ordered to establish a team consisting of a principal, a guidance counselor, a psychologist, a social worker, an educational evaluator, and regular or special education teachers to serve all children who were in need of evaluation and placement. Moreover, the court ordered that students with limited English proficiency were to be evaluated in their native language or "mode of communication." Parents were to be informed of their children's rights under the laws. In addition, the school system was ordered to make all facilities housing handicapped children accessible to the physically and mentally handicapped. The school system was ordered to provide a plan which assured that "all students have full access within a reasonable distance from their homes to all services from which they are capable of benefitting including, but not limited to, gymnasiums, libraries, lunchrooms, auditoriums and other mainstreaming opportunities. . . ." Finally, the school system was ordered to prepare monthly reports on the plans and their progress and to assess staff needs for preservice and inservice training of all newly hired persons who were to work with the handicapped. In sum, the school system was ordered to come up with a specific and detailed plan which would provide substantially equal educational opportunities for all handicapped children in the system.

PLACEMENT AND PROGRAMMING

A major problem which has developed as school officials have attempted to implement state and national laws on special education and education for the handicapped is the misplacement of students. Many school officials have been somewhat loose in their identification of special education students. In hundreds of schools, normal minority children have been classified as special education students. Those who have felt victimized by these practices have sued.

In *Hernandez v. Porter* (1975, 1978),[4] a class action suit in Michigan, Spanish-speaking students alleged that they were incorrectly placed in special education classes and as a result were damaged by the experience. They demanded remedial education services and money damages. Although in this case the court ruled for the defendants and decided that school officials had acted within their legal rights, the court did order the Detroit school system to initiate a series of actions designed to protect students against misclassification. These included such things as reevaluation of Latino students by a Latino psychologist, provision for some remedial services to get students back into the regular program, and correction of student records where errors had been made. The case was back in court in 1978 when plaintiffs charged school officials with neglect in implementing the order. In a similar case, *Lora v. Board of Education of the City of New York*,[5] action was brought on behalf of emotionally disabled black and Hispanic students in need of special education. They alleged that the special day schools established for them were "dumping grounds" for minorities. Claiming that procedures for assignment were vague and subjective, they alleged that their civil rights were being violated. The court declared that recommendation for placement in special schools could be justified only if the treatment provided there was appropriate for the needs of the child. This finding was based on law, i.e., the Education For All Handicapped

Children Act of 1975. There was, in the court's view, both a constitutional and a statutory right to adequate treatment. In this instance, the court found that there was a prima facie case of racial discrimination in violation of the Constitution and an unacceptable educational program in violation of the law.

State and federal courts may be willing to become deeply involved in determining what schools must do in order to meet the requirements of P.L. 94–142. Such was the case of a Colorado district court in *Lopez v. Salida School District* (1977).[6] Lopez, identified as a handicapped student, had been excluded from school for three years. He claimed he was denied a free public education, an appropriate program written especially for his needs, and due process of law. The court agreed on all counts. It directed the Salida school system to provide Lopez with a program designed for his needs as well as tutorial, psychological, and counseling services. Moreover, the local school board was directed to provide Lopez' attorneys with periodic progress reports twice each academic school year.

A landmark case on placement occurred in California in the late seventies. In *Larry P. v. Riles*,[7] the parents of black children challenged the placement process for classes for the educable mentally retarded (EMR) for the entire state of California. California was using standardized individual intelligence tests as a means of classifying students. As it turned out, black students were overrepresented in EMR classes. Although black students in California constituted only 10 percent of the school population, 22.6 percent of them were enrolled in EMR classes. In this case, the court found prima facie evidence that placement of students in EMR classes was discriminatory. The court found that IQ testing had a history of racial prejudice. Even worse, once students were placed in EMR classes, they were neglected. According to the court's findings, the program in California operated not to correct deficiencies and return students to regular programs, but to segregate and trap students in the EMR program. The court determined from the evidence presented that the overrepresentation of blacks in the EMR classes was not a result of chance and could not be explained by a slightly higher incidence of mild retardation on the part of black children. The court pointed out that Section 504 of the Rehabilitation Act of 1973 prohibited discrimination against the handicapped and specifically "seeks to protect students from erroneously being denied admission to regular classes." The court also found that Public Law 94–142 provided procedural protections, including protections against the use of racially or culturally discriminatory evaluation techniques. The court held that it was the responsibility of the school system to demonstrate that the evaluation tools were valid and suited for the purposes for which they were used. California failed to do this. The court found discriminatory intent in the California program and charged that it reflected an intent to segregate students by race.

DUE PROCESS

There have been hundreds of cases in recent years involving due process. Indeed, most of the cases cited above involved the claim on the part of the plaintiffs that their constitutional and legal rights to due process had been violated. Due process cases have involved teachers as well as students.

In *Hairston v. Drosick* (1974),[8] the Supreme Court of North Dakota ruled that due process had been denied a mentally competent student with spina bifida by excluding him from regular classes. In this case, the student was unable to control his bowels. The court reasoned that there "must be a compelling educational justification" to deny a handicapped student access to a regular class. The court found that exclusion of the student without notice and hearing denied procedural due process. Regulations formulated by HEW under the Rehabilitation Act of 1973 provide for full notice and an extensive hearing before an impartial person; these were not provided in this case. However, a Missouri court ruled against the plaintiff in a similar case in 1977 (*Sherer v. Waier*).[9]

In *Rainey v. Tennessee Department of Education* (1976),[10] the Chancery Court of Tennessee ruled that not providing a special education program for the handicapped was a violation of the plaintiff's due process of law. In answer to the plea by the state department of education that funds were not available, the court expressed the view (although it did not rule on the issue) that "where there is a shortage of funds the whole program must suffer without discrimination as to members of a minority class." This ruling was upheld in 1977 by the Tennessee Court of Appeals.

In *Frederick L. v. Thomas* (1977),[11] the district court for eastern Pennsylvania ruled that the failure of the Philadelphia schools to provide a suitable education for students with perceptual handicaps was a violation of equal protection of the laws and denied the plantiffs due process of law. The court observed that the school district was providing normal children with appropriate free public education while denying the same opportunity to the plaintiffs.

A case in Virginia, *Kruse v. Campbell* (1977),[12] involved a number of issues in addition to that of due process. This case challenged Virginia's program in special education, which provided up to 75 percent of the cost of special education. The plaintiffs in this case argued that the program was discriminatory since it subsidized the rich and provided nothing for the poor, who could not raise the additional 25 percent. The court agreed, indicating that the Virginia system was in violation of the Constitution as well as in conflict with P.L. 94–142. In citing *San Antonio Independent School District v. Rodriguez*,[13] in which the Supreme Court indicated that the absolute denial of public education would not be constitutionally acceptable, the court ruled that the Virginia program constituted "discriminatory exclusion from educational opportunity," violated the equal protection clause, and was "irrational and failed to further any legitimate state interest." This case went to the Supreme Court in October of 1977; the Supreme Court vacated and remanded the case with directions to the lower court to decide the claim based on Sec. 504 of the Rehabilitation Act of 1973.

In some due process cases the courts have relied on the Rehabilitation Act of 1973 in determining the justice of claims made by plaintiffs. Must a college provide deaf students with an interpreter? Yes, said the district court in South Carolina in *Barnes v. Converse College* (1977).[14] The court indicated that not providing the student with assistance constituted discrimination expressly prohibited by the Rehabilitation Act of 1973 as well as a denial of due process under the Fourteenth Amendment.

Due process has been involved in employment policies regarding handicapped persons. In *Gurmankin v. Costanzo* (1976),[15] the court ordered the school district to employ the plaintiff, a blind person, as an English teacher. The school had not permitted the plaintiff, Ms. Gurmankin, to take the employment examination. The court judged this action to be a violation of the Fourteenth Amendment and Section 504 of the Rehabilitation Act of 1973.

In another case involving employment,[16] a blind teacher charged school officials with discriminatory policies because they refused to hire him as a school administrator. The school district officials claimed that the reason they refused to hire Mr. Upshur was because he did not meet the qualifications for the position. In this case, the court supported the position of the school district since it found that the district had no policy which would discriminate against blind persons as a class.

P.L. 94–142 has extended the application of due process. In *Stuart v. Nappi* (1978),[17] a Connecticut district court made some interesting legal points. The court would not permit the expulsion of a handicapped student who had been disruptive in class on the grounds that "the right to education in the least restrictive environment may be circumvented if the schools are permitted to expel handicapped chidren." On disciplining the handicapped, the court said: "Handicapped children are neither immune from a school's disciplinary process nor are they entitled to participate in programs when their behavior impairs the education of other children." What was clear to the court in this case was that there was a procedure which was outlined by the Education For All Handicapped Children Act which had to be followed.

There have been a number of cases on the issue of due process as it relates to discipline in the schools. In *Mrs. A. J. v. Special School District No. 1*,[18] a junior high student was expelled for 15 days as a result of a fight at school. A conference was held with the student. It was the third time the student had been expelled during the school year for similar problems. During the suspension the student was evaluated, and the school officials recommended that she be placed in a special program. Her mother challenged the placement, arguing that her daughter had been denied due process of law in her dismissal from school and that the placement in the special program violated P.L. 94–142. The court found that the suspension process which was used was in violation of state statutes insuring adequate due process for cumulative suspensions. The court could find no violation of the student's constitutional rights or her rights under P.L. 94–142.

The major concerns of the courts in discipline issues seem to rest on the circumstances of the case. If the discipline problem is of such a nature as to create a serious threat to other children or to school property, and if the school officials observe due process and act in good faith in seeing that the suspended student is not deprived of educational opportunity, there is a good chance that the courts will support the schools. Lacking any of these conditions, the school is in a weak position vis-à-vis the courts. For example, in *Turlington*,[19] when nine handicapped students were expelled for almost two years without due process hearings and with no effort made to evaluate their emotional problems, the court ruled in favor of the students. The court said that, under the law, the schools were responsible for providing adequate due process hearings, for having students evaluated by competent persons, and for providing an educational program that would suit the students' particular needs.

ACCESSIBILITY

In recent years, several cases involving accessibility to programs and employment by handicapped persons have been brought to court. As in other areas involving the rights of handicapped persons, the courts have tended to view each case on its merits and have attempted to reach a reasonable conclusion in each case. In a case heard by the United States Supreme Court[20] in 1979, the Court supported Southeastern Community College in denying admission to its nursing program to a student with a serious hearing disability. The student charged that she was being denied her rights under Section 504 of the Rehabilitation Act. In reviewing the case, the Supreme Court said that Section 504 does not mean that "a person need not meet legitimate physical requirements in order to be . . . qualified." The student argued that Section 504 required that programs be modified in ways which would make it possible for handicapped persons to enter any program. In the absence of such effort, the student charged, the school was acting in a discriminatory manner. The Court pointed out that "the line between lawful refusal to extend affirmative action and illegal discrimination against handicapped persons will not always be clear," but in this case the school's unwillingness to make major adjustments in its nursing program did not constitute discrimination. The Court reasoned that "uncontroverted testimony established that the purpose of petitioner's program was to train persons who could serve the nursing profession in all customary ways, and this type of purpose, far from reflecting any animus against the handicapped individuals, is shared by many if not most of the institutions that train persons to render professional service . . ." The Court declared that "Section 504 imposes no requirement upon an educational institution to lower or to effect substantial modifications of standards to accommodate a handicapped person."

A Florida appeals court came to the same conclusion regarding the complaint of a blind physical education teacher who was denied a position because of his handicap.[21] School officials offered the position to Mr. Zorick but withdrew the offer after discovering that he was blind. They alleged that a blind person would be unable to perform adequately in the position. Zorick charged that this was a violation of his rights under the Fourteenth Amendment and Section 504 of the Rehabilitation Act. The court found that the plaintiff's due process rights under the Fourteenth Amendment had not been violated since he was refused the job because of job-related requirements. In ruling on Section 504, the court said that it could find no "indication that the primary objective of the financial aid to the school district is to provide employment." Section 504, the court reasoned, does not prevent federal aid recipients from enforcing standards for physical capacities which are reasonably related to the work or program involved. It found that the school's actions were "neither arbitrary, capricious, or groundlessly discriminatory against the blind."

CONCLUSIONS —SOME POLICY ISSUES

The Rehabilitation Act of 1973, Public Law 94–142, and the developing case law have initiated some sweeping changes in the educational treatment of handicapped children. It should be clear from the great volume of litigation which has developed under this legal framework that parents of handicapped children are interested in their rights and that the schools have a great deal to learn about their responsibilities. These responsibilities are awesome in scope and detail. They range from identification to observance of due process to the development of individual programs for every identified handicapped person.

The schools face serious problems in satisfying parents that they are meeting the basic requirements of the law. For example, a recent study reported in *Education Daily*[22] indicated that parents were dissatisfied with the progress schools were making in the development of individualized education plans (IEPs) required under P.L. 94–142. In a Texas survey by Randall Soffer, it was discovered that parents wanted to be more involved in decision making about their children's programs. They also expressed a desire to meet more frequently with school personnel.

If parents of handicapped children criticise the law because it doesn't go far enough, or because it is poorly enforced, others criticise it for other reasons. John Pittenger and Peter Kuriloff[23] referred to Public Law 94–142 as a "radical" law. They were concerned because the law promised so much and the political and educational systems would not be able to deliver. Their major concerns were the cost of the program, the growth of litigation and bureaucracy and loss of public confidence.

Pittenger and Kuriloff suggest that the costs could be staggering. They estimated that the cost of providing an education for handicapped children was approximately double that for other children. Since the national government in the 1982 fiscal year was only picking up about 5 percent of the cost, the major burden fell on the states and the local school districts. This occurs when state and local governments are facing hard times without additional burdens. In view of declining local and state government income and the pressures on the local and state levels to cut rather than raise taxes, it seems unlikely that the needed funds for the implementation of Public Law 94–142 will be available anytime soon.

This puts local school officials in a terrible bind since the law mandates certain programs be provided often at great cost. The courts, meanwhile, have overwhelmingly supported parents who want to see the law implemented. Some of these court decisions can put extreme pressures on local school budgets. For example, in *Armstrong v. Kline* the district court in Pennsylvania ruled that schooling must be provided on a year-round basis for handicapped children in Pennsylvania. The Supreme Court let this decision stand. What this means is that every state must provide year-round schooling. Pittenger and Kuriloff estimated the cost of this single decision for the 50 states at $830 million per year.

The litigation which has followed the law has resulted in a serious expansion of bureaucracy. The nature of Public Law 94–142 and the administrative guidelines which were developed to implement it have necessitated the creation of new bureaucracies on the local school level. This is particularly true of the due process aspects of the law. In order to insure due process local schools first must identify students. They must develop IEPs which can involve parents and a team consisting of the teacher, counselor, administrator, and the student. In some instances, a lawyer and psychologist may be present. Just the task of getting this many people together can be difficult. But this is merely the beginning. Detailed programs must be evaluated and reported. All this can have a devastating bureaucratic effect. In the words of Pittenger and Kuriloff:

> Superintendents and principals are increasingly surrounded by legalistic and bureaucratic restrictions . . . the danger arises that the cumulative effect of these restrictions is to prevent anyone from exercising any leadership at all. . . . What we may be doing, inadvertently, is creating an environment in which risk-avoidance, rather than risk-taking, is the norm—hardly a formula for curing what's wrong with the public schools.[24]

Not only are school administrators in danger of becoming functionaries in the process of implementing the provisions of Public Law 94–142, but everyone involved on the school level is. The guidelines for developing IEPs, the heart of the educational program for individual handicapped children, are very behavioral in nature. Shapiro describes the IEP in this way:

> Its goals are highly circumscribed, minutely fragmented, and quantifiable. Such an approach generally excludes a concern with imaginative, creative, or divergent thinking. Education becomes a process in which the student attempts to come as close as possible to the outcomes already anticipated by a teacher. It replaces a process that is open-ended and exploratory, with one that awards conformity with "correct" answers. Overall, the approach is clearly congruent with bureaucratic values . . . [25]

Finally, Pittenger and Kuriloff make the point that Public Law 94–142 may cause public confidence in the schools to decline even more. This could happen since the cost of meeting the mandates of the law will necessitate an increase in taxes on the local and state levels. Even with an increase in funding regular programs in the schools would not benefit since the increases would have to be used to provide for the handicapped. Thus, even though support for schools increase, the major problems of low achievement, discipline, the need to help the poor and minorities and others would not be addressed.

Pittenger and Kuriloff suggest that Public Law 94–142 could be reformed. Their suggestions include: (1) define the term "appropriate education" more narrowly, (2) eliminate the specific requirements on the IEP, (3) delay implementation of the mandates of the law until such time as federal appropriations reached a level of 20 percent, (4) amend the law to allow greater discretion on the local level for placement of students in separate facilities, and (5) make a distinction between severe and less severe handicaps and exempt the schools from legal mandates on the less severe cases. Pittenger and Kuriloff express little hope that these reforms will be forthcoming. What they predict is that Congress will cut funding while leaving the mandates in place.

There is some indication however, that the critics of the law are beginning to be heard. In *Board of Education of the Hendrick Hudson Central School Disrict v. Rowley*, while affirming most aspects of P.L. 94–142, the Supreme Court ruled that a New York school district did not have to provide a sign language interpreter for a deaf student. The central question involved the definition of "a free appropriate public education." In this case the court issued a two-pronged test of "appropriateness": (1) have the procedures outlined in the law been adhered to? and (2) are the individually designed program and related services of "educational benefit" to the child?

The Court declared further that "to require . . . the furnishing of every special service necessary to maximize each handicapped child's potential is, we think, further than Congress intended to go." What the impact of this decision will be is anybody's guess. It does, however vaguely, provide defendant school districts a little encouragement in that there appear to be some limits on the manner in which "appropriateness" is defined.

In addition, there is some indication that Congress may be pushed into a reconsideration of the law. In the summer of 1982 the secretary of education proposed new guidelines for education of the handicapped. Although the House of Representatives rejected them, the ideas they contained are not likely to disappear. Among other things, the new guidelines recommended by Secretary Bell included changing the rules on discipline and due process giving local authorities more discretion in these matters. Individual services required, including parental counseling, social-work services and school health services would have been eliminated. On placement the new rules would eliminate the requirement that children be placed in programs close to their homes. Also eliminated were the provisions requiring that handicapped children participate with the nonhandicapped in extracurricular activities. Bell would have eliminated the timetables presently required for developing IEPs. The new rules suggested that states be required to submit program plans every three years instead of every year. Finally changes were proposed which would not require the local school district to increase funding for handicapped programs over the previous year's level.

The immediate effect of these changes would be to greatly reduce the mandatory requirements placed on local schools. These proposals would also give local school districts a much stronger position in court cases. Indeed, the total effect might very well be to allow the schools to do what they were doing before there was a P.L. 94–142.

Yet the law, as it exists, presents formidable problems for local schools. About the only advice one could give those who are faced with decisions on the implementation of school programs and policies is to know the Fourteenth Amendment, follow the statutory and HEW guidelines, read *Matti T.* and *Larry P.*, and wait for a court suit.

•

The major issues in providing for the education of the handicapped appear to be:

1. How should a school identify the handicapped?
2. What kind of program will meet all the legal tests?
3. What kind of evaluation system should be used (to prove the school is meeting the needs of all handicapped children)?
4. What constitutes due process in any specific program?
5. How can legal challenges be avoided in the classification of minority children?

This is by no means a complete list, but it does suggest the complexity of the issues involved. By far the most complex issue is the one involving minority children. For years, schools have misclassified normal minority children as retarded, learning disabled, or otherwise handicapped. This is no longer legal. How to help minority children with genuine problems without being charged with direct violation of rights under the Fourteenth Amendment as well as violations of P.L. 94–142 is perhaps the most difficult problem facing school people. Progress has been made, but whether the schools can cope successfully with the legal mandates is as yet unclear. Future teachers and school administrators may have to be more concerned with whether they are violating the law and the Constitution than with helping children learn.

NOTES

1. The cases reported may be found in summary form in the *Education Law Bulletin*, no. 14 (Cambridge, Mass.: Center for Law and Education, July 1980), pp. 854–958.
2. *Mattie T. v. Holladay*, C. A. No. D. C. 75–31–S (N. D. Miss., 1977).
3. *Jose P. v. Ambach*, C. A. No. 79–3–270 (E. D. N. Y., December 14, 1979).
4. *Hernandez v. Porter*, C. A. No. 75–71532 (E.D. Mich., S. D. 1978).
5. *Lora v. Board of Education of the City of New York,* No. 75–C–917 (E. D. N. Y., 1978).
6. *Lopez v. Salida School District*, C. A. No. C–73078, Dist. Ct., City of Denver (1977).
7. *Larry P. v. Riles*, C. A. No. C–71–2270 RFP (N. D. Calif., 1979).
8. *Hairston v. Drosick*, 423 F. Supp. 180 (1976).
9. *Scherer v. Waier*, C. A. No. 787–0510–CV–W–4 (W. D. Mo., 1978).
10. *Rainey v. Tennessee Department of Education*, C. A. No. A–3100, Chancery Court at Nashville (1976).
11. *Frederick L. v. Thomas*, 577 F. Supp. 180 (1977).
12. *Kruse v. Campbell*, 431 F. Supp. 180 (1977).
13. *San Antonio v. Rodriguez*, 411 U.S. 1 (1973).
14. *Barnes v. Converse College*, C. A. No. 77–1116 (D. So. Car., 1977).
15. *Gurmankin v. Costanzo*, 411 F. Supp. 982 (1976).
16. *Upshur v. Love*, 474 F. Supp. 332 (N. D. Calif., 1979).
17. *Stuart v. Nappi*, C. A. No. B–77–381 (D. Conn., 1978).
18. *Mrs. A. J. v. Special School District No. 1*, C. A. No. 4–77–192 (D. Minn., 1979).
19. *S–1 v. Turlington*, C. A. No. 787–8020–Civ. Ca. WPB (S.D. Fla., 1979).
20. *Southeastern Community College v. Davis*, 99 S. Ct. 2361 (1979).

21. *Zorick v. Tynes*, 372 So. 2nd. 133 (Fla. App., 1979).
22. *Education Daily*, 2 December 1980, pp. 5–6.
23. John C. Pittenger and Peter Kuriloff, "Educating the Handicapped: Reforming a Radical Law." *The Public Interest*, no. 66 (Winter 1982): 73–96.
24. Ibid., p. 99.
25. H. S. Shapiro, "Society, Ideology and the Reform of Special Education: A Study in the Limits of Educational Change," *Educational Theory* 30 (Summer 1980): 217.

13

Equality of Education
and School Finance

The allocation of public funds for educational purposes has always been a problem in American society. There has never been a time in our history when policy makers were not forced to make hard choices on how public funds should be spent. There have always been great demands on public funds, and the distribution of tax money for various governmental purposes has been subjected to heated debates. Thus, by its very nature, the problem of educational expenditure is political in the American system. Most of the money for schools comes from local and state sources, and the decisions on how to spend this money are made by politically elected officeholders—from members of the local school board to state legislators.

In the early years, the matter of school finances was relatively simple. Schooling was simple—and it was controlled, financed, and administered locally. In any community, citizens could get together and, with minimal tax levies on their property, raise funds, build a small school, and hire a teacher. As the years passed, citizens demanded more of their schools, until the educational enterprise grew to be one of the largest of all public functions. As the demands for more schooling and a greater variety of schooling grew, the old systems of school finance became inadequate. Unfortunately, the demands for schooling always seemed to be far ahead of plans for adequately financing the system. As communities struggled to provide comprehensive educational systems, it became apparent that the most common source of funds—the local property tax—would be inadequate. Yet the system was so firmly entrenched that it was difficult to change.

The tradition of local funding resulted in serious problems. Supreme Court Justice Potter Stewart, commenting in the *Rodriguez* case, described the system of public education as "chaotic and unjust." He was referring to the system of local school finance. Nor is it difficult to find the major reason for the unjust nature of the system. As long as the major source of funding is the local property tax, inequities are sure to exist. Since the value of property varies greatly from one school district to another, any system with a major source of revenue based primarily on local property values is certain to reflect inequities. These inequities can be observed all over the United States. In rich property districts, one can find sparkling new schools with the latest equipment, well-trained faculties, and comprehensive educational programs. In other districts which are property poor, one can find deteriorating school buildings, inexperienced teachers, apathetic students, inadequate facilities, and poor programs. The contrast becomes even more dramatic in the very many localities in the United States where rich and poor school districts exist within the same state and often in close geographic proximity to each other. The problem is so serious that one can flatly conclude that the greatest single obstacle to equality of educational opportunity in the United States is the manner in which schools are financed. Perhaps even worse, the problem appears to be extremely resistant to reform efforts.

In an effort to determine how the problem of financial inequities developed, this chapter presents a brief history of school finance in the United States. This is followed by a brief overview of the system as it presently exists, a description of some of the major financial problems which plague the schools, and an outline of the major efforts to reform the system.

A BRIEF HISTORY OF SCHOOL FINANCE

The use of public money for the support of schools has been a long struggle in the United States. As a nation, we were not committed at the outset to a program of tax-supported schools. When we did move to provide tax-supported "free" public schooling, it was not a carefully planned process. Instead, it was more of a hit-or-miss process which grew out of an environment of need.

The tradition of school support in the United States is a tradition of local funding and local control. The first laws in Massachussetts in 1647 and Connecticut in 1650 left the matter of securing funds to provide schools entirely up to local citizens. It wasn't until more than a century later that Connecticut, in 1795, provided that money received from the sale of its western lands could be distributed for educational purposes. In the same year, the New York legislature provided that funds could be taken from its state revenues and given to municipalities for school use.

Even so, localism continued to be the major pattern for school finance throughout the nineteenth century. Although many efforts were launched during the nineteenth century to broaden the base for educational support, these efforts faced serious obstacles. There was deep feeling against providing broad public support for the schools. Referring to the attitude of the public toward school funding during much of the nineteenth century, Henry Morrison said:

> Less than half a century ago, citizens could be found in abundance who would sacrifice to the last dollar, sir, before they would submit to the injustice of being taxed for the benefit of other people's children. Much more recently, individuals would proclaim their willingness to "rot in jail before sending my boy to school, if I don't want to."[1]

Related to the issue of compulsory schooling is the fact that there were many rural people in the United States who could see no value in schooling beyond the three Rs. Children were needed to work on the farms and in the factories, and schooling beyond basic grammar school was an economic hardship in many cases. Why should the children idle away their time in the schoolroom when they could be profitably employed on the farm or in the factory? Always beneath this question was the feeling that a more comprehensive system of schooling would cost the taxpayer dearly.

Progress for tax-supported schooling was slow in this kind of an environment. In the early years, it seemed to be easier to get public funds to support only the children of the poor rather than all the children. Schooling was considered, except for the poor, to be the responsibility of the family or at best the local community—not the state. Thus, many of the common school laws which were passed in the early part of the nineteenth century provided minimal programs, largely for the poor. In 1802, Massachusetts provided for the education of the poor but stipulated that the money was to be raised within each township. In 1812, the legislature in New York established the office of State Superintendent of Common Schools and created a permanent school fund from money which was derived from the sale of public lands in the state. Even here, there was a provision for local participation. According to the provisions of the act, the interest from the school fund was to be distributed during February of each year on the basis of population. Moreover, the law required towns to raise a sum equal to that which was to be distributed by the state.

The Ordinances of 1785 and 1787 set a pattern for state support in education which was encouraged by national land policy. Ohio provided a precedent for many states when it was admitted to the union in 1803. The question arose in Congress as to whether Ohio ought to have the right to tax the public lands of the United States which were included within her proposed boundaries. The legislature of Ohio resolved this problem with Congress by agreeing not to tax the land owned by the United States. In return, Congress was to provide the new state with the sixteenth section of each township, to be used for educational purposes. This pattern was followed by all states admitted to the Union after Ohio, with the exceptions of Texas, West Virginia, and Maine.

In the 1820s, several New England states enacted school laws which provided for the supervision of local schools by state agencies and provided some state funds for the support of local schools. By the 1830s, the movement for state support for educational purposes had become almost a national phenomenon. By the time of the Civil War, most of the northern states had the beginnings of a system of state-supported free elementary schools. The South, however, continued for the most part to rely on local control and funding, a pattern which persisted in some southern states well into the twentieth century.

After the Civil War, rapid industrial growth, particularly in the Northeast, had the effect of forcing the states into a more active educational role. Early industrialization encouraged child labor, which had become such a serious problem by the end of the century that many groups were denouncing it. Interested groups, particularly the emerging labor union movement, along with a number of other allies brought enough pressure to bear in many state legislatures that child labor laws were enacted in a number of states. Accompanying this movement was pressure to expand compulsory school legislation and provide greater state support for local schools. By the turn of the century, the combined forces of education pressure groups, educational leaders, and a growing interest in basic schooling for the children of immigrants had succeeded in at least directing the attention of state legislatures to the consideration of greater state support for local schools.

In spite of these pressures, the major source of funds for schools continued to come from local property taxpayers. In 1905 Ellwood Cubberley, concerned about the inequities in a system which relied so heavily on local support, declared: "Justice and equity demand a rearrangement of the apportionment plan as to place a larger portion of aid where it is most needed."[2] Cubberley was concerned about the need to move away from predominantly local support because of the great differences in taxable wealth which existed among local school districts. Cubberley reasoned that schooling was not a local matter—as, for example, the maintenance of streets was—but that schools existed for the general good of the society and means should be found to provide a broader base of support for them. In reviewing data from several states, Cubberley found that school systems based almost completely on local support were grossly unequal in the potential funds they could raise. He found that property-poor districts had high taxes and poor schools, while rich districts tended to have low taxes and good schools—a problem which has yet to be solved in many states.

Cubberley's observations stimulated others to address the same problem. Harlan Updegraff reported on the sources of support for public schools in New York State in 1921. He found inequities related to local taxable wealth and recommended a program which would have provided more state aid for tax-poor school districts.[3] In a report on school finance in New York State, George Strayer suggested that the state make a serious effort to equalize educational opportunity. Strayer offered the view that "there exists today and has existed for many years a movement which has come to be known as the 'equalization of educational opportunity.'"[4] According to Strayer:

> The state should insure equal educational facilities to every child within its borders at a uniform effort throughout the state in terms of the burden of taxation; the tax burden of education should throughout the state be uniform in relation to tax-paying ability, and the provision of the schools should be uniform in relation to the educable population desiring education. Most of the supporters of this proposition, however, would not preclude any particular community from offering at its own expense a particularly rich and costly educational program. They would insist that there be an adequate minimum offering everywhere, the expense of which should be considered a prior claim on the state's economic resources.[5]

One of Strayer's students, Paul Mort, refined the Strayer proposal and suggested that the term "foundation program" be used to describe the basic state support system.[6] Coming as they did from the influential Teachers College at Columbia University in the 1920s and 1930s, the ideas from Strayer and Mort and their students were widely disseminated throughout the country and provided guidelines for state legislatures which were groping with the major problem of providing state support for local schools. By mid-century, some kind of basic state foundation program was in place in most of the states in the country.

It should not be concluded from this brief history that the problem of unequal school finance had been solved. In spite of the efforts of the early twentieth-century scholars and their students, in spite of the fact that many legislatures took their work seriously and made efforts to expand the state's contribution to education, American schools are still basically dependent upon local funding.

THE EXISTING SYSTEM

In a very general way, the public schools get their money from three major sources: intergovernmental revenue, borrowing, and taxation. Intergovernmental revenue includes the money provided for the local school district by the county or municipality as well as by the state and federal government. Funds raised locally, within the school district or on the county and municipal level, remain the major source of revenue for our schools. However, state and national support has become increasingly important. Table 13.1[7] illustrates the federal, state, and local share for the support of public elementary and secondary schools from 1942 to 1978.

Several things are apparent from an analysis of this table. Although the local share of support is obviously declining, it still constitutes the major source of funding. In the last decade, most of the decline in the percentage of local support has been absorbed by the state. Federal support increased dramatically during the sixties and tended to level off during the seventies. What these percentages repre-

TABLE 13.1
Sources of School Revenue, 1942–1978

	Percentage Distribution		
School year	*Federal*	*State*	*Local*
1942	1.4	31.5	67.1
1946	1.4	34.8	63.8
1950	2.9	39.8	57.3
1954	4.5	37.4	58.1
1958	4.0	39.4	56.6
1962	4.3	38.8	56.9
1966	7.9	39.1	53.0
1970	8.0	39.9	52.1
1974	8.5	41.7	49.8
1978	8.1	44.1	47.8

sent in dollars is even more revealing. The total from all sources—federal, state, and local—grew in current dollars from about 2.5 billion in 1942 to nearly 81 billion in 1978. Revenue more than doubled in the 1970s, from a little over 40 billion in 1970 to 80 billion in 1978. In current dollars, the states spent a little over 35.5 billion in 1978 and local revenues furnished approximately 38.7 billion.[8] Clearly, intergovernmental support is an important source of revenue for the schools, but local responsibility continues to be extremely important.

Local school districts continue to rely on borrowing to provide needed facilities for the local system. This has become an increasingly difficult problem for many school districts. The most common method used by school districts to provide the necessary plant and equipment is through the sale of bonds. A bond may be defined as "a legal instrument or contract in which a corporate body promises to pay within a certain time the amount borrowed with interest at some fixed rate payable at certain stated intervals."[9]

Historically, school disctricts have experienced very little difficulty in acquiring money for capital outlay needs through the sale of bonds. Every state, through constitutional provisions or statutes, determines the means by which bonds may be sold. Generally, the first step is to write a proposal in language required by the constitution or statutes. Usually, the language of the bond issue submitted to the voters must be clear as to the amount requested, the purposes for which it is to be used, and the method of repayment. In most states, bond issues must be approved by a majority of those voting in the election.

One of the most difficult problems facing school people in recent years has been the reluctance on the part of the voter-taxpayers to vote for an increase in their taxes to finance the acquisition of public school facilities. The number of bond issues proposed and the number approved declined sharply between 1967 and 1977. During this period, the proportion of bond issues approved ranged from a high of 68 percent in 1968 to a low of 46 percent in 1975. The number of bond elections in the country declined from 1,625 in 1967 to 858 ten years later.[10] By the early eighties, school officials could expect that only about half the bond issues proposed would be successful. Although this public resistance may be due to many factors, the drop in the number of bond issues is related to the fact that school enrollments have dropped and the demand for new facilities has decreased. In addition to this, even in school districts where new facilities are desperately needed, school officials, facing possible rejection of their plans, tend to become less anxious to submit bond issues to the public. In the case of bond issues which are rejected, the growing popular distaste for increasing taxes clearly must figure prominently among the reasons for rejection.

A third major source of revenue for the schools is public taxation. The most important taxes for educational purposes include the general property tax, state sales taxes, and state income taxes. Although there are numerous other kinds of taxes and fees collected by state and local governments for educational purposes, the property, sales, and income taxes are clearly the most important. Among these, the property tax is clearly the major source of local funding for schools. The sales tax is sometimes used to provide local school funds, but local sales taxes are

more often utilized to support other local governmental functions. Moreover, like
the income tax, the sales tax has always been more popular as a state revenue
source than as a local revenue source.

In theory, the property tax (or ad valorem tax, as it is frequently called) is
based on ability to pay and the direct benefit idea. Real and personal property has
long been considered an accurate measure of wealth in the United States. From
colonial times, property owners agreed to tax themselves for purposes of general
governmental support on the theory that property owners benefited directly from
services which government could provide. These services included such direct
functions as police protection, the building of roads and streets, and other activities which theoretically enhanced the value of real property. Later, in the nineteenth century, education came to be considered one of the benefits of organized
society.

Although no one likes to pay taxes, the property tax seemed more popular than
other forms of taxation because it was locally collected and could be controlled
by local citizens and spent for the purposes which they deemed to be necessary.
So long as the local community could pay the total cost of whatever activities
it desired, it need not fear interference from state or national levels of government. Hence, the idea of the property tax as a means of support for all functions
of local government, including education, became and still remains a strong part
of the idea of federalism, with its emphasis on local self-determination and local
control of the simple functions of government. When the United States was a
predominantly rural society and the needs for schooling were minimal, the inequities which existed because taxing ability varied and local support for education
varied were not considered a serious problem. Even where great inequities developed and were publicized by school finance scholars, the people seemed more
willing to live with the inequities than to risk the chance of losing local control.

As America became industrialized and urbanized, the inequities increased. In
the developing cities, great burdens were placed on local taxpayers to provide all
sorts of demanded services—including more and better schools. Paralleling industrial and urban development were demands for increasing the number of
years of schooling and developing more comprehensive educational programs.
The problem was complicated by the fact that urban development and the growth
of wealth were uneven. Not all cities grew at the same rate, nor was wealth
evenly distributed throughout the city. Added to this problem was the fact that
the idea of local control of the schools was moved from its rural environment to
the new urban environment. Thus, in a typical city in the early twentieth century,
public officials carved out a number of school districts for taxing purposes and for
administrative convenience. Those responsible for drawing these districts were
concerned more often with providing convenient "neighborhood" schools and
ease of administration than with providing equitable tax bases. Even worse, officials were also prone to divide school populations along racial or class lines. The
result was the creation of school districts, or separate taxing entities within cities,
with wide variations in taxable wealth. The notion of localism, combined with
rapid urban growth, uneven economic development, and a revenue-raising sys-

tem which depended on local assessed property valuations, resulted in a system in which pupil expenditures varied greatly from one district to the next. In a word, these forces encouraged the growth of a progressively unequal system of public schooling in America.

Although the problem of disparities in educational expenditures among states and within states did not go unnoticed, it continues to exist. For example, per-pupil expenditures in 1977 ranged from a low of $766 in Tennessee to a high of $3,049 in Alaska.[11] Even differences in the cost of living between Tennessee and Alaska cannot justify such a large variation. A more revealing comparison, perhaps, is the disparity that existed across all school districts in the United States that year. In 1977, 5.6 percent of all school districts in the United States spent less than $800 per pupil, while 3.1 percent of all districts spent $2,600 or more per pupil.[12] There are also serious differences in per-pupil expenditures within states. In 1977, the expenditures in nearly half the states ranged from a low of $800 to a high of $1,400.[13]

THE MAJOR CAUSES OF FINANCIAL INEQUITIES

Although there are many reasons why wide variations in school per-pupil expenditures exist between school districts within states and between states, most relate directly or indirectly to the method of school finance used in the United States. Some of the major causes for inequities relate to the following problems: growth, American values, political and geographic factors, and, of course, the property tax.

In addition to the growth of cities alluded to earlier, special growth problems were created after World War II. Beginning in the late forties and continuing through the seventies, the most notable demographic feature on the American landscape was the burgeoning growth of the suburbs. The flight to the suburbs, particularly during the fifties and sixties, coupled with a significant increase in births, placed a heavy burden on suburban school districts to provide funds for current operations as well as capital outlay for new schools and facilities. Added to this burden, during the 20-year period from 1950 to 1970, was inflation, which presented its own special problems. Although the value of property increased through growth and inflation, local revenues seemed somehow never able to keep pace with the demand. National birth rates declined significantly in the seventies, but the movement into the suburbs continued, and many suburban school districts, even with virtually zero population growth nationally, continued to be faced with growth problems. Shifting population patterns created special problems for the inner cities. Even though many inner cities experienced a slowed growth or even a decline in population, they experienced simultaneously a decline in business, industry, and middle-class homeowners and a subsequent loss of property tax revenues. The loss in revenue always seemed to outpace the loss of students. Further complicating an already difficult financial situation was the fact that the educational deficiencies of the inner-city children were so severe that more costly educational programs were needed to cope with the situation. Thus, the nature and character of the growth of suburbs and the decline of the inner city worked in tandem to exacerbate existing inequities.

Nor could the school officials readily turn for help to a receptive public. In spite of rhetoric to the contrary, Americans have not been overly enthusiastic about spending large sums of money on schooling, especially for the poor. In reality, traditional American values and attitudes have tended to make it difficult to raise needed funds. Even in the relatively affluent suburbs, it has always seemed easier to raise money for gyms than for libraries. Being a good football player seems to have a higher value attached to it than does reading. Being smart is not as good as being rich. This peculiar brand of anti-intellectualism clung to the myth which proclaimed that poverty was the fault of the poor. Until very recently, the notion that anybody with any gumption could escape the slums was widespread. This, coupled with the faith in localism and a certain amount of egocentrism, worked together to make it rather difficult to transfer funds raised locally to districts in desperate need. The idea that taxes raised locally should be spent locally was firmly entrenched.

Moreover, political and geographic conditions seemed to support the inequities. Any significant reform within states would certainly have to come from the state level. Unfortunately for the poor districts, local interests are strong in state legislatures. Typically, individual legislators are not known for their interest in voting funds away from their home districts to provide better funding for other districts. Governors are reluctant to assume leadership in schemes to redistribute tax wealth since this tends to make more enemies than friends. Even the courts are reluctant to disrupt long-standing existing systems. These political conditions are buttressed by geographic conditions. In most states, the richest school districts are located in suburban and rural areas which together account for a majority of the representation in most state legislatures. This makes genuine reform politically difficult.

Finally, the major source of local school support, the property tax itself, may be the major cause of financial and educational inequality in the United States. The system of property tax as it has developed in the United States is a rather simple one. First, a taxing jurisdiction is outlined, usually in the state constitution. The original base for property tax may have been the county or township, but as new needs developed, special taxing districts were created by constitutional amendment or statute. Assessors are appointed or elected to evaluate each parcel of property within the taxing district and to place these values on the tax rolls. The next step is for the people, or their elected representatives on the school board, the county commission, the city council, or some other representative body, to determine the amount of taxes which will be paid. Normally this is set as a mill levy or a certain number of dollars of tax to be paid by the property owner on each one thousand dollars of assessed valuation. For example, let us assume that the county is the local taxing unit. All property in the county is then assessed on the basis of some formula. Let us assume that the formula in our hypothetical county is 50 percent of the current market value of the property. Each taxing unit (such as the school district, the fire district, the police district, etc.) determines its budget for the fiscal year. The total cost of local government is then determined, and that share of it which must come from the property tax is set. Let us further assume that the mill levy is set at 90—that is, each taxpayer pays $90 per year in property taxes for every $1,000 of assessed valuation of his property. Let us further assume that the schools need more money than this will provide. The school's budget or finance officer has determined that school needs will require an additional five mills of property taxation. The voters (in some states, only the property owners) are then called upon to decide whether an additional five mills can be levied. Although this is a greatly oversimplified example, it is generally the way it works. The reader should check his own locality to determine how the assessment and collection of the property tax is determined. Teachers should become vitally concerned with this problem since the local property tax remains a major source of school support.

There have been many arguments, pro and con, concerning the property tax as a means of school support. It does have certain advantages. It is a stable tax which returns a fairly reliable yield, and if the ownership of property represents a reasonable measure of wealth, then the system is based to some extent on ability to pay. It is a fairly easy tax to collect. However, there are many disadvantages to the property tax. It is very inflexible. There are serious limits to it as a major source of income. Rates and assessments are traditionally difficult to change, and the source of revenue from the property tax grows slowly. In bad times, it becomes a very undependable source of income, and the burden of high property taxes has given rise in the past to bankruptcies, foreclosures, and forced sales. Property tax is a relatively expensive tax to collect, since it requires paid assessors and extensive records. Moreover, it is becoming increasingly evident that property ownership may not be the best measure of ability to pay. The fluctuations in property values have created certain serious problems in proper assessment. Taxes, particularly personal property taxes, are easy enough to evade by dishonest taxpayers who merely neglect to report all of their personal holdings. Finally, there are notorious examples of unequal assessments of property from one state to the next and frequently from one neighborhood to the next within the same taxing district. The greatest single problem is that a low tax rate in a district with much valuable property can raise many times more revenue than a high tax in a poor district. It is this basic inequity that has led citizens in several states to challenge the constitutionality of the property tax as a means of school support. As a result of these challenges, many state legislatures have been moved to reconsider their tax structure.

In their analysis of financial reform in American education, Charles Benson and his colleagues ask: "If the system is so bad, why has it lasted?"[14] Benson and his colleagues present three possibilities. First, the present system is a good revenue producer. Many school officials are willing to accept the inequities in the system as long as the dollars from local sources continue to pour in. A second reason for its stubborn resistance to change is the fact that the present system has the support and allegiance of affluent households. The property tax system does not penalize the rich districts, only the poor. Finally, the system continues because it preserves the values of localism in government. This point is a particularly strong one, for it argues for the status quo for all kinds of reasons. Local patrons argue that any change might diminish the high quality of their schools. Also, they don't want state or federal interference in their local schools. In some cases, the local supporters are interested in racial and social class separation in the public schools in their locality. Yet, in spite of these strong feelings, the tax system which supports schools has faced a struggle for its very existence.

THE ATTACK ON TAXES

Never enthusiastic about paying taxes, Americans in recent years have not only been reluctant to increase their taxes but have launched efforts to reduce them. The resistance to taxes had become so serious by the late seventies that it came to be called a taxpayer revolt. Politicians on the local, state, and national levels have always found that promises to reduce taxes have a great deal of political appeal. In recent years they seem to be more serious about keeping these promises. In nearly every state legislature in the country, efforts were made in the late seventies to provide some form of tax relief for citizens. Unhappy with the slow progress of state legislatures in their efforts to reduce taxes, the voters in many states, following California's lead in 1977, took the initiative for reducing taxes into their own hands.

In California, the voters approved a measure which was popularly known as Proposition 13. This was a tax measure enacted through an initiative referendum in which the people voted to severely limit the property tax as a means of funding state and local functions. Its general provisions limited property taxes to 1 percent of the market value of real property, reduced the assessed value of real property for tax purposes to 25 percent of the market value, and limited future increases to no more than two percent annually. In addition, it prevented the legislature from raising taxes unless the increase was approved by a two-thirds vote of the legislature.[15]

The effect in California was to reduce local revenues by about seven billion dollars in fiscal year 1978–79. School districts were the largest losers. They lost over 50 percent of their property tax and approximately 30 percent of their total revenue as a result of the measure. The state managed to soften the blow of such severe losses during the 1978–79 school year by appropriating about $5 billion of its surplus for schools. How the schools will cope with their needs in future years is anybody's guess.

The Proposition 13 idea was immensely popular, and citizens all over the country adopted the idea in their states. According to Kenneth Quindry, "Proposition 13 . . . was largely responsible for the appearance of tax or spending limitations on the ballots in fifteen states . . . in 1978 and possibly as many as thirty-six states in 1979."[16] In some states, efforts to limit or roll back taxes were successful; in others, the efforts failed. In Colorado, for example, voters placed a 7 percent lid on budget increases in 1978. Several states took action on taxes in the late seventies. Alabama passed a tax package which reduced assessments on homes and farms and provided a tax break for the elderly. Idaho passed a law almost identical to California's Proposition 13. Massachusetts gave some relief to homeowners while increasing taxes on commercial property. Michigan limited income taxes on individuals. Nevada passed a Proposition 13-type law. North Dakota cut personal income taxes, and Texas placed a lid on legislative spending. In other states, similar legislation was defeated.[17] What may be more significant than a listing of the states which have considered tax limits or reductions is the fact that it is a movement that is not likely to end soon—even in states where such measures have been defeated by the voters or by legislative action. Every state legislature in the Union is under some pressure to reduce taxes. If the tax reduction forces fail in one legislative session, they almost certainly try again the next year.

THE COURTS AND FINANCIAL REFORM

Beginning in the early seventies, the courts have become deeply involved in attempting to resolve conflicts over the manner in which schools should be financed. These cases arose primarily because there was an obvious conflict between the U.S. constitutional and state constitutional provisions and the tax programs used to finance schools. The Fourteenth Amendment to the U.S. Constitution, which provides, in part, that "No State" shall "deny to any person within its jurisdiction the equal protection of the laws," appeared to be in conflict with taxing systems within states which provided grossly unequal expenditures from one district to the next. Many states have similar provisions within their own constitutions. Thus, when students in one school district had significantly less money spent on their schooling than students in other districts in the state, parents or interested groups who lived in poor school districts felt that their constitutional rights were being violated. This feeling has resulted in a number of state court cases and one U.S. Supreme Court case which have challenged methods of school funding. An early major case which set the pattern for many other cases was *Serrano v. Priest* in California in 1971. This case is presented in detail here since it defines and discusses problems common to many states and deals with many of the legal issues which were to surface in later cases.

Serrano v. Priest
5 C3rd 582, 487, P2nd 1241, 96 Cal Rptr 601 (1971)

We are called upon to determine whether the California public school financing system, with its substantial dependence on local property taxes and resultant wide disparities in school revenue, violates the equal protection clause of the Fourteenth Amendment. We have determined that this funding scheme invidiously discriminates against the poor because it makes the quality of a child's education a function of the wealth of his parents and neighbors. Recognizing as we must that the right to an education in our public schools is a fundamental interest which cannot be conditioned on wealth, we can discern no compelling state purpose necessitating the present method of financing. We have concluded, therefore, that such a system cannot withstand constitutional challenge and must fall before the equal protection clause.

Plaintiffs, who are Los Angeles County public school children and their parents, brought this class action for declaratory and injunctive relief against certain state and county officials charged with administering the financing of the California public school system. Plaintiff children claim to represent a class consisting of all public school pupils in California, "except children in that school district, the identity to which is presently unknown, which school district affords the greatest educational opportunity of all school districts within California." Plaintiff parents purport to represent a class of all parents who have children in the school system and who pay real property taxes in the county of their residence.

The complaint sets forth three causes of action. The first cause alleges in substance as follows: Plaintiff children attend public elementary and secondary schools located in specified school districts in Los Angeles County. This public school system is maintained throughout California by a financing plan or scheme which relies heavily on local property taxes and causes substantial disparities among individual school districts in the amount of revenue available per pupil for the districts' educational programs. Consequently, districts with smaller tax bases are not able to spend as much money per child for education as districts with larger assessed valuations.

It is alleged that "As a direct result of the financing scheme . . . substantial disparities in the quality and extent of availability of educational opportunities exist and are perpetuated among the several school districts of the State. . . . The educational opportunities made available to children attending public schools in the District, including plaintiff children, are substantially inferior to the educational opportunities made available to children attending public schools in many other districts of the State. . . ." The financing scheme thus fails to meet the requirements of the equal protection clause of the Fourteenth Amendment of the United States Constitution and the California Constitution in several specified respects.

In the second cause of action, plaintiff parents, after incorporating by reference all the allegations of the first clause, allege that as a direct result of the financing scheme they are required to pay a higher tax rate than taxpayers in many other school districts in order to obtain for their children the same or lesser educational opportunities afforded children in those other districts.

In the third cause of action, after incorporating by reference all the allegations of the first two causes, all plaintiffs allege that an actual controversy has arisen and now exists between the parties as to the validity and constitutionality of the financing scheme under the Fourteenth Amendment of the United States Constitution and under the California Constitution.

Plaintiffs pray for: (1) a declaration that the present financing system is unconstitutional; (2) an order directing defendants to reallocate school funds in order to remedy this invalidity; and (3) an adjudication that the trial court retain jurisdiction of the action so that it may restructure the system if defendants and the state Legislature fail to act within a reasonable time. . . .

We begin our task by examining the California public school financing system which is the focal point of the complaint's allegations. At the threshold we find a fundamental statistic—over 90 percent of our public school funds derive from two basic sources: (a) local district taxes on real property and (b) aid from the State School Fund.

By far the major source of school revenue is the local real property tax. Pursuant to article IX, section 6 of the California Constitution, the Legislature has authorized the governing body of each county, and city and county, to levy taxes on the real property within a school district at a rate necessary to meet the district's annual education budget. . . . The amount of revenue which a district can raise in this manner thus depends largely on its tax base—i.e., the assessed valuation of real property within its borders. Tax bases vary widely throughout the state; in 1969–1970, for example, the assessed valuation per unit of average daily attendance of elementary school children ranged from a low of $103 to a peak of $952,156—a ratio of nearly 4 to 10,000. . . .

The other factor determining local school revenue is the rate of taxation within the district. Although the Legislature has placed ceilings on permissible district tax rates . . . these statutory maxima may be surpassed in a "tax override" election if a majority of the district's voters approve a higher rate. . . . Nearly all districts have voted to override the statutory limits. Thus the locally raised funds which constitute the largest portion of school revenue are primarily a function of the value of the realty within a particular school district, coupled with the willingness of the district's residents to tax themselves for education.

Most of the remaining school revenue comes from the State School Fund pursuant to the "foundation program," through which the state undertakes to supplement local taxes in order to provide a "minimum amount of guaranteed support to all districts. . . ." With certain minor exceptions, the foundation program ensures that each school district will receive annually, from state or local funds, $355 for each elementary school pupil . . . and $488 for each high school student.

The state contribution is supplied in two principal forms. "Basic state aid" consists of a flat grant to each district of $125 per pupil per year, regardless of the relative wealth of the district. . . . "Equalization aid" is distributed in inverse proportion to the wealth of the district.

To compute the amount of equalization aid to which a district is entitled, the State Superintendent of Public Instruction first determines how much local property tax revenue would be generated if the district were to levy a hypothetical tax at a rate of $1 on each $100 of assessed valuation in elementary school districts and $.80 per $100 in high school districts. . . . To that figure, he adds the $125 per pupil basic aid grant. If the sum of those two amounts is less than the foundation program minimum for that district, the state contributes the difference. . . . Thus, equalization funds guarantee to the poorer districts a basic minimum revenue, while wealthier districts are ineligible for such assistance.

An additional state program of "supplemental aid" is available to subsidize particularly poor school districts which are willing to make an extra local tax effort. An elementary district with an assessed valuation of $12,500 or less per pupil may obtain up to $125 more for each child if it sets its local tax rate above a certain statutory level. A high school district whose assessed valuation does not exceed $24,500 per pupil is eligible for a supplement of up to $72 per child if its local tax is sufficiently high. . . .

Although equalization aid and supplemental aid temper the disparities which result from the vast variations in real property assessed valuation, wide differentials remain in the revenue available to individual districts and, consequently, in the level of educational expenditures. . . . For example, in Los Angeles County, where plaintiff children attend school, the Baldwin Park Unified School District expended only $577.49 to educate each of its pupils in 1968–1969; during the same year the Pasadena Unified School District spent $840.19 on every student; and the Beverly Hills Unified

School District paid out $1,231.72 per child. . . . The source of these disparities is un-mistakable: in Baldwin Park the assessed valuation per child totaled only $3,706; in Pasadena, assessed valuation was $13,706; while in Beverly Hills, the corresponding figure was $50,885—a ratio of 1 to 4 to 13. Thus, the state grants are inadequate to offset the inequalities inherent in a financing system based on widely varying local tax bases.

Furthermore, basic aid, which constitutes about half of the state educational funds . . . is distributed on a uniform per pupil basis to all districts, irrespective of a district's wealth. Beverly Hills, as well as Baldwin Park, receives $125 from the state for each of its students.

Having disposed of these preliminary matters, we take up the chief contention underlying plaintiffs' complaint, namely that the California public school financing scheme violates the equal protection clause of the Fourteenth Amendment to the United States Constitution. . . .

. . . Plaintiffs contend that the school financing system classifies on the basis of wealth. We find this proposition irrefutable. As we have already discussed, over half of all educational revenue is raised locally by levying taxes on real property in the individual school districts. Above the foundation program minimun . . . the wealth of a school district, as measured by its assessed valuation, is the major determinant of educational expenditures. Although the amount of money raised locally is also a func-tion of the rate at which the residents of a district are willing to tax themselves, as a practical matter districts with small tax bases simply cannot levy taxes at a rate suf-ficient to produce the revenue that more affluent districts reap with minimal tax efforts. . . . For example, Baldwin Park citizens, who paid a school tax of $5.48 per $100 of assessed valuation in 1968–1969, were able to spend less than half as much on education as Beverly Hills residents, who were taxed only $2.38 per $100. . . .

But plaintiffs' equal protection attack on the fiscal system has an additional dimension. They assert that the system not only draws lines on the basis of wealth but that it "touches upon," indeed has a direct and significant impact upon, a "fun-damental interest," namely education. It is urged that these two grounds, particularly in combination, establish a demonstrable denial of equal protection of the laws. To this phase of the argument we now turn out attention. . . .

We therefore begin by examining the indispensable role which education plays in the modern industrial state. This role, we believe, has two significant aspects: first, education is a major determinant of an individual's chances for economic and social success in our competitive society; second, education is a unique influence on a child's political and community life. "[T]he pivotal position of education to success in Amer-ican society and its essential role in opening up to the individual the central experi-ences of our culture lend it an importance that is undeniable." . . . Thus, education is the lifeline of both the individual and society.

The fundamental importance of education has been recognized in other contexts by the United States Supreme Court and by this court. These decisions—while not legally controlling on the exact issue before us—are persuasive in their accurate factual description of the significance of learning. (Fn. omitted.)

The classic expression of this position came in *Brown v. Board of Education* (1954) 347 U.S. 483, which invalidated de jure segregation by race in public schools. The high court declared: "Today, education is perhaps the most important function of state and local governments. Compulsory school attendance laws and the great expenditures for education both demonstrate our recognition of the importance of education to our democratic society. It is required in the performance of our most basic public responsibilities, even service in the armed forces. It is the very foundation of good citizenship. Today it is a principal instrument in awakening the child to cultural values, in preparing him for later professional training, and in helping him to adjust normally to his environment. In these days, it is doubtful that any child may reasonably be expected to succeed in life if he is denied the opportunity of an education. Such an opportunity, where the state has undertaken to provide it, is a right which must be made available to all on equal terms." . . .

We are convinced that the distinctive and priceless function of education in our society warrants, indeed compels, our treating it as a "fundamental interest." (Fn. omitted.)

First, education is essential in maintaining what several commentators have termed "free enterprise democracy"—that is, preserving an individual's opportunity to compete successfully in the economic marketplace, despite a disadvantaged background. Accordingly, the public schools of this state are the bright hope for entry of the poor and oppressed into the mainstream of American society. (Fn. omitted.)

Second, education is universally revelant. "Not every person finds it necessary to call upon the fire department or even the police in an entire lifetime. Relatively few are on welfare. Every person, however, benefits from education. . . ." (Fn. omitted.)

Third, public education continues over a lengthy period of life—between 10 and 13 years. Few other government services have such sustained, intensive contact with the recipient.

Fourth, education is unmatched in the extent to which it molds the personality of the youth of society. While police and fire protection, garbage collection and street lights are essentially neutral in their effect on the individual psyche, public education actively attempts to shape a child's personal development in a manner chosen not by the child or his parents but by the state. (Fn. omitted.) "[T]he influence of the school is not confined to how well it can teach the disadvantaged child; it also has a significant role to play in shaping the student's emotional and psychological make-up."

Finally, education is so important that the state has made it compulsory—not only in the requirement of attendance but also by assignment to a particular district and school. Although a child of wealthy parents has the opportunity to attend a private school, this freedom is seldom available to the indigent. In this context, it has been suggested that "a child of the poor assigned willy-nilly to an inferior state school takes on the complexion of a prisoner, complete with a minimum sentence of 12 years. . . ."

We now reach the final step in the application of the "strict scrutiny" equal protection standard—the determination of whether the California school financing system, as presently structured, is necessary to achieve a compelling state interest.

The state interest which defendants advance in support of the current fiscal scheme is California's policy "to strengthen and encourage local responsibility for control of public education." . . . We treat separately the two possible aspects of this goal: first, the granting to local districts of effective decision-making power over the administration of their schools; and second, the promotion of local fiscal control over the amount of money to be spent on education.

The individual district may well be in the best position to decide whom to hire, how to schedule its educational offerings, and a host of other matters which are either of significant local impact or of such a detailed nature as to require decentralized determination. But even assuming arguendo that local administrative control may be a compelling state interest, the present financial system cannot be considered necessary to further this interest. No matter how the state decides to finance its system of public education, it can still leave this decision-making power in the hands of local districts.

The other asserted policy interest is that of allowing a local district to choose how much it wishes to spend on the education of its children. Defendants argue: "[I]f one district raises a lesser amount per pupil than another district, this is a matter of choice and preference of the individual district, and reflects the individual desire for lower taxes rather than an expanded educational program, or may reflect a greater interest within that district in such other services that are supported by local property taxes as, for example, police and fire protection or hospital services."

We need not decide whether such decentralized financial decision-making is a compelling state interest, since under the present financing system, such fiscal free-will is a cruel illusion for the poor school districts. We cannot agree that Baldwin Park residents care less about education than those in Beverly Hills solely because Baldwin Park spends less than $600 per child while Beverly Hills spends over $1,200. As defendants themselves recognize, perhaps the most accurate reflection of a community's commitment to education is the rate at which its citizens are willing to tax themselves to support their schools. Yet by that standard, Baldwin Park should be deemed far more devoted to learning than Beverly Hills, for Baldwin Park citizens levied a school tax of well over $5 per $100 of assessed valuation, while residents of Beverly Hills paid only slightly more than $2. . . .

We, therefore, arrive at this conclusion. The California public school financing system, as presented to us by plaintiffs' complaint supplemented by matters judicially noticed, since it deals intimately with education, obviously touches upon a fundamental interest. For the reasons we have explained in detail, this system conditions the full entitlement to such interest on wealth, classifies its recipients on the basis of their collective affluence and makes the quality of a child's education depend upon the resources of his school district and ultimately upon the pocketbook of his parents. We find that such financing system as presently constituted is not necessary to the attainment of any compelling state interest. Since it does not withstand the requisite "strict scrutiny," it denies to the plaintiffs and others similarly situated the equal protection of the laws. (Fn. omitted.) If the allegations of the complaint are sustained, the financial system must fall and the statutes comprising it must be found unconstitutional. . . .

. . . By our holding today we further the cherished idea of American education that in a democratic society free public schools shall make available to all children equally the abundant gifts of learning. This was the credo of Horace Mann, which has been the heritage and the inspiration of this country. "I believe," he wrote, "in the existence of a great, immortal immutable principle of natural law, or natural ethics,—a principle antecedent to all human institutions, and incapable of being abrogated by any ordinance of man . . . which proves the *absolute right* to an education of every human being that comes into the world, and which, of course, proves the correlative duty of every government to see that the means of that education are provided for all. . . ."

Two years after the decision in *Serrano*, the Supreme Court of the United States heard *San Antonio Independent School District v. Rodriguez.* Many of the issues in the two cases were similar. In *Rodriguez,* the Supreme Court addressed the issue of the Texas system of school finance, which was similar in some respects to the one in California. Since the Supreme Court elected not to hear an appeal in the *Serrano* case, thereby letting the California court decision stand, some were surprised with the findings in *Rodriguez*. Excerpts from *Rodriguez* are presented here.

San Antonio Independent School District v. Rodriguez
411 US 1 (1973)

Mr. Justice Powell delivered the opinion of the Court.

This suit attacking the Texas system of financing public education was initiated by Mexican-American parents whose children attend the elementary and secondary schools in the Edgewood Independent School District, an urban school district in San Antonio, Texas. They brought a class action on behalf of school children throughout the state who are members of minority groups or who are poor and reside in school districts having a low property tax base. Named as defendants were the state board of education, the commissioner of education, the state attorney general, and the Bexar County (San Antonio) Board of Trustees. The complaint was filed in the summer of 1968 and a three-judge court was impaneled in January 1969. In December 1971 the panel rendered its judgment in a per curiam opinion holding the Texas school finance system unconstitutional under the equal protection clause of the Fourteenth Amendment. The state appealed, and we noted probable jurisdiction to consider the far-reaching constitutional questions presented. . . . For the reasons stated in this opinion we reverse the decision of the district court. . . .

The school district in which appellees reside, the Edgewood Independent School District, has been compared throughout this litigation with the Alamo Heights Independent School District. This comparison between the least and most affluent districts in the San Antonio area serves to illustrate the manner in which the dual system of finance operates and to indicate the extent to which substantial disparities exist despite the state's impressive progress in recent years. Edgewood is one of seven public school districts in the metropolitan area. Approximately 22,000 students are enrolled in its twenty-five elementary and secondary schools. The district is situated in the core-city sector of San Antonio in a residential neighborhood that has little commercial or industrial property. The residents are predominantly of Mexican-American descent: approximately 90 percent of the student population is Mexican-American and over 6 percent is Negro. The average assessed property value per pupil is $5,960—the lowest in the metropolitan area—and the median family income ($4,686) is also the lowest. At an equalized tax rate of $1.05 per $100 of assessed property—the highest in the metropolitan area—the district contributed $26 to the education of each child for the 1967–68 school year above its local fund assignment for the Minimum Foundation Program. The Foundation Program contributed $222 per pupil for a state-local total of $248. Federal funds added another $108 for a total of $356 per pupil. (Fn. omitted.)

Alamo Heights is the most affluent school district in San Antonio. Its six schools, housing approximately 5,000 students, are situated in a residential community quite unlike the Edgewood District. The school population is predominantly Anglo, having only 18 percent Mexican-Americans and less than 1 percent Negroes. The assessed property value per pupil exceeds $49,000 and the median family income is $8,001. In 1967–68 the local tax rate of $.85 per $100 of valuation yielded $333 per pupil over and above its contribution to the Foundation Program. Coupled with the $225 provided from that program, the district was able to supply $588 per student. Supplemented by a $36 per-pupil grant from federal sources, Alamo Heights spent $594 per pupil. . . .

We must decide, first, whether the Texas system of financing public education operates to the disadvantage of some suspect class or impinges upon a fundamental right explicitly or implicitly protected by the Constitution, thereby requiring strict judicial scrutiny. . . .

Only appellees' first possible basis for describing the class disadvantaged by the Texas school finance system—discrimination against a class of definably "poor" persons—might arguably meet the criteria established in . . . prior cases. Even a cursory examination, however, demonstrates that neither of the two distinguishing characteristics of wealth classifications can be found here. First, in support of their charge that the system discriminates against the "poor," appellees have made no effort to demonstrate that it operates to the peculiar disadvantage of any class fairly definable as indigent, or as composed of persons whose incomes are beneath any designated poverty level. Indeed, there is reason to believe that the poorest families are not necessarily clustered in the poorest property districts. A recent and exhaustive study of school districts in Connecticut concluded that "it is clearly incorrect . . . to contend that the 'poor' live in 'poor' districts. . . . Thus, the major factual assumption of Serrano—that the educational financing system discriminates against the 'poor'—is simply false in Connecticut." Defining "poor" families as those below the Bureau of the Census "poverty level," the Connecticut study found, not surprisingly, that the poor were clustered around commercial and industrial areas—those same areas that provide the most attractive sources of property tax income for school districts. . . .

Second, neither appellees nor the district court addressed the fact that, unlike each of the foregoing cases, lack of personal resources has not occasioned an absolute deprivation of the desired benefit. The argument here is not that the children in districts having relatively low assessable property values are receiving no public education; rather, it is that they are receiving a poorer quality education than that available to children in districts having more assessable wealth. Apart from the unsettled and disputed question whether the quality of education may be determined by the amount of money expended for it, a sufficient answer to appellees' argument is that at least where wealth is involved the equal protection clause does not require absolute equality or precisely equal advantages. . . .

For these two reasons—the absence of any evidence that the financing system discriminates against any definable category of "poor" people or that it results in the absolute deprivation of education—the disadvantaged class is not susceptible of identification in traditional terms. . . .

However described, it is clear that appellees' suit asks this court to extend its most exacting scrutiny to review a system that allegedly discriminates against a large, diverse, and amorphous class, unified only by the common factor of residence in districts that happen to have less taxable wealth than other districts. The system of alleged discrimination and the class it defines have none of the traditional indicia of suspectness: the class is not saddled with such disabilities, or subjected to such a history of purposeful unequal treatment, or relegated to such a position of political powerlessness as to command extraordinary protection from the majoritarian political process.

We thus conclude that the Texas system does not operate to the peculiar disadvantage of any suspect class. But in recognition of the fact that this court has never heretofore held that wealth discrimination alone provides an adequate basis for invoking strict scrutiny, appellees have not relied solely on this contention. They also assert that the state's system impermissibly interferes with the exercise of a "fundamental" right and that accordingly the prior decisions of this court require the application of the strict standard of judicial review. . . . (Fn. omitted.)

The lesson of these cases in addressing the question now before the court is plain. It is not the province of this court to create substantive constitutional rights in the name of guaranteeing equal protection of the laws. Thus the key to discovering whether education is "fundamental" is not to be found in comparisons of the relative societal significance of education as opposed to subsistence or housing. Nor is it to be found by weighing whether education is as important as the right to travel. Rather, the answer lies in assessing whether there is a right to education explicitly or implicitly guaranteed by the Constitution. . . .

Education, of course, is not among the rights afforded explicit protection under our federal Constitution. Nor do we find any basis for saying it is implicitly so protected: As we have said, the undisputed importance of education will not alone cause this court to depart from the usual standard for reviewing a state's social and economic legislation. It is appellees' contention, however, that education is distinguishable from other services and benefits provided by the state because it bears a peculiarly close relationship to other rights and liberties accorded protection under the Constitution. Specifically, they insist that education is itself a fundamental personal right because it is essential to the effective exercise of First Amendment freedoms and to intelligent utilization of the right to vote. In asserting a nexus between speech and education, appellees urge that the right to speak is meaningless unless the speaker is capable of articulating his thoughts intelligently and persuasively. The "marketplace of ideas" is an empty forum for those lacking basic communicative tools. Likewise, they argue that the corollary right to receive information becomes little more than a hollow privilege when the recipient has not been taught to read, assimilate, and utilize available knowledge. . . .

Even if it were conceded that some identifiable quantum of education is a constitutionally protected prerequisite to the meaningful exercise of either right, we have no indication that the present levels of educational expenditures in Texas provide an education that falls short. . . . [N]o charge fairly could be made that the system fails to provide each child with an opportunity to acquire the basic minimal skills necessary for the enjoyment of the rights of speech and of full participation in the political process. . . .

[T]he justices of this court lack both the expertise and the familiarity with local problems so necessary to the making of wise decisions with respect to the raising and disposition of public revenues. Yet we are urged to direct the states either to alter drastically the present system or to throw out the property tax altogether in favor of some other form of taxation. No scheme of taxation, whether the tax is imposed on property, income, or purchases of goods and services, has yet been devised which is free of all discriminatory impact. In such a complex arena in which no perfect alternatives exist, the court does well not to impose too rigorous a standard of scrutiny lest all local fiscal schemes become subjects of criticism under the equal protection clause. (Fns. omitted.)

In addition to matters of fiscal policy, this case also involves the most persistent and difficult questions of educational policy, another area in which this court's lack of specialized knowledge and experience counsels against premature interference with the informed judgments made at the state and local levels. . . . On even the most basic questions in this area the scholars and educational experts are divided. Indeed, one of the major sources of controversy concerns the extent to which there is a demonstrable correlation between educational expenditures and the quality of education—an assumed correlation underlying virtually every legal conclusion drawn by the district court in this case. Related to the questioned relationship between cost and quality is the equally unsettled controversy as to the proper goals of a system of public education. . . . In such circumstances the judiciary is well advised to refrain from imposing on the states inflexible constitutional restraints that could circumscribe or handicap the continued research and experimentation so vital to finding even partial solutions to educational problems and to keeping abreast of ever changing conditions.

It must be remembered also that every claim arising under the equal protection clause has implications for the relationship between national and state power under our federal system. . . . [I]t would be difficult to imagine a case having a greater potential impact on our federal system than the one now before us, in which we are urged to abrogate systems of financing public education presently in existence in virtually every state.

The foregoing considerations buttress our conclusion that Texas' system of public school finance is an inappropriate candidate for strict judicial scrutiny. These same considerations are relevant to the determination whether that system, with its conceded imperfections, nevertheless bears some rational relationship to a legitimate state purpose. It is to this question that we next turn our attention. . . .

The Texas system of school finance . . . [w]hile assuring a basic education for every child in the state . . . permits and encourages a large measure of participation in and control of each district's schools at the local level. . . .

The persistence of attachment to government at the lowest level where education is concerned reflects the depth of commitment of its supporters. In part, local control means as Professor Coleman suggests, the freedom to devote more money to the education of one's children. Equally important, however, is the opportunity it offers for participation in the decision-making process that determines how those local tax dollars will be spent. . . .

Moreover, if local taxation for local expenditures were an unconstitutional method of providing for education then it might be an equally impermissible means of providing other necessary services customarily financed largely from local property taxes, including local police and fire protection, public health and hospitals, and public utility facilities of various kinds. We perceive no justification for such a severe denigration of local property taxation and control as would follow from appellees' contentions. . . .

In sum, to the extent that the Texas system of financing results in unequal expenditures between children who happen to reside in different districts, we cannot say that such disparities are the product of a system that is so irrational as to be invidiously discriminatory. Texas has acknowledged its shortcomings and has persistently endeavored—not without some success—to ameliorate the differences in levels of expenditures without sacrificing the benefits of local participation. The Texas plan is not the result of hurried, ill-conceived legislation. It certainly is not the product of purposeful discrimination against any group or class. . . .

(Dissent by Mr. Justice White omitted.)

Mr. Justice Marshall, with whom Mr. Justice Douglas concurs, dissenting.

The court today decides, in effect, that a state may constitutionally vary the quality of education which it offers its children in accordance with the amount of taxable wealth located in the school districts within which they reside. The majority's decision represents an abrupt departure from the mainstream of recent state and federal court decisions concerning the unconstitutionality of state educational financing schemes dependent upon taxable local wealth. More unfortunately, though, the majority's holding can only be seen as a retreat from our historic commitment to equality of educational opportunity and as unsupportable acquiescence in a system which deprives children in their earliest years of the chance to reach their full potential as citizens. The court does this despite the absence of any substantial justification for a scheme which arbitrarily channels educational resources in accordance with the fortuity of the amount of taxable wealth within each district. . . .

The court acknowledges that "substantial interdistrict disparities in school expenditures" exist in Texas . . . and that these disparities are "largely attributable to differences in the amounts of money collected through local property taxation." . . . But instead of closely examining the seriousness of these disparities and the invidiousness of the Texas financing scheme, the court undertakes an elaborate exploration of the efforts Texas has purportedly made to close the gaps between its districts in terms of levels of district wealth and resulting educational funding. Yet, however praiseworthy Texas' equalizing efforts, the issue in this case is not whether Texas is doing its best to ameliorate the worst features of a discriminatory scheme, but rather whether the scheme itself is in fact unconstitutionally discriminatory in the face of the Fourteenth Amendment's guarantee of equal protection of the laws. When the Texas financing scheme is taken as a whole, I do not think it can be doubted that it produces a discriminatory impact on substantial numbers of the school-age children of the state of Texas. . . .

[W]hile on its face the Texas scheme may merely discriminate between local districts, the impact of that discrimination falls directly upon the children whose educational opportunity is dependent upon where they happen to live. Consequently, the district court correctly concluded that the Texas financing scheme discriminates, from a constitutional perspective, between school children on the basis of the amount of taxable property located within their local districts. . . .

I believe it is sufficient that the overarching form of discrimination in this case is between the school children of Texas on the basis of the taxable property wealth of the districts in which they happen to live. To understand both the precise nature of this discrimination and the parameters of the disadvantaged class it is sufficient to consider the constitutional principle which appellees contend is controlling in the context of educational financing. In their complaint appellees asserted that the Constitution does not permit local district wealth to be determinative of educational opportunity. This is simply another way of saying, as the district court concluded, that consistent with the guarantee of equal protection of the laws, "the quality of public education may not be a function of wealth, other than the wealth of the state as a whole." . . . Under such a principle, the children of a district are excessively advantaged if that district has more taxable property per pupil than the average amount of taxable property per pupil considering the state as a whole. By contrast, the children of a district are disadvantaged if that district has less taxable property per pupil than the state average. . . . Whether this discrimination, against the school children of property poor districts, inherent in the Texas financing scheme is violative of the equal protection clause is the question to which we must now turn. . . .

The only justification offered by appellants to sustain the discrimination in educational opportunity caused by the Texas financing scheme is local educational control.

... On this record, it is apparent that the state's purported concern with local control is offered primarily as an excuse rather than as a justification for interdistrict inequality.

In Texas statewide laws regulate in fact the most minute details of local public education. For example, the state prescribes required courses. All textbooks must be submitted for state approval, and only approved textbooks may be used. The state has established the qualifications necessary for teaching in Texas public schools and the procedures for obtaining certification. The state has even legislated on the length of the school day.

Moreover, even if we accept Texas' general dedication to local control in educational matters, it is difficult to find any evidence of such dedication with respect to fiscal matters. It ignores reality to suggest ... that the local property tax element of the Texas financing scheme reflects a conscious legislative effort to provide school districts with local control. If Texas has a system truly dedicated to local fiscal control one would expect the quality of the educational opportunity provided in each district to vary with the decision of the voters in that district as to the level of sacrifice they wish to make for public education. In fact, the Texas scheme produces precisely the opposite result. Local school districts cannot choose to have the best education in the state by imposing the highest tax rate. Instead, the quality of the educational opportunity offered by any particular district is largely determined by the amount of taxable property located in the district—a factor over which local voters can exercise no control. ...

In conclusion it is essential to recognize that an end to the wide variations in taxable district property wealth inherent in the Texas financing scheme would entail none of the untoward consequences suggested by the court or by the appellants.

First, affirmance of the district court's decisions would hardly sound the death knell for local control of education. It would mean neither centralized decision-making nor federal court intervention in the operation of public schools. Clearly, this suit has nothing to do with local decision-making with respect to educational policy or even educational spending. It involves only a narrow aspect of local control—namely, local control over the raising of educational funds. In fact, in striking down interdistrict disparities in taxable local wealth, the district court took the course which is most likely to make true local control over educational decision-making a reality for all Texas school districts.

Nor does the district court's decision even necessarily eliminate local control of educational funding. The district court struck down nothing more than the continued interdistrict wealth discrimination inherent in the present property tax. Both centralized and decentralized plans for educational funding not involving such interdistrict discrimination have been put forward. The choice among these or other alternatives would remain with the state, not with the federal courts. ... I would therefore affirm the judgment of the district court.

Although the differences and similarities between *Rodriguez* and *Serrano* speak for themselves, a few observations might be appropriate. The facts in both cases were very similar. Both state finance programs resulted in serious inequities from one district to another in the tax burden as well as in the amount of revenue which could be raised from the tax effort. Even the foundation programs in California and Texas were similar, in that in both cases supplemental aid from the state provided more assistance to the rich districts than to the poor districts. However, that is where the similarities end. In California, the Supreme Court found that wealth was a suspect classification and that education was a fundamental right. In *Rodriguez*, the Supreme Court disagreed on both these points. The *Rodriguez* Court reasoned that wealth was not a suspect classification in Texas since there was no deliberate attempt in the tax program to single out the poor as a class. Indeed, they discovered that there were poor as well as rich students enrolled in both poor and rich districts in Texas. In spite of *Brown v. Topeka* and dozens of cases in which they ruled otherwise, in *Rodriguez* the Court could find nothing in the U.S. Constitution which afforded explicit or implicit protection to the plaintiffs. That is, under the Constitution, the right to an education was not a "fundamental" right as the *Serrano* Court said it was.

How does one reconcile these differences? Although it is impossible to look into the motives of the Supreme Court justices, the Supreme Court had taken on a more conservative tone after the Nixon appointees joined the Court in the early seventies. Perhaps a more compelling explanation is that the California Court ruled on both its own constitutional provisions and statutes which were different, however slightly, from those in Texas. This alone could explain some of the differences. Also, a decision of the Supreme Court on this issue in *Rodriguez* would have affected all the states in the Union except those with total state funding, while the California decision was limited to a single state. The effects of a U.S. Supreme Court ruling could have been devastating. A decision for *Rodriguez* would have created severe problems—and not only for school finance; in very many cases, it would have required a complete overhaul of state systems of taxation and finance. The Court, reluctant to open this can of worms, was content to allow individual states to solve their own problems. Whatever the reasons, the effect of *Rodriguez* was to dump the whole problem back into the laps of state officials and state courts.

Since the *Rodriguez* decision did not set a new national policy on school finance, it resulted in a large number of state-level lawsuits following a pattern similar to that in *Serrano*. Dozens of state cases have been heard since *Rodriguez*, and although the cases are widely diverse because of differences from state to state in the law and in school finance programs, it is fair to state that those challenging systems based on property tax inequities have been rather successful. From 1978 to 1980, for example, courts in Washington, New York, Colorado, Connecticut, Arizona, Idaho, New Jersey, and Ohio found their state systems of school finance to be unconstitutional. In other states, the courts upheld the state systems. Several cases were pending in 1982.[18]

Whether the courts uphold a state system of school finance or declare it to be a violation of the Constitution depends on the nature of the finance system and the state constitutional provisions. In most of the state cases, the state courts continue to utilize U.S. Supreme Court cases on integration which defined education as a fundamental right. If state constitutional provisions on equality are explicit on education or can be implied to apply to education, the courts generally rule that tax systems which do not provide substantial equality of expenditure on each child in the system are unconstitutional. In cases where the constitution and the laws are not clear or where statutes providing for funding are consistent with the constitution, the courts generally support the existing system. A number of states in recent years have managed to avoid litigation by taking legislative action to reform the system in ways which do not conflict with the state's constitution.

Thus, *Serrano* and the many state cases which have followed have provided great stimulus for legislative reform of school finance systems. The obvious inequities in many state systems have also stimulated a number of significant proposals for reform from scholars in the area of school finance. These reform proposals have been of great interest in states which face court action. Proposals for reform take on great significance in states where the courts void existing programs, because the courts rarely present the legislature with a plan that would satisfy constitutional provisions. Generally, the courts leave the specific method of reform to the state legislature.

REFORM PROPOSALS

Generally, the efforts for reform have followed three major patterns or variations of them. These include high-level foundation aid, augmented foundation, and district power equalization.[19]

High-level foundation programs usually provide for a minimum legal level of per-pupil support on a statewide basis. The money for the program comes from local and state sources. Normally there is a fixed and equitable rate of property taxation which all school districts must require. Where poor districts cannot raise the minimum required funds, the state makes up the difference. The most simple way to provide total equality is for the state to set the level of per-pupil expenditure and provide full funding for the program. In such cases the state might eliminate local fund raising for schools or collect and redistribute local taxes. By 1979, 11 states had installed a system of high-level foundation programs.[20] The system doesn't always reduce disparities. In seven states which moved to a high-level foundation program, the disparities were reduced; in three states, disparities increased; and in one state, they stayed the same.

Whether or not high-level foundation programs reduce disparities among districts depends on how the program is written. In considering statewide tax reforms, legislatures are often pressured by wealthy school districts, which have local pride in their "good" schools, to write a program which will enable the wealthy school districts to continue local funding at a level much higher than the minimum. If a maximum is not placed on local effort, or if some scheme is not devised which permits the state to collect local revenues which exceed a specific per-pupil amount, equalization is difficult. This is true because rich districts may be reluctant to tax local property more than is needed to maintain legally required, minimun per-pupil expenditures if the excess collected goes to the state for distribution to other districts.

District power equalizing forces wealthy districts to help poor districts. In district power equalizing, the state sets the basic expenditure level as well as the tax rate. Thus, the tax rate would be the same in all school districts. If the tax rate does not meet the basic expenditure level required by the state, the state makes up the difference. If the tax rate raises more than the basic expenditure level, the state collects the excess and distributes it to the poor districts.[21]

Augmented foundation focuses on a district's wealth and tax effort. In this system, the tax rate on the local level is determined by the state. Along with a basic tax rate, a guaranteed per-pupil expenditure is established. If local taxes do not raise enough to provide for the guaranteed per-pupil expenditure, the state makes up the difference. An added feature of this plan is an encouragement to local districts to increase their tax effort. If a local school district raises its rates above the minimum, it gets increased funds from the state. If the tax rate is set on a high level by the state, it tends to result in greater equalization. If it is set low, the problem of disparities continues to exist. Three of six states which adopted this plan in the seventies experienced an increase in disparities.

These descriptions of various kinds of school finance reform are greatly simplified. Indeed, most state efforts at reform are extremely complex. In many cases, bits and pieces from these reform plans are patched together with original ideas advocated by various state interests. (District power equalizing seems to be the least popular reform.) School finance reform is complex and difficult because existing programs have been years in development and have grown almost without direction. The result is that in most states school funding programs are supported by a myriad of sources with which school people and legislators are reluctant to tamper. Added to this is the fact that the politics of school finance is a complex and mysterious business. Representatives in the legislature from rich and poor districts always have conflicting views on how the problems should be solved. School pressure groups add to the confusion by pushing their own plans for reform. Professionals who might be consulted often present conflicting schemes. It might be fair to say that most legislatures would be reluctant to deal with the problem at all if it were not for the threat of court action.

Adding to the complexity of school financial reform is a confusion over the need to provide substantial equality, as required by most state constitutions, and at the same time attempt to meet the educational needs of children within school districts. Substantial equality is not hard to define if one assumes that equality means that every child is entitled to have spent on his schooling basically the same amount as is spent on every other child's schooling. Unfortunately, such a simple view is not possible. Existing federal and state programs which provide supplemental funds for the poor, for minorities and the handicapped, for children with language difficulties and learning problems do not permit anything even approaching absolute equality.

Equal educational opportunity, even as the courts have defined it, does not always mean that all students have equal amounts spent on their schooling. Parents and groups which represent them have demanded that special problems be given special treatment by the schools. Parents who have handicapped children or children with language difficulties demand that their children receive what is needed in order for them to obtain the same basic kind of education as other children. This creates problems, since special programs for the handicapped and special language programs, for example, simply cost more than "normal" programs. Moreover, the courts have tended to support parents in their quest for special programs where needed. Thus, states seeking to equalize educational opportunity are faced with Hobson's choice. If there are serious disparities in per-pupil spending for legally mandated programs, they are in trouble; if there is substantial equality which neglects special problems, they are in trouble.

Added to this problem is increasing concern on the part of parents with the achievement of equality of educational outcomes. Both the consumers of schooling and those who deliver it have come to realize that equality of input does not always result in equality of output (a point made in *Rodriguez*). For most students and parents, what really counts are results. Given the great range of individual differences which exist and the incredible variety of educational needs which must be met in any state, coupled with the inconclusive nature of how best to deal with children who have learning problems, it may be impossible to provide a system in which there is substantial equality of result. Balancing the demands for equality of input and equality of result will continue to plague the schools, even in states which have made good faith efforts to reform their school finance system.

NOTES

1. Henry C. Morrison, *School Revenue* (Chicago: University of Chicago Press, 1930), p. 84.
2. Ellwood P. Cubberley, *School Funds and Their Apportionment* (New York: Teachers College, Columbia University Press, 1905), p. 3.
3. Updegraff's plan is noted in Roe L. Johns and Edgar L. Morphet, *The Economics of Financing Education: A Systems Approach*, 3d ed. (Englewood Cliffs, N.J.: 1975), p. 209.
4. Ibid.
5. Ibid.
6. Descriptions of these early state support proposals may be found in Imogene K. Chambers, "The Evolution of School Financial Accounting in the United States from 1910–1980" (Ed.D. dissertation, Oklahoma State University, 1980), pp. 98–107.
7. National Center for Education Statistics, *The Condition of Education* (Washington, D.C.: Department of Health, Education, and Welfare, 1979), p. 149.
8. Ibid., p. 145.
9. Arvid J. Burke, *Financing Public Schools in the United States* (New York: Harper & Row, 1957), p. 195.
10. National Center for Education Statistics, *The Condition of Education*, p. 152.
11. Ibid., p. 139.
12. Ibid., p. 165.
13. Ibid., p. 139.
14. Charles S. Benson et al., *Planning for Educational Reform* (New York: Dodd, Mead & Company, 1974), p. 8.
15. L. Laszlo Ecker-Racz, "Coping with Proposition 13," *Today's Education* (a publication of the National Education Association) 67 (September/October 1978): p. 5.

16. Kenneth E. Quindry, "The State Local Tax Picture," *Journal of Education Finance* 4 (Summer 1979): 33.

17. For a complete listing in 1978–79, see *The American School Board Journal* 166 (January 1979): 23–29.

18. For recent data on the status of school finance cases, see *Update on State Wide School Finance Cases*. School Finance Project, Lawyers Committee for Civil Rights Under Law, 733 15th St. N.W., Suite 520, Washington, D.C.

19. These methods are briefly explained in the National Center for Education Statistics, *The Condition of Education* (Washington, D.C.: Department of Health, Education, and Welfare, 1979), p. 138. Benson et al., in *Planning for Educational Reform*, ch. 3, listed full state assumption, district power equalizing, and categorical aid as the major reform alternatives.

20. National Center for Education Statistics, *The Condition of Education*, p. 140.

21. For a good description of district power equalizing, see James Guthrie, *Equity in School Financing: District Power Equalizing* (Bloomington, Ind.: Phi Delta Kappa Fastback No. 57, 1975).

14

Zero Sum Schools, the Economy, and Computers

For anyone who works in the public sector and depends upon taxes for their livelihood, budget cutting and retrenchment on taxes can be discouraging almost to the point of despair. Understanding the nature of the problem sometimes helps. What follows are some observations on school problems as a "zero sum game" and some comments on the relationship between economic problems, computer technology, and the schools.

ZERO SUM SCHOOLS

Lester Thurow, in a book entitled *The Zero Sum Society*,[1] was concerned that America had become paralyzed. This had occurred, in Thurow's view, because there was little or no economic growth. Without growth, such serious problems as unemployment, illness, crime, poverty, the insecurity of the elderly, and failing schools cannot be addressed. The reason is simple. When there is no economic growth, the money to attack the problems is unavailable. This is all the more frustrating because there are solutions to these problems. However, if income is not increasing, problems must be solved either with what funds there are or by greatly increasing the national debt. Deficit financing is difficult politically because it means that, in order to satisfy one group clamoring for the solution to its problem, government must take funds away from some other group. This is a zero sum game, complicated by the fact that many of the groups petitioning for the solution to their problems are politically well organized. If finding solutions to any single problem means that somebody must lose, then it is impossible to solve the problem. That is true, according to Thurow, because "no one wants to volunteer for this role. . . . Everyone wants someone else to suffer the necessary economic losses, and as a consequence none of the possible solutions can be adopted."[2]

Along with every other institution in the society, education is affected by the zero sum game. Not only are the schools in competition with other political and social needs, for fixed available resources, such as those of defense, roads, and welfare, but there is disagreement within the educational establishment over what priorities should be addressed. Real economic growth is accompanied by increased tax resources for education, and nearly everyone's needs and demands can get a little attention. Some will get more than others, but in an expanding economy no single cause need be faced with a loss.

The problems facing the schools provide an excellent illustration of the impact of Thurow's thesis. In some states, local, state, and federal revenues have declined in absolute numbers. Meanwhile, school problems awaiting solution have grown more serious. The decline in enrollments in public schools and colleges has not helped much because of the nature of school financing. In most states, state funds are a very significant part of local school budgets, and state funding levels are often tied directly to the number of students enrolled. Thus, a decline in enrollment, rather than improving economic conditions, actually makes them worse.

What happens to the schools in an evironment of retrenchment and shrinking budgets? Strangely, the schools can hold their own and even make modest gains in this environment. In some instances they have actually come off as winners in the zero sum game. Even in some of those states faced with the triple ills of high unemployment, low productivity, and retrenchment on taxes, schools have somehow managed to gain a little. In others, schools have been the last to experience cuts. Perhaps this is because schooling has such great priority as a political issue. Where school funding manages to make small gains in depressed areas with shrinking budgets, obviously it has been accomplished only at the expense of lower priority items such as highways, prisons, and welfare.

However, when the increase in expenditures for schooling begins to level off, the zero sum game is then played out between school interests. Competition for available resources between conflicting groups within the school establishment becomes fierce.

Who are the winners and who the losers in the local-state zero sum game over available funds? The most obvious answer is that the winners are those with the most power and the losers are the powerless. There is some evidence to support this proposition in the recent history of governmental activity in education on the national, state, and local levels. There are clearly differences in the kinds of problems addressed by government on these levels. Beginning in the sixties and continuing until the present, the national government, as represented by both the White House and Congress, has expressed an interest in the powerless. Thus, legislation on civil rights had many school applications. The national bureaucracy became deeply involved in fighting discrimination against minorities, women, and the handicapped. There was concern for the poor. Urban school children in the inner city benefited. Integration was pushed through the courts with assistance from Congress in the form of sweeping legislation. The national bureaucracy developed and enforced the law and developed guidelines for local implementation. Hungry children, who constituted no real political constituency, were fed. Various programs for in-service training were provided for teachers.

Curriculum reform in almost every field was undertaken in the national interest. All of these programs suffer under the rules of the zero sum game as it is being played out on the national level.

What happens when the problems are shifted to the local-state level? There is evidence that the local-state decision makers are not interested in the same kinds of school problems that get the attention of the national government. One can judge this from looking at what the states and localities have done historically and what they have done in recent years. Historically, the states and local school districts have had to be dragged reluctantly into programs which provided direct assistance to the powerless. In nearly every area where the national government has provided categorical assistance to states and local districts, it did so partly because the state and local levels were doing nothing about the problems. States and local districts have historically expressed very little concern about segregated schools, the civil rights of students and teachers, equal opportunity for women, and equal opportunity for the handicapped. A review of recent local-state efforts provides little hope that local-state decision makers have changed their positions.

Local-state "reforms" generally ignore the kinds of problems and issues which the national government has addressed. When the local school boards and the state legislatures act to reform the schools clearly the top issue addressed is teacher pay. A companion issue in recent years in most states has been the reform of teacher education. Moreover, the reform legislation in this area appears to be developing a rather common pattern, which includes such things as mandated competency tests for teachers, new licensing and certification requirements, and better pay and fringe benefits for tenured teachers.

When local-state decision makers look at reforms which impact on students, they tend to deal with such issues as special programs for the gifted, smaller classes, and better buildings and equipment. Curriculum improvement is a major concern of the local-state arena, but it doesn't mean the same thing on the local-state level as it does on the national level. When local-state decision makers get into curruculum improvement, they tend to emphasize "back to basics" approaches, the teaching of "Americanism," and training children to become "employable." Employable very often means expansion of vocational-technical programs to provide trained workers for local and state business and industry.

Thus, "better local schools" tends to mean whatever the most influential groups in the local districts and on the state level think it means. In an incredible number of communities, good schools mean traditional and safe schools. Traditional means emphasis on the basics, discipline and authority, and "useful" training. Safe means uncontroversial texts and materials as well as a safe physical environment.

WINNERS AND LOSERS

The winners in this game are those with power. Clearly the teachers have power, because even in a zero sum environment where state budgets and local budgets are static or falling, they manage to hold on or to make advances. State educational officials in state education agencies are winners because of their special relationship with the state legislature and the convenience with which they can press their claims. Their power is enhanced by the fact that they are closely associated with their major clients, the teachers. Local pressure groups can also be winners. Well-funded and organized groups which represent the community establishment, such as local business organizations, are winners. Not only do such groups exercise power but their position is enhanced by the fact that they represent the heart and soul of conservative and traditional ideas. For the most part, they pose no threat to existing systems and ways of doing things.

On some single-issue causes, such as sex education, evolution, religion in the schools, and Americanism, local religious and patriotic groups are winners. A zero sum environment is made to order for such groups for several reasons. First, they very often are in the position of opposing new programs. What they advocate is not going to cost more; it will cost less. Second, they identify themselves closely with "true Americanism." They believe in God and Country and the great traditions of the past. It is difficult to argue with this. Finally, they are often extremely well organized. They know what they want, they have proven tactics, they are often well funded, and their membership is emotional and enthusiastic in support of the cause. They are winners.

The losers are not hard to identify. In zero sum games it is good to have both power and the right cause. The losers have neither. Women as a group are losers. They lack consensus and strong organization. Even though the law may be on their side, this is little help in a zero sum game because it costs money to provide equality. Equality means expanding traditional programs to let women in. It means developing new programs. It means setting aside years of discriminatory practices and doing what is fair. These things are not easily accomplished in a zero sum game on the state and local levels.

The minorities are losers. By definition they lack power on the local-state level. When decision makers in a zero sum game are faced with a choice between what is good for minorities and what is good for mainstream, white, middle-class majorities, there can be little doubt about the outcome. The handicapped are losers for the same reasons. The poor, the dropouts, and the alienated are losers. Totally disorganized and unrepresented, their situation in a zero sum game is hopeless.

There are other losers. In a zero sum game on the state level, school districts with little representation in the state legislature are losers. These districts include the poor ones in isolated rural areas and the poorest of the poor in the inner city.

The zero sum game thesis applied to the schools has serious implications for the nature and the direction of school reform. Simply stated, it means that the most serious continuing problems of the schools will not be solved. Without national mandates on the problems of the poor and minorities, major reforms are neglected and what little progress has been made can be reversed.

CAN TECHNOLOGY SAVE US?

The most obvious solution to the frustrations and difficulties presented by lack of economic growth is the return of growth. In any developed nation, growth in the public sector can be mandated. Unfortunately, unless there is real economic growth, the game is still zero sum. The questions which must then arise are: Is real economic growth possible, and if so, what is most likely to be the source of that growth? It is in this context that technology enters the picture. There is not space here for a lengthy, general discussion of technology, so the comments which follow will be limited to a single aspect of it: computer technology. Since this work deals with the schools, the discussion will be limited further to a brief discussion of the relationship between computer technology and the schools.

In any society there is a close relationship between education, politics, and the economy. The relationship becomes more noticeable and perhaps more vital in developing countries which are struggling to raise their standard of living and in highly developed nations which are experiencing economic difficulties. There is an overwhelming temptation in both cases to look to education as a means of solving problems. Yet the nature of political and economic difficulties is such that the schools cannot singlehandedly save the system. When the political system is operating smoothly and efficiently and the economy is prospering, the schools tend to follow. In the words of Heinz Eulau: "If the political order is sound, stable, legitimate, just, or whatever other criterion of 'goodness' one wishes to apply, education and all that is implied by education, such as creation of new knowledge or the transmission of traditional knowledge, flourishes. If the political order is in trouble, education is in trouble."[3] Eulau could easily have included the economic system as well. If the political system is in trouble, the economic system is likely to be, or vice versa. Politics, economics, and education are intricately woven together

In the United States, economic problems such as unemployment, a high rate of inflation, high interest rates which inhibit investment, a growing national debt, the inability of industry to compete with other nations are all problems with which political leadership has attempted to deal for more than a decade without notable success. This lack of success has obvious effects on what is happening in education. Although politicians and economists may disagree on the policies which should be followed to correct the problems, most agree that a most basic problem in the economic system is the low level of productivity of the industrial sector. If only some solution could be found to make workers more productive, to encourage investment in new industries and new jobs, many of our difficulties would disappear. The difficulties of capitalism in highly developed capitalist nations were posed in the so-called Schumpeter Question. Economist Joseph Schumpeter wondered if capitalism could thrive in a society which seems to have everything. To thrive, Schumpeter suggested, capitalism depends on a continuous demand for new products. When that demand no longer exists, what follows is a loss of jobs, a loss of income, and ultimately a serious decline in investment and the production of new goods.

Many economist would disagree. After all, there are always those who do not have plenty, and human wants are insatiable. For some economists, the solution to low productivity and all the ills which flow from this is to make decisions which will somehow stimulate existing producers to make their operations more efficient and to produce more things which are already available at a lower cost, thereby increasing demand for them. For these economists, low productivity in basic industries such as autos, steel, and energy from natural resources are temporary problems which can be corrected by manipulation of the political rules or by the provision of economic incentives. When operating at peak levels or somewhere near that, the old industries can provide more jobs, more income, and more tax revenues.

Those who write about the computer age see things differently. The industries which accounted for past prosperity are referred to as "sunset" industries. The implication, of course, is that those industries have seen their best days, and the future belongs to new industries and new products which are now possible because of the level of development of computer technology. The difference between the old industrial revolution and the computer age was nicely summarized by Amitai Etzioni. Etzioni suggested that the technological breakthroughs which marked the industrial revolution were basically extensions of muscle power. He characterized the steam engine, the electrical saw, the automotive lathe, and even missiles as a "duplication and magnification of muscle power."[4] The development of computers, on the other hand, represents the expansion of our brain power.

Computer technology has an entirely new and different potential when applied to economic productivity. While it can make the old industries much more productive, it can also, and more importantly, create new products and new processes that can't even be imagined. As great and sweeping as the changes were which grew out of the industrial revolution, the computer revolution could make these changes seem pale by comparison.

What is already beginning to happen is that ours is rapidly becoming an information society. Indeed, information is beginning to be regarded as the single most important resource. The advantages of an information society over the old industrial society, which depended on natural resources, were summarized by Harlan Cleveland writing in the *Christian Science Monitor*.[5] Unlike natural resources, information is "nondepletive." It is recyclable, like waste paper and aluminum cans. Computer technology already aids in the conservation of resources which are nonrenewable. Computer technology can help eliminate large inventories by speeding up the planning and ordering process. Available resources can be located and matched with needs almost instantly, reducing or eliminating costly and inefficient production delays. Computer technology can help consumers locate reusable items that might otherwise lie rusting and unused. It can reduce the quantities of natural resources needed in the old productive processes by reducing waste.

Another characteristic of information is that it is not scarce as natural resources are. According to Cleveland, information is in chronic surplus—what is scarce is time, and the computer can dramatically reduce the cost of research efforts and help us to create new combinations and processes which can be rapidly implemented.

The information society is not resource hungry according to Cleveland. In his words: "Compared to the processes of the steel-and-automobile economy the production and distribution of information are remarkably sparing in their requirements for energy and other physical and biological resources." Cleveland might have added that the use of computers to help solve energy problems and to create synthetics could greatly increase productivity in traditional products and at the same time actually decrease the use of existing natural resources. It is conceivable that, barring huge population increases, new processes made possible by the application of computer technology could facilitate the recycling of much of what we have already produced, thus vastly reducing the demand for further exploitation of existing natural resources.

Finally, and perhaps most importantly, information gives rise to sharing transactions not exchange transactions. The old industrial order is based on exchange transactions. For example, country A trades wheat to country B for autos. When this happens, as Cleveland correctly points out, country A no longer has the wheat and country B no longer has the autos. However, if we give or sell a piece of information, both the buyer and the seller have it. In Cleveland's words, "both . . . can replicate it, manipulate it, and pass it along at will."[6]

Of course, Cleveland sees marvelous things growing out of the information system. Information can be more equitably distributed than things; that is, its benefits can be more widely dispensed. An information society can maximize and enhance choice, since access to information enables everyone to make better choices. On the level of daily work, communications and computer technology have already permitted many to decide on their own workplace. They can work at home and determine their own work hours and working conditions.

Some futurists are even more enthusiastic. Toffler's *Third Wave*[7] examines some optimistic hopes for a computer society. The first two waves were the agricultural and industrial revolutions. Toffler's third wave sounds utopian. Mass production could give way to production of goods to meet individual demands: punch your desires into a computer and it will provide you with a customized product. In place of mass media there could be millions of video terminals where individuals would have a cornucopia of choices. We would no longer work in factories but at home, in an "electronic cottage" industry, on our own computers and at our own pace.

Even if one considers the hopes of futurists a bit overstated, it is true that the introduction of computers has already made an impact on the economy. It has created new products, such as home computers and video games, which are in great demand. The introduction of computers into banking and retail trade has been nothing short of revolutionary. The new computer industry has replaced workers, but at the same time it has created millions of new jobs. There is every reason to believe that a full-scale application of computers will have a positive effect on the economic system. It is a growth area which certainly has the potential of breathing new life into a declining industrial system.

Whether the various aspects of the application of computer technology are good or bad from a social point of view is almost an irrelevent question. Computers are here to stay. One might hope that we are wise enough to put the technology to use for the general benefit of mankind, but whatever course the application of computers takes, we probably have no choice. Anything as obviously useful as computers will be used.

THE IMPLICATIONS FOR SCHOOLING

The enthusiasm for the potential of computers in the schools seems to know no bounds. Even the late Robert Hutchins, a well-known advocate of the generally educated citizen, sang their praises. Looking into his crystal ball in the late sixties, Hutchins saw infinite educational possibilities in the computer. In Hutchins' view, our motives for implementing computer technology should be pure of heart. In his words: "The aim of society could be the fullest human development of the individual and the community." He saw in the computer the dream of creating a world society where the computer and other devices could make every home a learning unit. The extent to which computers might be used for this purpose was illustrated in a conversation he had with a dean at the University of California at Irvine. According to Hutchins, the dean had placed a computer on every floor of every dormitory on campus. Hutchins asked: "If you are prepared to put the computer on every floor of every dormitory, and ultimately, as the price declines . . . to put one in every room . . . why go to the trouble of maintaining the plant? Why not put the computer in every home?" "Oh," he said, "That's what I intend to do. The campus at Irvine will be obsolete in ten years."[8]

Although the dean may have erred in his prediction, since the campus at Irvine was still there after 10 years, he made a good point. His time schedule may have been off, but enthusiasm and hopes for computers have not diminished. In an obviously biased report, the *Data Communications Magazine* reported in mid-1982 that home computers are likely to change the entire educational system. The report suggested that with home computers it would no longer be necessary to segregate students by age; classes could be created on the bases of interests and skills; and teachers' roles could be vastly affected since they would no longer have to deal with rote learning and drill but could concentrate on more advanced problem-solving skills.

The editors of *Time Magazine* must agree with this. In a cover story entitled "Here Come the Microkids," *Time* reported in its May 3, 1982 issue that the new generation of kids who were fascinated with computers were the vanguard of an electronic revolution. *Time* reported that kids in computer camps had to be dragged, almost kicking and screaming, from their computer screens onto the playgrounds and into the swimming pools.

As more and more uses are found for computers in the classroom, the demand for them soars. The economic message is not lost on the computer industry. They are aggressively exploiting the educational market. There is nothing in history to compare with this demand. The market potential for school uses seems almost insatiable since computers, like textbooks, can be individual learning devices. The goal of aggressive computer salesmen is nothing less than an individual computer for every school child in America. Moreover, the companies are more than willing to provide suggestions for the many applications of computers in the school setting. One such example is a monograph published by The Association for Computing Machinery, Inc., which in 91 pages outlines the uses of computers in everything from art, music, and the humanities to developing skills for the handicapped. One of the most "dog-eared" books in any library frequented by teachers is a book edited by Robert Taylor entitled *The Computer in the School: Tutor, Tool, Tutee*. Taylor's "how to" book draws on the knowledge of several computer experts who instruct readers on everything from how to get their hands on some computers, to how to program the computer, to how to teach critical thinking.

There are a few critics. John Simon's criticism in the February 27, 1979 issue of *Esquire* is typical. Simon worried about computers creating an illiterate society. His criticism was directed at the overly enthusiastic advocates who claim that the computer will eliminate the need for people to learn to read or do simple math. Admitting that pushing buttons could provide useful information, Simon charged that what the computer produced was information not education. Information, he said, is not "knowledge and wisdom." The computer can produce only what it is programmed to produce, and, according to Simon, the computer can't ask good questions.

Regardless what Simon thinks; the computer is here to stay. As a genuine economic stimulus, it is difficult to imagine any serious, unfortunate long-range effects. It is a new industry, the forms of which are barely perceptible on the horizon. It will create new jobs and new economic arrangements. It can increase productivity and thus stimulate economic systems. What we are less sure about are the social effects of the computer age. There isn't any doubt that the industry has already been launched, and there is no stopping it. It is a useful product which will be utilized for all kinds of purposes. As has been the case in the past with new technology, the sociological implications will come as an afterthought. Communications computer technology can lead just as easily to a meaningless society with increasing alienation as it can to some form of a more equitable, just, and feeling society. One thing is certain—the schools will be affected in significant ways. Whether computers are used to reach Hutchins' goal of "the fullest human development of the individual" or for some less lofty purpose depends, to a great extent, on the manner in which the schools and the society approach them.

NOTES

1. Lester Thurow, *The Zero Sum Society* (New York: Basic Books, 1980).
2. Ibid., p. 11.

3. Heinz Eulau, *Technology and Civility* (Stanford: Hoover Institution Press, 1977), p. 36.
4. Amitai Etzioni, "Boosting Our Brain Power," *Human Behavior* 8 (May 1979): p. 16.
5. Harland Cleveland, "How Leaders Must Change in the Information Age," *The Christian Science Monitor*, 16 February 1982, p. 12.
6. Ibid.
7. Alvin Toffler, *The Third Wave* (New York: William Morrow, 1982).
8. Robert M. Hutchins, "Implications for Education," in *Technology, Human Values and Leisure*, ed. Max Kaplan and Phillip Bosserman (New York: Abingdon Press, 1971), pp. 121–122.
9. John Simon, "Compact with Computers," *Esquire*, 27 February 1979, p. 19.

Index